SUCCEEDING in the World of Work

SIXTH EDITION

Teacher's Manual

Grady Kimbrell
Educational Consultant
Santa Barbara, California

Ben S. Vineyard
Professor and
    Chairman Emeritus
Vocational and
    Technical Education
Pittsburg State University
Pittsburg, Kansas

 **Glencoe McGraw-Hill**

New York, New York   Columbus, Ohio   Woodland Hills, California   Peoria, Illinois

TABLE OF CONTENTS

Inside the *Student Edition* . . . . TM 4

Inside the *Teacher's Wraparound Edition* . . . . TM 10

Teacher's Classroom Resources . . . . TM 16

Professional Notes

    Developing a School-to-Work Program . . . . TM 20

    Integrating School-Based Learning . . . . TM 22

    Integrating Work-Based Learning . . . . TM 23

    Integrating Connecting Activities . . . . TM 24

    Teaching All Aspects of Industry . . . . TM 25

    Marketing Your School-to-Work Program . . . . TM 26

    Integrating Career Education Across the Curriculum . . . . . TM 28

    Addressing Cultural Diversity . . . . TM 29

    Integrating Technology into Your Career Education Program . . . TM 30

    SCANS and *Succeeding in the World of Work* . . . . TM 32

    Using Cooperative Learning . . . . TM 34

    Using Alternative Means of Assessment . . . . TM 36

    Teaching Critical-Thinking Skills . . . . TM 38

    Teaching Ethical Decision-Making Skills . . . . TM 40

    Meeting Individual Needs and Learning Styles . . . . TM 41

    Meeting Special Needs . . . . TM 42

    Meeting Individual Needs and Learning Styles . . . . TM 44

    Course Planning Guide . . . . TM 46

    Block Scheduling . . . . TM 48

Glencoe/McGraw-Hill

A Division of The **McGraw·Hill** Companies

Printed in the United States of America.

Send all inquiries to:
Glencoe/McGraw-Hill
21600 Oxnard Street, Suite 500
Woodland Hills, CA 91367

ISBN 0-02-814219-5 (Student Text)
ISBN 0-02-814221-7 (Teacher's Wraparound Edition)

5 6 7 8 9   004/043   03 02 01 00

To best research and address the needs of today's workplace, Glencoe/McGraw-Hill assembled an advisory board of industry leaders and educators. The board lent its expertise and experience to establish the foundation for this innovative, real-world, career education program. Glencoe/McGraw-Hill would like to acknowledge the following companies and individuals for their support and commitment to this project:

Mark Ballard
Director of Human Resources
Recruitment and Development
The Limited, Inc.
Columbus, OH

Michele Bina
Michele Bina and Associates
former Manager of Organizational Effectiveness
The Prudential Healthcare Group
Woodland Hills, CA

Joe Bryan
Industrial Cooperative Training Coordinator
Warsaw Community Schools
Warsaw, IN

Mary Sue Burkhardt
Career Specialist
Family and Consumer Sciences
Twin Lakes High School
Monticello, IN

Mable Burton
Career Development Specialist
Office of Education for Employment
Philadelphia, PA

Lolita B. Hall, Specialist
Program Improvement
Virginia Department of Education
Richmond, VA

Liz Lamatrice
Career Education Coordinator
Jefferson County, OH

Keith Mitchell
Manager, Testing and Assessment
Abbott Laboratories
Abbott Park, IL

James Murphy
Education Relations Manager
The Boeing Company
Seattle, WA

William M. Pepito
Manager, Lake County Skills Development Program
Abbott Laboratories
Abbott Park, IL

William J. Ratzburg
Director, Education for Work and Careers
Racine School District
Racine, WI

Gary Schepf
Business Education Department Chair
Nimitz High School
Irving, TX

Welcome to Succeeding in the World of Work!

Students with all kinds of career and academic goals share one important need: they must be prepared to succeed in the world of work. *Succeeding in the World of Work* presents information, explores ideas, and develops skills and competencies that will help all your students succeed in their careers.

This completely revised and up-to-date edition prepares students for the rapidly changing nature of the workplace. New emphasis on SCANS skills, on technology, and on understanding and working with cultural differences makes this text especially relevant and useful. A fresh new design, with attractive visuals, clear type, and an easy-to-read style invite students of all backgrounds and abilities to explore the content.

Succeeding in the World of Work places special emphasis on the skills and competencies identified in the SCANS report, *What Work Requires of Schools*. These skills and competencies are integrated into the student text and are highlighted in the teaching suggestions of the *Teacher's Wraparound Edition*.

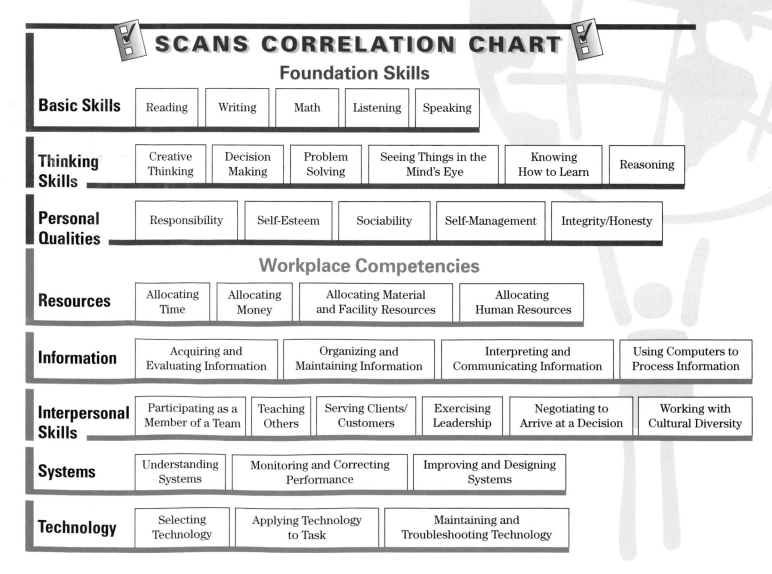

SCANS CORRELATION CHART

Foundation Skills

Basic Skills — Reading | Writing | Math | Listening | Speaking

Thinking Skills — Creative Thinking | Decision Making | Problem Solving | Seeing Things in the Mind's Eye | Knowing How to Learn | Reasoning

Personal Qualities — Responsibility | Self-Esteem | Sociability | Self-Management | Integrity/Honesty

Workplace Competencies

Resources — Allocating Time | Allocating Money | Allocating Material and Facility Resources | Allocating Human Resources

Information — Acquiring and Evaluating Information | Organizing and Maintaining Information | Interpreting and Communicating Information | Using Computers to Process Information

Interpersonal Skills — Participating as a Member of a Team | Teaching Others | Serving Clients/Customers | Exercising Leadership | Negotiating to Arrive at a Decision | Working with Cultural Diversity

Systems — Understanding Systems | Monitoring and Correcting Performance | Improving and Designing Systems

Technology — Selecting Technology | Applying Technology to Task | Maintaining and Troubleshooting Technology

Succeeding with Each Unit

The *Sixth Edition* of *Succeeding in the World of Work* contains seven units, which lead students from **Self-Assessment, Exploring Careers,** and **Finding a Job** through **Joining the Workforce** and **Professional Development,** and on to **Life Skills** and **Lifelong Learning**.

A relevant photograph prompts student discussion. Other photographs and exciting graphics throughout the text help maintain student involvement.

Predictable organization, readable type size, and attractive graphics invite all students to become involved and participate in classroom interaction.

The opening pages of each unit draw students into the contents.

UNIT 1
Self-Assessment

Chapter 1
You and the World of Work

Chapter 2
Getting to Know Yourself

A listing of chapter titles helps students anticipate the concepts to be presented in each unit.

UNIT 1 QUIZ:
What Do You Know About Self-Assessment?

• How is a job different from a career?
• Why do people work?
• How has the workplace changed in the last ten years?
• Picture yourself in five years. What will your life be like?
• What things are important to you?
• What do you want from a career?

UNIT QUIZ pretests students' familiarity with the content of the unit and helps them to anticipate topics contained in the unit's chapters.

UNIT 1 LAB

ASPECTS OF INDUSTRY:
Technical and Production Skills

Overview
In Unit One, you read about why people work, and focused on evaluating your skills and aptitudes. In this Unit Lab, you will use what you have learned while exploring one of the aspects of industry: **Technical and Production Skills**.

The Technical and Production Skills aspect of industry covers the actual techniques and abilities you'll need on the job. It also covers how you'll work—whether you'll time-share, telecommute, or rotate jobs with someone else.

Tools
1. *Occupational Outlook Handbook*
2. Trade and business magazines
3. Consumer magazines
4. Information on apprenticeship programs
5. College/Specialty school catalogs

Procedures
STEP A

Choose one of the following 15 job clusters that interests you: Agribusiness and Natural Resources; Business and Office; Communications and Media; Construction; Family and Consumer Services; Environment; Fine Arts and Humanities; Health; Hospitality and Recreation; Manufacturing; Marine Science; Marketing and Distribution; Personal Service; Public Service; Transportation.

Choose three jobs in the job cluster that you would seriously think about pursuing. Research each of the three, listing the skills you would need to perform the job (reading, computer use, carpentry, math, etc.). Use the *Occupational Outlook Handbook (OOH)* and other career references, trade and business magazines, and consumer magazines to get your information. Some of these sources are on the Internet.

In your research, look for comments that indicate how the work is performed by computer, individually, in groups, and so on. Mention if the way the work is done is changing.

STEP B

If you have not already done so, make lists of your skills, interests, aptitudes, and values. You may want to brainstorm with two or three classmates.

Compare the list of your skills, aptitudes, interests, and values to the lists of skills you made for the three jobs.

Choose the job that most closely matches your skills, interests, aptitudes, and values.

STEP C

Have your teacher, counselor, or parent help you arrange a short (20- to 30-minute) interview with a person in that job. If someone in your first choice job is not available, go on to your second choice.

During the interview, ask the following:

1. Which skills are most important in performing the job?
2. How did the person get the skills to perform the job? (Formal training? Experience?)

3. How have the job skill requirements changed in the past five to ten years? Are they expected to change in the next five to ten years?
4. How does the person perform his or her job? (Telecommuting? In groups? Alone?)

During the interview, take careful notes. Do not record the interview without permission. Be punctual and be courteous.

REPORT

Write a one-page, word-processed report using the information you gathered in your lists, your research, and the interview.

• Explain how the job skill requirements have changed in the last five to ten years. Predict how they may change in the future.
• Explain how your current skills, interests, aptitudes, and values suit the job choice, if in fact they do. If they do not, explain why.
• Note the skills you currently lack and how you could go about getting those skills.

Keep your lists, interview notes, and report in a folder entitled "Career Exploration."

UNIT LAB concludes each unit. Labs give students an opportunity to research all aspects of industry.

44

45

Succeeding with Each Chapter

Each unit of *Succeeding in the World of Work* includes two to six chapters. These chapters focus student attention on specific areas of learning, with special attention to SCANS skills and competencies.

Expanded content includes new chapters on ethics, attitude, legal issues in the workplace, thinking skills, technology, managing time and information, lifelong learning, and personal and career changes.

Revised chapters have been completely updated to help students explore current developments in the workplace. Special attention is given in each chapter to the SCANS skills and competencies.

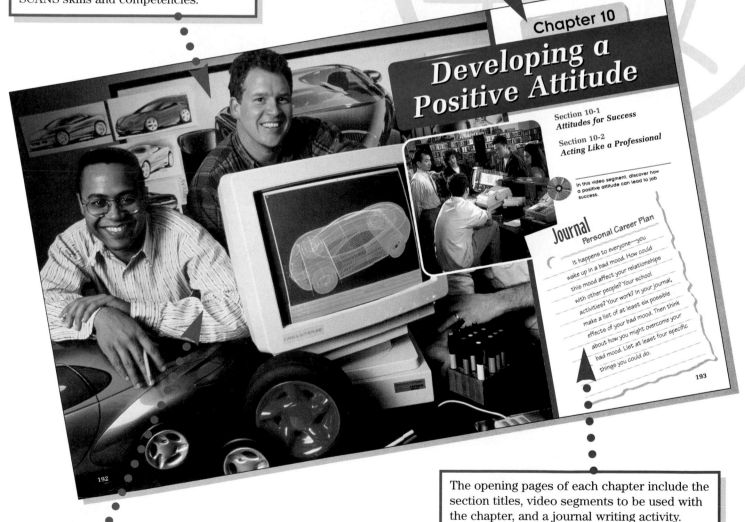

Chapter 10

Developing a Positive Attitude

Section 10-1
Attitudes for Success

Section 10-2
Acting Like a Professional

In this video segment, discover how a positive attitude can lead to job success.

Journal
Personal Career Plan

It happens to everyone—you wake up in a bad mood. How could this mood affect your relationships with other people? Your school activities? Your work? In your journal, make a list of at least six possible effects of your bad mood. Then think about how you might overcome your bad mood. List at least four specific things you could do.

192

193

The opening pages of each chapter include the section titles, video segments to be used with the chapter, and a journal writing activity.

Attractive photographs, clear organization, and easy-to-read type draw students into the content of each chapter.

Succeeding with Each Section

In the *Sixth Edition* of *Succeeding in the World of Work* each chapter is divided into two or three sections. Each section is carefully designed to introduce and develop material in comprehensible segments as well as to provide a review of that material.

Photographs, illustrations, charts, and graphs add visual impact and reinforce the content of each section. Captions guide students in recalling information, relating facts to real-world situations, and exploring their own ideas.

OBJECTIVES list the specific skills and knowledge students can expect to master as they study each section. These objectives guide students to read, discuss, and review the section, keeping specific goals in mind.

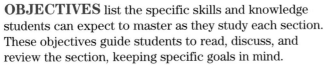

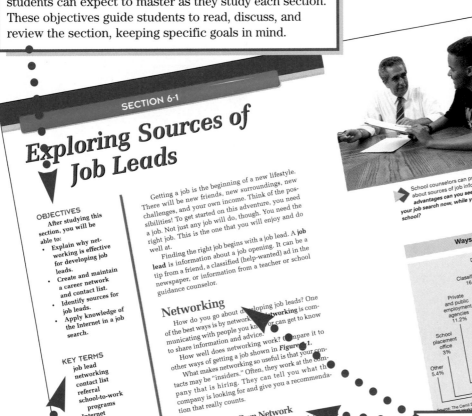

SECTION 6-1

Exploring Sources of Job Leads

OBJECTIVES
After studying this section, you will be able to:
- Explain why networking is effective for developing job leads.
- Create and maintain a career network and contact list.
- Identify sources for job leads.
- Apply knowledge of the Internet in a job search.

KEY TERMS
job lead
networking
contact list
referral
school-to-work programs
Internet

Getting a job is the beginning of a new lifestyle. There will be new friends, new surroundings, new challenges, and your own income. Think of the possibilities! To get started on this adventure, you need a job. Not just any job will do, though. You need the right job. This is the one that you will enjoy and do well at.

Finding the right job begins with a job lead. A **job lead** is information about a job opening. It can be a tip from a friend, a classified (help-wanted) ad in the newspaper, or information from a teacher or school guidance counselor.

Networking

How do you go about developing job leads? One of the best ways is by networking. **Networking** is communicating with people you know or can get to know to share information and advice.

How well does networking work? Compare it to other ways of getting a job shown in **Figure 6-1**.

What makes networking so useful is that your contacts may be "insiders." Often, they work at the company that is hiring. They can tell you what the company is looking for and give you a recommendation that really counts.

Creating Your Own Network

Networking is not as difficult as you might think. You know people, don't you? Those people will form the basis for your network.

School counselors can provide advice about sources of job information. *What advantages can you see in beginning your job search now, while you are still in school?*

To get started, make a **contact list**. This is simply a list of people you know. Include everyone—family friends, neighbors, classmates, friends of friends, and even casual acquaintances.

Now begin networking by contacting the people on your list. Ask for any information that will lead to a job. You may think your aunt doesn't know anything about job openings. Maybe she doesn't, but her neighbor might, so don't give up on your aunt. Ask whether she knows anyone who works in the business you're interested in or for a company you'd like to work for.

Build your contact list by getting a referral from everyone you talk to. A **referral** is someone such as your aunt's neighbor to whom you've been directed, or referred. By contacting referrals, you

Figure 6-1
The graph shows the proportion of jobs people get from different sources. Why do you think most people get jobs by networking and contacting employers directly?

Ways That People Get Jobs

- Direct employer contact 29.8%
- Classified ads 16.6%
- Private and public employment agencies 11.2%
- School placement office 3%
- Other 5.4%
- Networking 34%

Source: The Camil Study in *The Very Quick Job Search*, Inc., 1991, p. 26

Clear text headings help students recognize and organize information within each section.

with your school and public libraries. Many are already connected to the Internet. You might also check with community colleges, universities, copy shops, and your state employment office.

employment opportunities, job listing and *careers*.

Keywords will lead you to some of the many job-related sites on the Internet, such as America's Job Bank, Online Career Center, or Federal Job Openings.

KEY TERMS list major terms presented in each section. They are highlighted with boldface type as they are introduced in the chapter, and are accompanied by clear, in-context definitions.

SECTION 6-1 *Review*

Understanding Key Concepts

Using complete sentences, answer the following questions on a separate sheet of paper.

1. Explain why networking is one of the most effective means of finding a job.

2. Whom should you include on your contact list? Why?

3. Which source for job leads will you use first in job hunting? Why?

4. What are six keywords you might use in a job search on the Internet?

UNDERSTANDING KEY CONCEPTS presents factual recall questions to guide students in reviewing the major concepts developed in the section.

Focus on the Features

Special features in each chapter are designed to engage students' interest, increase their understanding of chapter content, and expand their involvement with real-world situations.

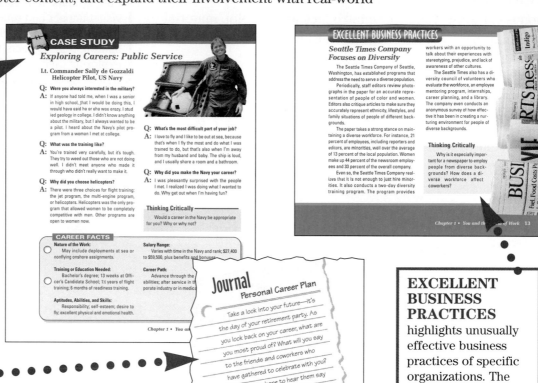

EXPLORING CAREERS

presents information about various careers and individuals who work in them. Students learn about necessary job skills, career paths, and advantages and disadvantages of a specific career.

PERSONAL CAREER PLAN

is a journal activity that helps students consider chapter content and apply it to their own career explorations.

CAREER DO'S AND DON'TS

provides helpful reminders for students to use in real-life situations.

YOU'RE THE BOSS: SOLVING WORKPLACE PROBLEMS

invites students to make decisions about challenging workplace situations.

EXCELLENT BUSINESS PRACTICES

highlights unusually effective business practices of specific organizations. The feature includes a follow-up critical thinking question.

ATTITUDE COUNTS

reinforces the importance of adopting a positive point of view at work.

ETHICS IN ACTION

presents students with real-life situations that may challenge their personal values and business ethics. This feature asks students to discuss and defend their ideas.

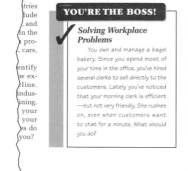

Reinforcing Chapter Concepts

Each chapter in *Succeeding in the World of Work* concludes with a thorough review designed to help students recall, use, and expand on the concepts presented in the chapter.

The review begins with **Chapter Highlights**, a full-page and clearly organized listing of the main points developed within that chapter.

A two-page **Chapter Review** presents activities that are flexible and address the varying levels of abilities.

CHAPTER 7 *Highlights*

SECTION 7-1 Summary
- Prepare carefully for an interview. Research the company and current events in the industry.
- Rehearse before an interview. Practice with a mirror and a tape recorder, and ask a friend for comments.
- Plan what you will wear at an interview. Dress conservatively and avoid flashy items. Appear neat and well-groomed.
- Arrive on time.

Key Term
interview (p. 132)

SECTION 7-2 Summary
- Employers will be evaluating your attitude and your communication skills. Be positive and enthusiastic.
- You will probably be asked some typical questions at an interview. Be prepared to answer them.
- You may be asked some tough questions designed to rattle you. Be prepared to respond to them with a calm and positive attitude.
- Some questions may involve role-playing or problem solving to evaluate your ability to think on your feet.
- Some questions are illegal for an employer to ask during an interview. You are not required to answer them.

Key Terms
body language (p. 136)
role-playing (p. 140)
problem solving (p. 141)
stress (p. 142)

SECTION 7-3 Summary
- Evaluate your performance after an interview. Send a follow-up letter.
- Follow standard procedures for accepting or rejecting employment. Don't say no during an interview. Always leave the door open for the future.

Chapter 7 • Interviewing 147

REVIEWING KEY TERMS
presents a game or other interesting activity that helps students review the Chapter Key Terms.

THINKING CRITICALLY
challenges students to use the higher-level thinking skills.

CHAPTER 7 *REVIEW*

Reviewing Key Terms
On a separate sheet of paper, write a paragraph describing how you would prepare for an interview. Use the terms below in your paragraph.
interview
body language
role-playing
stress
problem solving

Recalling Key Concepts
Choose the correct answer for each item below. Write your answers on a separate sheet of paper.
1. Researching a company before an interview enables you to ___.
   (a) ask intelligent questions
   (b) impress your friends
   (c) dress for success
2. Preparing a 30-second "commercial" about yourself is a good way to ___.
   (a) research a company
   (b) negotiate a salary
   (c) rehearse for an interview
3. Which of the following topics is illegal for an employer to ask about? ___
   (a) your skills   (b) your goals
   (c) your citizenship
4. Interviewers look for applicants ___.
   (a) wearing fashionable clothes
   (b) demonstrating a positive attitude
   (c) with a sense of humor
5. In a follow-up letter, you should ___.
   (a) restate your continued interest
   (b) invent additional references
   (c) apologize for being nervous

148 *Unit 3 • Finding a Job*

Thinking Critically
Using complete sentences, answer each of the questions below on a separate sheet of paper.
1. In what ways can you stand out positively at an interview?
2. Summarize the importance of body language at a job interview.
3. Compare rehearsing for an interview alone and rehearsing with a friend. Identify the advantages of each method.
4. What would you infer about a job applicant who asks questions about a job's responsibilities and chances for advancement in the company?
5. Imagine that you are an employer. List the five most important qualities of a great job applicant in order of priority. Give reasons for the order.

SCANS Foundation Skills and Workplace Competencies

Basic Skills: *Speaking*
1. Compose a 30-second "commercial" to summarize your abilities. In it, act as if you are being interviewed.

Thinking Skills: *Reasoning*
2. An interviewer asks Wendy: "Do you plan to have children anytime soon?" How should she answer this question?

Personal Skills: *Self-Esteem*
3. Michael is in the middle of a job interview. Suddenly, he feels very stressed. Write a paragraph telling what he can do to calm down and finish the interview successfully.

Interpersonal Skills: Exercising Leadership
4. An interviewer says to you: "You have no experience in this field. Why should I hire you?" In a few sentences, describe how you could answer this tough question in a way that shows maturity and ability to take charge of a situation.

Connecting Academics to the Workplace

Social Studies
1. Ella wants to research trends in the computer software company. Using the library, magazines, newspapers, or the Internet, find relevant information. Then describe some ways she might use this information in an interview.

Human Relations
2. Kyle has an interview scheduled with a company that is based in a foreign country. He wants to make sure he understands the body language in this country. Choose a country (such as Japan, Saudi Arabia, Kenya, Norway), and research its "rules" about body language. What movements and gestures should Kyle be aware of?

Math
3. It is a 20-minute ride to Laura's job interview. However, due to construction, she will have to take a detour that will add 15 minutes. If she wants to arrive 15 minutes early, how much time should she allow for the trip?

Developing Teamwork and Leadership Skills
You are part of a hiring team in charge of department stores. You need to hire a person for an entry-level position in sales. Describe the job and identify the skills it requires. Then create a four-person role-playing exercise that will enable candidates to display those skills. As a team, decide which person you would hire, and explain the reasons for your decision.

Real-World Workshop
In groups of three, identify a job that interests you. Then research skills involved in the job. Separately, develop interview questions. Have two members act as interviewer and applicant, while the third member evaluates the applicant. After each member of the team has served in each role, comment on each other's interview style.

School-to-Work Connection
Talk to an employer or a manager who has interviewed job applicants. Ask this person about common mistakes that people make during job interviews. What advice would this person give every applicant? Report your findings to the class.

Individual Career Plan
Using standard business style, write a thank-you letter to an employer. Mention your unique skills, and express your enthusiasm for the job. Proofread for standard English, spelling, and punctuation.

Chapter 7 • Interviewing 149

DEVELOPING TEAMWORK AND LEADERSHIP SKILLS
allows students to enhance their teamwork and leadership skills as they work in teams to complete specific projects.

REAL-WORLD WORKSHOP
presents practical situations in which students apply their career skills.

SCHOOL-TO-WORK CONNECTION
activities allow students to explore and experience the realities of the workplace.

RECALLING KEY CONCEPTS
helps students review and recall the most important ideas in the chapter.

BUILDING SCANS FOUNDATION SKILLS AND WORKPLACE COMPETENCIES
activities help students develop identified SCANS skills and competencies.

CONNECTING ACADEMICS TO THE WORKPLACE
asks students to apply academic skills in real-life work scenarios.

INDIVIDUAL CAREER PLAN
activities guide students in developing their own career plan.

Introducing the Teacher's Wraparound Edition

The *Teacher's Wraparound Edition* of *Succeeding in the World of Work* is a comprehensive resource designed to help you motivate and involve your students throughout the learning process. Suggestions and ideas "wrapped around" the actual student pages will guide you in reaching students of all levels of ability and backgrounds and will make the course more rewarding for you—and for your students.

Using the Four-Step Teaching Plan

Succeeding in the World of Work and its *Teacher's Wraparound Edition* have been carefully planned to make full and effective use of a mastery approach in four steps: focus, teach, assess, and close.

STEP 1: FOCUS

As a teacher, you know that the first step in presenting new material is to capture students' interest. Special features in the *Student Edition* are designed to engage students in the material to be presented within the coming unit, chapter, or section. In addition, the *Teacher's Wraparound Edition* suggests a variety of interesting motivational activities to focus students' interest.

STEP 2: TEACH

The second step in the instructional process involves the presentation and exploration of new material. The *Teacher's Wraparound Edition* of *Succeeding in the World of Work* presents a teaching plan designed to give you maximum flexibility in meeting the needs of your class. The variety of approaches, strategies, and activities allows you to help all students assimilate the content of each chapter.

STEP 3: ASSESS

This third step involves an assessment of students' learning. Because students have different learning styles and learn at different rates, the Assess section of the *Teacher's Wraparound Edition* provides a variety of evaluation and reteaching activities designed to accommodate a wide range of learning abilities.

STEP 4: CLOSE

In this final step of the instructional process, students look back over the new material presented in the lesson. This is an opportunity for them to summarize what they have learned, evaluate their own learning processes, and view the relevance of the new material to their own lives. The *Teacher's Wraparound Edition* suggests a variety of activities to facilitate this work with the entire class, with groups, and with individual students.

Teaching Each Unit

In the *Teacher's Wraparound Edition*, the opening pages of each unit provide information and ideas that will help you guide your students through the unit.

RESOURCES FOR ENRICHMENT is a list of relevant books, magazines, organizations, and Internet resources that students will find useful.

UNIT OVERVIEW offers helpful background information and a brief summary of the material included in the unit chapters.

INTRODUCING THE UNIT provides activities that will spark students' interest in the content of the unit.

UNIT CLOSURE provides a concluding activity for the unit.

DEVELOPING COMMUNITY INVOLVEMENT presents useful ideas and resources that will help you encourage student involvement in the community.

UNIT PROJECT is a hands-on activity that students can work on throughout the unit.

UNIT EVALUATION identifies the assessment instrument you can use to evaluate students' understanding of the unit.

BUILDING PARTNERS WITH INDUSTRY provides specific suggestions for developing school-business partnerships.

Using the Chapter Planning Guide

To help you select activities that will best meet the needs of your students, the *Teacher's Wraparound Edition* includes a two-page Planning Guide at the beginning of each chapter.

SECTION OBJECTIVES list the performance-based objectives for each section of the chapter. These objectives help both you and your students identify exactly what they are expected to know upon completion of the chapter.

SCANS CORRELATION CHART shows the specific SCANS skills and workplace competencies that students develop.

GUEST SPEAKER SUGGESTIONS present ideas for inviting practitioners to the classroom who can help bring the chapter to life.

SECTION FEATURES identify the specific features.

CLASSROOM RESOURCES provide information on the various support materials available to you and your students.

INTERNET CONNECTIONS guide you in using Internet resources to enhance chapter learning.

FIELD TRIP SUGGESTIONS include ideas for learning opportunities outside the classroom.

KEY TO ABILITY LEVELS explains the different levels of activities used throughout the *Teacher's Wraparound Edition*. These various levels help you customize activities to the needs of the class or to specific individuals.

Teaching Each Chapter

The chapter opener pages provide material to guide you in introducing and reviewing the chapter in ways suited to your students' needs.

WORK-BASED LEARNING STRATEGIES AND ACTIVITIES include suggestions for implementing work-based learning in school and in industry.

SCHOOL-TO-WORK CONNECTING ACTIVITIES offer ideas for providing a common thread between school-based and work-based learning.

CHAPTER OVERVIEW describes the purpose of the chapter and summarizes the content of each chapter section.

BACKGROUND INFORMATION suggests brief activities that will help students preview the content of the chapter.

MEETING SPECIAL NEEDS suggests activities designed to support students with special learning needs.

ADDRESSING LEARNING STYLES presents tips for focusing on students' individual learning styles.

WORKFORCE 2000 INTERACTIVE TRAINING VIDEO BAR CODE allows you to scan and locate the appropriate section on the videodisc.

PRETEACHING VOCABULARY presents an activity that will help introduce the Key Terms from each section of the chapter.

Teaching Each Section

Each chapter contains two or three sections. Each section follows the four steps of the teaching process—Focus, Teach, Assess, and Close.

FOCUS

BELL RINGER is an independent activity that helps students "switch gears" from their previous classes and focus on the material to be presented.

INTRODUCING THE SECTION provides an opportunity to preview the lesson topic.

MOTIVATIONAL ACTIVITY challenges students to begin thinking creatively about the lesson topic.

TEACH

Guided Practice

TEACHING TIPS offer a step-by-step approach to helping students read and think about the section.

DISCUSSION STARTER presents topics or open-ended questions that will involve students in comprehending and applying the concepts presented.

CRITICAL THINKING leads students to examine points of view; look for relationships, theories, and patterns; identify alternatives; and make judgments, choices, and decisions.

SCANS ACTIVITIES provide guided development in Foundation Skills and Workplace Competencies. These activities are written to suit varying student ability levels.

Independent Practice

These are practice activities that students can complete as homework or in class without your assistance. Specific assignments may focus on Reading, Research, Practice Skills, and Writing.

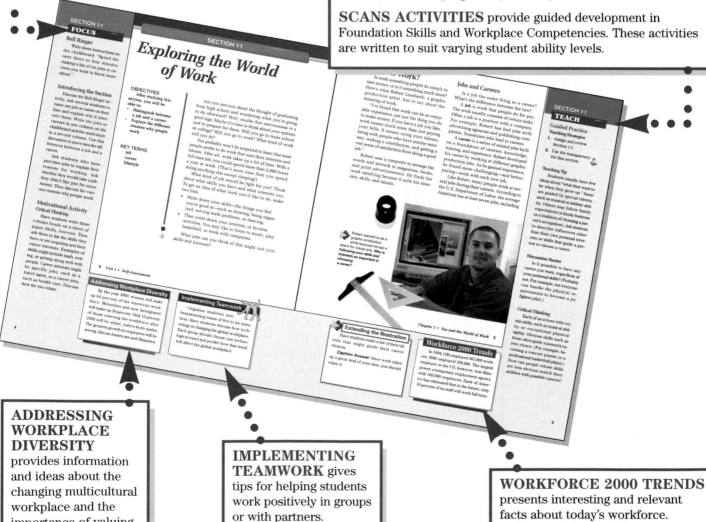

ADDRESSING WORKPLACE DIVERSITY provides information and ideas about the changing multicultural workplace and the importance of valuing cultural diversity.

IMPLEMENTING TEAMWORK gives tips for helping students work positively in groups or with partners.

WORKFORCE 2000 TRENDS presents interesting and relevant facts about today's workforce.

ASSESS

ASSESSMENT provides an activity for oral assessment, performance assessment, process assessment, or content assessment.

EVALUATION suggests uses for the UNDERSTANDING KEY CONCEPTS questions. In the final section of each chapter, a Mini Quiz is also included.

RETEACHING provides ideas for reinforcing the most important concepts of each section. These activities are most appropriate for students who have demonstrated difficulties with the lesson material.

EXTENDING THE CONTENT presents activities that help students explore the section in greater depth.

CLOSE

A final exercise helps students summarize key concepts or examine their own ideas during the last minutes of class discussion.

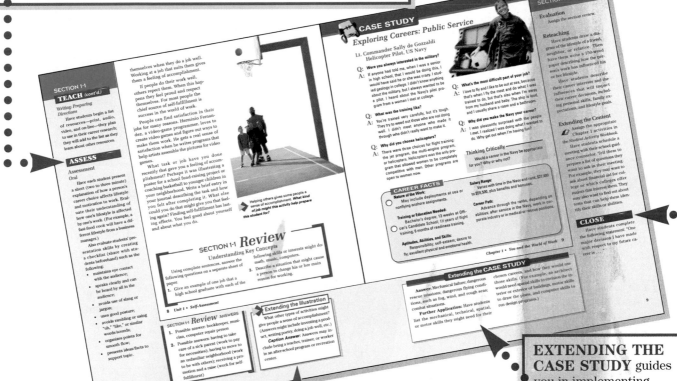

EXTENDING THE ILLUSTRATION suggests activities for using every photograph or illustration as a learning tool. In addition, responses to the caption questions are provided.

SECTION REVIEW ANSWERS lists short, clear answers to UNDERSTANDING KEY CONCEPTS questions.

EXTENDING THE CASE STUDY guides you in implementing EXPLORING CAREERS and EXCELLENT BUSINESS PRACTICES with the entire class or with small groups.

Meeting Every Classroom Need with Classroom Resources

The *Succeeding in the World of Work* program includes a complete selection of teacher support materials. Used in conjunction with the *Teacher's Wraparound Edition*, these materials will enable you to tailor the program to meet the specific needs of your classes, as well as to meet the varying needs of individual students. The program resources are specially developed to support you in meeting your course objectives and in maximizing student learning.

Student Activity Workbook presents SCANS Foundation Skills and Workplace Competencies, and Research Activities for each chapter.

Performance Assessment Binder is a complete assessment resource that will help you evaluate students' progress. This testing program includes: a set of reproducible Chapter, Unit, Midterm, and Final Tests, a printed testbank of all test questions, the Test Generator User's Guide, a DOS and MAC disk with a complete selection of test questions, and a booklet of chapter mini quizzes.

Teacher's Annotated Edition of the *Student Activity Workbook* includes answers and suggestions that will help you direct students in using the Workbook.

SPANISH RESOURCES

TRANSPARENCY PACKAGE

NEW! *Transparency Package* offers complete lesson plans as well as transparencies, which present the Objectives, Bell Ringer activities for each section, and chapter content material.

NEW! *Spanish Resource Binder* provides a teaching tool to be used with Spanish-speaking students. The *Spanish Resource Binder* presents a translation of all the section Objectives, Key Terms and their definitions, Chapter Highlights, Recalling Key Concepts questions and their answers, and the Glossary. Also included are two audiocassettes with pronunciation guides.

NEW! *Implementing Block Scheduling* provides detailed guidelines for using the text effectively in longer class periods (block scheduling). This booklet explains what block scheduling is, when and how it can be implemented, and what particular benefits it provides.

IMPLEMENTING BLOCK SCHEDULING

LESSON PLANS

Teacher's Lesson Plans give you a listing of all the objectives and teaching options available for every section within the chapters of the student text. This valuable reproducible resource simplifies lesson planning and saves you time.

NEW! *Print, Media, and Internet Handbook* offers a comprehensive list of resources corresponding to the contents of each chapter of *Succeeding in the World of Work*. Listings include book titles, media resources, and Internet addresses that enable you to support and supplement your students' learning.

PRINT, MEDIA, AND INTERNET HANDBOOK

SUCCEEDING in the World of Work

INCLUDES:
- Books
- Magazines
- Videos
- Internet Addresses

SIXTH EDITION

NEW! *Exploring the World of Work, An Interactive CD-ROM* delivers the latest career-planning information in an exciting yet easy-to-use CD-ROM format. This CD-ROM is designed to assist students in every aspect of career planning and research. Included on this CD-ROM are articles and videos on the career clusters, career success tips, career planning and assessment activities, a résumé builder, and a tic-tac-pros game.

NEW! *Workforce 2000 Video Library* provides exciting career exploration video segments to accompany every chapter in the textbook. A detailed Teacher's Manual provides instructions for incorporating the video into your career education program and activities for expanding and reinforcing the video content. The video program is available in English and Spanish as either a set of six videotapes or two level one videodiscs.

NEW! *School-to-Work Activity Handbook* is an invaluable resource for students in any kind of school-to-work program. The *Handbook* provides a selection of reproducible worksheets designed to help students relate their class work to their on-the-job experiences.

NEW! *Teacher's Manual* of the *School-to-Work Activity Handbook* provides guidelines that will help you integrate the various aspects of your school-to-work program. It also includes a Rubric Assessment for each Handbook activity and lists suggested student responses.

NEW! *Strategies for Implementing Connecting Activities* include a variety of proven approaches to integrating classroom learning with learning in the workplace.

NEW! *Strategies for Implementing Work-Based Learning* help you work with students, fellow teachers, mentors, employers, and government officials in implementing your work-based learning program.

Developing a School-to-Work Program

School-to-work programs have been one of the most important developments in recent educational reform. These programs assume many different forms in order to meet the particular needs of different communities, schools, and students; all forms offer the following benefits for students:

- an improved understanding of self,
- a clearer vision of a productive future and an understanding of how to make that vision a reality,
- familiarity with a wide range of career options,
- an appreciation of the relevance of school learning to "real life", and
- increased motivation to stay in and to succeed in school.

An effective school-to-work program involves a close relationship between local businesses and schools. This relationship, when thoughtfully developed and carefully tended, can result in benefits to schools and to businesses alike, as well as to parents and the community at large.

School-to-Work Opportunities Act of 1994

Much of the impetus for growth in school-to-work programs has been provided by the School-to-Work Opportunities Act of 1994. This legislation encourages states to create systems to implement school-to-work programs. The stated purposes of the Act help clarify the intent, as well as the benefits, of school-to-work programs.

PURPOSES OF THE SCHOOL-TO-WORK OPPORTUNITIES ACT

- To facilitate the creation of a universal, high-quality school-to-work transition system that enables youths in the United States to identify and pursue paths to progressively more rewarding roles in the workplace.

- To utilize workplaces as learning environments in the educational process by making employers and educators joint partners in providing opportunities for students to participate in high-quality, work-based learning.

- To promote the formation of partnerships dedicated to linking the worlds of school and work among secondary schools and private and public employers, labor organizations, government, community-based organizations, parents, students, state and local educational agencies, and training and human service agencies.

- To increase knowledge and improve skills of students by integrating academic and occupational learning and building links between secondary and postsecondary educational institutions.

- To motivate all students, including low-achievers, dropouts, and those with disabilities, to stay in or return to school or an alternative classroom setting and strive to continue their education in postsecondary institutions.

- To expose students to a broad array of career opportunities and facilitate the selection of major areas of study, based on individual interests, goals, and abilities.

Components of a School-to-Work Program

A school-to-work program has three essential elements:

- **School-Based Learning:** refers to all of the ways in which schools can prepare young people for their occupational future.
- **Work-Based Learning:** a program of job training that makes use of business and sites as part of a school's curriculum.
- **Connecting Activities:** the involvement of employers, schools, and students in such activities as matching students with appropriate work-based learning opportunities; providing in-service training for counselors, teachers, and mentors; helping with the placement of students in jobs; further education and/or training; and follow-up on students' progress after graduation.

Each of these aspects of a school-to-work program must be carefully developed, and all three aspects must support each other.

Making Choices

There is no single answer to the question, "What kind of school-to-work program do we need?" Rather, each school community must consider its own particular assets and needs in selecting a school-to-work learning model. Involving teachers, counselors, administrators, parents, students, businesspeople, and labor organizers at every step of the decision-making process can, in itself, be a unifying activity, and it will help you develop the school-to-work program best suited to your community and students.

Integrating School-Based Learning

In most cases, the development of a school-to-work program begins with the establishment of school-based learning. This preparatory aspect of the program provides various opportunities for students to explore the world of work without participating directly in it; the focus is on career exposure rather than on on-site education and training. In school-based learning, students consider their own abilities and interests, learn about various occupational options, develop appropriate skills and competencies, and practice making work-related decisions and doing work-related activities.

School-based learning assumes many forms. Each district, school, and sometimes even each group within a school must consider various options and select the one option—or the combination of options—that best meets its specific needs. School-based learning options are career exploration, service learning, and school-based enterprise.

Career Exploration

Career exploration develops awareness of various job and career opportunities for all students. Career exploration activities include career fairs, counseling, field trips, presentations by guest speakers, job shadowing, and unpaid work experience. Such activities help students develop a realistic understanding of the relationship between education and the world of work; the activities also guide students in making realistic academic and career plans.

Service Learning

A program of service learning provides service to the community and enhances students' academic learning, personal growth, and civic responsibility. Through this kind of program, students for varying periods of time serve as volunteers to help meet human needs, such as: caring for younger children, the sick,

the elderly, or the disabled; completing community improvement projects; or serving as reading or math tutors. Service learning enhances students' self-esteem, citizenship skills, and critical thinking. It provides both short- and long-term benefits to the community.

> In most cases, the development of a school-to-work program begins with the establishment of school-based learning.

School-Based Enterprise

In a program of school-based enterprise, students create and run their own businesses; in doing so, they become familiar with all aspects of entrepreneurship. Students who take part in this kind of program produce goods or services to sell to other students or members of the community. They may, for example, renovate houses, run a school store, or operate a repair shop. Participating in a school-based enterprise helps students link their school curriculum with work in a productive setting. It also promotes positive work attitudes and expands their understanding of business.

Integrating Work-Based Learning

The work-based learning component of a school-to-work program provides experiential education that makes use of business sites as part of a school's curriculum. Work-based learning, whether paid or unpaid, offers the following benefits to students:

- experiences that help them develop interests and abilities and guide them in the acquisition of skills;
- smooth transition from school to work; and
- improved human-relations skills.

Work-based learning also benefits participating employers in the following ways:

- Employers participating in school-to-work programs have relatively inexpensive and easy access to a pool of future employees—students in the community.
- Employers reduce training time and costs by hiring student workers full-time following graduation.
- Student workers often display increased productivity.
- Businesspeople and educators become active partners.
- The program fosters community and social involvement.

Work-Based Learning: One Part of the School-to-Work Program

Work-based education is effective only when it is thoughtfully coordinated with students' school-based programs, as well as with their traditional academic and career classes. To prepare for and benefit from work-based opportunities, students should first participate in career awareness programs, structured career planning and decision-making courses, and placement activities in both their academic and career/technical education programs. School-based career awareness programs help students reflect upon their interests and abilities so that, with guidance from teachers or counselors, they can identify the most appropriate work-based settings for their continued learning.

Work-based programs are not intended to replace any aspect of career or academic instruction; rather, the various forms of learning should support each other and thus enhance students' growth and development. Students who participate in work-based programs need appropriate classes in math, English, science, and social studies, as well as in technical studies. In these classes, students can develop and refine their skills and can recognize the applicability of this aspect of learning to their future in the workforce. In addition—and perhaps of greatest importance—they can develop the skills needed for lifelong learning, which will help them deal successfully with changes both in the workplace and society.

Glencoe Resources

The ancillary package for *Succeeding in the World of Work* includes *Strategies for Implementing Work-Based Learning*. This booklet provides valuable information on ways to integrate work-based learning into your school-to-work program.

Integrating Connecting Activities

A school-to-work program with strong school-based and work-based learning components cannot thrive without its third component: connecting activities. Connecting activities are considered so important that the School-to-Work Opportunities Act of 1994 lists the following as required elements:

- matching students with the work-based learning opportunities of employers;
- providing ... a school mentor to act as a liaison among the student, employer, teacher, school administrator, and parent;
- providing technical assistance and services to employers ... in designing learning components... and training teachers, workplace mentors, school mentors, and counselors;
- providing assistance to schools and employers to integrate school- and work-based learning, and integrate academic and occupational learning;
- encouraging the active participation of employers;
- providing assistance to students ... in finding appropriate jobs, continuing their education, or entering into additional training programs, and linking them with other community services necessary for a successful transition from school to work;
- following up to assess student performance in the program; and
- linking classroom development activities ... with employer-industry strategies for upgrading the skills of workers.

School-to-Work Coordinators

Because they are so diverse and so important, connecting activities are typically undertaken by a teacher or counselor—or by a group of teachers and counselors—serving as school-to-work coordinator(s) who are responsible for supporting students and employers in four areas:

- **Coordination activities** provide a direct linkage between the classroom and the work site. These activities include matching students with work-based learning opportunities, encouraging attendance at school and at the work site, and correlating the content of school instruction with work-site learning.
- **Liaison activities** keep the lines of communication open among employers, teachers, the school, parents, students, and other community partners.
  - **Technical assistance** involves school-to-work coordinators in the training of teachers, workplace mentors, school mentors, and counselors.
  - **Placement assistance** includes pre-employment activities such as career counseling, locating training stations, and monitoring student progress.

Glencoe Resources

The *Strategies for Implementing Connecting Activities* booklet will aid you in using connecting activities in your career program. The booklet provides proven approaches to integrating classroom learning in the workplace.

STRATEGIES FOR IMPLEMENTING CONNECTING ACTIVITIES

SUCCEEDING in the World of Work

SIXTH EDITION

Teaching All Aspects of Industry

The Carl D. Perkins Vocational and Applied Technology Education Act was passed by Congress in 1990 "to make the United States more competitive in the world economy by developing more fully the academic and occupational skills of all segments of the population." This legislation emphasizes the importance of "experience in and understanding of all aspects of the industry the student is preparing to enter." Both the Carl D. Perkins Act and the School-to-Work Opportunities Act of 1994 list these components of "all aspects of industry":

- planning;
- management;
- finances;
- technical and production skills;
- underlying principles of technology;
- labor and community issues;
- health and safety issues; and
- environmental issues.

Advantages of Teaching All Aspects of Industry

Teaching all aspects of industry provides important benefits to both students and employers.

Those students who have prepared for full-time employment by gaining an understanding of and experience in all aspects of the industry or industry sector that interests them are prepared to deal with changes in the workplace they will inevitably face. Their skills will enable them to move easily from one set of responsibilities to another; their competencies will allow them to transfer their skills to other, related industries. Students who have learned all aspects of an industry are prepared for change and are ready for lifelong learning; they can become productive workers in a variety of settings.

An industry clearly benefits from workers who bring these skills and competencies to the workplace. An industry cannot adapt to advancing technology and changing economic needs unless its workers are prepared and flexible—as are workers who have been taught all aspects of industry as students.

Experience—Not Exposure

To teach all aspects of an industry, it is essential to involve employers and mentors as well as counselors and classroom teachers, for students need to become actively engaged in all aspects of their chosen industry—planning, management, finances, technical and production skills, underlying principles of technology, labor and community issues, health and safety issues, and environmental issues. These goals can be met through job shadowing, workplace mentoring, paid or unpaid experience, and classroom programs in both technical and academic courses.

Unit Labs

New to this edition are **Unit Labs—Aspects of Industry**. These lab activities give students an opportunity to explore all aspects of industry in relation to specific careers. Students investigate the various areas through worksite learning experiences; Internet, magazine, book, and newspaper research; and through personal interviews.

Marketing Your School-to-Work Program

Your school-to-work program— however well planned and carefully administered—cannot succeed without the support of individuals and groups throughout the community. An essential step in developing and maintaining a school-to-work program is enlisting the support, enthusiasm, and participation of others, including:

- high school educators;
- elementary and junior high educators;
- postsecondary educators;
- local leaders of business and industry;
- local labor leaders;
- government officials;
- the student body; and
- parents.

Researching Expectations

As you and your colleagues begin developing your school-to-work program, you are bound to feel enthusiastic and optimistic. You understand that this special program offers unique advantages to all involved. Still, you must not assume that other educators, business and labor leaders, government officials, and parents and students share your enthusiasm.

Before you can effectively market your school-to-work program in the community, you have to learn about community members' interests, opinions, and expectations. For example:

- What do they think of current educational programs?
- How well do they think graduates are prepared for the world of work—whether or not those graduates go on to postsecondary education?
- What assistance are students currently given in planning their secondary courses? What other kinds of assistance do community members think students should have?
- What aspects of a school-to-work program do members of each group in the community find most appealing? Why?

- What sources of information— especially information about education—reach the members of each group most effectively?

Depending on your school's resources and needs, you can select one—or more than one—method of gathering this information from community members. Focus-group meetings can be especially effective; they offer you an opportunity to meet with people face-to-face, to share information directly, and to record and gauge participants' responses. You can also use telephone interviews, one-on-one conferences, mailed surveys using return letters or postcards, and electronic survey techniques. Whatever method you choose, be sure to reach a fair cross-section of each group; while gathering opinions from only those who are already

enthusiastic about school-to-work programs may be encouraging at first, it won't help you build that base of support your program will need in the months and years ahead.

Enlisting Support

Once you understand the opinions and expectations of community members, you'll be able to present your school-to-work program and inspire the support of various groups and individuals.

One proven method of engaging community members is to invite them to participate in planning and developing your program. Involve them in answering questions such as: What specific goals do you think we should have for our students? How can we help them meet those goals? What can parents do to support our school-to-work program? What connections can we make with local two-year colleges? Four-year colleges? Businesses? Industries? Labor organizations? Government agencies? Everyone whose responses to such

An essential step in developing and maintaining a school-to-work program is enlisting the support, enthusiasm, and participation of others.

questions have been taken seriously will be committed to helping make the school-to-work program succeed.

As you focus on developing community support, you will probably want to conduct a series of small group meetings with people who are—or should become—interested in the school-to-work program. Explain your program as it has been developed so far, and schedule a presentation by a speaker to whom the participants can relate. For example:

- Recent high school graduates— including some who have enrolled in college programs—might talk about the problems they have faced in finding and developing careers.
- An economist might discuss long-range employment trends and the kinds of preparation workers will need.
- Labor leaders—as well as business and industry leaders—could outline the kinds of training and preparation they feel are most useful.
- Mentors, employers, counselors, teachers, and student-workers from other schools might discuss their own experiences.

In each of these meetings, you will want to allow plenty of time for discussion, questions, and input from members of the community.

Maintaining Interest

Although a school-to-work program benefits everyone involved—teachers, students, parents, mentors, employers, and other employees—it is still useful to spend time and energy acknowledging their efforts. Banners, posters, and local advertisements can be effective means of expressing appreciation; so can awards, recognition meetings or banquets, and other social occasions.

It is also important that everyone involved—and everyone affected—be kept informed about your school-to-work program. You might use newsletters, regularly scheduled meetings, and conferences to stay in touch with parents and students. A brochure, video, a weekly or monthly newspaper column, and public service announcements on local radio and TV can help inform the community about your school-to-work program and its progress.

Integrating Career Education Across the Curriculum

In a recent survey of high school graduates—many of whom had gone directly to work rather than into postsecondary education—more than half the respondents said their high schools should have placed more emphasis on the following academic skills:

- communication;
- reading;
- mathematics; and
- science.

However, these students—like so many others—failed to recognize the relevance and value of much of their course work while they were in high school. Integrating students' academic and career/technical learning can make students more aware of the connections between school work and the real world—before it's too late to take advantage of those connections.

> **Integrating students' academic and career/technical learning can make students more aware of the connections between school work and the real world.**

In addition, a program that integrates career and academic learning is best able to foster students' development of the SCANS Foundation Skills and Workplace Competencies. Integrated learning offers the following additional benefits to students:

- It provides examples of real-world learning and thus establishes patterns of lifelong learning.
- It improves the academic achievement of all students—including those who will begin their careers directly after high school, those who will go on to postsecondary education or training, and those who will obtain four-year college degrees.
- It supports students in making realistic plans for their own careers and education.

Developing and implementing a program of integrated learning also offers important benefits to teachers. It can promote a heightened degree of professionalism among faculty members, reduce the sense of isolation many teachers feel, and encourage teachers to experiment with new teaching strategies.

Team Planning and Team Teaching

In many cases, integrated learning is developed through team planning. You might begin with the simplest possible team: just you and one teacher from another discipline—math or English, for example. Together, you can discuss your routine lesson plans and agree on simple changes that will connect the two disciplines. Eventually, teachers of career classes may meet with teachers from traditional academic areas—English, math, science, and social studies—to develop integrated curriculum plans for an entire semester.

Another approach to integrated learning is team teaching, in which you work with one other teacher—or even several others—to plan a presentation of interrelated materials from two (or more) fields. Then you work together in both classrooms, presenting and developing the materials in each area and integrating it with the materials your co-teacher presents.

Addressing Cultural Diversity

Your students are preparing to enter a workforce noted for its cultural diversity. For students to become productive workers and responsible citizens, it is essential that they be open to cultural differences.

The following chart shows major ethnic groups as percentages of the total population in 1995 and, as projected, in 2025.

MAJOR ETHNIC GROUPS IN THE UNITED STATES		
Percentage of the Total Population	**1995**	**2025**
African Americans	12.6%	14.2%
Asian Americans	3.7	7.5
European Americans (Non-Hispanic)	72.7	60.5
Hispanic Americans	10.2	16.8
Native Americans	0.8	1.0

Textbook Resources

The contents of *Succeeding in the World of Work*—including the photographs, the Case Studies, and other special features—have been selected to help students recognize and discuss issues of cultural diversity. In addition, each chapter in the *Teacher's Wraparound Edition* includes a special feature, **Addressing Workplace Diversity**, which you can use as the basis of class discussion. During class activities, you may also find it appropriate to integrate questions related to cultural diversity. For example, you might expand a discussion by asking:

- Would your response change if the customer were not a native speaker of English? If so, how?
- Would you direct your employee differently if she were an African American? An Asian American?
- Would your decision change if your co-worker were a male (female)? From your own ethnic background? From a different background? Why?

As students learn about skills and attitudes in the workplace, they should keep in mind the diversity of the people they are likely to encounter in every aspect of their working lives. In class and in one-on-one conferences, you can help students consider the diversity of the U.S. population, not only in terms of ethnicity, but also in terms of customs, attitudes, religious beliefs, language backgrounds, and physical capabilities. High school students should come to understand and put into practice throughout their careers that: *ability and success do not come packaged in one skin color or one gender.*

Addressing Workplace Diversity

By the year 2000, women will make up 64 percent of the American workforce. Minorities and new immigrants will make up 26 percent. Only 15 percent of those entering the workforce after 2000 will be white, native-born males. The greatest growth in employees will be among African Americans and Hispanics.

Integrating Technology into Your Career Education Program

Technology—particularly computers and computer-related technology—is changing the way people work, play, and live. Telecommuting allows people to work from home and spend more time with their families. Interactive educational software allows people to learn about the world around them as they "play" at exploring or designing. Access to the Internet allows people to do research and exchange ideas with others from all over the world.

Teaching students about technology is especially important in a career education program. Students must learn about technology in order for them to compete and succeed in the world of work.

Succeeding in the World of Work gives you a platform for teaching and integrating technology into your career education program. Updated text, end-of-chapter activities, and *Teacher's Wraparound Edition* activities place greater emphasis on the relationship between knowing about and understanding technology, and succeeding in the world of work.

> **Students must learn about technology in order for them to compete and succeed in the world of work.**

Student Text

The text reflects changes in technology. How modern technology affects not only what work people do, but how and where they work is discussed extensively.

In addition, Chapter 17, **Technology in the Workplace**, gives students specific information about technology as it applies to almost every aspect of their lives. The chapter describes how computer and communications technology affects us at home, school, and work. It also describes equipment that uses advanced technologies.

End-of-Chapter Activities

New to this edition are end-of-chapter activities, which include **SCANS Foundation Skills** and **Workplace Competencies**. The SCANS activities instruct students how to select technology, apply technology to task, and maintain or troubleshoot technology.

Teacher's Wraparound Edition

Teacher's Wraparound Edition activities also cover the SCANS workplace competencies for Technology. In every chapter, there are computer activity suggestions, including spreadsheets, databases, and word-processing. Also in every chapter, there are *Teacher's Wraparound Edition* activities called the **Internet Connection** that provide strategies for using the Internet in the classroom.

Other Resources

The ancillary package includes the *Workforce 2000 Interactive Training Library*. The training library includes a video that contains segments related to each chapter. A bar code in the *Teacher's Wraparound Edition* allows you to locate the chapter section on the video. *Career Exploration Software* is also available. Students can use the software for career planning and research. The program is further enhanced by *Career Exploration Videos* that provide insight into a variety of careers.

In addition the *Print, Media, and Internet Handbook* provides a comprehensive list of resources corresponding to the contents of each chapter in *Succeeding in the World of Work*.

Several outside resources also may be available to help you bring technology to your students. Among these resources are online services, newspapers, magazines, and school resources.

- **Online Services.** If your school or local library has access to an online service, schedule time to have the service demonstrated to students. Online services are an excellent way of showing students how to access a database and conduct research. One online service to check out is the National Students Research Center. Using the National Public Telecomputing Network (TELNET), students can visit an electronic library and review abstracts on a variety of topics.

- **Newspapers and Magazines.** Find newspaper and magazine articles that describe how technology has changed certain jobs or the way people do their jobs. For example, you might find an article about how electronic banking has affected bank tellers and account service representatives. Then, you could visit a local bank to talk to these workers about how their work has changed.

The business section of a newspaper is an excellent source for up-to-the-minute information about how technology is affecting jobs and businesses. Have students bring these sections to class and discuss at least one article per week. If your local newspaper doesn't have a business section, find out if your school or local library carries newspapers from a city in your area that does.

Also check libraries for *The Wall Street Journal*, *Business Week*, *Fortune*, and other major newspapers and magazines. Again, have students bring articles to class to discuss how technology is affecting jobs and the workplace.

- **School Resources.** Introduce students to technology by planning activities with other teachers and students responsible for computer and audio/visual equipment. For example, have students role-play job interviews with each other and videotape them. Other possibilities include using a computer to create a résumé or using an online newspaper to find interesting employment ads.

SCANS and Succeeding in the World of Work

In 1991, the U.S. Department of Labor released a report entitled, What Work Requires of Schools: A SCANS Report for America 2000. The SCANS report identified five competencies which, in conjunction with a three-part foundation of skills and personal qualities, lie at the heart of job performance and are needed by all workers in order to prosper in the emerging workplace. These skills and competencies have been integrated into the *Succeeding in the World of Work* program.

THE FOUNDATION	*Succeeding in the World of Work*	

Basic Skills—reading, writing, math, listening, and speaking.	The following chapters deal specifically with reading, writing, speaking, and listening:
	Chapters 1–25
		In the following activities, students demonstrate competency in basic skills:
		• Building SCANS Foundation Skills and Workplace Competencies
		   Math—Chapters 1, 9, 23, 24
		   Speaking—Chapters 2, 7, 16
		   Listening—Chapters 4, 15
		   Writing—Chapters 5, 12, 14–16, 22, 24
		   Reading—Chapter 12
		• Connecting Academics to the Workplace
		   Math—Chapters 1–4, 6–8, 13, 14, 17, 19–23, 25
		   Social Studies—Chapters 15, 18, 25
		   Language Arts—Chapters 15, 19
		• Real World Workshop—Chapters 6, 15

Thinking Skills—creative thinking, decision making, problem solving, seeing things in the mind's eye, knowing how to learn, and reasoning.	The following chapters deal specifically with thinking skills:
	Chapters 1–25
		In the following activities, students demonstrate competency in thinking skills:
		• Thinking Critically—Chapters 1–25
		• Building SCANS Foundation Skills and Workplace Competencies
		   Decision Making—Chapter 5
		   Knowing How to Learn—Chapters 6, 8, 10, 25
		   Reasoning—Chapter 7
		   Problem Solving—Chapters 11, 12, 20, 21
		   Seeing Things in the Mind's Eye—Chapter 18
		   Creative Thinking—Chapter 19
		• Real-World Workshop—Chapters 5, 16

Personal Qualities—responsibility, self-esteem, sociability, self-management, and integrity and honesty.	The following chapters deal specifically with personal qualities:
	Chapters 2, 4, 7, 8, 9, 10, 13, 14, 24, 25
		In the following activities, students demonstrate competency in the development of personal qualities:
		• Building SCANS Foundation Skills and Workplace Competencies
		   Self-Esteem—Chapters 3, 7
		   Integrity/Honesty—Chapters 6, 17
		   Sociability—Chapter 8
		   Self-Management—Chapter 13
		• Connecting Academics to the Workplace
		   Human Relations—Chapter 13

WORKPLACE COMPETENCIES	*Succeeding in the World of Work*	

Resources—allocate time, money, material and facility resources, and human resources.	The following chapters deal specifically with resources:
	
	Chapters
	2, 16, 18, 20
		In the following activities, students demonstrate competency with resources:
		• Building SCANS Foundation Skills and Workplace Competencies
		  Allocating Time—Chapters 3, 6
		  Allocating Money—Chapter 25
		• Connecting Academics to the Workplace
		  Social Studies and *Language Arts*—Chapter 18
		• Real-World Workshop—Chapter 18

Interpersonal Skills—work in teams, teach others, serve customers, lead, negotiate, and work with people from culturally diverse backgrounds.	The following chapters deal specifically with interpersonal skills:
	
	Chapters
	2, 4, 8, 10, 12,
	13, 14, 15, 16
		In the following activities, students demonstrate competency in interpersonal skills:
		• Building SCANS Foundation Skills and Workplace Competencies
		  Teaching Others—Chapters 1, 15
		  Serving Clients/Customers—Chapter 4
		  Participating as a Team Member—Chapters 5, 10
		  Exercising Leadership—Chapters 7, 14, 24
		  Working with Diverse Cultures—Chapter 13
		  Negotiating—Chapter 21
		• Connecting Academics to the Workplace
		  Foreign Language—Chapter 8
		  Computer Science—Chapter 13
		• Developing Teamwork and Leadership Skills—Chapters 1–25

Information—acquire and evaluate, organize and maintain, interpret and communicate, and use computers to process information.	The following chapters deal specifically with information:
	
	Chapters
	2, 3, 4, 5, 6, 7,
	12, 13, 15, 16,
	17, 23
		In the following activities, students demonstrate competency in information:
		• Building SCANS Foundation Skills and Workplace Competencies
		  Organizing and Maintaining Information—Chapters 2, 18, 20
		  Acquiring and Evaluating Information—Chapters 9, 16, 19, 23
		• Connecting Academics to the Workplace
		  Chapters 1, 3–7, 9–12, 14, 15, 17, 20–22
		• Real World Workshop—Chapters 12, 19–22
		• School-to-Work Connection—Chapters 1–25
		• Individual Career Plan—Chapters 1–25

Systems—understand systems, monitor and correct performance, and improve and design systems.	The following chapters deal specifically with systems: **Chapters 11, 12, 14,** **19, 20, 21, 23**	In the following activities, students demonstrate competency in systems: • Connecting Academics to the Workplace—Chapters 1–25

Technology—select technology, apply technology to task, and maintain and troubleshoot technology.	The following chapters deal specifically with technology:
	
	Chapters
	1, 3, 11, 15, 17
		In the following activities, students demonstrate competency in technology:
		• Building SCANS Foundation Skills and Workplace Competencies
		  Selecting Technology—Chapters 3, 8, 17
		  Maintaining and Troubleshooting Technology—Chapter 11
		• Connecting Academics to the Workplace
		  Computer Science—Chapters 6, 18, 23, 24
		• Real-World Workshop—Chapter 17

Using Cooperative Learning

Both in the workplace and the classroom, emphasis on teamwork is growing. Working in teams is so much a part of the workplace today that many employers give prospective employees inventories and assessments to determine their ability to function within a team framework.

In the classroom, teachers are moving away from the lecture format to more student involvement via learning teams. It makes sense for students to practice teamwork at school so that they can carry that skill to the workplace and to other areas of life.

> It makes sense for students to practice teamwork at school so that they can carry that skill to the workplace and to other areas of life.

Cooperative learning offers the classroom teacher a structured method of teaching team-building, collaborative social skills, and team decision making while teaching basic concepts.

Benefits of Cooperative Learning

Cooperative learning offers many benefits, including the following:

* Through higher level thinking, students are drawn into learning situations that require them to be directly involved. Each student must make a contribution as well as process input from others.
* Students discover how to work with people of all types. Schools with racially or ethnically mixed populations often improve interracial and multicultural relationships among students.
* The pressures of competition, common in many teaching situations, are diminished as students learn to work in a cooperative atmosphere.
* Empathy grows as students are compelled to consider the feelings of others when they work closely together.
* Communication and social skills are strengthened.

* Students learn to work through conflicts.
* Students develop self-esteem as they support and encourage each other in the pursuit of successful outcomes. Attitudes become more positive toward self and others.

Structures

A variety of structures can be used to implement cooperative learning. The following are some of the most widely used learning modes in cooperative learning. You can adapt these structures to fit course content and your own teaching style.

* *Student Teams Achievement.* Students are assigned to teams, the teacher presents the lesson to the class as a whole, then teams work together to make sure all members understand the information. Weekly quizzes assess achievement.
* *Team-Games Tournament.* The weekly quizzes of the Student Teams Achievement mode are replaced with weekly tournaments (or competitions).
* *Jigsaw I.* Divide an assignment into separate parts (one for each team member). Each team member works independently to gather the necessary information. Through the cooperation of everyone on the team, the information is collected, organized, and reported back to the class.
* *Jigsaw II.* This learning mode is more demanding than Jigsaw I because the team is given the entire assignment and team members determine how the tasks and responsibilities will be divided.
* *Learning Together.* Students work together to complete an activity and produce a finished product.
* *Group Investigation.* Students accept greater responsibility because they decide what they will learn, how they will organize their group to accomplish the task, and how they will share what they learn with the rest of the class.

Teacher Responsibilities

The teacher is responsible for preparing the students for the cooperative learning process. The following will help you establish an effective cooperative learning environment.

- Assign students to heterogeneous groups of four to six. Mix the group in ability, sex, and ethnicity.
- Coordinate the efforts of all participants in the group.
- Arrange the classroom so students can face each other as they work.
- Set the task and goal structure and make sure the team goal is well defined and understood.
- Provide the appropriate materials.
- Discuss cooperation and social skills, encourage all students to participate, and express the need to support team members.
- Monitor student interaction. Intervene when necessary to mediate or solve problems and teach skills.
- Evaluate student outcomes.

Student Responsibilities

Students also have responsibilities in cooperative learning. In order to accomplish a goal as a team, students must:

- work toward group goals, yet understand that individual accountability is expected;
- contribute their own ideas;
- understand that they are responsible for one another's learning as well as their own;
- have tolerance for individual differences;

- draw upon their own creativity and on the strengths of their teammates;
- communicate effectively with one another; and
- recognize that the differences among team members are a form of enrichment rather than deficits.

Cooperative Learning in this Text

Succeeding in the World of Work provides many opportunities for cooperative learning. Activities such as **Developing Teamwork and Leadership Skills** are designed as group activities; you can easily adapt others. For example, assign students to work in pairs to discuss and complete the activities **Reviewing Key Terms** and **Recalling Key Concepts**.

Cooperative learning is especially effective for more difficult learning tasks such as problem solving and critical thinking. Divide students into groups of four to complete the **Thinking Critically** activities or, activities that require research, and have them present their findings to the class.

The *Teacher's Wraparound Edition* also provides opportunities for cooperative learning with **Implementing Teamwork**. These activities allow students to help each other and increase their own self-esteem by working in teams or pairs.

Implementing Teamwork

Organize students into brainstorming teams of five to six members. Have students discuss how technology is changing the global workplace. Each group should choose one technological trend and predict how that trend will affect the global workplace.

Using Alternative Means of Assessment

Evaluation of student performance is fundamental to the teaching and learning process. As a teacher, you will need a variety of ways to assess what your students have learned.

One traditional method of measuring student progress is a written test that evaluates recall of subject content. Today, however, it is necessary to assess far more than students' rote learning skills. New curriculum objectives focus on the acquisition of knowledge and skills that will help students function in the work world, such as critical thinking, problem solving, communication, and human relations skills. The acquisition of those skills is not so easily evaluated using the traditional paper-and-pencil test.

> **As a teacher, you will need a variety of ways to assess what your students have learned.**

Performance Assessment

Performance assessment carries out a specific task, often through role-playing. For example, how does the student perform in an interview? Or, how does the student handle a work-related conflict with a co-worker? A paper-and-pencil test will not demonstrate your students' skills in these areas.

Succeeding in the World of Work provides you with many activities, projects, and situations that create opportunities for alternative assessment. Within the end-of-chapter activities are **Building SCANS Foundation Skills and Workplace Competencies**. Many of the skills and competencies, such as decision making and participating as a team member, are scenario-based. Students must write or demonstrate responses to real-life situations. **Connecting Academics to the Workplace** links various academic areas to work scenarios that students

might actually encounter. In **Developing Teamwork and Leadership Skills**, students work in teams to complete a project. With **Real-World Workshop** students apply learned skills to potential career situations. **School-to-Work Connection** takes students out of the classroom and provides practical work experience, and **Individual Career Plan** allows students to develop their own career plan.

Assessment Strategies

The aforementioned activities require students to demonstrate learned skills and apply ideas, and provide you the opportunity to use alternative assessment strategies. Additionally, the *Teacher's Wraparound Edition* includes an assessment section for each chapter. Each assessment activity is broken down into one of the following subheads: oral, performance, process, and content.

The chart on the next page can help you determine which assessment strategies will work best for you and your students. By comparing the advantages and disadvantages of different strategies, you will be able to make this text's variety of assessment strategies work to your advantage.

PROFESSIONAL NOTES

ASSESSMENT STRATEGIES

STRATEGIES	ADVANTAGES	DISADVANTAGES

Objective measures
Multiple choice
Matching
Item sets
True/False
	Reliable, easy to validate
	Objective, if designed effectively
	Low cost, efficient
	Automated administration
	Lends to equating
		Measures cognitive knowledge
		  effectively
		Limited on other measures
		Not a good measure of overall
		  performance

Written measures
Essays
Restricted response
Written simulations
Case analysis
Problem-solving exercises
	Face validity (real life)
	In-depth assessment
	Measures writing skills and higher level
	  skills
	Reasonable developmental costs and
	  time
		Subjective scoring
		Time consuming and expensive to score
		Limited breadth
		Difficult to equate
		Moderate reliability

Oral measures
Oral examinations
Interviews
	Measures communications and
	  interpersonal skills
	In-depth assessment with varied
	  stimulus materials
	Learner involvement
		Costly and time consuming
		Limited reliability
		Narrow sample of content
		Scoring difficult, need multiple raters

Simulated activities In-basket Computer simulations	Moderate reliability Performance-based measure	Costly and time consuming Difficult to score, administer, and develop

**Portfolio and product
  analysis**
Work samples
Projects
Work diaries and logs
Achievement records
	Provides information not normally
	  available
	Learner involvement
	Face validity (real life)
	Easy to collect information
		Costly to administer
		Labor and paper intensive
		Difficult to validate or equate
		Biased toward best samples or
		  outstanding qualities

Performance measures Demonstrations Presentations Performances Production work Observation	Job-related Relatively easy to administer In-depth assessment Face validity	Rater training required Hard to equate Subjective scoring Time consuming if breadth is needed
Performance records References Performance rating forms Parental rating	Efficient Low cost Easy to administer	Low reliability Subjective Hard to equate Rater judgment
Self-evaluation	Learner involvement and empowerment Learner responsibility Measures dimensions not available otherwise	May be biased or unrealistic

Source: *Business Education Forum*, April 1996.

Teaching Critical-Thinking Skills

The teaching of critical-thinking skills is a goal of all educational disciplines. Today's business environment—be it a corporate setting, self-employment, or a small business—is highly competitive and demands skilled employees. One of the factors in achieving success in the workforce is an individual's ability to deal with the varied demands of the fast-paced world of business, which requires insightful decision making, creative problem solving, and interacting with diverse groups—be it employees, management, investors, customers, or clients. By teaching students critical thinking, you are equipping them with essential skills necessary for achieving success in today's workforce.

Critical thinking, which is the process of reasonably or logically deciding what to do or believe, involves the ability to:

- compare and contrast,
- solve problems,
- make decisions,
- analyze and evaluate,
- synthesize and transfer knowledge, and
- conduct metacognitive exercises.

> **By teaching students critical thinking, you are equipping them with essential skills necessary for achieving success in today's workforce.**

Critical-thinking skills are important for the following reasons:

- Critical-thinking skills help students investigate their own ways of solving problems and finding creative resolutions.
- Critical-thinking skills lead students to investigations that compare and contrast what they know with unknowns.
- Critical-thinking skills allow students to make decisions about their own learning and also make them aware of the processes they use.

How to Teach Critical Thinking

How, then, do we teach critical thinking? Doesn't all learning require thinking? What is meant by higher-level thinking? These questions and questions like them require teachers to reflect on the instructional strategies used in daily lessons and include opportunities for students to reason and think about what is being learned.

All learning requires thinking. Benjamin Bloom's Taxonomy of the Cognitive Domain is probably the most widely recognized schema for levels of thinking.

Each of Bloom's cognitive categories includes a list of a variety of thinking skills and indicates the kind of behavior students are expected to perform at the objectives or goals of specific learning tasks. Here are some examples.

- *Knowledge:* define, recognize, recall, identify, label, understand, examine, show, collect
- *Comprehension:* translate, interpret, explain, describe, summarize, extrapolate
- *Application:* apply, solve, experiment, show, predict
- *Analysis:* connect, relate, differentiate, classify, arrange, check, group, distinguish, organize, categorize, detect, compare, infer
- *Synthesis:* produce, propose, design, plan, combine, formulate, compose, hypothesize, construct
- *Evaluation:* appraise, judge, criticize, decide

The wealth of activities and guidance provided both in the student text and this *Teacher's Wraparound Edition* will help you integrate critical-thinking skills into your daily plans. Each chapter includes the case studies **Exploring Careers** and **Excellent Business Practices** with critical thinking questions relevant to the topic presented; as part of the end-of-chapter activities there are also a series of critical thinking questions. In the *Teacher's Wraparound Edition*, the **Guided Practice** activities provide critical thinking questions for every section of the chapter. These questions ask students to:

- understand meaning and views;
- look for relationships, causes, patterns, and alternatives; and
- make judgments, choices, and decisions based on information.

Below are some guidelines for integrating and teaching critical-thinking skills.

- *Let students know* they are engaging in aspects of critical thinking. For example, if students are to research a given topic and answer questions about it or report on it (as students are asked to do throughout end-of-chapter activities), tell them that they are analyzing and evaluating. Extend the application of this skill to other areas of students' lives; tell them that they constantly analyze and evaluate music, conversations with friends, magazine or newspaper articles, and television programs. This will help demonstrate to students that they have had experience in using the skill.

- *Use activities that focus* on open-ended problems. Activities with no "right answers" open up the possibilities and foster greater growth and a safe environment for using creative approaches to problem solving. For example, in the chapter feature **Ethics in Action**, students are given a hypothetical business situation and asked to make a decision. When possible, have them share their ideas and discuss how they arrived at their decisions. In this way, you can point out that different people use different thought processes to arrive at solutions to problems.

- *Organize students* in cooperative learning groups so that they can see how others solve problems, give each other feedback, and try out new ideas in a safe environment. For example, every chapter has a **Developing Teamwork and Leadership Skills** activity that provides students with opportunities for cooperative learning.

- *Provide feedback* and use assessments that measure students' growth and performance in their newly acquired skills. Your feedback is important in encouraging students to feel comfortable experimenting with new ideas and new ways to look at problem solving and critical thinking. For example, by using alternative assessments, such as interviews and simulated activities, you can better track each student's growth and understanding of critical thinking skills.

All the above suggestions, and others you find throughout this resource, will help you guide your students to perform more productively and successfully in their professional lives.

Teaching Ethical Decision-Making Skills

Why do you need to teach ethical decision-making skills in your career education classes? During the course of your students' work lives, they will encounter many situations that will require them to make decisions about their actions. Often, the ethical aspects of a decision are not even considered until after the decision has been made. However, at that point it is often too late to consider the consequences and see how the decision will affect the people involved. Helping students learn about ethical behavior and how to consider the effects of a decision before it is made are important topics for your course.

The goal of teaching ethical decision-making skills is not to teach values, but rather to help students clarify their ethical beliefs and to learn how to evaluate ethical situations in light of their personal beliefs. Students need to learn how to evaluate their actions and to ask questions such as, "Will I think well of myself if I take this action?" "Would I want others to know about my actions?"

The Ethical Decision-Making Model

Your students will learn to analyze the ethics of a situation better if they have a model to use in deliberating the issues and considering the welfare of the people affected by a decision. The following basic decision model has five steps to help students with the decision-making process.

1. What are the ethical issues?

2. What are the alternatives?

3. Who are the affected parties?

4. How do the alternatives affect the parties?

5. What is your decision?

There are ethics features, entitled **Ethics in Action**, in every other chapter of this text. These features provide students with a hypothetical situation in which they are asked to make a decision. Use the first ethics feature as a sample and help students build the decision model. The *Teacher's Wraparound Edition* includes teaching strategies for each **Ethics in Action** feature in **Teaching Ethics in Action**.

Classroom Strategies

You may want to use these features for class discussion or have your students develop their writing skills by requiring them to write short reports. In either case, students need to understand that there is no right or wrong answer. As they discuss or consider each feature, they are discussing and considering possibilities. Students should feel that the classroom is a relatively risk-free environment in which to make ethical decisions.

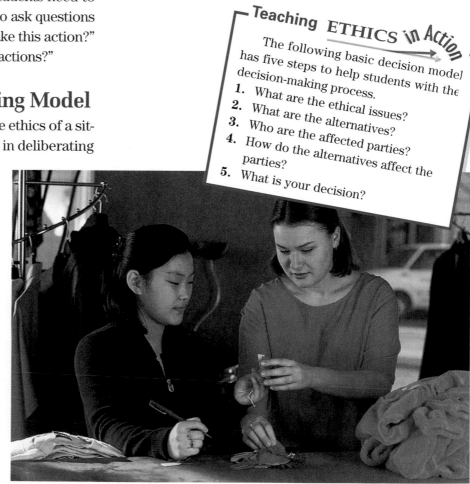

Teaching ETHICS in Action

The following basic decision model has five steps to help students with the decision-making process.

1. What are the ethical issues?
2. What are the alternatives?
3. Who are the affected parties?
4. How do the alternatives affect the parties?
5. What is your decision?

Meeting Individual Needs and Learning Styles

One of your greatest challenges as a teacher is to provide a positive learning environment for *all* students in your classroom. Because each student has his or her own unique set of abilities, perceptions, and needs, the learning styles and physical abilities of your students may vary widely.

Assisting Students with Individual Needs

In order to help you provide all your students with a positive learning experience, this text provides a variety of activities. This diversity will stimulate student interest, motivate learning, and facilitate understanding.

The *Teacher's Wraparound Edition* provides additional individualized activities. Each section will include SCANS activities at three levels. Each of these activities is specifically designed and coded for a variety of student ability levels.

- *Level 1* designates basic activities designed for the ability range of all students.
- *Level 2* activities provide practical applications designed for students who have mastered the concepts presented. Average to above-average students should be able to complete Level 2 activities.
- *Level 3* activities challenge students to expand their perspectives of the basic concepts learned. Level 3 activities are designed for the ability range of above-average students.

Also included in the *Teacher's Wraparound Edition* are **Independent Practice** activities. These activities provide additional reinforcement and allow students to progress at their own pace.

Teaching Students with Special Needs

Students in your classroom may be physically challenged. They may have impaired hearing or vision, learning disabilities, or behavior disorders (all of which may interfere with their ability to learn). Learning styles of your students can also vary. Some students may be visual

learners; others may learn more effectively through hands-on activities. Some students may work well independently, while others need the interaction of others. Students may come from a variety of cultural backgrounds, and some students may have limited English proficiency.

Once you determine the special needs of your students, you can identify the areas in the curriculum that may present barriers to them. In order to remove those barriers, you may need to modify your teaching methods.

In the bottom columns of every chapter opener of the *Teacher's Wraparound Edition* are **Meeting Special Needs** and **Addressing Learning Styles**. **Meeting Special Needs** provides tips on how to teach students with various special needs, and **Addressing Learning Styles** focuses on ways to teach students based upon their various learning styles.

On the following pages are two charts. The first chart, **Meeting Special Needs**, describes some of the special needs you may encounter with students in your classroom and identifies sources of information. Also provided are tips for modifying your teaching style to accommodate the special needs of your students and locations of teaching tips with the *Teacher's Wraparound Edition*.

The second chart, **Seven Ways of Learning**, will help you identify your students' learning styles. The chart gives a description of each type of learner; describes the likes of each type, what each type is good at, and how each learns best; and names some famous learners.

MEETING SPECIAL NEEDS

SUBJECT	DESCRIPTION	SOURCES OF INFORMATION
Limited Proficiency in English	Certain students often speak English as a second language, or not at all. Customs and behavior of people in the majority culture may be confusing for some of these students. Cultural values may inhibit some students from full participation in the classroom.	*Teaching English as a Second Language* *Mainstreaming and the Minority Child*
Behaviorally Disordered	Children with behavior disorders deviate from standards or expectations of behavior and impair the functioning of others and themselves. These children may also be gifted or learning disabled.	*Exceptional Children* *Journal of Special Education*
Visually Impaired	Children who are visually disabled have partial or total loss of sight. Individuals with visual impairments are not significantly different from their sighted peers in ability range or personality. However, blindness may affect cognitive, motor, and social development.	*Journal of Visual Impairment and Blindness* *Education of Visually Handicapped* *American Foundation for the Blind*
Hearing Impaired	Children who are hearing impaired have partial or total loss of hearing. Individuals with hearing impairments are not significantly different from their peers in ability range or personality. However, the chronic condition of deafness may affect cognitive, motor, social, and speech development.	*American Annals of the Deaf* *Journal of Speech and Hearing Research* *Sign Language Studies*
Physically Challenged	Children who are physically disabled fall into two categories—those with orthopedic impairments (use of one or more limbs severely restricted) and those with other health impairments.	*The Source Book for the Disabled* *Teaching Exceptional Children*
Gifted	Although no formal definition exists, these students can be described as having above average ability, task commitment, and creativity. They rank in the top five percent of their classes. They usually finish work more quickly than other students, and are capable of divergent thinking.	*Journal for the Education of the Gifted* *Gifted Child Quarterly* *Gifted Creative/Talented*
Learning Disabled	All learning disabled students have a problem in one or more areas, such as academic learning, language, perception, social-emotional adjustment, memory, or ability to pay attention.	*Journal of Learning Disabilities* *Learning Disability Quarterly*

MEETING SPECIAL NEEDS

TIPS FOR INSTRUCTION	CHAPTER
• Remember that students' ability to speak English does not reflect their academic ability. • Try to incorporate students' cultural experiences into your instruction. The help of a bilingual aide may be effective. • Include information about different cultures in your curriculum to help build students' self-image. • Avoid cultural stereotypes. • Encourage students to share their cultures in the classroom.	2, 3, 4, 12, 13, 21, 24, 25
• Work for long-term improvement; do not expect immediate success. • Talk with students about their strengths and weaknesses, and clearly outline objectives and tell how you will help them obtain their goals. • Structure schedules, rules, room arrangement, and safety for a conducive learning environment. • Model appropriate behavior for students and reinforce proper behavior. • Adjust group requirements for individual needs.	19
• Modify assignments as needed to help students become independent. • Teach classmates how to serve as guides for the visually impaired; pair students so sighted peers can assist in cooperative learning work. • Tape lectures and reading assignments for the visually impaired. • For the benefit of the visually impaired, encourage students to use their sense of touch; provide tactile models whenever possible. • Verbally describe people and events as they occur in the classroom for the visually impaired. • Limit unnecessary noise in the classroom.	23
• Provide favorable seating arrangement so hearing-impaired students can see speakers and read their lips (or interpreters can assist); avoid visual distractions. • Write out all instructions on paper or on the board; overhead projectors enable you to maintain eye contact while writing. • Avoid standing with your back to the window or light source.	1, 5, 15
• With the student, determine when you should offer aid. • Help other students and adults understand physically disabled students. • Learn about special devices or procedures and if any special necessary safety precautions are needed. • Allow students to participate in all activities including field trips, special events, and projects.	9, 22
• Emphasize concepts, theories, relationships, ideas, and generalizations. • Let students express themselves in a variety of ways including drawing, creative writing, or acting. • Make arrangements for students to work on independent projects. • Utilize public services and resources, such as agencies providing free and inexpensive materials, community services and programs, and people in the community with specific expertise. • Make arrangements for students to take selected subjects early.	11, 17
• Establish conditions and create an environment that leads to success. • Provide assistance and direction; clearly define rules, assignments, and duties. • Allow for pair interaction during class time; utilize peer helpers. • Practice skills frequently. • Distribute outlines of material presented in class. • Maintain student interest with games. • Allow extra time to complete tests and assignments.	6, 7, 8, 10, 14, 16, 18, 20

Meeting Individual Needs and Learning Styles

SEVEN WAYS OF LEARNING

TYPE	DESCRIPTION	LIKES TO...
Verbal/Linguistic Learner	Intelligence is related to words and language, written and spoken.	read, write, tell stories, play word games, and tell jokes and riddles.
Logical/Mathematical Learner	Intelligence deals with inductive and deductive thinking and reasoning, numbers, and abstractions.	perform experiments, solve puzzles, work with numbers, ask questions, and explore patterns and relationships.
Visual/Spatial Learner	Intelligence relies on the sense of sight and being able to visualize an object, including the ability to create mental images.	draw, build, design, and create things, daydream, do jigsaw puzzles and mazes, watch videos, look at photos, and draw maps and charts.
Musical/Rhythmic Learner	Intelligence is based on recognition of tonal patterns, including various environmental sounds, and on a sensitivity to rhythm and beats.	sing and hum, listen to music, play an instrument, move body when music is playing, and make up songs.
Bodily/Kinesthetic Learner	Intelligence is related to physical movement and the brain's motor cortex, which controls bodily motion.	learn by hands-on methods, demonstrate skill in crafts, tinker, perform, display physical endurance, and challenge self physically.
Interpersonal Learner	Intelligence operates primarily through person-to-person relationships and communication.	have lots of friends, talk to people, join groups, play cooperative games, solve problems as part of a group, and volunteer help when others need it.
Intrapersonal Learner	Intelligence is related to inner states of being, self-reflection, metacognition, and awareness of spiritual realities.	work alone, pursue own interests, daydream, keep a personal diary or journal, and think about starting own business.

SEVEN WAYS OF LEARNING

IS GOOD AT...	LEARNS BY...	FAMOUS LEARNERS	CHAPTER
memorizing names, dates, places, and trivia; spelling; using descriptive language; and creating imaginary worlds.	saying, hearing, and seeing words.	Maya Angelou—poet Abraham Lincoln—U.S. President and statesman Jerry Seinfeld—comedian Mary Hatwood Futrell—international teacher, leader, orator	6, 8, 21, 23, 25
math, reasoning, logic, problem solving, computing numbers mentally, moving from concrete to abstract, thinking conceptually, and organizing thoughts.	categorizing, classifying, and working with abstract patterns and relationships.	Stephen Hawking—physicist Albert Einstein—theoretical physicist Marilyn Burns—math educator Alexa Canady—neurosurgeon	3, 11, 18, 20, 24, 25
understanding the use of space and how to get around in it, thinking in three-dimensional terms, and imagining things in clear visual images.	visualizing, dreaming, using the mind's eye, and working with colors and pictures.	Pablo Picasso—artist Maria Martinez—Pueblo Indian famous for black pottery I. M. Pei—architect	1, 9, 16, 19, 25
remembering melodies; keeping time; mimicking beat and rhythm; noticing pitches, rhythms, and background and environmental sounds; and differentiating patterns in sounds.	rhythm, melody, and music.	Henry Mancini—composer Marian Anderson—contralto Midori—violinist Paul McCartney—singer, song writer, musician	10, 15, 25
physical activities such as sports, dancing, acting, and crafts.	touching, moving, interacting with space, and processing knowledge through bodily sensations.	Marcel Marceau—mime Jackie Joyner-Kersey—Olympic gold medalist in track and field Katherine Dunham—modern dancer and choreographer	7, 13, 17, 22, 24, 25
understanding people and their feelings, leading others, organizing, communicating, manipulating, mediating conflicts, and understanding and recognizing stereotypes and prejudices.	sharing, comparing, relating, cooperating, and interviewing.	Jimmy Carter—U.S. President and statesman Eleanor Roosevelt—First Lady and social reform advocate Lee Iacocca—President of Chrysler Corp. Mother Teresa—winner of Nobel Peace Prize	4, 12, 14, 25
understanding self, focusing inward on feelings/dreams, following instincts, pursuing interests, setting goals, and being original.	working alone, doing individualized projects, engaging in self-paced instruction, and having own space.	Admiral Richard E. Byrd—naval flier and Antarctic explorer Maria Montessori—educator and physician Sigmund Freud—psychotherapist Arnold Adoff—author and poet	2, 4, 5, 14, 25

Course Planning Guide

Full-Year Course Six-Week Grading System	

Grading Period	Chapter	Chapter Title
FIRST		*Self-Assessment*
	1	You and the World of Work
	2	Getting to Know Yourself
		Exploring Careers
	3	Researching Careers
	4	Entrepreneurship
SECOND	5	Developing an Individual Career Plan
		Finding a Job
	6	Finding and Applying for a Job
	7	Interviewing
		Joining the Workforce
	8	Beginning a New Job
THIRD	9	Workplace and Ethics
	10	Developing a Positive Attitude
	11	Workplace Health and Safety
	12	Workplace and Legal Matters
FOURTH		*Professional Development*
	13	Interpersonal Relationships at Work
	14	Teamwork and Leadership
	15	Professional Communication Skills
	16	Thinking Skills on the Job
FIFTH	17	Technology in the Workplace
	18	Time and Information Management
		Life Skills
	19	Economics and the Consumer
	20	Managing Your Money
SIXTH	21	Banking and Credit
	22	Buying Insurance
	23	Taxes and Social Security
		Lifelong Learning
	24	Adapting to Change
	25	Balancing Work and Personal Life

Full-Year Course
Nine-Week Grading System

WEEK 1 WEEK 2 WEEK 3 WEEK 4 WEEK 5 WEEK 6 WEEK 7 WEEK 8 WEEK 9

Grading Period	Chapter	Chapter Title
■ FIRST		*Self-Assessment*
	1	You and the World of Work
	2	Getting to Know Yourself
		Exploring Careers
	3	Researching Careers
	4	Entrepreneurship
	5	Developing an Individual Career Plan
■ SECOND		*Finding a Job*
	6	Finding and Applying for a Job
	7	Interviewing
		Joining the Workforce
	8	Beginning a New Job
	9	Workplace Ethics
	10	Developing a Positive Attitude
	11	Workplace Health and Safety
	12	Workplace Legal Matters
■ THIRD		*Professional Development*
	13	Interpersonal Relationships at Work
	14	Teamwork and Leadership
	15	Professional Communication Skills
	16	Thinking Skills on the Job
	17	Technology in the Workplace
	18	Time and Information Management
■ FOURTH		*Life Skills*
	19	Economics and the Consumer
	20	Managing Your Money
	21	Banking and Credit
	22	Buying Insurance
	23	Taxes and Social Security
		Lifelong Learning
	24	Adapting to Change
	25	Balancing Work and Personal Life

Block Scheduling

In most high schools in the United States, the typical school day is made up of six, seven, or eight class periods of 40 to 50 minutes that meet 180 days a year. In "block scheduling", class sessions are scheduled for longer periods of time over fewer days. For example, a school day of block scheduling might consist of four blocks of 90-minute sessions that run for 90 days, or half a school year.

In the following planning guide for *Succeeding in the World of Work*, to the right of each unit title is the suggested total number of days for that unit, based on a 90-minute class period; this number is the sum of the days suggested to teach each chapter in that unit. This schedule includes the presentation of the features provided in the *Teacher's Wraparound Edition* and end-of-chapter activities, as well as **Unit** and **Chapter Tests**, **Transparencies**, and **Student Activity Workbook**.

Optional activities, which enhance that particular chapter, are not listed but include **The School-to-Work Activity Handbook, Spanish Resources, Workforce 2000 Interactive Training Library,** and

the **Career Exploration Software**. These optional activities, of course, will require more time than given here for each chapter. Typically, optional activities take from one-third to one-half a day each. You may wish to include these optional activities if you find you have some extra time. Or, if you want your students to do one of the optional activities, you could do less of something else, say, fewer end-of-chapter activities.

As part of the ancillary package, you will find the **Implementing Block Scheduling** handbook. This booklet provides detailed guidelines for using *Succeeding in the World of Work* in a block scheduling environment.

UNIT/CHAPTER		DAYS
Unit 1: Self-Assessment		10
Chapter 1:	You and the World of Work	5
Chapter 2:	Getting to Know Yourself	5
Unit 2: Exploring Careers		10
Chapter 3:	Researching Careers	2½
Chapter 4:	Entrepreneurship	2½
Chapter 5:	Developing an Individual Career Plan	5
Unit 3: Finding a Job		10
Chapter 6:	Finding and Applying for a Job	5
Chapter 7:	Interviewing	5
Unit 4: Joining the Workforce		15
Chapter 8:	Beginning a New Job	3
Chapter 9:	Workplace Ethics	3
Chapter 10:	Developing a Positive Attitude	3
Chapter 11:	Workplace Health and Safety	3
Chapter 12:	Workplace Legal Matters	3

UNIT/CHAPTER		DAYS
Unit 5: Professional Development		20
Chapter 13:	Interpersonal Relationships at Work	3
Chapter 14:	Teamwork and Leadership	3
Chapter 15:	Professional Communication Skills	3
Chapter 16:	Thinking Skills on the Job	3
Chapter 17:	Technology in the Workplace	4
Chapter 18:	Time and Information Management	4
Unit 6: Life Skills		15
Chapter 19:	Economics and the Consumer	3
Chapter 20:	Managing Your Money	3
Chapter 21:	Banking and Credit	3
Chapter 22:	Buying Insurance	3
Chapter 23:	Taxes and Social Security	3
Unit 7: Lifelong Learning		10
Chapter 24:	Adapting to Change	5
Chapter 25:	Balancing Work and Personal Life	5

SUCCEEDING
in the
World
of Work

SIXTH EDITION

Grady Kimbrell
Educational Consultant
Santa Barbara, California

Ben S. Vineyard
Professor and
    Chairman Emeritus
Vocational and
    Technical Education
Pittsburg State University
Pittsburg, Kansas

Glencoe
McGraw-Hill

New York, New York   Columbus, Ohio   Woodland Hills, California   Peoria, Illinois

Glencoe/McGraw-Hill

A Division of The **McGraw·Hill** *Companies*

Send all inquiries to:
Glencoe/McGraw-Hill
21600 Oxnard Street, Suite 500
Woodland Hills, California 91367

ISBN 0-02-814219-5 (Student Text)
ISBN 0-02-814221-7 (Teacher's Wraparound Edition)

1 2 3 4 5 6 7 8 9   004   01 00 99 98 97

To best research and address the needs of today's workplace, Glencoe/McGraw-Hill assembled an advisory board of industry leaders and educators. The board lent its expertise and experience to establish the foundation for this innovative, real-world, career education program. Glencoe/McGraw-Hill would like to acknowledge the following companies and individuals for their support and commitment to this project:

Mark Ballard
Director of Human Resources
Recruitment and Development
The Limited, Inc.
Columbus, OH

Michele Bina
Michele Bina and Associates
former Manager of Organizational
 Effectiveness
The Prudential Healthcare Group
Woodland Hills, CA

Joe Bryan
Industrial Cooperative Training Coordinator
Warsaw Community Schools
Warsaw, IN

Mary Sue Burkhardt
Career Specialist
Family and Consumer Sciences
Twin Lakes High School
Monticello, IN

Mable Burton
Career Development Specialist
Office of Education for Employment
Philadelphia, PA

Lolita B. Hall, Specialist
Program Improvement
Virginia Department of Education
Richmond, VA

Liz Lamatrice
Career Education Coordinator
Jefferson County, OH

Keith Mitchell
Manager, Testing and Assessment
Abbott Laboratories
Abbott Park, IL

James Murphy
Education Relations Manager
The Boeing Company
Seattle, WA

William M. Pepito
Manager, Lake County Skills
 Development Program
Abbott Laboratories
Abbott Park, IL

William J. Ratzburg
Director, Education for Work and Careers
Racine School District
Racine, WI

Gary Schepf
Business Education Department Chair
Nimitz High School
Irving, TX

Reviewers

Debra Brewster
Local Vocation Educator/Coordinator
DeForest High School
DeForrest, WI

Annie Hunter Clasen
Diversified Cooperative Training
 Coordinator
Bloomingdale Senior High School
Valrico, FL

Robert P. Dasco
Occupational Work Experience
 Coordinator
McKinley Senior High School
Canton, OH

Karen Ann Altfilisch Ellis
School-to-Career Program Director
Manual High School
Denver, CO

James R. Flanigan
English Teacher
McGuffey High School
Claysville, PA

Anthony M. Kemps
Technology Education Supervisor
Ramsey Public Schools
Ramsey, NJ

Albert A. Kennedy, Jr.
Industrial Cooperative Training
 Coordinator
Stephen F. Austin High School
Houston, TX

LouGene McKinney
Teacher/Coordinator Business and
 Marketing
Laramie High School
Laramie, WY

Lyn Flammia McMillan
Industrial Cooperative Training Teacher
Millbrook High School
Raleigh, NC

Mary Ann Carey-Nelson
Business Teacher
Ken-Ton School District
Kenmore West High School
Kenmore, NY

Ted Pietrzak
Marketing/Management Coordinator
Hayward High School
Hayward, CA

David E. Renkenberger
Construction Trades Department Head,
 Co-op Coordinator
Anthis Career Center
Fort Wayne, IN

Pam Schaffer
Vocational Education Coordinator
Utic Schools
Sterling Heights, MI

Jay L. Smith
I.C.E. Director
Lakeland High School
La Grange, IN

Table of Contents

To the Student   xviii

UNIT 1   **Self-Assessment**   xx

Chapter 1   *You and the World of Work*   2

    SECTION 1-1   Exploring the World of Work   4

    SECTION 1-2   The Changing Workplace   10

CASE STUDY
Exploring Careers: Public Service   9

EXCELLENT BUSINESS PRACTICES:
Seattle Times Company Focuses on Diversity   13

Chapter Review and Applications   20

Chapter 2   *Getting to Know Yourself*   22

    SECTION 2-1   **Decision Making**   24

    SECTION 2-2   **Setting Lifestyle Goals**   30

    SECTION 2-3   **Are Your Goals Realistic?**   36

CASE STUDY
Exploring Careers: Communications and Media   35

EXCELLENT BUSINESS PRACTICES:
Personal Empowerment   27

Chapter Review and Applications   42

UNIT 2 Exploring Careers   46

Chapter 3 *Researching Careers*   48

▪ SECTION 3-1   Exploring Careers   50
▪ SECTION 3-2   What to Research   57

CASE STUDY
   Exploring Careers: Marine Science   56

EXCELLENT BUSINESS PRACTICES:
   Looking at a Career in Tourism   61

Chapter Review and Applications   64

Chapter 4 *Entrepreneurship*   66

▪ SECTION 4-1   What Is Entrepreneurship?   68
▪ SECTION 4-2   Ways of Becoming a
                Business Owner   73
▪ SECTION 4-3   Getting Started in
                Your Own Business   78

CASE STUDY
   *Exploring Careers: Hospitality
   and Recreation*   77

EXCELLENT BUSINESS PRACTICES:
   Responsibility to the Planet   81

Chapter Review and Applications   84

| Chapter 5 | Developing an Individual Career Plan | 86 |

SECTION 5-1   **Evaluating Career Choices**   **88**

SECTION 5-2   **Your Plan of Action**   **93**

CASE STUDY
Exploring Careers: Agribusiness   **92**

EXCELLENT BUSINESS PRACTICES:
Providing a Second Chance   **95**

Chapter Review and Applications   **104**

| UNIT 3 | Finding a Job | 108 |

| Chapter 6 | Finding and Applying for a Job | 110 |

SECTION 6-1   **Exploring Sources of Job Leads**   **112**

SECTION 6-2   **Applying for a Job**   **119**

CASE STUDY
Exploring Careers: Construction   **118**

EXCELLENT BUSINESS PRACTICES:
Interactive Technology That Lists Your Résumé   **121**

Chapter Review and Applications   **128**

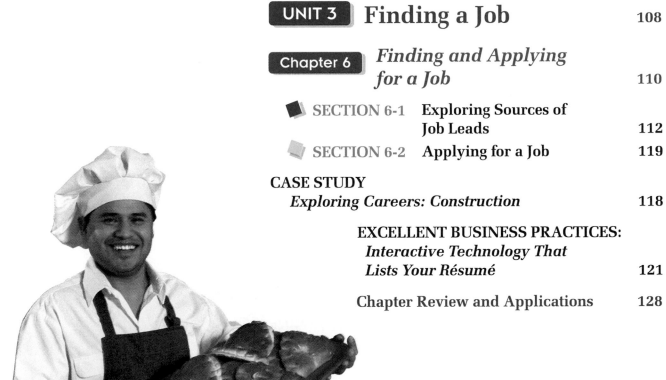

Chapter 7 *Interviewing*   130

■ SECTION 7-1   Before an Interview:
Getting Ready   132

■ SECTION 7-2   During an Interview:
It's Show Time   136

■ SECTION 7-3   After an Interview:
Following Up   144

CASE STUDY
Exploring Careers: Personal Service   143

EXCELLENT BUSINESS PRACTICES:
Exploring Opportunities   141

Chapter Review and Applications   148

UNIT 4   Joining the Workforce   152

Chapter 8 *Beginning a New Job*   154

■ SECTION 8-1   Preparing for Your
First Day on the Job   156

■ SECTION 8-2   What You Can Expect
From Your Employer   164

CASE STUDY
Exploring Careers: Health   163

EXCELLENT BUSINESS PRACTICES:
Employing the Older Worker   159

Chapter Review and Applications   170

Chapter 9 *Workplace Ethics* 172

   ■ SECTION 9-1 **Desirable Employee Qualities** 174

   ◆ SECTION 9-2 **Ethical Behavior** 181

CASE STUDY
*Exploring Careers: Fine Arts
and Humanities* 180

EXCELLENT BUSINESS PRACTICES:
Reaching the Global Marketplace 178

Chapter Review and Applications 190

Chapter 10 *Developing a Positive
Attitude* 192

   ■ SECTION 10-1 **Attitudes for Success** 194

   ◆ SECTION 10-2 **Acting Like a Professional** 203

CASE STUDY
Exploring Careers: Marketing and Distribution 202

EXCELLENT BUSINESS PRACTICES:
Stress Reduction in the Workplace 204

Chapter Review and Applications 210

Chapter 11   *Workplace Health and Safety*   **212**

SECTION 11-1   **Becoming a Healthy Worker**   **214**

SECTION 11-2   **Safety on the Job**   **222**

CASE STUDY
Exploring Careers: Communications and Media   **221**

EXCELLENT BUSINESS PRACTICES:
The Effect of Fitness Screenings   **225**

Chapter Review and Applications   **230**

Chapter 12   *Workplace Legal Matters*   232

SECTION 12-1   **Laws About the Workplace**   **234**

SECTION 12-2   **You and the Legal System**   **242**

CASE STUDY
Exploring Careers: Construction   **241**

EXCELLENT BUSINESS PRACTICES:
Resolving Conflicts   **237**

Chapter Review and Applications   **250**

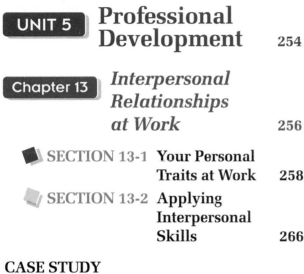

| UNIT 5 | Professional Development | 254 |

| Chapter 13 | *Interpersonal Relationships at Work* | 256 |

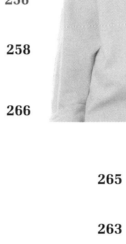 SECTION 13-1 **Your Personal Traits at Work** 258

SECTION 13-2 **Applying Interpersonal Skills** 266

CASE STUDY
Exploring Careers: Family and Consumer Services 265

EXCELLENT BUSINESS PRACTICES:
Networking 263

Chapter Review and Applications 272

| Chapter 14 | *Teamwork and Leadership* | 274 |

SECTION 14-1 **Teamwork** 276

SECTION 14-2 **Leadership** 285

CASE STUDY
Exploring Careers: Fine Arts and Humanities 284

EXCELLENT BUSINESS PRACTICES:
Building Teamwork Through Experiential Training 281

Chapter Review and Applications 292

| Chapter 15 | Professional Communication Skills | 294 |

SECTION 15-1 Speaking and Listening 296
SECTION 15-2 Writing and Reading 305

CASE STUDY
Exploring Careers: Public Service 304

EXCELLENT BUSINESS PRACTICES:
Working with Visual Impairments 309

Chapter Review and Applications 312

| Chapter 16 | *Thinking Skills on the Job* | 314 |

SECTION 16-1 Making Decisions on the Job 316
SECTION 16-2 Solving Workplace Problems 324

CASE STUDY
Exploring Careers:
Transportation 323

EXCELLENT BUSINESS PRACTICES:
Total Quality Management 318

Chapter Review and Applications 332

Chapter 17 *Technology in the Workplace* 334

SECTION 17-1 **Changing Technology in Everyday Living** 336

SECTION 17-2 **Computer Software and Its Applications** 344

CASE STUDY
Exploring Careers: Business and Office 343

EXCELLENT BUSINESS PRACTICES:
Preparing Students for Working with Technology 347

Chapter Review and Applications 352

Chapter 18 *Time and Information Management* 354

SECTION 18-1 **Using Time Effectively** 356

SECTION 18-2 **Organizing Your Work** 366

CASE STUDY
Exploring Careers: Hospitality and Recreation 365

EXCELLENT BUSINESS PRACTICES:
On-Site Child Care 369

Chapter Review and Applications 372

| UNIT 6 | Life Skills | 376 |

| Chapter 19 | Economics and the Consumer | 378 |

SECTION 19-1 Our Economic System 380
SECTION 19-2 You, the Consumer 388

CASE STUDY
Exploring Careers:
Communications and Media 387

EXCELLENT BUSINESS PRACTICES:
Ribs 101 385

Chapter Review and Applications 394

| Chapter 20 | *Managing Your Money* | 396 |

SECTION 20-1 Budgeting 398
SECTION 20-2 Coping with Financial
Responsibility 409

CASE STUDY
Exploring Careers:
Communications and Media 408

EXCELLENT BUSINESS PRACTICES:
Choose Your Own Benefits 404

Chapter Review and Applications 414

Chapter 21	*Banking and Credit*	416

SECTION 21-1 **Saving Money** **418**

SECTION 21-2 **Checking Accounts and Other Banking Services** **423**

SECTION 21-3 **Using Credit Wisely** **429**

CASE STUDY
Exploring Careers: Manufacturing **428**

EXCELLENT BUSINESS PRACTICES:
A Slice of the Pie **426**

Chapter Review and Applications **434**

Chapter 22	*Buying Insurance*	436

SECTION 22-1 **Insurance Basics** **438**

SECTION 22-2 **Home and Automobile Insurance** **441**

SECTION 22-3 **Health and Life Insurance** **449**

CASE STUDY
Exploring Careers: Office and Business **448**

EXCELLENT BUSINESS PRACTICES:
Reducing Injury on the Job **451**

Chapter Review and Applications **454**

Chapter 23 *Taxes and Social Security*   456

   ■ SECTION 23-1 **All About Taxes**   458
   ■ SECTION 23-2 **All About Social Security**   471

CASE STUDY
   Exploring Careers: Manufacturing   470

EXCELLENT BUSINESS PRACTICES:
   Protecting Your Privacy   463

Chapter Review and Applications   476

UNIT 7 **Lifelong Learning**   480

Chapter 24 *Adapting to Change*   482

   ■ SECTION 24-1 **Managing Your Career**   484
   ■ SECTION 24-2 **Changing Jobs or Careers**   491

CASE STUDY
   Exploring Careers: Environment   490

EXCELLENT BUSINESS PRACTICES:
   Environmental Concerns   487

Chapter Review and Applications   500

Chapter 25 *Balancing Work and Personal Life* 502

   ■ SECTION 25-1 **Setting Up Your Own Household** 504

   ■ SECTION 25-2 **Managing Work, Family, and Community Life** 511

CASE STUDY
   Exploring Careers: Public Service 510

EXCELLENT BUSINESS PRACTICES:
   Career Management 517

Chapter Review and Applications 520

Glossary 524
Index 538

Welcome to *Succeeding in the World of Work!*

What do you want to do with your life? What do you dream of becoming? What are you good at? What do you enjoy? This book will help you find the answers to these questions.

If you really think about it, there is at least one thing, if not several things, you really enjoy—things that make the time fly and make you feel good about yourself. Maybe you love playing sports or acting in plays. Maybe you like working with computers or writing stories. Throughout this course, your challenge is to convert the things that interest you into a satisfying career. This book will help you do just that.

First, you'll take a look at yourself. You'll determine your interests, values, and ideal life-style and consider how they will influence your career choice. You'll then explore the many career areas and decide which careers best suit you. For example, if you love animals and value education, you may decide a career working as an exhibit interpreter at a zoo or aquarium is right for you.

Next, you will develop your individual career plan. You will look at the type of education you will need, and how to find, apply, and interview for a job.

From there, you'll take a good look at the skills you'll need on the job and gain valuable insight into how to develop these professional skills.

You'll also take an in-depth look at what to expect once you're living on your own. You'll learn how to manage your money,

make wise consumer purchases, and meet your adult responsibilities.

Finally, you'll focus on the importance of lifelong learning. You'll receive valuable advice on how to get ahead on the job and how to put your career on the fast track. You'll also learn tips on how to balance your work and personal life to achieve career and personal success.

Understanding the Text Structure

You'll find the structure of *Succeeding in the World of Work* easy to read and comprehend. The text is divided into seven units. Each unit covers a distinct area of career exploration: Self-Assessment, Exploring Careers, Finding a Job, Joining the Workforce, Professional Development, Life Skills, and Lifelong Learning.

Within each unit there are chapters. Each chapter is broken down into two or three short sections. The sections begin with a list of **Objectives** that tell you the skills and knowledge you will have mastered once you complete the section. The section's **Key Terms** are also listed. Each section concludes with a **Section Review** that helps to reinforce your understanding of section concepts.

At the end of the chapter, a **Highlights** page summarizes the chapter information. You can use this summary to review chapter content. A two-page **Chapter Review**

and journal writing as you apply chapter content to your own career explorations. This activity appears on the opening pages of each chapter.

• **Exploring Careers** presents information about various careers and individuals who work in them.

• **Excellent Business Practices** highlights unusually effective business practices of specific business organizations.

• **Career Do's and Don'ts** provides helpful tips to use in real-life situations.

• **Attitude Counts** stresses the importance of adopting a positive viewpoint at work.

• **Ethics in Action** gives you the opportunity to consider what ethical decision you would make given specific real-life situations.

• **You're the Boss: Solving Workplace Problems** invites you to make managerial decisions about challenging workplace situations.

• The **Glossary** and **Index** allow you to quickly access definitions to terms and locate career subjects. The **Glossary** provides definitions for more than 200 terms. Following each definition in parentheses is the chapter page number on which the term is explained. The **Index** lists key terms and concepts along with important graphs, charts, and other chapter illustrations.

Get ready for an exciting career exploration adventure with *Succeeding in the World of Work*. An adventure that will prepare you for a lifetime!

follows the Highlights page. The review provides extensive questions and activities designed to help you check your understanding of the chapter.

Chapter Features

Text features provide further insight into career topics and challenge your creativity and imagination.

• The **Workforce 2000 Video** explores career material related to the chapter content. There is a video segment for every chapter. A scene from the chapter video segment appears on the chapter opener pages.

• The **Unit Quiz** gives you a chance to pretest your familiarity with the unit material you are about to explore.

• The **Unit Lab** gives you an opportunity to research all aspects of industry.

• **Journal: Personal Career Plan** gives you an opportunity to do some creative thinking

Unit Overview

Unit 1 introduces the world of work and shows how career choices affect lifestyle. Students will also learn how global economic interests and rapidly changing technology will affect future careers.

As they begin to assess their own skills and aptitudes, students will learn more about themselves and match their personal interests with career options.

Introducing the Unit

Ask students to list five of their values, interests, aptitudes, and abilities. Then have them list the training and/or education they have had so far in connection with these characteristics.

Is there a correlation between their interests and aptitudes and educational choices they have made?

Finally, have students identify three or four careers they find attractive.

Unit Project

Over a period of time, have students conduct interviews of six friends or family members, asking these questions:

• Are you living the lifestyle you had planned in high school?

• Are you doing the work you had expected to do when you were in high school?

After students read Chapter 2, have them report the results of their interviews to the class.

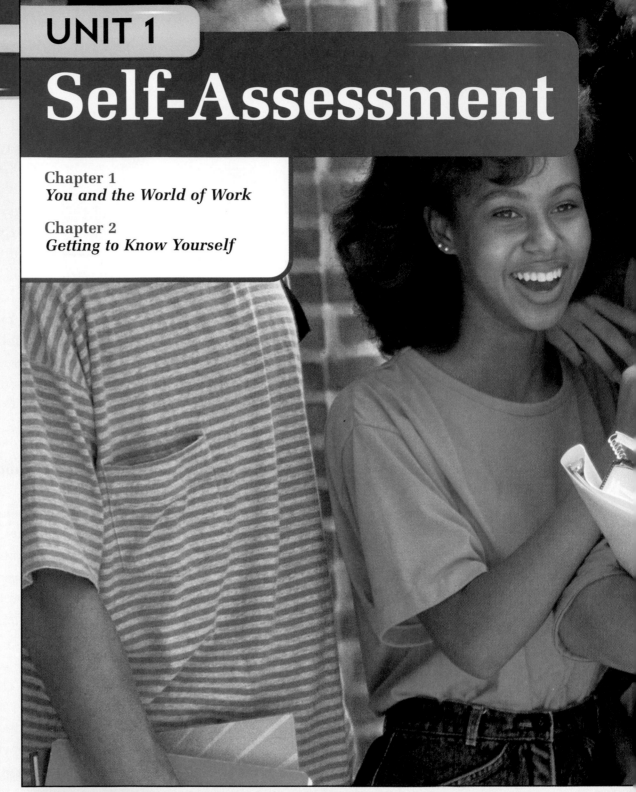

UNIT 1
Self-Assessment

Chapter 1
You and the World of Work

Chapter 2
Getting to Know Yourself

Developing Community Involvement

Have students brainstorm ways they could contribute to the community in a weekend project. Ideas might include collecting toys and personal items for a shelter, clearing a vacant lot of debris, or removing grafitti in the school neighborhood. The class should choose three of the most enthusiastically supported ideas, rescarch the project—identifying who needs to give permission for a lot clean-up, for example—then document their work with photographs, a notebook, or scrapbook.

UNIT 1 QUIZ:

What Do You Know About Self-Assessment?

- How is a job different from a career?
- Why do people work?
- How has the workplace changed in the last ten years?
- Picture yourself in five years. What will your life be like?
- What things are important to you?
- What do you want from a career?

1

Resources for Enrichment

Books

- *Occupational Outlook Handbook* U.S. Dept. of Labor
- *Every Student's Guide to the Internet* by Pitter, *et al.*
- *Career Choices* by Bingham & Stryker
- *Using the Internet in Your Job Search* by Jandt & Nemnich

Magazines and Newsletters

Career Opportunities News, Choices, Careers and Colleges, Career Success

Organizations

- American Vocational Association
- U.S. Department of Labor

Internet

JobHunt—Lists job resource sites for on-line career searches: http://rescomp. stanford.edu/jobs

America's Job Bank—Job listings from public employment service job banks: http:// www.ajb.dni.us

Unit Closure

Have students write a 150–250 word paragraph describing the steps they will take to research and plan their careers.

Unit Evaluation

Administer the reproducible test for Unit 1, which you will find in your Performance Assessment Binder, or construct your own test using the IBM Testmaker Software.

Building Partners in Industry

As you begin to establish school-business partnerships, you may want to focus on direct contact with local business and industry leaders. That's an excellent idea—but don't forget to contact your students' parents as well. Parents—and other family members—can be especially important allies in this venture. By using letters, notes, or even conferences, share your ideas and aims with as many parents as possible. Encourage their responses and input—and be prepared for some excellent ideas and leads!

• • • PLANNING GUIDE • • •
Chapter 1

SECTION 1 *Exploring the World of Work*

SECTION OBJECTIVES	SECTION FEATURES	SECTION RESOURCES
• Distinguish between a job and a career.	Personal Career Plan, p. 3	 Workforce 2000 Videodisc and Videotape
• Explain the different reasons why people work.	Attitude Counts, p. 6	Section 1-1 Review, p. 8
	Exploring Careers, p. 9	Student Activity Workbook

SECTION 2 *The Changing Workplace*

SECTION OBJECTIVES	SECTION FEATURES	SECTION RESOURCES
• Describe how the global economy affects jobs in the United States.	Career Do's and Don'ts, p. 12	Workforce 2000 Videodisc and Videotape
• Explain how technology is changing the workplace.	Excellent Business Practices, p. 13	Section 1-2 Review, p. 18
• Explain how the job outlook will affect your career plans.	You're the Boss!, p. 17	Chapter 1 Review, pp. 20–21
		Student Activity Workbook

CHAPTER 1

CHAPTER RESOURCES

- Chapter Transparencies and Lesson Plans
- Chapter 1 Test
- Spanish Resources, Chapter 1
- School-to-Work Activity Handbook, Chapter 1 Activity
- Teacher's Lesson Plans, Chapter 1
- Implementing Block Scheduling, Chapter 1
- Print, Media, and Internet Handbook
- Strategies for Implementing Work-Based Learning
- Strategies for Implementing Connecting Activities

Career Notes

SCANS CORRELATION CHART

Foundation Skills

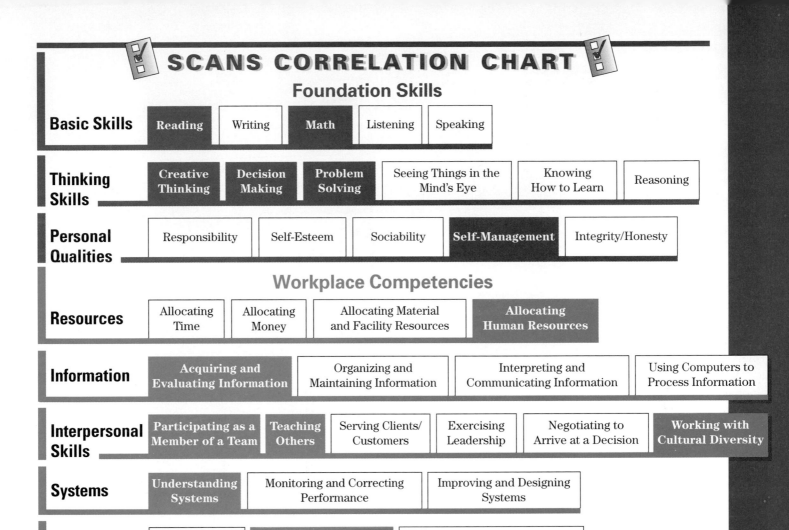

Basic Skills | Reading | Writing | Math | Listening | Speaking

Thinking Skills | Creative Thinking | Decision Making | Problem Solving | Seeing Things in the Mind's Eye | Knowing How to Learn | Reasoning

Personal Qualities | Responsibility | Self-Esteem | Sociability | Self-Management | Integrity/Honesty

Workplace Competencies

Resources | Allocating Time | Allocating Money | Allocating Material and Facility Resources | Allocating Human Resources

Information | Acquiring and Evaluating Information | Organizing and Maintaining Information | Interpreting and Communicating Information | Using Computers to Process Information

Interpersonal Skills | Participating as a Member of a Team | Teaching Others | Serving Clients/Customers | Exercising Leadership | Negotiating to Arrive at a Decision | Working with Cultural Diversity

Systems | Understanding Systems | Monitoring and Correcting Performance | Improving and Designing Systems

Technology | Selecting Technology | Applying Technology to Task | Maintaining and Troubleshooting Technology

Highlighted blocks indicate areas covered in the Chapter.

Additional Activities

Internet Connection

Ask students to use the Internet to find information on trade schools, community colleges, or universities in their chosen career. They should look for admission requirements, costs, length of the program, and the types of certification that are available on graduation.

Field Trip Suggestions

Arrange to take students to the offices of a company that specializes in temporary workers. Ask someone at the office to talk to students about what kinds of skills are most in demand, what kind of work is available, and what kind of educational background most temporary workers have.

Guest Speaker Suggestions

Locate persons in your community who really love what they do, and ask them to address the class about how they started in their careers, what they get out of working, and what advice they have for students starting into the workplace.

Key to Ability Levels

Each section gives skill-building activities. Each activity has been labeled for use with students of various learning styles and abilities.

L1 Level 1 activities are basic activities and should be within the range of all students.

L2 Level 2 activities are average activities and should be within the range of average and above average students.

L3 Level 3 activities are challenging activities designed for the ability range of above average students.

You and the World of Work

Chapter Overview

In this chapter, students learn that personal and economic factors influence career choice decisions.

Section 1-1 focuses on the difference between a job and a career and how lifestyle and personal motivation steer people to different careers.

Section 1-2 explains how global economic interests and changing technology affect careers and the skills workers will need to succeed in future jobs.

Background Information

Write chapter objectives (Sections 1-1 and 1-2) on the chalkboard or use the chapter objective transparency for class discussion.

Choose assignments from the *Student Activity Workbook* and write them on the chalkboard.

Have students preview the chapter, looking at pictures, and reading captions and content headings. Ask what types of things they can expect to learn in this chapter.

As a study aid, have students prepare an outline of the chapter.

Preteaching Vocabulary

Write the Key Terms from Sections 1-1 and 1-2 on the chalkboard. Ask students to describe how each term could affect career choice decisions.

2

Meeting SPECIAL Needs

Hearing Impaired

Avoid talking while writing on the chalkboard, whenever your back is turned to the classroom, or while looking down at your text or desk. You may want to repeat questions or answers given by other students. If you are working with an interpreter, leave adequate time for him or her to interpret your words and those of other students. When you talk to a hearing impaired student, be sure to speak clearly and look directly at the student.

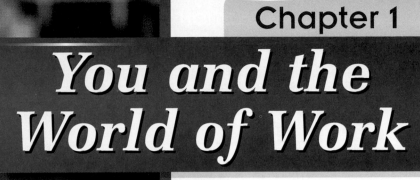

Chapter 1

You and the World of Work

Section 1-1
Exploring the World of Work

Section 1-2
The Changing Workplace

In this video segment, find out why success means something different to everyone.

Journal
Personal Career Plan

Take a look into your future—it's the day of your retirement party. As you look back on your career, what are you most proud of? What will you say to the friends and coworkers who have gathered to celebrate with you? What do you hope to hear them say about you and your work? Write a journal entry about your feelings and ideas.

3

School-to-Work Connecting Activities

Have students choose a local business for which they might like to work. Tell them to interview the human resources director, either in person or on the telephone. Students are to find out about the types of jobs the company offers, the training each job requires, and the personal qualities the company looks for when interviewing potential employees. Have students write a brief report about the interview.

Work-Based Learning Strategies and Activities

Bring real-world examples into your classroom discussions by inviting local employers to talk about the jobs they offer and the skills they seek in their employees.

Form liaisons with HR departments, and ask them to be available when students need information. You might also set up a business advisory council that can serve as resources both for in-class presentations and interviews and for work-site student observations.

WORKFORCE 2000 Training Video

Have students view the video and perform the interactive exercises to reinforce important chapter concepts and thinking processes.

Chapter 1

Addressing LEARNING Styles

Visual/Spatial Learner

Have students assemble words and images from magazines, personal photos, and personal objects into a collage that illustrates the things they enjoy doing. Encourage them to include as many things as possible from babysitting, to rollerblading, to computer games. The images, words, and objects should be grouped according to similar skills or interests. The finished collages may reveal areas of interest students had not previously considered as career possibilities.

FOCUS

Bell Ringer

Write these instructions on the chalkboard: "Spend the next three to four minutes making a list of ten jobs or careers you want to know more about."

Introducing the Section

Discuss the Bell Ringer activity. Ask several students to name one job or career on their lists and explain why it interests them. Write the jobs or careers in one column on the chalkboard and the motivation in a second column. Use this discussion to move into the differences between a job and a career.

Ask students who have part-time jobs to explain their reasons for working. Ask whether they would take a job they didn't like just for more money. Then discuss the various reasons why people work.

Motivational Activity
Critical Thinking

Have students write these column heads on a sheet of paper: *Skills, Interests*. Then ask them to list the skills they have or are acquiring and their career interests. Examples of skills might include math, writing, or getting along well with people. Career interests might be specific jobs, such as a travel agent, or a career area, such as health care. Discuss how the two relate.

Exploring the World of Work

OBJECTIVES

After studying this section, you will be able to:

- **Distinguish between a job and a career.**
- **Explain the different reasons why people work.**

KEY TERMS

job
career
lifestyle

Are you nervous about the thought of graduating from high school and wondering what you're going to do afterward? Well, maybe that nervousness is a good sign. Maybe it's time to think about your options and to prepare for them. Will you go to trade school or college? Will you go to work? What kind of work will you do?

You probably won't be surprised to learn that most people prefer to do work that uses their interests and talents. After all, work takes up a lot of time. With a full-time job, you could spend more than 2,000 hours a year at work. (That's more time than you spend doing anything else except sleeping!)

What kind of job would be right for you? Think about what skills you have and what interests you. To get an idea of what work you'd like to do, make two lists.

- Write down your *skills*—the things you feel you're good at—such as drawing, being organized, solving math problems, or dancing.

- Then write down your *interests*, or favorite activities. You may like to listen to music, play basketball, or work with computers.

What jobs can you think of that might suit your skills and interests?

Addressing Workplace Diversity

By the year 2000, women will make up 64 percent of the American workforce. Minorities and new immigrants will make up 26 percent. Only 15 percent of those entering the workforce after 2000 will be white, native-born males. The greatest growth in employees will be among African Americans and Hispanics.

What Is Work?

Is work something people do simply to earn money, or is it something much more? Here's what Robert Lombardi, a graphic production artist, has to say about the meaning of work.

"I've found that work can be an enjoyable experience, not just the thing you do to make money. If you have a job you like, work means much more than just paying your bills. It means using your talents, being with people who have similar interests, making a contribution, and getting a real sense of satisfaction from doing a good job."

Robert uses a computer to arrange the words and artwork in magazines, books, and print advertisements. He finds his work satisfying because it suits his interests, skills, and talents.

Jobs and Careers

Is a job the same thing as a career? What's the difference between the two?

A **job** is work that people do for pay. The work usually consists of certain tasks. Often a job is a position with a company. For example, Robert has had jobs with advertising agencies and publishing companies. Sometimes jobs lead to careers.

A **career** is a series of related jobs built on a foundation of interest, knowledge, training, and experience. Robert developed his career by working at different graphic production jobs. As he gained experience, he found more challenging—and better-paying—work with each new job.

Like Robert, many people work at several jobs during their careers. According to the U.S. Department of Labor, the average American has at least seven jobs, including

Robert wanted to be a graphic production artist because he had a talent for visual arts. *Why is following your skills and interests so important in choosing a career?*

Chapter 1 • You and the World of Work **5**

Discussion Starter

Name a celebrity, such as an athlete or entertainer, and speculate on what special talents that person has and how the person's career affects her or his circle of friends, time spent with family, standard of living, and lifestyle.

SCANS Foundation Skills Connection

L1 Reading

Have students read the help-wanted ads in your local newspaper. Discuss which types of occupations have the most openings.

L2 Decision Making

Have students go to the school or local library and find books on choosing a career. Tell them to scan several books, evaluating whether the books contain information that they think would be helpful in making a career decision. Students are to make a list of at least three books. Their lists should include the title, author(s), publisher, and copyright year.

L3 Self-Management

Tell students to choose a career that interests them. Have them map out a plan for researching that career. Their plans should include a description of the career, the type of information they want to research, a goal for completing the research, and the specific times/dates they will do the research.

part-time jobs as teenagers, before age 30. Other recent reports show that those beginning their first jobs in the mid-1990s will change employers six or seven times before retirement.

Impact on Lifestyle

Your **lifestyle** is the way you use your time, energy, and resources. Many people use much of their time and energy and many of their resources at work. The work you do affects other parts of your life. It can determine how much time you have to spend with friends and family and how much money and energy you have to

Attitude Counts ✔

"Stop bragging!" That's good advice—as far as it goes. Remember, though, that bragging is not the same as recognizing and appreciating your own good qualities. Take the time to recognize and appreciate your own special abilities and talents. That's not bragging—that's positive thinking.

pursue your favorite activities. Your lifestyle may vary according to changes in your career.

To see how work affects lifestyle, read about Amelia. Amelia Sanchez is studying for her associate degree in early childhood education. Her goal is to work at a day care center, but for now she baby-sits for two elementary school children in the afternoons and on weekends.

Amelia's baby-sitting schedule frees her to take classes in the morning. She also is gaining experience working with children. Between going to school and working, though, she

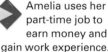

Amelia uses her part-time job to earn money and gain work experience. *How can your job affect your lifestyle?*

Extending the Illustration

Think of jobs in two different locations, such as a big city versus a small town. How is lifestyle affected with each job?

Caption Answer: It can affect the amount of leisure time and the amount of money you have.

Teaching Attitude Counts ✔

Have students meet in small groups to discuss their responses to these questions:

• What is the difference between bragging and positive thinking?

• What examples of bragging can we offer? What are some related examples of positive thinking?

doesn't have much free time to spend with her friends and family. In addition, she spends most of her income and energy on getting her training. However, Amelia knows that she'll soon have the career she wants. She's willing to make sacrifices now. She knows that they are only temporary.

What kind of lifestyle do *you* want in the future? What things are important to you? Make a list of how you'd like to spend your time, resources, and energy. Look back at the lists you made earlier about your skills and interests. These lists can help you find out the kind of work you'd like to do and the kind of lifestyle you'd like to have.

Why People Work

Why do people work? Why do your family members work? Why do your friends work? If you have an after-school job, why do *you* work?

That's a no-brainer, you say—to make money! That's the most basic reason, of course, but can you think of other reasons for having a job? Here's a short list of why people work:

- People work to earn money to pay for housing, transportation, food, and clothes. There are other expenses, too, such as health care, insurance, education, and taxes. That's not all. Most people want money to pay for movies, gifts, travel, and other extras. Look at *Figure 1-1* below to see how consumers spend their money.

- People also work because they want to be with other people. They may enjoy working with a group of people, helping others, or just being in an environment with people who have similar interests.

- Self-fulfillment is another reason why people work. They feel good about

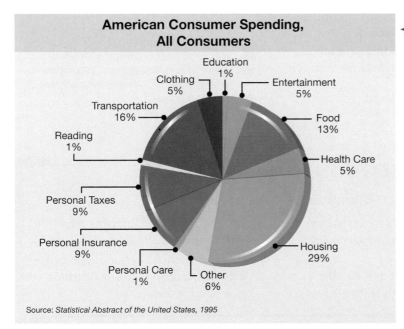

American Consumer Spending, All Consumers

- Education 1%
- Clothing 5%
- Entertainment 5%
- Transportation 16%
- Food 13%
- Reading 1%
- Health Care 5%
- Personal Taxes 9%
- Personal Insurance 9%
- Personal Care 1%
- Other 6%
- Housing 29%

Source: *Statistical Abstract of the United States, 1995*

 Figure 1-1

American consumers spend more than half their money in three areas. What are they? Why do you think this fact is a real eye-opener to people just starting out on their own?

Chapter 1 • You and the World of Work **7**

☑ **SCANS Workplace Competencies Connection**

L1 **Acquiring and Evaluating Information**

Have students interview their school guidance counselor or librarian to find resources for career research.

L2 **Participating as a Member of a Team**

Students who have similar career interests should work together to create a chart showing career progression (from entry-level to top-level titles) for three different careers.

L3 **Applying Technology to Task**

If your school has access to the Internet, have students learn how to use on-line services to conduct career research. If you do not have Internet access, have students visit the public library to learn how to use their computer databases for career research.

Independent Practice

✍ Assign as homework the chapter activity in the *School-to-Work Activity Handbook*.

Reading

Have students read an article about career exploration in magazines, such as *Choices* and *Career Success*. Have them list ideas for career opportunities they might use in choosing their own careers.

▶▶ **Extending Figure 1-1** ◀◀

Give an example of a full-time job (40 hours/week) paying the minimum wage. Have students apply the percentages in the figure to this income. Discuss the amount available for housing, for example, and the actual cost of housing in your area.

Caption Answer: housing, transportation, and food; they probably think they'll be able to use most of their money to buy clothes, eat out, see movies, etc.

Writing: *Preparing Directions*

Have students begin a list of resources—print, audio, video, and on-line—they plan to use in their career research; they will add to the list as they learn about other resources.

ASSESS

Assessment
Oral

Have each student present a short (two to three minute) explanation of how a person's career choice affects lifestyle and motivation to work. Evaluate their understanding of how one's lifestyle is affected by one's work. (For example, a fast-food cook will have a different lifestyle from a business manager.)

Also evaluate students' presentation skills by creating a checklist (share with students beforehand) such as the following:

- maintains eye contact with the audience;
- speaks clearly and can be heard by all in the audience;
- avoids use of slang or jargon;
- uses good posture;
- avoids rambling or using "uh," "like," or similar words/sounds;
- organizes points for smooth flow;
- presents ideas/facts to support topic.

themselves when they do a job well. Working at a job that suits them gives them a feeling of accomplishment.

If people do their work well, others repect them. When this happens they feel proud and respect themselves. For most people the chief source of self-fulfillment is success in the world of work.

People can find satisfaction in their jobs for many reasons. Herminio Fernandez, a video-game programmer, loves to create video games and figure out ways to make them work. He gets a real sense of satisfaction when he writes programs that help artists assemble the pictures for video games.

What task or job have you done recently that gave you a feeling of accomplishment? Perhaps it was illustrating a poster for a school fund-raising project or coaching basketball to younger children in your neighborhood. Write a brief entry in your journal describing the task and how you felt after completing it. What else could you do that might give you that feeling again? Finding self-fulfillment has lasting effects. You feel good about yourself and about what you do.

Helping others gives some people a sense of accomplishment. ***What kind of job might this activity help prepare this student for?***

SECTION 1-1 *Review*

Understanding Key Concepts

Using complete sentences, answer the following questions on a separate sheet of paper.

1. Give an example of one job that a high school graduate with each of the following skills or interests might do: math, music, computers.

2. Describe a situation that might cause a person to change his or her main reason for working.

SECTION 1-1 *Review* ANSWERS

1. Possible answer: bookkeeper, musician, computer repair person
2. Possible answers: having to take care of a sick parent (work to pay for necessities); having to move to an unfamiliar neighborhood (work to be with others); receiving a promotion and a raise (work for self-fulfillment)

Extending the Illustration

What other types of activities might give people a sense of accomplishment? (Answers might include inventing a product, writing poetry, doing a job well, etc.)

Caption Answer: Answers may include being a teacher, trainer, or worker in an after-school program or recreation center.

CASE STUDY

Exploring Careers: Public Service

Lt. Commander Sally de Gozzaldi
Helicopter Pilot, US Navy

Q: **Were you always interested in the military?**

A: If anyone had told me, when I was a senior in high school, that I would be doing this, I would have said he or she was crazy. I studied geology in college. I didn't know anything about the military, but I always wanted to be a pilot. I heard about the Navy's pilot program from a woman I met at college.

Q: **What was the training like?**

A: You're trained very carefully, but it's tough. They try to weed out those who are not doing well. I didn't meet anyone who made it through who didn't really want to make it.

Q: **Why did you choose helicopters?**

A: There were three choices for flight training: the jet program, the multi-engine program, or helicopters. Helicopters was the only program that allowed women to be completely competitive with men. Other programs are open to women now.

Q: **What's the most difficult part of your job?**

A: I love to fly and I like to be out at sea, because that's when I fly the most and do what I was trained to do, but that's also when I'm away from my husband and baby. The ship is loud, and I usually share a room and a bathroom.

Q: **Why did you make the Navy your career?**

A: I was pleasantly surprised with the people I met. I realized I was doing what I wanted to do. Why get out when I'm having fun?

Thinking Critically

Would a career in the Navy be appropriate for you? Why or why not?

CAREER FACTS

Nature of the Work:
May include deployments at sea or nonflying onshore assignments.

Training or Education Needed:
Bachelor's degree; 13 weeks at Officer's Candidate School; 1½ years of flight training; 6 months of readiness training.

Aptitudes, Abilities, and Skills:
Responsibility; self-esteem; desire to fly; excellent physical and emotional health.

Salary Range:
Varies with time in the Navy and rank; $27,400 to $59,500, plus benefits and bonuses.

Career Path:
Advance through the ranks, depending on abilities; after service in the Navy, work in corporate industry or in medical or rescue positions.

Chapter 1 • You and the World of Work **9**

Extending the CASE STUDY

Answer: Answers will vary but should include specific reasons why a career in the Navy would or wouldn't be appropriate.

Further Application: Have students list the mechanical, technical, spatial, or motor skills they might need for their chosen careers, and how they would use those skills. (For example, an architect would need spatial skills to envision the interior or exterior of buildings, motor skills to draw the plans, and computer skills to run design programs.)

Evaluation
Assign the section review.

Reteaching
Have students draw a diagram of the lifestyle of a friend, neighbor, or relative. Then have them write a 150-word paper describing how the person's work has influenced his or her lifestyle.

Have students describe their career interests and the influences that will impact their career decisions, including personal skills, family expectations, and lifestyle goals.

Extending the Content
Assign the appropriate Chapter 1 activities in the *Student Activity Workbook.*

Have students schedule a meeting with their school guidance counselor. Tell them to prepare a list of questions they want to ask in their meeting. For example, they may want to ask about financial aid for college or which colleges offer majors that interest them. They may also want to find out about tests that can help them identify their skills or abilities.

CLOSE

Have students complete the following statement: "One major decision I have made with respect to my future career is . . . ."

SECTION 1-2

The Changing Workplace

OBJECTIVES

After studying this section, you will be able to:

- **Describe how the global economy affects jobs in the United States.**
- **Explain how technology is changing the workplace.**
- **Explain how the job outlook will affect your career plans.**

KEY TERMS

economy
global economy
job market
team
outsourcing
telecommute

Your place in the world of work will influence every aspect of your life. This is why choosing the kind of work you will do is one of the most important decisions you will ever make. So far, you've been thinking about the kind of work that might fit your interests and skills. You've also been thinking about the kind of lifestyle you'd like to have and how your work would affect it. What else might be important to consider when thinking about the work you'd like to do?

Well, there's the workplace itself. Today, however, the workplace is constantly changing. Changes in the world affect what work is available for people to do and the way in which they do it. Knowing about these changes can help you make sound decisions about your job, your career, and your future. How can you keep up with all these changes?

You can follow trends in the world of work the same way you keep up with what's happening in music, fashion, sports, and entertainment. Which are the up-and-coming industries and occupations? Which ones are on the way out? To find out, read newspapers and magazines and watch the news on television. Talk to people who work in the field that you're interested in and ask them questions about the changes and opportunities in their workplace.

The Global Economy and the Job Market

Look at a few of the things you own—a pair of pants, a book, a CD, a bicycle—and check their labels or packaging. Where were the objects made? At least some of your possessions were probably made in other countries. Because of what you buy, you are part of the global economy. The term **economy** refers to the ways in which a group produces, distributes, and consumes its goods and services. *Goods* are the items that people buy. *Services* are activities done for others for a fee. The term **global economy** refers to the ways in which the world's economies are linked.

The global economy has a direct impact on the **job market**, or the demand for particular jobs, in each country. How does the global economy affect the job market in the United States—the job market you will probably be entering?

Some critics say that the global economy is bad for this country. Trade with foreign countries, they argue, can lead to American workers losing their jobs to workers overseas. For instance, some American computer software companies hire workers in India and Pakistan—where labor costs are cheaper—to do basic programming.

On the other hand, many people believe that the global economy is good for the United States. Many American businesses export goods (sell goods to other countries), and these exports create jobs. In fact, the export business accounted for one of every six new manufacturing jobs in this country in a recent year. Also, foreign firms employ more than 10 million Americans in their U.S.-based offices.

Keeping abreast of the global economy can help you learn more about the worldwide job market. For example, which jobs

As a part of the global economy, consumers can buy products from around the world. **What are the advantages?**

Chapter 1 • You and the World of Work **11**

Guided Practice
Teaching Strategies

1. Assign and review Section 1-2.
2. Use the transparency for this section.
3. Assign and review the Case Study.

Discussion Starter

Ask students what skills or knowledge they might need to work for a global company. (Possible answers include ability to adapt to living in another country, learning to speak and write another language, being aware of cultural differences, and understanding different business practices.)

Teaching Tip

Ask students what they think when they see merchandise stamped "Made in Spain" (or any other country). How does the import of such items affect the U.S. economy? (On the positive side, imports create jobs for those who bring items into the country. They also help keep prices low because they add to competition in the U.S. marketplace. On the negative side, imports can contribute to a high trade imbalance. Jobs can also be lost when U.S. companies cannot compete with lower-cost foreign goods.)

Extending the Illustration

Teenagers in other countries can also buy U.S. products. What are the advantages for U.S. businesses? (Answers might include greater sales growth and ability to hire more people for products made in the U.S.)

Caption Answer: Consumers probably have more choices and better prices because of the competition.

TEACH (cont'd.)

Skills Practice

Have students research at least three countries with different cultural backgrounds and write a short paper describing how communication styles and traditions vary among the three. (For example, students might describe how people greet each other, or how gestures and facial expressions are interpreted.)

SCANS Foundation Skills Connection

L1 Reading

Have students go to their local library and ask for business annual reports. They are to find a company that operates in other countries and read about its business activities. Have students share their findings in class.

L2 Creative Thinking

Suppose you want to work in a job that involves interacting with people in other countries or even working in another country. How would you prepare for such a job?

L3 Self-Management

Tell students to choose a software program that they want to learn. Have them make a list of the things they want to be able to do with this program. Then have them develop a list of goals for learning the program, including a time for meeting the goal.

Career Do's & Don'ts

When Entering the Workplace...

Do:
- define your goals.
- be informed.
- expect the best.
- learn from others.

Don't:
- be influenced by negative people.
- let failure stop you.
- be self-critical.
- limit your thinking.

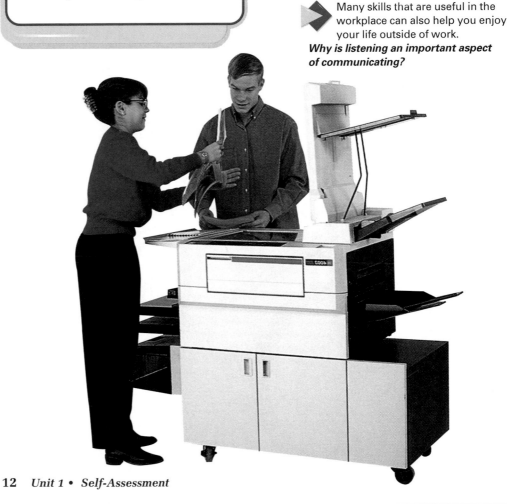

will be sent abroad? Which jobs will be created because of the changing economy? Which jobs will involve trade with foreign countries? Which jobs will be available to American workers in foreign countries?

Impact on Today's Workers

The global economy creates stiff competition for businesses. Just as you want to do well in your career, an employer wants his or her business to do well. As a result,

Many skills that are useful in the workplace can also help you enjoy your life outside of work.
Why is listening an important aspect of communicating?

12 *Unit 1 • Self-Assessment*

Extending the Illustration

Ask students to discuss the difference between hearing and listening.
Caption Answer: You can learn from listening to others; you appreciate people listening to you when you speak.

the employer will need employees who can do a variety of tasks and who possess a variety of skills.

How can you meet the demands put on workers in a global economy? You can develop skills—many of which you are already learning—and apply them in your job. The U.S. Labor Department Secretary's Commission on Achieving Necessary Skills (SCANS) has identified the following workplace skills:

- *basic skills*, such as reading, writing, mathematics, listening, and speaking;
- *thinking skills*, such as creative thinking, decision making, problem solving, seeing things in the mind's eye (picturing things in your mind), knowing how to learn, and reasoning; and
- *personal qualities*, such as responsibility, self-esteem, sociability, self-management, integrity, and honesty.

SECTION 1-2

SCANS Workplace Competencies Connection

L1 **Allocating Human Resources**

Have students imagine that they work for an export company that needs to hire additional staff. Currently, two employees handle export orders. Each person can process approximately 12 orders per day. The company is receiving an average of 55 orders per day. Decide the number of people to hire.

L2 **Understanding Systems**

Have students contact a local or state office dealing with business exports (or perhaps the local Chamber of Commerce). Tell them to ask for information about procedures a company must follow to export its products. Have them draw a flow chart illustrating each step in the export process.

L3 **Working with Cultural Diversity**

Have teams of students discuss the meaning of cultural diversity, using library research, if necessary. Each team should prepare a class presentation, describing cultural diversity in the United States. Have them give examples (from their research and their own personal experience) of how people can better work together.

EXCELLENT BUSINESS PRACTICES

Seattle Times Company Focuses on Diversity

The Seattle Times Company of Seattle, Washington, has established programs that address the need to serve a diverse population.

Periodically, staff editors review photographs in the paper for an accurate representation of people of color and women. Editors also critique articles to make sure they accurately represent ethnicity, lifestyles, and family situations of people of different backgrounds.

The paper takes a strong stance on maintaining a diverse workforce. For instance, 21 percent of employees, including reporters and editors, are minorities, well over the average of 13 percent of the local population. Women make up 44 percent of the newsroom employees and 33 percent of the overall company.

Even so, the Seattle Times Company realizes that it is not enough to just hire minorities. It also conducts a two-day diversity training program. The program provides workers with an opportunity to talk about their experiences with stereotyping, prejudice, and lack of awareness of other cultures.

The Seattle Times also has a diversity council of volunteers who evaluate the workforce, an employee mentoring program, internships, career planning, and a library. The company even conducts an anonymous survey of how effective it has been in creating a nurturing environment for people of diverse backgrounds.

Thinking Critically

Why is it especially important for a newspaper to employ people from diverse backgrounds? How does a diverse workforce affect coworkers?

Chapter 1 • You and the World of Work **13**

Extending EXCELLENT BUSINESS PRACTICES

Answer: Having a diverse workforce helps the newspaper portray cultural diversity in its articles. Cultural diversity helps to educate and helps others to understand and work effectively together.

Further Application: Have students research the level of diversity in your school. Is it reflective of the community, the state, or the nation? Does your school emphasize recruiting employees from diverse backgrounds?

Independent Practice
Reading

Have students read an article about a company that is part of the global economy in several business magazines (such as *Business Week*, *Forbes*, or *Fortune*) in your local or school library.

Students should take notes about the business activities of the company. Hold a class discussion about the different ways a business can participate in the global economy and the jobs that result.

Skills Practice

Tell students to go to a local store and count the number of products whose labels indicate their country of origin, including the United States. What proportion of products are made in the United States versus those made in other countries?

Research

Have students research the countries to which the United States exports the most goods (by dollar amount). Have them find out the countries from which the United States imports the most goods, also by dollar amount. Finally, they should create a table of imports and exports, by country and ranked from largest to smallest dollar amount.

Changing Technology

Not long ago, floppy disks were still floppy, laptops had not been invented, there were no CD-ROMs, and the Internet did not exist. Desktop personal computers were just coming into common use. Such advances in technology are constantly—and rapidly—changing how people work. As *Figure 1-2* shows, people working in very different fields use a wide range of technology to help them do their work more quickly and efficiently.

▶ Figure 1-2

Technology in the Workplace

Modern technology enables a variety of workers to do their jobs quickly and efficiently.

A Sales workers in stores wave wands over goods so that lasers can read prices. The sale is instantly fed into a computerized database that tracks the store's inventory. Sales workers can help customers complete their shopping more quickly. Stores keep better track of how each item sells and when they need to reorder.

B Repair workers out on calls communicate with the home office via cellular phones. In this way they can quickly learn of homes or offices they must visit to make repairs. The company saves time. Customers get faster service.

14   *Unit 1 • Self-Assessment*

◀ Extending Figure 1-2 ▶

Think of several other ways in which people use technology to do their jobs. (Some examples are airline pilots and train operators, auto manufacturers, laser surgeons, international bankers.)

Today's Workplace

Modern technology affects not only what work you do but how and where you do it. Trends that you'll probably encounter in the workplace include the use of teams, outsourcing, and telecommuting.

* A **team** is an organized group that sets goals, makes decisions, and implements actions within a company. As companies increase their use of technology, some new jobs are created (such as technical jobs), and others

A business team may have a facilitator rather than a leader. ***How can you develop teamwork skills?***

C The most widespread technology, though, is the computer. Millions of workers now use computers. Office workers use them to prepare letters and reports. Manufacturing workers use them to run robots and to test products. Farmworkers use them to test the soil and to keep track of livestock.

are eliminated. Many companies have eliminated the position of middle manager—a job that involves directing other workers. As a result, workers are collaborating on projects rather than just doing what a manager tells them to do.

* Another practice is **outsourcing**. In this practice, businesses hire other companies or individuals to produce their services or goods. For example, airline companies often contract with individuals or other companies to provide baggage handling and meals for their customers.

Chapter 1 • You and the World of Work   **15**

▶ Extending the Illustration

What do you consider to be teamwork skills? (Possible answers include communicating clearly with others, being cooperative, doing your fair share of the work, accepting other people's ideas.)

Caption Answer: play sports, volunteer for organizations

SECTION 1-2

Teaching Tip

Invite a prominent woman in your community to speak about the challenges women face in business. Try to find a woman who has been successful in a male-dominated field. Ask her to discuss how the challenges are different for men.

Also invite a man who works in a traditionally female field (for example, a male nurse) to speak to your class. Ask him to discuss the special challenges he faces.

Another option is to use the following case with students:

"It's nearing the end of Jeremy's first week of work as an administrative assistant at Moran's Temporary Services. For the past four days, Jeremy has heard jibes about being a man in a woman's job and listened to comments about his skills.

"Jeremy likes using a computer to perform clerical tasks, and this is his second job as an administrative assistant. He took this new job when his former employer had to lay off 200 workers. How would you feel if you were Jeremy? How would you deal with this situation? Would you give up a career you really like just because other people make comments?"

(Students' responses to this case will vary, but many may see the situation as a threat to self-esteem.)

Discussion Starter

Ask students to think of the ways they use technology in their daily lives. Did they use a microwave oven today, operate a computer program, put one call on hold while answering another?

Have students brainstorm ways they can learn about technology and keep up with future changes. Emphasize that students will be responsible for much of their own learning, and they will need to develop a habit of lifelong learning if they are to maintain job skills.

(Possible ways to keep up with technology are to take computer and software courses, participate in work-training programs, read computer magazines, and use the Internet.)

Skills Practice

Have students imagine they supervise volunteers at a local hospital. Ask them to list four ways they could acknowledge their volunteers' work and thus boost their self-esteem.

Teaching Tip

Bring a copy of your Yellow Pages to class and choose several businesses at random. Ask students whether each business they chose produces goods or services.

• More than 24 million workers do not work at a company's work site. Instead they **telecommute**, or work at home, using a computer, fax (facsimile), and telephone to perform their jobs.

Impact on Today's Workers

The workplace may be changing, but one thing is certain. You'll be involved with technology in some form—especially computers—in whatever career you choose. Does that mean you need to know what goes on inside a computer? No, says one expert: "After all, you don't have to know how to design a car to drive one." You will need to know how to *use* one, though.

You'll also probably continue learning for as long as you work—not just about new technologies but also about new ways of working. While advanced technology offers you many different opportunities for work, it also means you'll need to keep up with the changes.

The Job Outlook

What can you expect jobwise when you graduate from high school? The good news is that nearly 25 million new jobs are predicted to be created by the year 2005. However, these jobs will not be evenly distributed across industries. Most of the work will be in the service-producing

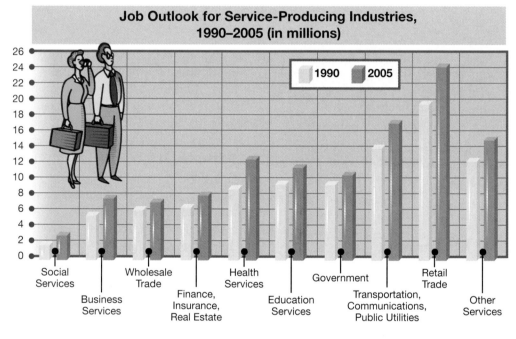

Job Outlook for Service-Producing Industries, 1990–2005 (in millions)

1990   2005

Industry   Source: Bureau of Labor Statistics

▲ **Figure 1-3**   Why do you think the service sector—health, business, education, social services—is creating so many jobs?

▶▶ Extending Figure 1-3 ◀◀

Choose one area of service and think of the types of jobs that might be available in that area.

Caption Answer: Health care—improvements in medical technology and an aging population; business—the rise of temporary-help agencies and the growth of computer services; education—rising enrollments in elementary, secondary, and postsecondary schools and rising enrollments of older, foreign-born, and part-time students; social services—an aging population and an economy in which more mothers work outside the home.

Job Outlook for Goods-Producing Industries, 1990–2005 (in millions)

Legend: 1990, 2005

Y-axis: 0, 2, 4, 6, 8, 10, 12, 14, 16, 18, 20

X-axis (Industry): Mining; Agriculture, Forestry, Fishing; Construction; Manufacturing

Source: Bureau of Labor Statistics

◀ Figure 1-4

Some jobs in manufacturing are expected to decline. Why do you think this is so?

industries. *Service-producing industries* provide services for a fee. These include medical care, travel accommodations, and education. Fewer jobs are expected in the *goods-producing industries*, which provide goods such as stereo systems, cars, and buildings.

Figure 1-3 and *Figure 1-4* identify these different industries and show expectations for their growth or decline. Read the graphs to find out which industries are growing and which are declining. How does this information affect your ideas about a career? Think about your skills and interests. Which industries do you think would be appropriate for you?

YOU'RE THE BOSS!

✓ *Solving Workplace Problems*

You own and manage a bagel bakery. Since you spend most of your time in the office, you've hired several clerks to sell directly to the customers. Lately you've noticed that your morning clerk is efficient —but not very friendly. She rushes on, even when customers want to chat for a minute. What should you do?

▶▶ Extending Figure 1-4 ◀◀

Goods-producing industries are manufacturers. What types of manufacturing jobs are available in these industries?

Caption Answer: Technology has replaced some jobs.

Teaching YOU'RE THE BOSS!

✓ Possible responses: Talk with the clerk about the importance of maintaining friendly relationships so that customers will keep coming back. Perhaps role-play some situations with the clerk to help her practice. Spend some time working side-by-side with her to model effective customer relations.

Skills Practice

Rita and Pedro plan to get married this summer. Rita wants to live in the suburbs, have two children, and work full-time. Pedro also wants to live in the suburbs and have two children. Once they have children, though, Pedro does not want Rita to work. What do Pedro and Rita need to discuss regarding their future careers and lifestyle plans?

(Possible answers include how to meet two sets of conflicting career needs, how to juggle child-care responsibilities, and how to negotiate a solution that both can accept.)

Discussion Starter

Give students this scenario: "Health-care is one of the fastest-growing career areas. Your interests and skills are not particularly suited for this career area, but you wonder whether you should go in this direction so that you'll be assured of having a job."

Ask students to argue the pros and cons of pursuing a health-care career when one lacks real interest in that area. (Pros: Potentially a lot of job openings, demand may increase earnings, jobs may be more secure than in other industries. Cons: Lack of interest may mean one does a poor job and is not paid as well; it could also cause dissatisfaction in other parts of life because work consumes a major portion of one's time; lost opportunity to work in a career that would make one happier.)

Assessment

Content

Have students explain what is meant by a "global economy" and describe the advantages and disadvantages facing the United States as a part of that economy.

Evaluation

Assign the section review.

MINI QUIZ

True-False

1. Most people will change employers at least nine or ten times before retirement. (false)

2. Elements of lifestyle include friends, family, and where and how you live. (true)

3. Most people spend a larger percentage of their earnings on housing than on other items. (true)

4. The job market in this country is not affected by the global economy. (false)

5. Three future trends in the workplace are the use of teams, outsourcing, and telecommuting. (true)

Use the Testmaker to create a customized test for Chapter 1.

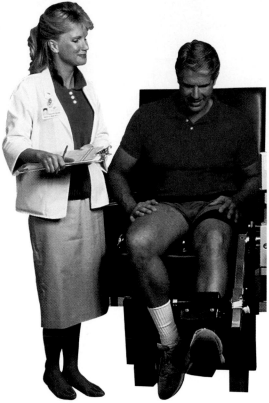

A physical therapy aide helps people recover their strength after orthopedic surgery. **Why does a physical therapy aide need to have a sense of responsibility and self-esteem?**

Impact on Today's Workers

You don't have to choose a career just because it seems to offer the best job prospects. Even though you're learning to follow trends in the job market, you still want to find work that matches your interests, skills, personality, and abilities. Whatever occupation you choose, though, you *will* need certain basic skills, thinking skills, and personal qualities. In addition, you'll probably need specific task-related skills.

For example, suppose you decide to become a physical therapy aide. What interests, skills, and personal qualities would you need for this occupation? Here are a few:

- a desire to help and motivate people,

- good listening skills in order to learn what your patients' needs are,

- good speaking skills in order to explain the exercises to your patients, and

- the ability to work under the supervision of a physical therapist.

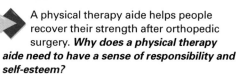

SECTION 1-2 *Review*

Understanding Key Concepts

Using complete sentences, answer the following questions on a separate sheet of paper.

1. How does the global economy affect the job market?

2. Choose a career you're interested in, and describe how technology may affect it.

3. Which do you consider more important in choosing a career—following your own interests or following the job outlook? Why?

Extending the Illustration

What other traits might be needed by a physical therapist? (Answers might include physical strength, compassion for others, and patience.)

Caption Answer: He or she needs to be responsive to patients' needs and be able to take direction from a supervising physical therapist.

SECTION 1-2 *Review* ANSWERS

1. The job market has become much more competitive.

2. Answers will vary, but students should mention computers' effects on their occupations.

3. Answers will vary. Some students will emphasize job satisfaction or lifestyle desires. Others will stress the importance of the job outlook.

Highlights

SECTION 1-1 **Summary**

- Consider your interests and skills when planning the kind of work you'd like to do.

- A job is work that people do for pay. The work usually consists of certain tasks. A career is a series of related jobs built on a person's interests, knowledge, training, and experience.

- Your lifestyle is the way you use your time, energy, and resources.

- Three important reasons why people work are (1) to earn money to pay expenses, (2) to fulfill their need to be with other people, and (3) to receive satisfaction from doing a job well.

Key Terms

job *(p. 5)*
career *(p. 5)*
lifestyle *(p. 6)*

Key Terms

economy *(p. 11)*
global economy *(p. 11)*
job market *(p. 11)*
team *(p. 15)*
outsourcing *(p. 15)*
telecommute *(p. 16)*

SECTION 1-2 **Summary**

- The global economy has a direct impact on the job market. You need basic skills, thinking skills, and personal qualities to meet the demands of the job market.

- Rapidly advancing technology has changed the workplace. Trends in the workplace include the use of teams, outsourcing, and telecommuting.

- Most of the new jobs predicted for 1990 through 2005 will fall in the service-producing sector. While you need to be aware of trends, seeking job satisfaction is also very important.

Chapter 1 • You and the World of Work **19**

Reteaching

1. Ask students to look at the label on an item of clothing they are wearing or a product they have with them to see where it was made. List on the chalkboard the different countries represented. Ask students why they bought items made in other countries. Then discuss the popularity of items made in the United States with consumers in other countries. For example, Levi's jeans are especially popular with European consumers. What foreign products are especially popular in this country? (Some examples might include televisions, VCRs, CD players, autos.)

2. Assign and review vocabulary terms, chapter questions, and activities from the Chapter Review.

Extending the Content

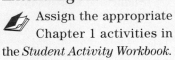 Assign the appropriate Chapter 1 activities in the *Student Activity Workbook*.

Have students think of a product or service they would like to sell to teens in another country. Have them list the ways they could use technology to sell their products or services.

CLOSE

Ask students to write a short paragraph describing how their study of this chapter has changed their ideas about the technological skills they will need in the future.

Computer Activity

Using the column feature of a word processing software package, have students set up a three-column document. Title one column *Skills*, the second column *Interests*, and the third column *Jobs*. Have students key in their list of skills, interests, and jobs under each heading. Save this document on disk and have them add to the columns as they discover new areas under those headings. Once completed, have them title the document "My Career Match" and print it out.

CHAPTER 1 REVIEW

Answers

Reviewing Key Terms

Paragraphs will vary.

Recalling Key Concepts

1. c
2. b
3. c
4. a
5. c

Thinking Critically

1. Possible answers: to learn from people on the job, to gain both work and workplace experience, to learn about possibilities for advancement

2. Higher-income jobs provide more money for essentials and other items.

3. Possible answer: Goods and services must compete with those made in other countries, so businesses need to provide products of high quality and low cost.

4. Possible answer: You might not learn of challenging careers that you would enjoy.

5. Possible answer: They must organize their own workday and be responsible for their own tasks.

Reviewing Key Terms

Write a short paragraph about the world of work, using the terms below.

job	job market
career	team
lifestyle	outsourcing
economy	telecommute
global economy	

Recalling Key Concepts

Choose the correct answer for each item below.

1. Work that you do for pay is ____.

   (a) a career (b) an industry (c) a job

2. American consumers spend the most money on ____.

   (a) food (b) housing (c) health care

3. Why do some people think the global economy is good for the United States?

   (a) Some jobs go to workers overseas.

   (b) Foreign products are of a higher quality.

   (c) The U.S. export business creates new jobs here at home.

4. Telecommuting means ____.

   (a) working at home, using a computer, fax, and telephone

   (b) transporting manufactured goods

   (c) communicating by television

5. By 2005, most new jobs will be in ____.

   (a) manufacturing (b) entertainment

   (c) services

Thinking Critically

Using complete sentences, answer each of the questions below on a separate sheet of paper.

1. Why is it an advantage to have several jobs while you are building your career?

2. How does your job's income affect other aspects of your lifestyle?

3. Do you agree that the global economy makes businesses more competitive? Explain.

4. What is the danger of limiting your career opportunities to only those you have heard about or been trained for?

5. Why do people who telecommute need good organizational and management skills?

SCANS Foundation Skills and Workplace Competencies

Basic Skills: *Math*

1. Your clothing store is open seven days a week from 9 a.m. to 9 p.m. You are the manager of three employees, each of whom wants to work at least 24 hours a week. Each employee can work the 9:00 a.m. to 3:00 p.m. shift or the 3:00 p.m. to 9:00 p.m. shift and at least one weekend day. No one can work both shifts on the same day. Make up a schedule that will meet these requirements.

Interpersonal Skills: *Teaching Others*

2. Sherry works as an administrative assistant for a small law firm. Today she needs to explain to a new lawyer how to use the office's voice mail

SCANS Foundation Skills and Workplace Competencies

1. Possible answer: Ray—9:00 to 3:00 on Sun., Mon., Tues., Thurs., and Fri.; Nicki—3:00 to 9:00 on Tues. through Sat.; Jan—9:00 to 3:00 on Wed. and Sat. and 3:00 to 9:00 shift on Sun. and Mon. Two

employees can work 30 hours; the other employee can work 24 hours.

2. Possible answer: She might first show the lawyer how to use it. Then she might ask the lawyer to use it himself. In this way, the lawyer would get valuable hands-on experience.

system. Prepare an outline of one good way for Sherry to teach the lawyer the system so that he fully understands it.

Connecting Academics to the Workplace

Health

1. Anita works as a bookkeeper for an insurance company. One day, she notices a loose telephone wire on the floor. Research workplace safety in the library, via the Internet, or by speaking to an employer. Is there a safety law that protects workers? Then explain what you think Anita should do.

Math

2. Rick is an intern in a restaurant. He wants to become a chef. It takes three workers 20 minutes each to prepare the vegetables for the salad bar. If the salad bar is filled four times a night, on average, how much worker time is required to keep it filled?

Social Studies

3. Sarah is a hot-line computer trouble-shooter for a manufacturer in the United States. She is interested in living and working in Japan. Research the current job outlook in Japan. Which industries and occupations are growing and which are declining? What openings are there for foreigners?

Developing Teamwork and Leadership Skills

Divide into teams of four. Select one member as the facilitator to keep the team

organized. Assume that you all work in the personnel department of a publishing company. There is an opening for a receptionist. First, work together to write a job description. Then write a classified ad.

Real-World Workshop

Develop a list of jobs that you've had— volunteer and for pay. For each job, list the tasks you had to complete. Then list the skills you used to perform each task.

School-to-Work Connection

Think of an industry that you are interested in. Identify someone who works in that industry, and discuss with that person the impact of the global economy and technological changes on that industry. Ask what impact these changes have had—and are expected to have—on the training needed by workers in that industry. Prepare a brief report on your findings.

Individual Career Plan

Select an industry that you are interested in working in. Locate the most recent Bureau of Labor Statistics report analyzing future employment trends. Find your industry in the report, and note how much jobs in that industry are expected to grow or decline in the future. Explain in a paragraph how the trends you read about affect your interest in that industry. Keep this and other information about the industry in order to maintain a personal update on your future career.

Chapter 1 • You and the World of Work **21**

Real-World Workshop

Students should add to their lists whenever possible. They should also be encouraged to refer to the lists when they assess themselves (Chapter 2), explore careers (Chapters 3–5), and find a job (Chapters 6 and 7).

School-to-Work Connection

Answers will be specific to the person's chosen industry. However, general comments may include the following: The global economy has increased competition for (1) quality products at low prices, (2) less expensive and more efficient labor, and (3) highly educated, technical-minded workers.

Individual Career Plan

Students may rethink their choice of career if the most recent Bureau of Labor Statistics report shows that the industry they are interested in is expected to decline. On the other hand, if they have such a strong interest in their choice, they may stick with it.

Connecting Academics to the Workplace

1. Possible answer: The Occupational and Safety Act of 1970 requires companies to provide safe workplaces. Anita should report the problem to her supervisor.

2. Four hours—three workers times 20 minutes each times four occasions

3. Answer will vary according to the materials students research.

Developing Teamwork and Leadership Skills

The classified ad should include skills and personal qualities needed, responsibilities, hours, and salary. It should also be written in the format and language of classified ads.

··· PLANNING GUIDE ···
Chapter 2

SECTION 1 *Decision Making*

SECTION OBJECTIVES	SECTION FEATURES	SECTION RESOURCES
• Follow the seven steps in the decision-making process. • Follow an effective strategy for choosing a career.	Personal Career Plan, p. 23 You're the Boss!, p. 25 Excellent Business Practices, p. 27	Workforce 2000 Videodisc and Videotape Section 2-1 Review, p. 29 Student Activity Workbook

SECTION 2 *Setting Lifestyle Goals*

SECTION OBJECTIVES	SECTION FEATURES	SECTION RESOURCES
• Identify your values and describe how they affect your career choices. • Identify your interests and describe how they affect your career choices. • Determine whether you prefer working with data, people, or things.	Ethics in Action, p. 34 Exploring Careers, p. 35	Workforce 2000 Videodisc and Videotape Section 2-2 Review, p. 34 Student Activity Workbook

SECTION 3 *Are Your Goals Realistic?*

SECTION OBJECTIVES	SECTION FEATURES	SECTION RESOURCES
• Identify your aptitudes and abilities and describe how they affect your career choice. • Identify and match your personality and learning style to career choices.	Career Do's and Don'ts, p. 40	Workforce 2000 Videodisc and Videotape Section 2-3 Review, p. 40 Chapter 2 Review, pp. 42–43 Student Activity Workbook

CHAPTER 2

CHAPTER RESOURCES

- Chapter Transparencies and Lesson Plans
- Chapter 2 Test
- Spanish Resources, Chapter 2
- School-to-Work Activity Handbook, Chapter 2 Activity
- Teacher's Lesson Plans, Chapter 2
- Implementing Block Scheduling, Chapter 2
- Print, Media, and Internet Handbook
- Strategies for Implementing Work-Based Learning
- Strategies for Implementing Connecting Activities

SCANS CORRELATION CHART

Foundation Skills

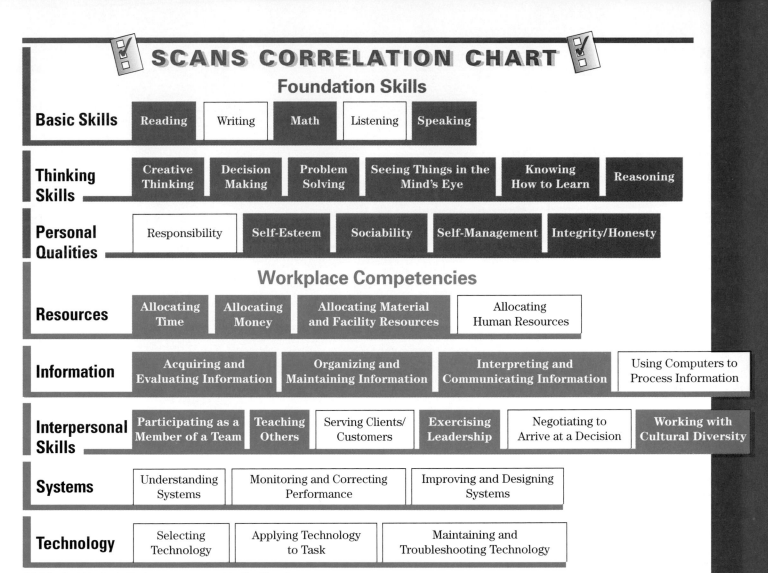

Basic Skills	Reading	Writing	Math	Listening	Speaking		

Thinking Skills	Creative Thinking	Decision Making	Problem Solving	Seeing Things in the Mind's Eye	Knowing How to Learn	Reasoning

Personal Qualities	Responsibility	Self-Esteem	Sociability	Self-Management	Integrity/Honesty

Workplace Competencies

Resources	Allocating Time	Allocating Money	Allocating Material and Facility Resources	Allocating Human Resources

Information	Acquiring and Evaluating Information	Organizing and Maintaining Information	Interpreting and Communicating Information	Using Computers to Process Information

Interpersonal Skills	Participating as a Member of a Team	Teaching Others	Serving Clients/ Customers	Exercising Leadership	Negotiating to Arrive at a Decision	Working with Cultural Diversity

Systems	Understanding Systems	Monitoring and Correcting Performance	Improving and Designing Systems

Technology	Selecting Technology	Applying Technology to Task	Maintaining and Troubleshooting Technology

Highlighted blocks indicate areas covered in the Chapter.

Additional Activities

 ### Internet Connection

Ask students to use the Internet to find what kinds of career planning information is available on-line. They should note what kinds of career aptitude tests are available on-line (and take those that are free), what kinds of counseling are available, and make note of appropriate Web sites.

 ### Field Trip Suggestions

Take students to a college placement service office. Have them find out what kinds of audio/visual materials, brochures, and catalogs are available to research their careers. Have students write a couple of paragraphs on the kinds of information available on careers that interest them.

 ### Guest Speaker Suggestions

Ask someone at a placement center to talk about the types of tests available to help students determine what their aptitudes and abilities are. Have them explain that these are often available, for a fee, at college and university placement centers.

Key to Ability Levels

Each section gives skill-building activities. Each activity has been labeled for use with students of various learning styles and abilities.

L1 Level 1 activities are basic activities and should be within the range of all students.

L2 Level 2 activities are average activities and should be within the range of average and above average students.

L3 Level 3 activities are challenging activities designed for the ability range of above average students.

School-Based Learning

Chapter Overview

Chapter 2 emphasizes students' need to reflect on personal values and lifestyle goals as they make decisions about potential careers.

Section 2-1 presents a decision-making activity that students can use for self-evaluation and career selection.

Section 2-2 helps students identify how individual values and the role values and lifestyle goals play in career decisions.

Section 2-3 focuses on how aptitudes and abilities affect career choices.

Background Information

Write chapter objectives (Sections 2-1, 2-2, and 2-3) on the chalkboard or use the chapter objective transparency for class discussion.

Choose assignments from the *Student Activity Workbook* and write them on the chalkboard.

Have students preview the chapter, looking at pictures, and reading captions and content headings. Ask students to describe what they might learn in this chapter.

Preteaching Vocabulary

Write the Key Terms from Sections 2-1, 2-2, and 2-3 on the chalkboard. Have students describe how each term relates to learning about personal interests and career choices.

22

Meeting SPECIAL Needs

Limited Proficiency in English

Have a language specialist help you prepare exams and review reading assignments. Specialists can identify potential problems with language used in an exam. They can offer suggestions on wording, sentence structure, and vocabulary level that will increase students' comprehension without compromising the integrity of the exam. They can also help identify where students are having trouble with the material versus having trouble with the language.

Getting to Know Yourself

Section 2-1
Decision Making

Section 2-2
Setting Lifestyle Goals

Section 2-3
Are Your Goals Realistic?

In this video segment, explore why it's important to consider your personality, interests, and abilities, when choosing a career.

Journal
Personal Career Plan

Think about all your activities during a typical week—at school and work, with your friends, with your family, and alone. Which particular activity do you find most satisfying? What makes that activity especially satisfying for you? What does this tell you about your values and your interests? Record your ideas in your journal.

23

Addressing LEARNING Styles

Intrapersonal Learner

Have students research the background of someone they admire—musician, scientist, teacher, actor, or community leader, for example—through books, magazines, videos, or personal interviews. Students should focus on the kinds of jobs the person has had over the course of his or her career as well as the skills the person has acquired, including any that are not directly job related. Ask students to write a résumé for the person they researched.

FOCUS

Bell Ringer

Ask students to list three situations in which they have made a decision or will soon need to make a decision.

Introducing the Section

Ask for volunteers to read items on their lists. Ask what process the students used to make their decisions. As you obtain information, write it on the chalkboard. Use this to introduce the decision-making process, relating each step to things students may have done in making their own decisions. As you discuss each step, ask students to name things they would do to make a career decision.

Motivational Activity

Discussion

Have students imagine they have just won $10,000 in a contest. They can buy anything they want with the money. Ask students to tell you each step in the decision-making process regarding their purchases and write them on the chalkboard.

Have students describe what they would do at each step and list this information on the board. After discussing each step in the decision-making process, ask volunteers to explain how using such a process for deciding what to buy might help them make a better decision. How would they relate this process to other decisions they make?

Decision Making

OBJECTIVES

After studying this section, you will be able to:

• Follow the seven steps in the decision-making process.
• Follow an effective strategy for choosing a career.

KEY TERM

decision-making process

How do you make decisions? Do you flip a coin? Consult friends? Make lists of pros and cons? If you're the kind of person who waits for someone else to make decisions for you, you may not be very happy with the outcome.

Maybe you've been putting off deciding what to do after graduation. If so, keep the following fact in mind: Most people don't plan to fail; they just fail to plan. The truth is, half of all employed people simply fall into their jobs—out of laziness or luck or from being unaware of other options. If you'd rather have a say in your future, it's time to take control of your own life.

A Seven-Step Process

If you've ever made an important decision, you know that good decision making doesn't just happen. The longer a decision will affect your life, the more time you need to think about possible consequences. Decisions that will affect your life for many years should be made carefully and logically. One of the biggest decisions in your life—your career choice—will require serious planning. This will be easier if you follow a **decision-making process**—a logical series of steps to identify and evaluate possibilities and to arrive at a good choice.

Workforce 2000 Trends

In the 21st century, full-time jobs may largely disappear. Instead, work will be done by temporary workers, consultants, and sub-contractors. In the late 1990s, approximately one-third of American industries sub-contracted manufacturing, clerical, and even management work.

TEACH

Guided Practice

Teaching Strategies

1. Assign and review Section 2-1.
2. Use the transparency for this section.

Teaching Tip

People who make decisions too quickly or without considering the impact on long-term goals may find that their actions are not helping them achieve what they want. Help students understand that using a systematic approach to making decisions can help them consider a wider range of alternatives and make decisions that better fit both short-term and long-term goals.

Discussion Starter

Find out how many students have made decisions only to later change their minds or wish they could reverse their decisions. How could they avoid such situations in the future?

Critical Thinking

Using the decision-making process may not be necessary for all decisions that students make. Have students prepare a list of ten types of situations requiring decisions (such as which movie to see or which car to buy). Then have them identify which of the ten decisions would benefit from the decision-making process.

Breaking It Down

Like learning a new dance, following a decision-making process may feel awkward at first as you work through the basic steps. Once you have learned them, however, you can add variations of your own to adapt the process to different life situations. Here, then, are the seven basic steps in a typical decision-making process:

1. Define your needs or wants.
2. Analyze your resources.
3. Identify your choices.
4. Gather information.
5. Evaluate your choices.
6. Make a decision.
7. Plan how to reach your goal.

Now take a look at **Figure 2-1** on the next page to see how these seven steps can be applied to buying a car.

> Some decisions are more important than others. **Why might these newlyweds take a long time to decide which house to buy?**

YOU'RE THE BOSS!

Solving Workplace Problems

As the owner of a fast-food franchise, you have trouble keeping reliable employees. This is the first job for most of the young people you hire, and they need weeks of training. You often feel that, once your employees are well trained and productive, they move on to other jobs. What will you do about this situation?

Chapter 2 • Getting to Know Yourself **25**

Extending the Illustration

Ask students to explain to a friend when to use the decision-making process and when not to use it.

Caption Answer: Buying a house is a major decision that will probably affect their lives for years to come.

Teaching YOU'RE THE BOSS!

Possible responses: Accept and plan for the situation. Screen applicants more carefully and select only those who do not need much training. Offer pay increases and supervisory opportunities to encourage good employees to stay.

TEACH *(cont'd.)*

SCANS Foundation Skills Connection

L1 Math

Anna wants to buy a car from a family friend who is selling it for $6,000. Anna earns $115 a week from her part-time job and has $2,500 as a down payment. The owner will let her pay the remainder over 18 months without interest.

Calculate the amount of the payments. Decide whether you would buy the car if you were Anna. ($200. Students would probably buy the car because the payments are affordable for Anna and no interest is being charged.)

L2 Knowing How to Learn

One of the steps in the decision-making process is to gather information. Tell students that they need to buy camping equipment. What resources would they use to decide what type of equipment they need?

(Possible answers include books, experienced campers, trade shows, magazine articles, advertisements, and the Internet.)

L3 Decision Making

Have students create a career plan using the seven-step decision-making process. Students should list each step, then write answers as they relate to a future career.

Would You Buy This Car?
How to Use a Seven-Step Decision-Making Process

Step 1	**Define Your Needs or Wants**	Chances are, you want a car that is not too expensive and is in reasonably good condition.
Step 2	**Analyze Your Resources**	Your main resource in this case is money. How much do you have? How much do you need to buy the car?
Step 3	**Identify Your Choices**	Now it's time to think about where you will get the car. You might make a list of sources, including new-car dealers, used-car dealers, owner-advertised cars in the classified ads, and your second cousin Ellen, who offered to sell you her 1985 station wagon for "next to nothing."
Step 4	**Gather Information**	Next, you must take time to evaluate each source on your list. Call each person or place, and make an appointment. Look at each available car, and ask questions. Take notes on such factors as cost, condition, insurance, warranty, and appearance. Take test drives. Draw sketches. At this point, you may eliminate some choices. For example, a new car may be too expensive.
Step 5	**Evaluate Your Choices**	Now is the time to review your notes. You might make a chart rating each car on the basis of four or five factors. In evaluating your choices, you will need to consider which factors are most important to you.
Step 6	**Make a Decision**	Working from your notes or chart, decide which car you want to buy.
Step 7	**Plan How to Reach Your Goal**	Focusing now on the car you have chosen, list the steps you need to take before you can actually drive the car home. These may include informing the dealer that you want the car, making a down payment, arranging a loan, and buying insurance.

▲ **Figure 2-1** A seven-step decision-making process can help you make informed choices. Why is it important to make conscious decisions?

Extending Figure 2-1

What role do feelings or intuition play in decision making? (Some decisions just "feel" right, perhaps because the decision maker has studied the issues and weighed alternatives.)

Caption Answer: Making conscious decisions allows you to exert greater control over the course of your life.

Extending the Illustration

Why do you think you might be more successful doing a job you enjoy? (You're likely to put in more effort and work better with others if you enjoy your work.)

Caption Answer: They probably enjoy working with their hands, spending time outdoors, being part of a team, and derive satisfaction from making something from scratch.

 What you enjoy doing is an important personal resource that needs to be considered as you plan your career. *What do you think these carpenters enjoy about their work?*

Choosing a Career

You can also use the seven-step process in choosing a career. However, since the stakes are much higher than they are in buying a car, the process will be more complex. You will work through each of the following steps in detail as you proceed through this and the next three chapters.

EXCELLENT BUSINESS PRACTICES

Personal Empowerment

Rhino Foods Inc. of Burlington, Vermont, a small frozen-dessert company, has a "wants" program designed to help employees achieve their life goals. All employees are encouraged to work with "wants coordinators" who coach employees in identifying what they want and setting steps to achieve goals or to cultivate skills. These wants may range from buying a house to writing a book or seeking a promotion. The program helps workers develop strong connections between their work and personal lives.

The company also takes a personal interest in employees. When Rhino Foods faced a temporary overload of 25 percent of its workforce, the company helped employees find temporary work at local companies. If the other companies paid them lower wages, Rhino paid the difference. Employees kept their seniority, benefits, and accrued vacation, and came back to Rhino when jobs opened up again.

Thinking Critically

How can a job be an essential component to attaining specific "wants"?

Chapter 2 • Getting to Know Yourself **27**

Extending EXCELLENT BUSINESS PRACTICES

Answer: A job can provide the income and skills to attain wants.

Further Application: Have students make a "wants" list that includes items they might want to have within the next month or six months, or goals they want to achieve within five years. Ask students to list the steps they can take to bring them closer to getting what they want.

Independent Practice

Assign as homework the chapter activity in the *School-to-Work Activity Handbook.*

Skills Practice

Have students construct a time line that charts their predicted wants and needs over the next ten years.

Writing: *Directions*

Tell students they have a friend who is considering a job as a salesperson. The job pays $4.75 per hour plus a 3 percent commission on all sales. Have students write directions for calculating total potential weekly earnings if the job requires 40 hours a week and typical sales are $3,200 each week.

Research

Have students learn more about personality and learning styles by researching and taking tests that measure these attributes. A guidance counselor or librarian are good resources.

ASSESS

Assessment
Process

Have students apply the decision-making process to choosing an apartment. Collect rental ads from the local newspaper or have students bring ads to class. Set an amount students can spend, then have them follow the process to make a decision.

Step 1. Define Your Needs by Using Your Hopes and Dreams

The path to a career starts with considering your hopes and dreams for the future. Where will you want to live? Do you want a job that will allow you to travel or to stay at home? How much money will you need to earn? How much of your time and energy will you be willing to devote to your job? Later in this chapter, you will explore such questions and generate information about your personal goals.

Step 2. Analyze Your Personal Resources

In choosing a career, your resources relate to who you are and what you have to offer. Such resources include your values, interests, aptitudes and abilities, and personality traits and styles of learning. By being aware of all that you are, you will be more likely to make a realistic career choice. In the next sections of this chapter, you will examine these various aspects of yourself.

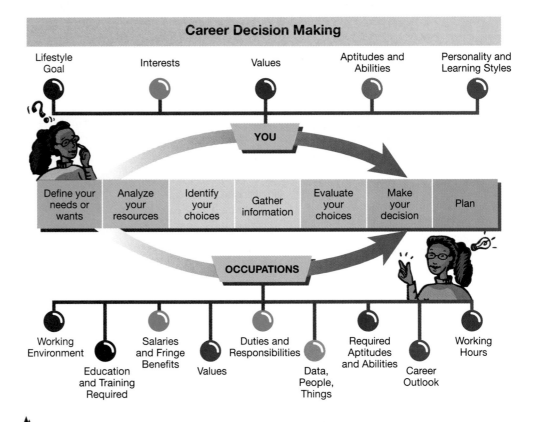

▲ **Figure 2-2** Over the next few chapters, you will be proceeding through the seven-step decision-making process, trying to choose a career for yourself. This diagram previews your course. What two general areas will you be exploring before you actually make a career decision and begin to plan for it?

▶▶ **Extending Figure 2-2** ◀◀

Why is it important to make a career decision rather than haphazardly trying different careers until you find one you like? (Studying your interests and career areas that fit those interests can help you find a more satisfying career than you are likely to find by following a hit-or-miss approach.)

Caption Answer: your personality and the various occupations

Step 3. Identify Your Career Choices

This step involves selecting several possible careers that you think may match your personal goals and resources. If you are like many teenagers, you may not be able to think of a career you would enjoy. You can jump-start your thinking by increasing your awareness of life's possibilities. Keep your eyes and ears open to discover "what's out there." Even if you decide not to follow certain paths, at least you will know your options. Chapters 3 and 4 will help you uncover many career possibilities.

Step 4. Research Your Career Choices

Have you ever heard the phrase "research and development"? The two terms go together because successful people know that there is no development without research. Chapter 3 will show you how to go about researching the careers you've identified as possible choices for yourself. In Chapter 4, you will see if being in business for yourself is the right path for you.

Step 5. Evaluate Your Career Choices

By the time you reach this fifth step, you will have gathered much information both about yourself and about various career possibilities. Evaluating your career choices involves systematically looking at them to see whether they match your personal goals and resources. *Figure 2-2* shows how the decision-making process is central to career evaluation. If the process looks complicated, don't worry. Chapter 5 will suggest a helpful strategy for making this evaluation process manageable.

Steps 6 and 7. Make Your Decision and Plan How to Reach Your Goal

Though you may change your career goal several times, it is still important to make a decision and a plan. You may also discover at some point that your career goal is unrealistic or undesirable. You can then repeat the decision-making process to arrive at a new goal. Chapter 5 will help you focus on these last two steps.

SECTION 2-1 *Review*

Understanding Key Concepts

Using complete sentences, answer the following questions on a separate sheet of paper.

1. Imagine that you've won a $1,000 gift certificate for buying audio/video equipment at a local store. Explain how you would use the seven steps in the decision-making process to decide what to buy.

2. Explain the importance of having a strategy for choosing a career.

Chapter 2 • Getting to Know Yourself **29**

SECTION 2-1 *Review* ANSWERS

1. Answers should demonstrate, through relevant and concrete examples, students' understanding of the seven steps in the decision-making model.

2. A strategy makes decision-making easier by breaking it down into logical steps so that possible courses of action can be identified and evaluated and a good choice can be made.

Evaluation

Assign the section review.

Reteaching

Have students write a paragraph listing each step in the decision-making process. Then have students write a sentence or two explaining the actions to be taken at each step. Next, have them explain why following each step in the process is important in making a good career choice.

Extending the Content

Assign the appropriate Chapter 2 activities in the *Student Activity Workbook*.

Ask students to write a paragraph or two beginning with this sentence: "If I could be anything, I would be . . . ." Tell students to expand the paragraph by describing their hopes and dreams for the future.

CLOSE

Have students explain this statement: "No decision is the same as a 'no' decision."

FOCUS

Bell Ringer

Ask students to make a list of five people they admire and tell why they admire each one.

Introducing the Section

Have students share their lists of people they admire from the Bell Ringer activity. What values do they think each person possesses? Discuss how students' choices of people reflect their own values. Use this discussion to talk about lifestyle goals and how they are influenced by individual values.

Next, discuss individual interests and how they relate to career choices. Give several examples and ask students to give examples also. After discussing interests, ask students to give you examples of different kinds of jobs—working with data, people, and things. Finish this section by discussing interest surveys and how they can help guide a person's career choice. You may want to have your school's guidance counselor talk to your class about the surveys they can take.

Motivational Activity

Writing

Have students list five interests or aptitudes they would like to pursue in a future career. For each interest or aptitude, have them identify a possible career.

Setting Lifestyle Goals

OBJECTIVES

After studying this section, you will be able to:

- Identify your values and describe how they affect your career choices.
- Identify your interests and describe how they affect your career choices.
- Determine whether you prefer working with data, people, or things.

KEY TERMS

lifestyle goals
values
data

"Know thyself!" This inscription was carved at the Ancient Greek temple in Delphi, where people once traveled seeking advice about their futures. This bit of ancient wisdom is no less valid today. By getting to know yourself, you can plot your future better and choose a career you'll be interested in pursuing. A good place to begin this inward exploration is by considering lifestyle goals.

Lifestyle goals are the way you want to spend your time, energy, and resources in the future. Brainstorm about the lifestyle you'd like to have someday. Ask yourself a few questions.

- What do you want to accomplish in life?
- Do you want to raise a family?
- Where would you like to live—in a house or in an apartment? In a city or in the country?
- How would you like to spend your free time?
- Do you want a high income or just enough money to be comfortable?

Now imagine your life 5 or 10 years from today. Write down or sketch the way you'd like to be living. What career would make this lifestyle possible? To begin to see whether this career would be a realistic choice for you, you'll need to take a closer look at yourself.

30 *Unit 1 • Self-Assessment*

Addressing Workplace Diversity

In the 21st century, as more women make up the workforce, child care, elder care, job sharing, flexible work schedules, and telecommuting will become important benefits for companies to offer in order to retain valuable employees.

Many people prefer a career that allows them to live near their family and friends. **What kind of career might give you a chance to work in your community?**

listening to music, you probably would say that one of your values is artistic expression.

Besides principles and beliefs, your values may also include concrete things, such as money and fine clothing. As you think about a future career, you should consider how well it suits your values.

Six General Values

Your values may change as you go through life. However, you will probably keep a core set of basic values that you learned early on from the people who were most important to you. To help determine your current values, think about the following list of six general values. Which ones are very important to you, and which ones concern you less? Can you think of any careers especially suited to each of these values?

1. *Responsibility.* Being responsible means fulfilling obligations in a dependable and trustworthy way. You may decide to take on responsibilities, such as caring for a sick friend. Other responsibilities may be automatically expected of you as part of your position in life, say, as a parent or team leader.

2. *Relationships.* If you value relationships, your family and friends are important to you. You may then make career decisions that will allow you to work with people you like or to live near your family.

What Are Your Values?

Becoming aware of your values is an important way of getting to know yourself. Your **values** are the principles that you want to live by and the beliefs that are important to you. For example, if you spend a good deal of time playing your guitar and

This woman works as an aide in a veterinary clinic. **What other career would be appropriate for a person who cares about animals?**

Chapter 2 • Getting to Know Yourself **31**

Guided Practice
Teaching Strategies
1. Assign and review Section 2-2.
2. Use the transparency for this section.
3. Assign and review the Case Study.

Teaching Tip

Bring several magazines to class that show people in a variety of lifestyles. Have students go through the magazines and identify lifestyles that appeal to them. Discuss how having a lifestyle goal can help guide the choice of a career.

Discussion Starter

Individual interests often lead people to their careers. Have students name as many hobbies as they can think of while you write them on the chalkboard. Then ask students to suggest possible careers related to each hobby.

Teaching Tip

Write each of the six general values on the chalkboard. Have students give examples of each value. Discuss how people's values affect the choices they make. For example, a person who values good grades might pass up a movie to study for a test.

Next, ask students to add other values to the list. (For example, some students might value art or music; others might value physical fitness or punctuality.)

Extending the Illustration

How do personal preferences affect career decisions? (Personal interests and values help you determine the jobs you might enjoy as well as guide your decision to seek jobs in certain areas.)

Caption Answer: Possible answers include owning a neighborhood business; or working in a local company, school, or hospital.

Extending the Illustration

Would a person who likes taking care of animals enjoy taking care of people just as well? (Not necessarily. People who are shy around others may be more comfortable working with animals.)

Caption Answer: pet walking and pet care, training seeing-eye dogs, working in a wildlife conservancy

3. *Compassion.* Having compassion means you care deeply about people and their well-being. You may also feel compassion for other creatures, such as threatened animals. A compassionate person may choose a career that would help people lead better lives.

4. *Courage.* Courage is the ability to conquer fear or despair. You use courage, for example, when you speak up for an unpopular cause. It may take courage to follow your values!

5. *Achievement.* Valuing achievement means you want to succeed in whatever you do, whether you are an artist, an auto mechanic, a wilderness guide, or a computer programmer.

6. *Recognition.* If you value recognition, you want other people to appreciate and respect your accomplishments. You want to be rewarded for your work in some noticeable way—with a good salary, through job promotions, or with approval and praise.

Now make your own list, ranking your values in order of importance. You may include some or all of the six general values, and you may add as many others as you wish. (Keep this list for later use.) Can you imagine a career that would satisfy your particular mix of values?

Putting Your Values into Practice

While many people may share the same value—such as believing it is important to help others—each person may put that value into practice in a different way. For example, Chris Watson is a paraprofessional at an elementary school in suburban Chicago. He helps disabled children get around by assisting them

Chris works at a school for children with special needs. He makes friends with all the children at the school. This behavior helps students with disabilities become more a part of things. *How else could Chris help the children he works with?*

with their wheelchairs and walkers. Through his work, Chris helps one person at a time. Janet Gregory, in contrast, helps others indirectly by working as an administrator for a charity organization that shelters the homeless in the Bronx, New York. In trying to match a career to your own set of values, you will probably find that you have a range of choices. Narrowing your choices will mean looking even deeper into yourself.

What Are Your Interests?

In addition to recognizing your values, you need to pay attention to your interests when considering a career. Your interests are the things you enjoy doing. You may, for example, like singing in a choir or doing dissections in biology class. If you aren't sure what your interests are, one way to find out is to try activities you haven't done before. You might try, for example, taking karate classes or volunteering at a hospital.

Favorite Activities

You probably already enjoy a variety of activities, so make a list of your 10 favorite ones and try to rank them. Think of activities you like to do with friends or quietly by yourself—at school, at home, at work, or outdoors. (Keep this list for later use.)

Careers Related to Data, People, and Things

Data	People	Things
Web site designer	Fitness trainer	Video producer
Bookkeeper	Nurse	Computer service technician
Translator	Sales representative	Landscaper
Statistical clerk	Psychiatric aide	Recording engineer
Proofreader	Hairstylist	Cabinetmaker

Figure 2-3 This chart shows some careers in each of three categories. Which career interests you the most? Why? You can find other listings at your library in the U.S. Department of Labor's <u>Dictionary of Occupational Titles.</u>

SCANS Workplace Competencies Connection

L1 **Participating as a Member of a Team**

Group students in teams of three or four. Tell each team to discuss their individual career interests, then list them on a sheet of paper. Each team is to then watch one or more popular television program and identify the occupations of the characters that might correspond to their list of interests. Ask the teams to share their lists and observations in class.

L2 **Organizing and Maintaining Information**

Have students create a chart of their personal values and interests. Students can use these charts as they study later chapters and as they research careers that match their values and interests.

L3 **Working with Cultural Diversity**

Tell students they are working in a large city hospital admissions office. Many of the patients speak little or no English. What special values and interests might students need to work in this career? (Values might include compassion, patience, and interest in helping others. Special interests might include health care, clerical work, or learning other languages.)

Teaching ETHICS in Action

Have students follow these steps to help them make a decision.
1. What are the ethical issues?
2. What are the alternatives?
3. Who are the affected parties?
4. How do the alternatives affect the parties?
5. What is your decision?

Extending Figure 2-3

Think of people you know who have full-time jobs. Which of them work with people? With data? With things?

Caption Answer: Answers will vary, but students should explain their choices.

TEACH *(cont'd.)*

Critical Thinking

Ask students to discuss whether their values will change as they get older and have more life experience.

Independent Practice
Reading

Have students read the classified section of your local newspaper to find three jobs they consider intriguing. Have students make a list of at least three values and three interests a person would need to succeed in each of these jobs.

Writing: *Informational*

Have students write at least 10 activities they like to do. Beside each activity, they are to indicate whether it involves primarily data, people, or things. Have students write a paragraph regarding the possible career based on their preferences for working with data, people, or things.

Skills Practice

Tell students they work with someone whose values are very different from theirs. For example, the coworker is often late to meetings and rarely finishes work on time, which is detrimental to students' performance. Have students discuss how they would handle this situation. (Some possibilities are to discuss the problem with the coworker, try to negotiate changes in work behavior, try to get assigned to a different team.)

34

Data, People, or Things?

Identifying your interests can help you recognize whether you would prefer to work with data, people, or things. These three categories described below can form the basis for describing different kinds of careers.

- The **data** category involves working with information, ideas, facts, symbols, figures, or statistics.
- The people category includes working with people *and* animals.
- The things category involves working with physical objects of any size, such as instruments, tools, machinery, equipment, raw materials, and vehicles.

Since any career you choose would probably involve an overlapping of these categories, think about which category you are *most* interested in. Look at *Figure 2-3* on page 33 to see some careers in which people work primarily with data, people, or things.

ETHICS in Action

You're a newly hired sales clerk in an office supply store. A group of students comes into the store regularly. You've seen these students steal several small items. When you mention this to a more experienced employee, she just shrugs. Will you discuss your observations with anyone else? Why or why not?

Interest Surveys

Another helpful way to identify and assess your interests is to take an interest survey, which is like a test that has no right or wrong answers. You choose from a long list of activities to determine which ones appeal to you and then match your interests to possible careers. Ask your teacher or guidance counselor for help in finding an interest survey.

SECTION 2-2 *Review*

Understanding Key Concepts

Using complete sentences, answer the following questions on a separate sheet of paper.

1. Choose a value that is important to you. Discuss how you developed this value and how you might put it into practice in a career.

2. Choose one of your interests, and write down reasons why you enjoy this activity. Suggest what career might let you develop this interest further.

3. Choose a career from Figure 2-3. Describe how the categories data, people, and things might overlap for a person working in that career.

SECTION 2-2 *Review* ANSWERS

1. Answers will vary. Possible response: I developed compassion after helping a neighbor care for an injured stray cat.

2. Answers will vary. Possible response: I love playing basketball because I like physical activity and the challenge of making a basket. I might use this interest in a career in recreation.

3. Answers will vary. Possible response: A sales representative, while working mainly with people, would also use things, such as computers, and data connected with the product he sells.

CASE STUDY

Exploring Careers: Communications and Media

Carolina Narváez
Public Relations Specialist

Q: What *is* public relations?

A: My company deals with corporate public relations. We try to build a positive public image of each client's company or corporation. We do that by writing press releases about things going on in the company—new products, staff changes, policy changes, events that promote the company's image. We contact the media; such as television, radio, newspapers, or magazines.

Q: What skills are most useful in your job?

A: The most useful skills are people skills. I work with the client and with others at the company who are on the client's team. I have to be able to communicate clearly. I also have to be detail-oriented, organized, and patient. Writing, editing, and proofreading skills are also necessary.

Q: What background did you have before going into public relations?

A: I majored in communications in college and had some experience in the communications field. I thought it would be interesting and a good learning experience to handle multiple tasks and accounts at once.

Thinking Critically —————

What types of companies need public relations specialists? Explain.

CAREER FACTS

Nature of the Work:
Develop and maintain a favorable public image for a client through media contacts, public events, and publications.

Training or Education Needed:
English, journalism, or communications degree preferred; experience working in a related field.

Aptitudes, Abilities, and Skills:
Math, listening, speaking, and interpersonal skills; problem-solving skills; decision-making and reading and writing

skills; ability to allocate time, material, and human resources; ability to work under pressure; skills in persuasion; creativity; self-reliance; attention to detail.

Salary Range:
Start $15,000 to $20,000; up to $50,000 or more.

Career Path:
Start at a newspaper or as a secretary or research assistant at a public relations firm, gradually taking on a wider range of responsibilities; advance within the firm or by moving to other firms.

Chapter 2 • Getting to Know Yourself **35**

Extending the CASE STUDY

Answer: any large corporation; city and state governments; museums, zoos, aquariums, symphonies; universities; environmental organizations; political organizations

Further Application: Have students discuss other fields they might explore in

which they could learn skills to complement their chosen careers. (For example, someone interested in environmental issues might volunteer in a political campaign; someone interested in fashion might work in a fabric store or with a photographer.)

Assessment
Oral

Divide students into two panels. Panel 1 is to discuss information related to values and how individual values affect career choices. Panel 2 is to focus on interests and how they can lead to career preferences, and preferences for working with data, people, or things.

Evaluation

Assign the section review.

Reteaching

To help reinforce the six general values, have students write each value on a separate sheet of paper and then draw a picture or clip one from a newspaper or magazine to show what the value represents to them.

Extending the Content

Assign the appropriate Chapter 2 activities in the *Student Activity Workbook*.

Have students list at least two values, interests, and lifestyle goals that might draw people to the following types of work: dancer, pet store owner, chemistry teacher, jeweler, electrician.

CLOSE

Have students draw a pyramid of their personal values.

FOCUS

Bell Ringer

Have students write a list of five jobs. For each job, have them describe a basic personality type that might be good at the job (for example, an outgoing person in a sales job). Ask them to list other character traits a person doing each job should have.

Introducing the Section

Have volunteers share their lists from the Bell Ringer activity and their reasons for matching personality types and character traits to each job. Point out that personality types directly relate to career choices. Ask students if their "dream jobs" suit their personalities.

Discuss the role that skills and aptitudes play in career choice. Ask students for examples (for example, musical ability is required to be a rock singer, and good hand-eye coordination is needed for sports careers).

Finally, discuss how knowing your personal style can help you learn more efficiently.

Motivational Activity

Critical Thinking

Although people fall into broad, general personality types, each person is unique. Ask students whether they can change elements of their personalities and if so, how?

Are Your Goals Realistic?

OBJECTIVES

After studying this section, you will be able to:

- **Identify your aptitudes and abilities and describe how they affect your career choice.**
- **Identify and match your personality and learning style to career choices.**

KEY TERMS

aptitude
ability
personality
self-concept
learning styles

Now that you have identified some of your values and interests, what's next? You'll want to consider your skills and personality.

Aptitudes and Abilities

Aptitude and ability are the "before and after" of a skill. An **aptitude** is your potential for learning a certain skill. An **ability** is a skill you have already developed. Suppose you discover that you have the knack for training your new pet dog. If you continue to study and work with other dogs to become a professional trainer, then your aptitude will become your ability.

How do you discover your own aptitudes and abilities? First, you need to realize that there are many kinds of skills. Look at these general examples from the list of SCANS Skills:

creative thinking	decision making
knowing how to learn	seeing things in the mind's eye
responsibility	self-esteem
friendliness	adaptability
honesty	self-control

What other skills can you think of?

What Are *Your* Aptitudes and Abilities?

To get a clear picture of your aptitudes and abilities, make a list of all your skills that you can think of. Need help? Try these techniques:

36 *Unit 1 • Self-Assessment*

Implementing Teamwork

Using the lists of aptitudes and abilities above, organize students into pairs. Ask each pair to exchange lists and review the items identified. Once the lists are reviewed, have each reviewer provide additional positive information about his or her partner. Lead a discussion about constructive criticism.

- Make a chart with the headings Mental, Physical, and Social. List your aptitudes and abilities in each category.
- Meet with a friend, family member, neighbor, or anyone else you trust. Talk about what you think your aptitudes and abilities are, and ask the other person to write them down. After you finish, discuss the list. Does this person agree with your evaluation? What ideas does he or she have about your aptitudes and abilities?

Matching Your Aptitudes and Abilities to Careers

Now review your list of aptitudes and abilities, and try to think of at least one career that requires each of your skills. For example, if one of your aptitudes is caring for children, a good match might be a career as a day care provider or teacher. Finding a realistic career match for your aptitudes and abilities will make your working life more enjoyable.

Once you have identified some of your aptitudes and abilities, you will probably feel that you are really getting to know yourself. Next, look at how your personality influences your career choice.

Your Personality and Learning Styles

All the special qualities that make you an individual form your personality. **Personality** is the combination of your attitudes, behaviors, and characteristics. To explore your personality, you need to examine your self-concept and styles of learning.

Self-Concept

The way you see yourself is your **self-concept**. When you look in the mirror, do you see someone who is confident, curious, dependable, funny, observant, sympathetic? You may have some or all of these traits, and more. Some of your personality traits may even seem to contradict one another. You may, for example, feel shy in new situations but outgoing in familiar surroundings. On some days you may think you're a fairly interesting person, and on other days, you may think you're not that interesting. Everyone has highs and lows. However, you probably do have a fairly consistent self-concept—a feeling that you know the kind of person you are.

Personality Types and Learning Styles

The way you interact with the world around you to gather information and turn it into knowledge is a key component of your personality. The different ways that people naturally think and learn are called **learning styles** (see *Figure 2-4*). When you are aware of your own learning styles, you are able to determine the best approach for you to learn something new. You also can judge what kind of field would be good for your particular personality type, because you'd probably do well in a career that used your strongest learning style.

TEACH

Guided Practice
Teaching Strategies
1. Assign and review Section 2-3.
2. Use the transparency for this section.

Discussion Starter
Tell students they have focused on the following three want ads: public relations director for an airline, computer programmer for a software company, and carpenter for a construction company. Which job would best suit their personalities (not necessarily their aptitudes or abilities)? Why?

Critical Thinking
How does a person with a good self-concept differ from one who is conceited?

Interview
Have students interview five people regarding their learning styles. Tell students to share the information in Figure 2-4 with their subjects. Do most people identify one particular style, or do they use different styles depending on what they need to learn?

SCANS Foundation Skills Connection

L1 Reasoning
Have each student list 10 adjectives that describe his or her personality. Have students use this description in matching personal traits to career interests.

SCANS Foundation Skills Connection (cont'd.)

L2 Self-Esteem

Have students present their special skills and aptitudes to the class. The presentation can take the form of a poster, flyer, magazine ad, picture, or other medium.

L3 Self-Management

Amy is a smart, hardworking student who wants to be a lawyer. She has a visual learning style and has some difficulty learning from reading. Amy is concerned that it may take too much reading for her to achieve her career goal. How would you feel if you were Amy? Would you give up or would you still pursue your dream?

SCANS Workplace Competencies Connections

L1 Interpreting and Communicating Information

Have students imagine that they are managers dealing with an employee who is outgoing and confident but who has weak job skills. The employee has just asked for a large raise, which you feel he or she doesn't deserve. Have students brainstorm ways they could communicate the appropriate message without being negative or demoralizing the person.

Read the list of the seven styles of learning given in *Figure 2-4.* Which ones apply to you? Which one do you think is your main style of learning?

Being aware of all the aspects of yourself that make you who you are will give you a great advantage as you explore career choices. Look at *Figure 2-5* on page 39 to see how one person developed her special qualities on the path to a career. Then write a description of yourself in your journal, adding drawings if you wish. Include at least some of your values, interests, aptitudes and abilities, and personality traits and learning styles.

In Chapter 3, you will find out how to research careers—and you will come closer to knowing what you want to do.

Seven Styles of Learning

Type of Learner	Likes	Best Ways to Learn
Linguistic	Likes to read, write, and tell stories; good at memorizing names and dates.	Learns best by saying, hearing, and seeing words.
Logical/ Mathematical	Likes to do experiments, work with numbers, explore patterns and relationships; good at math, logic, and problem solving.	Learns best by making categories, classifying, and working with patterns.
Spatial	Likes to draw, build, design, and create things; good at imagining, doing puzzles and mazes, and reading maps and charts.	Learns best by using the mind's eye and working with colors and pictures.
Musical	Likes to sing, hum, play an instrument, and listen to music; good at remembering melodies, noticing pitches and rhythms, and keeping time.	Learns best through rhythm and melody.
Bodily/ Kinesthetic	Likes to touch and move around; good at hands-on activities and crafts.	Learns best by interacting with people and objects in a real space.
Interpersonal	Likes having lots of friends, talking to people, and joining groups; good at understanding people, leading, organizing, communicating, and mediating conflicts.	Learns best by sharing, comparing, and cooperating.
Intrapersonal	Likes to work alone and pursue interests at own pace; good at self-awareness, focusing on personal feelings, and following instincts to learn what needs to be known.	Learns best through independent study.

 Figure 2-4 Although most people may have a preferred style of learning, they can usually shift between styles to acquire new skills and knowledge. Can you think of a career that would be especially suited to each type of learner?

 Extending Figure 2-4

Read the chart and decide your own preferred style of learning. What other learning styles do you use?

Caption Answer: Possible answers include: linguistic—journalist; logical/ mathematical—accountant; spatial—visual artist; musical—sound engineer; bodily/ kinesthetic—physical therapist; interpersonal—politician; intrapersonal—scholar

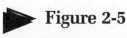

Figure 2-5

The Path to a Career

Sasha's awareness of her values, interests, aptitudes and abilities, and personality and learning styles helped her develop a career as an event planner.

A **Values and Interests.** Sasha always valued her friends. She was a "people" person. She also loved to play sports.

$$a^2 + b^2 = c^2$$

B **Aptitudes and Abilities.** In school, Sasha developed her talent for creative thinking and problem solving. She also had a knack for seeing things in her mind's eye.

C **Personality and Learning Styles.** Sasha was outgoing and liked to be in groups of people. She is an interpersonal learner and enjoys working with people.

D Sasha now has her own business, planning banquets, corporate events, and fund-raisers.

Chapter 2 • Getting to Know Yourself **39**

Extending Figure 2-5

Have students draw their own possible career paths. On their drawings, have them portray their values, interests, aptitudes and abilities, personality, and learning styles.

L2 **Exercising Leadership**

Have students imagine that they work on a team with an employee who has a difficult personality. The person always wants to do things his or her way. As a result, the team does not function very well. Have students discuss ways they can change working relations with the difficult team member and improve the efficiency of the team.

L3 **Participating as a Member of a Team**

Divide the class into pairs. Have each pair choose two jobs and "create" a person to fill each job. Have students write a description of each person that includes name, gender, personality type, special aptitudes and skills, career, lifestyle, marital status, number of children, area of residence, and hobbies.

Encourage students to paint a vivid picture of each person. Have each team read its descriptions to the class. Then discuss why students chose such images. What role did stereotyping play in their choices?

Independent Practice

Have students write six experiences that made them feel good or proud (such as doing well on a school project or helping another person). Then have them write at least three personal aptitudes and/or abilities they displayed in each situation.

39

TEACH *(cont'd.)*

Writing: *Preparation for Oral Presentations*

Have students take notes and prepare visuals for a short presentation regarding what a person needs to know about himself or herself to research and choose a rewarding career.

ASSESS

Assessment

Oral

Have students present what they prepared for the previous activity. See if they understand the relationship between knowledge of self and career interests and goals.

Evaluation

Assign the section review.

MINI QUIZ

Short Answer

1. The first step in the decision-making process is to define your ____. (needs)

2. Beliefs that are important to you are your ____. (values)

3. If you try to succeed in whatever you do, you value ____. (achievement)

4. An ____ is your potential for learning a specific skill. (aptitude)

5. The way you sell yourself is your ____. (self-concept)

Brainstorming about your aptitudes and abilities with a person you trust can help you learn more about yourself. **Why is it useful to get suggestions or advice about careers from an older person?**

Career Do's & Don'ts

To Find Out More About Yourself...

Do:
- spend quiet moments to identify what is important to you.
- keep an open mind to all ideas, people, and opportunities.
- make a list of personal strengths and weaknesses.
- start something you always wanted to do.

Don't:
- place more importance on personal appearance than on who you are inside.
- reject criticism unless it is totally unfounded.
- believe that your way is the only right way.
- make excuses for your behavior.

SECTION 2-3 *Review*

Understanding Key Concepts

Using complete sentences, answer the following questions on a separate sheet of paper.

1. Name something you feel you have an aptitude for. Design a plan for developing it into an ability.

2. Choose a learning style and name a career that you think would match it. Explain why that career would be appropriate for the learner.

40 *Unit 1 • Self-Assessment*

Extending the Illustration

Ask three friends what they think your strongest abilities are. Do their answers match your own perception of your abilities?

Caption Answer: An older person has experience in the workplace and with life in general and may share valuable tips and information.

SECTION 2-3 *Review* ANSWERS

1. Answers will vary. Possible response: I can fix bicycles. I plan to read books on bikes until I can build a bike from scratch.

2. Answers will vary. Possible response: A linguistic learner would be a good tour guide, because he or she is good at memorizing names, places, and dates.

SECTION 2-1 Summary

- Careful planning for your future career will allow you to be in control of one of the biggest decisions in your life.
- The longer a decision will affect your life, the more time you need to think about the consequences beforehand.

Key Terms

decision-making process
(p. 24)

SECTION 2-2 Summary

- When beginning to think about a career, consider your lifestyle goals. Imagine how you would like to spend your time, energy, and resources in the future.
- Consider your values, or the principles that you want to live by, when you are planning for a career. General values include responsibility, relationships, compassion, courage, achievement, and recognition.
- Your interests are your favorite activities. You probably want to plan for a career that would involve your interests. You need to determine whether you prefer working with data, people, or things.

Key Terms

lifestyle goals *(p. 30)*
values *(p. 31)*
data *(p. 34)*

SECTION 2-3 Summary

- An aptitude is your potential for learning a certain skill. An ability is a skill you have already developed. You want to discover your aptitudes and abilities because you will want to use them in the career of your choice.
- Your personality and main learning style can influence the kind of career that would be right for you. Personality includes your attitudes, behaviors, and characteristics. There are seven learning styles, which relate to how you think and learn.

Key Terms

aptitude *(p. 36)*
ability *(p. 36)*
personality *(p. 37)*
self-concept *(p. 37)*
learning styles *(p.37)*

Chapter 2 • Getting to Know Yourself **41**

Computer Activity

Using a word processing software package, have students start an outline titled, "A Seven-Step Career Plan." Students will add to this document in the next two chapters. Ask them to key in a list using the following subheadings: Define Needs/Wants; Analyze Resources; Identify Choices; Gather Information; Evaluate Choices; Make a Decision; Plan Goal.

Use the Testmaker to create a customized test for Chapter 2.

Reteaching

1. Have students identify a favorite activity or hobby. Then have them write answers to these questions: What *values* do you express through this hobby? What *interests* help you enjoy it? What skills with *data, people, or things* does it demand? What *aptitudes* or *abilities* do you bring to it? How does it fit your personality?

2. Assign and review vocabulary terms, chapter questions, and activities from the Chapter Review.

3. Assign and review the Unit Project located on the unit opener pages.

Extending the Content

Assign the appropriate Chapter 2 activities in the *Student Activity Workbook*.

Ask students to decide which of these careers suits them *least*: accountant, park ranger, social worker, plumber, salesperson, poet, astronomer, teacher, athletic coach. Have students write a 200-word report explaining why the career does not suit them.

CLOSE

See the Unit Closure and Unit Evaluation located on page 1.

Answers
Reviewing Key Terms

Profiles will vary but should incorporate all seven headings.

Recalling Key Concepts

1. False: The first step in the seven-step decision-making process is defining wants and needs.
2. True
3. False: People who share the same values can put them into practice in different ways.
4. True
5. False: Working with data means you are working with information, ideas, facts, symbols, figures, or statistics.
6. False: Abilities are skills you have already developed.
7. True

Thinking Critically

1. Possible answer: Instincts are important but should not override following a logical strategy.
2. Possible answer: Settling on a career that opposes your values might result in mental anguish.
3. data—designing, organizing; people—supervising, communicating; things—repairing, operating
4. Possible answer: Would you prefer to work with data, people, or things? What activities do you enjoy at school, at home, and with your friends?

Reviewing Key Terms

On separate paper, write a yearbook profile of yourself using the following terms as headings.

lifestyle goals   aptitudes
values   abilities
data   self-concept
learning styles   personality

Recalling Key Concepts

On a separate sheet of paper, tell whether each statement is true or false. Rewrite any false statements to make them true.

1. The first step in the seven-step decision-making process is to gather information.
2. In choosing a career, your resources pertain to who you are and what you have to offer.
3. People who share the same values always practice them in the same way.
4. Your interests are the things you like to do.
5. Working with data means you are working with things.
6. Aptitudes are skills you have already developed.
7. Learning styles are the different ways that people think and learn.

Thinking Critically

Using complete sentences, answer each of the questions below on a separate sheet of paper.

1. What role do you think your instincts should play in the decision-making process when considering possible careers?

2. What consequences might result from settling on a career that conflicts with your personal values?
3. Classify the following skills according to data, people, or things and explain your reasoning: supervising, repairing, communicating, designing, organizing, operating.
4. Volunteer to help a friend discover his or her aptitudes and abilities. What questions would you ask to encourage your friend to become better aware of his or her personal skills?
5. Think of three people you know well, and decide which learning styles fit them. Explain your choices.

 SCANS Foundation Skills and Workplace Competencies

Basic Skills: *Speaking*

1. Decide on three values that you feel are important. Give a brief talk to the class explaining why you care about these values. Give examples to illustrate each value. You may want to write out your whole speech and practice at home before speaking to the class.

Information: *Organizing and Maintaining Information*

2. Create a chart to help you keep track of what you have learned about yourself. Use these column headings: Lifestyle Goals, Values, Interests, Aptitudes, Abilities, and Learning Styles. Write or brainstorm to fill in the chart. You can add to it as the year goes on.

5. Possible answer: My mother is a spatial learner because she is a sculptor; my grandfather is a linguistic learner because he likes to tell stories; my friend is an intrapersonal learner because he prefers to work on projects alone.

 SCANS Foundation Skills and Workplace Competencies

1. Possible values may include responsibility, relationships, compassion, courage, achievement, recognition, or any other values. Students should explain their choices and give examples of the values.

Connecting Academics to the Workplace

Social Studies

1. Research the system of values in another culture. Look in library books, an encyclopedia, or CD-ROM, or interview someone who grew up in a different culture. Name and describe three values. How do these values affect the world of work in that culture? Share your findings in a report to the class.

Math

2. Conduct a study on the learning styles in your class. Follow these steps:

- Take a survey. Ask each student to identify his or her main learning style. Record the total number of students for each style.

- Make a bar graph showing the number of students for each learning style.

- Write up a brief report of your class's learning styles. Is there one main style? Are all the learning styles represented?

Art

3. Draw a picture that reflects one (or some) of your values or interests. Use a pencil, markers, watercolors, or collage techniques. Make the picture abstract or realistic, but be prepared to explain your artwork.

Developing Teamwork and Leadership Skills

Work with a small group and decide on a value that you can put into practice that will benefit your community. Brainstorm about different values and various possible projects you could do as a group. Then choose one project, plan how to go about doing it, and get to work—as a team.

Real-World Workshop

With a partner, role-play abilities as they might be used in the workplace. Each of you can choose an ability, such as adaptability or decision making. Improvise situations until you feel comfortable that you are expressing the ability, then show your role-play to the class. Can the others guess what ability you are acting out?

School-to-Work Connection

Interview the director of human resources at a local business to find out what methods the company uses to match applicants to particular jobs. Does the company use interest surveys or other means of assessing aptitudes and abilities? Prepare questions in advance, and take a pen and notebook to write down the responses. Write what you learned in an interview format, showing your questions and the director's answers.

Individual Career Plan

Look at Figure 2-5. Then make a chart for yourself similar to this one showing Sasha's steps. Does this give you an insight into a career choice? If not, show your chart to a family member, friend, or teacher. Ask the person to suggest an appropriate career.

Chapter 2 • Getting to Know Yourself **43**

learning style and explaining how the styles are spread out among the students.

3. Answers will vary, but students should try to explain how their artwork reflects their values or interests.

Developing Teamwork and Leadership Skills

Answers will vary. For example, if students chose environmental protection as their value, they might plan a community project to plant trees or flowers in a park or other public space. Team members should work collaboratively, dividing up tasks as they choose.

Real-World Workshop

Students should be as specific as possible in order to make the ability clear when they act it out.

School-to-Work Connection

Students should arrange the interview, plan the questions, and practice asking the questions with a partner before going on the interview.

Individual Career Plan

Students' charts should show their values, interests, aptitudes and abilities, and personality and learning styles. Students should try to decide on an appropriate career to consider.

2. Answers will vary, but students should list several entries under each column heading.

Connecting Academics to the Workplace

1. Answers will vary, depending on the culture that students research.

2. Students should make a survey sheet that lists the seven learning styles and the total number of students for each style. The bar graph should have the learning styles listed on the horizontal side and the number of students on the vertical side. Students should write about their results identifying the main

Aspects of Industry: Technical and Production Skills

Students who are fairly sure of their future careers may use all the Labs to investigate all the aspects of industry for one career. Other students may want to investigate a different job cluster with each Lab.

STEP A

To develop a list of three job possiblities in each job cluster, students may brainstorm with other students or research the possibilities in the *Occupational Outlook Handbook (OOH)* or other career references.

Students should be able to relate the skills described in the references and other publications to basic **SCANS (Secretary's Commission on Achieving Necessary Skills)** skill groups: reading, math, speaking, and so on. Be sure students are considering all the SCANS groups.

Students should pay attention to how and where the work is performed. A student interested in writing, for example, might work alone at home, or in a busy newspaper office. One situation or the other might not suit the student.

Recommend that students not limit themselves to current trade and business periodicals. By looking at periodicals that are five to ten years old, they may be able to see how the field has changed, what has not changed, and what predictions about the field have come true. They can use this information in their reports.

ASPECTS OF INDUSTRY: *Technical and Production Skills*

Overview

In Unit One, you read about why people work, and focused on evaluating your skills and aptitudes. In this Unit Lab, you will use what you have learned while exploring one of the aspects of industry: **Technical and Production Skills.**

The Technical and Production Skills aspect of industry covers the actual techniques and abilities you'll need on the job. It also covers how you'll work—whether you'll time-share, telecommute, or rotate jobs with someone else.

Tools

1. *Occupational Outlook Handbook*
2. Trade and business magazines
3. Consumer magazines
4. Information on apprenticeship programs
5. College/Specialty school catalogs

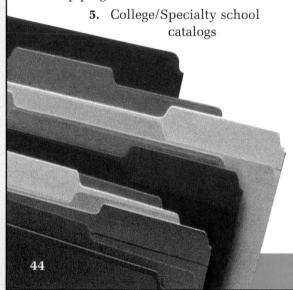

Procedures

STEP A

Choose one of the following 15 job clusters that interests you: Agribusiness and Natural Resources; Business and Office; Communications and Media; Construction; Family and Consumer Services; Environment; Fine Arts and Humanities; Health; Hospitality and Recreation; Manufacturing; Marine Science; Marketing and Distribution; Personal Service; Public Service; Transportation.

Choose three jobs in the job cluster that you would seriously think about pursuing. Research each of the three, listing the skills you would need to perform the job (reading, computer use, carpentry, math, etc.). Use the *Occupational Outlook Handbook (OOH)* and other career references, trade and business magazines, and consumer magazines to get your information. Some of these sources are on the Internet.

In your research, look for comments that indicate how the work is performed by computer, individually, in groups, and so on. Mention if the way the work is done is changing.

STEP B

If you have not already done so, make lists of your skills, interests, aptitudes, and values. You may want to brainstorm with two or three classmates.

STEP B

This step should build on lists students have already made and exercises they have already done. They should expand their lists, if possible, to give their potential careers greater breadth.

Working in teams may help students discover skills, aptitudes, and interests they were not aware could translate into job skills. Encourage students to ask family members, coworkers, and friends outside of class for suggestions on possible careers.

Compare the list of your skills, aptitudes, interests, and values to the lists of skills you made for the three jobs.

Choose the job that most closely matches your skills, interests, aptitudes, and values.

STEP C

Have your teacher, counselor, or parent help you arrange a short (20- to 30-minute) interview with a person in that job. If someone in your first choice job is not available, go on to your second choice.

During the interview, ask the following:

1. Which skills are most important in performing the job?

2. How did the person get the skills to perform the job? (Formal training? Experience?)

3. How have the job skill requirements changed in the past five to ten years? Are they expected to change in the next five to ten years?

4. How does the person perform his or her job? (Telecommuting? In groups? Alone?)

During the interview, take careful notes. Do not record the interview without permission. Be punctual and be courteous.

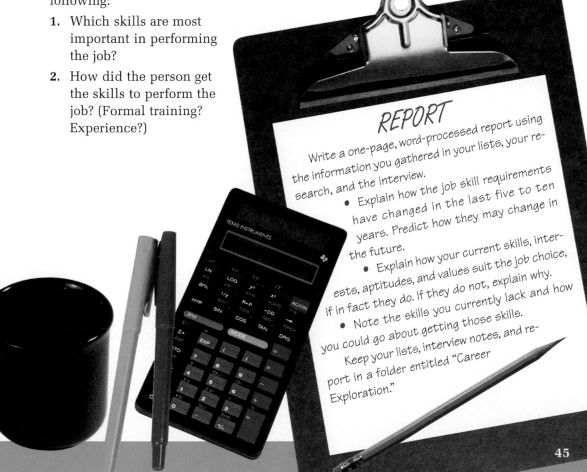

REPORT

Write a one-page, word-processed report using the information you gathered in your lists, your research, and the interview.

- Explain how the job skill requirements have changed in the last five to ten years. Predict how they may change in the future.
- Explain how your current skills, interests, aptitudes, and values suit the job choice, if in fact they do. If they do not, explain why.
- Note the skills you currently lack and how you could go about getting those skills.

Keep your lists, interview notes, and report in a folder entitled "Career Exploration."

45

Report

Students should use the Lab to begin to refine their job searches; at the same time, they should be keeping their options open. Encourage them to think broadly; have them discuss how the skills they might acquire for their first choice jobs would transfer to another job within the job cluster they have chosen. How might those skills transfer to another job cluster?

Have students discovered a lack of compatibility between the jobs they chose to investigate and their skills/interest list? How will they use this knowledge to refine their job search?

Have students discuss the ways they might acquire the skills they need for their jobs. (Part-time jobs now? Apprentice programs? Specialty schools?) Have them begin to collect catalogs and brochures on different types of training available for jobs in their chosen clusters.

STEP C

Students may get help setting up the interview, but encourage them to personally make phone contact with the interviewee. They should confirm the time of the interview, explain what information they will be asking for, and ask to see the job site.

Students should write their interview questions out in advance, arrive at the interview promptly, be courteous and professional, ask their questions clearly, and follow up the interview with a thank you.

If students are interested or have the time, they may want to interview a person in each of the other two jobs they have chosen. All persons interviewed may act as future references or networking contacts when the student begins looking for a job.

Unit Overview

In this unit, students begin their personal searches for rewarding careers. Students learn about methods for researching careers and ways to compare the requirements of different careers.

Students also learn about entrepreneurship as a career option and ways of starting a business. The unit concludes with strategies for setting career goals and developing individual career plans.

Introducing the Unit

Ask students what self-assessment means to them. As students talk, write their ideas on the chalkboard. Discuss how each relates to learning about oneself.

Discuss ways students can learn more about themselves (tests, discussions with family and friends, introspection).

Unit Project

Before beginning this unit, have students start a notebook entitled "Goals for My Chosen Career." Have students choose a business that they might like to work in or own. After you complete each chapter, have students think about the skills and/or knowledge outlined in that chapter and write in their notebook how it applies to the particular career they have chosen. If students identify skills they lack, have them write those in their notebooks and their goals for gaining the skills. At the end of the unit, collect and evaluate the notebooks.

UNIT 2
Exploring Careers

Chapter 3
Researching Careers

Chapter 4
Entrepreneurship

Chapter 5
Developing an Individual Career Plan

46

Developing Community Involvement

Host a pancake breakfast or barbecue to raise money for a charitable cause chosen by the class. Get permission to use a recreation hall or park, and arrange to have food donated. Have students divide into teams to take on tasks such as cooking, serving, clean-up, and advertising. Afterward, the class should send thank-you notes to those who donated time and materials. The class may want to start small, hosting this kind of event for the school only.

UNIT 2 QUIZ:

What Do You Know About Exploring Careers?

- **What is the difference between job shadowing and an internship?**
- **What kind of job benefits are important to you?**
- **Would you want to start your own business or work for someone else?**
- **What career interests you?**

47

Resources for Enrichment

Books

- *Adventure Careers* by Hiam and Angle
- *The Career Guide for Creative and Unconventional People* by Eikleberry
- *Electronic Job Search Revolution* by Kennedy and Morrow

Magazines

Inc., Entrepreneur, Success, Business Week, Forbes, Fortune

Organizations

- Better Business Bureau
- Chamber of Commerce
- Small Business Administration

Internet

E-span—Job-search service with job listings: http://www.espan.com/js/js.html

U.S. News **College Fair**—Reviews of schools, best education buys, career tips: http://www.usnews.com/usnews/fair/home.html

Unit Closure

Have students create a one- or two-page newsletter describing career research techniques, personal career profiles, career goals, and entrepreneurship as a career option.

Unit Evaluation

Administer the reproducible test for Unit 2, which you will find in your Performance Assessment Binder, or construct your own test using the IBM Testmaker software.

Building Partners in Industry

When you're first establishing contact with local business people, it is essential to emphasize common goals. How can a school-business partnership benefit both the school's students and the business's management and workers? You probably have several good answers to that question. However, it's also important to find out what individual business leaders want to gain from the partnership. Only by recognizing and working toward their goals will you be able to build a strong, lasting relationship.

SECTION 1 *Exploring Careers*

SECTION OBJECTIVES	SECTION FEATURES	SECTION RESOURCES
• Research careers informally, using people you know and media resources. • Research careers formally, using libraries, the Internet, and exploratory interviews. • Explain how you can explore careers through part-time work.	Personal Career Plan, p. 49 Attitude Counts, p. 55 Exploring Careers, p. 56	Workforce 2000 Videodisc and Videotape Section 3-1 Review, p. 55 Student Activity Workbook

SECTION 2 *What to Research*

SECTION OBJECTIVES	SECTION FEATURES	SECTION RESOURCES
• Target key questions that you can ask in researching careers. • Examine some of the characteristics that make up a career profile.	Career Do's and Don'ts, p. 60 Excellent Business Practices, p. 61 You're the Boss!, p. 62	Workforce 2000 Videodisc and Videotape Section 3-2 Review, p. 62 Chapter 3 Review, pp. 64–65 Student Activity Workbook

CHAPTER 3

CHAPTER RESOURCES

- Chapter Transparencies and Lesson Plans
- Chapter 3 Test
- Spanish Resources, Chapter 3
- School-to-Work Activity Handbook, Chapter 3 Activity
- Teacher's Lesson Plans, Chapter 3
- Implementing Block Scheduling, Chapter 3
- Print, Media, and Internet Handbook
- Strategies for Implementing Work-Based Learning
- Strategies for Implementing Connecting Activities

Career Notes

SCANS CORRELATION CHART

Foundation Skills

Basic Skills	Reading	Writing	Math	**Listening**	**Speaking**

Thinking Skills	**Creative Thinking**	**Decision Making**	**Problem Solving**	Seeing Things in the Mind's Eye	**Knowing How to Learn**	Reasoning

Personal Qualities	Responsibility	**Self-Esteem**	Sociability	**Self-Management**	Integrity/Honesty

Workplace Competencies

Resources	**Allocating Time**	Allocating Money	Allocating Material and Facility Resources	**Allocating Human Resources**

Information	**Acquiring and Evaluating Information**	**Organizing and Maintaining Information**	**Interpreting and Communicating Information**	Using Computers to Process Information

Interpersonal Skills	**Participating as a Member of a Team**	Teaching Others	Serving Clients/ Customers	Exercising Leadership	Negotiating to Arrive at a Decision	Working with Cultural Diversity

Systems	**Understanding Systems**	Monitoring and Correcting Performance	Improving and Designing Systems

Technology	Selecting Technology	**Applying Technology to Task**	Maintaining and Troubleshooting Technology

Highlighted blocks indicate areas covered in the Chapter.

Additional Activities

 ### Internet Connection

Have students choose a job that interests them, using the Internet. Have them find a company hiring persons for that kind of job. Students should note where the job is available, what the job requirements are, and the pay. They should locate at least three to five open positions.

 ### Field Trip Suggestions

Arrange a trip to a large, local corporation that performs a variety of operations on site. Ask for brief visits to the accounting, manufacturing, computer networking, food service, shipping, and/or training areas. Later, ask students to write a paragraph about the section that interested them the most.

 ### Guest Speaker Suggestions

To find out what they really want from life, people may turn to professional career planning counselors. Ask a career planning counselor to talk to the class, giving students ideas on determining what they really enjoy, and how to turn that into a career.

Key to Ability Levels

Each section gives skill-building activities. Each activity has been labeled for use with students of various learning styles and abilities.

L1 Level 1 activities are basic activities and should be within the range of all students.

L2 Level 2 activities are average activities and should be within the range of average and above average students.

L3 Level 3 activities are challenging activities designed for the ability range of above average students.

Chapter 3

Researching Careers

School-Based Learning

Chapter Overview

Chapter 3 explores ways to do career research.

Section 3-1 presents methods of conducting career research. This section also discusses the value of part-time work as a means of exploring a career.

Section 3-2 looks at ten factors that affect career decisions.

Background Information

Write chapter objectives (Sections 3-1 and 3-2) on the chalkboard or use the chapter objective transparency for class discussion.

Choose assignments from the *Student Activity Workbook* and write them on the chalkboard.

Have students preview the chapter, looking at pictures, reading captions, and section heads.

Ask students how the information in this chapter might help them choose a career.

Preteaching Vocabulary

Write the Key Terms from Sections 3-1 and 3-2 on the chalkboard. Conduct a class discussion on how each term relates to learning how to research career areas.

Meeting SPECIAL Needs

Limited Proficiency in English

Give students with a limited understanding of English the course outline and schedule that tells them when you are likely to cover a chapter. The students can prepare by reading the chapter ahead of the class, looking up words that are new or difficult.

Spanish-speaking students will benefit from the translations in the *Spanish Resource Binder*.

Researching Careers

Section 3-1
Exploring Careers

Section 3-2
What to Research

In this video segment, learn how your friends can help you research careers.

Journal
Personal Career Plan

You come into contact with people involved in many different careers—teachers, salespeople, police officers, and administrators, to name just a few. In your journal, write a list of the careers represented by people you meet or observe in a single day. Then review your list. Which of the careers might interest you? Why?

49

One skill future workers will need is the ability to continue learning new skills throughout their careers due to changing technology.

Assign students to groups of four or five. Have each group choose a formal research method mentioned in this chapter and find information on future work trends and job skills. Tell students to include in their reports a purpose, the research method used, the findings, and conclusions.

Work-Based
Learning Strategies
and Activities

Choose a local business that provides training programs for its employees. Arrange for students to visit the business and listen to a trainer describe the company's training programs. Ask whether students could participate in one of the training programs for a short time.

As follow-up, have students write a paragraph or two identifying the job skills they need to develop.

WORKFORCE 2000
Training Video

Have students view the video and perform the interactive exercises to reinforce important chapter concepts and thinking processes.

Chapter 3

Addressing **LEARNING** Styles

Logical/Mathematical Learner

Have students choose five or more careers that interest them. Ask them to list the ways that the jobs are similar—the kind of working environment; working with people, data, or things; the potential for telecommuting; the pay scale; deadline pressure, and so on. Drawing parallels between dissimilar careers can help students understand what their interests are and what aspects of working are important to them. It can also give them flexibility in their career planning.

Bell Ringer

Ask students to respond in writing to this question:

"If money were not an issue and you could work at anything you wanted, what would you do?"

Allow students five minutes to write their responses.

Introducing the Section

Ask for volunteers to share what they wrote for the Bell Ringer activity. Tell students to think about what they enjoy doing and whether they would want to turn an interest into a career. Ask how they would go about finding information on careers.

Use this discussion to lead into methods of conducting career research. Ask students if they have ever engaged in informal research. Then discuss the methods for conducting formal research.

Motivational Activity

Demonstration

If your school is connected to the Internet, have students do on-line research by visiting one or more Internet sites providing career or job information. Refer to the list of Internet resources on the unit opener page for sites to visit.

50

GERSTENBLATT
Exploring Careers

OBJECTIVES

After studying this section, you will be able to:

- **Research careers informally, using people you know and media resources.**
- **Research careers formally, using libraries, the Internet, and exploratory interviews.**
- **Explain how you can explore careers through part-time work.**

KEY TERMS

Internet job services
exploratory
    interview
cooperative program
job shadowing
internship
service learning

Now that you've thought about your own interests and abilities, it's time to learn more about the real world of work. The U.S. Office of Education lends a hand by dividing careers into 15 clusters. Look at *Figure 3-1.* Which cluster—or clusters—seems to fit the kind of person you are? Narrow your search by choosing a cluster. Then start exploring related careers that might be right for you.

Research—It's Right Before Your Very Eyes

You can discover what the world of work has to offer by simply keeping your eyes and ears open. Look around as you travel to school, as you play, eat, shop, or just hang out with friends. During the next week, list all the careers that you notice. You'll be amazed at how effective this kind of informal research can be.

Been There, Done That

Talk to people you know about their career experiences. Just ask a few basic questions.

- What was your favorite job?
- What was your least favorite job?
- What was your most unusual job?
- How do you like your current job?

Put your SCANS listening skills to work as you gather firsthand information.

50   *Unit 2 • Exploring Careers*

Implementing Teamwork

Organize your class into four teams. Assign each team one formal research tool: books, videotapes, Internet job search, or exploratory interviews. They can use the library or technology in the classroom to research a career. Ask each team to present its data and explain how it used their research tools.

Workforce 2000 Trends

Temporary workers in the future will not only provide clerical and assembly-line skills, but they will also include electrical engineers, accountants, and managers. As temporary workers take over a larger portion of the workforce, permanent, full-time workers will dwindle in number.

The U.S. Office of Education Job Clusters

Career Clusters	Job Examples
Agribusiness and natural resources	Small-animal breeder, horse groomer, poultry farmer, forestry technician
Business and office	Receptionist, bookkeeper, computer servicer, claim examiner
Communications and media	Cable television technician, book editor, computer artist, technical writer
Construction	Air-conditioning, heating, and refrigeration mechanic; roofer; building inspector; surveyor
Family and consumer services	Child-care worker, pet-care worker, jeweler, floral designer
Environment	Environmental technician, hazardous waste management technician, pollution-control technician, sanitary engineer
Fine arts and humanities	Actor, cartoonist, dancer, musician
Health	Operating-room technician, dental hygienist, nurse's aide, home health aide
Hospitality and recreation	Cruise director, fitness instructor, park ranger, pastry chef, baker
Manufacturing	Industrial laser machine operator, toolmaker, stationary engineer, production supervisor
Marine science	Ocean technician, diver, fish culture technician, marine engineer
Marketing and distribution	Insurance agent, real estate agent, auto sales worker, retail buyer
Personal service	Barber and hairstylist, cosmetologist, massage therapist, bridal consultant
Public service	Teacher, member of the armed services, firefighter, paralegal aide
Transportation	Airline reservations agent, airline pilot, railroad conductor, automotive mechanic

Figure 3-1 The U.S. Office of Education has grouped careers into 15 clusters based on similar job characteristics. Which areas appeal to you? Why?

TEACH

Guided Practice
Teaching Strategies

1. Assign and review Section 3-1.
2. Use the transparency for this section.
3. Assign and review the Case Study.

Teaching Tip

Help students understand that research can be a part of everyday life by asking them for information about a favorite music group or television star. Ask how they learned the information.

Discussion Starter

Have students assume that they enjoy taking care of animals. Ask them how they might use informal research to find out about related jobs. (Some ideas are talking with veterinarians, observing the operations at an animal shelter, visiting zoos, or asking questions at a pet-grooming business.)

Ask students to imagine that they have career interests in physical performance (sports, dance, or gymnastics, for example). What career clusters include these types of jobs? (Fine arts and humanities, and hospitality and recreation.) How does researching a career cluster help you identify a possible career? (A career cluster contains many different types of jobs that may require similar skills and aptitudes.)

▶▶ Extending Figure 3-1 ◀◀

Read the title of each career cluster and ask for a show of hands of students interested in that cluster. Tally responses and identify the most popular career cluster. Discuss why that may be the case.

Caption Answer: Students may respond that business and office workers deal with information and money, that fine arts and humanities workers are interested in creative expression, or that health and public service workers are directly involved with helping people.

Critical Thinking

Pose this situation to students: Suppose you take a job as a sales representative. This type of job appealed to you because of its potentially high earnings and the opportunity to travel. You've been in the job for a year and you've traveled to many different cities. In fact, you feel you have to travel too much and have little time for friends or family.

In this situation, how has career choice affected lifestyle? What research could you have done to learn more about the drawbacks of this type of job? Under what conditions might you still have taken the job?

Teaching Tip

Schedule a session with your school's librarian as well as a visit to the local public library to guide students through the career reference materials available—in print format, digital media, or on-line resources.

What's Happening?

Have you ever seen a situation in a movie and thought, "Wow, that's the job I want"? Think about movies and TV shows that you've seen and magazines and newspapers that you've read. Are people doing things you'd like to do? If so, learn more about them. That's how Jen Kizer found her career. She never missed her favorite TV program—real-life rescues of people in danger. When she stopped to think about it, she realized that emergency rescue work was exactly what she wanted to do with her life.

Formal Research

Consider yourself a detective, hot on the trail of a satisfying career. While informal research gives you some clues, formal approaches yield even more.

Libraries—Check Them Out

Your first stop might be your school or public library. Many libraries have job information or career centers. The information is well organized, and it's free. You'll find reference books, magazines, videotapes, and other sources of career information. You can also search the card catalog or electronic catalog.

Books. Look for three useful books published by the U.S. Department of Labor.

- The *Dictionary of Occupational Titles* describes more than 20,000 jobs.

- The *Occupational Outlook Handbook*, updated every two years, describes the type of work, the training and education required, and the future outlook for hundreds of careers.

- The *Guide for Occupational Exploration* groups careers into categories, such as mechanical careers and careers protecting people,

Libraries have a broad range of career materials, including videotapes and audiotapes. *Why do you think a videotape that shows someone at work might be more engaging than reading about someone at work?*

Extending the Illustration

Check with your school or local public library and find out what career videotapes are available. Make a list to hand out to students, and have them review one or more.

Caption Answer: A videotape would allow a person to see exactly how the work is performed and what the workplace looks like.

and describes many careers within each category.

Additional Print Resources. Libraries also contain other print resources, including magazines, government reports, and newspapers.

- With the *Reader's Guide to Periodical Literature*, locate magazine articles on specific industries and career trends. Business magazines, such as *Forbes, Business Week, Entrepreneur,* and *Wired,* cover the hot topics and inside news of many industries.

- The *Occupational Outlook Quarterly,* published by the Department of Labor, provides up-to-date information on employment trends.

- Job listings in your local newspaper show what is available in your local job market.

VCR Resources. Many labor organizations and industry service groups produce audiotapes and videotapes of workers in action. The library collects them for you, so take advantage of them.

Computerized Guidance. Some libraries also offer special computer programs that can speed up your career search. These programs let you call up detailed information on particular occupations. You can also do some career browsing: Tell the program what you like doing, and it suggests possible careers. In the process, you'll grow more skilled at using computers, a SCANS competency.

Internet Job Services

Computer users can find huge amounts of career information on the Internet, particularly on the World Wide Web. The Web offers such **Internet job services** as Web sites, newsgroups, and bulletin boards created by trade organizations, companies, and individuals—all designed for job recruitment and career research. You can surf the Net to find everything from global statistics (How many plumbers are there in India?) to occupational chat rooms ("Let me tell you about the design problem I solved today!").

Exploratory Interviews

Ask your family, friends, neighbors, teachers, and counselors to help you build a list of people who work in careers that

An exploratory interview is a perfect opportunity to let your personal qualities shine. *Name at least three social skills that will help make an interview go smoothly.*

Chapter 3 • Researching Careers **53**

SCANS Foundation Skills Connection

L1 Creative Thinking

Have students make a list of all the careers they hear of during the course of a designated day—while attending class, watching television, listening to the radio, and reading books and magazines. Have students share their lists with the class.

L2 Speaking

Have students research a career area of interest to them and give three- to five-minute talks on the job skills and training needed for the career. Tell students to include information about the wide range of jobs within a career area.

L3 Knowing How to Learn

Have students choose an unusual job or career area. Some examples might include a personal shopper, a golf pro, an animal trainer, a movie stunt person, or an agribusiness technician. Have students research the career and create a profile of a person working in that career. The profile should include education required, special skills, prior job experience, and personal traits that would help a person succeed. Ask students to share their research in a class discussion.

Extending the Illustration

Ask another teacher or a local businessperson to help you role-play an exploratory interview for students.

Caption Answer: Answers may include politeness, friendliness, interest, or enthusiasm.

SCANS Workplace Competencies Connection

L1 Participating as a Member of a Team

Assign students to teams of two or three. Have each team choose a career they want to learn more about through an exploratory interview. Tell the teams to write a list of at least ten questions they would ask in such an interview.

L2 Acquiring and Evaluating Information

For one week, have students take notes on the positive and negative things they hear people say about their own careers. Have them draw conclusions about the information they gained. Then ask them how one can decide if the negatives outweigh the positives? (What is negative to one person may be positive to another.)

L3 Understanding Systems

Have students visit their local library and find out about its career information resources. Tell them to write a paragraph for each type of resource available, describing how to use the resource and the type of information it provides.

Independent Practice

Assign as homework the chapter activity in the *School-to-Work Activity Handbook.*

54

you find interesting. After doing some initial research into a career, call the appropriate person and arrange an **exploratory interview**. That's simply a short, informal talk with someone who works in a career that appeals to you.

Ask questions such as these:

- How did you start your career?
- What education and training did it require?
- What do you like about your job?
- What do you do on a typical day at your job?

Don't be afraid to ask people for interviews. They may have started out by receiving someone else's help and may be more than happy to pass the favor along.

The story of John Liu is a great example. When he was a teenager, John thought he wanted a career in retailing. He asked everyone he knew until he found the perfect contact—a friend's aunt who worked as a department store buyer. "I learned more about buying and selling in an hour with her than I could have imagined. She was smart, savvy, and she loved her work." The interview paid off. John went on to become a well-known marketing consultant. "I'm really grateful for her advice, and I help students today whenever I'm asked."

Part-Time Work

The most direct way to learn about a career is to work. If your schedule allows it, working part-time will enable you to observe a career from the inside. You'll gain experience, make personal contacts, and put some money in your pocket at the same time. Paula Terrano started doing part-time work after school setting up displays at a

convention center. Her carefulness and enthusiasm, she says, were noticed, and she moved up the ladder of responsibility. She eventually accepted full-time work at the center as assistant event coordinator.

Work Experience Programs

You may find a part-time job through a vocational education program. Such programs are designed to give you a chance to learn job skills while you are still in high school. As a bonus, the work also earns you class credit and a grade.

Some local corporations team up with schools, hiring students to perform jobs that are taught in their high school classes. This is called a **cooperative program**. A high school in California, for example, used math and science classes to prepare students for work at a local chemical company.

Some schools create school-based businesses. One enterprising high school in Minnesota bought a grocery store that was going out of business. Students learned

You can learn about careers through part-time work. *What job skills might be needed for the job pictured here?*

Extending the Illustration

Ask students who have or have had part-time jobs to name the companies for which they work or worked. Ask students to identify the types of careers available at these businesses.

Caption Answer: Answers may include waiting on customers, stocking shelves, and preparing bank deposits.

Teaching Attitude Counts ✓

Ask students to free-write about a recent undertaking that they considered a failure.

- How did you feel at first?
- Specifically, what can you learn from your "failure?"
- How have your feelings about your "failure" changed?

marketing and retailing in classes and then applied their knowledge working at the school store.

Job Shadowing

You don't need to be a spy to "shadow" someone. **Job shadowing,** which involves following a worker for a few days on the job, means learning the ropes by watching and listening.

Today Elena Kazinski is a television camera operator for a major production company, but when she was a student she didn't know anyone in the industry. As she tells it, "I was always hanging around our local TV studio, and one day I just asked the camera operator if I could talk to her about her job. She offered to let me shadow her. I got the OK from the station, and I stuck to her like glue for a week. I even helped with some equipment. After that, I was hooked. TV production has been my life ever since."

Volunteering and Internships

You may think that volunteers don't get paid. True, they don't usually draw a salary, but they are paid in valuable experience. Don't underestimate the value of volunteering as another way to explore

careers. What you learn can help you make major decisions later. Hospitals, senior citizen centers, and museums are just a few places that use volunteers.

An **internship** is a more formal position and usually requires a longer-term commitment than volunteering. Like volunteers, interns are usually unpaid, but they learn vital job skills. An intern is on the spot, working where the action is. With one foot in the door, interns who work hard can sometimes step into full-time paying positions.

In addition, many communities and schools offer **service learning**. In such programs, community service—for example, cleaning up a neighborhood—becomes part of your schoolwork.

Skills Practice

Have students imagine that they are interested in a career as a hospice worker. Have students list skills needed to care for terminally ill patients. Do these skills differ from those needed to be a salesclerk?

Writing: *Informational*

Have students start a notebook of career information. To begin the notebook, have students research the *Dictionary of Occupational Titles* (or a similar reference) and choose three growing career areas that interest them.

Tell students to write descriptions of each career area in their notebooks. They should include data about potential new openings in the field, percentage growth over the next five years, and training needed to work in the field.

ASSESS

Assessment
Oral

1. What is the difference between informal and formal research? (Informal research is done by observing other people and asking questions. Formal research uses a variety of resources to collect data.)

2. How might formal research help you find a career? (Research helps you identify skills and aptitudes needed for a variety of jobs. It also helps you identify potential careers that you may never have considered.)

SECTION 3-1 *Review*

Understanding Key Concepts

Using complete sentences, answer the following questions on a separate sheet of paper.

1. Why are talking to people and using media resources called informal methods of researching jobs?

2. What kinds of career information can you find in libraries and on the Internet?

3. What are some benefits of doing unpaid part-time work?

Chapter 3 • Researching Careers 55

SECTION 3-1 *Review* ANSWERS

1. The information is not organized the way it would be in library or computer reference materials.

2. You can find books, articles, and announcements about specific careers and industries. The information

available includes everything from specific job tasks and salaries to discussions of career prospects.

3. You gain on-the-job experience, make contacts, possibly get school credit, and help a company or community.

ASSESS (cont'd.)

3. What are some ways you could you learn about a career other than through informal or formal research? (part-time jobs, cooperative programs, job shadowing, internships, service learning)

Evaluation

Assign the section review.

Reteaching

Choose a career area and write it on the chalkboard. (For example, high school band director.)

Ask students to tell you resources they would use to find out about that career. List each resource on the chalkboard, categorizing them by type of resource (on-line, books, interviews, etc.). Leave space for category headings and ask students to supply them.

Extending the Content

Assign the appropriate Chapter 3 activities in the *Student Activity Workbook*.

Ask students to choose three methods they will use to conduct career research and describe why they chose each method.

CLOSE

Now that students have learned about the different types of careers available, have them complete this statement, "I plan to research the following careers . . . ."

CASE STUDY

Exploring Careers: Marine Science

Dawn Murray
Biologist/Senior Interpreter,
Monterey Bay Aquarium

Q: What is your work like?

A: I work with the interpretive programs in the aquarium's education department. We interpret—or explain—marine science to aquarium visitors. I train 750 volunteers in shifts, three times a day, seven days a week, working with a different group of volunteers each shift. I tell them what's new at the aquarium, or give them information on anything from how birds fly to how a mollusk makes its shell.

Q: How did you get into this field?

A: When I was eight, I went with my family to the Great Barrier Reef in Australia. I'll never forget the manta rays and the turtles. I remember thinking, "This is what I want to do—study marine life." So I studied biology in college and started working as an intern at the aquarium after graduation. The aquarium kept rehiring me, first part-time, then full-time.

Q: What makes your work important to you?

A: The fact that I can have such an impact. People don't know much about marine biology. We're just now beginning to figure out what it's like out in the ocean. I can take a class at the university, write a lecture about what I've learned, and teach it to the volunteers, who teach it to the public. If I can get my spark into the volunteers, they can get that spark into the public.

Thinking Critically

What are some other kinds of jobs that might use educational interpreters?

CAREER FACTS

Nature of the Work:
   Enrich visitors' experiences through tours, lectures, classes. Design training and public programs; teach.

Training or Education Needed:
   Bachelor's or master's degree in education or in science; experience working in aquariums, museums, zoos.

Aptitudes, Abilities, and Skills:
   Math, listening, speaking, and interpersonal skills; self-management skills; problem-solving and decision-making skills; reading and writing skills.

Salary Range:
   Start at $28,000; up to $65,000; depends on the institution.

Career Path:
   Start as a volunteer or an intern; take on more responsibility as an instructor, a resource coordinator, or an education director.

56 *Unit 2 • Exploring Careers*

Extending the CASE STUDY

Answer: zoos, museums, libraries; educational or historical theme parks or attractions; historical societies; theme parks such as Disneyland and Epcot Center; historical monuments and buildings

Further Application: Have students discuss why particular careers are important to them. For example, people in fashion or personal service careers can make clients feel good about themselves; those in health professions can help heal; workers in computer-oriented services can help businesses grow and prosper or can provide timely information for customers.

What to Research

OBJECTIVES

After studying this section, you will be able to:

- **Target key questions that you can ask in researching careers.**
- **Examine some of the characteristics that make up a career profile.**

KEY TERMS

**work environment
flextime
fringe benefits**

Once you know *where* to get career information, the next question is *what* information should you get? You'll want to know what the career is like and whether it is right for you. You can find that out by examining careers in terms of these 10 characteristics:

1. values,
2. tasks and responsibilities,
3. working with data-people-things,
4. work environment,
5. working hours,
6. aptitudes and abilities,
7. education and training,
8. salary and fringe benefits,
9. career outlook, and
10. international career outlook.

Try to gather information on each of these factors for each career you investigate. This will enable you to compare careers directly and make a wise career decision.

Values

When you look into a career, ask yourself if your values match the values that will help you in that career. What do you really care about? What do people in that career really care about? Justice? Art? Money? Health? Fame?

Chapter 3 • Researching Careers **57**

Addressing Workplace Diversity

Companies that honor diversity have lower turnover rates, less absenteeism, increased production and efficiency, fewer legal costs from employee grievances, and they also use fewer outside consultants.

SECTION 3-2
FOCUS

Bell Ringer

For five minutes, have students write a list of all the things they would want to know about a job that interests them.

Introducing the Section

Write students' answers to the Bell Ringer activity on the chalkboard.

If students have not mentioned all of the ten items on this page, add the missing items to the list. Then discuss each topic and how it relates to a person's career choice.

Explain that most people have aptitudes for many different kinds of work; using the ten steps listed here can help narrow choices.

Discussion Starter

Have students assume that they love to buy clothes, and enjoy wearing the latest styles. Would they enjoy a career in retailing? How could they decide whether a retailing career would be satisfying? (Research the career, take a part-time retailing job, shadow one or more retail workers.)

Motivational Activity
Writing

After presenting this section, have students write a few paragraphs describing their personal aptitudes and abilities. Tell students to describe how they plan to use these aptitudes and abilities in choosing a future career.

Teaching Strategies

1. Assign and review Section 3-2.
2. Use the transparency for this section.

Discussion Starter

Draw an empty room with ten closed doors on the chalkboard or transparency. Each door represents one of the ten characteristics to research for career information. Have students tell you the name of each characteristic before you write it on a door.

Critical Thinking

Give students this scenario: Suppose you decide to become an elementary teacher. After four years of college, you discover that the outlook for this career is not promising because your local area is small and few teaching jobs become available. What could you have done before deciding on this career? What compromises might you have to make now?

(Possible answers include researching the local market for openings and also learning about the jobs that are available in the area. Compromises might include taking a non-teaching job for a while or moving to an area where a teaching job is available.)

Tasks and Responsibilities

When you go to work each day, what will you actually be doing? Find out by asking basic questions, such as these:

- What specific tasks do workers in this career perform?
- Are the workdays repetitive or full of new experiences?
- Is the pace easy, or is the career a high-pressure one?
- Is the work primarily physical or mental?

Working with Data-People-Things

Careers involve working with data, people, and things. Many careers entail working with all three categories, as *Figure 3-2* shows. For any given career, though, one area tends to predominate. Statisticians, for example, work mainly with data, home health aides work primarily with people, and technicians usually work with things.

 **Figure 3-2**

Working with Data-People-Things

Many careers involve working with data, people, and things.

A **Data.** The dental hygienist uses information — what she learned in her training plus her knowledge of this particular patient from past cleaning sessions.

B **People.** The hygienist spends most of her day working with people. A hygienist with a friendly manner will help patients feel comfortable.

C **Things.** The hygienist works with things — the tools that she uses to clean the patient's teeth. A hygienist has to use dental tools carefully and keep all equipment clean.

▶▶ Extending Figure 3-2 ◀◀

Have students take an informal survey of their friends and relatives, asking whether they work with people, data, or things. Tally the responses in class. Do most people work with one more than the other? Students' answers will vary.

Work Environment

Because you'll be spending about 40 hours a week at work, do yourself a favor: Consider your **work environment**. Your physical and social surroundings can affect your well-being. Do you want to work indoors or outdoors? Would you rather work alone or with other people?

Take a few minutes to visualize your ideal work environment. Then draw a picture or write a paragraph describing what you envisioned. As you research careers, try to find those that match that image.

Working Hours

When you think about work, do you assume you'll be starting at 9:00 A.M. and quitting at 5:00 P.M.? Of course, many people do work those hours—but in the world of work, variety rules. Andrew Barros, a restaurant host, starts work at 3:00 P.M. and leaves after the last guest does at about 11:00 P.M. Andrew's restaurant buys produce from Janet Cho, who works from 4:00 A.M. to noon. Many careers are simply not 9-to-5 careers. When are you at your best? Are you a night owl or a morning person?

Some careers allow flexible scheduling. With **flextime**, workers construct their work schedules to suit their lives. Some people work four 10-hour days and enjoy three-day weekends. Some work from 7:00 A.M. to 3:00 P.M. so that they can be home when their children return from school. Some people telecommute: They work at home and communicate with clients and colleagues by phone, fax, and computer.

 Flextime scheduling allows some workers to more easily match their work schedules with the demands of family life. Many employers that offer flextime require workers to be on-site during certain core hours, typically from 10:00 A.M. to 4:00 P.M. **Why do you think this is the case?**

Aptitudes and Abilities

As you know, skills for any kind of work are more easily learned if you have an aptitude for learning them. In Chapter 2 you analyzed your own aptitudes and abilities. As you do your research, find out

Chapter 3 • Researching Careers **59**

Teaching Tip

Ask students who have part-time jobs to share their thoughts about their work environment. How does it affect their attitudes toward their jobs?

SCANS Foundation Skills Connection

L1 Listening

Ask your school's guidance counselor to speak to your class about aptitude and interest tests. Have students write summaries. Follow up by urging students to take the tests that interest them.

L2 Creative Thinking

Tell students to think about their personal values. Have them list things they do that exemplify values, such as physical health, friendship, honesty, education, and so on.

L3 Self-Management

Ask students to think about the role that talent plays in a career decision. Use an example of a famous musician, singer, or sports figure. Is that person naturally gifted or did he or she develop talent through great effort and sacrifice? (Students might mention devoting a great deal of time to practicing, studying for many years, giving up entertainment and time with friends and family, and observing healthy habits to maintain strength.)

Extending the Illustration

Ask students to think about the benefits to the employer of offering flextime. (Possible answers include more satisfied, productive workers; and fewer commuting problems as workers can choose less busy times to travel to and from work.)

Caption Answer: Having the entire staff on site during core hours ensures that workers have the opportunity to communicate and work together when necessary.

SCANS Workplace Competencies Connection

L1 Allocating Human Resources

Assign students the project of planning a career day. Let the class brainstorm about how to organize the day and which businesses to invite. List students' ideas on the chalkboard and discuss the issues involved.

When they have decided the basic structure of the day, divide students into teams of four or five. Have each team select a leader and choose what part of the planning they will do. Give each team time to complete its planning and to write a brief summary of its part of career day. Ask the team leaders to share each team's plans with the class.

L2 Interpreting and Communicating Information

Have students implement their plans and hold the career day. Afterwards, ask students to choose three career areas they found to be interesting. Have students use the information they learned on the career day and list the things they would need to do to prepare for each of the jobs.

Set aside class time and have students present their information about careers and preparing for them.

Career Do's & Don'ts

To Identify a Career Path ...

Do:
- visualize yourself doing every job you come across.
- acknowledge that developing a career is a process.
- seek personal satisfaction.

Don't:
- underestimate the skills and discipline required to do any job well.
- be discouraged by the long educational process or years of experience required for some careers.
- consider a field you would not like even if it's known for high pay.
- choose a career path only because family members have that career.

which aptitudes and abilities are needed for each career. You can then match your natural talents with careers that require those same abilities. Anthony McCabe was a high school student who loved to talk. He talked about anything to anybody, and he had the knack of getting people to relax and open up to him. When it dawned on him that talking was what he was really good at, his career started to take shape, and today he hosts his own radio talk show.

Education and Training

Careers demand different kinds and levels of education and training. You may need a two-year associate's degree, a four-year bachelor's degree, or a technical or business school license or certificate. As you research, note how much time, money, and effort it will take to get the necessary education and training for various careers.

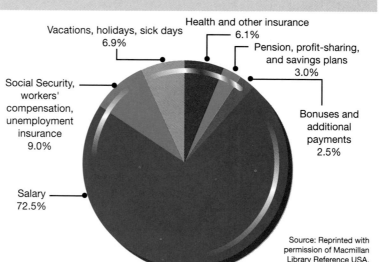

Salary and Fringe Benefits

Vacations, holidays, sick days 6.9%

Health and other insurance 6.1%

Pension, profit-sharing, and savings plans 3.0%

Social Security, workers' compensation, unemployment insurance 9.0%

Bonuses and additional payments 2.5%

Salary 72.5%

Source: Reprinted with permission of Macmillan Library Reference USA. Copyright 1996.

Figure 3-3

This chart shows salary and fringe benefits in relation to overall employee compenstion. What is the difference between a salary and a fringe benefit?

Extending Figure 3-3

Ask students who have part-time jobs what an average weekly salary would be. Based on this salary, have students apply the percentages and calculate what it costs the employer in addition to salary.

Caption Answer: Salary: cash payment for work performed. Fringe benefit: extra beyond salary.

Salary and Fringe Benefits

Occupational directories often include general information on what careers pay. They list an hourly rate or a weekly or annual salary, as well as ranges based on national averages.

Of course, many company employees receive more than their paychecks. **Fringe benefits** may include health insurance, paid vacation and holiday time, and a retirement plan. As *Figure 3-3* shows, fringe benefits can add substantially to what you earn.

Career Outlook

What will your career area be like in 10 years? Many of the research materials described in Section 3-1 can tell you about industry prospects and help you make big decisions.

Kathy Silno's research helped her. Kathy was mechanically inclined, and she considered a career in manufacturing. Her research, however, pointed to an upcoming increase in service jobs. Kathy decided on automotive repair and found a service job with a good future.

SECTION 3-2

L3   **Applying Technology to Task**

If possible, have students create their presentations from the preceding activity with a software presentation program, such as Powerpoint or Persuasion.

Independent Practice

Reading

Have students list one career they are exploring and evaluate it based on the ten factors listed on page 57. Have them note in which areas the career ranks highest. Do the areas that rank lowest make this a poor career choice? Why or why not?

Skills Practice

Ramon is considering two jobs. The first pays $22,500 per year plus a health and benefits package worth $95 per month. The second pays $22,200 per year plus a health and benefits package of $115 a month. Which job has a higher total yearly value? (first job: $22,500 + ($95 × 12) = $23,640; second job: $22,200 + ($115 × 12) = $23,580)

Research

Obtaining specialized training or attending a college or university may be beyond the financial resources of many students. Have students research financial aid, grants, and other programs that provide assistance for gaining some type of postsecondary education or training. Ask students to share the results of their research in class.

EXCELLENT BUSINESS PRACTICES

Looking at a Career in Tourism

Century Plaza Hotel and Tower in Los Angeles, California, has made a commitment to help high school students learn about the tourism industry. The 1,072-room hotel gives teenagers from two inner-city high schools an opportunity to experience the behind-the-scenes workings of a luxury hotel.

During the two-day program, managers provide information about opportunities in the hotel industry, including educational requirements, professional careers, and rates of pay. They also discuss the hotel's standards.

Students choose the department they want to "work" in and are fitted with uniforms they wear while shadowing an employee through his or her shift.

The program has helped students understand more about the working world and visualize themselves making tourism their career.

Thinking Critically

How does following someone through a day's work give you a more complete understanding of that person's job than just talking about it?

Chapter 3 • Researching Careers **61**

Extending EXCELLENT BUSINESS PRACTICES

Answer: This hands-on approach allows you to view and experience what that person does in a given day.

Further Application: Ask students to contact companies, associations, or other organizations they would like to visit. They should explain that they are interested in exploring careers and would like to arrange a tour.

TEACH *(cont'd.)*

Teaching Tip

Many new careers are the result of the growing global economy. Your local library should have several books on finding an international job. Suggest that students consult these books to help them decide whether an international career is of interest to them.

If you have access to the Internet, see the Internet resources listed on the unit opener page for a couple of sites to visit.

ASSESS

Evaluation

Assign the section review.

MINI QUIZ

True-False

1. An exploratory interview is a formal meeting through which you apply for a job. (false)

2. Observing a worker on the job is called job shadowing. (true)

3. Service learning involves selling a company's services to its customers. (false)

4. Values are the things we believe because they are true. (false)

5. Fringe benefits add to what you earn because the employer pays costs that you would otherwise have to pay. (true)

Use the Testmaker to create a customized test for Chapter 3.

YOU'RE THE BOSS!

Solving Workplace Problems

You manage a used car lot, and your salespeople are rewarded with commissions. Your top-selling employee has asked to work only on weekends. Your other employees object, since this would give them fewer opportunities to work weekends, when the majority of sales are made. How will you deal with this situation?

International Career Outlook

With growth in the global economy, more and more careers involve working internationally. Brainstorm with your friends and family. Do they know someone who has worked in a foreign country? Pool your resources with other students and make a list of international career possibilities, such as English teacher, civil engineer, or health-care worker.

You can find plenty of international jobs by using library resources. Browse the Web as well.

In today's global economy, many jobs are opening up in foreign countries. *In what foreign country do you think you might like to work? Why?*

SECTION 3-2 *Review*

Understanding Key Concepts

Using complete sentences, answer the following questions on a separate sheet of paper.

1. What aspects of the work environment are important when evaluating a career?

2. Why should you consider a career's outlook?

Extending the Illustration

Ask students to name U.S. companies in other countries that might be a source of a job abroad. (Some of the best-known companies are McDonald's, KFC, Coca-Cola, the Disney Company.)

Caption Answer: Answers will vary, but students should indicate the reasons for their choices, including adventure, advancement, and a good salary.

SECTION 3-2 *Review* ANSWERS

1. The physical and social surroundings of a career are important, whether the job is indoors or outdoors and whether the work is done primarily alone or with others.

2. Knowing a career's outlook is vital to knowing whether the career has long-term stability.

Key Terms

Internet job services *(p. 53)*
exploratory interview
(p. 54)
cooperative program *(p. 54)*
job shadowing *(p. 55)*
internship *(p. 55)*
service learning *(p. 55)*

SECTION 3-1 Summary

- The U.S. Office of Education divides careers into 15 clusters.
- You can research careers informally from the world around you, friends and family, and media resources.
- You can research careers formally in books, magazines, and other printed matter; videotapes and audiotapes; and in computerized job resources.
- You can obtain a wealth of up-to-date information on the Internet, especially the World Wide Web.
- You can research a career and then interview someone who works in that field.
- You can obtain part-time work in many different ways: through educational programs, job shadowing, volunteering, internships, and service learning.

Key Terms

work environment *(p. 59)*
flextime *(p. 59)*
fringe benefits *(p. 61)*

SECTION 3-2 Summary

- Consider whether the values that a career reinforces match your values.
- Investigate exactly what tasks and responsibilities a career entails.
- Look for a career that balances working with data, people, and things in a way that suits you.
- Evaluate the work environment a career offers.
- Find out what scheduling flexibility is possible within a career.
- Determine what aptitudes and abilities you have that a career requires.
- Investigate what education and training you need for a career.
- Many career resources describe the salary ranges of different careers.
- Consider whether the number of people working in a career is expected to increase or decrease in the future.
- Consider international careers in the growing global economy.

Chapter 3 • Researching Careers **63**

Reteaching

1. Have students consider two jobs at an airline: airplane mechanic and reservation agent. Ask them to find a profile of the two jobs. Then have them list the values; relationship among data, people, and things; work environment; working hours; and the aptitudes and abilities required for each job. Also have them compare average salaries, as well as the career outlook for both jobs.

2. Assign and review vocabulary, chapter questions, and activities from the Chapter Review.

Extending the Content

 Assign the appropriate Chapter 3 activities in the *Student Activity Workbook*.

Have students obtain a copy of a company newsletter, annual report, and/or magazine article on a company of their choice. Or, they may use a reference book describing U.S. companies. (The local public library should have several of these.) Have them use these references to write a 250-word report describing the company with respect to the 10 characteristics listed on page 57.

CLOSE

Tell students to think of three jobs that would be unsuitable to them because of their personal values. Have them share their thoughts with a classmate.

Teaching YOU'RE THE BOSS!

✓ Possible responses: Reward the best employee with the opportunity to work weekends only, or negotiate a compromise.

Computer Activity

Have students open the outline document they created in Chapter 2. Add the sections, "Identify Choices" and "Gather Information." Students should refer to the 10 characteristics of examining careers as they gather information for these two sections.

Answers
Reviewing Key Terms

Examples will vary but should reflect an understanding of the meanings of the terms.

Recalling Key Concepts

1. b
2. a
3. c
4. c
5. a

Thinking Critically

1. Formal career research is comprehensive and provides a depth of information. Sources consulted during formal research tend to be more knowledgeable and organized.

2. By researching a career first, you can learn basic background information which you can use to develop more useful interview questions.

3. A professional might allow job shadowing to repay past favors or simply to help an eager young person learn about the profession.

4. In addition to patriotism, responsibility and courage are likely values for someone who enters the military.

5. Working in an environment suited to one's personality makes work more pleasant and increases one's job satisfaction.

Reviewing Key Terms

Work with a partner to practice your vocabulary. On a separate sheet of paper, write an example of each term, and see if you and your partner can match each other's examples with the correct terms.

Internet job services
exploratory interview
cooperative program
service learning
work environment
flextime
fringe benefits
job shadowing
internship

Recalling Key Concepts

Choose the correct answer for each item below. Write your answers on a separate sheet of paper.

1. The *Dictionary of Occupational Titles* is a guide to ____.
   (a) employers (b) job titles
   (c) career magazines

2. The *Reader's Guide to Periodical Literature* helps in finding ____.
   (a) magazine articles (b) career videos
   (c) Internet listings

3. Working in a homeless shelter as part of course work is called ____.
   (a) an internship (b) fringe benefits
   (c) service learning

4. Driving a tow-truck and repairing engines are examples of ____.
   (a) a career outlook (b) values
   (c) tasks and responsibilities

5. One characteristic that makes up a career profile is ____.
   (a) salary (b) internships (c) data

Thinking Critically

Using complete sentences, answer each of the questions below on a separate sheet of paper.

1. What are some advantages of doing formal career research?

2. Why is it a good idea to research a career before having an exploratory interview?

3. What might motivate a career professional to allow a student to shadow him or her on the job?

4. What personal values would match someone to a career in the military?

5. How might a compatible work environment contribute to job satisfaction?

 ## SCANS Foundation Skills and Workplace Competencies

Personal Qualities: *Self-Esteem*

1. List qualities that make you a good candidate for a part-time job.

Resources: *Allocating Time*

2. Imagine that you have volunteered for after-school service learning. Estimate how many hours per week and on which days you could work. What factors influenced your estimate?

Technology: *Selecting Technology*

3. Compare searching for career information using the *Reader's Guide to Periodical Literature* with searching on the Internet.

 ## SCANS Foundation Skills and Workplace Competencies

1. Students' answers should reflect desirable workplace qualities.

2. Students' answers should reflect balancing school, work, and family.

3. Using the *Reader's Guide* costs nothing, whereas searching the Internet entails phone charges. The Internet covers more sources and is faster. An Internet search should yield many years' worth of sources whereas the *Reader's Guide* provides only one year's worth at a time.

Connecting Academics to the Workplace

Art

1. Henry volunteers at the Mayfield Senior Citizen Center. He is in charge of publicity for a yard sale intended to raise funds for a group trip. Design a flyer, by hand or with a computer, advertising the event.

Social Studies

2. Eriko is an intern at the local radio station, which is doing market research for a station profile. Its listening audience is mostly 30- to 40-year-olds. Eriko must research the major historical and cultural events that occurred when these listeners were teenagers. What five events would you suggest?

Math

3. A listing in the *Occupational Outlook Handbook* puts the average weekly salary range for a career at $250 to $300. What would the yearly salary range be? If a worker earning the minimum of this range received a 5 percent raise, what would the new weekly salary be?

Developing Teamwork and Leadership Skills

Join forces with three other students to form a career recruitment team. Choose one of the U.S. Office of Education career clusters shown in Figure 3-1. Each team member should research one career within that cluster. Then pool information and work together to create posters, brochures, and other materials that explain the characteristics of each career. Present the materials to the class.

Real-World Workshop

Using one of the resources mentioned in the chapter or another resource that you locate, identify five employers in your area who hire part-time workers. (Do not use fast-food restaurants, service stations, or supermarkets for any of the examples.)

School-to-Work Connection

Find someone who will agree to allow you to job shadow over a weekend or a holiday. Make notes on the career in terms of the 10 characteristics described in this chapter. Report to your class about the career.

Individual Career Plan

Write a letter introducing yourself to someone working in a career that interests you. In your letter, describe your interest in the career and request an exploratory interview. Supplement your letter with a list of questions for your interview subject.

Chapter 3 • Researching Careers **65**

Developing Teamwork and Leadership Skill

This is a good activity to assess students' ability to apply the research tools presented in the chapter. Students should be able to identify the distinguishing features of each career, including tasks and responsibilities, work environment, education and training, salary, and outlook.

Real-World Workshop

Students' research should reveal more potential employers than they thought would be available. The research compiled by the class could become a part-time job bank.

School-to-Work Connection

Reports should include information on all 10 characteristics listed on page 57.

Individual Career Plan

Letters will vary but should reflect an ability to combine formal language with a polite, friendly tone. Letters should also imply an understanding of what an exploratory interview entails. Questions may be based on the list of interview questions in Section 3-1.

Connecting Academics to the Workplace

1. Flyers will vary. Use the activity as an opportunity to discuss marketing strategies and graphic design skills.

2. Answers will vary. They should reflect the student's ability to calculate the correct era based on the ages of the listening audience, and to identify the relevant major issues.

3. yearly: $13,000 to $15,600; weekly, after raise: $262.50

• • • PLANNING GUIDE • • •
Chapter 4

SECTION 1 *What is Entrepreneurship?*

SECTION OBJECTIVES	SECTION FEATURES	SECTION RESOURCES
• Define entrepreneurship and identify the traits of successful entrepreneurs. • Explain the advantages and disadvantages of becoming an entrepreneur.	Personal Career Plan, p. 67 Ethics in Action, p. 69 Career Do's and Don'ts, p. 72	Workforce 2000 Videodisc and Videotape Section 4-1 Review, p. 72 Student Activity Workbook

SECTION 2 *Business Owner*

SECTION OBJECTIVES	SECTION FEATURES	SECTION RESOURCES
• Identify the four main ways of becoming a business owner. • Explain the advantages and disadvantages of each major route to business ownership.	Exploring Careers, p. 77	Workforce 2000 Videodisc and Videotape Section 4-2 Review, p. 76 Student Activity Workbook

SECTION 3 *Getting Started in Your Own Business*

SECTION OBJECTIVES	SECTION FEATURES	SECTION RESOURCES
• Describe the different legal forms of business ownership. • Identify key factors in selecting a business location. • Describe the documents needed when financing a new business.	You're the Boss!, p. 80 Excellent Business Practices, p. 81	Workforce 2000 Videodisc and Videotape Section 4-3 Review, p. 82 Chapter 4 Review, pp. 84–85 Student Activity Workbook

CHAPTER 4

CHAPTER RESOURCES

- Chapter Transparencies and Lesson Plans
- Chapter 4 Test
- Spanish Resources, Chapter 4
- School-to-Work Activity Handbook, Chapter 4 Activity
- Teacher's Lesson Plans, Chapter 4
- Implementing Block Scheduling, Chapter 4
- Print, Media, and Internet Handbook
- Strategies for Implementing Work-Based Learning
- Strategies for Implementing Connecting Activities

SCANS CORRELATION CHART

Foundation Skills

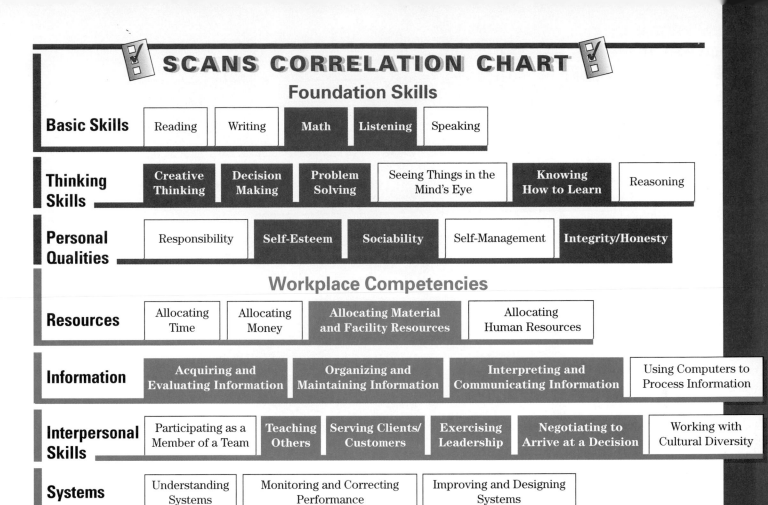

Basic Skills: Reading | Writing | Math | Listening | Speaking

Thinking Skills: Creative Thinking | Decision Making | Problem Solving | Seeing Things in the Mind's Eye | Knowing How to Learn | Reasoning

Personal Qualities: Responsibility | Self-Esteem | Sociability | Self-Management | Integrity/Honesty

Workplace Competencies

Resources: Allocating Time | Allocating Money | Allocating Material and Facility Resources | Allocating Human Resources

Information: Acquiring and Evaluating Information | Organizing and Maintaining Information | Interpreting and Communicating Information | Using Computers to Process Information

Interpersonal Skills: Participating as a Member of a Team | Teaching Others | Serving Clients/Customers | Exercising Leadership | Negotiating to Arrive at a Decision | Working with Cultural Diversity

Systems: Understanding Systems | Monitoring and Correcting Performance | Improving and Designing Systems

Technology: Selecting Technology | Applying Technology to Task | Maintaining and Troubleshooting Technology

Highlighted blocks indicate areas covered in the Chapter.

Additional Activities

Internet Connection

Ask students to consider becoming entrepreneurs in a field that interests them. Have them use the Internet to find out what types of training are available for entrepreneurs in general and their field specifically. What kind of support and mentoring is available for entrepreneurs? Where is funding available?

Field Trip Suggestions

Get permission to attend a local Chamber of Commerce meeting. Ask members to sponsor a student during the meeting, and be willing to introduce the student to other business people there. Later, discuss how meetings such as these help an entrepreneur's business.

Guest Speaker Suggestions

Through local business groups, locate a young entrepreneur. Ask the guest to talk about the attributes a successful entrepreneur should have, and the advantages and disadvantages of running one's own business.

Key to Ability Levels

Each section gives skill-building activities. Each activity has been labeled for use with students of various learning styles and abilities.

L1 Level 1 activities are basic activities and should be within the range of all students.

L2 Level 2 activities are average activities and should be within the range of average and above average students.

L3 Level 3 activities are challenging activities designed for the ability range of above average students.

Chapter Overview

Chapter 4 explores the personal characteristics of entrepreneurs and the elements involved in starting and maintaining a business.

Section 4-1 describes entrepreneurship and highlights the traits entrepreneurs need to be successful.

Section 4-2 looks at different ways to enter business other than starting from scratch.

Section 4-3 describes the legal matters of business and explores the factors that must be considered before starting a business.

Background Information

Write chapter objectives (Sections 4-1, 4-2, and 4-3) on the chalkboard or use the chapter objective transparency for class discussion.

Choose assignments from the *Student Activity Workbook* and write them on the chalkboard.

Have students preview the chapter, looking at pictures, reading captions, and noting content headings. Ask students to describe what they might learn in the chapter.

Preteaching
Vocabulary

Write the Key Terms from Sections 4-1, 4-2, and 4-3 on the chalkboard. How does each term relate to an entrepreneur's personal traits and business activities?

66

Meeting SPECIAL Needs

Limited Proficiency in English

Students with limited English language skills will be helped by a review of the vocabulary used in the chapter. Focus not only on the new terms introduced in the chapter, but on the other more complex words that may be unfamiliar, such as competition and self-motivation. Some ways to review are: to go over the broad concepts; define concepts and words in more than one way; or have students define the terms in their own words, helping them correct or revise their definitions.

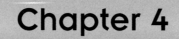

Chapter 4

Entrepreneurship

Section 4-1
What Is Entrepreneurship?

Section 4-2
Ways of Becoming a Business Owner

Section 4-3
Getting Started in Your Own Business

In this video segment, find out how your interests may lead to entrepreneurial opportunities.

Journal
Personal Career Plan

Entrepreneurs create and develop their own businesses. It's an exciting undertaking—but it's not for everyone. How does the prospect of entrepreneurship fit your own values, interests, and abilities? In your journal, list the advantages entrepreneurship might offer you as an individual. Then write a list of the disadvantages.

67

School-to-Work Connecting Activities

Invite a local entrepreneur to visit your class. Have students prepare interview questions that focus on the personal traits, business organization, and operation issues described in the chapter.

After the interview, have students apply what they have learned by "creating" their own business. Have students write a mini-business plan describing their business idea, their product or service, their customers, and how they will operate the business.

Work-Based Learning Strategies and Activities

Have students do an informal survey of businesses at a local mall and write a brief report of their findings. Students should count the number owned by corporations (such as department store chains) and the number owned and operated by entrepreneurs.

Have students analyze how entrepreneurial opportunities may affect their own career choices.

WORKFORCE 2000 Training Video

Have students view the video and perform the interactive exercises to reinforce important chapter concepts and thinking processes.

Chapter 4

Addressing **LEARNING** Styles

Intrapersonal and Interpersonal Learners

Break students into groups. By pooling its skills, ask each group to decide what kind of business it could open. Students should do the following: select a site, envision the advertising, figure out where they would get funding, decide who would be best for which positions, and so on. Try to see that the groups are balanced, containing both outgoing, interpersonal learners and reflective intrapersonal learners.

FOCUS

Bell Ringer

Write this ad on the chalkboard: *Business opportunity. Good location, discount store in well-established shopping mall. 65K purchase price.*

Have students write answers to these questions: Would you buy this business? Why or why not? What else would you want to know about this business? What personal values would you consider in making your decision?

Introducing the Section

Write students' answers from the Bell Ringer activity on the chalkboard. Introduce the concept of entrepreneurship and the traits of entrepreneurs. Review the importance of personal values and lifestyle goals when making a career decision to become an entrepreneur.

Ask students if working on their own appeals to them. Use this question to lead into a discussion of the advantages and disadvantages of being an entrepreneur.

Motivational Activity
Critical Thinking

Have students imagine that they work for themselves. They need to create a schedule of their activities for a day. Using their schedules, have them tally the total number of hours they would spend working during the week.

Ask students if they could support themselves and a family working that number of hours. Then discuss the number of hours most people work during a week (40 or more, in general).

68

What Is Entrepreneurship?

OBJECTIVES

After studying this section, you will be able to:

* Define *entrepreneurship* and identify the traits of successful entrepreneurs.
* Explain the advantages and disadvantages of becoming an entrepreneur.

KEY TERM

entrepreneur

Are you a fan of the *Star Trek* movies and TV programs? In this sci-fi adventure, the crew of a starship travels across the universe, exploring places where no one has gone before. The starship is called the *Enterprise*—and for good reason. The word comes from an Old French word, meaning "to take action, take risks, take responsibility."

You might be surprised to learn that the word *entrepreneur* comes from the same root as *enterprise*. An **entrepreneur** is someone who organizes and then runs a business. An entrepreneur's life is challenging. The risks can be high, but the rewards can also be great. Entrepreneurs must make wise decisions and search out inventive solutions.

Does this adventure appeal to you? Are you willing to set off into the unknown and find your way? Maybe your career path leads to entrepreneurship.

Advantages of Entrepreneurship

If you think entrepreneurship would demand a great deal from you, you're right. What, then, are the advantages?

* *You're in charge.* Entrepreneurs decide when and how hard to work and how their businesses will operate.
* *There is great job satisfaction.*
* *Entrepreneurship can lead to a good income.*

68 *Unit 2 • Exploring Careers*

Implementing Teamwork

Divide your class into teams of three to four students and tell them to form business partnerships. Have each partnership decide on a type of business, a location, and the start-up costs they may incur. Ask them to put this information in outline form that could be used to create a business plan.

Entrepreneurs can't go home at 5:00 P.M. if there's still work to be done. **What rewards does the entrepreneur reap for all the long hours put in?**

Disadvantages of Entrepreneurship

Entrepreneurship can be exciting and rewarding, but there are also drawbacks.

- *There is financial risk.* You can lose your investment and sometimes more.

- *Entrepreneurs often work long hours.*

- *Competition can be stiff.*

- *There are no guarantees of success.* Almost two of every three new businesses fail within their first four years.

ETHICS in Action

For years, you've worked in your town's only copy shop. The owner has trained you well and given you unusual opportunities and responsibilities. Now a financial backer offers to help you open your own copy shop—in direct competition with your current employer. Will you take advantage of this opportunity? Why or why not?

Chapter 4 • Entrepreneurship **69**

Extending the Illustration

More people have started their own businesses in the last few years. Ask students why people may be starting their own businesses. (Downsizing hit a number of people with significant job skills that could be used in starting a business.)

Caption Answer: Answers may include job satisfaction, high income, a successful business, and independence.

Teaching ETHICS in Action

Have students follow these steps to help them make a decision.

1. What are the ethical issues?
2. What are the alternatives?
3. Who are the affected parties?
4. How do the alternatives affect the parties?
5. What is your decision?

Guided Practice

Teaching Strategies

1. Assign and review Section 4-1.
2. Use the transparency for this section.

Teaching Tip

Lead students in a discussion of why they think some people pursue their ideas to become entrepreneurs and others do not. (Possible answers include lack of money, doubting one's ability to be successful, low priority for being an entrepreneur, bad timing in the market.)

Discussion Starter

According to an article in *U.S. News and World Report,* the average entrepreneur in this country began working full-time at age 18, and owned a business by age 29. Have students discuss how age may affect the decision to become an entrepreneur. (Young people are not as established in their careers, so they have less to lose; they may be willing to take more risks because they do not yet have families to support.)

Critical Thinking

Women are starting new businesses at a rate almost twice that of men. Have students speculate on reasons why this might be happening. (Possible reasons include desire for independence, difficulty of securing top management positions in existing businesses, and avoidance of workplace gender discrimination.)

SCANS Foundation Skills Connection

L1 Math

Have students assume that they are entrepreneurs employing three people in addition to themselves. Each employee earns $350 a week. The business pays social security taxes of 7.65 percent on employee earnings. As the owner, you pay yourself $500 a week and set aside 15.3 percent of that amount for social security taxes. How much money is spent for employee salaries and taxes in a year? ($350 × 3 × 52 = $54,600 × .0765 = $4,177; $54,600 + $4,177 = $58,777)

L2 Knowing How to Learn

Have students use the library to find information on a well-known entrepreneur. Tell students to write a profile of the person, including educational background, when and why the business was started, and factors contributing to the person's success.

L3 Creative Thinking

Have students write their own autobiographies as entrepreneurs from the perspective of 10 years in the future. Have them include the type of business they started, how successful it has been, the number of people it employs, and plans for the future.

Traits of Entrepreneurs

Most entrepreneurs share certain behaviors and attitudes. If the ones described below don't quite match traits you see in yourself, you can develop them.

Motivation

Successful entrepreneurs are very self-motivated. They know what they want to achieve, and they believe in their ability. They keep themselves motivated by setting short- and long-term goals. Then they make and follow a plan for achieving those goals.

Sight and Foresight

Entrepreneurs recognize opportunities (see *Figure 4-1*). They see problems and find a way to build success on them. That's how Daryl Bernstein got his start when he was 17 years old.

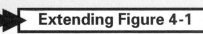

▶ **Figure 4-1**

Viewing Problems as Opportunities

For the entrepreneur, every problem is an opportunity.

A Entrepreneurs are alert to situations around them. The difference between the advertisements produced by major corporations and those produced by small businesses is apparent. The entrepreneur might ask, "What is the difference between these ads? How can I help make small businesses more competitive?"

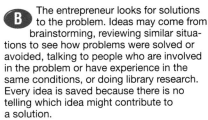

B The entrepreneur looks for solutions to the problem. Ideas may come from brainstorming, reviewing similar situations to see how problems were solved or avoided, talking to people who are involved in the problem or have experience in the same conditions, or doing library research. Every idea is saved because there is no telling which idea might contribute to a solution.

70   *Unit 2 • Exploring Careers*

▶▶▶ **Extending Figure 4-1** ◀◀◀

Have students discuss the role attitude plays in determining success, whether as an entrepreneur or as an employee. Can someone with a negative attitude learn to be more positive?

(Attitude is a key ingredient in any kind of business arrangement. Having a positive attitude is an attribute that many employers look for in their employees. Through consistent reinforcement, a negative attitude can be changed to be more positive.)

Pros and Cons of Logo Business	
Pros	**Cons**
Do it myself.	Selling to small businesspeople will be hard.
I have computer and software.	
Low overhead.	No one to advise me on logo design.

C Each idea is evaluated to see whether it represents the best solution. The evaluation may include research into the costs of implementing the idea, surveys to learn customer preferences, and interviews with experts. When the facts are gathered, the entrepreneur compares the pros and cons of each idea to find the best solution.

D If the solution ideas have been fully researched, nothing remains but to put the idea into action. Implementation may reveal more problems. The entrepreneur uses the problems as a springboard for making adjustments to the solution.

Chapter 4 • Entrepreneurship **71**

SCANS Workplace Competencies Connection

L1 Exercising Leadership

Have students work in pairs to create a list of leadership skills they think an entrepreneur would need. Have students share their lists in class.

L2 Interpreting and Communicating Information

Have students choose a personal interest that they think they could turn into a business. Tell students to create a flyer or a newspaper ad describing the type of their business.

L3 Negotiating to Arrive at a Decision

Have teams brainstorm ideas for starting a new business in your area. From their lists, team members must choose one business that they think could be successful. Have students share their ideas in class.

Independent Practice

Assign as homework the chapter activity in the *School-to-Work Activity Handbook.*

Reading

Have students read an article about an entrepreneur. Magazines such as *Entrepreneur, Success,* or *Inc.* are good sources.

Computer Activity

Have students open the outline document they created in Chapters 2 and 3. Under the section titled "Gather Information" have them add to their existing list.

Using the desktop publishing features of their software program, create a business card illustrating a type of business they would like own or operate.

Writing: Persuasion

Have students write newspaper ads seeking partners with whom to start a business. Students should list the traits they think are necessary for their business partners to have.

ASSESS

Assessment

Content

Have students create flip charts describing the advantages and disadvantages of entrepreneurship.

Evaluation

Assign the section review.

Reteaching

Have students create a bulletin board display on entrepreneurship, with these elements: a definition/description of entrepreneurship, advantages and disadvantages of entrepreneurship, traits needed for business success, and names of some famous entrepreneurs along with their photos from magazines and newspapers.

Extending the Content

Assign the appropriate Chapter 4 activities in the *Student Activity Workbook*.

CLOSE

Have students make a list of as many famous entrepreneurs as they can name.

Daryl noticed that large companies used logos to promote their services and products. He thought logos would also benefit small companies. As a result, he started a business creating logos for small companies. It took a while, but his business became a success. In the process, he helped his clients increase their profits by giving them a greater identity and ultimately more recognition.

Viewing problems as opportunities can be seen as a process. *Figure 4-1* on pages 70–71 shows how Bernstein might have used this skill to develop the idea for his business.

Decision Making

Entrepreneurs make business decisions every day, and the decisions must be good ones. Refer back to Section 2-1 of Chapter 2 for more information on how to make decisions.

Career Do's & Don'ts

When Starting Your Own Business...
Do:
- talk to several people who started their own businesses.
- make a plan for starting a business.
- be open to even the craziest ideas.
- make having your own business an ongoing lifetime goal if you know it's right for you.

Don't:
- limit yourself by thinking all the "good ideas are already taken."
- hold yourself back from working hard.
- get involved with "partners" who can't contribute their share.
- let others crush your dreams.

SECTION 4-1 *Review*

Understanding Key Concepts

Using complete sentences, answer the following questions on a separate sheet of paper.

1. Give an example of a successful business in your community. How might the traits of an entrepreneur have helped this business succeed?

2. Are the advantages or the disadvantages of entrepreneurship more important to you? Why?

SECTION 4-1 *Review* ANSWERS

1. Businesses named will vary. Students should describe how motivation, goal setting, and the ability to recognize and take advantage of opportunities helped make the entrepreneur's business a success.

2. Answers will vary. Students should discuss the advantages and disadvantages of entrepreneurship and tell which are more important to them and why.

Ways of Becoming a Business Owner

OBJECTIVES

After studying this section, you will be able to:

- Identify the four main ways of becoming a business owner.
- Explain the advantages and disadvantages of each major route to business ownership.

KEY TERMS

start-up costs
lease
goodwill
market outlook
franchise

If you decide entrepreneurship is for you, you'll have to decide how you're going to get your own business. Here are the four main ways of doing so:

1. starting a new business,
2. buying an existing business,
3. buying a franchise, and
4. taking over the family business.

Starting a New Business

Starting a new business is a dream many people share. What an exciting adventure! If you start a new business, look for challenges as well as rewards.

The Challenges

No matter how you get into business, you will face challenges. If you're starting a new business, you'll face a few additional ones.

- A new business requires more time and effort than an established business.
- Start-up costs are often high. **Start-up costs** are the expenses involved in going into business. Examples include renting or buying space and buying equipment, office supplies, and insurance.
- If you borrow money, you'll have to convince lenders that your business idea will work.
- It's risky. No matter how well you plan, you won't know if the business will succeed until you've tried it.

Chapter 4 • Entrepreneurship **73**

Workforce 2000 Trends

Scientific discoveries are being made so fast that most of what we know now was discovered in the past *decade*. Many of these discoveries have the potential to change whole portions of the economy. Workers of the future will have to constantly update their education and keep their skills flexible.

FOCUS

Bell Ringer

Write the words *new businesses, existing businesses,* and *franchises* on the chalkboard. Have students make lists of local businesses that come to mind for each category.

Introducing the Section

Ask students to share their lists. Write the names of the businesses under each category. Use these lists to begin the discussion of the ways an entrepreneur can become a business owner.

Find an example of a new business that may have opened recently in your area. Ask students how the challenges faced by a new business owner compare to the challenges faced by someone who chooses to enter a new career field as an employee. Also discuss the differences in possible rewards in each situation.

Motivational Activity
Critical Thinking

Have students complete the following in paragraph form: "I think becoming an entrepreneur would be . . . ."

Ask volunteers to read their paragraphs to the class and give reasons for their thinking. Then ask students to discuss how the goal of becoming an entrepreneur might affect the short-term goals they set for themselves.

Guided Practice
Teaching Strategies

1. Assign and review Section 4-2.
2. Use the transparency for this section.
3. Assign and review the Case Study.

Discussion Starter

Share this anecdote with students: Paul Orfalea became an entrepreneur in college when he borrowed $5,000 to open a copy shop near campus. Today he has stores throughout the country. The name of the store? Kinko's.

Paul Orfalea saw a need and built a business around that need. Discuss with students how entrepreneurs find ideas for businesses. (Some possibilities include looking for services that aren't being provided, thinking about ways to improve people's lives or save time.)

Critical Thinking

Is the location of a business as important in our present age of almost instant worldwide communication and rapid transportation as it once was? Give examples to support your answer.

SCANS Foundation Skills Connection

L1 Listening

Invite a local entrepreneur to speak to your class. Ask the person to talk about how he or she came up with the idea for the business.

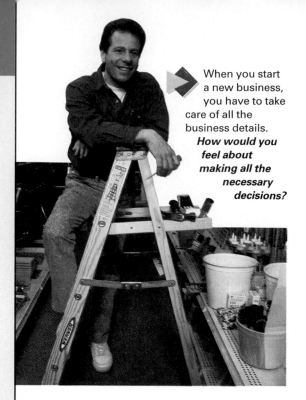

When you start a new business, you have to take care of all the business details. *How would you feel about making all the necessary decisions?*

The Rewards

Tough challenges await those who build a business. What are the rewards? Besides those enjoyed by all entrepreneurs, consider these benefits:

- You don't inherit a previous owner's mistakes.
- You can try fresh ideas and build your business your way.
- You get personal satisfaction from knowing you built the business yourself.

Buying an Existing Business

If you don't want to start a new business, you might buy an existing one. There

are many reasons why a business might be for sale. A successful one may be for sale because the owners are retiring or entering a new business. Perhaps business is so good, they can't handle it all anymore.

There may also be many reasons why an unsuccessful business is for sale. The bottom line, however, is that it is losing money. Perhaps it's still a good investment, if it can be turned around.

A Fast Start

Buying an existing business can put you several steps ahead. First, you can save on start-up costs by taking advantage of the previous owner's business agreements, such as a lease signed when rents were lower. A **lease** is a contract to use something for a specified period of time.

When buying an existing business, check out customer goodwill. *Why should you think twice about buying a business that lacks goodwill?*

Extending the Illustration

Ask students how entrepreneurs develop the self-confidence needed to go into business for themselves. (Through successful work experiences, a positive attitude, and learning what is needed to operate a business.)

Caption Answer: Possible answers include proud, satisfied, or independent.

Extending the Illustration

Keeping customers satisfied is a major part of staying in business. Ask students to think of examples of how some local businesses keep their customers satisfied.

Caption Answer: An existing business without customer goodwill is one that is not successful. The business may not be worth buying.

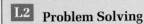

There are more than 500,000 franchised businesses in the United States.
Why do you think such businesses are so popular with entrepreneurs?

If the business has been successful, you can build on that success. The **goodwill**, or loyalty, of customers is one of a business's most valuable assets. You may also benefit from an established reputation and a trained staff.

Drawbacks

Every business has its problems, but if it's struggling, look for the reasons.

- The location may be poor.
- The competition may be taking business away.
- The **market outlook**, or potential for future sales, may have changed.
- The building or equipment may need expensive repairs or replacement.
- The business may have a reputation for poor products.

Buying a Franchise

A type of existing business that offers specific advantages is the franchise. A **franchise** is the legal right to sell a company's goods and services. Many fast-food restaurants and real estate offices are franchises.

When you buy a franchise, you are actually buying the right to sell another company's products. In addition to paying for the franchise, you will continue to pay a percentage of your profits to the parent company.

Like any business owner, you are in charge. However, you must follow the parent company's guidelines. These may dictate how to make or distribute the goods or services.

Less Risk

A franchise may be a wise choice for people with limited business experience. Here are some other benefits you'll gain:

- a recognized product name,
- established management systems,
- a business reputation and customer goodwill,
- training and support services,
- advertising, and
- financing.

Less Gain

A franchise is not the right choice for everyone. A franchise may be less profitable because you pay a portion of your profits to the parent company. Since you didn't build the company from scratch, there may be less satisfaction.

Taking Over the Family Business

Does your father, mother, or another relative own a business? If so, it might be a shortcut into entrepreneurship.

Chapter 4 • Entrepreneurship **75**

Extending the Illustration

Ask students to make a list of the franchises in your community. Most of the fast-food restaurants will be franchises. You may also have copy shops and hardware stores that are franchises.

Caption Answer: Buying a franchise removes much of the risk of investing in a business.

SCANS Workplace Competencies Connection (cont'd.)

L3 Organizing and Maintaining Information

Have students visit the local Chamber of Commerce to find out about programs that are geared toward entrepreneurs and small business owners. Have students organize the information into categories and share their information in class.

Independent Practice

Reading

Have students read ads for business opportunities in the local paper and bring in at least five different ads. Have them decide which of the four methods for starting a business applies to each ad.

Research

Have students assume that they want to open a business in your area. Tell them to select a location for their business, then determine how much it costs to lease space there.

Have students make a list of information they would need to provide a bank's loan officer when asking for a loan for start-up costs. (Information would include monthly rent, maintenance costs, cost of store or office furnishings, inventory costs, typical selling/ marketing expenses, employees' salaries, and projections for earnings with data supporting the projections.)

Joining a family business can be an easy entry into business. Relatives provide emotional as well as professional support. *What do you think would be the hardest part of joining a family business?*

Smoothing the Way

Taking over a family business can have the advantages of the franchise without the fees.

- Your relatives might help you finance the business.
- Family members tend to be loyal and to trust each other.
- Family members working as a team can achieve more than individuals.
- Relatives can teach you the business.

Bumps in the Road

In addition to the usual hazards of business ownership, a family business presents special ones. To begin with, it's sometimes hard to have normal business relationships with relatives. Moreover, when the family is part of the business, you can't always go home and leave the business behind.

SECTION 4-2 *Review*

Understanding Key Concepts

Using complete sentences, answer the following questions on a separate sheet of paper.

1. Describe four ways to enter the fast-food business. Which one do you think would offer you the best chance for success? Why?

2. State the advantages and disadvantages of buying an existing business rather than starting a new business.

Extending the Illustration

Ask whether any students in your class work in a family business. Ask them to share their ideas about the advantages and disadvantages of doing so.

Caption Answer: Answers will vary. Students may say it would be difficult to manage a business when an older family member is looking over their shoulders.

SECTION 4-2 *Review* ANSWERS

1. start a new business, buy an existing business, purchase a franchise, or enter the family business

2. advantages: save on start-up costs, build on a successful business's success; disadvantages: won't get the satisfaction of starting a business from scratch, location may be poor

CASE STUDY

Exploring Careers: Hospitality and Recreation

Ben Abebe
Travel Agent

Q: Why did you become a travel agent?

A: First of all, I love to travel. Travel is always exciting. As a travel agent, I send people to places they've been waiting to visit for a long time. It always makes me happy to see my customers happy.

Q: What training did you have?

A: I had a year of training as a ticket reservationist at Ethiopian Airlines, where I worked before coming to this country. That helped me in this business because the basic principles are the same.

Q: What skills are important for a travel agent?

A: I think you need to know the specific areas your clients are going to. For example, I book people who want to go to Africa, especially Ethiopia. I know the area and what airlines are going there. Knowing your own product really helps you promote yourself.

Q: What is the future like for travel agents?

A: Many airlines have cut the commissions they pay travel agents. Most people book their own travel with their personal computers. Electronic ticketing is crippling for travel agents. However, the business will probably continue to be good for experienced agents.

Thinking Critically

People are traveling more than ever before. Can you name ways that a travel agent might go into the business despite the restrictions mentioned above?

CAREER FACTS

Nature of the Work:
Help clients plan trips; make reservations; write tickets.

Training or Education Needed:
Training in a travel school or experience in a related travel field.

Aptitudes, Abilities, and Skills:
Math, listening, speaking, and interpersonal skills; problem-solving skills; reading and writing skills; interest in travel, world cultures, and geography; sales ability; detail-oriented; decision-making skills; office skills; foreign language skills.

Salary Range:
Salary, commission, or a combination. Start at $13,000; average $20,000 with 5 years of experience; up to $65,000 or more with 10 years of experience.

Career Path:
Start in a related travel field or a travel agency office. Because of shrinking demand, work may be scarce.

Chapter 4 • Entrepreneurship **77**

Extending the CASE STUDY

Answer: Work for a large corporation making travel arrangements for employees; specialize in package tours, where you put together itineraries, make reservations, plan sight-seeing side trips, and take care of special needs; specialize in exotic tours to rarely visited places; offer your outstanding Internet surfing skills to book trips.

Further Application: Have students discuss the future of their chosen fields. What changes can they see that may eliminate or reduce their jobs in the next 10 years? How will they change and grow to stay in their chosen careers?

Assessment

Performance

Assign students to four teams. Have each team take one method of becoming a business owner and prepare a three-minute presentation describing the method, its advantages and disadvantages, and the risk the business owner faces when choosing that method.

Evaluation

Assign the section review.

Reteaching

Have students prepare a bulletin board display on the methods for starting a business. The display should list each method and its advantages and disadvantages, along with the names of local businesses in each category.

Extending the Content

Assign the appropriate Chapter 4 activities in the *Student Activity Workbook*.

Obtain from a bank a personal information form used for business loan applications. Reproduce the form and have students imagine they are entrepreneurs of a small business and fill out the form. Have them discuss each other's completed forms in class.

CLOSE

Have students complete this statement: "Many experts agree that the single most important factor in determining the success or failure of a new business is . . . ."

FOCUS

Bell Ringer

Tell students to assume that they have decided to invest money in a business. Have them write a sentence or two telling whether they prefer to start a business on their own, with one partner, or with several partners.

Introducing the Section

Write on the chalkboard *sole proprietorship, partnership,* and *corporation.* Tally students' responses from the Bell Ringer activity. Give a definition of each form of business ownership and have students briefly describe what they think are the advantages and disadvantages of each.

Ask an attorney to visit your class to talk about the legal issues involved in setting up a business. Have the attorney discuss the pitfalls partners face when they do not have a partnership agreement. Set aside time for students to ask questions.

Motivational Activity
Critical Thinking

Have students prepare a list of the personal qualities they would want in a business partner. Beside each quality, ask them to write a reason for choosing that quality. Have students share their lists with classmates. Then ask them to describe how their own personal qualities would mesh with the qualities they described for a partner.

Getting Started in Your Own Business

OBJECTIVES

After studying this section, you will be able to:
- **Describe the different legal forms of business ownership.**
- **Identify key factors in selecting a business location.**
- **Describe the documents needed when financing a new business.**

KEY TERMS

sole proprietorship
partnership
corporation
operating expenses
income statement
revenue
gross profit
net profit

Let's say that you've decided to become an entrepreneur. Will you own the business by yourself, or do you want someone to share the work and the risks? Where will you locate your business—in your home or in a building elsewhere? Think about the business you'd like to start. How would you answer these questions?

Forms of Legal Ownership

Suppose you decide that you want to own a business. You must now decide what form the ownership will take. This is a legal issue, so think carefully about it. You have three choices: sole proprietorship, partnership, or corporation. *Figure 4-2* compares the advantages and disadvantages of each form of ownership.

Sole Proprietorship

Most businesses begin as a **sole proprietorship**. This means the business is completely owned by one person. About 75 percent of all U.S. businesses are sole proprietorships.

Partnership

A **partnership** is a legal arrangement in which two or more people share ownership. Control and profits are divided between or among partners, according to

Addressing Workplace Diversity

Diversity covers not only gender and culture, but employees' attitudes, capabilities, backgrounds, learning and behavior styles, and work habits. A diverse workforce improves an organization's flexibility and creativity, and ensures its long-term health and survival.

Form of Legal Ownership	Advantages	Disadvantages
Sole Proprietorship 	• Owner makes all decisions • Easiest form of business to set up • Least regulated of the three forms of business	• Limited by the skills, abilities, and financial resources of one person • Difficult to raise funds to finance business • Owner has sole financial responsibility for company; personal assets sometimes at risk
Partnership 	• Can draw on the skills, abilities, and financial resources of more than one person • Easier to raise funds than in sole proprietorship	• More complicated than sole proprietorship • Tensions and conflicts may develop among partners • Owners liable for all business losses; personal property sometimes in jeopardy
Corporation 	• Easier to finance than other forms of business • Financial liability of shareholders limited (usually, can lose only what they've invested)	• Expensive to set up • Record keeping often time-consuming and costly • Often pays more taxes than other forms of business

Figure 4-2 Every form of business ownership has its advantages and disadvantages. What business do you know of that is owned as a sole proprietorship? A partnership? A corporation?

a partnership agreement. A partnership is the least common of the three forms of business ownership.

Corporation

A **corporation** is a business chartered by a state that legally operates apart from the owner(s). The owners buy shares, or parts, of the company. They are called *shareholders* and earn a profit based on the number of shares they own.

Location, Location, Location

Suppose you want to open a fast-food restaurant. Is location important? Of course! You've got to be near your customers. What about a mail-order business? As long as a good postal service is available, you can ship goods from anywhere. In this case, location may not be so important.

Chapter 4 • Entrepreneurship **79**

SCANS Foundation Skills Connection

L1 Sociability

Being a sole proprietor requires skill in getting along with all types of people. Have the class generate a list of the human relations skills needed to deal with the general public. (Possible skills include sociability, ability to communicate clearly, helpful attitude, honesty, and reliability.)

L2 Self-Esteem

Have students reflect on themselves as business partners. What personal qualities do they have that would be valued in a business relationship? Do they like to share responsibility, help solve problems, and help make decisions? Ask each student to write a 100-word essay telling whether they are suited to being a partner in a business.

L3 Creative Thinking

Tell students that they and a friend want to start an advertising business. One person knows advertising and printing and will be responsible for producing advertising brochures. The other person has the money to start the business and will be responsible for finding clients. When the partners meet with an attorney to draw up a partnership agreement, what should be ⌐ated about each person's ⌐nsibilities?

Good locations are usually expensive, yet business owners usually choose the best location they can afford. *What advantages does this site offer the business owner?*

When location is important, consider these factors:

- the type of businesses in the area,
- the condition of streets and buildings,
- the cost of property,
- the location of the competition, and
- the location of your customers.

Working at Home

What about working out of your home? It's cheaper than leasing a location and more convenient. You'll also enjoy more flexibility and a relaxed atmosphere.

What about the problems? First, some communities restrict the kinds of businesses that can operate in residential areas. In addition, the isolation of working at home troubles many business owners. Jean Ainsworth left a large office to start a home-based business. "I hadn't realized how much I enjoyed saying 'Good morning' to

80 *Unit 2 • Exploring Careers*

people, sharing the weekend, hearing about the football games," says Ainsworth. "I had a grandchild last August and I didn't have a set of people to show the pictures to."

Financing

Whatever type of business you launch, you'll need money to get it going. You might draw on your savings or get a loan from friends. More likely, you'll need to borrow money from a commercial lender. To apply for a loan, you'll need a business description and a financial plan.

A *business description* gives specific information about your business. It describes your product and states where your business will be located. It specifies how many employees you will hire and what their salaries will be. It describes your competitors and points out their strengths and weaknesses. It also describes your timetable for starting the business.

YOU'RE THE BOSS!

✓ Solving Workplace Problems

You've developed a successful business designing and selling T-shirts. One of your regular customers places an unusually large order for special T-shirts. However, the customer has requested a slogan that goes against your most basic values; making and selling these shirts would be difficult for you. How will you respond?

Extending the Illustration

Have students think about a local business that has recently opened or one that recently closed because of the lack of business. Why is its location good or not so good?

Caption Answer: Many potential customers work in the area or drive through it. The neighborhood is well maintained and appears safe.

Teaching YOU'RE THE BOSS!

✓ Possible responses: Put business before values and fill the order. Discuss your reservations with the customer and try for a compromise (depending on the topic). Discuss your values with the customer and suggest that another designer work on these shirts.

A *financial plan* spells out your start-up costs, operating expenses, and other costs for the first few months. **Operating expenses** are the costs of doing business, such as the costs of manufacturing and selling the product.

Producing these reports will require you to apply the SCANS skills of math and writing. If you're planning on entrepreneurship, now is the time to master these skills.

Operating Your Own Business

Whatever business you choose, you will use many of the SCANS skills and competencies. These include reading, writing, math, listening, and speaking skills.

Africa Brown started a business called Africa's Clothing when she was a 16-year-old high school student in Washington, D.C. She got the idea after participating in an entrepreneurship program offered by the Business Kids Institute and the city of Washington, D.C. Brown makes clothing to order, mainly for her classmates. She must listen effectively to take orders accurately and to get the job done right. She must speak well so that she can explain her service. Think about the business you'd like to start. How will you use listening, speaking, reading, writing, and math skills?

EXCELLENT BUSINESS PRACTICES

Responsibility to the Planet

Ben & Jerry's Homemade, Inc. of Burlington, Vermont, manufactures and markets ice cream and franchises shops. Part of the company's mission is to initiate innovative ways to improve the quality of life on local, national, and international levels.

The company created a foundation that sets aside 7.5 percent of pretax profits to support progressive social change by funding small grassroots organizations.

In manufacturing its product, Ben & Jerry's also supports small businesses. During a period of volatile prices in the dairy industry, Ben & Jerry's paid a dairy premium totaling a half million dollars to the Vermont family farmers who supply the milk for their products. Brownies used in one product come from a bakery which employs disadvantaged people from the local community. Nuts used in another product are imported directly from South American rain forests, supporting the local industry.

Ben & Jerry's opened shops in Petrozavodsk and Kondopaga, Russia. Profits from the shops are designed to fund cross-cultural exchanges.

Thinking Critically

If you operated your own successful company, what values would you support and which activities would you fund?

Extending EXCELLENT BUSINESS PRACTICES

Answer: Answers will vary.

Further Application: Have students call the public relations department of a local company or any corporation they're curious about. What is the company's "mission statement"? How does the company support quality of life on local, national, or international levels?

SCANS Workplace Competencies Connections

L1 Serving Customers

Studies show that it costs businesses less money to keep their existing customers than to find new ones. Have students brainstorm ways to provide good service.

L2 Interpreting and Communicating Information

Divide the class into teams and have them choose a business they would like to promote. Have them create posters advertising its products or services.

L3 Teaching Others

Divide students into five groups and assign each group one of these information sources: the local Chamber of Commerce, the Small Business Administration, the library, an accountant, and a bank loan officer. Have the groups gather information about the needs of a new business and then have them teach others what they learned.

Independent Practice

Writing: *Informational*

Have students write a letter to the Better Business Bureau asking about the services it provides to businesses and consumers. Discuss responses in class.

Have students read the annual report of a corporation that interests them and summarize the kinds of information provided in the report. Would this information be enough for them to decide whether to buy stock in the company? What else would they want to know? (Buying decisions would vary. Students should also want to know the market outlook for businesses in this industry and to study data from similar companies to compare operating results.)

Research

Many magazines and newspapers carry ads aimed at people who want to start home-based businesses. Some ads offer nothing more than a list of ideas for a fee. Others may require the purchase of products or equipment. Some ads are scams. Tell students to find several types of ads and contact the advertisers to find out about the offer. Have students compare their information in class and decide whether the ads offer real business opportunities.

ASSESS

Assessment
Content

Have students create posters defining entrepreneurship, showing ways of starting a business, and showing the various forms of business ownership. Have students illustrate ~h poster with photos of en- ~neurs or businesses or ~ own graphics.

 Entrepreneurs whose businesses are based on technical or mechanical skills need good communication skills. *What are some situations in which listening is important in business?*

Mountain Air Bikes Income Statement

Year Ended December 31		
Revenue:		
Sales	$212,015	
Cost of goods sold	109,614	
Gross profit		**$102,401**
Operating expenses:		
Salaries	$24,019	
Rent	11,211	
Utilities	4,514	
Advertising	2,422	
Total operating expenses		$42,166
Net profit (before taxes)		$60,235

▲ **Figure 4-3** An income statement shows whether a company has made a profit or suffered a loss. If this business had lost money, how would the entries on the income statement be different?

You'll need math skills for almost every aspect of business, from setting prices and calculating payroll to balancing your business checking account.

One essential record for business owners is the **income statement**. This document shows how much the business has earned or lost. *Figure 4-3* shows such a statement. The first item in the income statement is **revenue**, or income from sales. Another item is **gross profit**, or the difference between the cost of goods and their selling price. **Net profit** is the amount left after operating expenses are subtracted from the gross profit.

SECTION 4-3 *Review*

Understanding Key Concepts

Using complete sentences, answer the following questions on a separate sheet of paper.

1. Imagine that you are starting a trucking company. What form of ownership will you choose? Why?

2. What should you consider in choosing a location for this business?

3. You have decided to organize your trucking company as a corporation. How will you go about financing it?

SECTION 4-3 *Review* ANSWERS

1. Answers will vary. Students should give reasons why they would choose a sole proprietorship, partnership, or corporation.

2. Possible answers: the location of customers, condition of streets, proximity to thoroughfares, types of other businesses in the neighborhood

3. Possible answers: sell shares to shareholders, prepare a business description and financial plan and then apply to lender for financing

SECTION 4-1 Summary

- Entrepreneurship offers you the chance to run your own business, to enjoy job satisfaction, and to earn a high income. The downside is financial risk, long hours, and no *guarantee* of success.

- Entrepreneurs are self-motivated and recognize opportunities around them.

Key Term

entrepreneur *(p. 68)*

SECTION 4-2 Summary

- If you start a new business, you don't inherit problems. However, it's risky, takes time, effort, and money.

- If you buy an existing business, you may have low start-up costs, an operating business, and goodwill. However, you may inherit a poor location, stiff competition, a dwindling market, bad equipment, or a poor reputation.

- When you buy a franchise, you get a proven product, established systems, and company support. However, a franchise can be expensive, and you must pay part of your profits to the parent company.

- If you enter a family business, relatives may help you finance it and may teach you the business. However, having normal business relationships with relatives is often difficult.

Key Terms

start-up costs *(p. 73)*
lease *(p. 74)*
goodwill *(p. 75)*
market outlook *(p. 75)*
franchise *(p. 75)*

Key Terms

sole proprietorship *(p. 78)*
partnership *(p. 78)*
corporation *(p. 79)*
operating expenses *(p. 81)*
income statement *(p. 82)*
revenue *(p. 82)*
gross profit *(p. 82)*
net profit *(p. 82)*

SECTION 4-3 Summary

- There are three legal forms of business ownership: sole proprietorships, partnerships, and corporations.

- Location is extremely important for many businesses.

- A home-based business has low costs and flexible working conditions. However, you may feel isolated.

- A business loan application requires a business description and a financial plan.

Chapter 4 • Entrepreneurship **83**

Evaluation

Assign the section review.

MINI QUIZ

True-False

1. One advantage of being an entrepreneur is to reduce business risk. (false)

2. Entrepreneurs view problems as opportunities. (true)

3. Buying an existing business that is losing money is never a good investment. (false)

4. Buying a franchise gives you the right to sell someone else's products. (true)

5. Operating expenses are one-time costs of setting up a business. (false)

Use the Testmaker to create a customized test for Chapter 4.

Reteaching

Assign the vocabulary, chapter questions, and activities from the Chapter Review.

Extending the Content

Assign the appropriate Chapter 4 activities in the *Student Activity Workbook*.

CLOSE

Have students complete this sentence, "If I were going into business for myself, I would like to . . . ."

▶ Extending the Illustration

Caption Answer: Possible answers: listening to a customer's needs, resolving conflicts among employees, hiring employees, learning about new projects from factory experts, taking orders, learning from suppliers of business services, and understanding the costs and benefits of banking, insurance, and other services.

▶ Extending Figure 4-3

Inadequate cash flow is one of the causes of business failure. Ask students why financial statements are important to review frequently. (to know what the business's cash flow is)

Caption Answer: The gross profit would be less than the total operating expenses. The net profit entry would be a negative number.

Answers

Reviewing Key Terms

Descriptions will vary but should incorporate all terms listed.

Recalling Key Concepts

1. True
2. False: Once a franchise is paid for, a percentage of profits must be paid to the parent company.
3. True
4. False: In a partnership, the owners can sometimes lose their personal property if the business fails.
5. False: An income statement shows how much a business has earned or lost.

Thinking Critically

1. Possible answer: It's more like a franchise because it's a proven business with existing management and operating systems. Also, relatives may help financially and teach you the business.
2. Possible answer: In a partnership, there is someone else to help share the responsibility, the work, and the risk of business ownership.
3. He should understand that his goods cost more to sell than he is charging for them.

Reviewing Key Terms

On separate paper, describe a business you would like to own. Use the following key terms in your description.

entrepreneur	partnership
start-up costs	corporation
lease	operating expenses
goodwill	income statement
market outlook	revenue
franchise	gross profit
sole proprietorship	net profit

Recalling Key Concepts

On a separate sheet of paper, tell whether each of the following statements is true or false. Rewrite any false statements to make them true.

1. Entrepreneurs often work long hours, but they enjoy great job satisfaction.
2. Once a franchise is paid for, all profits go to the entrepreneur.
3. Entrepreneurs who plan to work out of their homes should consider whether they can take the isolation.
4. In a partnership, the owners can never lose their personal property if the business fails.
5. A financial plan shows how much a business has earned or lost.

Thinking Critically

Using complete sentences, answer each of the questions below on a separate sheet of paper.

1. Is a family business more like a franchise or more like a business you might start from scratch? Explain your answer.

2. Why would someone wish to enter into a partnership instead of operating as a sole proprietor?
3. After six months of operation, an entrepreneur prepares an income statement. It shows that while he has had strong sales and high revenue, instead of a gross profit, he has a gross loss. What should he understand about the cost of the goods he is selling?

SCANS Foundation Skills and Workplace Competencies

Basic Skills: *Listening Skills*

1. Work with a group of four or five other students. Individually, prepare a detailed message. Give the message orally to a group member, who should pass it on to the next group member, who should also pass it on. When you receive a message, write it down before passing it on. When all messages have returned to their authors, discuss with your group the accuracy of the messages given and received. Write a one-paragraph summary of your conclusion.

Interpersonal Skills: *Serving Clients/Customers*

2. Alicia owns a bakery. During busy hours, she and her one employee cannot serve customers quickly enough. The customers become upset when she waits on them out of order. Sometimes they leave if the line is too long. Without hiring more employees, what might Alicia do to keep her customers happy?

SCANS Foundation Skills and Workplace Competencies

1. Answers will vary. Students should note the accuracy of the messages that were returned to them and the effect of writing down the messages before passing them on.

2. Possible answers: Alicia might provide for some kind of customer self-service. She might provide customer numbers so that customers are served in order.

Connecting Academics to the Workplace

Math

1. Brad sells ice cream and soft drinks at outdoor festivals. He buys soft drinks for 50 cents per can and ice-cream bars for $75 per hundred. He marks up all items by 100 percent, selling the drinks for $1.00 and ice-cream bars for $1.50. One day, he sold 100 cans of soft drinks and 90 ice-cream bars. Expenses totaled $31.50. What was his net profit?

Social Studies

2. Carlos wants to operate a landscaping business out of the garage behind his house. In your neighborhood, would it be legal to run such a business at home? Research your community's guidelines for home businesses.

Human Relations

3. Because of a downturn in business, Christy must lay off three employees. What local or state agencies can help them find new jobs or provide training for new careers? Research services provided in your area.

Developing Teamwork and Leadership Skills

With a team of four people, create a plan for a T-shirt shop. Decide what products to sell, what prices to charge, and where to locate the shop. What other decisions must be made? Select one team member as a facilitator to keep the team on target. Give a formal presentation of your plan to the rest of the class. Include visuals.

Real-World Workshop

Write a business description of a small business you would like to start. Include the goods or services to be provided, your business location, number of employees and their salaries, and your competitors' strengths and weaknesses. Choose a business that fits your interests, skills, and work experience. Research if necessary.

School-to-Work Connection

Identify one small business in your community that interests you. Interview the owner about the business. Ask questions about how and why the owner got into the business. What does he or she like about it? What are some problems? What special skills are needed? What advice would the owner give someone who wanted to get into the business? Prepare a brief report to share with the class.

Individual Career Plan

Choose a business that interests you. Research the skills and experience you would need to get into the business and be successful. Finally, develop short-term and long-term goals for learning those skills and getting the necessary experience.

Connecting Academics to the Workplace

1. $86.00
2. Answers will vary, according to local zoning laws and ordinances.
3. Answers will vary. Students should identify local and state job-placement agencies and job-training resources.

Developing Teamwork and Leadership Skills

Team members should come up with a detailed plan for the T-shirt shop. The presentation should include visuals as well as an oral report.

Real-World Workshop

The business description should describe a real-world business the student might enter. It should include details about the goods or services; the number of employees, if any, and their salaries; and the location of the business. The description should also identify and discuss competitors. Finally, it should be compatible with the students' interests, skills, and experience.

School-to-Work Connection

Student reports should be specific and detailed and give an insightful look at the advantages, disadvantages, challenges, and opportunities of the business.

Individual Career Plan

Students should set both short-term and long-term goals that will help them gain experience and master skills necessary to succeed in the business they have chosen. The goals should reflect detailed knowledge of the business, and they should be specific and realistic.

···PLANNING GUIDE···
Chapter 5

SECTION 1 *Evaluating Career Choices*

SECTION OBJECTIVES	SECTION FEATURES	SECTION RESOURCES
• Evaluate various career possibilities.	Personal Career Plan, p. 87 Attitude Counts, p. 90 You're the Boss!, p. 91 Exploring Careers, p. 92	💿 Workforce 2000 Videodisc and Videotape 📁 Section 5-1 Review, p. 91 📖 Student Activity Workbook

SECTION 2 *Your Plan of Action*

SECTION OBJECTIVES	SECTION FEATURES	SECTION RESOURCES
• Establish a plan of action and intermediate career goals. • Identify the education and training you will need. • Develop an individual career plan.	Excellent Business Practices, p. 95 Career Do's and Don'ts, p. 100	💿 Workforce 2000 Videodisc and Videotape 📁 Section 5-2 Review, p. 102 📁 Chapter 5 Review, pp. 104–105 📖 Student Activity Workbook

CHAPTER 5

CHAPTER RESOURCES

- Chapter Transparencies and Lesson Plans
- Chapter 5 Test
- Spanish Resources, Chapter 5
- School-to-Work Activity Handbook, Chapter 5 Activity
- Teacher's Lesson Plans, Chapter 5
- Implementing Block Scheduling, Chapter 5
- Print, Media, and Internet Handbook
- Strategies for Implementing Work-Based Learning
- Strategies for Implementing Connecting Activities

Career Notes

SCANS CORRELATION CHART

Foundation Skills

Basic Skills

Reading	Writing	Math	Listening	Speaking

Thinking Skills

Creative Thinking	Decision Making	Problem Solving	Seeing Things in the Mind's Eye	Knowing How to Learn	Reasoning

Personal Qualities

Responsibility	Self-Esteem	Sociability	Self-Management	Integrity/Honesty

Workplace Competencies

Resources

Allocating Time	Allocating Money	Allocating Material and Facility Resources	Allocating Human Resources

Information

Acquiring and Evaluating Information	Organizing and Maintaining Information	Interpreting and Communicating Information	Using Computers to Process Information

Interpersonal Skills

Participating as a Member of a Team	Teaching Others	Serving Clients/ Customers	Exercising Leadership	Negotiating to Arrive at a Decision	Working with Cultural Diversity

Systems

Understanding Systems	Monitoring and Correcting Performance	Improving and Designing Systems

Technology

Selecting Technology	Applying Technology to Task	Maintaining and Troubleshooting Technology

Highlighted blocks indicate areas covered in the Chapter.

Additional Activities

Internet Connection

Ask students to choose three careers that interest them. Using the Internet, they should find out what training is available or required, the costs of education, and the availability of work in that career. Students should note the addresses of the Web sites at which they find it.

Field Trip Suggestions

Take students for a bus tour around the community. Have them look for examples of businesses that offer jobs in which they could use the skills they now have, and for businesses that might give them the skills they need to proceed with their career. Encourage them to think broadly.

Guest Speaker Suggestions

Contact an armed services recruiter. Ask the guest to speak to the class about the requirements for military service, the kinds of training available, the pay and rank advancement, and the advantages and disadvantages of life in the military.

Key to Ability Levels

Each section gives skill-building activities. Each activity has been labeled for use with students of various learning styles and abilities.

L1 Level 1 activities are basic activities and should be within the range of all students.

L2 Level 2 activities are average activities and should be within the range of average and above average students.

L3 Level 3 activities are challenging activities designed for the ability range of above average students.

School-Based Learning

Chapter Overview

Chapter 5 guides students through the process of evaluating career choices, deciding on a career, and then developing an individual career plan.

Section 5-1 helps students learn how to evaluate career choices by analyzing their personal values; personality; preferences for working with data, people, or things; skills and aptitudes; and education.

Section 5-2 teaches students how to set goals and meet their goals.

Background Information

Write chapter objectives (Sections 5-1 and 5-2) on the chalkboard or use the chapter objective transparency for class discussion.

Choose assignments from the *Student Activity Workbook* and write them on the chalkboard.

Have students preview the chapter, looking at pictures, and reading captions and content headings. Ask students to describe what they expect to learn in this chapter.

Preteaching Vocabulary

Write the Key Terms from Sections 5-1 and 5-2 on the chalkboard. Have students describe how the terms relate to making a career decision.

86

Meeting SPECIAL Needs

Hearing Impaired

Hearing-impaired students may need someone to take notes for them so they can concentrate on lip-reading your presentation or following an interpreter. Try to help these students identify a reliable classmate who takes good notes. Contract with that student to provide a duplicate set of notes for the hearing-impaired student. You might arrange for the notetaker to use the school photocopier for this purpose.

Developing an Individual Career Plan

Section 5-1
Evaluating Career Choices

Section 5-2
Your Plan of Action

In this video segment, learn how to develop your own individual career plan.

Journal
Personal Career Plan

Think of a goal you've set for yourself. Once you set that goal, what steps did you take toward achieving it? What progress have you made? Why? Record your experiences and ideas in your journal.

87

School-to-Work ◄
Connecting Activities

Three ways students can gain workplace learning are actual work experience, work training programs, and career exposure activities.

Work with local businesses to provide on-site work experiences by having students perform job duties alongside an experienced worker. Some employers may also be willing to provide entry-level job training to students. Others may be interested in having students observe workers in a variety of jobs to gain exposure to a number of different career areas.

Work-Based Learning Strategies and Activities

As students narrow their choices for future careers, make arrangements to have them visit local or regional businesses that offer jobs in their career areas as well as to speak with the company's Director of Human Resources.

After their on-site visits, have students create a chart for each career area and enter data they learned at each company.

WORKFORCE 2000 Training Video

Have students view the video and perform the interactive exercises to reinforce important chapter concepts and thinking processes.

Chapter 5

Addressing LEARNING Styles

Intrapersonal Learner

Encourage students to keep notebooks throughout the year. They should be unstructured journals of thoughts or job hunting ideas which students can constantly expand. They should record all career possibilities, schooling needs, desires, lifestyle plans, personal contacts, and so on. They should look at how what they're doing now—in and out of school—will contribute to a career.

SECTION 5-1

FOCUS

Bell Ringer

Have students write a 50-word paragraph explaining the problems that could result from not analyzing career choices and making a decision to pursue a specific career.

Introducing the Section

List on the board some of the problems students identified in the Bell Ringer activity. Some of the problems might include missed opportunities, not getting the training needed, or being stuck in unappealing jobs or careers.

Stress the importance of making career decisions early so that students have time to find out what training they will need and how they can get it. Remind students that they always have the option of later changing their minds and pursuing a different career.

Motivational Activity
Oral Presentation

Have all students complete personal career profiles for each career that interests them. Divide students into groups of three or four. Have them present their career profiles to each other and evaluate their choices by answering aloud the questions on pages 90–91.

Encourage group members to offer suggestions regarding each other's career plans.

Evaluating Career Choices

OBJECTIVE

After studying this section, you will be able to:
- **Evaluate various career possibilities.**

KEY TERMS

evaluation
personal career profile form

Throughout Chapters 2, 3, and 4, you have been completing the first four steps in the decision-making process to explore career possibilities. This process began in Chapter 2 with your taking a close look at your own personal needs and resources. You then identified your choices and began gathering information as part of your career research.

If you've done your research well, you've turned up many career choices. Narrowing these choices to a few "winners" involves comparing your personal data with the career information you've gathered. This step needs to be done with special care.

Evaluate Your Choices

Evaluation can take several forms. Usually it involves comparing and contrasting sets of data to rank them and determine winners. You will do this to find the best possible match between yourself and a career. Why is choice A better than choice B? Why is choice C less realistic than choice D?

Evaluation can also involve weighing possible outcomes. If I take this course of action, what will happen?

Finally, evaluation can involve thinking about your choices in light of your values. If I make this choice, will I be living up to what I truly believe in?

88 *Unit 2 • Exploring Careers*

Implementing Teamwork

Divide students into small teams to design posters or bulletin boards highlighting at least three non-traditional careers (for example, men in nursing; women in construction). Use the illustrations to lead a discussion about breaking down career stereotypes.

Personal Career Profile Form

Name _Gloria Perry_   **Date** _December 14_   **Career** _Fashion Industry Publicist_

Personal Information	Career Information	Match (1–10)
Your Values I believe in equal opportunities for all people, especially women! I like to do creative things too.	**Career Values** All kinds of people work in fashion. As a publicist, I would be able to use my creativity, as well as work with other creative people.	9
Your Interests My hobbies include reading Victorian novels. I love fashion and keep very up-to-date on the new styles, but I hate sewing! I also enjoy parties.	**Career Duties and Responsibilities** As a fashion publicist, I would make contacts with stores and buyers, arrange fashion shows and launch parties, and send out press releases.	8
Your Personality I'm very outgoing and enjoy having lots of friends. I get bored just sitting in class, unless there are open discussions. I have a good imagination.	**Personality Type Needed** A publicist must be outgoing and friendly. She must also be responsible and keep on top of things. Communication skills are important.	6
Data-People-Things Preferences I like being with people best of all. I find people fascinating. Sometimes facts interest me, too, but I prefer spending time with people!	**Data-People-Things Relationships** Publicists work mostly with people. In the fashion industry, you must be on top of trends, which are constantly changing. You don't work much with things—except for clothes and accessories!	9
Skills and Aptitudes My best subject is history. I have a natural sense of design and color, but I'm about average at actually drawing. My teacher says I'm "excellent" at reading comprehension, but I hate grammar.	**Skills and Aptitudes Required** Good verbal and writing skills are essential for a publicist. You also must be a good "people person." History doesn't matter so much, but you never know—it could help.	7
Education/Training Acceptable I would love to go to fashion school in New York City. I suppose I need some business training as well.	**Education/Training Required** I guess a four-year fashion school would be best—one that has a good business department.	9

▲ **Figure 5-1**   Gloria Perry completed a personal career profile form for each career possibility that she researched. Do you think Gloria would be successful as a fashion industry publicist?

A good tool to use in evaluating your choices is the **personal career profile form** shown in *Figure 5-1.* This is a chart in which you can arrange side by side what you have learned about yourself and what you have learned about a career possibility. In the third column, you are asked to use a 1-to-10 rating system to express how

Chapter 5 • Developing an Individual Career Plan   **89**

Extending Figure 5-1

Ask students what other possible careers might appeal to someone with this type of personal profile. (Possibilities include being a personal shopper or a wardrobe consultant.)

Caption Answer: Gloria may well be on the right track since the ratings in most of the categories are high.

SECTION 5-1
TEACH

Guided Practice
Teaching Strategies
1. Assign and review Section 5-1.
2. Use the transparency for this section.
3. Assign and review the Case Study.

Teaching Tip
Write each of the headings from the personal career profile on the chalkboard. Use the career of teacher as an example. Ask students to describe the values, interests, personality traits, data-people-things preferences, skills and aptitudes, and education/training needed to be a teacher.

Discussion Starter
Tell students to think of someone they know who dislikes his or her career. Ask students to share the advice they would give the person about changing careers and making a more positive career choice.

Critical Thinking
Have students identify possible negative aspects of any or all of the career choices they made for their personal career profiles. Have them write one thing they could do to improve or eliminate each unfavorable factor.

SCANS Foundation Skills Connection

L1 Reading

Have students look at professional journals or career magazines to find articles about unusual careers. Discuss findings in class.

L2 Self-Esteem

Ask students to think about a career that interests them. Have students write a 100–150 word essay describing how their skills would help them succeed.

L3 Decision Making

Have students choose two or three careers that interest them. Ask students to make a list of pros and cons for each career.

SCANS Workplace Competencies Connection

L1 Math

Tell students that they have decided to attend a local community college and get a two-year degree. They plan to borrow $4,000 the first year and $5,500 the second year. The interest on a student loan is 8 percent. Have students calculate the total amount they will owe at the end of two years. ($4,000 × 0.08 = $320 × 2 = $640 + $4,000 = $4,640; $5,500 × 0.08 = $440 × 2 = $880 + $5,500 = $6,380; $4,640 + $6,380 = $11,020)

Attitude Counts ✔

Your current project—whatever it is—will never be completely perfect. For that matter, neither will you! Of course, that's no reason to stop trying. Keep striving to improve your work—and yourself. However, don't expect yourself or the people around you to be perfect. If only perfection can satisfy you, you'll always be disappointed.

closely your personal and career information match. A perfect 10 (or as close as possible) in all six categories wins the gold.

Use the following questions to help you assign a score for each category:

- *Values.* Does this career match up well with my values?

- *Interests Versus Responsibilities.* Will the day-to-day responsibilities interest me? Will I be good at them?

- *Personality.* Will I be happy with the work environment and hours?

Choosing the right career path can seem bewildering. *Why is it important to keep your career plans flexible at this stage in your life?*

Teaching Attitude Counts ✔

Use these questions to lead a brief class discussion.

- What is perfectionism?

- What problems can perfectionism cause?

- How do perfectionists affect themselves? The people around them?

Extending the Illustration

Ask students how they could reduce the confusion of making a career choice. (By researching several different careers, talking to people about what they do, and trying different work through part-time jobs or volunteer activities.)

Caption Answer: Sticking to only one career path may mean that you never get to explore other possibilities.

- *Data-People-Things.* Do the data-people-things requirements of this career match up well with my own preferences?
- *Skills and Aptitudes.* Do I have the skills I need for this career—or the aptitudes to develop them?
- *Education/Training.* Am I willing to get the education and training necessary for this career?

You should complete a personal career profile form for each career choice you have identified for yourself. Then you should tally the scores on all the forms and see which career choice ranks the highest. You are now ready for the next step.

Make Your Decision

Now's the time to make a choice. Which career will you pursue? You may be afraid to commit yourself, but try to have confidence in your research and evaluations. Remember: Unless you define a goal, you are unlikely to reach it. Also, remember that your choice is flexible—one that you will probably change as your life develops.

In the next section, you will work on the final step in the decision-making process: drawing up your plan of action.

YOU'RE THE BOSS!

✓ *Solving Workplace Problems*

As a vet, you run your own small animal clinic. Recently, a customer's sick cat was so frightened by another customer's dog that the cat ran out the door and was lost. The owner of the missing cat is very angry. How will you respond to the cat owner? What changes should you make to prevent this kind of problem from recurring?

L2 Allocating Money

Have students research the cost of education or training for a career that interests them. Have them create a list of expenses including tuition, fees, and average living expenses for each year of education or training.

L3 Using Computers to Process Information

Have students download information they find on the Internet they'll want to use for future career reference. Then have them write a summary of how to find career information on the Internet.

Independent Practice

✏ Assign as homework the chapter activity in the *School-to-Work Activity Handbook.*

Writing: *Persuasion*

Have students write a script for a telephone call they might make to the human resource department of a company of their choice. The purpose is to ask for information about career opportunities with that company.

SECTION 5-1 *Review*

Understanding Key Concepts

Using complete sentences, answer the following question on a separate sheet of paper.

1. Your uncle has been urging you to pursue a career as a real estate broker. However, you feel you'd prefer working as a sales representative for a sporting goods manufacturer. How would you go about evaluating these two career possibilities to see which one might be better for you?

SECTION 5-1 *Review* ANSWERS

Answers will vary, but students should demonstrate familiarity with the seven steps outlined in choosing a career, especially using the Personal Career Profile form to match personal preferences to career requirements.

Teaching YOU'RE THE BOSS!

✓ Possible responses: Be as reassuring and as comforting to the cat owner as possible; offer to look for the cat and/or provide a reward for the return of the cat. Introduce waiting-room rules such as all dogs must be on leashes and all cats must be in carriers.

Assessment

Content

Ask students to write two or three paragraphs describing the elements of a personal career profile and how preparing such a profile will help them make a career decision.

Evaluation

Assign the section review.

Reteaching

Write each of the elements of the personal career profile on the chalkboard, leaving space between the elements to fill in information. Ask students to name someone who has a high-profile career and devise a personal career profile for the person.

As you discuss each profile element, ask students to give examples of what they think the person's characteristics are. (For example, what values the person might have that are evident in her or his career.)

Extending the Content

Assign the appropriate Chapter 5 activities in the *Student Activity Workbook*.

CLOSE

Have students discuss how making a comparison of career options will help them make a career choice.

CASE STUDY

Exploring Careers: Agribusiness

Jean Lesley
Farrier

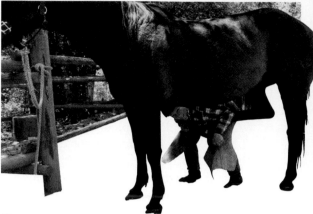

Q: **Have you always worked with horses?**

A: I had horses until I was 22. Then I sold them and went to college. Though I worked in stables in my 20s and loved it, I thought I should do something traditional, more white-collar. I worked as a graphic designer for 15 years before realizing the position didn't suit my personality. I wanted to be outside with horses.

Q: **What drew you to horseshoeing?**

A: When you train horses or teach riding, you deal more with the person, not the horse. As a farrier, I work directly with the horse.

Horseshoeing requires craftsmanship. I have a lot of ability with my hands, and I enjoy working with my hands. I like creating shapes—as I did as a graphic designer. Now, however, I work in three dimensions with metal instead of two-dimensional shapes.

Farrier work is also very independent. You work for yourself. You're not in a team situation. In an office, you work with other people.

Q: **How do you train to be a farrier?**

A: I went to the farrier school at Oregon State University. It's a three-month program in which students work every day, eight hours a day, with horses. It gives you a lot of hands-on experience. Others become farriers by apprenticing with other farriers.

Thinking Critically

Where is a farrier likely to work and under what kinds of conditions?

CAREER FACTS

Nature of the Work:
Fit shoes to horses with tools; keep careful notes on each horse.

Training or Education Needed:
Experience working with other farriers; training in a specialty trade school.

Aptitudes, Abilities, and Skills:
Ability to work with tools; decision-making and problem-solving skills; ability to work intuitively; self-management skills; responsibility; ability to work with large animals; patience; riding skills.

Salary Range:
$20,000 first five years; after five years: average $50,000 to $60,000; up to $100,000.

Career Path:
Start in a training or apprenticeship program; work for stables; work for self.

92 *Unit 2 • Exploring Careers*

Extending the CASE STUDY

Answer: In rural areas where people use horses; in suburbs where wealthier clients might keep horses in stables for weekend riding; in areas surrounding large cities where there are racetracks or rodeos. Conditions are often dirty, muddy, and wet.

Further Application: Have students choose two very diverse careers that interest them—freelance writer and airline pilot, for example. Ask them to evaluate and determine which skills would apply to both fields. (For example, a freelance writer has to meet deadlines, and a pilot has to meet schedules; a writer may have some computer skills, and so will a pilot.)

Your Plan of Action

OBJECTIVES

After studying this section, you will be able to:

- Establish a plan of action and intermediate career goals.
- Identify the education and training you will need.
- Develop an individual career plan.

KEY TERMS

individual career
   plan
on-the-job training
apprentice
vocational-technical
   center
trade school
continuing education

Making your career goals a reality means planning a course of action, called an **individual career plan**. This is the seventh and final step in the decision-making process leading to a career. There is no substitute for planning if you want to be successful and happy. Having a plan doesn't guarantee success, but it greatly improves your chances. You may get help from many sources, but the most workable plan will probably be the one you design yourself. Consider, for example, how Ronald Jones of Chelsea, Massachusetts, is planning for his future.

Since graduating from high school, Ron has been working five nights a week as a waiter at a French restaurant in Boston. During the day, he attends a culinary arts institute, where he is learning to become a gourmet chef. He describes his job as follows:

"It's a little hectic most of the time, but when things slow down, I can watch how the kitchen is run and how various dishes are prepared. I'm making good tips, which is helping me pay for school. I wouldn't want to have this waitering job forever, but the restaurant experience I'm getting—not to mention the cash—is helping me prepare for the career I really want."

Like Ron, it's time for you to start making plans. How will you begin?

Chapter 5 • Developing an Individual Career Plan **93**

Addressing Workplace Diversity

Emphasizing diversity makes good business sense. Increasing numbers of customers, clients, and investors expect their particular cultural backgrounds to be represented in the businesses from which they get supplies and services, and which they support with capital.

Bell Ringer

Have students write their ultimate career goal and the steps they plan to take to achieve that goal.

Introducing the Section

Ask students to share their career goals and their future plans. Make a list on the chalkboard as students share their information.

Discuss the need for putting goals in writing and updating them as you move from one stepping-stone to another. Then ask students to interpret this comment: "Making a plan is half the battle in accomplishing what you want." Have students give you examples of what happens in their lives when they plan (for example, plans to meet friends at a certain time and place) versus what happens when they fail to plan (no particular place to go or person to meet).

Motivational Activity
Oral Presentation

Have students make notes about goals they set, how they set them, and whether they reached their goals. Tell them they will be sharing these goals with the class.

Ask students to comment about whether goals are too general, too broad, or unrealistic. How could they have set better goals?

Teaching Strategies

1. Assign and review Section 5-2.
2. Use the transparency for this section.
3. Assign and review the Case Study.

Discussion Starter

Ask students to name some well-known people who overcame great odds to pursue their career choices. (For example, you might mention Max Cleland, elected to Congress from Georgia, who is a quadriplegic.) Students may know someone in your community who fits this description.

Query students on their thoughts about the role that setting goals played in these people's achievements.

Teaching Tip

Setting goals can be a difficult task for students, who may have too little experience to know what their possibilities are. With your students, work through a goal-setting exercise by having them plan how to turn a summer job into a career. Have students choose a career area, then write the goal on the chalkboard. Ask students to suggest steps they would take to reach the goal.

Broad steps include deciding the training or education needed to work in this career, completing the training, researching companies that offer the career, preparing a résumé, applying for a job, and interviewing for the job.

Plan How to Reach Your Goal

To reach your ultimate career goal, you will first need to establish some intermediate planning goals. These are the steps you will take to get from where you are now to where you want to be. For example, if your career goal is to be a real estate broker, one intermediate goal is to find out what training you will need to qualify for a real estate license in your particular state.

Taking Aim

The more specific your intermediate career targets, the more likely you are to hit the bull's-eye. If your ultimate career goal is to become a medical technician, it is not enough to say your intermediate goal is "to get a job working in a hospital." That's like throwing a dart in the general direction of the board. Instead, "to enroll in a program that will train me to be an emergency room technician" is much closer to the mark.

In your journal, write down a few intermediate goals for your particular career choice. Then see if you can make each one more specific.

With Your Feet on the Ground

Besides being specific, your planning goals should be realistic. To plan realistic goals

Ron dreams of becoming a great chef. *How do you get from where you are now to your ultimate goal?*

Extending the Illustration

Ask students to discuss why some people are afraid to pursue their interests or to take career risks. (Possible answers include fear of the unknown, fear of a loss of security, or simply the lack of self-confidence.)

Caption Answer: You must identify and act on specific, intermediate planning goals.

for the future, you must think about who and where you are today.

It would be almost impossible to hit that bull's-eye if you didn't know where you were standing in relation to the dartboard. It would be just as difficult to reach your career goals if you were not honest with yourself about where you are starting from on your career path.

For example, if you dislike math, you may not be happy as an engineer. On the other hand, even if your math skills are weak right now, you may still strongly believe that you would enjoy being an engineer. Therefore, a realistic—and

necessary—intermediate goal would be to strengthen your math skills in the near future.

An important note: Be careful not to confuse the words *realistic* and *traditional*. For example, women were traditionally more limited in their job options than men. Today, however, it is realistic for women to consider all available jobs. Also, since you will be developing your career in the years to come, do not limit yourself by the current reality of the world. Be creative in your thinking. You may end up starting a trendsetting business, as Meredith Hunter has done. (See **Figure 5-2** on page 96).

Critical Thinking

Have students imagine that they dropped out of high school two years ago and have been unable to find employment. Give students a few minutes to think of the alternatives for getting further education or finding employment. Then discuss their ideas in class.

SCANS Foundation Skills Connection

L1 **Listening**

Invite representatives of local educational/training organizations (e.g., vocational, military, technical, college, university) to serve as speakers in a panel discussion about educational and training opportunities in your area.

L2 **Reasoning**

Urge students to be open to a broad range of career ideas and to list a variety of activities that are personally appealing. Have students evaluate their lists and determine a priority for their career goals.

L3 **Self-Management**

Have students evaluate their personal attitudes toward work and study and how they manage their time. Have them determine whether they need to make changes in their personal habits or attitudes and, if so, create a plan for making these changes.

EXCELLENT BUSINESS PRACTICES

Providing a Second Chance

The DELSTAR Group of Phoenix, Arizona, believes in giving people a chance to rebuild their lives after having experienced personal problems. DELSTAR owns and operates retail specialty shops in airports and resorts. The company lists openings at nonprofit agencies and recruits job candidates from various community groups.

DELSTAR's special program provides meaningful work and creates an environment for growth and achievement. Participants receive training, evaluation, and support on a one-to-one basis. They learn about certain personal issues, such as how to manage finances or use a checking account.

A special training program teaches employees how to become small-business entrepreneurs. Employees take the course on

their own time. More than a dozen have used the training to open their own businesses.

Thinking Critically

How can organizing your personal life help you do well at work? How can a steady job help you in your personal life?

Chapter 5 • Developing an Individual Career Plan **95**

Extending EXCELLENT BUSINESS PRACTICES

Answer: By limiting stress in your personal life, you can stay focused at work, thus achieving success. By maintaining a steady job, your sense of worth or self-esteem will be high. High self-esteem will lead to self-confidence, which will carry over to your personal life.

Further Application: Have students identify careers that have set educational and training patterns, and careers that can be pursued via different paths. Have them contact individuals who have reached high levels in such careers and ask those people how they got there and what the advantages and disadvantages of their jobs are.

L1 **Allocating Time**

Have students choose a career and determine the training or education they need. Tell students that they will be working part-time (probably 20 hours a week) during this training. Provide a list of courses they will need to take or number of weeks in a training program for students to allocate their time and determine how long it will take them to complete their training.

L2 **Acquiring and Evaluating Information**

Have students learn about on-the-job training opportunities, apprentice-ships, and vocational train-ing programs in your area by conducting research. Di-vide students into groups and assign each group one of these types of training. The local Chamber of Com-merce or other business or-ganization should be able to provide some help in identi-fying companies offering training or apprenticeship programs. The local public library may also have books on apprenticeships. The school guidance counselor should be able to help with local and regional voca-tional schools. Students may also search the Internet for training and educational programs.

Stepping-Stone Goals

Think of your ultimate goal as a green meadow on the far side of a river. If you simply plunge into the river, chances are you will be carried way off course. Now imagine a series of stepping-stones. By using each one in turn, you will be able to cross the river safely—and relatively quickly. Think of the stepping-stones as your short-, medium-, and long-term plan-ning goals.

Ronald Jones, whom you read about earlier, has established several stepping-stone goals. While his ultimate career goal is to be head chef at a fine restaurant, he is currently working on a short-term goal: to get practical restaurant experience while serving as a waiter. He is also working on a medium-term goal: to earn a certificate within a few years from the culinary institute he attends. One long-term goal he has is to study with a master chef in France.

 Figure 5-2

Setting Planning Goals

Stepping-stone goals are short-, medium-, and long-term goals that can help you reach your ultimate career goal in realistic stages.

A Several years ago, Meredith Hunter made a career decision. She wanted to start a company that would create computer games based on well-known, high-quality children's books. Since she had little experience with business or computers, she knew that she had a long way to go before she could achieve her goal. However, she also knew that listing specific planning goals was a good place to start.

B Meredith's first short-term goal was to attend business school to acquire the knowledge and skills she would need to start her own business. She planned to take courses in business incorporation, management, and law, as well as in computer programming.

Extending Figure 5-2

Ask students whether they think their goals will remain the same for the next five years? Ten years? (Goals change as life circumstances change; stu-dents' goals will likely change as well.)

Having stepping-stone goals will also allow you to make a "course correction" if you decide your ultimate goal is not right for you. At any point along the way, you can change your mind and head off in a different direction. On the basis of his waitering experience, for example, Ron might decide he would prefer to own and operate a restaurant. He could then revise his medium-term goals to include taking business courses.

C One of Meredith's medium-term goals was to get a job with a successful computer game company—preferably one in which she would have some creative input. She accomplished that goal. At this job, she learned as much as she could about how games are researched, developed, manufactured, and distributed.

D Another medium-term goal of Meredith's was to find out which children's books were the most popular. During her time off from work, she did research at libraries and bookstores.

E Meredith has reached her long-term goal. Having found businesspeople willing to invest in her idea, she hired a creative team of artists. Today she runs a company that creates computer games.

Chapter 5 • Developing an Individual Career Plan **97**

L3 **Using Computers to Process Information**

Have students use a database program to create a file of career references. For each career choice, have them collect the following information: schools/training programs; names and addresses of companies offering jobs, and names and telephone numbers of human resource personnel; career counseling contacts, such as teachers, school counselors, friends, relatives, or businesspeople; Internet addresses for helpful sites; job search references, including books, magazines, and databases; and any other category students want to include.

Have students print out their databases and discuss how to use them to access career search information in an organized fashion.

Teaching Tip

Invite one or more successful businesspeople in the community to speak to your class about setting goals. Ask the speakers to share with students when they made career decisions, what goals they set at the time, the plans they made for accomplishing their goals, and how they implemented their plans. Also ask them to share their current goal-setting procedures and how they use goals to stay successful in business.

Computer Activity

Have students open the outline document they used in Chapters 2, 3 and 4. Students should add to the section titled "Make a Decision." In this section, have students list a number of careers that match the research previously recorded. Have students print out the document.

Teaching Tip

Students need to set personal goals along with their career goals. Some students may need to improve communication skills or their attitudes. Others may want to become more aware of how others perceive them. Discuss how students can set personal goals and work toward achieving them. (For example, someone who wants to improve communication skills might ask parents or friends to help remind them when they are not communicating effectively.)

Independent Practice
Writing: *Informational*

Ask students to respond in writing to these questions:

1. Why do some people call an investment in education an investment in one's future?

2. Why do state colleges and universities charge nonresidents more for tuition than they charge state residents?

> This person is working part-time to learn more about the restaurant business. In the future, she would like to own a restaurant. **Why is it helpful to have stepping-stone goals in planning for a career?**

Deciding on Education and Training

One of your first stepping-stone goals should be receiving the education and training you will need to achieve your ultimate career goal. Almost every job requires some special training, and having advanced education and training means more career opportunities to choose from. *Figure 5-3* shows that workers who have more than a high-school diploma are generally better prepared to succeed at their jobs than those who do not.

Many options are available for getting the education and training you will need.

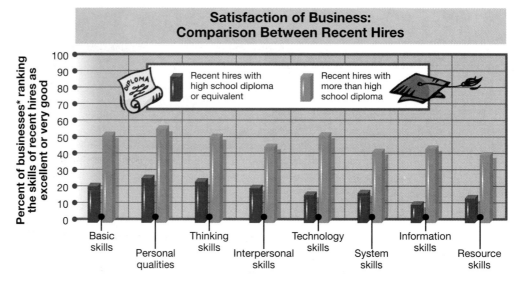

Satisfaction of Business: Comparison Between Recent Hires

Percent of businesses* ranking the skills of recent hires as excellent or very good

- Recent hires with high school diploma or equivalent
- Recent hires with more than high school diploma

Basic skills · Personal qualities · Thinking skills · Interpersonal skills · Technology skills · System skills · Information skills · Resource skills

*Racine Area Manufacturing and Commerce (RAMAC) Members, Racine County, Wisconsin
Source: RAMAC Education Committee Workforce Survey

Figure 5-3 A survey by the Racine Area Manufacturers and Commerce Education Committee found that employers tend to be more satisfied with workers who have received some post–high school training. How do you suppose such extra training affects an employee's wages over the course of a career?

Extending the Illustration

Ask students why it is important to break long-term goals into shorter steps. (To allow for changes in how you reach a long-term goal or to make different goals your priority.)

Caption Answer: Stepping-stone goals are short-, medium-, and long-term goals that can help you reach your ultimate career goal in realistic stages.

Extending Figure 5-3

Future careers are expected to require more training and technical job skills. Ask students how they plan to acquire needed skills. (Students' answers will vary but might include technical schools, college programs, or special training programs.)

Caption Answer: Those with better training and skills generally earn more.

On-the-Job Training: Learning by Doing

Offered by many companies, **on-the-job training** is on-site instruction in how to perform a particular job. It may consist of a few days of orientation for new employees or more formal long-term instruction. Workers at nuclear power plants, for example, undergo continual training in technical and safety procedures.

The need to be on the cutting edge of new trends makes many large companies stress ongoing training for their employees. For instance, companies that use computer networks generally offer courses to keep their workers up-to-date with the latest software and computer technology.

Apprenticeship

The practice of training young people through apprenticeship to master a craft goes back many hundreds of years. Today an **apprentice** is someone who learns how to do a job through hands-on experience under the guidance of a skilled worker.

Kattai Wendall of Pittsburgh, Pennsylvania, for example, found her apprenticeship as a sheet-metal worker through her state apprenticeship agency. Although she does not make very much money now working at a manufacturing plant, she feels lucky because she is getting paid to learn a trade that will eventually earn her a better position and salary.

Vocational-Technical Centers

You can prepare for many careers by attending a **vocational-technical center.** This is a school that offers a variety of

The practice of serving as an apprentice to learn a craft from a master is centuries old. *What advantages does this form of training have?*

Chapter 5 • Developing an Individual Career Plan **99**

Skills Practice

Write the following excerpt by the 18th century Scottish poet Robert Burns on the chalkboard:

"O wad some Power the giftie gie us,

"To see oursels as ithers see us!"

Ask students how they would respond if someone said the above to them. Then ask students to make a list, in one column, of the slang words and jargon they use in their conversations. In a second column, have students write words that mean the same thing but are more understood by a broader segment of the population. How can they use this example to improve their own communication skills?

Research

Have students research the educational and training possibilities for their personal interests. Have them identify the schools or training programs where they can acquire a degree or skills needed to pursue the interest. Have students set up a table comparing the education or training options, including the type of school or training program, length of training, and costs. Discuss their findings in class.

Extending the Illustration

Ask students what businesses would be most likely to provide apprenticeship training. (Likely businesses include electrical, construction, plumbing, and manufacturing companies.)

Caption Answer: Possible answers include one-on-one instruction, practical hands-on experience, or earning a salary while learning a craft.

Skills Practice

If your school is connected to the Internet, set aside time for students to participate in an electronic "chat." One site that provides information and ideas to teens is at this address: http://www.taponline.com

This site provides information about job resources, technology review and jargon, entertainment, and sports. A chat group is also available.

Teaching Tip

Some students may feel that their grades are not good enough or that they lack the finances to attend college. Have your school guidance counselor discuss the types of financial aid that are available, including direct aid from a school, work-study programs, educational grants from government, private sources, and education loans.

Discussion Starter

Ask students to respond to this sentence: "Attitude is everything." Ask students to give you words that reflect a person's attitude. Possible words include *anger, negative, positive, determined, easygoing, open, closed.*

Have students discuss how attitude either helps them achieve or miss their goals.

Career Do's & Don'ts

When Finding the Right Career ...
Do:
- talk to people about their career choices.
- work at a job in the field you are interested in to see if it feels right.
- recognize that you may choose several careers in your lifetime.
- map out the steps to achieving the level you want to attain in each career path you identify.

Don't:
- overlook internships or volunteer work.
- limit your options because some of the academic requirements are not your strongest subjects.
- be discouraged by job outlooks in a particular career; there's room for you if you want to do it.
- get sidetracked by a job that won't help you reach your goals.

skills-oriented programs, such as courses in automotive or computer technology. Most vocational-technical centers have evening classes and are relatively inexpensive.

Trade Schools

The culinary arts institute that Ronald Jones attends in Massachusetts is an example of a trade school. A **trade school** is a privately run institution that trains students for a particular profession. Trade schools are usually more expensive than vocational-technical centers. However, they sometimes offer programs that vocational-technical centers do not.

Community and Technical Colleges

Community colleges and technical colleges offer two-year and certificate programs in many occupational areas, such as accounting, tourism management, paralegal work, retailing, and desktop publishing. These colleges usually offer night and weekend classes and are less expensive than trade schools or four-year colleges. One who graduates from a community or technical college with a two-year associate's degree can usually transfer his or her credits to a four-year college or university.

Four-Year Colleges and Universities

Some careers—such as teacher and physical therapist—require a minimum of a bachelor's degree from a four-year college or university. Other careers—such as those in law, architecture, and medicine—require even more advanced degrees. In choosing a college, you will want to consider such factors as location, size, cost, the quality of your particular program, entrance requirements, and the availability of financial aid.

Continuing Education

Many adults return to school at some point in their lives to complete their education, brush up on old skills, or pursue

100 *Unit 2 • Exploring Careers*

Workforce 2000 Trends

In the 21st century, companies will continue to expand their use of work teams and self-management. Emphasizing employee involvement improves quality, productivity, customer service, and employee morale; it decreases grievances, absenteeism, and turnover.

 The military is one place you can get post–high school training. *Why might the armed forces be a good career choice for some and not for others?*

new paths. Many high schools, colleges, and universities offer **continuing education**—programs geared toward adult students. Some even offer correspondence courses. Some of these programs lead to academic degrees.

Military Service

Did you know that the military is the largest employer in the United States? If you think you might be cut out for the military, you may be able to receive training in one of more than 200 different occupations, including health technician and air-traffic controller. Depending on the career you choose, you must enlist for up to six years of active duty.

Sometimes you can attend school before or during your service. At other times, the military will pay for your education after you serve.

Committing Yourself on Paper

Are you feeling overwhelmed? That's only natural when faced with so many career options, but don't waste your energy worrying. Instead, take out a large notebook and begin formulating your individual career plan on paper.

Questions and Answers

Start by creating a list of questions to answer about your career goals, education, and training. You might begin with these questions and add others that you feel apply to your particular situation:

- What is my ultimate career goal?

- What is my first "stepping-stone" or short-term goal?

- Which educational programs offer the training I need to prepare for my career?

- How much money will I need to pay for my education and training? Where will this money come from?

Chapter 5 • Developing an Individual Career Plan **101**

Extending the Illustration

Ask students how the military has broadened career options for many people. (By providing training for programs that have counterparts in civilian life, as well as offering benefits that pay for education after leaving the military.)

Caption Answer: Some people may not be suited for the rigors and dangers of military life. Others may have moral or religious reservations.

SECTION 5-2

Creative Thinking

Share the following information with students. Fifty years ago, Dr. William P. Foster invented a new career: leading a marching band for Florida A&M University. Today most colleges and universities have marching bands.

Have students invent their own careers by thinking about the things they enjoy doing and how they want to live their lives. Ask them to write a 50-word paragraph describing the career they invent.

Role-Play

Ask the director of human resources for a local company to role-play conversations with students about technological skills future employees will need. Ask for two to three volunteers to participate in the role-plays. Have the volunteers prepare their list of questions beforehand.

You may first want to model a conversation with the speaker. As follow up, ask students how they will apply communication and interviewing skills as they research career opportunities.

Teaching Tip

Poll students to find out how many of them might be interested in either a military career or education and training through the military. If a significant number are interested, invite representatives of one or more of the military branches to speak to your class about career and education opportunities in the military.

Assessment

Process

Have students complete personal career profiles for a career of their choice. After completing the profile, have them write their goals for gaining the education or training needed and the steps they plan to take to achieve their goals.

Evaluation

Assign and review the section review.

MINI QUIZ

True-False

1. A rating of 1 on a personal career profile means that a career closely matches your personal career interests. (false)

2. A long-term goal is one that must be accomplished within five years. (false)

3. Short-term goals are stepping-stones to achieving your longer term goals. (true)

4. Once you complete school, you will not need any further education or training in the future. (false)

5. An apprenticeship offers a person the opportunity to learn a trade on the job. (true)

Use the Testmaker to create a customized test for Chapter 5.

Where Do You Go from Here?

Now write up your individual career plan, such as Ronald Jones's shown in **Figure 5-4** below. In chronological order, write your short-, medium-, and long-term goals. Make sure to include your projected starting and ending dates. You can modify the goals and dates as you get closer to your ultimate goal.

Also, remember that your decisions and plans are flexible. They are not set in stone. Expect to change them. The advantage to having a plan, though, is that you will continue to move ahead until you find the career that is right for you.

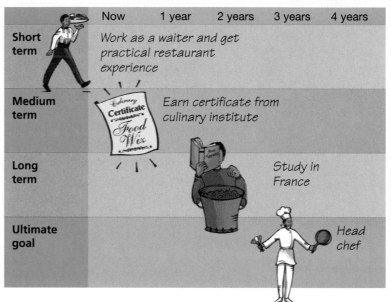

An Individual Career Plan

	Now	1 year	2 years	3 years	4 years
Short term	Work as a waiter and get practical restaurant experience				
Medium term	Earn certificate from culinary institute				
Long term	Study in France				
Ultimate goal	Head chef				

Figure 5-4

Putting his short-, medium-, and long-term plans in chronological order allowed Ronald Jones to visualize his career goals. Which plans will Ronald be working on simultaneously for a while?

SECTION 5-2 *Review*

Understanding Key Concepts

Using complete sentences, answer the following questions on a separate sheet of paper.

1. Explain why having "stepping-stone" planning goals is important for reaching your ultimate career goal.

2. Suppose that you have a friend who wants to be a fashion designer. What education or training options would you advise your friend to explore?

3. What is the advantage of committing your career plans to writing?

SECTION 5-2 *Review* ANSWERS

1. Possible answer: "Stepping-stone" planning goals establish a path to the ultimate goal by identifying intermediate steps along the way. They also allow for "course corrections" along the path if the ultimate goal becomes undesirable or unattainable.

2. Possible answer: I'd advise the friend to get some practical on-the-job training in fashion design and perhaps to enroll in a trade school specializing in the fashion industry.

3. Possible answer: Formulating an individual career plan on paper helps the writer develop specific goals while allowing for revision as the plan proceeds.

SECTION 5-1 **Summary**

- In evaluating possible careers, you should match the career information you've gathered to your personal interests and resources.
- Using a personal career profile form allows you to analyze career possibilities in a systematic way.

Key Terms

evaluation *(p. 88)*
personal career profile
    form *(p. 89)*

SECTION 5-2 **Summary**

- The most workable career plan will probably be the one you design for yourself.
- Establishing intermediate career goals will make your ultimate goal easier to reach.
- For your planning goals to be realistic, you must be honest with yourself about your personal strengths.
- Setting short-, medium-, and long-term goals will enable you to evaluate your career path as you go along.
- Acquiring more education and training means having more career opportunities to choose from. Your options include on-the-job training, apprenticeship, vocational-technical programs, trade schools, community and technical colleges, four-year colleges and universities, continuing education programs, and military service.
- Committing your plan of action to paper will help you develop specific career plans. It will also allow you to revise your plans while you continue to move ahead toward a career that will be right for you.

Key Terms

individual career
    plan *(p. 93)*
on-the-job training *(p. 99)*
apprentice *(p. 99)*
vocational-technical
    center *(p. 99)*
trade school *(p. 100)*
continuing education
    (p. 101)

Chapter 5 • Developing an Individual Career Plan   **103**

Reteaching

1. Ask students to interview an adult who enjoys his or her work. Ask: "How did you chose your career? What career goals did you set, and how did you plan to reach your goals? If you had it to do again, would you do anything different? If so, what and why?" Have students share their responses in class.

2. Assign and review vocabulary terms, chapter questions, and activities from the Chapter Review.

3. Assign and review the Unit Project located on the unit opener pages.

Extending the Content

Assign the appropriate Chapter 5 activities in the *Student Activity Workbook*.

Have students choose a training program or major offered by an educational institution or the military that might help them succeed in their chosen career. Have students write a 50-word paragraph telling why they would or would not enroll in the program to reach their career goal.

CLOSE

See the Unit Closure and Unit Evaluation located on page 47.

▶▶ **Extending Figure 5-4** ◀◀

Have students draw their own career plans following this model.

Caption Answer: He will be working on his short- and medium-range plans at the same time.

Answers

Reviewing Key Terms

Articles will vary but should include all key terms listed.

Recalling Key Concepts

1. True
2. False: A career plan is flexible and should be changed as circumstances change.
3. False: Vocational-technical centers are less expensive than trade schools.
4. True.

Thinking Critically

1. Possible answer: Settling on a career that conflicts with your values may result in considerable stress and mental anguish. An example would be a pacifist who takes a job in a weapons factory.
2. Possible answer: If you were asked to plan an event, for example, it would be helpful to be able to see in the mind's eye such details as how many people would attend, how large the room had to be, how much food had to be catered, and so forth. The same would be true for designing a room or building a house.

Reviewing Key Terms

Write a one- or two-page article for your school newspaper about how a typical high school senior might go about making a career decision. Use the following terms in your article:

evaluation	on-the-job training
personal career profile form	vocational-technical center
	trade school
individual career plan	continuing education
apprentice	

Recalling Key Concepts

On a separate sheet of paper, tell whether each statement is true or false. Rewrite false statements to make them true.

1. You can use a personal career profile form to match what you know about yourself with what you know about different careers.
2. Once you establish an individual career plan, you should not change it.
3. Vocational-technical centers are more expensive than trade schools.
4. An individual career plan should include short-, medium-, and long-term goals.

Thinking Critically

Using complete sentences, answer each of the questions below on a separate sheet of paper.

1. What consequences might result from settling on a career that conflicts with your personal values?

---

2. When evaluating your hopes and dreams, it helps to visualize your future. How might good visualization skills help you in your job or career?

SCANS Foundation Skills and Workplace Competencies

Basic Skills: *Writing*

1. Determine your top three career choices. Research the education and training needed for each career. Summarize your findings in a 150-word report.

Thinking Skills: *Decision Making*

2. Andrew just graduated from high school. His interests are radio and television, and he plans to build a career in the communications industry. He has just been offered an excellent job as publicity coordinator for a local radio station. The problem is that it is a full-time job with irregular hours and Andrew has been planning to attend college full-time. How should Andrew reach a decision? What do you think a good decision might be?

Interpersonal Skills: *Participating as a Team Member*

3. As a class make a list of the names and addresses of vocational-technical centers, trade schools, community and technical colleges, and four-year colleges and universities. Then, break the class down into teams of three students. Each team should select a

---

SCANS Foundation Skills and Workplace Competencies

1. Reports will depend on the careers selected.
2. Responses should indicate awareness of decision-making strategies and how

short-term decisions can affect long-term goals.
3. Materials should be displayed so they are available to all students.

different institution. As a team write a letter requesting information from the institution you have selected. Send your letter to the institution. When you receive the material, use it to create a class display.

Connecting Academics to the Workplace

Vocational Education

1. Lynn recently graduated from high school. Her career goal is to become a computer programmer. She is interested in learning computer programming. However, she must stick to a very strict budget. Using the library, the Internet, or the telephone, research the costs of computer-training programs in your area. Determine which program offers the best training for the lowest cost.

Art

2. You have been told you have excellent art skills and should pursue a career in the art field. Using resources in your school library, develop a list of five careers that require artistic skills. Explain the job task involved in each career that would require your art skills.

Science

3. You are interested in becoming a physical therapist. Research the career to find out more about it. Then develop a list of short-, medium-, and long-term goals that would help you reach this ultimate career goal.

Developing Teamwork and Leadership Skills

Working with a classmate, select several careers you are each interested in. Then help each other establish a list of intermediate planning goals to reach your ultimate career goals.

Real-World Workshop

Use copies of the personal career profile form shown in Figure 5-1 to compare four or more possible careers within your general area of interest. For example, if your interests lie in the area of fine arts, you might use the forms to evaluate and then compare such careers as individual artist, art gallery owner, museum tour guide, and state art council program administrator. After you complete your evaluations, write a summary in which you identify the most promising career choice for you.

School-to-Work Connection

Arrange to spend a day at an apprentice program, vocational-technical center, trade school, or one of the other kinds of education or training sites discussed in this chapter. If possible, arrange to sit in on a typical class, and take notes on what you observe. Give an oral presentation on your findings to the class.

Individual Career Plan

Using Figure 5-4 as a guide, create your own individual career plan. Include your short-, medium-, and long-term goals.

Chapter 5 • Developing an Individual Career Plan **105**

medium-term: intern in a health care clinic; long-term: after high school receive formal training in an accredited program at a four-year college and take the national test administered by the state.

Developing Teamwork and Leadership Skills

Team planning goals will vary.

Real-World Workshop

Students' evaluation forms should demonstrate care in the gathering of the information for each of the four or more career possibilities. The forms should also demonstrate a realistic matching of personal preferences to each of the career requirements.

School-to-Work Connection

Presentations will vary. Students may comment on the various types of programs offered, the facilities available, and the job-placement success rate that each school or program provides.

Individual Career Plan

Students' career plans should show careful thought and present realistic plans for students' ultimate careers.

Connecting Academics to the Workplace

1. Students will probably discover that private trade schools are considerably more expensive than public vocational-technical programs.

2. Careers might include graphic artist, computer animator, individual artist, or illustrator.

3. Goals might include short term: to receive more education and training in health and science in high school;

Aspects of Industry: Planning

Students who are fairly sure of their future careers may use the Labs to investigate all the aspects of industry for one career. Other students may want to investigate a different job cluster with each Lab.

STEP A

To find two job possibilities in each job cluster, students may brainstorm with other students, or research the possibilities in the *Occupational Outlook Handbook (OOH)* or other career references.

To help students prepare for the research project, be sure they understand the difference between a corporation and a sole ownership. In class, brainstorm a variety of economic, political and social decisions and conditions that affect business in general. (For example, tax cuts may help some businesses but have serious consequences for public services; changing social views forces changes in hazardous waste disposal or working conditions; plant closures or strikes affect businesses throughout the industry.)

In small groups, have students focus on the industries they have chosen, looking at the forces that affect them. Groups may focus on one particular industry, or divide into smaller brainstorming groups to help each student with his or her particular needs. You may want to have students bring in daily newspaper or magazine articles that reflect the influences on the industries chosen.

ASPECTS OF INDUSTRY: *Planning*

Overview

In Unit Two, you began thinking about what kind of work is right for you and developing your career plan. In this Unit Lab, you will use what you have learned about careers while exploring another aspect of industry: **Planning.**

The Planning aspect of industry covers the various types of business ownership— sole ownership (proprietorship), partnership, cooperative, corporation—and how businesses of all types affect and are affected by the economy, politics, and society.

Tools

1. Internet
2. Trade and business magazines
3. Business newspapers
4. Personal interviews

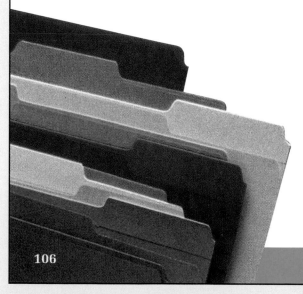

106

Recommend that students not limit themselves to current trade and business periodicals. By looking at periodicals that are five to ten years old, they may be able to see what forces have influenced the industries in the past, and how industry was changed as a result. They may use this information both in their interviews and their reports.

Procedures

STEP A

Choose one of the 15 job clusters from Figure 3-1 in Chapter 3. You may choose the same cluster you explored in the previous Lab, or a different one.

Choose two jobs in the job cluster that you would seriously think about pursuing. Using trade and business magazines, newspapers, and the Internet, research how the industry represented by the jobs you have chosen is affected by economic, political, or social changes.

STEP B

Identify a local corporation that employs people in one of the jobs you have chosen. Ask friends, family, teachers, and counselors for leads. You may also check with your local Chamber of Commerce, which may have a directory of member businesses.

If possible, research that particular corporation. The Chamber of Commerce may have profiled the business in its newsletter, or the local newspaper may have run stories about the business.

Contact a manager at the corporation and ask permission to do a short (20- to 30-minute) interview. You want to find out why the business is organized as a corporation and what the advantages and disadvantages are of that form of business.

STEP B

The purpose of this exercise is to get students to understand the complexity of corporate organization. They should try to get a sense of why corporations make the decisions they do, and how those decisions affect employees and the industry at large.

Students should look at the information in the interview both from the viewpoint of a

Some of the questions you might ask at the interview are:

1. How does the corporate form of business allow the company to expand, change, and meet challenges?

2. How are important decisions made in the corporation?

3. What are the advantages and disadvantages of working for a corporation?

Write out your questions beforehand. If you are doing the interview in person, be prompt and courteous, and dress appropriately.

STEP C

You will now repeat instructions for Step B, but for a sole proprietorship. Identify a sole proprietorship that employs people in the other job you have chosen.

Contact the business owner, and ask permission to do a short (20- to 30-minute) interview. Find out why the owner

chose sole proprietorship. What are the advantages and disadvantages of that form of business? Some of the questions you might ask are:

1. How does being a sole proprietorship allow the company to expand, change, and meet challenges?

2. What are the advantages and disadvantages of being a sole proprietorship?

3. How are important decisions made in a sole proprietorship?

REPORT

Write a one-page, word-processed report using the information you gathered in your research and interviews.

- Compare the advantages and disadvantages of corporate organization versus sole proprietorships in terms of flexibility in the face of economic, political or social change, and the responsibility for decision making.

- Discuss the advantages and disadvantages of working for each type of business. Why would you—or would you not— want to run your own business?

Keep your research, interview notes, and report in a folder entitled "Career Exploration."

107

corporate manager and of a corporate employee. How would they fit into a corporate structure as an employee? As a manager? If time permits, encourage students to interview a manager of at least one more corporation, since not all corporations are the same.

Students may need help formulating questions that elicit this kind of information.

STEP C

In this exercise, students should understand the flexibility of a sole proprietorship, and the ability to change quickly as markets change. However, they should also realize that sole proprietorship entails much more risk, financially and personally. (For example, when government regulations, economic conditions, or social views change, small, sole proprietorships are often most hard hit.)

If time permits, encourage students to interview more than one sole proprietor. People who run their own businesses are often full of enthusiasm and ideas. Their stories are often inspiring.

Students should write out their interview questions in advance, arrive at the interview promptly, be courteous and professional, ask their questions clearly, and follow up the interview with a thank you.

Remind students that persons interviewed may in the future act as references or networking contacts when they begin looking for a job.

Report

Students should use the Lab to further refine their job searches. In their reports, they should explore why the type of business one works for may be just as important as the job one chooses. They should also have a feel for the stability of the industry.

If students are inclined to go into business for themselves, encourage them to think about what might make their businesses flexible enough to survive change. (Product diversity, continuing education, and strong financial planning might be some ideas.)

Have students discuss their interviews. What information did they find surprising? How has this new information affected the way they look at their potential careers?

Unit Overview

Unit 3 teaches students the skills needed to enter the world of work. Students will learn how to network and use other resources for identifying potential jobs. They'll also learn information needed to apply for a job.

Good interviewing skills are key to getting the job offer, and students will learn a variety of interviewing techniques.

Introducing the Unit

Ask students how many of them enjoy looking for jobs and going for interviews. Tell them that knowing what to expect, preparing to answer a variety of questions, and knowing how to dress will help relieve a lot of the stress of interviewing for jobs.

Unit Project

Throughout the unit, as students learn each element of a job search, have them place related documents in folders; for example, a blank job application form to fill out in class, a calendar for making appointments, a résumé, personal references, employer contacts, and telephone numbers.

UNIT 3

Finding a Job

Chapter 6
Finding and Applying for a Job

Chapter 7
Interviewing

108

108

Developing Community Involvement

There may be a park, nature trail, or bike trail in your area that needs grooming or repair. Working with park officials, divide the class into teams to pick up litter, repair or build trails, put up signs, plant trees, remove non-native species, or build walls. This work may be done on weekends or during the summer. One national group that coordinates this kind of activity at the local level is the Student Conservation Association in Arlington, Virginia. For further information, call (703) 524-2441.

Resources for Enrichment

Books

- *Graduating to the 9 to 5 World* by Bouchard
- *Knock'Em Dead* by Yate
- *The Guide to Internet Job Searching* by Riley, Roehm, and Oserman

Magazines

Emerge, Hispanic, American Employment Weekly, Federal Jobs Digest

Organizations

- Local career counseling/ search agencies
- Employment agencies

Internet

Career Magazine—Job listings, employer profiles, job hunt news, and articles: http://www.careermag.com/ careermag

Saludos Web Site—*Saludos Hispanos* magazine; job listings, career information: http://www.hooked.net/ saludos

UNIT 3 QUIZ:

How Do You Find and Apply for a Job?

- What are job leads?
- What do you include in a résumé?
- How should you dress for an interview?
- What should and shouldn't you do in an interview?

109

Unit Closure

Have students write articles of 150–200 words for the school newspaper. Have them describe methods of finding job leads, suggest techniques for applying for a job, and outline strategies for successful job interviews.

Unit Evaluation

Administer the reproducible test for Unit 3, which you will find in your Performance Assessment Binder, or construct your own test using the IBM Testmaker software.

Building Partners in Industry

Making speeches—attending meetings—joining committees—participating in panel discussions—responding to questionnaires —taking part in workshops—going to business openings and open houses: these are just some of the things you and other teachers and administrators can do to help develop school/business partnerships. You and your program must be visible and effective in a variety of business settings. The time you spend establishing friendly, effective relationships will benefit your program and your students.

• • • PLANNING GUIDE • • •
Chapter 6

SECTION 1	*Exploring Sources of Job Leads*		CHAPTER 6

SECTION OBJECTIVES	SECTION FEATURES	SECTION RESOURCES
• Explain why networking is effective for developing job leads. • Create and maintain a career network and contact list. • Identify sources for job leads. • Apply knowledge of the Internet in a job search.	Personal Career Plan, p. 111 Career Do's and Don'ts, p. 115 You're the Boss!, p. 116 Exploring Careers, p. 118	Workforce 2000 Videodisc and Videotape Section 6-1 Review, p. 117 Student Activity Workbook

CHAPTER RESOURCES

- Chapter Transparencies and Lesson Plans
- Chapter 6 Test
- Spanish Resources, Chapter 6
- School-to-Work Activity Handbook, Chapter 6 Activity
- Teacher's Lesson Plans, Chapter 6
- Implementing Block Scheduling, Chapter 6
- Print, Media, and Internet Handbook
- Strategies for Implementing Work-Based Learning
- Strategies for Implementing Connecting Activities

SECTION 2	*Applying for a Job*

SECTION OBJECTIVES	SECTION FEATURES	SECTION RESOURCES
• Outline procedures for applying for a job: filling out applications, preparing a résumé and cover letter, and taking tests.	Excellent Business Practices, p. 121 Ethics in Action, p. 126	Workforce 2000 Videodisc and Videotape Section 6-2 Review, p. 126 Chapter 6 Review, pp. 128–129 Student Activity Workbook

Career Notes

109a

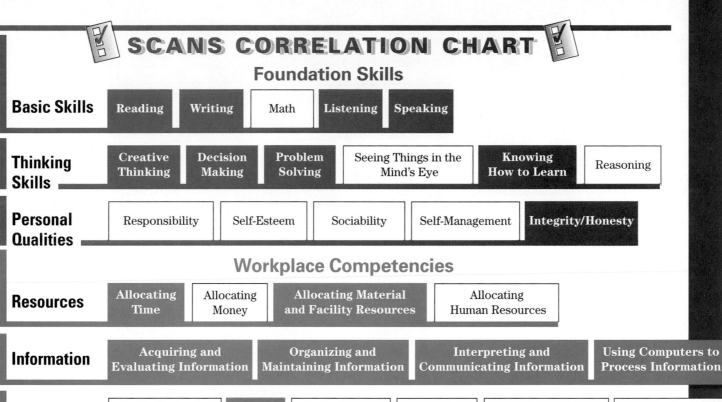

SCANS CORRELATION CHART

Foundation Skills

Basic Skills	Reading	Writing	Math	Listening	Speaking

Thinking Skills	Creative Thinking	Decision Making	Problem Solving	Seeing Things in the Mind's Eye	Knowing How to Learn	Reasoning

Personal Qualities	Responsibility	Self-Esteem	Sociability	Self-Management	Integrity/Honesty

Workplace Competencies

Resources	Allocating Time	Allocating Money	Allocating Material and Facility Resources	Allocating Human Resources

Information	Acquiring and Evaluating Information	Organizing and Maintaining Information	Interpreting and Communicating Information	Using Computers to Process Information

Interpersonal Skills	Participating as a Member of a Team	Teaching Others	Serving Clients/ Customers	Exercising Leadership	Negotiating to Arrive at a Decision	Working with Cultural Diversity

Systems	Understanding Systems	Monitoring and Correcting Performance	Improving and Designing Systems

Technology	Selecting Technology	Applying Technology to Task	Maintaining and Troubleshooting Technology

Highlighted blocks indicate areas covered in the Chapter.

Additional Activities

 Internet Connection

Writing a résumé can be daunting. Have students use the Internet to find out what resources are available to help them. They should list books and publications. They should also check out résumé writing services and compare the fees, the services offered, and the "sales pitch."

 Field Trip Suggestions

Arrange to take students to the local branch of your state employment agency. Have someone there explain what kinds of services are available, and what kinds of counseling, if any, are available. Have students take home a copy of the agency's application form and go over it with a copy of their résumé.

 Guest Speaker Suggestions

Invite representatives from unions, state agencies, and/or businesses that have apprenticeship programs. Have them discuss how to find and apply for apprenticeships, length of the programs, qualifications necessary, and what to expect from an apprenticeship.

Key to Ability Levels

Each section gives skill-building activities. Each activity has been labeled for use with students of various learning styles and abilities.

L1 Level 1 activities are basic activities and should be within the range of all students.

L2 Level 2 activities are average activities and should be within the range of average and above average students.

L3 Level 3 activities are challenging activities designed for the ability range of above average students.

Finding and Applying for a Job

School-Based Learning

Chapter Overview

Chapter 6 introduces effective methods for finding and getting jobs.

Section 6-1 emphasizes the importance of developing a job information network and helps students identify sources of job leads.

Section 6-2 covers the steps in applying for a job.

Background Information

Write chapter objectives (Sections 6-1 and 6-2) on the chalkboard or use the chapter objective transparency for class discussion.

Choose assignments from the *Student Activity Workbook* and write them on the chalkboard.

Have students preview the chapter, looking at pictures, reading captions, and noting content headings. Ask students to describe what they expect to learn in this chapter.

As a study aid, have students outline the chapter using the chapter headings.

Preteaching Vocabulary

Write the Key Terms from Sections 6-1 and 6-2 on the chalkboard. Have students describe how each term relates to identifying potential jobs and applying for a job.

110

Meeting SPECIAL Needs

Learning Disabled

Certain students may have trouble with sequential tasks involving numbers and following step-by-step instructions. They may have trouble preparing a résumé, for example. For these students, it may be helpful to break the task into smaller parts. You may want to give them a list of all the steps they need to follow to complete the task. Or, in the case of a résumé, you might design a form or template that they can follow.

Finding and Applying for a Job

Section 6-1
Exploring Sources of Job Leads

Section 6-2
Applying for a Job

In this video segment, discover how practicing with friends can help you improve your interview techniques.

Journal
Personal Career Plan

During the next week, explore as many sources of job leads as possible. Record your explorations in your journal, noting details about each job opening and how you learned about it. At the end of the week, write a paragraph summarizing what you have learned from this exploration.

111

School-to-Work Connecting Activities

Have students write letters to a local or regional company of their choice to request information about how the company fills its job openings. Tell students to ask questions such as whether openings are first posted for current employees, advertised in newspapers, advertised in on-line forums, or placed with job-search and employment agencies. Have students share the responses to their letters with the class.

Work-Based Learning Strategies and Activities

Have students schedule exploratory interviews with at least two local companies. For each interview, tell students to find out what openings the company anticipates during the next year. What skills will those jobs require?

Also have students ask about job interviews conducted by the company. Who conducts initial interviews? Have students share their findings with the class.

WORKFORCE 2000 Training Video

Have students view the video and perform the interactive exercises to reinforce important chapter concepts and thinking processes.

Chapter 6

Addressing LEARNING Styles

Linguistic Learner

Students are often embarrassed or uncomfortable telling prospective employers about their achievements and positive qualities. Ask students to prepare two- to three-minute speeches about themselves. Have them write them in the third person, as if they were introducing themselves at an awards banquet. They should highlight their education, achievements, skills, and the things that give them the most pride. Then have them give the speeches, still in the third person, to the class.

SECTION 6-1

FOCUS

Bell Ringer

Ask students to list a local or regional newspaper that runs employment ads, an employment agency, a friend or family member who knows about job openings, and a company that hires students.

Introducing the Section

Review students' answers from the Bell Ringer activity. Then have students describe the kind of summer job they would like to have. Ask which sources they might use to try to find such a job.

Then discuss networking with students and how important it can be to finding out about job openings.

Motivational Activity
Critical Thinking

Ask students to explain how networking with a wide variety of people could help them find out about jobs that are never advertised. An example of such jobs are those that companies post only on their bulletin boards and fill either with current employees or with people recommended by employees. Discuss students' ideas in class.

Exploring Sources of Job Leads

OBJECTIVES

After studying this section, you will be able to:

- Explain why networking is effective for developing job leads.
- Create and maintain a career network and contact list.
- Identify sources for job leads.
- Apply knowledge of the Internet in a job search.

KEY TERMS

job lead
networking
contact list
referral
school-to-work
   programs
Internet

Getting a job is the beginning of a new lifestyle. There will be new friends, new surroundings, new challenges, and your own income. Think of the possibilities! To get started on this adventure, you need a job. Not just any job will do, though. You need the right job. This is the one that you will enjoy and do well at.

Finding the right job begins with a job lead. A **job lead** is information about a job opening. It can be a tip from a friend, a classified (help-wanted) ad in the newspaper, or information from a teacher or school guidance counselor.

Networking

How do you go about developing job leads? One of the best ways is by networking. **Networking** is communicating with people you know or can get to know to share information and advice.

How well does networking work? Compare it to other ways of getting a job shown in *Figure 6-1.*

What makes networking so useful is that your contacts may be "insiders." Often, they work at the company that is hiring. They can tell you what the company is looking for and give you a recommendation that really counts.

Creating Your Own Network

Networking is not as difficult as you might think. You know people, don't you? Those people will form the basis for your network.

Implementing Teamwork

Organize students into teams based on these broad occupational clusters: business, health care, agriculture, engineering, human and public service, computer science, entertainment and sports. Using the *Dictionary of Occupational Titles* or the Internet, do a job search and identify at least five careers in each cluster.

Extending the Illustration

Ask students what their counselors can provide regarding career plans. (Information on colleges, financial aid and loan programs, aptitude tests, background information on careers.)

Caption Answer: Students will have more time to find the best jobs. If they need additional skills, they can learn them while still in school.

School counselors can provide advice about sources of job information. *What advantages can you see in beginning your job search now, while you are still in school?*

To get started, make a **contact list**. This is simply a list of people you know. Include everyone—family friends, neighbors, classmates, friends of friends, and even casual acquaintances.

Now begin networking by contacting the people on your list. Ask for any information that will lead to a job. You may think your aunt doesn't know anything about job openings. Maybe she doesn't, but her neighbor might, so don't give up on your aunt. Ask whether she knows anyone who works in the business you're interested in or for a company you'd like to work for.

Build your contact list by getting a referral from everyone you talk to. A **referral** is someone such as your aunt's neighbor to whom you've been directed, or referred. By contacting referrals, you

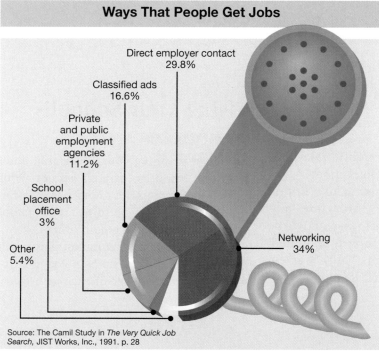

Ways That People Get Jobs

Direct employer contact
29.8%

Classified ads
16.6%

Private and public employment agencies
11.2%

School placement office
3%

Other
5.4%

Networking
34%

Source: The Camil Study in *The Very Quick Job Search*, JIST Works, Inc., 1991. p. 28

Figure 6-1

The graph shows the proportion of jobs people get from different sources. Why do you think most people get jobs by networking and contacting employers directly?

Chapter 6 • Finding and Applying for a Job **113**

▶▶ Extending Figure 6-1 ◀◀

Ask students to speculate about the impact the Internet may have as a source of job information. (Use of the Internet will likely increase in the future because of handier access of information and because it is less expensive for businesses to use online ads than printed ones.)

Caption Answer: A possible answer might include the greater competition for advertised jobs. In addition, employers prefer hiring people who are referred to them or who show the initiative to seek them out directly.

Guided Practice
Teaching Strategies

1. Assign and review Section 6-1.
2. Use the transparency for this section.
3. Assign and review the Case Study.

Teaching Tip

Students often underestimate the number of resources available to them to find a job. Have each student make a list of his or her resources, then share them with a classmate. After sharing the lists, have students revise their own lists to add other resources resulting from their discussions. Tell students to keep these lists as reminders for their own job search plans.

Discussion Starter

The saying that "It's not what you know but who you know" often applies to finding a job. Ask students if they agree or disagree.

Skills Practice

Kim's parents have arranged for her to work in the family hardware store after school—without asking Kim whether this is the type of part-time job she wants. Kim would prefer to work with a local musical group. If you were Kim, what would you tell your parents?

SCANS Foundation Skills Connection

L1 **Decision Making**

Have students create networking charts containing names of people who might be sources of job leads. Tell students to list each person's occupation, employer, address, and telephone number. They should also tell how they know the person (for example, they might use headings such as *School, Family, Church, Work, Clubs, Friends, Former Employers, Junior Achievement,* and so on).

L2 **Speaking**

Have students create a list of job leads, either from people they know or from newspaper articles about businesses that are or will be hiring. For each job lead, students are to write a list of questions to ask the appropriate person for each job lead over the telephone.

Have students report on their experiences: how they started their conversations, whether they were able to obtain answers to all their questions, and how they ended the conversations. Then ask about the follow-up actions they plan to take. Suggest that they schedule a time for a follow-up.

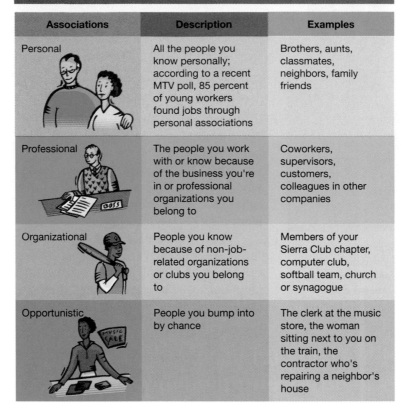

Associations in Successful Networks		
Associations	**Description**	**Examples**
Personal	All the people you know personally; according to a recent MTV poll, 85 percent of young workers found jobs through personal associations	Brothers, aunts, classmates, neighbors, family friends
Professional	The people you work with or know because of the business you're in or professional organizations you belong to	Coworkers, supervisors, customers, colleagues in other companies
Organizational	People you know because of non-job-related organizations or clubs you belong to	Members of your Sierra Club chapter, computer club, softball team, church or synagogue
Opportunistic	People you bump into by chance	The clerk at the music store, the woman sitting next to you on the train, the contractor who's repairing a neighbor's house

Figure 6-2

Successful networks include four types of associations: personal, professional, organizational, and opportunistic. Why should you try to include all four in your network?

build your network. (See *Figure 6-2*.) Eventually, networking will lead to a job.

Take Carrie Lannon, for example. She found her job in hotel public relations through networking. She had an interview with a promotions director of a hotel. Nothing came of that interview, but she added the director to her network. A month later, the director telephoned Lannon with a job lead. There was an opening at another hotel. Lannon got an interview and the job.

Using Your School's Resources

When planning your job search, don't overlook resources at your school. Your school has a counselor or teacher who can guide you in your job hunt. Your school may even have a placement office.

A counselor can set up interviews with employers. He or she can help you identify and follow leads in specific career areas.

 Extending Figure 6-2

Have students discuss the actual process of networking; for example, when, how, and where. (People network whenever they come into contact, whether in person or electronically. They use the telephone, conversations, letters, E-mail, and so on to exchange information.)

Caption Answer: Including all four types of associations will provide more opportunities to find a good job. It will give you contact with people from many different backgrounds and associations, which increases your opportunities.

Your school counselor may also be able to help you get into **school-to-work programs**. These programs bring schools and local businesses together. Students gain work experience and training. When they graduate, they usually get preference for jobs at the businesses.

Job Advertisements

The classified ads can be one part of your job search, but it should not be the only one. Only a small percentage of job seekers find their jobs through ads.

In pursuing this method of job hunting, don't limit yourself to newspaper classifieds. There are many other sources. Check these out:

- *National Business Employment Weekly*;

- *Black Enterprise*, *Hispanic Business*, and similar publications that are geared to specific ethnic groups; and

- magazines that specialize in particular industries, such as *Advertising Age* and *Computerworld*.

Using the Telephone

The telephone is one of your most useful job-hunting tools. Use it to make hot calls. A *hot call* is a call to a referral or a call to follow up a lead. It's *hot* because you know whom you're

 You can begin networking with your friends. **How can they help you find a job?**

Career Do's & Don'ts

When Looking for a Job...
Do:
- make it a top priority.
- create a professional résumé.
- tell everyone you know that you're looking for a job.
- be prepared to sell yourself on the phone to get an interview.

Don't:
- accept a job until you clearly understand the position.
- forget to ask questions about the company, the opportunities, and the benefits.
- put yourself down.
- ignore the importance of making a good first impression.

Chapter 6 • Finding and Applying for a Job **115**

L3 **Knowing How to Learn**

Have students make appointments to visit local employment agencies. They may choose from various professional/technical, government, or temporary agencies. Students should interview staff members to gather information on how each particular agency assists job seekers.

Tell students to prepare their questions beforehand. They should ask about fees, educational requirements, training opportunities, and the types of jobs offered. Have students write a 150-word summary describing what they learned.

 SCANS Workplace Competencies Connection

L1 **Interpreting and Communicating Information**

Have students cut job advertisements from newspapers that interest them and paste them in a notebook.

Under each ad, have students write a brief summary of the type of job described, the educational requirements, whether previous experience is required, the responsibilities of the job, salary ranges, and any other information that would be helpful in deciding whether to respond to the ad.

Extending the Illustration

Have students practice career networking by role-playing conversations in which they discuss their career interests and ask for help or information.

Caption Answer: They can tell you about jobs they've heard of and introduce you to family or friends who have jobs in a field you're interested in.

SCANS Workplace Competencies Connection (cont'd.)

L2 **Acquiring and Evaluating Information**

Tell students to talk to people who can provide job leads, such as the guidance counselor, principal, vocational and business teachers, and so on. Have students decide which leads they will pursue and in what order.

L3 **Using Computers to Process Information**

Have students do a job search on the Internet. Have them download useful information, which they will organize according to career areas and analyze its relevancy to their individual career interests. Have them use a word processing program to write a brief summary and share their information with the class.

Independent Practice

Assign as homework the chapter activity in the *School-to-Work Handbook*.

Skills Practice

Yoko has found 27 job leads. She believes she has a 65 percent chance of getting an interview for each job for which she applies. If Yoko applies for all 27 jobs, how many interviews will she be offered based on her assumption? Round answers to the nearest whole number. (27 × 0.65 = 17.55, or 18 interviews)

116

YOU'RE THE BOSS!

Solving Workplace Problems

You and a partner run a small but thriving repair business. You've agreed that it's time to hire an assistant to handle most of the office duties. You're about to place an ad at the local newspaper when your partner says, "Don't bother with the ad. My cousin can do the work, and we won't have to pay him as much." How do you respond?

When making cold calls, plan your conversation carefully. **Why is it helpful to write a script?**

calling and you know there's a job or information at the other end of it.

You may also make *cold calls*. These are blind calls. You're not calling to follow up on a specific job lead or a referral but just to get information. Does the company have any openings? Whom can you talk to there? If you make cold calls, plan them carefully.

- Scan the Yellow Pages for companies you might want to work for, and call them. Ask for the personnel director or the supervisor of a department.

- Write an introductory script to use when calling. Tell who you are, why you're calling, and what you want.

- Write questions that will get you information about job openings. Be sure to request referrals.

116 Unit 3 • *Finding a Job*

A telephone call may be your first personal contact with an employer. Make it effective. Practice the SCANS skills of speaking and listening.

Employment Agencies

An employment agency is a matchmaker between job seekers and companies with job openings. Job seekers fill out applications at the agency. Businesses call the agency when they have openings. The agency brings the two together.

There are two kinds of employment agencies—public and private. Public agencies provide free placement services. Private agencies charge a fee, which may be paid by either the job seeker or the employer. Private agencies may give more

---

Teaching YOU'RE THE BOSS!

Possible responses: Suggest that you run the ad and let your partner's cousin go through the application process. Or find out why your partner thinks his or her cousin won't have to be paid as much as another employee.

Extending the Illustration

Have students choose a networking call they want to make and write a script for the call.

Caption Answer: You will have more confidence because you will know what you're going to say. You're more likely to include all the information you need and to ask all the necessary questions.

personal service and list jobs not on file with the public agency.

Using the Internet

Using the job-hunting tactics discussed so far, you can contact hundreds of potential employers. That's not bad, but there's a way to reach thousands. It's the **Internet**, a worldwide electronic community that links millions of computers and computer users. You can view on-line job ads, post your résumé, and find advice and information at career centers.

Getting on the Internet

What do you need to get hooked up to the Internet? A computer, a modem, a telephone line, and an account with an on-line server, such as America Online, CompuServe, or Prodigy.

Even if you don't have a computer, access to the Internet is available. Check with your school and public libraries. Many are already connected to the Internet. You might also check with community colleges, universities, copy shops, and your state employment office.

 The Internet is the newest tool for finding jobs. *What keywords might lead you to jobs in the field you're interested in?*

Navigating the Internet

Once you're on-line, hundreds of job-listing sites are just a few keystrokes away. To find them, type in keywords. *Keywords* are descriptive words that tell your computer what to search for. Examples are *employment opportunities*, *job listings*, and *careers*.

Keywords will lead you to some of the many job-related sites on the Internet, such as America's Job Bank, Online Career Center, or Federal Job Openings.

SECTION 6-1 *Review*

Understanding Key Concepts

Using complete sentences, answer the following questions on a separate sheet of paper.

1. Explain why networking is one of the most effective means of finding a job.

2. Whom should you include on your contact list? Why?

3. Which source for job leads will you use first in job hunting? Why?

4. What are six keywords you might use in a job search on the Internet?

Chapter 6 • Finding and Applying for a Job **117**

SECTION 6-1

Writing: *Informational*

Have students choose three companies for which they might like to work and prepare for a phone call to each one. Tell students to consider:

- what information to give about themselves;
- the position or type of job they are seeking;
- how to ask about available positions; and
- how they will show appreciation for the person's time, information, and cooperation.

ASSESS

Assessment
Performance

Divide students into six teams. Assign each team one of the following: *Networking, School Resources, Job Advertisements, Using the Telephone, Employment Agencies,* and *Using the Internet.* Have students prepare short presentations explaining how each of the above might be used in a job search.

Also, have students do role-plays. For example, students on the Networking team might role-play a conversation in which one person expresses an interest in working for the other person's employer and asks about current job openings.

Evaluate teams on accuracy and completeness of information as well as the relevancy of their role-plays.

SECTION 6-1 *Review* ANSWERS

1. By networking, you have access to inside information about openings.
2. Include everyone you know. You never know who will be helpful.
3. Answers will vary.
4. Possible answers: employment, jobs, job offerings, job-seeking strategies, job openings, career development

Extending the Illustration

Relate Internet searches to the print searches students do. For example, to find information on a topic, you might look in the index of a book under all related terms; for a computer database, you might enter related terms.

Caption Answer: Answers will vary, depending on the field of interest.

ASSESS (cont'd.)

Evaluation

Assign the section review.

Reteaching

Have students write a definition of the term "job lead" and then draw a graphic representation of the different sources of job leads available to them.

Extending the Content

Assign the appropriate Chapter 6 activities in the *Student Activity Workbook*.

Have students make appointments with the school guidance or career counselor or with a teacher they know well and ask him or her to help them generate a list of five part-time jobs for which they could apply. Then have students select three family members and/or friends who can help them identify three potential employment opportunities in their career interest areas. Finally, have students cut out three newspaper ads for jobs in their career areas. Have them develop a plan for responding to the ads and applying for a job.

CLOSE

Have students think of former jobs, even casual ones such as mowing lawns or babysitting, and write a short paragraph about the leads they used to find that job.

CASE STUDY

Exploring Careers: Construction

**Bill Jagger
Building Contractor**

Q: What's an average day like for a contractor?

A: I'm up at 6:00 or 6:30 A.M. and start working about 7:00 A.M. Once the crew is rolling, I take inventory to be sure we have enough supplies for the next few days. I answer questions and coordinate the work of subcontractors. If people don't show up for work, quite often I'll fill in. In the evenings or on weekends, I do the paperwork: pay bills, send bills, type contracts. Ten-hour days are not uncommon.

Q: How did you acquire your skills?

A: I worked for a friend's father in high school—pounding nails, cleaning up job sites. I ended up going to technical college and earning an associate degree in building construction. I've worked for many contractors over the years. Being a contractor is an acquired trade. The more you do, the better you are. I've worked at it about 20 years.

Q: What are some of the difficulties?

A: We sometimes have problems with labor. Sometimes lumber doesn't show up, or the order is wrong. There's a lot of risk. You're dealing with large sums of money. People don't forget if something goes wrong. But it's gratifying to stand back and look at a house you've built and say you've had a part in it.

Thinking Critically

What are the many ways that contractors use math skills on a daily basis?

CAREER FACTS

Nature of the Work:
Order supplies for construction jobs; coordinate work crews and subcontractors; work on the job; bill clients; pay invoices.

Training or Education Needed:
Experience on construction sites; work with other contractors; business skills.

Aptitudes, Abilities, and Skills:
Math and interpersonal skills; problem-solving and decision-making skills; ability to read blueprints and diagrams; ability to

work with tools and equipment; ability to work intuitively; reading and writing skills; ability to allocate resources.

Salary Range:
Average starting salary—$30,000; average top salary—$60,000.

Career Path:
Start on the job; develop skills in one or more trades; learn business of contracting; act as subcontractor; start own business or work for a large contracting firm.

118   *Unit 3 • Finding a Job*

Extending the CASE STUDY

Answer: billing clients for work provided; paying subcontractors and suppliers; measuring lumber, and figuring amounts of cement needed for foundations; reading blueprints and determining that all measurements are correct; figuring the time necessary to finish a job; figuring out costs for supplies, labor, and equipment; figuring payroll taxes

Further Application: Have students discuss the ways they will acquire the skills they will need for their future careers. Are they learning any of those skills now? How long will it take them to acquire those skills? Do any of them have long-range (10 years or more) estimates of the time it will take them to become proficient in their careers?

Applying for a Job

OBJECTIVE

After studying this section, you will be able to:

*   Outline procedures for applying for a job: filling out applications, preparing a résumé and cover letter, and taking tests

KEY TERMS

Social Security number
work permit
standard English
references
résumé
cover letter

Think of a personnel director with three piles of applications before him. One pile is labeled "Yes." One is labeled "Maybe." One is labeled "No." Your job is to get your application into the "Yes" pile. How will you do that?

It comes down to how well you present yourself in your phone calls, job application, résumé, and cover letter. Your knowledge of the SCANS skills of writing, problem solving, creative thinking, and reasoning will show.

Employers are looking for the best person to fill the job. They want to know whether or not you have the ability to do the work. They will be influenced by the way you dress and whether or not you are well-groomed. They will also notice if you use slang or any other language that is not standard English. In fact, they will want to know everything about you that relates to the job.

Be Confident and Be Prepared

You may feel anxious and insecure when applying for a job. That's natural, but don't show it. Project confidence and a positive, businesslike image. Display this image every time you communicate with an employer by phone, in writing, or in person.

Chapter 6 • Finding and Applying for a Job **119**

Tell students to imagine that they have been called for a job interview. Have them make a list of the information and documents they will need to take to the interview as well as what they will be asked to perform.

Introducing the Section

As students share their lists from the Bell Ringer activity, write each item on the chalkboard. Items may include a social security card, résumé, and a work permit. At the interview, students may be asked to fill out a job application form and to complete a performance test of some type. Briefly discuss each item and why it is needed for an interview.

Motivational Activity
Oral Presentation

Have students practice what they wish to say about themselves in a job interview in front of the class. Have students respond to this typical interview question: "Tell me about yourself." Suggest that students focus on their skills and interests, their current and previous work experience, any special subjects they've studied, and what they hope to do for a career.

Workforce 2000 Trends

In the future, one of the most important skills will be the ability to work without a stable "job." As more work becomes temporary, workers will spend more time trying to find work. To do this, workers will have to be flexible, creative, and independent.

Addressing Workplace Diversity

A more diverse workplace makes a company better able to do business worldwide. Feedback from diverse employees gives a company a broader base for its marketing decisions. For example, female managers may create more appropriate policies to serve a growing female workforce.

Be Prepared

An employer will require you to have certain documents. If you don't have them when you apply for a job, it shows you aren't prepared. Get them before you go job hunting.

First, you'll need a **Social Security number**. You probably already have one. If not, you can get one at the post office. This number is issued by the federal government.

If you are under 16, you will also need a work permit. Some states require work permits for workers under 18. A **work permit** shows that you have been advised of laws restricting the hours young people can work and the kinds of jobs they can hold. You should be able to get a work permit at your school's guidance office.

Communicating Effectively

The way you talk and write is one of the first and strongest impressions you'll make, so use **standard English**. This is the form of writing and speaking you've learned in school. It is the form used in newspapers and on television news programs. If you have trouble with grammar and usage, now is the time to polish these SCANS skills.

Filling Out the Job Application

A *job application* is one way an employer screens applicants. This form asks questions about your skills, work experience, education,

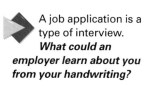

A job application is a type of interview. *What could an employer learn about you from your handwriting?*

and interests. Always fill out a job application completely and accurately. Keep these additional suggestions in mind:

- Read and follow directions exactly.
- Keep the application neat and clean.
- Make your statements positive. If you believe that answering a question might disqualify you, write "Will explain in interview."
- Keep your options open. Do not state the salary you want. Write "Negotiable." If you are asked whether you will work nights, write "Will consider."
- Prepare any lists of information in advance. Many applications, for example, ask for a list of schools

attended. If you've attended a number of schools, you might prepare this information in advance for your own reference. Then you can enter the information quickly and accurately.

Applications often request **references.** These are people who will recommend you to an employer. Choose references carefully and be prepared to list them on the application. Employers trust teachers or former employers the most. Make sure you ask permission to use people as references.

Employers don't have a right to ask about your race, religion, sex, children, or marital status. You don't have to tell if

SCANS Foundation Skills Connection

L1 Speaking

Mock interviews are a good way to prepare students for future job interviews. Assemble a panel of "experts" and conduct an interview with each student. After the interview, discuss areas in which the student excelled and areas that need improvement.

L2 Writing

A good cover letter plays an important role in determining whether an employer chooses to read further or decides to go on to the next applicant. Have students write a cover letter to send along with their résumés. Evaluate letters for accuracy of grammar, spelling, and punctuation.

L3 Reading

Career experts suggest that job applicants should learn about companies to which they are applying for a job. Assign a company—either local or national—to each student. Have students research the company, then write a summary of about 100 words describing what the company does, the jobs it provides, the number of people it employs, positions within its industry, economic outlook, and current business events that may positively or negatively affect the company.

EXCELLENT BUSINESS PRACTICES

Interactive Technology That Lists Your Résumé

Texas Instruments of Dallas, Texas, manufactures electronic components, defense electronics, and digital products. Texas Instruments designed a method of helping students list their qualifications on the company's employment database. During visits to college campuses or by mail, the company distributes a brochure and interactive floppy disks with a program called "Engineer Your Future." The interactive program was designed to streamline the recruitment process and teach job-searching skills.

Using the disks, students identify work styles and preferences with a career-mapping feature. They can then create résumés that will be submitted to the company.

Students return completed profiles on disk. When the company receives the information, it is entered into the employment database and reviewed, as appropriate, when job positions need to be filled. Each student receives a copy of the career profile generated by the program.

Thinking Critically

How would a recruitment tool designed specifically for one company help you in a job search at other companies?

Extending EXCELLENT BUSINESS PRACTICES

Answer: It would allow you to see the type of information companies are interested in knowing about you. It would be especially helpful for learning about wants and needs of companies in similiar fields.

Further Application: Have students contact companies they might like to work for. Have them ask if each company has any special recruitment policies. What information is provided for any open employment opportunities? Does the company have a method of keeping track of individuals who have applied for positions, or is it necessary to reapply for each opening?

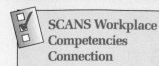

L1 Organizing and Maintaining Information

Have students collect samples of different types of résumés. Have them choose styles that best fit their own experience and job goals.

L2 Teaching Others

Working in teams of three or four, have members collect a job application from a local employer. Have team members discuss the form, then have each person fill out the form with help from their team members. Ask teams to discuss do's and don'ts in completing the form, as well as whether all questions on the forms are legal and non-discriminatory. Have each team present its form and comment on any difficulties.

L3 Acquiring and Evaluating Information

Have students contact an employer or employment agency that administers tests to job applicants. Tell students to interview over the telephone or in person and ask questions such as the following: What skills does the test measure? What do test scores reveal? How are scores used? If an applicant does poorly on a test, can he or she retake it?

you've been arrested, although you are required to tell if you've been convicted of a felony. If you are asked for this information on an application form, you might indicate that you'll explain in the interview.

Preparing a Résumé

A **résumé** is a brief summary of your personal information, education, skills, work experience, activities, and interests. You will send it to an employer when applying for a job by mail or via the Internet. An employer may also request that a copy be attached to your job application or brought to an interview. A résumé can get you an interview or kill your chance for a job. Don't be shy. Make yourself look good!

You do this by carefully choosing what you'll include, what you'll emphasize, and how you'll describe your experience. Do not include any negative information. If you don't have work experience, don't mention it. Focus on the skills, education, and training you do have. Don't hesitate to include awards, hobbies, or activities. References can be included, or you can indicate you'll provide them on request.

The best résumés are brief. Keep yours to one or two pages. It must be typed or computer generated. Of course, it must be neat, and there should be no errors in spelling, grammar, or usage. There are two basic forms of résumés.

A *chronological résumé* gives your experience in time order. You list your most recent job first, then your previous job, and so on. You organize your education and other information in the same reverse time order. *Figure 6-3* shows an example of a chronological résumé.

The advantage of a chronological résumé is that it shows your growth in experience. It works best for a person with continuous work experience.

A *skills résumé* highlights your skills and accomplishments. It is organized around skills or strengths, such as attention to detail or interpersonal skills. After each heading is a description. The advantage

 The information you include on a résumé must be accurate and true. What you include and how you state it is up to you. *What can you do to make yourself look good on a résumé?*

▶ Extending the Illustration

Remind students that it is important to use *accurate* information in emphasizing their strengths in their résumés.

Caption Answer: Possible answers are to highlight personal strengths and to de-emphasize weaknesses.

Figure 6-3

Chronological Résumé

Résumés may be organized in different formats. However, most will include the following kinds of information. Keep your résumé brief. An outline form is best because it is easy to read. Use titles and spacing to identify major categories of information.

1 **Name and Address.** Give your name, full address, and telephone number (with area code) at the top of your résumé.

2 **Job Objective.** State the job you are applying for. Be sure to change this item if you are using the same résumé when applying for different jobs.

3 **Work Experience.** List your work experience, beginning with your most recent job. Include volunteer work if it relates to the job you are applying for.

4 **Education.** List the schools you have attended and diplomas or degrees you have received. You may also include any subjects or programs you specialized in.

5 **Honors and Activities.** Include any honors or awards you have received or activities you have participated in that relate to the job you want.

6 **Special Skills and Abilities.** Identify any business or other skills and abilities that you have gained in school, on a job, or in other situations.

7 **References.** If your résumé is short, you may include references. If not, say "Available upon request."

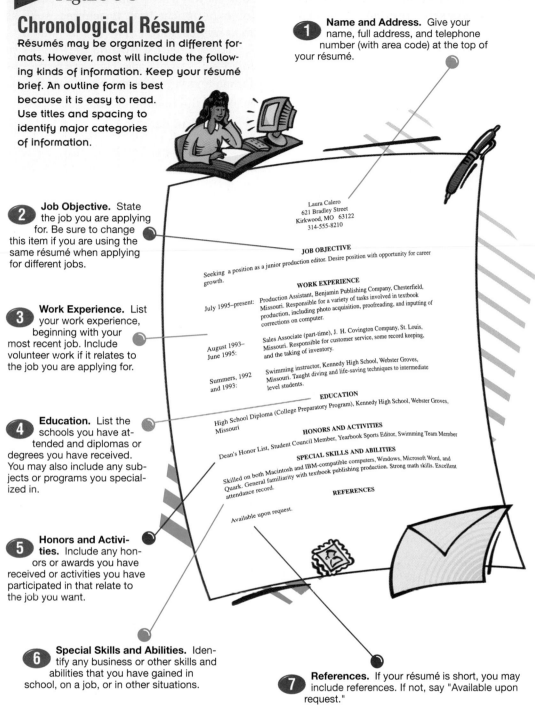

Laura Calero
621 Bradley Street
Kirkwood, MO 63122
314-555-8210

JOB OBJECTIVE

Seeking a position as a junior production editor. Desire position with opportunity for career growth.

WORK EXPERIENCE

July 1995–present: Production Assistant, Benjamin Publishing Company, Chesterfield, Missouri. Responsible for a variety of tasks involved in textbook production, including photo acquisition, proofreading, and inputting of corrections on computer.

August 1993–June 1995: Sales Associate (part-time), J. H. Covington Company, St. Louis, Missouri. Responsible for customer service, some record keeping, and the taking of inventory.

Summers, 1992 and 1993: Swimming instructor, Kennedy High School, Webster Groves, Missouri. Taught diving and life-saving techniques to intermediate level students.

EDUCATION

High School Diploma (College Preparatory Program), Kennedy High School, Webster Groves, Missouri

HONORS AND ACTIVITIES

Dean's Honor List, Student Council Member, Yearbook Sports Editor, Swimming Team Member

SPECIAL SKILLS AND ABILITIES

Skilled on both Macintosh and IBM-compatible computers, Windows, Microsoft Word, and Quark. General familiarity with textbook publishing production. Strong math skills. Excellent attendance record.

REFERENCES

Available upon request.

Chapter 6 • Finding and Applying for a Job   **123**

Teaching Tip

Invite a human resources representative or career counselor to talk to your students about résumé writing. Have the speaker discuss how to prepare a résumé and show samples of particularly effective ones. Give students time to work on their own résumés, then have the speaker review individual résumés and offer advice.

Independent Practice
Reading

Have students identify books in the school or public library on writing effective résumés. Have students make lists of at least five points they should consider when creating their own résumés.

Writing: *Résumé*

Have students handwrite their personal résumés—either a chronological résumé or a skills-based résumé. Have students critique other classmates' résumés.

► Extending Figure 6-3 ◄

Ask a local business person who regularly reviews résumés to give tips to students about the information he or she looks for in a résumé.

Skills Practice

Have students use a word-processing program to create professional looking résumés using the résumés in their text-books as models. Have them proofread their résumés, then print out a copy.

Critical Thinking

Ask students whether they should send the same résumé to all companies, regardless of the position for which they are applying.

Teaching Tip

Divide students into groups of two or three. Have groups share their résumés and ask for feedback about format and content. Tell each group to an-swer these questions about each résumé:

- Does it adequately detail the student's skills, work experience, activities, and interests?
- Is it grammatically cor-rect and free of spelling errors?
- Does it highlight work experience and academic strengths?

Writing: *Persuasion*

Have students write cover letters to the Simpson Depart-ment Store, applying for jobs as sales associates. Students can choose which departments of the store they wish to work in.

of this résumé is that you can emphasize your strengths. *Figure 6-4* shows one way to organize a skills résumé.

Electronic Résumés

Increasingly, companies *scan* résumés into their computers. That is, they copy and store them in their computers. When companies need to hire someone, they do an electronic search of the résumés. They look for keywords that describe skills or job experiences they're seeking, such as *food service*, *mathematics*, and *French*.

Try to create a résumé that works in today's electronic age. Here are some tips for making your résumé "scannable":

- Keep the résumé clean.
- Use crisp, dark type.

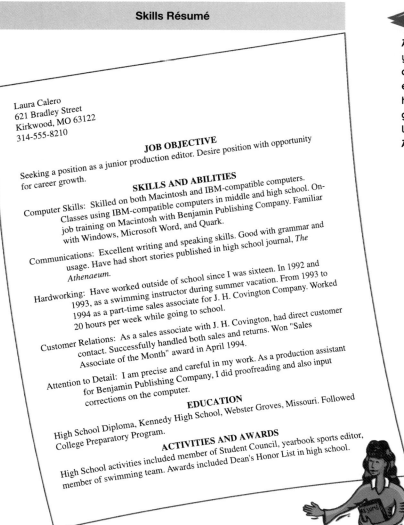

Skills Résumé

Laura Calero
621 Bradley Street
Kirkwood, MO 63122
314-555-8210

JOB OBJECTIVE

Seeking a position as a junior production editor. Desire position with opportunity for career growth.

SKILLS AND ABILITIES

Computer Skills: Skilled on both Macintosh and IBM-compatible computers. Classes using IBM-compatible computers in middle and high school. On-job training on Macintosh with Benjamin Publishing Company. Familiar with Windows, Microsoft Word, and Quark.

Communications: Excellent writing and speaking skills. Good with grammar and usage. Have had short stories published in high school journal, *The Athenaeum.*

Hardworking: Have worked outside of school since I was sixteen. In 1992 and 1993, as a swimming instructor during summer vacation. From 1993 to 1994 as a part-time sales associate for J. H. Covington Company. Worked 20 hours per week while going to school.

Customer Relations: As a sales associate with J. H. Covington, had direct customer contact. Successfully handled both sales and returns. Won "Sales Associate of the Month" award in April 1994.

Attention to Detail: I am precise and careful in my work. As a production assistant for Benjamin Publishing Company, I did proofreading and also input corrections on the computer.

EDUCATION

High School Diploma, Kennedy High School, Webster Groves, Missouri. Followed College Preparatory Program.

ACTIVITIES AND AWARDS

High School activities included member of Student Council, yearbook sports editor, member of swimming team. Awards included Dean's Honor List in high school.

▶ **Figure 6-4**

A skills résumé lets you highlight skills, aptitudes, and experience that you have. What cate-gories would you list under Skills and Abilities?

▶▶ Extending Figure 6-4 ◀◀

Ask students to think about jobs in which a chronological résumé might be more effective versus jobs in which a skills résumé might be more effective. (A chrono-logical résumé might be better for jobs re-quiring a broad range of knowledge, such as teaching. A skills résumé would be bet-ter for jobs requiring employees to perform technical skills, such as using a computer or working in the construction industry.

Caption Answer: Answers will vary.

- Avoid italics, underscores, and other fancy type.
- Use white paper.
- Use keywords in describing your experience.

Writing Cover Letters

Do not send your résumé by itself. Always include a **cover letter**. This is a one-page letter telling the employer who you are and why you're sending the résumé. It is sometimes called an *application letter*. Keep it concise and to the point. A cover letter has three parts. (See *Figure 6-5* below.)

- The opening explains why you are writing. Drop names! Say where, or from whom, you learned about the job.

Cover Letter

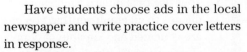

621 Bradley Street
Kirkwood, MO 63122
November 16, 1997

Mr. David Schweizer
Managing Editor
Premiere Publishing Company, Inc.
St. Louis, MO 63108

Dear Mr. Schweizer:

Ann Leiter, the editorial director for Sunshine Publishing, suggested I contact you about the position of junior production editor that is open with your company. Please consider me an applicant for this position.

I have been working since July 1995 as a production assistant for Benjamin Publishing Company in Chesterfield, Missouri. I've had an opportunity to develop skills in desktop publishing and to learn about many aspects of textbook publishing. Please review my résumé, which is enclosed. It provides more details about my experience and the skills I can bring to your company.

I am especially interested in pursuing a career with Premiere Publishing because of your reputation for creative use of graphics and page design. I believe employment with your company would offer me a wonderful opportunity to use my skills and advance in my career.

May I have an interview? I shall be glad to call at your convenience. My home telephone number is (314) 555-8210.

Sincerely,

Laura Calero

Laura Calero

Chapter 6 • Finding and Applying for a Job **125**

Figure 6-5

Make the purpose of your cover letter clear. Let your personality come through. How has this writer included the key elements of the three parts of the cover letter?

SECTION 6-2

Research

Have students study electronic résumés, both those that appear on the Internet and those that are intended to be scanned into computer systems. Tell them to list at least five suggestions on how to create an effective electronic résumé.

Discussion Starter

Write this sentence on the chalkboard: "You have only one opportunity to make a good first impression." Ask students to discuss how their résumés create an impression of them. For example, a letter that is poorly written indicates someone who lacks good writing skills. A letter with misspelled words creates the impression that the writer was careless and failed to proofread and correct errors.

Teaching Tip

Have students imagine they are writing letters of application for the following jobs:
- part-time retail sales clerk at MacArthur's Department Store,
- part-time plant tender at Harvest Garden Center,
- part-time clerk at the Super Seven Gasoline service station.

For each job, have students prepare a list of skills or work experience they could include in a letter of application.

▶▶ Extending Figure 6-5 ◀◀

Have students choose ads in the local newspaper and write practice cover letters in response.

Caption Answer: The first paragraph is the opening: it tells why she is writing (to apply for the position); it identifies the source of the lead (Ann Leiter). Paragraphs 2 and 3 are the body of the letter: The writer tells how her experience suits her to the job she's applying for; she explains why this job especially interests her. Paragraph 4 is the closing: it asks for an interview and includes her phone number.

ASSESS

Assessment
Process

Have students create a list of steps to take in applying for a job and preparing for an interview. Tell them to include documents needed for each step. Evaluate students' work for completeness of information. (Typical steps: (1) collect information, such as a Social Security card and work permit; (2) fill out application form, including a list of references; (3) write résumé; (4) write cover letter; (5) take any required tests.)

Evaluation

Assign the section review.

MINI QUIZ

Short Answer

1. Communicating to share information and advice is called ____. (networking)

2. Calling a person you know about a job lead is a ____ lead. (hot)

3. ____ employment agencies provide free job placement services. (Public)

4. A ____ résumé is organized by work experience and education, all listed in reverse time order. (chronological)

5. A ____ résumé is organized by skills and accomplishments. (skills-based)

- The body is your sales pitch. It tells why you are right for the job.
- The closing tells how you will follow up. Include your phone number so the employer can contact you.

Try to personalize your letter. One woman applied for a job with Playskool. As a child, she had loved the company's toys. She mentioned this fact in her cover letter. It helped her get the job.

Taking Tests

When you apply for a job, you may have to take one or more tests.

- A performance test evaluates how well you can do a particular task. An example is a typing test.
- A drug test is a blood or urine test for illegal drugs. Most companies in the nuclear power and transportation industries use drug tests.
- A polygraph test is a lie detector test. It may be required if you are applying for a job in law enforcement or government.

 When taking a test for a job, relax, stay calm, and keep focused. *What techniques do you have that help you relax during tests?*

ETHICS in Action

You've been looking for a part-time job, but you haven't had much luck. A classmate mentions a job you hadn't known about. "They said they'd call back tomorrow, and I really think I'll be hired. It's just the job I've been looking for." It's just what you've been looking for, too. Will you go and apply for the job this afternoon? Why or why not?

SECTION 6-2 *Review*

Understanding Key Concepts

Using complete sentences, answer the following question on a separate sheet of paper.

1. Why should you use standard English throughout the job application process?

Extending the Illustration

Discuss with students both positive and negative stress and how each can affect performance. (For example, stress can be positive when it helps an athlete run faster. Stress is negative when it causes worry and agitation.)

Caption Answer: Possible answers include deep breathing, stretching, or clearing the mind of distractions.

SECTION 6-2 *Review* ANSWERS

1. Your use of standard English indicates to an employer that you are educated and capable of communicating effectively in a work environment.

Key Terms

job lead *(p. 112)*
networking *(p. 112)*
contact list *(p. 113)*
referral *(p. 113)*
school-to-work
　programs *(p. 115)*
Internet *(p. 117)*

SECTION 6-1 **Summary**

- There are numerous sources for job leads. They include networking, employment agencies, school placement centers, classified ads, and the Internet.

- Networking means talking with people who can help you in your job search. Contact lists provide the foundation of networks.

- You build a network by getting referrals from people you know.

- School counselors and placement centers can help you identify and apply for jobs.

- You can find classified ads in newspapers and a variety of other publications. They should not be the only method for finding job leads.

- Employment agencies match job seekers with businesses seeking new employees. There are public and private employment agencies.

- The Internet has job lists, on-line career centers, and sites where you can post your résumé.

Key Terms

Social Security
　number *(p. 120)*
work permit *(p. 120)*
standard English *(p. 120)*
references *(p. 121)*
résumé *(p. 122)*
cover letter *(p. 125)*

SECTION 6-2 **Summary**

- Before you apply for a job, you should get a Social Security number, and you may need a work permit.

- When you apply for a job, use standard English, the form of speaking and writing that you learned in school.

- Employers screen applicants through job applications, résumés, and cover letters. You want to project a positive image of yourself in these documents.

- Some employers require tests—such as performance tests, drug tests, or polygraph tests—as part of the application process.

Chapter 6 • Finding and Applying for a Job **127**

Use the Testmaker to create a customized test for Chapter 6.

Reteaching

1. Have students generate a list of how employers may form impressions of them regarding whether or not they are suitable for a particular job.

2. Assign the vocabulary, chapter questions, and activities from the Chapter Review.

Extending the Content

Assign the appropriate Chapter 6 activities in the *Student Activity Workbook.*

Have students research a local company and determine the types of performance tests that are given to job applicants for three specific jobs within the company (for example, a warehousing worker who must lift heavy loads, an administrative assistant, or a telephone customer service specialist).

CLOSE

Have students write a chronological or a skills-based résumé that suits the types of jobs for which they are applying and explain why they chose to use that type of résumé.

Teaching ETHICS in Action

Have students follow these steps to help them make a decision.

1. What are the ethical issues?

2. What are the alternatives?

3. Who are the affected parties?

4. How do the alternatives affect the parties?

5. What is your decision?

Computer Activity

Using a database software package, have students create a bank of names, addresses, and phone numbers of people who could help them find a job. Create a list or report from that database and title it "My Job Networking List." Have students print out the list. You might suggest they verify the information to make sure it is accurate.

Answers
Reviewing Key Terms

Paragraphs will vary but should show an understanding of the terms included in them.

Recalling Key Concepts

1. b
2. c
3. a
4. b
5. b

Thinking Critically

1. Employers like to hire people they know. Referrals are more trustworthy sources than classified ads, employment agencies, or other sources.

2. The applicant is careless, not well educated, doesn't know what is expected in a work environment, and is not motivated to succeed.

3. Possible answer: skills such as typing to show tasks that you can perform; activities or accomplishments that show leadership or social skills

4. The employer would probably want to see whether applicants could perform the tasks required on the job.

5. Possible answers: the use of standard English, whether the applicant has researched the company, and what the applicant's level of interest and personality are like

Reviewing Key Terms

On a separate sheet of paper, write one or two paragraphs describing how you would conduct a job search. Use the terms below in your description.

job lead	Social Security
networking	number
contact list	work permit
referral	standard English
school-to-work	references
programs	résumé
Internet	cover letter

Recalling Key Concepts

Choose the correct answer for each item below. Write your answers on a separate sheet of paper.

1. Getting a job lead is the first step in ____.
   (a) building a network (b) finding a job
   (c) locating a school-to-work program

2. You build your network by asking for ____.
   (a) contact lists (b) job leads
   (c) referrals

3. A fee may be charged by a ____.
   (a) private employment agency
   (b) public employment agency
   (c) school placement center

4. When completing a job application, you should ____.
   (a) make it scannable
   (b) make your statements positive
   (c) ask for referrals

SCANS Foundation Skills and Workplace Competencies

1. Paragraphs should describe how it may provide job leads, advice on job hunting, and access to a school-to-work program.

2. She should be honest. She might write "Will discuss in interview" on the

5. A résumé that lists your last job first is a ____.
   (a) skills résumé
   (b) chronological résumé
   (c) electronic résumé

Thinking Critically

Using complete sentences, answer each of the questions below on a separate sheet of paper.

1. Many employers like to hire people referred to them through a network. Why do you think this is so?

2. If you were an employer, what would you think of an applicant who did not use standard English?

3. List information you would include on your résumé, and explain why.

4. Why would an employer give applicants a skill test before hiring them?

5. If you were an employer, what would you look for in an applicant's cover letter?

SCANS Foundation Skills and Workplace Competencies

Thinking Skills: *Knowing How to Learn*

1. In a paragraph, describe how your school placement office can help you find job leads.

application and explain in person what happened.

3. Possible answer: 9:00–10:00, read classified ads; 10:00–12:00, make networking calls; 1:00–3:00, research companies with openings; 4:00–5:00, write personalized cover letters

Personal Qualities: *Integrity/Honesty*

2. Jennifer is filling out a job application. She was fired from her last job. She wants to answer no to the question "Have you ever been fired?" What should she do and why?

Resources: *Allocating Time*

3. Imagine you are looking for a job. Prepare a daily schedule for your job search.

Connecting Academics to the Workplace

Mathematics

1. Bill has 20 people on his first contact list. If each person on his list refers him to two more people, and each of those people refers him to one more person, how many people will be on his new list?

Social Studies/Language Arts

2. Laura is interested in sending a résumé to a corporation. Choose a corporation she might be applying to and do research to learn about it. Then write a cover letter she might send to the corporation. Use your research in your letter.

Computer Science

3. Sheila wants to find out about opportunities in nursing in Texas. Use the Internet to find some on-line job bulletin boards. Find some jobs for Sheila. Contact an on-line career service to get some advice for her.

Developing Teamwork and Leadership Skills

Pair up with another student in a job-search team. As a team, choose a particular job and research openings through methods described in the chapter. Then present your findings to the class.

Real-World Workshop

Collaborate with a classmate to research ways to write résumés. You might read career books or find information on the Internet. Then write your résumé. Exchange résumés with your partner for review and proofreading. Check each other's résumé for standard English.

School-to-Work Connection

Call an employment agency or a business and ask to speak to the personnel director. Interview this person about common mistakes that people make on their job applications, cover letters, and résumés. What advice would this person give for preparing these documents? Present your findings to the class.

Individual Career Plan

Select a field that interests you. Do research to learn about companies that employ people in this field. Interview a person who knows about work in the field. This might be an employer or an employee in the field. Present your findings to the class in an illustrated oral report.

Real-World Workshop

Résumés should be accurate and functional. They should include paid and unpaid employment, school activities, transferable skills, education, and so on.

School-to-Work Connection

Answers will vary but should specify in detail common mistakes made on application documents and the advice the students received.

Individual Career Plan

Students should use visuals and an oral report to describe their findings. They should discuss current trends in the field, salaries, and ways to prepare for a job in the field.

Chapter 6 • Finding and Applying for a Job **129**

Connecting Academics to the Workplace

1. 20 + 40 + 40 = 100
2. Letters will vary, depending on the company chosen and the information learned through research.
3. Possible jobs and advice will vary, depending on the Internet resources used.

Developing Teamwork and Leadership Skills

Students should explain how they divided the work, chose a particular job, and used methods described in the chapter to find job leads. They should then describe what the most effective strategy was and why it was effective.

···PLANNING GUIDE···
Chapter 7

SECTION 1 — *Before an Interview: Getting Ready*

SECTION OBJECTIVES	SECTION FEATURES	SECTION RESOURCES
• Identify methods of preparing for interviews, including researching and rehearsing. • Recognize how to dress for success.	Personal Career Plan, p. 131 Career Do's and Don'ts, p. 134	⊙ Workforce 2000 Videodisc and Videotape 📁 Section 7-1 Review, p. 135 📖 Student Activity Workbook

SECTION 2 — *During an Interview: It's Show Time*

SECTION OBJECTIVES	SECTION FEATURES	SECTION RESOURCES
• Recognize the importance of displaying the proper attitude. • Practice clear and accurate communication. • Answer typical and tough questions. • Identify strategies for dealing with interview stress.	Excellent Business Practices, p. 141 You're the Boss!, p. 142 Exploring Careers, p. 143	⊙ Workforce 2000 Videodisc and Videotape 📁 Section 7-2 Review, p. 142 📖 Student Activity Workbook

SECTION 3 — *After an Interview: Following Up*

SECTION OBJECTIVES	SECTION FEATURES	SECTION RESOURCES
• Apply procedures for following up on an interview, including self-evaluation. • Recognize proper methods of accepting and rejecting employment.	Attitude Counts, p. 146	⊙ Workforce 2000 Videodisc and Videotape 📁 Section 7-3 Review, p. 146 📁 Chapter 7 Review, pp. 148–149 📖 Student Activity Workbook

CHAPTER 7

CHAPTER RESOURCES

- Chapter Transparencies and Lesson Plans
- Chapter 7 Test
- Spanish Resources, Chapter 7
- School-to-Work Activity Handbook, Chapter 7 Activity
- Teacher's Lesson Plans, Chapter 7
- Implementing Block Scheduling, Chapter 7
- Print, Media, and Internet Handbook
- Strategies for Implementing Work-Based Learning
- Strategies for Implementing Connecting Activities

SCANS CORRELATION CHART

Foundation Skills

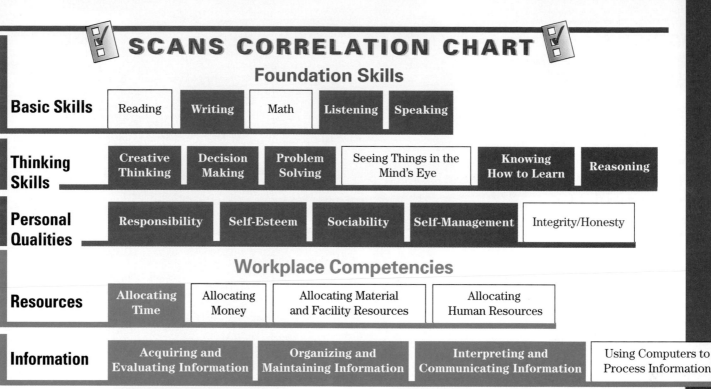

Basic Skills	Reading	Writing	Math	Listening	Speaking

Thinking Skills	Creative Thinking	Decision Making	Problem Solving	Seeing Things in the Mind's Eye	Knowing How to Learn	Reasoning

Personal Qualities	Responsibility	Self-Esteem	Sociability	Self-Management	Integrity/Honesty

Workplace Competencies

Resources	Allocating Time	Allocating Money	Allocating Material and Facility Resources	Allocating Human Resources

Information	Acquiring and Evaluating Information	Organizing and Maintaining Information	Interpreting and Communicating Information	Using Computers to Process Information

Interpersonal Skills	Participating as a Member of a Team	Teaching Others	Serving Clients/ Customers	Exercising Leadership	Negotiating to Arrive at a Decision	Working with Cultural Diversity

Systems	Understanding Systems	Monitoring and Correcting Performance	Improving and Designing Systems

Technology	Selecting Technology	Applying Technology to Task	Maintaining and Troubleshooting Technology

Highlighted blocks indicate areas covered in the Chapter.

Additional Activities

 Internet Connection

When interviewing, forewarned is forearmed. Ask students to use the Internet to find samples of interview questions (and suggested answers) they may be asked when applying for a job. Have them write out their answers to the five most commonly asked questions, and three unusual ones.

 Field Trip Suggestions

To help students put their best foot forward at an interview, arrange to take them to a modeling and/or cosmetology school. Ask someone there to give students a brief, informal and fun introduction into posture, movement, personal grooming, and hairstyles.

 Guest Speaker Suggestions

Invite representatives from temporary agencies that place everyone from assembly line workers to executives. Ask them to discuss the special concerns of temporary workers, the advantages and disadvantages of such an employment method.

Key to Ability Levels

Each section gives skill-building activities. Each activity has been labeled for use with students of various learning styles and abilities.

L1 Level 1 activities are basic activities and should be within the range of all students.

L2 Level 2 activities are average activities and should be within the range of average and above average students.

L3 Level 3 activities are challenging activities designed for the ability range of above average students.

School-Based Learning

Chapter Overview

In this chapter, students will learn how to put their best foot forward in an interview.

Section 7-1 teaches students to prepare for interviews by researching companies and rehearsing.

Section 7-2 focuses on proper attitude, good communication skills, and typical interview questions.

Section 7-3 deals with following up an interview: self-evaluation, thank-you letters, and how to accept or reject a job offer.

Background Information

Write chapter objectives (Sections 7-1, 7-2, and 7-3) on the chalkboard or use the chapter objective transparency for class discussion.

Choose assignments from the *Student Activity Workbook* and write them on the chalkboard.

Have students preview the chapter, looking at pictures, reading captions, and noting content headings.

Preteaching Vocabulary

Write the Key Terms from Sections 7-1, 7-2, and 7-3 on the chalkboard. Have students describe how each term relates to an effective interview.

130

Meeting SPECIAL Needs

Learning Disabled

Many teachers have found that it is important to give students with special needs frequent, specific feedback about how their work is progressing. When you meet with these students, emphasize how their work has improved in many ways compared to previous evaluations.

Interviewing

Section 7-1
*Before an Interview:
Getting Ready*

Section 7-2
*During an Interview:
It's Show Time*

Section 7-3
*After an Interview:
Following Up*

In this video segment, learn the right way to interview for a job.

Journal
Personal Career Plan

In your journal, write three or four questions you would want to ask a job applicant. Think of questions that would help you understand the applicant as an individual and as a possible employee, regardless of particular job skills. Now switch roles from interviewer to applicant; record your ideas for answering the questions.

131

Addressing **LEARNING** Styles

Kinesthetic Learner

Ask students to role-play an interview in pairs, one acting as the interviewer, one as the job seeker. Each job seeker should use different body language and tone of voice to suggest nervousness, confidence, dishonesty, honesty, selfishness, suspicion, arrogance, and so on. Other students should write down what they think the job seeker's body language portrays.

SECTION 7-1

FOCUS

Bell Ringer

Tell students they are interviewing for a job as a sales trainee for a local computer store. Have them list the steps they should take to look their best for their interview.

Introducing the Section

As students share their lists from the Bell Ringer activity, write the steps on the chalkboard. Display pictures of appropriate and inappropriate styles of dress and ask why each one is good or bad for an interview.

Motivational Activity
Discussion

Divide students into teams of four or five. Have each team choose a local job for which they might interview and discuss how to dress, research the company, and prepare for questions they might be asked.

Have each group use cutouts from magazines or other visuals to create a poster illustrating steps they recommend to prepare for the interview.

TEACH

Guided Practice
Teaching Strategies

1. Assign and review Section 7-1.
2. Use the transparency for this section.

Before an Interview: Getting Ready

OBJECTIVES

After studying this section, you will be able to:

- **Identify methods of preparing for interviews, including researching and rehearsing.**
- **Recognize how to dress for success.**

KEY TERM
interview

Your heart's pounding and your palms are sweaty. You're feeling that mix of confidence and excitement that is part of your first job interview. You prepared well, and you're ready to shine!

The **interview**—a formal meeting between an employer and a job applicant—is the employer's chance to meet you as a person, not just as a name on a résumé. Here's where research and rehearsal pay off.

Know Before You Go

How can you stand out in a job market packed with qualified people? Cheryl Nickerson of Nike says, "Please do your research. Be able to ask intelligent questions about the company and what's going on in the industry." Employers, Nickerson adds, want people with a "willingness to learn and grow."

Here are some smart ways to research a company before an interview:

- Use the library for books, magazines, and newspaper articles about the company and current industry events.

- Ask the public relations department for the annual report or press kit to check out the company's history.

- Visit the company's Internet site for up-to-the-minute information.

- Talk to people who work for the company.

Implementing Teamwork

Form research teams of four to five students. Have each team locate information about the fastest growing careers. Ask them to gather information on the education required and the potential income for various positions. Each team should present their findings and give a recommendation about job possibilities.

 Do your homework before you go to an interview. ***What is the advantage of reading articles in current magazines?***

Do these techniques work? Absolutely. The more you know about a company, the better you can showcase your ideas.

Rehearsal Time

Think of a television comedy. The program lasts less than half an hour, but it takes days of rehearsal to get it right. In an interview, you're the cast, and practice will improve your performance.

- **Practice your telephone skills.** When you request an interview, speak clearly and repeat the appointment time and location. Remember: You make your first impression on the telephone.

- **Interview with a friend.** Have a friend ask you typical questions and comment on your interview style.

Chapter 7 • Interviewing **133**

 Extending the Illustration

Have students make a list of ways they can learn about a company in addition to reading magazine articles. (Possibilities include researching business references, such as Dun & Bradstreet, talking with people who buy from or sell to the company, or talking with current or former employees.)

Caption Answer: You will get the latest information and appear knowledgeable at your interview.

Discussion Starter

Ask students what they would do if someone accidentally spilled coffee on them two minutes before an interview. (Interviewers would be impressed with an applicant who explained the situation and conducted the interview with poise.)

✓ SCANS Foundation Skills Connection

L1 **Speaking**

Have students practice speaking skills by having a friend or relative ask them questions and tape their responses.

L2 **Listening**

Have students listen to their taped interviews from the preceding exercise, or tape mock interviews in class. Tell students to listen for inappropriate utterances (for example, "um," "uh") and for the tone in which they answer questions. Are they answering politely? Do they sound self-assured? Have students list things they need to practice and discuss their lists in class.

L3 **Writing**

Have students use the school or public library to find books on successful interviewing and make a list of 20 questions that are typically asked in an interview. Tell students to write answers to each question. Set aside class time to discuss the questions and answers.

SCANS Workplace Competencies Connection

L1 Allocating Time

Tell students that they have three days to prepare for an interview with a local company. Have students prepare a time schedule of what they need to do to prepare for the interview.

L2 Teaching Others

Have students cut pictures from various magazines depicting proper and improper ways to dress for an interview and explain why each one is appropriate or inappropriate.

L3 Acquiring and Evaluating Information

Ask students to look for a job ad that gives a telephone number to call and find out additional information. Then have students write a 50-word paragraph describing how their specific skills would benefit the company.

Independent Practice

Assign as homework the chapter activity in the *School-to-Work Activity Handbook.*

Reading

Have students read an article about a local company and explain how the information might help them in a job interview with that company.

- **Use a mirror.** Are you sitting straight? Are you fidgeting? Is your facial expression alert and pleasant?
- **Use a tape recorder.** Are your words clear? Do you sound confident?
- **Prepare answers to typical questions.** For example, "What can you tell me about yourself?" One clever strategy is to prepare a 30-second "commercial" that highlights your unique talents and skills.

 Rehearsing before an interview will make the interview less stressful. *What should you practice?*

Dress for Success

What does an employer see first when you walk through the door? Not your great personality or your long list of accomplishments. It's your clothes.

Carefully plan what you will wear to your interview. Dress as you would for an actual day on the job, but a little bit better. Match your clothes to the job and, if you can, visit the workplace to see what other workers are wearing.

When in doubt, think conservative. Let your skills stand out, not your tie or dress. Be sure you're neat, clean, and well-groomed, with shined shoes and no fancy jewelry. What would an employer think of the Don'ts in *Figure 7-1?*

134 *Unit 3 • Finding a Job*

Career Do's & Don'ts

When at the Interview...

Do:
- arrive on time and alone.
- have a positive attitude.
- act enthusiastically.
- make sure you are up on current events.

Don't:
- make yourself at home in someone's office until you have been invited.
- chew gum.
- give one-word, yes-or-no answers.
- appear desperate.

Extending the Illustration

Divide students into pairs and have them take turns role-playing the initial greeting between an interviewer and the interviewee. Give students a specific job for which they are applying, or let them choose a job offered by a local company.

Caption Answer: You should practice answering questions, sitting up straight, and speaking clearly.

Extending Figure 7-1

Give students several different interview situations (for example, interviewing for a position in a bank, a construction position, or a retail sales associate position) and have them discuss appropriate dress for each situation.

Caption Answer: You can send the message that you understand what's required in the workplace.

Dressing for Success

Do's	Don'ts
• Make sure hair is clean and combed.	• Use lots of hair spray.
• Shower; use deodorant.	• Use perfume or cologne.
• Shave.	• Use heavy makeup.
• Wear clean shoes.	• Wear sandals.
• Wear conservative and appropriate clothes, neatly pressed.	• Wear clothes that will wrinkle easily.
• Trim fingernails.	• Wear bright nail polish.

▲ **Figure 7-1** Dressing for success means following a certain dress code. What is the most important message you can send with this code?

From Door to Door

Here's a simple but vital tip: Arrive at the interview alone and on time (maybe even make a trial run the day before). It's the mark of a responsible individual.

Bring a pen, a notepad, and two copies of your résumé—even if you've already sent one. Be prepared to fill out an application too, with Social Security number and references ready.

SECTION 7-1 *Review*

Understanding Key Concepts

Using complete sentences, answer the following questions on a separate sheet of paper.

1. How can you research an employer?

2. What methods can you use to rehearse an interview?

3. Why is it important to dress for success at a job interview?

SECTION 7-1 *Review* ANSWERS

1. Use the library to check current magazines and newspapers, visit Internet sites, talk to people who have worked at the company, or call the company for an annual report or a press kit.

2. Rehearse with a friend and ask for comments, practice in front of a mirror, or use a tape recorder.

3. Your clothes will make the first impression. Appropriate dress can help make you feel confident.

ASSESS

Assessment
Content

Have students write two or three sentences describing what to do under each heading: *Before the Interview, Preparing to Interview,* and *Dressing for the Interview.* Evaluate students' papers for accuracy; completeness; and for correct grammar, punctuation, and spelling.

Evaluation

Assign the section review.

Reteaching

Choose a well-known company and have students suggest ways to learn about the company (public library, annual reports, Internet sites, employees). Using the sources suggested in class, have students research the company and discuss their findings in class.

Extending the Content

Assign the appropriate Chapter 7 activities in the *Student Activity Workbook.*

Have students find a book in the school or public library about how to dress for success and make a list of at least five pointers.

CLOSE

Have students respond in writing to how the following comment applies to a job interview: "First impressions are lasting impressions."

FOCUS

Bell Ringer

Tell students to imagine they are interviewing for a job they would like to get. Have them write answers to these questions: Why should I hire you? What could you do for this company that someone else could not?

Introducing the Section

Ask for volunteers to read their answers to the Bell Ringer activity. Then discuss the attitudes that employers look for in employees. Tell students to put themselves in the place of the interviewer and try to phrase their answers to interview questions by identifying personal skills that will help the employer solve problems.

Rehearse typical interview questions with students.

Motivational Activity

Oral Presentation

Have students find job ads they may want to answer. Tell them to prepare three-minute presentations about themselves, responding to the skills and duties described in the ad. Ask students to think of the employer's requirements and see if their skills and abilities can help meet those requirements.

During an Interview: It's Show Time

OBJECTIVES

After studying this section, you will be able to:

- Recognize the importance of displaying the proper attitude.
- Practice clear and accurate communication.
- Answer typical and tough questions.
- Identify strategies for dealing with interview stress.

KEY TERMS

body language
role-playing
problem solving
stress

By preparing for an interview carefully, you can meet the challenge of the interview itself with confidence. With practice, you will be able to project a positive attitude, communicate effectively, and lessen the level of stress.

At the Top of the List: Attitude

When James Coblin of Nucor Steel interviews applicants for a mill in South Carolina, he doesn't focus on job skills. Coblin knows that he can teach workers how to make steel. What he looks for is the right *attitude*. He wants people who can speak honestly to each other, understand other people's feelings, and pitch in to solve problems together.

Let your smile and enthusiasm project your positive attitude. As Brian Johnson of the Dogwater Cafe, a Florida restaurant chain, puts it, "When I'm interviewing, I'm looking for someone with a lot of energy who wants this job more than anything." What do you think *Figure 7-2* says about attitude?

Body Talk

When you interact with people, you communicate through **body language**—the gestures, posture, and eye contact you use to send messages.

Eye contact, for example, shows that you're paying attention. A firm handshake signals self-confidence. Nodding your head shows that you are thinking, while

136 *Unit 3 • Finding a Job*

Addressing Workplace Diversity

Often white males are hired and promoted because they have had previous experience. Some companies correct this by hiring entry-level people who come from all backgrounds. The company then has a large, diverse pool of people from which to promote when the time comes.

What Teachers Believe Is Most Important in Career Success

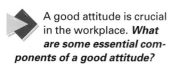

Being persistent
42%

Knowing the
right people
4%

Getting an excellent
academic education
21%

Knowing how
to deal well
with people
32%

Source: *Vocational Education Weekly*

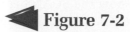 **Figure 7-2**

Persistence is one part of a good attitude. How can you demonstrate to an interviewer that you're persistent?

biting your nails may suggest that you're too nervous to handle the job. What message is body language sending in *Figure 7-3* on pages 138–139?

Good manners count too. Don't chew gum or eat during the interview. Don't throw your coat or papers on the interviewer's desk, and wait until the interviewer asks you to be seated.

Speaking for Success

Interview success depends not only on what you say but also on how you say it. Saying "Hello, it's nice to meet you" in a clear, confident voice immediately creates a positive, adult impression. Listen attentively too. Listening can calm you and keep you focused.

When you speak, use standard English, as you did on your résumé. Don't speak too quickly; enunciate so that the interviewer doesn't have to strain to understand you.

A good attitude is crucial in the workplace. *What are some essential components of a good attitude?*

Chapter 7 • Interviewing **137**

TEACH *(cont'd.)*

L1 Speaking

Have students rehearse introducing themselves during an interview. They should mention their goals, education, skills, and career interests. Have them present introductions to the class.

L2 Creative Thinking

Ask pairs of students to prepare a list of tough interview questions and discuss how to answer those questions. Have students switch partners to take turns asking and answering the questions.

L3 Decision Making

The Equal Employment Opportunity Commission and Title VII of the Civil Rights Act makes it illegal for employers to ask job applicants the following questions.

1. Are you married?

2. How old are you?

3. Do you have any health problems?

4. Have you been convicted of any crimes?

5. Do you plan to have children within the next two years?

6. Do you own a car?

Discuss students' responses to these questions in class and offer suggestions on how they could field them with poise.

Show the SCANS communication skills that employers look for.

Typical Questions

At an interview, an employer tries to find out who you are and what you can do for the company. Be ready to answer standard interview questions such as the following:

- What goals have you set for yourself?
- What do you think are your greatest strengths? Your greatest weaknesses?
- Why did you apply to our company?
- Why would you be right for this job?

▶ **Figure 7-3**

Body Language

At a job interview, make sure your body language says that you're a positive, confident person.

A Establish eye contact. If the interviewer holds out a hand, give it a firm handshake, and be sure to smile. Practice your handshake beforehand, making sure it's firm but not crushing.

B Lean forward slightly in your chair. Look at the interviewer, and listen to questions. Nod your head, when appropriate, as you listen to the interviewer.

▶▶ **Extending Figure 7-3** ◀◀

Ask students to brainstorm a list of actions that might be inappropriate during an interview. (Possible answers include chewing gum, smoking, nervously playing with one's hair, shuffling your feet as you sit, drumming your fingers on a chair, staring out a window.)

Honesty is the best policy. If you don't understand a question, ask the interviewer to clarify it. Interviewers also prefer specific answers that show you think clearly. Compare these answers:

Question: "Do you enjoy working with others or on your own?"

Answer 1: "I enjoy working with others."

Answer 2: "Well, that depends. Some tasks demand teamwork. Our soccer team, for example, won the city tournament because we worked together to put our strategy into action."

Which answer do you prefer? Why?

C Think about your hands as you speak. Don't clench your fists or bite your nails. Use your hands in a relaxed, confident way.

D Be friendly as the interview closes. Shake the interviewer's hand. Even if you don't get this job, the interviewer may be able to refer you to someone else.

Chapter 7 • Interviewing **139**

 SCANS Workplace Competencies Connection

L1 Teaching Others

Tell students they are about to have their first interview. Divide students into groups of three or four and have each person teach the others some techniques for handling stress. After all groups have discussed the issue, have the class select the best techniques.

L2 Exercising Leadership

Have students imagine they are being interviewed for a position as assistant to an executive who travels a lot. The assistant will need to take initiative in running the office smoothly during the executive's absence.

Tell students the interviewer has just asked this question: "Your boss is traveling and cannot be reached until 7 P.M. Tell me what you would do if you received an urgent message for your boss to contact the president of the company immediately." Have students write how they would answer this question, then discuss in class.

Extending the Illustration

(see illustration on top of page 140)
Have students who have part-time jobs and have interviewed before share questions they thought were tough to answer.

Caption Answer: You can brainstorm a list of possible questions and practice answering them with a friend.

L3 **Selecting Technology**

Tell students that an interviewer has just presented this situation: "One of your first duties is to prepare an employee handbook for your department. People have been assigned to write the different parts of the handbook, but you will be responsible for reminding them to turn their work in on time, putting the manuscript on disk and preparing an attractive format. How would you go about doing this job?" Have students write a description of the steps they would take.

(Steps might include writing a memo reminding people of deadlines, asking writers to submit disks instead of hard copy, and studying other companies' handbooks.)

Independent Practice
Reading

Have students choose a book from the school or local library that offers suggestions on how to handle tough interviewing questions. Examples might be *Knock'Em Dead* by Martin Yate, or *What Color Is Your Parachute?* by Richard Nelson Bolles. Ask students to choose five questions that they think they might be asked during an interview. Have them write the answers to each question.

Tough Questions

Sometimes an interviewer may toss a tough question your way. Don't be surprised. The interviewer might want to see how you respond, how you act when you're rattled, or how you think under pressure. You might hear eyebrow raisers such as these:

- How can the company be assured that you'll give us your best effort?

- What qualities do you have that offset your lack of experience?

- Are you going to move to a better job as soon as you gain experience here?

You may want to storm out of the office, but stay calm and don't get defensive. Turn the question around to focus on your skills. For example: "You're right. I'm not experienced, but my work on the Smith project proves that I'm a great organizer!"

If a panel of several people interview you simultaneously, stay calm and address

 Don't panic under tough questioning. *How can you prepare for tough questions?*

one question at a time. You may also face think-on-your-feet questions designed to stump you. Remember: There's often no right answer. It's how you react that counts.

Be prepared to ask your own questions too. Asking nuts-and-bolts questions can demonstrate genuine interest.

- What are the employee benefits?

- What does the health plan cover?

- Does the company pay for training?

Standing in the Spotlight

Some interviews include **role-playing**, in which you are asked to play a role in an invented situation and are evaluated on the skills

Role-playing means acting out a role assigned to you during your interview. *What can an interviewer learn about you through this technique?*

140 *Unit 3 • Finding a Job*

▶ Extending the Illustration

(see illustration above)

Have students think of ways they can improve their presentation skills. (A possible way is to volunteer to speak at assemblies.)

Caption Answer: By observing the way you act out the role, an interviewer can learn about your creative thinking, communication, and leadership skills.

▶ Extending the Illustration

(see illustration on top of page 141)

Have students brainstorm a list of actions they can take before the interview to help reduce their stress. (practicing interviews with teachers, researching about the company)

Caption Answer: deep breathing, reminding yourself that you're doing well, and maintaining perspective

you display. Microtraining Plus in Connecticut, for example, trains people to use computers. Job candidates, however, play the role of teachers and make a presentation on a topic other than computers. David Knise, the company's CEO, says, "We're hiring people for their ability to get up in front of six people they don't know and present material."

You also may face a question that requires **problem solving**. For example, "If you faced a deadline you couldn't meet, what would you do?" Remember that the interviewer is evaluating your thinking skills and your attitude (SCANS skills), not looking for one right answer.

 Interviewing can be stressful. The key is handling it well. *Can you think of some techniques for relaxing?*

Skills Practice

Have students imagine that they work in the human resources department of a business that has received a letter of application that uses slang and does not specify the job the writer of the letter wants or describe the person's education and work experience. What would students say to this person to help improve his or her potential for getting an interview in the future?

Writing: *Memo*

Have students write a memo to a friend giving tips for dressing for an interview, preparing for an interview, and behaving during an interview. Also have them suggest typical questions that may be asked and possible answers.

Teaching Tip

Tell students that on a day you select, they must come to class dressed to interview for a job they especially want. Encourage students to follow the tips given throughout the chapter. On the selected day, divide students into pairs. Have each pair write a 50-word description of each other's appearance and attire.

EXCELLENT BUSINESS PRACTICES

Exploring Opportunities

Patagonia, Inc. designs and distributes clothing for the outdoors. The company has an internship program that allows employees to take paid leaves-of-absence from their jobs for one week to one month and work for a nonprofit organization of their choice.

Employees identify and secure the internships on their own. They also design plans to cover their own job while they are absent.

Employees have volunteered for such diverse tasks as tagging and tracking salmon, monitoring growth of trees in a rain forest, and working at a family planning agency.

All parties involved benefit from this program. The company can support nonprofit groups with labor. Employees get time away from their regular jobs and can add to their personal growth and knowledge of issues important to them and the company.

Thinking Critically

What are the benefits—both to you and to the nonprofit organization—of volunteering your time?

Chapter 7 • Interviewing **141**

Extending EXCELLENT BUSINESS PRACTICES

Answer: To you: opportunity to help others, use talents and explore new interests.

To organization: can expand services without relying on additional funds, can benefit from diverse expertise of volunteers.

Further Application: Have students investigate several nonprofit organizations where they might like to volunteer. Have them find out the guidelines for part-time or summer internships.

Discuss ways students can research companies. For large corporations, the public library will have references such as *Dun & Bradstreet Million Dollar Directory; Thomas Register of American Manufacturers;* and *Standard & Poor's Register of Corporations, Directors, and Executives.*

ASSESS

Assessment

Content

Have students write answers to this question: "Your best friend is going for a first interview tomorrow. What advice would you give him or her?" Have them list at least five suggestions.

(Suggestions might include: display the right attitude, make eye contact and avoid nervous habits, speak clearly and avoid slang, practice answers to anticipated questions.)

Can They Ask You That?

An interviewer does not have the right to ask you about certain matters. For example, you don't have to answer questions about children or child care, age, disabilities, citizenship, lawsuits, or AIDS or HIV status.

If an interviewer asks you a question that isn't job-related, you might say, "I assure you that this area is not a problem. Let me tell you about the skills I have that fit this job."

The Stress Factor

During an interview, you may experience **stress**—mental or physical tension that is the body's natural response to conflict. You may feel stress before you perform in a concert or play in a big game. What should you do?

First of all, tell yourself you're doing well. (You probably are.) Don't worry about saying "the right thing." That can make you more tense. Stop trying so hard—relax and be yourself.

Most important, keep the experience in perspective. The worst thing that can happen is that you don't get the job. There are other jobs. Besides, if the interviewer does not think you're right for the company, the company may not be right for you.

Wrapping It Up

At the end of the interview, you may be offered the job on the spot. If not, thank the interviewer and come up with a reason to check back soon. You might say, "What is a convenient time to call you if I have other questions?"

YOU'RE THE BOSS!

✓ **Solving Workplace Problems**

You are a computer consultant, looking for a part-time employee to help with office chores; you are definitely not looking for an assistant or a trainee. During the interview, the most promising applicant tells you, "I'm so glad to find an opportunity to train as a computer consultant. It's what I've always wanted to do!" How do you respond?

SECTION 7-2 *Review*

Understanding Key Concepts

Using complete sentences, answer the following questions on a separate sheet of paper.

1. Why is a positive attitude essential to succeeding in the workplace?

2. Where in the job market do you see yourself in five years?

3. Why do you think employers ask tough questions?

4. How do you control interview stress?

SECTION 7-2 *Review* ANSWERS

1. People with positive attitudes do not create conflicts at work.

2. Answers will vary.

3. to see how the applicant responds to difficult situations

4. by reminding yourself that you're doing well, by relaxing and being yourself

Teaching YOU'RE THE BOSS!

✓ Possible responses: Explain clearly that the applicant will not have an opportunity to train as a computer consultant. Be prepared for him or her to withdraw his or her application as a result. Consider changing your plans and discuss with the applicant some possibilities for training after an initial work period.

CASE STUDY

Exploring Careers: Personal Service

Helen Choi
Hairstylist

Q: **How did you get interested in hairstyling?**

A: My profession in Korea was painting. It was hard to use my painting skills here, in the United States. I had a friend who was in beauty school. I used to take her to school and pick her up. As I waited for her, I thought, "I could do this. I could go to beauty school."

Q: **Was beauty school your only training?**

A: Most of my classmates got out of beauty school, got their licenses, and went to work, but I wanted to learn more. I decided to be a hairstylist's assistant and to learn from more experienced people. I was lucky. I had the best teachers. I spent about a year as an assistant. I started out sweeping the floor. It was hard work but good experience. Eventually, the boss said I could begin cutting customers' hair. When I didn't have customers, I watched the other hairstylists. I came in early and stayed late. The customers appreciated that. You build a business relationship and clientele that way.

Q: **What do you like about your work?**

A: It's exciting, challenging, and stimulating. It's creative. It's nonstop studying. Hairstyles change when the fashion changes.

Thinking Critically

What kinds of personal services do you think might grow in demand in the future?

CAREER FACTS

Nature of the Work:
Counsel clients about hairstyles; keep up on styles; cut hair; schedule appointments; maintain customer relations.

Training or Education Needed:
Approximately one year of beauty school; licensing may be required.

Aptitudes, Abilities, and Skills:
Listening, speaking, and interpersonal skills; problem-solving and decision-making skills; self-management skills; ability to work with your hands; an interest in trends and fashion; an enjoyment working with people; detail-oriented; ability to stand for hours.

Salary Range:
Average starting salary—$15,000; average salary after 5 to 10 years—$30,000-$50,000.

Career Path:
Work as an assistant to a hairdresser; rent space in a salon; start own salon.

Chapter 7 • Interviewing **143**

Evaluation
Assign the section review.

Reteaching
Tell students to ask classmates, teachers, and administrative staff at least ten questions about how to prepare for an interview as well as what to do during the interview. Have students compile answers, then write a list of at least ten responses. Discuss the results in class.

Extending the Content
Assign the appropriate Chapter 7 activities in the *Student Activity Workbook*.

Have students create their own personal press kits announcing their career goals, personal traits, work skills and knowledge, and career experience.

CLOSE
Have students complete this statement: "I can make a difference in how an employer sees me during a job interview by . . . ." (Students should stress highlighting their skills, demonstrating a positive attitude, and being a team player.)

Extending the CASE STUDY

Answer: Some examples are the beauty fields, child care, massage therapy, personal shopping, interior decorating, personal training, small party catering, tutoring, private lessons of all types, pet care, and gardening and home care.

Further Application: Have students discuss why they might pursue self-imposed apprenticeships in their chosen careers after they complete their initial training. Assisting well-known professionals in their fields might give them insight into the field, give them techniques to help them earn more, and give them recognition for their initiative.

SECTION 7-3

FOCUS

Bell Ringer

Have students make a list of at least five criteria they would use in deciding whether or not to accept a job offer.

Introducing the Section

Ask students to share their lists from the Bell Ringer activity. Then discuss the details of a job offer, such as the time generally given for the applicant to think over the offer, how to handle additional questions, and writing an acceptance letter.

Motivational Activity
Writing

Tell students they have just been interviewed for jobs as real estate sales associates. Have students write follow-up letters expressing interest in the positions and emphasizing why their skills can benefit the company.

TEACH

Guided Practice
Teaching Strategies

1. Assign and review Section 7-3.
2. Use the transparency for this section.

SCANS Foundation Skills Connection

L1 Self-Esteem

Have students write a brief paragraph describing the skills they already have and how they can gain new ones.

After an Interview: Following Up

OBJECTIVES

After studying this section, you will be able to:

- **Apply procedures for following up on an interview, including self-evaluation.**
- **Recognize proper methods of accepting and rejecting employment.**

The interview process doesn't end when you walk out the door of an employer's office. It's important to consider how you did at the interview. What went well? What skills do you need to sharpen? Another major consideration is how you will follow up on the interview. For example, how will you thank the interviewer? How will you get the interviewer to remember you? Most important, of course, is what you'll do if you're offered a job—or rejected.

Tying Up the Loose Ends

You've gotten through the interview! Now's the time to evaluate your own performance.

- Jot down some notes. Did you speak clearly? Did you use standard English? Show enthusiasm? Forget something important? Can you think of any additional information about yourself that you should have provided? Use the notes to improve your next interview.

- Send a follow-up letter soon—even the same day as the interview—in which you thank the interviewer, reinforce how your skills can benefit the company, and restate your continued interest in the job.

- Don't forget to call back.

Workforce 2000 Trends

New technology can generate new jobs. In 1986, one survey showed that 43 percent of employees working for companies employing 20–99 workers had jobs that had not existed four years before. Most of the new jobs of the future will be found in small to medium-sized companies.

Everyone likes to be thanked, even an interviewer.
What might you mention about the interview in your letter?

Accepting: See You Monday Morning

You hear those magic words: "The job's yours." Now what do you do? Believe it or not, you don't have to say yes immediately. If you want time to think about it, ask the employer if you can take a day to decide. List the job's pros and cons before calling back to accept the job. Ask for a formal offer letter for your files. Send an acceptance letter, and keep a copy.

Rejecting: Thanks, But No Thanks

Suppose an employer wants to hire you, but the salary is low or the job isn't exactly what you were looking for. Don't say no at the interview. Take a day to think about it, and talk it over with other people. You might change your mind, or you might be able to negotiate the salary. When you call back, thank the interviewer, give a reason for your answer, and keep your

Chapter 7 • Interviewing **145**

Extending the Illustration

Have students tell what follow-up letters say about them as job applicants. (They indicate to the interviewer that they are interested in the job, follow through on their actions, and know the proper post-interview etiquette.)

Caption Answer: You might mention topics discussed during the interview, how your skills would benefit the company, and how much you're interested in the job.

Assessment

Performance

Divide students into pairs and have each pair role-play a follow-up telephone call for a job interview of the students' choice. Evaluate students' understanding of why follow-up is important and determine whether their comments are appropriate and helpful.

Evaluation

Assign the section review.

MINI QUIZ

True-False

1. You can learn everything you need to know about a company during the interview. (false)

2. An interviewer who is concerned about an applicant's attitude wants to know how well the person will work with others. (true)

3. If an interviewer asks a question you know is not legal, it's best to answer it anyway. (false)

Attitude Counts ✓

Ready—set—relax! Those are good starting instructions for a job interview, a major test, or any other potentially stressful situation. Take the time to prepare yourself in advance. Shortly before the interview or test, review carefully. Then relax; feeling calm and confident will help you do your best.

options open. Who knows what the future may bring?

Handling Rejection

If an employer turns you down, consider it a learning experience. Ask why you weren't hired. Do you need more training? How did you come across in your interview? Feedback will help you in future interviews.

Sometimes it helps to make a pro/con list before deciding whether to take a job. **What might be on such a list?**

SECTION 7-3 *Review*

Understanding Key Concepts

Using complete sentences, answer the following questions on a separate sheet of paper.

1. What questions could you ask yourself to evaluate an interview?

2. What are some disadvantages to instantly accepting or rejecting a job?

146   *Unit 3 • Finding a Job*

SECTION 7-3 *Review* ANSWERS

1. Was I enthusiastic enough? Did my body language convey confidence? Did I speak clearly? Did I listen carefully?

2. Possible answers: After talking to people, you might find out negative points about the employer. You should never shut the door on opportunities at any company.

Extending the Illustration

Ask students what else they might do to help them make a job decision. (Possible answers include discussing the job offer with parents, a friend or relative, or a career counselor and evaluating how the job fits one's overall career plan.)

Caption Answer: The list might include salary, job duties, commuting time, and what potential colleagues are like.

SECTION 7-1 Summary

- Prepare carefully for an interview. Research the company and current events in the industry.
- Rehearse before an interview. Practice with a mirror and a tape recorder, and ask a friend for comments.
- Plan what you will wear at an interview. Dress conservatively and avoid flashy items. Appear neat and well-groomed.
- Arrive on time.

Key Term

interview *(p. 132)*

SECTION 7-2 Summary

- Employers will be evaluating your attitude and your communication skills. Be positive and enthusiastic.
- You will probably be asked some typical questions at an interview. Be prepared to answer them.
- You may be asked some tough questions designed to rattle you. Be prepared to respond to them with a calm and positive attitude.
- Some questions may involve role-playing or problem solving to evaluate your ability to think on your feet.
- Some questions are illegal for an employer to ask during an interview. You are not required to answer them.

Key Terms

body language *(p. 136)*
role-playing *(p. 140)*
problem solving *(p. 141)*
stress *(p. 142)*

SECTION 7-3 Summary

- Evaluate your performance after an interview. Send a follow-up letter.
- Follow standard procedures for accepting or rejecting employment. Don't say no during an interview. Always leave the door open for the future.

Chapter 7 • Interviewing **147**

Use the Testmaker to create a customized test for Chapter 7.

Reteaching

1. Arrange for a group of local businesspeople (four or five) to conduct interviews with your students (one per student). Then have students list the name of the interviewer, the job duties described, the job skills needed, and other notes that might be helpful for a future interview. Have students write a follow-up letter to the person who interviewed them.

2. Assign and review the vocabulary, chapter questions, and activities from the Chapter Review.

Extending the Content

Assign the appropriate Chapter 7 activities in the *Student Activity Workbook*.

Have students learn from rejection by writing follow-up letters to an interviewer who did not offer them the job they wanted. Tell students to thank the interviewer for the opportunity to meet with her or him and to ask for comments about the specific skills the company is seeking.

CLOSE

See the Unit Closure and Unit Evaluation located on page 109.

Teaching Attitude Counts ✓

Let students meet in small groups and brainstorm a list of relaxation techniques; encourage them to list both techniques they have tried and those they may have read or heard about. Then ask group members to discuss the listed techniques: Which would you like to try? Why?

Computer Activity

Have students research the five fastest growing careers to find out how many new jobs may be created within the next four years. Using a spreadsheet software package and the charting function, have students design a chart or graph to illustrate the numerical data from their research.

Answers

Reviewing Key Terms

Paragraphs will vary, but students should demonstrate awareness of the correct definitions of terms.

Recalling Key Concepts

1. a
2. c
3. c
4. b
5. a

Thinking Critically

1. You can dress properly, express enthusiasm, be honest and specific in answering questions, and remain calm when asked tough questions.

2. You can send positive messages by maintaining good eye contact, by shaking the interviewer's hand firmly, and by sitting up straight. You can send negative messages by twitching nervously, by avoiding eye contact, by slouching, and by invading the interviewer's personal space.

3. Rehearsing alone may help you feel less nervous, concentrate more fully, and speak more naturally. Rehearsing with a friend may help you see yourself as others see you, think on your feet, and adjust to constructive criticism.

4. An applicant who asks such questions would appear to be ambitious

Reviewing Key Terms

On a separate sheet of paper, write a paragraph describing how you would prepare for an interview. Use the terms below in your paragraph.

interview   stress
body language   problem solving
role-playing

Recalling Key Concepts

Choose the correct answer for each item below. Write your answers on a separate sheet of paper.

1. Researching a company before an interview enables you to ____.
   (a) ask intelligent questions
   (b) impress your friends
   (c) dress for success

2. Preparing a 30-second "commercial" about yourself is a good way to ____.
   (a) research a company
   (b) negotiate a salary
   (c) rehearse for an interview

3. Which of the following topics is illegal for an employer to ask about? ____
   (a) your skills   (b) your goals
   (c) your citizenship

4. Interviewers look for applicants ____.
   (a) wearing fashionable clothes
   (b) demonstrating a positive attitude
   (c) with a sense of humor

5. In a follow-up letter, you should ____.
   (a) restate your continued interest
   (b) invent additional references
   (c) apologize for being nervous

148   *Unit 3 • Finding a Job*

Thinking Critically

Using complete sentences, answer each of the questions below on a separate sheet of paper.

1. In what ways can you stand out positively at an interview?

2. Summarize the importance of body language at a job interview.

3. Compare rehearsing for an interview alone and rehearsing with a friend. Identify the advantages of each method.

4. What would you infer about a job applicant who asks questions about a job's responsibilities and chances for advancement in the company?

5. Imagine that you are an employer. List the five most important qualities of a great job applicant in order of priority. Give reasons for the order.

SCANS Foundation Skills and Workplace Competencies

Basic Skills: *Speaking*

1. Compose a 30-second "commercial" to summarize your abilities. In it, act as if you were being interviewed.

Thinking Skills: *Reasoning*

2. An interviewer asks Wendy: "Do you plan to have children anytime soon?" How should she answer this question?

Personal Skills: *Self-Esteem*

3. Michael is in the middle of a job interview. Suddenly, he feels very stressed. Write a paragraph telling what he can do to calm down and finish the interview successfully.

and energetic, seriously interested in performing well, and planning to make a long-term commitment to the company.

5. Possible answers: a positive attitude, a sense of responsibility, ability to deal with pressure, flexibility, and leadership skills; reasons will vary, but students should emphasize the importance of a positive attitude by listing it first.

SCANS Foundation Skills and Workplace Competencies

1. "Commercials" will vary but should be positive, honest, and enthusiastic.

2. This is an illegal question. She should turn the conversation back to skills.

3. He should tell himself he's doing fine, and keep the interview in perspective.

Interpersonal Skills: *Exercising Leadership*

4. An interviewer says to you: "You have no experience in this field. Why should I hire you?" In a few sentences, describe how you could answer this tough question in a way that shows maturity and ability to take charge of a situation.

Connecting Academics to the Workplace

Social Studies

1. Ella wants to research trends in the computer industry before her job interview at a software company. Using the library, current magazines, newspapers, or the Internet, find relevant information. Then describe some ways she might use this information in an interview.

Human Relations

2. Kyle has an interview scheduled with a company that is based in a foreign country. He wants to make sure he understands the body language in this country. Choose a country (such as Japan, Saudi Arabia, Kenya, Norway), and research its "rules" about body language. What movements and gestures should Kyle be aware of?

Math

3. It is a 20-minute ride to Laura's job interview. However, due to construction, she will have to take a detour that will add 15 minutes. If she wants to arrive 15 minutes early, how much time should she allow for the trip?

Developing Teamwork and Leadership Skills

You are part of a hiring team for a chain of department stores. You need to hire a person for an entry-level position in sales. Describe the job and identify the skills it requires. Then create a four-person role-playing exercise that will enable candidates to display those skills. As a team, decide which person you would hire, and explain the reasons for your decision.

Real-World Workshop

In groups of three, identify a job that interests you. Then research skills involved in the job. Separately, develop interview questions. Have two members act as interviewer and applicant, while the third member evaluates the applicant. After each member of the team has served in each role, comment on each other's interview style.

School-to-Work Connection

Talk to an employer or a manager who has interviewed job applicants. Ask this person about common mistakes that people make during job interviews. What advice would this person give every applicant? Report your findings to the class.

Individual Career Plan

Using standard business style, write a thank-you letter to an employer. Mention your unique skills, and express your enthusiasm for the job. Proofread for standard English, spelling, and punctuation.

Chapter 7 • Interviewing **149**

---

2. Answers will vary, depending on choice of country. Students might focus on rules concerning hand gestures, customs of dress, and interactions between men and women.

3. Laura should allow at least 50 minutes.

Developing Teamwork and Leadership Skills

After "hiring" a classmate, the team should describe the job, explain what skills it requires, how they came up with the exercise, what skills the exercise was supposed to reveal, and explain why they made the decision they did.

Real-World Workshop

Each student should evaluate how well the others answered the interviewer's questions, how well they projected a positive attitude, and how effective their speaking style and body language were.

School-to-Work Connection

Responses and reports will vary, but students should clearly identify their sources, specify the questions asked, and present the answers in a clear and organized way.

Individual Career Plan

Letters should use standard English and follow business format. Students should remind employers of their skills and be sure to leave the door open for future contact.

---

4. You could admit that you are not experienced but that you do have skills that would make you right for the job and emphasize, for example, your leadership of other projects, which shows that you are organized, a quick learner, or a good motivator.

Connecting Academics to the Workplace

1. Answers will vary depending on sources used. Ella might, for example, find articles about technology that will combine computers and television, then offer her own suggestions for ways to improve or market that technology.

Aspects of Industry: Management

Students who are fairly sure of their future careers may use the Labs to investigate all the aspects of industry for one career. Other students may want to investigate a different job cluster with each Lab.

STEP A

To find two job possibilities in each job cluster, students may use existing lists of jobs, brainstorm with other students, or research the possibilities in the *Occupational Outlook Handbook (OOH)* or other career references.

You might want to have them read the classifieds over a period of weeks, looking for jobs that interest them. How do their skills and experiences fit those jobs?

STEP B

The purpose of the interview is two-fold. First, students add to their contact lists. Second, they get invaluable information about hiring and working practices, benefits, and what is expected of employees.

To help students prepare for this interview and all the others that will follow in their lives, you may want to have them do practice interviews. Have them do the interview in front of the class with other teachers playing the role of the employer. Emphasize that students should regard this as their dress rehearsal and take it seriously. Students should

ASPECTS OF INDUSTRY: *Management*

Overview

In Unit Three, you learned about the process of finding, applying for, and interviewing for a job. In this Unit Lab, you will use what you have learned while exploring another aspect of industry: **Management.**

The Management aspect of industry covers the decisions managers make about their products and services, company growth, and profitability. It also includes managing employees—not only assigning and overseeing their work, but also planning how to keep employees interested in and enthusiastic about their work. Continuing education, involvement in company decisions, and flexible working schedules are a few ways to achieve that goal.

Tools

1. Internet

2. Trade and business magazines

3. Business newspapers

4. Personal interviews

Procedures

STEP A

Choose one of the 15 job clusters from Figure 3-1 in Chapter 3 that interests you. You may choose the same cluster you explored in the previous Lab, or a different one. Choose two jobs in the job cluster that you would seriously think about pursuing.

Using trade and business magazines, newspapers, and the Internet, research how the industry represented by the jobs you have chosen is affected by new management practices.

STEP B

Identify a local corporation that employs people in one of the jobs you have chosen. Ask friends, family, teachers, and counselors for leads. You may also check with your local Chamber of Commerce, which may have a directory of member businesses.

If possible, research that particular corporation. The Chamber of Commerce may have profiled the business in its newsletter, or the local newspaper may have run stories about the business.

Contact the personnel manager at each company. This should not be the same manager that you interviewed in previous

150

dress appropriately for the job they're applying for, have their résumé prepared, and ask appropriate questions. After the interview is over, have other students critique—not criticize—the student's performance. Emphasize that all comments are to be constructive. Comments such as "Your voice sounded weak and uncertain," are allowable. "You sounded like a wimp," is not.

If one of the students can operate a video camera, or if the school has a video program, you might want to tape the interviews. Watching themselves on videotape can help students become aware of their undesirable habits.

assignments. Ask permission to do a 20- to 30-minute interview. Make it clear that you are not interviewing for a job, but that you are seeking information for a class presentation.

Some of the questions you might ask are:

1. What qualities are most important in an employee?

2. What does the employer look for during an interview?

3. What might convince a manager to hire a student with little experience?

4. What kind of training/ education program does the company offer, if any?

5. Do employees participate in company decision or policy making?

6. What kinds of benefits do employees receive?

Remember, you are building your contact list through these exercises. Present yourself in as positive a light as possible.

STEP C

Working in groups of three or four, compare notes on your interviews. On what topics did the managers agree? On what did they disagree? What suggestions did the managers make? What kinds of attitudes did they display?

REPORT

Write a one-page, word-processed report using the information you gathered in your research.

- First, mention all the important information from the interview and discussions. What did you learn that will help you prepare for a future job interview?
- Then, focus on the personnel manager's perspective. Why does the company manage employees the way that it does? How do its management policies affect its products, service, marketing ability, and profitability? Does this give you insight into what will be expected of you as an employee?

Keep your research, interview notes, and report in a folder entitled "Career Exploration."

151

STEP C

Students should work together to discuss their findings. In many kinds of work, particularly in managerial positions, students will be called on to work in teams to discuss viewpoints.

After the teams have discussed their findings, open the class to a discussion. Are students surprised by any information? Encouraged? Discouraged? What would the benefits be of working for each company? What might the drawbacks be?

Report

Students should begin to evaluate their own strengths and weaknesses as a potential interviewee, and as a potential employee.

By looking at the decisions managers must make regarding employees, students better understand their roles in the workplace. You may want to have students role-play a management situation such as the following: a decision to lay off employees, a decision to promote an employee, or the setting up of a training or education program. Have them think in terms of what is best for the company while making their decisions.

Unit Overview

Unit 4 teaches students the skills they need to enter and succeed in the world of work. Students will learn how to make a good first impression. They will also learn what to expect from an employer in terms of salary and benefits. This unit will help students clarify their thoughts about ethical behavior. Finally, they will learn how to stay fit and healthy and to deal with legal issues in the workplace.

Introducing the Unit

Ask students to make two lists of expectations: first, have them write what they expect from a job, such as salary, working conditions, fairness; second, have them write what they think an employer expects of them, such as ethical behavior, reliability, honesty, and good work skills and habits.

Write students' responses on the chalkboard and discuss overlaps between employer and employee expectations.

Unit Project

Have students develop relationships with local employers. As you work through the unit, give students specific questions to ask employers that relate to chapter content. Have students keep notebooks of the questions and answers and turn them in, completed and signed by each employer, at the end of the unit.

UNIT 4

Joining the Workforce

Chapter 8
Beginning a New Job

Chapter 9
Workplace Ethics

Chapter 10
Developing a Positive Attitude

Chapter 11
Workplace Health and Safety

Chapter 12
Workplace Legal Matters

152

Developing Community Involvement

As a class, work with social service agencies to identify elderly or disabled people who need work done around their homes. Working in teams, students could clean gutters, rake leaves, mow lawns, etc. There may already be organizations in your area (such as Christmas in April) that offer such services and which would be glad of your help.

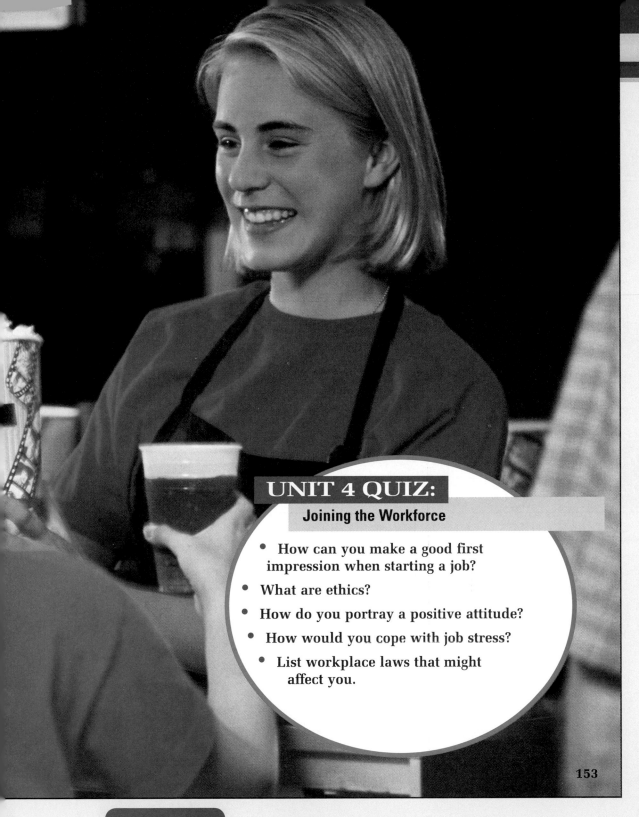

Resources for Enrichment

Books

- *First Job* by Fein
- *Martindale-Hubbell Law Directory*
- *Young Person's Occupational Outlook Handbook* JIST

Magazines

Prevention, Health, Psychology Today

Organizations

- American Bar Association
- (Your State) Bar Association
- Legal Aid Society

Internet

FitnessLink—health, fitness, and wellness information: http://www.fitnesslink.com

American Dietetic Association—information about diet and nutrition: http://www.eatright.org

Directory of Attorneys—listing of lawyers throughout the United States: http://www.lawyerlink.com/listusa.html

Unit Closure

Have students write a 250–300 word summary of what they learned by working with local employers to complete their unit projects.

Unit Evaluation

Administer the reproducible test for Unit 4, which you will find in your Performance Assessment Binder, or construct your own test using the IBM Testmaker Software.

UNIT 4 QUIZ:

Joining the Workforce

- How can you make a good first impression when starting a job?
- What are ethics?
- How do you portray a positive attitude?
- How would you cope with job stress?
- List workplace laws that might affect you.

153

Building Partners in Industry

Your school will want to offer its partners in business and industry as much positive recognition as possible. Here are a few suggestions:

- Ask students to write school newspaper articles about those businesses.

- Invite coverage from local media (newspapers, TV).

- Send memos or newsletters to parents about your business partners.

- Ask students to create posters or banners acknowledging the support of those businesses.

• • • PLANNING GUIDE • • •
Chapter 8

SECTION OBJECTIVES	SECTION FEATURES	SECTION RESOURCES
• Anticipate and manage the anxieties and challenges of a first day at work. • Discuss the proper ways to dress for work. • Understand company policies.	Personal Career Plan, p. 155 Ethics in Action, p. 157 You're the Boss!, p. 158 Excellent Business Practices, p. 159 Career Do's and Don'ts, p. 162 Exploring Careers, p. 163	Workforce 2000 Videodisc and Videotape Section 8-1 Review, p. 162 Student Activity Workbook

SECTION 2 — *What You Can Expect from Your Employer*

SECTION OBJECTIVES	SECTION FEATURES	SECTION RESOURCES
• Describe typical ways that employers pay workers. • Explain benefits that employers offer workers. • Discuss the significance of employee performance reviews.		Workforce 2000 Videodisc and Videotape Section 8-2 Review, p. 168 Chapter 8 Review, pp. 170–171 Student Activity Workbook

CHAPTER 8

CHAPTER RESOURCES

- Chapter Transparencies and Lesson Plans
- Chapter 8 Test
- Spanish Resources, Chapter 8
- School-to-Work Activity Handbook, Chapter 8 Activity
- Teacher's Lesson Plans, Chapter 8
- Implementing Block Scheduling, Chapter 8
- Print, Media, and Internet Handbook
- Strategies for Implementing Work-Based Learning
- Strategies for Implementing Connecting Activities

Career Notes

SCANS CORRELATION CHART

Foundation Skills

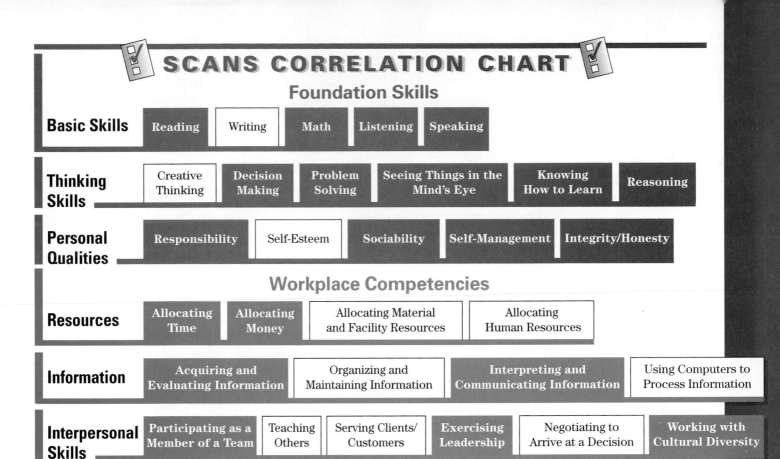

Basic Skills	Reading	Writing	Math	Listening	Speaking

Thinking Skills	Creative Thinking	Decision Making	Problem Solving	Seeing Things in the Mind's Eye	Knowing How to Learn	Reasoning

Personal Qualities	Responsibility	Self-Esteem	Sociability	Self-Management	Integrity/Honesty

Workplace Competencies

Resources	Allocating Time	Allocating Money	Allocating Material and Facility Resources	Allocating Human Resources

Information	Acquiring and Evaluating Information	Organizing and Maintaining Information	Interpreting and Communicating Information	Using Computers to Process Information

Interpersonal Skills	Participating as a Member of a Team	Teaching Others	Serving Clients/ Customers	Exercising Leadership	Negotiating to Arrive at a Decision	Working with Cultural Diversity

Systems	Understanding Systems	Monitoring and Correcting Performance	Improving and Designing Systems

Technology	Selecting Technology	Applying Technology to Task	Maintaining and Troubleshooting Technology

Highlighted blocks indicate areas covered in the Chapter.

Additional Activities

Internet Connection

Ask students to scan the Internet to find at least two companies they might like to work for. They should look at the company's mission/vision statement, number of employees, product, benefits and training. They should include only companies that suit their lifestyle choices and values.

Field Trip Suggestions

Work with another high school and arrange a "first work day" tour of the facility. Ask staff to take groups of "new employees" around the school and show them the ropes: introduce them to appropriate personnel, show them the staff lounge, give them an outline of their schedules and duties, and so on.

Guest Speaker Suggestions

Invite young middle managers— one male, one female—from a local company to speak to your class about how they started their careers, how they have advanced, and what their plans are for the future.

Key to Ability Levels

Each section gives skill-building activities. Each activity has been labeled for use with students of various learning styles and abilities.

L1 Level 1 activities are basic activities and should be within the range of all students.

L2 Level 2 activities are average activities and should be within the range of average and above average students.

L3 Level 3 activities are challenging activities designed for the ability range of above average students.

Beginning a New Job

Chapter Overview

In this chapter, students learn how to start their jobs on the right foot by learning what the employer expects from them and what they, in turn, can expect from the employer.

Section 8-1 examines dressing appropriately, company orientation programs, and company policies.

Section 8-2 covers what employees can expect from their employers.

Background Information

Write chapter objectives (Sections 8-1 and 8-2) on the chalkboard or use the chapter objective transparency for discussion.

Choose assignments from the *Student Activity Workbook* and write them on the chalkboard.

Have students preview the chapter, looking at pictures and reading captions, and noting content headings. Ask students to describe what they expect to learn in this chapter.

Preteaching Vocabulary

Write the Key Terms from Sections 8-1 and 8-2 on the chalkboard. Have students describe how each term relates to what they need to know before starting their first job.

154

Meeting SPECIAL Needs

Learning Disabled

Many teachers find that students with special needs understand visually presented materials more readily than isolated numbers. For example, if students' progress is presented in graph form, as opposed to numerical grades, the students are better able to understand how they are doing.

Chapter 8

Beginning a New Job

Section 8-1
Preparing for Your First Day on the Job

Section 8-2
What You Can Expect from Your Employer

In this video segment, find out what to expect on the first days of your new job.

Journal
Personal Career Plan

The first day on a new job is a time of excitement and anxiety. In your journal, write a list of questions and concerns you might have on your first day of work. Then think about the facts and ideas that might give you confidence on your first day. Write another list of your confidence-inspiring ideas.

155

School-to-Work Connecting Activities

Students can prepare for future careers by enrolling in technology or vocational courses. Have students chart their career options based on their personal goals, financial means, and plans to attend college or enter the workforce after high school. For their charts, tell students to identify each option and describe what they would be doing (for example, live at home and work at a local company, or attend community college and work part-time). Have students evaluate options to make decisions about further high school courses they should take.

Work-Based Learning Strategies and Activities

Work with your local Chamber of Commerce and several business executives to identify jobs that will need to be filled by employers in your area over the next several years. Identify the most common skills and begin incorporating the teaching of those skills into your school's curriculum.

WORKFORCE 2000 Training Video

Have students view the video and perform the interactive exercises to reinforce important chapter concepts and thinking processes.

Chapter 8

Addressing **LEARNING** Styles

Linguistic Learner

Have students imagine their first day at work in great detail. They should write down what they'll wear, how they'll get to work, who their coworkers will be, what their orientation will be like, what will be expected of them and how they think they'll feel. They should also include how they will feel and what they will do at the end of the day.

Preparing for Your First Day on the Job

OBJECTIVES

After studying this section, you will be able to:

- Anticipate and manage the anxieties and challenges of a first day at work.
- Discuss the proper ways to dress for work.
- Understand company policies.

KEY TERMS

company culture
orientation
mentors

Getting a new job is like moving to a different country. Who knows what's waiting for you there? Many unexpected things can happen. What can you do to prepare? What do employers expect from you? How can you deal with first-day anxieties?

Having a Good First Day

Your first day on the job can be exciting. Enjoy it. It will almost certainly be stressful as well. You can't avoid the stress, but you can prepare yourself for it.

Figure out how long it will take you to get ready and to get to work. Then get up even earlier. Don't make yourself more nervous by running late and then hurrying to get to your job on time.

At work, you'll be introduced to your new coworkers. You'll probably forget their names. Don't worry. You can't be expected to remember everyone's name at first. Just ask again. A simple trick that may help you remember is to repeat each person's name out loud as you're introduced. Then use the name again while talking to the person.

Company Culture

As soon as you walk in to work as an employee, you'll become immersed in the **company culture**. This is the behavior, attitudes, values, and habits of the employees and owners that are unique to a particular company.

156 *Unit 4 • Joining the Workforce*

Plan to get to your new job early. **What would your new supervisor think if you were late?**

Learning the company culture will take you a while. Until you understand it, take your time trying to fit in. You don't have to do a lot of talking your first few days. Concentrate on listening and observing. Watch your coworkers to learn how they work and interact. The SCANS skills of listening, knowing how to learn, and sociability will help you.

Dressing for the Job

One anxiety about your first day of work may concern how to dress. What's appropriate? How dressed up should you get? What makes this matter even more

ETHICS in Action

You and your best friend are trainees with a large corporation. Everything has gone well for both of you—until the company announces a drug test. Your friend says, "I can't do a drug test today. I'm taking lots of allergy medications. I've got a plan to get out of the test, but I need your help." How will you respond? Why?

confusing is that dress codes keep changing. Unless your job calls for a uniform, it's hard to know what to wear.

Office workers once wore suits and ties, skirts and high heels. That rule no longer applies in most places. The majority of companies are now moving toward more casual dress. Unfortunately, there's no "norm." What's correct in one office is inappropriate in another. Jeans and a rugby shirt might be fine at one place but too casual at another.

To complicate matters further, many companies now have "casual Fridays" and "jeans days." These allow even more casual dress. Even on these days, though, not everything goes.

If you work in a manufacturing plant, in a garage, or on a construction site, your choices may be more predictable. Even dress codes for these jobs have changed in recent years, however.

How do you know what to wear? When you show up for your interview, observe what other people are wearing. Make a point of asking about the dress code. It's

Chapter 8 • Beginning a New Job **157**

Guided Practice

Teaching Strategies

1. Assign and review Section 8-1.

2. Use the transparency for this section.

3. Assign and review the Case Study.

Teaching Tip

According to one survey, one of the major weaknesses that corporations find in first-time employees is that their expectations are unrealistic. To help students learn what is expected of them, and what they can expect, ask three or four of your former students who have been working full-time for at least a year to serve on a panel to discuss workplace expectations. Have them talk about how their expectations and employers' differed, and what they did to adjust.

Discussion Starter

Ask students how they would respond in this situation: "After finishing your own work for the day, you notice something else that needs to be done. You go ahead and do it. Your boss thanks you for your initiative, but a coworker later accuses you of trying to become the boss's pet."

Teaching ETHICS in Action

Have students follow these steps to help them make a decision:

1. What are the ethical issues?

2. What are the alternatives?

3. Who are the affected parties?

4. How do the alternatives affect the parties?

5. What is your decision?

Extending the Illustration

(see illustration on page 158)

Ask students to discuss what they are saying about themselves with the way they dress.

Caption Answer: wrong: oversized earrings, bright or garish colors, faddish cap; right: conservative colors, simple jewelry, clean clothing

TEACH *(cont'd.)*

Critical Thinking

Ask students to write a brief response to the following scenario:

Coworker: Did you hear the latest gossip about Susan? Alena saw her at the movies on Friday with Ms. Evans' assistant. She's probably trying to find a way to get a raise or promotion.

Discuss how office gossip can undermine their careers.

SCANS Foundation Skills Connection

L1 Reading

Obtain a portion of an employee manual from a local business. Have students list questions they have about the company's policies. Ask a representative of the company to speak to your class to answer questions.

L2 Seeing Things in the Mind's Eye

Have students visualize themselves in the following workplace situations: (1) a coworker is rude to them, (2) at the end of the day the boss asks why the work they were given isn't finished yet, (3) they observe a coworker sneaking out early.

Office casual means casual "business" clothing, not casual wear. You may need a separate wardrobe of work clothing. **What's wrong with the clothing these people are wearing? What's right?**

also a good idea to ask for examples because "office casual" means different things in different companies.

Still uncertain? Consider these pointers:

- Err on the side of conservative dress.
- Avoid bright or garish colors and clothes that are faddish.
- Keep jewelry simple and not too large.
- Wear clean clothes, and never wear clothes that are frayed or worn out.
- If you're meeting the public, wear more traditional business clothing. A business suit might be right if you're in sales, for example.

YOU'RE THE BOSS!

Solving Workplace Problems

Your growing mail-order business has two new employees who take orders over the phone and process orders received by phone, fax, or mail. One is charming and efficient on the phone, but not very organized in processing orders; the other is very organized, but too shy to be very effective on the phone. What will you do?

Learning the Ropes

You'll have a lot to prepare for and to think about on your first day. Your employer will also be preparing for you.

Orientation

To help new employees get started, companies provide **orientation**. This is a program that will introduce you to the company's policies, procedures, values, and benefits. You may get a tour of the company, meet coworkers, and be shown where the lunchroom and restrooms are.

At a small company, orientation may be informal. You may simply meet with the office manager to talk about benefits, have lunch with your supervisor, and tour the workplace. Most large companies have more elaborate orientations. You

Teaching YOU'RE THE BOSS!

Possible responses: Take time to train and encourage both employees; arrange a shift in responsibilities so that each spends most of his/her time doing what he/she does best.

Extending the Illustration

(see illustration on page 159)

Ask students who have part-time jobs whether they have or have had a mentor.

Caption Answer: The younger worker receives in-depth advice based on solid experience. The older worker gains self-esteem, develops teaching skills, and adds the new experience to his or her daily routine.

may receive a company manual and hear formal presentations. Orientation may last a few hours, all day, or much longer.

At some companies, the new employee may be paired with a senior coworker who acts as a mentor. **Mentors** are informal teachers. They introduce new employees to their coworkers and coach

 Even if a company does not assign a mentor to young workers, it is a good idea to look to experienced workers for advice. *How could this arrangement benefit the new and the experienced worker?*

EXCELLENT BUSINESS PRACTICES

Employing the Older Worker

The McDonald's Corporation, of Oak Brook, Illinois, is known for its success in employing workers who are 55 years of age and older. The fast-food company developed specific recruiting materials to sell McDonald's as a career opportunity for older workers. The materials emphasized flexibility in scheduling and working within government regulations so that older workers wouldn't jeopardize their Social Security benefits.

These new hires receive the same training as other workers. But special programs were established, for example, to teach computer skills to people who had never worked with computers before. McDonald's also sets up a buddy system so that each older worker has someone to help him or her learn the way things are done at McDonald's.

More than 40,000 older employees serve McDonald's customers worldwide. Older workers are known for better attendance, lower turnover rates, and lower accident rates. They also tend to excel in hospitality skills and customer service.

Thinking Critically

Which jobs are more suitable for younger workers and which might need workers with more experience? Why is attitude more important than age?

Chapter 8 • Beginning a New Job **159**

Extending EXCELLENT BUSINESS PRACTICES

Answer: Younger workers: jobs requiring physical strength, agility; older workers: jobs requiring varied experiences, a long-term viewpoint. Attitude determines dedication to job, commitment to excellence, desire to cooperate, and ability to overcome obstacles.

Further Application: Have students contact the school's employment office. Does the school have a specific hiring policy with regard to a worker's age? Do the ages of employees at the school reflect the ages of the workforce in the community?

L3 **Sociability**

One way to gain work skills is to get to know people in other departments and find out what they do and how their jobs fit within the organization. Have students list ways they can get to know others. (Suggestions include joining new groups in the cafeteria, inviting one new person you don't know well to lunch each week, asking coworkers to introduce you to friends in other departments, volunteering for assignments involving other departments, reading a company newsletter and asking for introductions to people you read about.)

SCANS Workplace Competencies Connection

L1 **Reasoning**

Have students decide how to dress for a new job. (Students might ask the person making the job offer about appropriate dress or observe how coworkers dress.)

L2 **Applying Technology to Task**

Assign students to teams of four or five. Tell each team to write and produce a one-page career newsletter with at least three short articles on adjusting to the world of work and making a good impression.

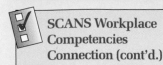
SCANS Workplace Competencies Connection (cont'd.)

L3 Understanding Systems

Have students choose a local business and interview the director of human resources to learn about job titles and overall organization. Have students use their information to draw an organization chart from the president down to entry-level employees. Students should include at least five levels of employees.

Independent Practice

Assign as homework the chapter activity in the *School-to-Work Activity Handbook.*

Skills Practice

Tell students to imagine that while they are interviewing an employee for a promotion, the employee begins describing all the negative aspects of the way the department operates and how he would make it operate more smoothly. Ask students how they would react to this. Would they promote the employee?

Writing: *Memo*

Tell students that they work for a new company doing the same kind of work they did in their old job. They feel that the work flow was more efficient at the old company. Have students write a memo asking for a meeting with the supervisor to discuss this issue.

them in the skills and procedures needed for their jobs. Mentors help new employees learn the company culture and company policies.

Figure 8-1
Orientation Programs

About 85 percent of businesses with more than 100 employees have an orientation program for new workers. Such programs differ in length and in type, but they all have a dual purpose: to make newly hired workers feel at home and to sharpen their job skills to fit their new employer's needs.

A In the past, orientation often consisted of filling out insurance forms and reading lengthy company policy manuals. At some companies today, this is what you will still find.

B Many companies now offer interactive training programs. The programs enable new workers to ask questions and to meet each other as they learn about their employer.

After three months, new employees often meet with their supervisors to talk about their new jobs, the company, and their future. *Figure 8-1* gives you an idea of the scope of some orientation programs.

160   *Unit 4 • Joining the Workforce*

Extending Figure 8-1

Formal orientation programs usually are offered only in large companies. Ask students how they think small companies provide orientation. (Someone in the human resources department or an experienced employee explains policies and procedures; in some cases, new employees learn by doing.)

However your company handles orientation, use it to get a clear idea of your responsibilities and the company goals. Get answers to the following questions:

- What is the company's mission, or purpose? How do your job and your department fit into the mission?
- What are your exact job responsibilities? What should you do first? Next?
- How will your performance be evaluated? When?

C Some employers even use games such as scavenger hunts to help introduce their new employees to the workplace.

D Employers may also include team-building activities to help new employees develop their abilities to work together.

E Orientation does not necessarily stop with new employees. Employers often "reorient" their entire staff to boost morale and to help employees keep up with changes within the company.

Chapter 8 • Beginning a New Job **161**

Addressing Workplace Diversity

Self-managed or self-directed teams are responsible for figuring out how to work together to achieve goals. As a result, team members have to build intercultural bridges among themselves by recognizing each other's differences and strengths.

Workforce 2000 Trends

Working in self-management teams means that employees of the future will take on greater responsibility for their own work and company productivity. However, in some companies, it also means that employees will share directly in the profits saved through increased efficiency.

SECTION 8-1

Teaching Tip

Ask students who have work experience to share a negative experience they had with a coworker. Discuss how they handled the situation and what the results were. Then have students offer suggestions for how the situation could have been avoided or turned into a positive experience.

Discussion Starter

In their careers, students will most likely work with people of all ages and ethnic groups. Ask students to list three to five ways they can foster good relations with fellow employees. List students' responses on the chalkboard and discuss. (Possible responses include being open to others' ideas, being friendly, avoiding work cliques, staying neutral in personal disputes, learning about cultural differences, showing appreciation for help or advice given, showing a willingness to learn from others.)

Critical Thinking

Tell students that in school they are the only ones responsible for their success or failure. On the job, however, other individuals can contribute to their success or failure. Have students write one or two paragraphs describing how coworkers might contribute to their success and how they might contribute to someone else's success. (Ideas include working as part of a team so that all can be successful or sharing information and ideas that help others do a better job.)

161

Role-Play

Divide students into pairs. Have them role-play a meeting in which a supervisor is laying off an employee because the business needs to reduce its workforce. Have students discuss what questions would be appropriate to ask at this kind of meeting.

What problems might the supervisor have to deal with regarding the employee's fears for his or her future or resentment toward the company? Have students incorporate as many ideas as possible into their role-plays. After the role-plays, discuss the issue in class.

ASSESS

Assessment
Performance

Divide students into groups of three or four. Have each group prepare and perform a skit demonstrating help offered by two (or three) friends to another friend who has just taken a new job. Skits should include what the new employee should expect on the job, how to dress, what will take place during orientation, and suggestions for making a good impression.

Evaluate students skills for inclusion of topics taught in this section and for effectiveness of their advice. Also evaluate teams on both group and individual effort.

Company Policies

Every company has specific policies that spell out what the company expects of you and what you can expect of the company. You will probably be given a company manual or other written statement of official policies. You should learn about these policies right away. Following are questions about just a few company policies.

- When will you be paid?
- What happens if you're late for work?
- How many sick days will you be paid for each year? What happens if you need more days than you're allowed?
- How much vacation time will you get, and when can you take it?
- What paid holidays does the company grant?
- When will you receive a raise? What will be the basis for it?

Career Do's & Don'ts

When Starting a New Job...
Do:
- learn the organization's corporate culture or rules.
- understand what your boss expects from you.
- be tactful.
- express interest in all aspects of the company and coworkers' jobs.

Don't:
- act like a know-it-all.
- constantly explain how things were done at your other job.
- complain or demand.
- sit there with nothing to do unless you've been instructed to.

SECTION 8-1 *Review*

Understanding Key Concepts

Using complete sentences, answer the following questions on a separate sheet of paper.

1. What worries you about starting a new job? How can you prepare for your first day at work?

2. How will knowing about your new employer's dress code help make your first day on the job successful?

3. Why should you learn about company policies as soon as possible?

SECTION 8-1 *Review* ANSWERS

1. Answers will vary. Anticipate and know the challenges of the first day at work.

2. Knowing the dress code will reduce anxiety the first day. It will help you fit in and be more comfortable. You will make the correct impression on coworkers and supervisors.

3. Knowing company policies will help you avoid misunderstandings about what is expected of you and what you can expect from the company.

CASE STUDY

Exploring Careers: Health

Marcelitte Failla, D.C.
Chiropractor

Q: Why did you choose chiropractic over conventional medicine?

A: My parents and grandparents in Louisiana used natural plant substances to cure illnesses. I realized that responding to illness with natural foods was better than trying to cover up symptoms with medicines. As a health-care professional, I wanted to go back to the way my parents had cared for our health. Chiropractic makes that possible.

Q: What kind of training have you had?

A: I have a bachelor's degree in pre-med. Then I went through a four-year chiropractic college program.

Q: What's involved in chiropractic treatment?

A: I interview a patient to get a medical history. Then I give an exam, looking for signs of injury to the spine. If the patient is in a lot of pain, I usually don't adjust him or her then. I give other treatments instead. I keep asking questions to help me rule out other things that could be causing the pain.

Q: In addition to having diagnostic skills, do you have to be strong?

A: You do need a certain amount of upper-body strength. I'm only 5 feet 3 inches tall, so I work out. I also use some of the tools and techniques that chiropractors have available to them to make things easier.

Thinking Critically

Why would chiropractors take pre-med programs in college if they are not going to be doctors?

CAREER FACTS

Nature of the Work:
Diagnose illness and injury; treat patients with adjustment and exercise.

Training or Education Needed:
A minimum of two years of college, or a bachelor's degree; training at an accredited chiropractic college.

Aptitudes, Abilities, and Skills:
Math, listening, speaking, and interpersonal skills; physical strength; an aptitude for the sciences; a strong desire to help people; ability to work well with hands.

Salary Range:
Average starting salary—$20,000 to $30,000; average top salary—$90,000.

Career Path:
Start as vacation relief for other chiropractors; work in a chiropractic clinic; go into partnership with other chiropractors, or start a practice.

Chapter 8 • Beginning a New Job **163**

Evaluation
Assign the section review.

Reteaching
Have students write 100-word papers describing why making a good first impression is so important to job success. Tell students to describe how they would go about making a good impression.

Extending the Content
Assign the appropriate Chapter 8 activities in the *Student Activity Workbook*.

Ask a representative from a local company to speak to students about orientation programs and to offer advice about beginning a new job. Have the speaker describe a typical first day on the job. Have students write summaries of the speaker's comments. Discuss comments in class.

CLOSE
Have students complete this sentence: "When I start a new job, I will . . . ."

Extending the CASE STUDY

Answer: Since they deal with patients' health, chiropractors need to have the same understanding of the human body and human health that doctors have; and they need to know medical terminology to talk to doctors when referring patients to them.

Further Application: Have students make a list of influences from family that affect the choice of careers they are considering. (For example, they may have helped in a family business, they may have admired a relative in a particular career, their families may have encouraged them in particular talents or skills.)

FOCUS

Bell Ringer

Have students list three things an employee should be able to expect from an employer.

Introducing the Section

Ask students to share their Bell Ringer lists with the class. Write their responses on the chalkboard and discuss.

One major item from students' lists will likely be payment for work. Use this discussion to introduce various forms of payment.

Motivational Activity
Critical Thinking

Tell students that they work in sales jobs. Ask them to discuss the pros and cons of working for a straight salary versus working for a reduced salary plus a commission on all sales.

Skills Practice

Rosanna delivers packages for a delivery service. She earns $7.50 an hour. Last week she worked 44 hours. The normal work week is 40 hours. How much did Rosanna earn? ($345: 7.50 × 40 = $300 + ($7.50 × 1.5) × 4 = $45 + $300 = $345)

Jamal is a computer salesperson. He earns a base salary of $1,100 a month plus a 5 percent commission on his sales. Last month his sales totaled $11,240. How much did Jamal earn last month? ($1,662: $1,100 + ($11,240 × .05))

What You Can Expect from Your Employer

OBJECTIVES

After studying this section, you will be able to:

- Describe typical ways that employers pay workers.
- Explain benefits that employers offer workers.
- Discuss the significance of employee performance reviews.

KEY TERMS

hourly wages
overtime
nonexempt
   employees
exempt employees
salary
commission
profit-sharing plan
performance bonuses
pension plan
probation
layoff

Every employee works for a reason. What's yours? A salary? Health insurance? A pension? The challenge of interesting work? Job security? You may want and expect these and other things from your employer.

The answers keep changing as business moves closer to the global market. Companies must be more efficient and more competitive. The result is a changing relationship between workers and their employers. *Figure 8-2* shows how the relationship has changed in recent years.

Payment

Of course, you expect to get paid for the work you do. This is one aspect of the employer-employee relationship that has not changed. However, your pay may be calculated in any number of ways.

Basic Payment Methods

Most entry-level employees receive **hourly wages**. In other words, the employer pays a fixed amount of money, such as $7, for each hour worked. At the end of each week, pay is calculated by multiplying the number of hours worked times the hourly rate.

Hourly wages may be affected by whether or not workers are paid **overtime** for working more than 40 hours in a week. Usually workers on overtime are paid one and one-half times their normal pay for each hour in excess of 40 hours. For example, if workers are normally paid $10 per hour, they will get $15 when working overtime.

▶ Extending the Illustration

Ask students who have part-time jobs to describe how and when they earn overtime pay.

Caption Answer: None. Workers receive overtime only for hours in excess of 40 hours in any single week.

Changing Worker Expectations

	In the Past	Today
Job Security	• Lifetime job security • Length of time with a company or experience in a career field guarantees job security • Company responsible for worker's security	• Limited job security • Continuing training provides job security • Current job skills allow mobility among companies and careers • Freedom from company ties
Salary	• Based on experience • Based on number of years with company	• Based on current value of the work

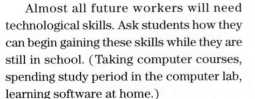

Source: "The New Deal" by Brian O'Reilly, *Current*, October 1994

◀ Figure 8-2

The competitive global and technology-based economy has changed the expectations of the American worker. What are the advantages for today's worker? What are the disadvantages?

Not everyone gets paid overtime. Who does? A federal law requires that certain types of workers must be paid overtime. Workers who are covered by this law are called **nonexempt employees**. These workers are normally paid an hourly wage. Workers who are not covered by the law are **exempt employees**. Most exempt employees earn a **salary**. That is, they are paid a fixed amount for a certain period of time, usually a month or a year. Exempt employees do not have to be paid overtime.

Workers in some kinds of jobs—such as sales or telemarketing—may be paid a **commission**. These workers' earnings are based on how much they sell. They might, for example, earn 2 percent of the value of the merchandise they sell. By basing pay directly on their performance, this system aims to motivate salespeople to work harder.

 Many workers who are paid an hourly wage must "clock in" at a time clock. This worker normally works seven hours per day, five days per week. This week she has worked eight hours per day for five days. ***How many hours of overtime is she entitled to?***

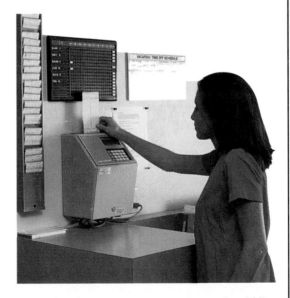

Chapter 8 • Beginning a New Job **165**

Extending Figure 8-2

Almost all future workers will need technological skills. Ask students how they can begin gaining these skills while they are still in school. (Taking computer courses, spending study period in the computer lab, learning software at home.)

Caption Answer: Advantages: Today's workers have greater independence and more control over their future. They can improve their income by improving their skills. Disadvantages: There are no guarantees about job security.

SECTION 8-2

TEACH

Guided Practice

Teaching Strategies

1. Assign and review Section 8-2.
2. Use the transparency for this section.

Discussion Starter

Ask students what they think *proactive* means. Write students' suggestions on the chalkboard. Then give students the dictionary definition or have them look it up in a dictionary. The *American Heritage Dictionary* defines *proactive* as "acting in advance to deal with an expected difficulty."

Discuss with students how they can be proactive in gaining job skills and keeping themselves "marketable" throughout their careers.

☑ SCANS Foundation Skills Connection

L1 Math

Have students provide answers to these problems: (1) If Malory is paid $18,000 a year, how much is she earning per hour for a 40-hour week? (2) Denzel worked Monday through Saturday, eight hours each day. A regular work week is 40 hours. If Denzel's annual salary is $21,000, how much did he earn for this week?

(Answers: (1) $8.65: ($18,000 ÷ 52) ÷ 40; (2) $525.20: ($21,000 ÷ 52) ÷ 40 = $10.10; ($10.10 × 40) + 8 × ($10.10 × 1.5))

165

SCANS Foundation Skills Connection (cont'd.)

L2 Knowing How to Learn

Have students learn about fringe benefits by asking parents to talk about the benefits their employers provide. Have them create a table listing the different types of benefits by category, such as health care, vacation, incentive bonuses, and so on.

L3 Decision Making

Tell students to imagine that they have been offered a job by two different companies. The first job pays a good starting salary, but potential raises will be in the 3 to 4 percent range. The second job pays a lower starting salary, but there is the possibility of a promotion and a higher salary within two years. What lifestyle factors might influence which job they would accept?

SCANS Workplace Competencies Connection

L1 Acquiring and Evaluating Information

Many federal laws exist to protect employee rights. Have students research the protection offered and the agencies and legislation created to ensure fair treatment. Tell students to write a one-page report.

These four members of a magazine advertising sales team have been offered a sales incentive. If the team can sell $200,000 worth of advertisements, each member will receive $1,000. *What are the benefits of a sales incentive such as this one?*

Incentive Plans

One change in how workers are paid is in incentive plans. These plans reward workers for achievement.

In a **profit-sharing plan**, workers receive a share of the company's profits. The better the company performs, the more the workers receive.

Performance bonuses reward workers for high levels of performance. Some companies pay bonuses to workers who increase the quantity or quality of their work. These bonuses vary greatly in amounts and how they are awarded. At Dow Brands, for example, employees may receive cash awards of several hundred dollars for doing good work. At Steelcase, factory workers are paid relatively low salaries, but their bonuses can almost double their incomes.

Fringe Benefits

The rewards for working are not limited to a paycheck. Various fringe benefits may come with a job. Fringe benefits are the "extras" that a company provides in

addition to pay. Usually there is a waiting period for many of these benefits.

The kinds and value of fringe benefits vary dramatically from employer to employer. However, they can be substantial. A recent study showed that benefits average about 40 percent of employers' payrolls.

Health Benefits

Health insurance is probably the most sought after benefit. It's also the most costly one for employers. Health-care costs have risen sharply over the past 20 years, and the trend is likely to continue. *Figure 8-3* shows the expected increase in these costs for the nation's 500 largest companies. Employers sometimes change their health insurance plans to find lower-cost alternatives.

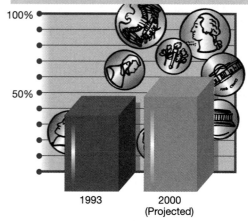

Employer Health-Care Costs*

1993   2000 (Projected)

* As a percentage of annual profits

Source: Joseph Pizzorno, M.D., *Total Wellness.* Prima Publishing, Rocklin, CA, 1996, p. 7

Figure 8-3 These graphs show the projected growth in health-care costs for the nation's 500 largest companies. How might this rising expense affect workers in a negative way?

Extending the Illustration

Ask students for examples of other types of jobs in which they might earn incentive pay. (sales jobs paying a commission, manufacturing jobs with bonuses for high productivity)

Caption Answer: The team members benefit by interacting more and helping each other; if they succeed, they earn extra money.

Extending Figure 8-3

Ask students to think of other benefits the employer helps to pay for. (Social Security, workers' compensation, unemployment insurance, sick days)

Caption Answer: Companies might be forced to reduce the number of medical benefits they offer workers, or reduce wages to accommodate rising health-care costs.

Retirement Plans

Many companies offer a **pension plan** that builds a retirement fund for each worker. Some employers make contributions for each worker. Some plans allow workers to contribute a portion of each paycheck to the fund. Many companies match the amount of each worker's contribution up to a certain percentage of his or her salary.

Convenience Benefits

Some employers also provide *convenience benefits*—services that make workers' lives easier. There is great variety in the types of convenience benefits. They range from flexible work hours and legal counseling services to on-site oil changes for employees' cars. Quad/Graphics, Inc., provides an accredited kindergarten for employees' children, a fitness center, and popcorn carts, where employees can get a

Some workers receive health-club memberships as an employee benefit. **How does this service benefit these employees? How does it benefit their employer?**

snack for a quarter. Hallmark Cards provides twice-monthly seminars to help employees handle family issues, such as elder care and parenting. Such benefits are designed to reduce employee stress, improve workers' health, and make workers more productive, loyal, and satisfied.

Cafeteria Plan

A *cafeteria plan* is not a benefit but a policy that lets employees choose the benefits they want. Employers realize that not all employees want or need the same benefits, so they let employees choose those they do want. For example, rather than vacation time, an employee may prefer disability insurance.

Honest and Fair Treatment

You have a right to expect your employer to be honest with you. You should be paid the amount you agreed to. You should receive all the benefits promised when you were hired. If your work situation changes, you should be told as soon as possible.

You also have a right to be treated fairly by your employer, supervisor, and coworkers. If you feel you have been treated unfairly, discuss it with the person involved or with your supervisor. Try to resolve the problem before it gets out of hand. Chapter 12 discusses additional options you have if your rights are violated.

Evaluations

How well are you succeeding at your work? Many companies have formal, scheduled *performance reviews*. These are

Chapter 8 • Beginning a New Job **167**

SECTION 8-2

L2 **Interpreting and Communicating Information**

Have students survey at least five local businesses and determine whether they complete annual reviews of their employees job performance. Tell students to ask for general categories on which employees are evaluated (for example, reliability, quality of work, attitude, teamwork, and so on). Ask them to share their results.

L3 **Allocating Money**

Students may believe that they're too young to think about retirement, but that isn't so. For this activity, have students use interest tables calculating the compound sum of a $1 annuity (check with a math teacher or refer to math or investments books). Have students calculate how much money they would have in 30 years if they saved $100 a month from age 20 on and invested it at 8 percent. ($135,939.60: $100 \times 12 = $1,200 \times 113.283$ (the factor for $1 at 8 percent for 30 years))

Independent Practice
Reading

Have students read an article in a current magazine about health care. Ask students to write a brief summary of the main points in the article and also describe how these points might affect their own health benefits.

▶ Extending the Illustration

Ask students what role benefits should play in their decision about accepting a job offer. (If everything else is equal, the company offering the better benefits will result in higher real earnings. If the jobs or the opportunities are unequal, choosing the job based on benefits may be short-sighted.)

Caption Answer: The employees benefit from exercise, which reduces stress and improves their health. The employer benefits by gaining employees who are healthier, which reduces medical costs and employee absenteeism and improves performance.

Writing: *Letters*

Public corporations have a board of directors to help make corporate decisions. Have students create their own personal "advisory boards" to help them make career decisions. Have students write letters that might be used to recruit advisory board members.

ASSESS

Assessment

Content

Have students list the things they can expect from an employer. Evaluate for accuracy and completeness.

Evaluation

Assign the section review.

MINI QUIZ

True-False

1. Companies have formal training that takes place during an orientation. (false)

2. Mentors are informal teachers. (true)

3. Paid holidays are part of a company's policies. (true)

4. A person who works for a salary plus commission will earn more than one who works for hourly wages. (false)

5. Regular performance evaluations should give you feedback to help you build your career. (true)

When businesses are forced to lay off workers, they often lay off more recently hired workers before those who have worked for the company longer. **Why do you think this is so?**

meetings between you and your supervisor to evaluate how well you're doing your job.

Reviews are important to you and to your supervisor. Promotions, pay increases, new responsibilities, and your future with the company may be based on these evaluations. If your company does not have regular evaluations, ask for one. You need feedback to improve your performance and build your career.

In some companies, new employees are put on **probation**. This is the period after you are first hired when you are "on trial."

During your probation period, your employer will decide whether you are suited to the job. When you are hired, ask if your company has a probation period policy. If it does, ask what guidelines will be used for the evaluation.

Standard Separation Procedures

Most people, at some time during their careers, will lose their jobs. There are several reasons why a company will *terminate*, or end, a worker's employment.

Employees may be terminated, or fired, for poor job performance. Your employer should have a clear policy for handling these situations.

Sometimes companies have to terminate employees because business is slow. This kind of job loss, which often affects many workers at once, is a **layoff**. Workers who are laid off may be rehired once a company's business improves.

Because you can't always avoid job loss, you should prepare for it. Keep your job-hunting network active and your skills up-to-date. Put aside money to help you through a time of unemployment.

SECTION 8-2 *Review*

Understanding Key Concepts

Using complete sentences, answer the following questions on a separate sheet of paper.

1. Why does working for a commission offer less financial security than working for a salary?

2. How do fringe benefits improve employee morale?

3. Why are performance reviews as important to workers as to their employers?

168   *Unit 4 • Joining the Workforce*

SECTION 8-2 *Review* ANSWERS

1. When you work for a commission, your income will vary on the basis of your day-to-day performance. A salary guarantees you a steady income.

2. Fringe benefits help employees with health, retirement, and other matters.

With fewer worries, employee morale improves.

3. Such reviews help employers see how well employees are doing their jobs. The reviews help employees improve their skills and job security.

Highlights

SECTION 8-1 **Summary**

- Reduce anxiety on the first day of work by giving yourself ample time to get ready and to get to work.

- Learn the company culture by listening and observing how your coworkers work and interact.

- Dress codes for work are changing, and different companies have different standards. Ask about the dress code at your interview. Observe what other workers are wearing.

- Companies help new employees learn policies, procedures, values, and benefits through orientation programs.

- Company policies spell out what the company expects of new employees and what employees can expect from the company. Learn these policies as soon as possible.

Key Terms

company culture *(p. 156)*
orientation *(p. 158)*
mentors *(p. 159)*

SECTION 8-2 **Summary**

- The basic methods of payment include hourly wages, salary, and commission.

- Incentive programs such as profit-sharing plans and performance bonuses offer workers a chance to share in their company's success.

- Workers usually receive fringe benefits, such as health insurance and a retirement plan. They may also receive convenience benefits.

- Employees have a right to honest and fair treatment from their employer.

- Employers and employees both benefit from performance evaluations.

- Some employers have probation periods for new employees.

- Employers sometimes terminate a worker's employment. This may be because of poor worker performance or bad business. Companies should have a clear termination policy.

- You can prepare for possible job loss by maintaining your network of contacts, keeping your skills up-to-date, and having some money saved.

Key Terms

hourly wages *(p. 164)*
overtime *(p. 164)*
nonexempt
employees *(p. 165)*
exempt employees *(p. 165)*
salary *(p. 165)*
commission *(p. 165)*
profit-sharing plan *(p. 166)*
performance
bonuses *(p. 166)*
pension plan *(p. 167)*
probation *(p. 168)*
layoff *(p. 168)*

Chapter 8 • Beginning a New Job **169**

Use the Testmaker to create a customized test for Chapter 8.

Reteaching

1. Without looking at their textbooks, have students write definitions for *wages*, *overtime*, *nonexempt employees*, *exempt employees*, *commission*, *profit-sharing plans*, and *performance bonuses*. Then have them list types of benefits an employer may offer.

2. Assign and review vocabulary terms, chapter questions, and activities from the Chapter Review.

Extending the Content

Assign the appropriate Chapter 8 activities in the *Student Activity Workbook*.

Have each student make a list of the advantages and disadvantages of receiving each type of pay discussed in this section.

Ask why a person might prefer a wage to a salary or commission. Discuss why some people might prefer working on commission. Also discuss why managers usually receive a salary instead of an hourly wage.

CLOSE

Have students interpret the sentence "Everyone has to pay his or her dues in a career." (Most workers will spend some time during early years doing work they may think is tedious.)

▶ **Extending the Illustration**

Discuss with students what they should do if they get a job and are laid off shortly afterwards. (try to gain technological skills that are valuable)

Caption Answer: Those who have worked for the company longer are more experienced. Also, labor agreements often require that layoffs be made on the basis of seniority.

Computer Activity

Have students create a spreadsheet to illustrate the income potential of two jobs. Give them the following. Company A: base salary, $20,000; health benefits, $1,500; education reimbursements, $4,000. Company B: base salary, $18,500; health benefits, $2,000; education reimbursements, $5,000. Discuss which company has the better financial offer.

Answers
Reviewing Key Terms

Employee manuals will vary but should use each of the key terms correctly.

Recalling Key Concepts

1. False: Companies are moving toward more casual clothing.
2. True
3. True
4. False: A cafeteria plan is a program that allows workers to select which benefits they would like to receive from their employer.
5. False: Probation is a period when new employees show whether they are suited to their jobs.

Thinking Critically

1. By seeing how others behave, a worker can learn the company culture.
2. They want employees to be successful in their jobs because successful workers make companies successful.
3. Employers know that if their employees are free from worry about health care and other matters, they will be more productive in their work.
4. Workers who are treated fairly and honestly will feel committed to an employer.
5. They want to be sure the new employees will fit in

Reviewing Key Terms

On a separate sheet of paper, write a one- to two-page employee manual. Use the terms listed below to explain the policies of an imaginary employer.

company culture
mentors
overtime
exempt employees
commission
performance bonuses
pension plan
orientation
hourly wages
nonexempt employees
salary
profit-sharing plan
probation
layoff

Recalling Key Concepts

On a separate sheet of paper, tell whether each statement is true or false. Rewrite any false statements to make them true.

1. Companies are beginning to insist on more formal business clothing.
2. During orientation, new employees are introduced to the company's policies, procedures, values, and benefits.
3. Typically, workers are paid an hourly wage, a salary, or a commission.
4. A cafeteria plan is a convenience benefit that allows workers to eat free meals while at work.
5. If you are on probation, it means that you are being considered for a pay raise.

Thinking Critically

Using complete sentences, answer each of the questions below on a separate sheet of paper.

1. How can watching other employees help a worker succeed on the job?
2. Why do some companies devote so much time to new-employee orientation?
3. If fringe benefits are so expensive, why do companies provide so many for employees?
4. How does fair and honest treatment contribute to a good workplace?
5. Why do some companies place new employees on probation?

SCANS Foundation Skills and Workplace Competencies

Thinking Skills: *Knowing How to Learn*

1. Working with a partner, role-play your first conversation with your new employer, who has called to congratulate you and answer any questions you may have about your first day at work. What questions will you ask?

Personal Qualities: *Sociability*

2. Brainstorm a list of suggestions for ways to get to know coworkers.

Technology: *Selecting Technology*

3. Your employer plans to link the personal computers in the accounting department. What issues should the employer address in making this change?

---

and do a good job before making a final decision about keeping them.

SCANS Foundation Skills and Workplace Competencies

1. What are my work hours? To whom will I report? What is my salary? What is the dress code?

2. Possible answers: Talk with them on work breaks. Ask them to have lunch with you. Offer to help them with their tasks if you have time.

3. What equipment is needed to link the computers? What software is required? What training will the workers need?

Connecting Academics to the Workplace

Math

1. Kumar earns $7.00 per hour. If he works an average of 40 hours a week, what does he earn a week? How much does he earn a year if he works 50 weeks? One week he worked 10 hours of overtime, for which he earned time-and-a-half pay. What were his total earnings that week?

Health and Physical Education

2. Your employer has decided to create a company wellness program to improve employee health and fitness. Write a one-page questionnaire for workers to complete that will inform your employer about the habits that affect their health and general well-being.

Foreign Language

3. You work in a company's shipping room. You have been assigned to be a mentor for a new employee whose native language is not English. Her duties include copying order forms, filling out address labels, and wrapping packages. How would you explain these tasks to her?

Developing Teamwork and Leadership Skills

Working with a group, prepare an orientation program for a company. You can make up the company or choose an existing one. Design an informative presentation using any combination of skits, talks, and written or audiovisual materials to welcome new employees (your classmates) to their new jobs.

Real-World Workshop

Your school is your present workplace and has a "company culture." Students and teachers have specific ways of behaving, interacting, talking, and doing work. If a new student entered this workplace and you were appointed his or her mentor, what would you tell the student about the company culture? Write a description of your school's culture.

School-to-Work Connection

Choose a local company and research its fringe benefits. You might call the human resources department or interview someone who works there. Write a report that outlines the benefits that the employer offers.

Individual Career Plan

What job would you like to have? For what company? Look through your wardrobe. Which outfits would you consider appropriate for the job? What additional clothing would you need to get to have a good work wardrobe? Create a list indicating your current work-appropriate clothing and what you would need to add.

Developing Teamwork and Leadership Skills

Students' presentations should reflect an understanding of what new workers need and want to know about a workplace.

Real-World Workshop

Answers will vary, depending on your school's culture. Students should describe the behavior, attitudes, values, and habits of students and staff. They should provide specific examples.

School-to-Work Connection

Reports will vary but should include a comprehensive overview of the various fringe benefits offered.

Individual Career Plan

Students' lists should reflect an awareness of appropriate business dress.

Chapter 8 • Beginning a New Job **171**

Connecting Academics to the Workplace

1. weekly: $280 ($7.00 per hour × 40 hours); yearly: $14,000 ($280 per week × 50 weeks); overtime week: $385 ($280 regular pay + $105 in overtime (10 hours × $10.50 per hour))

2. Questionnaires should ask questions such as these: How tall are you? How much do you weigh? How often do you exercise? What kind of exercise do you prefer? Are you a smoker?

3. Students may say they would demonstrate the steps in completing each of the tasks.

• • • PLANNING GUIDE • • •
Chapter 9

SECTION 1 · *Desirable Employee Qualities*

SECTION OBJECTIVES	SECTION FEATURES	SECTION RESOURCES
• Identify the qualities that employers look for in employees. • Describe ways that employees can become self-managing.	Personal Career Plan, p. 173 You're the Boss!, p. 177 Excellent Business Practices, p. 178 Exploring Careers, p. 180	Workforce 2000 Videodisc and Videotape Section 9-1 Review, p. 179 Student Activity Workbook

SECTION 2 · *Ethical Behavior*

SECTION OBJECTIVES	SECTION FEATURES	SECTION RESOURCES
• Explain why ethics are important in the workplace. • Describe ways to behave ethically in the workplace.	Attitude Counts, p. 185 Career Do's and Don'ts, p. 186	Workforce 2000 Videodisc and Videotape Section 9-2 Review, p. 188 Chapter 9 Review, pp. 190–191 Student Activity Workbook

CHAPTER 9

CHAPTER RESOURCES

- Chapter Transparencies and Lesson Plans
- Chapter 9 Test
- Spanish Resources, Chapter 9
- School-to-Work Activity Handbook, Chapter 9 Activity
- Teacher's Lesson Plans, Chapter 9
- Implementing Block Scheduling, Chapter 9
- Print, Media, and Internet Handbook
- Strategies for Implementing Work-Based Learning
- Strategies for Implementing Connecting Activities

Career Notes

SCANS CORRELATION CHART

Foundation Skills

Basic Skills
Reading	Writing	Math	Listening	Speaking

Thinking Skills
Creative Thinking	Decision Making	Problem Solving	Seeing Things in the Mind's Eye	Knowing How to Learn	Reasoning

Personal Qualities
Responsibility	Self-Esteem	Sociability	Self-Management	Integrity/Honesty

Workplace Competencies

Resources
Allocating Time	Allocating Money	Allocating Material and Facility Resources	Allocating Human Resources

Information
Acquiring and Evaluating Information	Organizing and Maintaining Information	Interpreting and Communicating Information	Using Computers to Process Information

Interpersonal Skills
Participating as a Member of a Team	Teaching Others	Serving Clients/ Customers	Exercising Leadership	Negotiating to Arrive at a Decision	Working with Cultural Diversity

Systems
Understanding Systems	Monitoring and Correcting Performance	Improving and Designing Systems

Technology
Selecting Technology	Applying Technology to Task	Maintaining and Troubleshooting Technology

Highlighted blocks indicate areas covered in the Chapter.

Additional Activities

 Internet Connection

Ask students to use the Internet to find out how people feel about work ethics. What do employers consider ethical behavior? Employees? How do different people define work ethics? Students can look up business articles about work ethics or use chat rooms to find their information.

 Field Trip Suggestions

Arrange for students to sit in on a class on business ethics at a local community college. Work with the instructor to choose a session that will be of interest to your students. Beforehand, discuss the ethical questions that will be brought up. Have students take careful notes during the lecture.

 Guest Speaker Suggestions

Invite to class a representative of an environmental organization, community policy agency, or human services agency. Ask your guest to describe the ways that individuals and corporations can contribute to the welfare of the community.

Key to Ability Levels

Each section gives skill-building activities. Each activity has been labeled for use with students of various learning styles and abilities.

L1 Level 1 activities are basic activities and should be within the range of all students.

L2 Level 2 activities are average activities and should be within the range of average and above average students.

L3 Level 3 activities are challenging activities designed for the ability range of above average students.

School-Based Learning

Chapter Overview

Learning to be an effective employee involves more than just knowing how to do a certain job. In this chapter, students learn about personal skills that also contribute to career success.

Section 9-1 presents the qualities employers look for in employees.

Section 9-2 focuses on ethical behavior.

Background Information

Write chapter objectives (Sections 9-1 and 9-2) on the chalkboard or use the chapter objective transparency for class discussion.

Choose assignments from the *Student Activity Workbook* and write them on the chalkboard.

Have students preview the chapter, looking at pictures, reading captions, and noting content headings. Ask students to describe what they expect to learn in this chapter.

Preteaching Vocabulary

Write the Key Terms from Sections 9-1 and 9-2 on the chalkboard. Have students describe how each term relates to developing the personal skills they will need in their future careers.

172

Meeting SPECIAL Needs

Physically Challenged

Physically handicapped students are sometimes slow or awkward writers. Encourage them to use a tape recorder to record class lectures. Urge them to bring a typed résumé when they go to apply for a job. These students should emphasize their computing and word-processing skills, which may be very strong.

Chapter 9

Workplace Ethics

Section 9-1
Desirable Employee Qualities

Section 9-2
Ethical Behavior

In this video segment, explore the importance of workplace ethics.

Journal
Personal Career Plan

What basic ethics should guide the behavior of a well-known business leader? In what ways—if any—should that leader's ethics differ from those of a part-time worker in that leader's company? How do the leader and the part-time worker affect each other's work ethics? Write a journal entry discussing your ideas.

School-to-Work Connecting Activities

Have students research local companies that provide employment in one or more of the career areas in which they are interested. (For example, a student interested in veterinary work might talk to a veterinarian or someone at an animal shelter. Someone interested in health care might visit a hospital or a nursing care facility.) Have students arrange to observe work activities for at least one full day and make a list of the job skills—both personal and professional—they will need to work in that particular field.

Work-Based Learning Strategies and Activities

Work with local employers to create summer internships for students. With employers, identify the skills students will need to work in those jobs. Then identify academic and/or vocational courses students can take to learn the necessary skills.

WORKFORCE 2000 Training Video

Have students view the video and perform the interactive exercises to reinforce important chapter concepts and thinking processes.

Chapter 9

Addressing LEARNING Styles

Visual/Spatial Learner

Ask students to use photos and type from magazines to create posters showing ethical work conflicts: taking small items, such as desk supplies or hardware; using the phone or fax for personal use; having a coworker punch their time-cards for them if they come in late or leave early. Brainstorm unethical work practices beforehand, then afterward discuss the posters and the cost of white collar crime to business.

SECTION 9-1

FOCUS

Bell Ringer

Have students visualize themselves in the workplace in five or six years. Ask them to write a list of at least five positive traits or characteristics as employees.

Introducing the Section

Ask for volunteers to read their lists from the Bell Ringer activity. Write students' responses on the chalkboard. Then discuss the traits that help make a person a desirable employee.

Tell students that they will learn about many of the traits employers look for in employees in this chapter.

Motivational Activity

Discussion

Divide the class into seven panels. Assign each panel one of the following characteristics: *cooperativeness, willingness to follow directions, willingness to learn, initiative, willingness to take on more responsibility, self-management,* and *loyalty.* Have each panel gather information from families and friends who work about how the topic relates to success in the workplace. Discuss each topic.

Desirable Employee Qualities

OBJECTIVES

After studying this section, you will be able to:

- Identify the qualities that employers look for in employees.
- Describe ways that employees can become self-managing.

KEY TERMS

cooperativeness
initiative
responsibility
self-management

In the past, employers looked for workers with specific skills. They wanted people who excelled at computer keyboarding, bookkeeping, or graphic art, for example. Skills such as these may still get you a job, but the workplace is changing. According to Raymond Brixley, director of human resources for the Quaker Oats Company, employers are beginning to ask for more. " ... we look for someone capable of doing lots of things well," he says, "and more importantly, someone who 'fits' into the organization's structure."

How do you prepare for doing lots of things well and fitting in? Master the SCANS skills. Solid thinking skills, skills in math and communications, and strong personal qualities will help you adapt to the changing needs of today's workplace.

Cooperativeness

One of an employee's most valued qualities is cooperativeness. **Cooperativeness** is a willingness to work well with everyone else on the job to reach a common goal. Cooperativeness is part of several of the SCANS skills, including listening skills, responsibility, self-esteem, and self-management.

Be forewarned. Your first job will put your cooperativeness to the test. You may get the worst tasks and little responsibility. If this happens, all you can do is smile, do the job well, and demonstrate a spirit of cooperativeness.

Addressing Workplace Diversity

Businesses that use self-managed work teams see English language skills improve among non-native employees. As team leaders, these employees must be able to communicate clearly to team members who do not speak their language.

How can you be cooperative?

- Do tasks you don't like without complaining or trying to avoid them.
- Do your fair share of a job when working with others.
- Pitch in to help a coworker who has a tough job or has fallen behind.
- Volunteer to help coworkers meet a deadline or reach a goal.

Willingness to Follow Directions

On the job, you will be asked to complete many tasks. To complete a task, you must first follow directions. This is a vital skill on any job.

Following directions requires many SCANS skills. Listening is one of the most important ones. These suggestions may help you follow directions:

- Stop whatever you are doing, and listen to the directions being given.
- Listen carefully, even if you think you already know the procedure. Some details might surprise you.
- Take notes, if possible. Even simple directions can become murky if you or your supervisor is hurried.
- Identify the goal or purpose of the task. Then try to visualize the steps leading to the goal.
- If you do not understand the directions, don't guess at what is needed. Ask questions!

Workers can show cooperation by willingly doing whatever tasks they are assigned. *Why is it important to demon–strate cooperation?*

Chapter 9 • Workplace Ethics **175**

Guided Practice

Teaching Strategies

1. Assign and review Section 9-1.
2. Use the transparency for this section.
3. Assign and review the Case Study.

Discussion Starter

Have students think of a famous person, television character, friend, or relative whom they admire. List personal traits students mention on the chalkboard.

Teaching Tips

Personal traits will determine how well they get along with others and how well students perform in their jobs. Using the list of traits from the preceding Discussion Starter, discuss with students how each trait affects their personal effectiveness.

One of the primary reasons employers give for firing new employees is their inability to get along with coworkers. Help students understand that developing strong personal traits will help them improve their interpersonal skills and thus their careers.

Extending the Illustration

Have students write lists of at least three other ways workers can show cooperation. (Listening carefully to work assignments, volunteering to help others, or learning about the company so as to be more productive workers.)

Caption Answer: A spirit of cooperation makes the work environment more pleasant. Supervisors appreciate cooperation and will value the worker more.

Model Cindy Crawford attended Northwestern University for one semester on a full-tuition scholarship to study chemical engineering. Obviously, she put aside her early career interests to pursue other opportunities. Have students write a paragraph about career flexibility and how they can develop skills to take advantage of alternative opportunities.

SCANS Foundation Skills Connection

L1 Listening

Have students practice their listening skills by listening to an audiotape of a self-improvement course. Your school or public library should have such tapes available. Have them write 50-word paragraphs enumerating and describing the points made in a five-minute segment of the tape.

L2 Problem Solving

Read this scenario to students: "This morning, your supervisor, who was in a hurry to leave the office for a business trip, asked you to finish a report you've been working on and fax it to her hotel this afternoon. She then left. You realize later that you do not have the hotel's fax number. What would you do?"

(Check her itinerary to see whether the hotel telephone and fax numbers are there. If not, call the hotel and get the fax number.)

Asking questions is the best way to learn a new job. It's also a good way to avoid making embarrassing mistakes. *What should you do if you ask a question and, after receiving an answer, still don't understand what to do?*

Willingness to Learn

Think ahead a few months or years. You've completed your education and walked into your first full-time job. You may think you're done with learning. You're not. You'll have lots to learn about your new job, even if the job is one you've been trained for. Every company has its own ways of doing things. You'll have to learn the system and how to work with your coworkers.

Because you're a new employee, your employer will not expect you to know everything. So don't pretend to know something you don't. Ask questions.

Be willing to learn any job, no matter how small. When the copier gets jammed, watch how to fix it. Next time, you can take care of it yourself.

Learn all you can about your job and about the company. This information will help you do your job better and will prepare you for a promotion.

Look for opportunities to get more training. Many companies will pay for their employees to attend workshops, training programs, or college. Take advantage of any chance to learn more.

Initiative

You may get by, just by doing what you're told. Employers expect more from you, however. They want employees to show **initiative**. Taking initiative means doing what needs to be done without being told to do it.

Disney World deliberately seeks out employees who have initiative. Robert Sias, a trainer for Disney, gives an example of what it wants. A mother had just bought her son a box of popcorn, he explains. The child, about four years old, stumbled and dropped the popcorn, spilling it all over. The little boy burst into tears, and the mother became upset. Just at that moment, a costumed employee who

 Extending the Illustration

Have students describe ways to help them learn new tasks or procedures. (Take notes about tasks, read procedure manuals, review previous work that can be used as a model, or observe coworkers.)

Caption Answer: Explain what remains confusing to you, or ask the supervisor or a coworker to demonstrate what you are to do.

was on his way to another attraction walked by. Without a pause, he scooped up the empty popcorn box, got it refilled by the vendor, handed it to the little boy, and went on his way.

The employee showed initiative. He saw a problem and fixed it. It was no big deal, but it made a customer happy. That's what employers want.

Willingness to Take on More Responsibility

Business today is more competitive than ever. Companies must do more to satisfy customers. Employers know the key is empowered employees. They want employees to take more responsibility. **Responsibility** is the willingness to accept an obligation and to be accountable for an action or situation.

YOU'RE THE BOSS!

✓ *Solving Workplace Problems*

A review of the records of your CD/tape store shows unusual losses of inventory. You have six employees, all of whom seem loyal and reliable. The losses seem to have begun around the time your newest employee started work, but you have no evidence that she has been dishonest. What will you do?

Marriott Hotels has this attitude. One of its employees is Tony Prsyszlak (Prush-lak). If he worked for another hotel, he might be called a doorman. At Marriott, he's called a "guest service associate." The difference is more than the title. Prsyszlak picks up a guest's luggage at the curb and carries it up to the room. He can also check the guest in, obtain theater tickets for a play, reserve a table at a restaurant, or provide other services for the guest.

"I'm a bellman, a doorman, a front-desk clerk, and a concierge all rolled into one," Prsyszlak says. "I have more responsibilities. I feel better about my job, and the guest gets better service."

 Human resource managers look for employees who help customers without being told to do so. *How can workers prepare themselves for showing initiative on their jobs?*

Chapter 9 • Workplace Ethics **177**

L3 Self-Management
Have students create tables for the seven headings in Section 9-1. Have them rate themselves from 1 to 10 on each trait. Tell students to determine which traits they could improve and to devise plans for improvement.

SCANS Workplace Competencies Connection

L1 Working with Cultural Diversity
Divide students into groups of three or four. Write this list on the chalkboard: *fire fighter, company president, handicapped person, doctor, lawyer, teacher, engineer, secretary, health care worker.* Have each group brainstorm a list of at least four terms that describe each person.

When groups complete their lists, discuss any stereotypes that arise and how they affect people's perceptions (for example, describing a fire fighter as "male"). Have students discuss how to overcome stereotypes.

▶ Extending the Illustration

Ask students who have part-time jobs to share examples of initiative they have taken at work. What were the results?

Caption Answer: by thinking about how their jobs fit the broad purpose of the company and then looking for ways to help fulfill that purpose

Teaching YOU'RE THE BOSS!

✓ Possible responses: Talk with each employee individually, trying to identify the source of the losses; institute new policies, review or reinforce existing policies; spend more time working with the employees as a role-model.

SCANS Workplace Competencies Connection (cont'd.)

L2 **Teaching Others**

Have students choose local charity or volunteer groups in the community. Tell them to talk with an employee to find out the group's purpose, who benefits from the group's work, and the types of work volunteers do. Then set aside class time for each student to teach classmates about the group he or she chose.

L3 **Serving Clients/ Customers**

Have students interview customer service personnel at two or three local businesses to determine personal traits someone needs to work in that job. Have them make lists of the traits and share them in class.

Independent Practice

Assign as homework the chapter activity in the *School-to-Work Activity Handbook.*

Reading

Willingness to learn means keeping an open mind. Have students read an editorial in a local or regional newspaper, summarize the viewpoint of the editorial, and tell whether they agree or disagree with the writer. Ask them what they learned from reading the editorial and how they might use that knowledge.

What do you get out of taking on more responsibility? Your job becomes more interesting. You gain experience and a chance at better jobs. You increase your value to the company and earn job security.

Prove to your employer that you can accept greater responsibility. Show that you're not afraid of change. Volunteer for new jobs. Look for opportunities to do more than you were hired to do. Practice looking ahead. Don't think about extra work as just unpaid overtime. Think about where the added responsibility will get you in a year.

Self-Management

Who do you think is going to get you a job, a promotion, a raise? Only you. You've got to take responsibility for the work you do and the career you want. This is called **self-management**. It means doing the things necessary to build a better career. Here are some tips:

- Set career goals, and develop a plan for reaching them. As you achieve goals, or as your situation changes, set new goals.

- Monitor your work habits and performance. For example, you might keep

EXCELLENT BUSINESS PRACTICES

Reaching the Global Marketplace

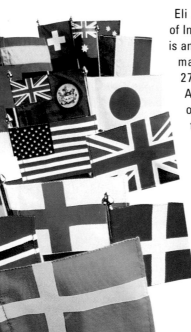

Eli Lilly and Company of Indianapolis, Indiana, is an international pharmaceutical firm with 27,700 employees. About 12,700 work overseas in 90 countries.

Lilly has made an effort to communicate the corporate strategy and company values to all employees worldwide. Employees learn to be sensitive to local differences and creative about finding ways to do business.

In some instances, however, Lilly does not want employees to follow the local culture. In some countries, "payoffs" are common, where a drug company representative pays doctors a fee every time they prescribe the company's product. Lilly does not allow this practice.

To help families of workers from other countries assimilate to American culture, Lilly has provided funds to the International School of Indiana. There, children of international workers can attend a special school that offers a cross-cultural curriculum.

Thinking Critically

In what ways does an international company have more challenges to maintain a firm position on ethics?

Extending EXCELLENT BUSINESS PRACTICES

Answer: An international company is likely to encounter more cultural differences that affect ethical decisions.

Further Application: Have students speak to someone who grew up in a country or a region of the United States different from their own. Can they identify three areas in which their backgrounds might differ with regard to acceptable standards of conduct?

a diary to track how you spend your time. Then you can identify ways to be more time-efficient.

- Ask for feedback on how you're doing your job. Ask coworkers and supervisors. Act on what you learn to improve your work habits and skills.

Loyalty

You know what it means to be loyal to your country and your school. It's also important to be loyal to your company. After all, you, your coworkers, your supervisors, and the owners are all in the business together. You're a team working toward a common goal.

How do you show loyalty at work? Don't run down the company or a supervisor in conversation. Be positive. Look for solutions. Don't point fingers.

When there's a crisis, pitch in and help the company get through it. This may involve self-sacrifice, some overtime, maybe even unpaid overtime. Remember you're doing it for yourself, too.

 Business owners today know they must do more to earn customer loyalty. *How does empowering employees with greater responsibility improve customer service?*

Writing: *Journal*

Have students write a 50-word entry in their career journals describing a personal or job-related experience requiring them to apply the personal traits listed in Section 9-1. Tell students to emphasize how the traits contributed to their success or lack of success in the situation.

ASSESS

Assessment

Content

Have students list the personal traits described in this section and give an example of how each trait applies to the workplace and helps make a person a more desirable employee. Evaluate for accuracy.

Evaluation

Assign the section review.

Reteaching

Tell students that they are being interviewed for a job as assistant to the animal trainer at a local aquatic park. The job involves feeding the animals, keeping track of props used in the shows, keeping the training area neat, and assisting the director in training exercises. Have students describe how their personal traits would help them do this job.

SECTION 9-1 *Review*

Understanding Key Concepts

Using complete sentences, answer the following questions on a separate sheet of paper.

1. Consider the qualities employers are seeking in employees. How will employees with these qualities allow companies to do less "managing"?

2. How is self-management good for you and good for your employer?

Chapter 9 • Workplace Ethics **179**

Extending the Illustration

Have students think of situations where they were displeased with the service they received from a business.

Caption Answer: If employees can do what's necessary to help customers, they can respond quickly and make customers happy.

SECTION 9-1 *Review* ANSWERS

1. Employees with these qualities will need less managing because they can work independently.

2. Self-management will help you become more skilled and disciplined. As a result, you will advance in your career.

ASSESS (cont'd.)

Extending the Content

Assign the appropriate Chapter 9 activities in the *Student Activity Workbook.*

Have students assume that they are considering two employees for a promotion to a supervisory job. One is a good worker and gets along well with coworkers but does not show a great deal of initiative. The second person shows initiative, gets a lot of work done, but sometimes shows impatience with coworkers who are not as energetic or dedicated to their jobs. Which person would students promote?

(Answers will vary, but most business owners would choose the second person because of the need for initiative in a supervisory job. The person could then get training to improve interpersonal skills.)

CLOSE

Have students explain what they think this statement means: "The best job security is your good reputation." (Students' interpretations will vary but should include that demonstrated job skills and ability to work well with people will be in demand by many employers.)

CASE STUDY

Exploring Careers: Fine Arts and Humanities

Erica Eysenbach
Graphic Designer

Q: How did you get your job as an art director?

A: I sort of slipped in the back door. I had an art history education and took a lot of art design and studio classes. I wanted to work at L. L. Bean, so I started as a customer service representative. Because of my background in art and my experience in working with the customers, I was eventually given the opportunity to work with the catalog. I started as an editor, then worked as an artist and editor, and finally became an art director.

Q: What skills are most important in your work?

A: You have to be a logical thinker. It's important to be able to juggle a lot of tasks. You have to be flexible and accept change because so many people have input into what you do. You should be able to work with many different people—from copywriters to corporate vice presidents to models.

Q: What are some of the changes you've seen in eight years?

A: The biggest change is the use of computers. We no longer draw everything by hand. We don't paste up the design. Typesetting is done directly on the computer. I think the use of computers will grow as computers develop.

Thinking Critically

What are some of the many ways graphic design is used today?

CAREER FACTS

Nature of the Work:
Use a variety of media and methods to communicate the client's ideas.

Training or Education Needed:
Bachelor's degree in art, specializing in graphic design; computer-design experience or training.

Aptitudes, Abilities, and Skills:
Math, listening, speaking, and interpersonal skills; problem-solving and decision-making skills; self-management skills; a good design sense, including an eye for color, form, and layout; the ability to work under deadline pressure; the ability to work alone and as part of a team; computer skills.

Salary Range:
Average starting salary—$18,000; average top salary—$50,000.

Career Path:
Start in a graphic design firm, publishing house, or advertising firm; take on more complex work and responsibility as an assistant art director and then as an art director; possibly open own business.

180   *Unit 4 • Joining the Workforce*

Extending the CASE STUDY

Answer: magazine, newspaper, and television advertising; direct-mail advertising; catalogs; package design; book design; billboards; corporate annual reports; brochures; posters for cultural events; letterheads

Further Application: Have students discuss the ways in which they might break into their chosen careers "through the back door." Such paths might involve starting in the restaurant business by waiting tables or designing menus; going into computer software design by selling software or designing web pages; becoming a journalist by working as an editor's assistant or doing computer layout at a newspaper.

Ethical Behavior

OBJECTIVES

After studying this section, you will be able to:

- **Explain why ethics are important in the workplace.**
- **Describe ways to behave ethically in the workplace.**

KEY TERMS

ethics
confidentiality
prejudice

Ethics are the principles of conduct that govern a group or society. How crucial are ethics in the workplace? Is it important for employees to behave ethically toward one another? Toward their company?

Many businesspeople think ethical behavior is critically important to success. Why? *Figure 9-1* on pages 182–183 shows how unethical behavior can have repercussions throughout a company.

Some companies have created programs to promote ethics. Do you think this is a good idea? Write down your answer to this question in your journal. List reasons for your opinion. As you read this section, add other reasons you discover.

Honesty

Employers expect their employees to be honest. Often, they're disappointed. Dishonesty is at the root of most ethics problems in the workplace.

What's the penalty for dishonesty? On a personal level, it can be devastating. One lie can destroy your reputation. How much does your reputation matter? If you were an employer, would you hire someone with a reputation for dishonesty? Be honest with your employer and your company. As an honest worker you will have a much better chance of being successful in your work.

Chapter 9 • Workplace Ethics **181**

Guided Practice

Teaching Strategies

1. Assign and review Section 9-2.

2. Use the transparency for this section.

Discussion Starter

Ask students to explain how they would handle this situation: You are listening to an experienced coworker explain a procedure to several new employees. You know that the coworker gave some erroneous information. When the person asks whether anyone has a question, what do you say? Is it dishonest to say nothing?

(Use tact and ask the coworker to clarify the point; perhaps he or she will state it correctly this time. If the statement still is wrong, wait and ask for clarification in private to avoid embarrassing him or her, who can then clear up the issue with the new employees. It isn't dishonest to say nothing, but you are not helping to clear up confusion that others may have.)

Critical Thinking

Tell students that they are small business owners ten years in the future. They are interviewing to hire three employees. What are the top three personal traits they are looking for? Discuss the choices in class, and have the class vote on the personal traits they believe to be most important. Ask for reasons why.

Honesty About Time

One of the most common ways in which employees can demonstrate honesty concerns their work hours. This is especially true for employees whose work takes them away from the company, who work at home, or who work on flextime, or flexible schedules. In each case, employees are trusted to work the hours they say they will. What might be the consequence if employees are dishonest about the time they work?

 Figure 9-1

The Effects of Unethical Behavior

Unethical behavior in the workplace has a spiraling effect. A single act can affect many people.

A There are many forms of unethical behavior. These workers have a responsibility to ship quality products. By deliberately shipping damaged goods, they're cheating their employer and the customer.

B Unethical behavior rarely goes unnoticed.

Extending Figure 9-1

Have students scan current issues of newspapers or magazines to find one example of unethical behavior on the part of both an employer and an employee. What actions were taken in response to the behavior?

Honesty About Money

Taking money out of the cash drawer is clearly dishonest. In many instances, the issue is more subtle. Consider the following case.

Juanita Benes is a salesperson. On a business trip, she spent more for meals than her expense account allowed. She thought she'd have to pay the difference out of her own pocket. On the other hand,

C The owners of Quality Televisions, Inc., will replace the damaged television sets, but they can't repair their reputation. Word of the problem spreads among customers. Customers will purchase television sets from another supplier.

D A company's reputation is its most important asset. Once the reputation is lost, business will be lost. Eventually, everyone who depended upon the company for a living will be affected.

Chapter 9 • Workplace Ethics **183**

Implementing Teamwork

Organize students into four groups to research unethical behavior in these four career areas: banking/finance, computer technology, government, and sports/entertainment. From their research, ask each group to present one case of unethical behavior for their career field.

☑ **SCANS Foundation Skills Connection**

L1 Math

Barbara, a clerk at Fran's Frame Shop, sold three picture frames to a customer for a total of $78.99. The shop was running a sale of four frames for $99.99. Did Barbara charge the correct amount for the three frames? If not, how much should she have charged? ($75: $99.99 ÷ 4 = $24.9975, or $25; $25 × 3 = $75)

L2 Integrity/Honesty

Tell students that one of their coworkers asks their opinion of a project he or she has been working on. After reviewing it, students think it isn't very good. They want to be honest with the coworker but also tactful. Ask students to write ideas on how to respond.

L3 Reasoning

Shoplifting and other forms of theft cost businesses millions of dollars each year. Have students write 100-word papers tracing the effect of these costs on consumers, employees, local government, and business owners. (Consumers pay higher prices, employees earn lower wages or have fewer jobs, local government gets less money from income taxes because the business hires fewer people, and business owners make less money and thus reinvest less in the business.)

SCANS Workplace Competencies Connection

L1 **Interpreting and Communicating Information**

Tell students to imagine that a new worker has made a fairly serious but not uncommon error. A second employee who notices the error waits until a supervisor is present, then says to the new worker, "You're making too many errors. Let me show you what to do before you make a mess."

Have students discuss how the supervisor might interpret the situation. Was the coworker's behavior ethical? (Probably not, the comment might make the supervisor think badly of the new worker.)

L2 **Understanding Systems**

In any organization, peer pressure can cause people to behave in ways they normally would not. Have students discuss how peer pressure in school affects their behavior. How might coworkers' attitudes cause someone to behave unethically? (An example is taking company supplies because "everyone does it.") How could students avoid such situations when they are employed? (By having a positive self-image and following their own beliefs when making choices.)

▶ **Figure 9-2**

A recent study by the Ethics Resource Center revealed that one-third of all employees interviewed observed some kind of unethical behavior during a one-year period. This graph shows the most common observations. Does the information on this chart surprise you? Why or why not?

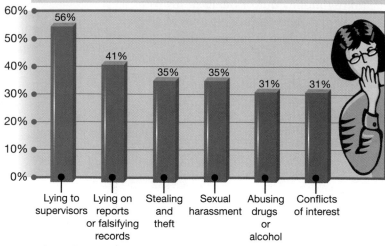

Observed Unethical Behavior

Category	Percentage
Lying to supervisors	56%
Lying on reports or falsifying records	41%
Stealing and theft	35%
Sexual harassment	35%
Abusing drugs or alcohol	31%
Conflicts of interest	31%

Source: Ethics Resource Center survey in Flynn, Gillian. "Make Employee Ethics Your Business," *Personnel Journal*, June 1995, v74 n6 p. 30.

International Passengers

Please Check-in At Ticket Counter

she thought she could make up the difference by adding the amount to two blank taxi receipts. Would this be dishonest?

Benes at first reasoned that it was only a technicality. Other employees probably did it. She wouldn't feel guilty telling her husband. Then she thought about telling her children. She realized that in their eyes, it would be dishonest.

Often you may think there is a thin line between honesty and dishonesty. As you reason through such cases in your career, think how your action might appear to others. *Figure 9-2* shows the types of unethical behavior observed during a one-year period.

▶ Business travelers have expense accounts. Their employers will pay for transportation, meals, and other job-related expenses. *Why do employers set limits for travel expenses?*

184 *Unit 4 • Joining the Workforce*

▶▶ **Extending Figure 9-2** ◀◀

Have students interview five people regarding examples of unethical behavior they have observed in their own work.

Caption Answer: Answers will vary. Many students may respond that they are surprised by how common unethical behavior is.

▶▶ **Extending the Illustration**

Ask students to make lists of ways employees can help their employers save money. How does saving money benefit employees? (Saving money benefits employees because the employer can afford to pay higher wages or offer better benefits.)

Caption Answer: Employers have to control the cost of doing business.

Respecting Employers' Property

Another way to risk your reputation and job is to be careless with company property. Don't illegally copy company software for your personal use. Don't take office supplies home for your own use. These items may seem petty, but the small costs do add up. Also, think about it from your supervisor's point of view. If he or she knows you're stealing stamps, will he or she put you in charge of more costly items?

Interacting with Others

Whatever business you enter, you'll be talking and working with others. Occasionally, your interactions may involve ethical issues.

Confidentiality

As an employee, you may have information that would harm the company if others learned about it. This information might have to do with new products, expansion plans, promotions, and so on. Your company will expect you to observe **confidentiality**. In other words, don't tell secrets to people who are not supposed to know them.

Confidentiality is behavior your friends, family, and coworkers also expect from you. They don't want their secrets told either.

▶ Any business may face a crisis from time to time. When it happens, everyone needs to pull together. *Why is it important to have a good attitude, even if you don't like the extra work?*

Chapter 9 • Workplace Ethics **185**

L3 Acquiring and Evaluating Information

Have students read a news article describing either a local or a regional company that is laying off workers or closing a plant. Have them write brief summaries of the main point of the article, then write whether they think the company's actions are ethical or unethical. Have students give reasons for their stance.

Independent Practice
Role-Play

Have pairs of students role-play making requests in these situations:

- asking a coworker to switch shifts,
- telling a coworker that his or her voice is loud and disturbing,
- asking a coworker for help with a client who speaks only Spanish, and
- refusing to gossip about another coworker.

You may also want to have pairs of students perform these role-plays:

- asking a supervisor to repeat directions,
- informing a supervisor of problems with a supplier,
- asking a supervisor for a raise or a promotion, and
- making a suggestion to a supervisor to improve the department.

Extending the Illustration

Ask students how they can turn crisis situations into opportunities for learning new skills. (Supervisors notice people who willingly try to learn new skills.)

Caption Answer: When people work under stress, a bad attitude only makes the situation worse.

Teaching Attitude Counts ✔

After students have read and discussed the "Attitude Counts" paragraph, let them write journal entries recording their own ideas about boring duties. For example:

- What school- or work-related duties do you find especially boring?
- Why are those duties important?

Teaching Tip

Have students read the boxed text "Career Do's & Don'ts." For the "Do's," ask students to describe how they would apply each item to their personal lives. For example, how do they develop and maintain integrity?

For the "Don'ts," have students explain why they should not do each of the items. For example, what are the consequences of revealing information that should not be made public? Also ask students to give strategies for how they can avoid these situations.

Critical Thinking

Ask students to write a paragraph describing the difference between trying to convince someone about something and arguing with that person. (Convincing someone usually requires citing facts or reasons; arguing is more emotional and may be based more on personal wants than on logical reasons.)

Interview

Invite a local business person whose company has a formal ethics (written) policy to speak to your class. If possible, ask the speaker to provide copies of the policy. Have students prepare questions in advance. After the interview, ask students what one item of information was most surprising to them. Have students explain the benefits of working in a company that has a formal ethics policy.

Career Do's & Don'ts

When Balancing What Feels Right To You...

Do:

- develop and maintain integrity.
- respect the values of other people, even if you don't agree.
- communicate openly without distorting information.
- speak to a counselor if you have an ethical decision to make.

Don't:

- say or do anything you wouldn't feel comfortable with being made public.
- go along with other people because they pressure you.
- send mixed messages, so others don't know where you stand.
- hesitate leaving the job if the company's ethics don't match yours.

On the surface, confidentiality seems easy. Sometimes, though, there are conflicting interests. Take the situation involving Sheila Williams.

Williams ran into a former coworker and friend at a seminar. They had dinner together. While talking, Williams learned about a new product her friend's company was developing. It was a product similar to one Williams's own company was working on. Not only that, but her friend's company had solved a problem that Williams's company was stuck on. Her friend didn't know Williams's company was a rival. Should Williams use the information to help her company beat out the rival?

The Ethics Quiz in *Figure 9-3* may help you with such decisions. Use it to resolve Williams's dilemma.

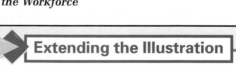

Coworkers often become good friends. *Why is confidentiality especially important when one of the friends moves to a new job?*

186 *Unit 4 • Joining the Workforce*

Extending the Illustration

Have students decide in which of the following situations they should keep the information confidential: (1) You see a memo naming a coworker who is to be fired; (2) Annual sales for a public corporation are $140 million; (3) You overhear a conversation between two executives about a new project that will be announced to the public in six months. (Items one and three.)

Caption Answer: As coworkers, people become accustomed to sharing information about their jobs and work situation. When one moves on, the friendship continues. Confidentiality ensures that the friendship isn't marred by rivalry or distrust.

Ethics Quiz

✓ Is this action against the law?
If it is, don't do it.

✓ Do you know the action is wrong?
If so, don't do it.

✓ Is the action contrary to company values?
*Every company has a set of values.
Sometimes they are written policy.
Sometimes they are not written but are
part of an unwritten code of behavior.*

✓ Will you feel bad if you perform this action?
If so, don't do it.

✓ Are you unsure if the action is wrong?
*Ask someone. Check with coworkers, your
supervisor, friends or associates outside
of work.*

✓ If this action were reported on the five
o'clock news, what would viewers think
about it?

✓ If you asked an eight-year-old about the
action, what would he or she tell you to do?

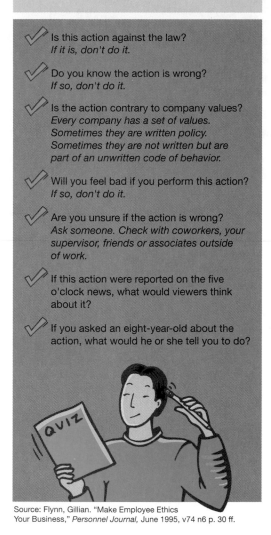

Source: Flynn, Gillian. "Make Employee Ethics
Your Business," *Personnel Journal,* June 1995, v74 n6 p. 30 ff.

▲ **Figure 9-3** Questions about
ethical issues often do not have definite or
clear-cut answers. You must simply use your
best judgment. Why does it help to try to
see the situation through a child's eyes?

Fairness

Virtually every business includes men and women of different races and religions. You'll interact with them as customers, owners, and coworkers. Treat everyone fairly, openly, and honestly.

Prejudice—an unjustifiable negative attitude toward a person or group—is an ethical issue. Prejudice comes in many forms, including racist or sexist comments, stereotyping, name calling, and generalizations. Prejudice in any form, however, is hurtful, offensive, and unacceptable; it cannot be tolerated in today's workplace. Not only can employees be fired for prejudicial comments, but they and their companies can be sued.

Handling Unethical Practices

What if you're the victim of unethical practices? What if you experience prejudice in the workplace? What if you observe unethical business practices?

Consider whether it was an isolated incident or an ongoing practice. Maybe it can be cleared up by a calm, open discussion.

If the offense is deliberate, don't ignore it. Don't act rashly either. First, consider your options. If you're dealing with a customer, you might simply walk away. You don't have to sell a product to an abusive or dishonest customer. Report the incident to your supervisor.

If you're dealing with a coworker, you might tell him or her you will not tolerate his or her prejudiced behavior. If that does not work, talk to your supervisor. Look for solutions, not revenge.

Chapter 9 • Workplace Ethics **187**

Discussion Starter

Prejudice is not always negative. You can be prejudiced in someone's favor, for example, by always viewing their actions as positive. Ask students how many of them think they have been the subject of prejudice—either negative or positive. Have them describe their experience. How did they handle the situation?

Teaching Tip

Write the following sentence on the chalkboard: *It's 30 minutes before the end of the work day. A coworker wants to leave early and has asked you to tell your supervisor, if asked, that he or she is in another department.*

Read each item in the ethics quiz (Figure 9-3). As you read the item, have students apply it to the above situation. (The action is not illegal; it is dishonest and most likely against company values. Students may or may not feel bad about doing this. The action is wrong and certain people might say the coworker should leave on time. A child might say it's wrong to cheat.)

Now tell students the coworker who wants to leave early is a parent who has been called to pick up a sick child and the supervisor is nowhere to be found. Does that change the ethics of the situation?

▶▶ Extending Figure 9-3 ◀◀

Have students write a paragraph describing a work situation involving ethics and their recommendation for how the situation should be handled. (Examples might include how to talk with a friend who breaks work rules or how to respond to a coworker who takes supplies or urges others to do so.)

Caption Answer: A possible answer is that a child sees things more simply and honestly than adults do. The child is less likely to realize that people cheat or to use what other people do as an excuse to justify unethical actions.

ASSESS

Assessment

Content

Tell students that they are entrepreneurs who believe they need a company policy on ethical behavior. Have students write 250-word policy manuals dealing with this issue.

(Evaluate students' manuals for accuracy of grammar, spelling, and punctuation. Students should write policies relating to honesty, confidentiality of company information, company attitude toward fairness, and equal opportunity for all employees.)

Evaluation

Assign the section review.

MINI QUIZ

Short Answer

1. Working well with coworkers is an example of _____. (cooperativeness)

2. Taking _____ means seeing something that needs to be done and doing it. (initiative)

3. Being responsible for building your own career is a part of _____. (self-management)

4. Lying to _____ is one of the most common forms of unethical behavior. (supervisors)

5. Racist or sexist comments are an example of _____. (prejudice)

Use the Testmaker to create a customized test for Chapter 9.

What if your employer is unethical? You can choose to live with the situation. You can keep quiet and find another job. You can report it to the appropriate authority. The choice may not be easy. If you decide to take action, these pointers may help:

- Keep a written record as shown in *Figure 9-4*. Describe each incident. Record the date and time.

- Check your observations with others. Maybe they can explain matters. Maybe they will help.

- Get advice from people you trust.

- Check your motives. Are you acting for the right reasons?

- Collect any evidence you can, such as receipts, invoices, or contracts.

- Decide whether you want to remain anonymous or to speak up openly.

- Report only facts or observations. Don't exaggerate or speculate.

> **July 23, 10:45 A.M.**
> I saw Mr. Jones meeting with Andrew Mathes, a sales representative for XYZ Company. They met in his office for 25 minutes. When they left, Mr. Jones said, "I'll take care of it. When I get your company's bid, I'll see it's given preferential treatment."
>
> **July 27, 3:30 P.M.**
> A courier arrived with an envelope for Mr. Jones. I signed for the envelope. It was from Mr. Mathes. Mr. Jones opened the envelope in front of me. It contained two play-off tickets.

Figure 9-4 Accurate, complete records of unethical behavior can serve as partial proof of the events. Why would it be a good idea to have a coworker keep additional records?

SECTION 9-2 *Review*

Understanding Key Concepts

Using complete sentences, answer the following questions on a separate sheet of paper.

1. Imagine that you've observed a coworker lying to a customer. How might this unethical behavior affect you?

2. Of the different kinds of ethical behavior, which do you think will be your biggest challenge? Why?

SECTION 9-2 *Review* ANSWERS

1. It might result in a loss of business, which could cause a loss of jobs.

2. Possible answer: It will be blowing the whistle on a coworker's unethical behavior. It might be hard to work with that person in the future. There might be other workplace consequences.

Extending Figure 9-4

Have students brainstorm actions they could take if they worked for a chemical manufacturer that they think is illegally dumping toxic wastes. (Contact the Environmental Protection Agency.)

Caption Answer: Each record would support the other. Employees might have different interpretations of what they saw.

Key Terms

cooperativeness *(p. 174)*
initiative *(p. 176)*
responsibility *(p. 177)*
self-management *(p. 178)*

SECTION 9-1 Summary

- Today's employers want employees who can do many things and who will fit into the company's structure. A key is cooperativeness. This means working well with coworkers and managers.

- Employees must be skilled at listening to and following directions.

- You should be prepared to continue learning throughout your working career.

- Businesses are looking for employees who show initiative. These are people who will step forward and do what needs to be done without having to be told.

- Most employers want workers to take on more responsibility. Taking on additional responsibility will make your work more interesting and make you more valuable to your employer.

- To succeed in the world of work, you must manage your own career.

Key Terms

ethics *(p. 181)*
confidentiality *(p. 185)*
prejudice *(p. 187)*

SECTION 9-2 Summary

- Ethics are the moral rules of society. Ethics are very important because unethical behavior can have negative repercussions throughout a company.

- As an employee, you should strive to be honest, especially as this relates to time, money, and your employer's property.

- Every career involves interactions with other people. Respecting the confidentiality of your employer and coworkers and acting fairly with everyone are critical to your success.

- You must maintain your own values. When you are the victim or observer of unethical behavior, there are several ways to respond. Choosing the correct response can be a difficult decision.

Chapter 9 • Workplace Ethics **189**

Reteaching

1. Have students choose a work experience where they think unethical behavior may have taken place. Ask students to answer these questions about the situation: (a) What was unethical? (b) Was the person involved dishonest and if so, how? (c) How could the person have handled this situation in a more ethical way?

2. Assign and review vocabulary terms, chapter questions, and activities from the Chapter Review.

Extending the Content

Assign the appropriate Chapter 9 activities in the *Student Activity Workbook.*

Tell students to imagine that they are a supervisor working with an employee whose work is not up to par. To cover mistakes, the employee often lies about the work. Have students write what they would say to this employee to try to improve both his or her work and behavior.

CLOSE

Have students complete this sentence: "One way I can demonstrate ethical behavior in the workplace is to . . . ."

Computer Activity

Have students use a spreadsheet software package to prepare a personal inventory form that could be used to assess an individual's personal qualities. Students should select at least five different personal qualities and design an evaluation scale for assessment (for example, poor–excellent; 1–5; unimportant–very important). After they have finished the forms, have them exchange them with a partner. Ask students to use the forms to take their own personal inventory.

Answers
Reviewing Key Terms

Paragraphs will vary but should include all of the key terms.

Recalling Key Concepts

1. b
2. a
3. b
4. c
5. c

Thinking Critically

1. Cooperativeness involves doing any tasks that are assigned. Sometimes you may feel that such tasks are beneath you. You have to feel good about yourself to do them anyway and without complaining.

2. It will demonstrate your initiative, that is, that you are willing to learn, to take on new jobs, and to accept additional responsibilities. These are qualities an employer values.

3. Answers will vary. Positives include feeling you have done the right thing, a more successful company, or more job security. Negatives include an angry confrontation with the coworker, distrust or dislike from other coworkers, or feelings of guilt at getting a coworker in trouble.

Reviewing Key Terms

On a separate sheet of paper, write a paragraph about the qualities employers seek in employees. Use each of the key terms.

cooperativeness   initiative
responsibility   self-management
ethics   confidentiality
prejudice

Recalling Key Concepts

Choose the correct answer for each item below. Write your answers on a separate sheet of paper.

1. A willingness to work with others is ____.
   (a) initiative   (b) cooperativeness
   (c) ethics

2. When you are given directions, you should ____.
   (a) listen   (b) show initiative
   (c) experiment

3. When you take on unassigned tasks, you are demonstrating ____.
   (a) honesty   (b) initiative   (c) caution

4. The ethics of your coworkers ____.
   (a) cannot affect a business's success
   (b) should not concern you
   (c) can affect your job security

5. If you observe confidentiality, you ____.
   (a) report a coworker's dishonesty
   (b) work the hours you are expected to work
   (c) don't tell company secrets

190   *Unit 4 • Joining the Workforce*

Thinking Critically

Using complete sentences, answer each of the questions below on a separate sheet of paper.

1. Why might you need a strong sense of self-esteem to be cooperative in the workplace?

2. How might learning tasks that are not part of your regular job make you a more valuable employee?

3. What are some positive and some negative consequences that might result from reporting a coworker's unethical behavior?

SCANS Foundation Skills and Workplace Competencies

Information: *Acquiring and Evaluating Information*

1. Employees in retail stores spend time at a variety of tasks, such as helping customers, checking them out at the cash register, stocking shelves, taking inventory, and ordering products. To operate efficiently, store managers must know how much time employees spend at each task. Create a chart that might be used to collect and record this information.

Basic Skills: *Math*

2. Because retail stores are busier at certain times of the day, more employees are needed to run the cash registers at different hours. Construct a line graph that presents the following information: one employee at 8:00 A.M.,

SCANS Foundation Skills and Workplace Competencies

1. Students may produce a chart with various tasks listed as column heads and rows labeled with times of the day, perhaps in 15-minute intervals.

2. Students should construct a line graph accurately recording the information provided. The y-axis should be labeled to

show the number of employees working at the cash registers. The x-axis should be labeled with the hours.

Connecting Academics to the Workplace

1. Answers will vary, depending on waste disposal laws and resources in the students' area. Students should investigate

two at 9:00, two at 10:00, three at 11:00, four at 12:00, five at 1:00 P.M., two at 2:00, one at 3:00, one at 4:00, two at 5:00, five at 6:00, six at 7:00, six at 8:00, four at 9:00, two at 10:00.

Connecting Academics to the Workplace

Science

1. Li works for a small manufacturing company in your area. The owner has 50 cans of latex paint stored in the back of his warehouse. The paint is no longer good, and the owner wants to dispose of it. He has asked Li to investigate options for safely disposing of the paint. Find out how old paint can be legally disposed of in your area, and provide two practical options.

Social Studies

2. Andrew works in the human resources department of a small publishing company. The owners have asked Andrew to investigate the pros and cons of flextime. They also want to know if flextime is suitable for their kind of business. Do research to learn the answers. You might use library resources or the Internet or talk with human resource managers whose companies have flextime.

Developing Teamwork and Leadership Skills

Work with four or five other students. Assume that your group works in the human resources department of a company that is participating in a job fair at your high school. As a group, select a business. Then develop and give a presentation in which you describe three openings in your company and the skills and personal behavior required.

Real-World Workshop

Imagine that you work for a company that is no longer profitable. Layoffs are possible, and morale is low. Work with four classmates, who will be your coworkers. Choose a business and create a list of problems you have witnessed. Examples include lack of training, bad morale, and poor customer service. Then brainstorm solutions to this question: What can we, as employees, do to improve morale and protect our job security?

School-to-Work Connection

Interview the owner or human resource manager of a local business. Find out what skills and personal behavior the company is looking for in a person just entering the workforce. Does the company provide training for new employees? Report your findings to your class.

Individual Career Plan

What job would you like to have when you finish school? What skills and personal qualities will this job require? How do you measure up right now? Do you have the skills needed? Write an assessment of your skills and personal qualities.

Developing Teamwork and Leadership Skills

The presentation should include realistic skills and personal qualities needed for the business selected.

Real-World Workshop

Students should brainstorm a list of solutions that employees might implement to improve workplace efficiency and morale. These may include giving more responsibility to employees, beefing up training to improve job skills, and providing better customer service.

School-to-Work Connection

Answers will be specific to the company students learn about and to the individual interviewed.

Individual Career Plan

Students should write an honest appraisal of their current level of skills and their personal qualities.

Chapter 9 • Workplace Ethics **191**

and provide two options for disposing of the old paint.

2. Answers will vary. Pros include improved employee morale, resulting in a better work environment. Cons include problems of internal communication because everyone would not work the same hours and potential problems if employees did not work the hours agreed upon.

Flextime is successful with companies in which employees often work independently. It is usually not suitable for businesses such as retailers, who must have employees available at regular hours to serve customers, or in factories where the work is interconnected.

· · · PLANNING GUIDE · · ·
Chapter 10

SECTION 1 *Attitudes for Success*

SECTION OBJECTIVES	SECTION FEATURES	SECTION RESOURCES
• Discuss how a positive attitude and high self-esteem lead to success on the job. • Explain the value of enthusiasm at work. • Describe how to assert yourself at work.	Personal Career Plan, p. 193 You're the Boss!, p. 198 Ethics in Action, p. 201 Exploring Careers, p. 202	Workforce 2000 Videodisc and Videotape Section 10-1 Review, p. 201 Student Activity Workbook

SECTION 2 *Acting Like a Professional*

SECTION OBJECTIVES	SECTION FEATURES	SECTION RESOURCES
• Describe how to accept criticism at work. • Give examples of how to professionally handle workplace pressure and gossip. • Explain how to control anger on the job.	Excellent Business Practices, p. 204 Career Do's and Don'ts, p. 208	Workforce 2000 Videodisc and Videotape Section 10-2 Review, p. 208 Chapter 10 Review, pp. 210–211 Student Activity Workbook

CHAPTER RESOURCES

- Chapter Transparencies and Lesson Plans
- Chapter 10 Test
- Spanish Resources, Chapter 10
- School-to-Work Activity Handbook, Chapter 10 Activity
- Teacher's Lesson Plans, Chapter 10
- Implementing Block Scheduling, Chapter 10
- Print, Media, and Internet Handbook
- Strategies for Implementing Work-Based Learning
- Strategies for Implementing Connecting Activities

Career Notes

SCANS CORRELATION CHART

Foundation Skills

Basic Skills

Reading	Writing	Math	Listening	Speaking

Thinking Skills

Creative Thinking	Decision Making	Problem Solving	Seeing Things in the Mind's Eye	Knowing How to Learn	Reasoning

Personal Qualities

Responsibility	Self-Esteem	Sociability	Self-Management	Integrity/Honesty

Workplace Competencies

Resources

Allocating Time	Allocating Money	Allocating Material and Facility Resources	Allocating Human Resources

Information

Acquiring and Evaluating Information	Organizing and Maintaining Information	Interprêting and Communicating Information	Using Computers to Process Information

Interpersonal Skills

Participating as a Member of a Team	Teaching Others	Serving Clients/ Customers	Exercising Leadership	Negotiating to Arrive at a Decision	Working with Cultural Diversity

Systems

Understanding Systems	Monitoring and Correcting Performance	Improving and Designing Systems

Technology

Selecting Technology	Applying Technology to Task	Maintaining and Troubleshooting Technology

Highlighted blocks indicate areas covered in the Chapter.

Additional Activities

 ### Internet Connection

Ask students to use the Internet to find discussion groups or chat rooms where they can talk about work. Have them note the kinds of gripes that arise, ask questions about the work, and so on. After students have gone on-line at least three times, have them compare their findings in class.

 ### Field Trip Suggestions

Arrange to take students to a local business show. Have them look closely at the booths that interest them. They should write down what attracted them—the person, displays, brochures, slogans. They should also note the impression they had of the business or the product as the result of the booth.

 ### Guest Speaker Suggestions

Invite a corporate workshop leader who specializes in stress management. Ask the guest to talk about the kinds of stress in the workplace, and offer suggestions on how workers can manage the stress of daily work, and rapid workplace change.

Key to Ability Levels

Each section gives skill-building activities. Each activity has been labeled for use with students of various learning styles and abilities.

L1 Level 1 activities are basic activities and should be within the range of all students.

L2 Level 2 activities are average activities and should be within the range of average and above average students.

L3 Level 3 activities are challenging activities designed for the ability range of above average students.

Chapter 10

Developing a Positive Attitude

 ### School-Based Learning

Chapter Overview

Attitude plays an important role in initial job success. In this chapter, students will learn how to develop a positive attitude and to demonstrate professional behavior on the job.

Section 10-1 presents strategies for developing a positive attitude and self-esteem.

Section 10-2 explores methods of accepting and responding to criticism and learning to handle emotions at work.

Background Information

Write chapter objectives (Sections 10-1 and 10-2) on the chalkboard or use the chapter objective transparency for class discussion.

Choose assignments from the *Student Activity Workbook* and write them on the chalkboard.

Have students preview the chapter, looking at pictures, reading captions, and noting content headings. Ask students to describe what they expect to learn in this chapter.

Preteaching Vocabulary

Write the Key Terms from Sections 10-1 and 10-2 on the chalkboard. Have students describe how each term relates to developing a positive attitude and dealing with criticism and emotions on the job.

192

Meeting SPECIAL Needs

Learning Disabled

It is common to grade students on participation in class. However, students who have difficulties expressing themselves find class participation hard. These students need encouragement and patience. For example, ask them factual questions and give them time to find the answers in the textbook.

Chapter 10

Developing a Positive Attitude

Section 10-1
Attitudes for Success

Section 10-2
Acting Like a Professional

In this video segment, discover how a positive attitude can lead to job success.

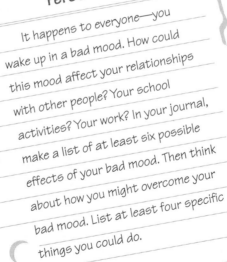

Journal
Personal Career Plan

It happens to everyone—you wake up in a bad mood. How could this mood affect your relationships with other people? Your school activities? Your work? In your journal, make a list of at least six possible effects of your bad mood. Then think about how you might overcome your bad mood. List at least four specific things you could do.

193

⮞ School-to-Work ⮜ Connecting Activities

Invite a human resources manager and a counselor or psychologist to speak to your class. First, ask the manager to talk about how he or she views employees who respond inappropriately in difficult situations, giving examples of such behavior. Then have the counselor or psychologist discuss skills for learning to handle emotions. Reserve time for questions, then have students write summaries.

Work-Based Learning Strategies and Activities

Meet with representatives of nonprofit organizations and arrange for students to volunteer. Review the skills needed for volunteer work and try to arrange for a variety of activities. (For example, animal care through the Humane Society or health care through a hospital.) Weekly, have students discuss their experiences and give methods for applying the skills they are learning to a career.

WORKFORCE 2000 Training Video

Have students view the video and perform the interactive exercises to reinforce important chapter concepts and thinking processes.

Chapter 10

Addressing **LEARNING** Styles

Musical Learner

Ask students to choose favorite songs or TV jingles. Have them write new words to the jingle that would remind themselves or others who hear the song to have a positive attitude. Naturally the tunes they choose should be upbeat. Students may want to work in teams of two or three to do this. Have the most confident students perform their "attitude" songs.

193

SECTION 10-1

FOCUS

Bell Ringer

Have students identify a person whom they consider to be successful and write at least ten words that describe the characteristics or traits that help make her or him successful.

Introducing the Section

As students share their answers from the Bell Ringer activity, write the traits on the chalkboard. Use this discussion to introduce attitude, and how someone with a positive attitude reacts to work situations. Discuss strategies for building a positive attitude and the effect that attitude has on developing self-esteem.

Motivational Activity
Role-play

Choose a student or ask another teacher or an assistant to help you model negative behavior by doing a role-play and then role-playing a positive reaction to the same situation. This siutation could be, for example, an announcement that new computer software is being purchased and that all employees must be trained to use it.

Have students respond to the two role-plays from the viewpoint of the person announcing the change. Which response made them feel more favorably toward the employee? Discuss responses with students.

Attitudes for Success

OBJECTIVES

After studying this section, you will be able to:

- **Discuss how a positive attitude and high self-esteem lead to success on the job.**
- **Explain the value of enthusiasm at work.**
- **Describe how to assert yourself at work.**

KEY TERMS

attitude
self-esteem
enthusiasm
assertiveness
arrogance

School-to-work students Roy Marcus and Gary Sikes have just received some surprising news. Amy Ngo, their coworker at the administrative offices of LaSalle Industries, is moving to another city. She will be leaving in two weeks and will not be replaced. After celebrating with Amy over lunch, Roy and Gary discuss their reactions in private.

Roy thinks the news is great—not only for Amy but also for himself and Gary. Without Amy, they will have the opportunity to learn more about running the business. They will be able to prove themselves to the company. They may even earn permanent positions at LaSalle.

Gary, on the other hand, considers the situation a problem. "What's so great?" he scowls. "All this means is we'll be doing more work for the same pay."

Does this scene sound familiar? If not, be prepared. You may face a similar one at work. While you can't control everything that happens on the job, you can control how you react.

If you are more a "Gary" than a "Roy," pay special attention to this section. Your **attitude,** or basic outlook on life, matters. It determines how you react to certain situations and, often, how you are perceived by others. It is your way of looking at the world and the people in it. How well you get along with your employer and your coworkers will depend on your attitude. If you have a positive attitude, you are already on your way to success on the job.

194 *Unit 4 • Joining the Workforce*

Workforce 2000 Trends

In the future, a company's success will depend on its employees' ability and willingness to learn. The competitive edge will depend on whether a business puts new ideas into effect, learns from multi-disciplinary points of view, and is able to learn from smaller businesses.

Building a positive attitude is like climbing a spiral staircase. *How can positive thinking help you get ahead?*

I'm Positive!

The first step in building a positive attitude is to think positively. When you think positively, you reap many rewards.

What Positive Thinking Can Do for You

Have you ever heard people attribute their success to "the power of positive thinking"? Well, they may be right. Evidence shows that thinking positively can bring you power—in your life and on the job. Think back to Roy and Gary. Whom do you think is more likely to succeed at work? Why?

Here are some ways that positive thinking can lead you to positive results:

- *Positive thinkers get along better with others.* When you think positively, you are more receptive, or open, to the people around you.

- *Others feel more comfortable with positive thinkers.* Whom would you rather be around: someone who is optimistic or someone who is negative?

Chapter 10 • Developing a Positive Attitude **195**

SCANS Foundation Skills Connection

L1 Self-Esteem

For at least a week, have students note when someone compliments them on an action. Tell students to write the action and the person's comment in notebooks. At the end of the week, have them review the comments. How did their actions reflect positive thinking?

L2 Listening

Obtain a tape from your school or public library on how to develop positive thinking skills. Play the tape (or a segment of it) for students, then have them write a list of the major points made in the tape.

L3 Self-Management

Almost everyone can improve their powers of positive thinking. Have students take an informal survey of at least 10 people, (friends, family, or teachers) asking two questions to each person: How have you observed me being positive? How have you observed me being negative? Tell students to write each person's comments and create lists or charts of all positive and negative comments. Have students refer to the information in Figure 10-1, then create a plan to improve the negative actions or attitudes.

- *Positive thinkers handle problems more effectively.* Consider this "upward spiral": When you think positively, you elevate your mood. When you elevate your mood, you make better decisions. When you make better decisions, you feel even better, and so forth.

- *Positive thinking can help you reach your goals by motivating you to act.* As Les Brown, author of *Live Your Dreams*, explains: "People who expect to achieve their goals don't

 Figure 10-1

Building a Positive Attitude

If you want to build a positive attitude, it helps to practice the four steps shown here.

B Surround yourself with positive thinkers. Positive energy is contagious. Unfortunately, negative energy can be as well. You should not make a practice of deserting friends in need. However, if most of your friends are in a negative place, and particularly if they are bringing you down, it may be a good idea to seek out new friends.

A Promote positive thoughts by taking positive actions. Instead of sitting around complaining about problems, mobilize and act. Join or form a group or club for a one-time or ongoing action.

196 *Unit 4 • Joining the Workforce*

Extending Figure 10-1

Choose a recent news event in your community and describe it in negative terms. Have students analyze how the event could be interpreted in a more positive light.

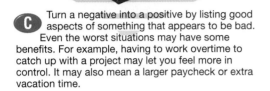

D Present your ideas positively, without apologizing. Attending a school-, job-, or community-related meeting offers an excellent opportunity to work on this step. Remember to speak slowly and clearly and to watch your body language.

C Turn a negative into a positive by listing good aspects of something that appears to be bad. Even the worst situations may have some benefits. For example, having to work overtime to catch up with a project may let you feel more in control. It may also mean a larger paycheck or extra vacation time.

stand around talking about them. They're engaged in action."

- *Positive thinkers are healthier.* In fact, a study has shown that pessimistic students get sick twice as often as optimistic ones.

How to Build a Positive Attitude

OK, you may be thinking, a positive attitude is good. Now how do I go about getting one? The answer is you must build one, step-by-step. *Figure 10-1* shows some of the steps in the process.

Developing Self-Esteem

As *Figure 10-1* shows, when you present your ideas without apologizing, you show **self-esteem**, or a recognition and regard for yourself and your abilities. Self-esteem is essential for a positive attitude.

Here's another "upward spiral": Self-esteem breeds confidence. Confidence generates success. Success boosts self-esteem.

Overcoming Doubt

Do you have a little voice inside your head? Does it sometimes whisper negative messages, such as "You don't deserve to get that new job" or "You're not smart enough to pass that test"? Most people suffer twinges of inner doubt. Would you like to get rid of that voice? One technique that works for many people is called positive self-talk.

Positive self-talk means you "outtalk" your negative inner voice. When the voice says, "You can't," you answer, "I can—and

Chapter 10 • Developing a Positive Attitude **197**

Implementing Teamwork

Divide your class into groups of five to six students. Have the groups discuss a hypothetical problem related to low morale in the workplace. Ask the groups to brainstorm possible solutions to the problem. Some students should assume the role of management and others the role of hourly wage earners.

SCANS Workplace Competencies Connection (cont'd.)

L3 Applying Technology to Task

After students complete the preceding activity, have the same groups write their business plans about how much they can earn, what it will cost to operate, and estimate salaries for each member. Have students use a word processing program to create the narrative and a spreadsheet program to create the financial assumptions. If students need help on the financials, have them check the public library for books on writing business plans.

Discussion Starter

Ask students what expression they usually have on their faces. Are they smiling, grumpy, sad? Have students ask classmates what they usually see. Then discuss how facial expressions can convey messages to employers.

Teaching Tip

Have students suggest at least three ways they can demonstrate enthusiasm on the job. (Examples might include smiling, being open to suggestions or volunteering to learn new techniques.)

Independent Practice

Assign as homework the chapter activity in the *School-to-Work Activity Handbook.*

YOU'RE THE BOSS!

Solving Workplace Problems

You've had your own law practice for nearly 10 years. Originally, you planned to defend the interests of children in family and criminal court. Recently, however, you've felt dissatisfied; you realize that you're making a lot of money, but you aren't working for or with children at all. What changes will you make?

I will!" Making a list of positive statements also can help. Statements might include "I am in charge of my life" and "I can achieve whatever I want." Try repeating these statements to yourself throughout the day.

How to Build Self-Esteem

Once that negative voice is on its way out, self-esteem is on its way in. Here are some ways you can speed its arrival:

- Make lists of your abilities and successes. Look at them often.

- Set reachable goals, and work to achieve them.

- Think about how you have made a difference in someone else's life.

The Importance of Enthusiasm

What do employers look for in their employees? Experience? Skills? Many employers value an upbeat attitude most. They look for enthusiastic people who take pride in their work and show initiative.

It's easy to have **enthusiasm,** or eager interest, when you love your work. However, even your dream job will have its down moments. What then?

You may have to push yourself to act with enthusiasm. While this may not feel natural, it's worth the effort. An upbeat attitude will help you develop a reputation as a hard and willing worker. When you act with enthusiasm, you are more likely to end up really feeling enthusiastic.

Dealing with Mistakes

No one is perfect. Everyone makes mistakes. The difference between highly successful people and those who are less successful is not that the successful people make fewer mistakes. It's that

Your negative inner voice is like a bully who is always putting you down. *How can positive self-talk help you get rid of that "bully"?*

Teaching YOU'RE THE BOSS!

Possible responses: Focus on improving attitude toward current work. Expand practice to include a few child-advocacy cases. Change practice back to original intentions.

Extending the Illustration

Have students think of real-life examples of how positive thoughts can aid achievement (such as Olympic sports figures who envision perfect performances throughout their competitions).

Caption Answer: When you repeat positive statements to yourself, the negative voice eventually disappears.

While this woman had less experience than some of the other applicants, she got the job because of her outgoing manner. **Why do employers value enthusiasm?**

they don't give up. Instead of letting mistakes bring them down, they use them as opportunities to learn and grow.

Remember: Whenever you make a mistake, be patient with yourself. You will probably have the opportunity to correct the mistake. Also, you will have other opportunities to succeed.

Once you have accepted that you will make mistakes from time to time, you can prepare yourself to act effectively when you do. When you think you have made a mistake, try following these steps:

1. Make sure it's really a mistake. Because a project didn't turn out the way you planned doesn't mean it's wrong.

2. It's easier to handle a mistake you acknowledge than one you try to hide. Tell your supervisor immediately, and accept responsibility.

3. Offer a way to solve the problem.

4. Find a lesson you can learn from your mistake.

5. Forgive yourself. Don't dwell on your mistake. Learn from it, and move on.

Chapter 10 • Developing a Positive Attitude **199**

 Extending the Illustration

Have students think of situations where they were not enthusiastic about doing something, but they still had to do it (perhaps household chores or a school project). Did they procrastinate? Would a positive attitude have helped them finish faster?

Caption Answer: Enthusiastic people are likely to work hard and they interact effectively with their coworkers.

Teaching Tip

Point out that there is a difference between being assertive and being arrogant. Most people accept assertiveness but someone who is arrogant rubs people the wrong way. Ask students for examples of assertive and arrogant behaviors. For each example of arrogant behavior they mention, ask how that behavior could be made assertive instead.

Discussion Starter

Ask students how many of them have been in situations where someone else took credit for their work or their ideas. How did they react? How could they have taken due credit without making the other person look bad?

Research

Have students research the topic of assertiveness training. They should be able to find a number of books in the school or public library dealing with this topic. Tell students to write one-page reports describing techniques to use in learning to be assertive.

Asserting Yourself

Most people who work hard to do a good job want to be recognized for their efforts. How do you get the credit you deserve from those around you? You do it by practicing **assertiveness**. When you confidently present yourself and your abilities to those around you, you are showing assertiveness.

Representing Yourself

In some cultures, asserting individuality is frowned upon. In the United States, however, especially in the business world, presenting yourself confidently is usually admired. How should you go about it?

The first step in practicing assertiveness is to be friendly and outgoing. When you notice a coworker you haven't met, find a good moment and introduce yourself. Use positive body language and speak with confidence.

Make an effort to get to know your supervisor better too. If he or she has an "open door" policy, take advantage of it. Offer your opinions or suggestions from time to time. Asking for advice is also an excellent way to let your supervisor know that you care about your job.

Here are some other ways to make yourself better known:

- Volunteer for committees and projects.
- Keep informed. Become an expert on your job or company.
- Keep a journal of your accomplishments. Include the date, what you did, and how it helped your employer. Bring your journal to performance reviews.

This person has made a mistake pricing merchandise. He is informing his supervisor. *Why is it important to admit mistakes you make at work?*

200 Unit 4 • *Joining the Workforce*

Extending the Illustration

A negative attitude may cause a person to blame others for his or her mistakes. Have students give examples of such situations.

Caption Answer: Mistakes that you hide have a way of catching up to you later on. By that time, they may well have had negative repercussions that you could have avoided.

Teaching ETHICS in Action

Have students follow these steps to help them make a decision.

1. What are the ethical issues?
2. What are the alternatives?
3. Who are the affected parties?
4. How do the alternatives affect the parties?
5. What is your decision?

ETHICS in Action

You work as an assistant to a technical writer. Recently, you suggested a major reorganization of the manual your boss was writing, and she agreed to adopt your ideas. Now you've heard that your boss has received special recognition, and a bonus for her work on that manual. What will you do?

This woman keeps a record of her accomplishments on the job. *How can keeping a journal help your reputation as a good worker?*

Assertiveness—Not Arrogance

Here's an important distinction to remember: Most employers will accept, and even admire, employees who confidently indicate their real accomplishments and abilities. That is assertiveness. However, no one likes employees who are overbearing and full of self-importance. That is **arrogance**, which you want to avoid. The difference has to do with respecting other people and *their* abilities. It's a question of using the proper attitude and tone.

Critical Thinking

Tell students to imagine this scenario: "You have been asked to meet with your supervisor to discuss a work issue, but you were not told what the issue is. When you arrive at the supervisor's office at the appointed time, you find that she has not returned from lunch. The supervisor's assistant tells you to wait. When the supervisor returns 15 minutes later, she first reads her telephone messages and then talks with her assistant for several minutes. Finally she turns to you and says, 'Now what can I do for you?'"

Ask students how they would respond to the supervisor. Evaluate their responses for either assertiveness or aggressiveness.

ASSESS

Assessment
Content

Have students write a paragraph on each of these topics: the role that positive thinking plays in career success, tactics for developing self-esteem, how to admit mistakes and move beyond them.

Evaluate students' paragraphs for accuracy of grammar, spelling, and punctuation as well as correct interpretation of each topic.

Evaluation

Assign the section review.

SECTION 10-1 *Review*

Understanding Key Concepts

Using complete sentences, answer the following questions on a separate sheet of paper.

1. How might having a positive attitude help an employee get a raise or a promotion?

2. On Sheila's second day on her new job at an accounting firm, her supervisor asks her to reorganize the storage closet. Sheila knows this will involve many hours of tedious work. How should she respond to the request? Why?

3. Marco's supervisor is about to prepare her quarterly evaluation of him. He is fairly sure she doesn't realize that he worked much harder than his coworkers on a recent team project. How can Marco get the credit he deserves?

Chapter 10 • Developing a Positive Attitude **201**

SECTION 10-1 *Review* ANSWERS

1. Positive thinkers handle problems well, and show they care about their jobs. Positive qualities are likely to be rewarded at work.

2. She should respond with an enthusiastic attitude. It will help her develop a good reputation.

3. He can share his work journal that explains his contributions.

Extending the Illustration

Ask students to brainstorm a list of attitudes that contribute to developing a good reputation. (eagerness to learn, willingness to take on more responsibility)

Caption Answer: A supervisor may not be aware of all that you do. The journal might show that you care about your job.

Reteaching

Have students prepare flip charts or posters for a seminar on developing good work skills (you may want to have them work in groups for this activity). Have students include a poster or chart for each of the major topics in this section. Have them make at least three suggestions for how to develop each skill and present their posters or charts to the class.

Extending the Content

Assign the appropriate Chapter 10 activities in the *Student Activity Workbook*.

According to one estimate, U.S. businesses now employ more than a million temporary workers each day. Projections are that this trend will increase in the next few years. Temporary workers are much easier to dismiss than permanent employees. Have students research the use of temporary workers and write one or two paragraphs about the importance of the right attitude and good job skills to a temporary worker.

CLOSE

Have students write their interpretations of this sentence: "To be successful, you need to be part of the solution, not part of the problem."

CASE STUDY

Exploring Careers: Marketing and Distribution

John Gabaldon
Internet Specialist in Marketing

Q: What kind of background do you have as an Internet specialist?

A: In college I worked with computers a lot, doing everything—word processing, programming, desktop publishing. Much of the time I felt isolated. So I focused on a career in marketing because of the interaction with people. I taught myself about the Internet—reading all the good books on it, learning about the programs.

Q: What do you do for your clients?

A: I help them market their products on-line through promotions and Web pages. I can help them link with other Web sites that get lots of hits so that they get more exposure.

When people give us information on the Internet, we can keep track of the statistics. We can then target markets for them when there are future products. It can be a real cost-cutter for the client.

With the new programs it's so much easier for people to find things out about a product. For example, you can get a video that can show you a car, interior and exterior, from all angles.

Q: What's the future for someone who wants to do Internet marketing?

A: All the big companies are getting a Web site presence. In the future, small- to medium-size companies will be getting into this kind of marketing.

Thinking Critically

What are the advantages of marketing through the Internet?

CAREER FACTS

Nature of the Work:
Develop and maintain Web sites; devise marketing plans for clients.

Training or Education Needed:
Training in computer programming; experience using various programs.

Aptitudes, Abilities, and Skills:
Very strong computer skills; listening,

speaking, and interpersonal skills; problem-solving and decision-making skills.

Salary Range:
Average starting salary—$30,000; average top salary—$65,000.

Career Path:
Work as a programmer or in traditional marketing fields; freelance; start own business.

---

202   *Unit 4 • Joining the Workforce*

Extending the CASE STUDY

Answer: Internet marketers can compete with larger companies; they can target their markets carefully and waste less money on inappropriate marketing; they can reach large numbers of clients; they can link to other Web pages that get a lot of hits and get more exposure than they might by conventional advertising alone.

Further Application: Have students discuss what kinds of information and design they would put on a Web page to promote a product related to their careers (for example, in health insurance, graphic design work, or environmental cleanup work). Have them investigate what information is currently on-line.

Acting Like a Professional

OBJECTIVES

After studying this section, you will be able to:

- **Describe how to accept criticism at work.**
- **Give examples of how to professionally handle workplace pressure and gossip.**
- **Explain how to control anger on the job.**

KEY TERMS

professionalism
constructive criticism
defensiveness
gossip

Think back to a difficult time at school or work. Maybe you had a classmate who challenged you every time you spoke up. Perhaps you were so overworked you felt you would explode if someone told you to do just one more thing.

Now divide a sheet of paper into three columns. In the first column, briefly describe the *situation* you recalled. In the second, list the *feelings* you experienced. In the third, describe the *action* you took. Turn the paper over. Then answer these questions: Was your reaction a mature response to your problem? Was your answer constructive? What could you have done differently?

When you experience difficulties, these will be important questions to ask yourself. Particularly in the workplace, you should question yourself before you react to a problem. At work, you will need to show **professionalism**. That is, you will need to handle problems and criticism gracefully and maturely. Instead of reacting prematurely, think things through before you take any action.

Accepting Criticism

You already know that properly handling criticism can be difficult. However, it is vital to your survival in any job.

Chapter 10 • Developing a Positive Attitude **203**

Addressing Workplace Diversity

Seventy percent of employees are fired each year because they cannot work well with their coworkers or superiors. As ethnic and gender balances change, it will become even more important to learn the skills and develop the attitudes that will help you work with others effectively.

Have you ever had a day like this? *Why should you learn to handle pressure gracefully?*

Guided Practice

Teaching Strategies

1. Assign and review Section 10-2.
2. Use the transparency for this section.

Discussion Starter

Ask students to give examples of a "win-win" situation, then a "win-lose (either I win, you lose or you win, I lose)" situation. Use the win-lose examples and have students discuss how they could have been turned into win-win situations.

Teaching Tip

Accepting and responding appropriately to criticism can be easier if students keep in mind ways to make winners of both parties. Ask students how they can be a winner if someone is criticizing them (by learning from the criticism).

Critical Thinking

Some employers criticize workers because they allow their personal lives to spill over to the workplace. Have students write 50-word responses to this comment: "Good employees leave their personal lives at home each morning."

What Makes Criticism Constructive?

Criticism that is presented in a way that can help you learn and grow is **constructive criticism**. When you see criticism as potentially helpful, it becomes easier to handle. Believe it or not, some employees welcome criticism. They have found that it teaches them better ways to succeed at their jobs.

EXCELLENT BUSINESS PRACTICES

Stress Reduction in the Workplace

Cigna Corporation, a Philadelphia-based health-care, insurance, and financial services organization, has a stress-reduction program for employees. Called "Fast Break," the program is designed to help employees manage tension and focus their energies, whether they are stressed from personal issues or work pressures.

Employees decide if they need to relax or energize and can choose a break of 5, 10, or 15 minutes. Employees can relax with New Age music, meditation, and stretching, or they can increase their energy levels by listening to tapes of empowering thoughts or by moving to upbeat music.

Some of the breaks are conducted by instructors from Cigna's Employee Wellness Center, an on-site health and fitness center which offers free confidential counseling (for employees and their families) and classes on stress reduction, tai chi, and yoga.

Thinking Critically

How does stress affect a person's job performance?

Extending EXCELLENT BUSINESS PRACTICES

Answer: Stress can contribute to reduction in efficiency; increase in illnesses, accidents, and injuries; poor communication between coworkers; increase in absenteeism; increase in job turnover rates.

Further Application: If students have jobs, do they take breaks to relax or energize themselves? Have them ask family members or friends who work if their employers recommend or require breaks for relaxing or energizing.

Of course, not all criticism is equally productive. *Figure 10-2* compares constructive criticism to less helpful criticism. You can use the standards in this figure to evaluate criticism you receive. You can also use them if your job requires you to evaluate employees.

Responding to Criticism

What does the term *defensiveness* bring to mind? Consider this situation:

Janet's coworker Paolo has been late many times. Recently, Janet overheard her supervisor tell a colleague that if Paolo continued to be late, he would lose his job. After work, Janet told Paolo what she had heard and suggested he try to get to work on time. Paolo snapped back, "But it's not my fault! My car is always breaking down. Besides, who are you to judge me?" Janet understood why Paolo was upset. However, she wished that he had really listened to what she had to say. After all, she felt the criticism had been for his own good.

Defensiveness means putting up an emotional guard against negative opinions. Remember the upward spirals from Section 1? Here's a downward spiral: When Paolo reacts defensively, he becomes closed. When he is closed, he cannot listen. When he cannot listen, he cannot grow. The only way he could have benefited from Janet's criticism was to be receptive and not defensive.

What Makes Criticism Constructive?	
Constructive Criticism	**Less Helpful Criticism**
Addresses behavior	Addresses attitude
Is specific	Is general
Is offered immediately	Is not offered immediately
Makes some mention of positive points	Focuses exclusively on negative points
Offers specific actions to solve the problem(s)	Offers no solution to the problem(s)
Is given in private	Is announced in public

Figure 10-2

You can learn to give and accept constructive criticism. Why is it easier to accept <u>constructive</u> criticism?

Chapter 10 • Developing a Positive Attitude **205**

SCANS Foundation Skills Connection (cont'd.)

L3 **Sociability**

Present the following scenario to students. "Some of your coworkers have been avoiding you at lunch and refusing to acknowledge your hellos. You wonder what is going on but then overhear a conversation identifying you as the person who complained and got smoking banned from the office. You did complain because you have asthma, but you asked only to be moved into a clearer area and for some smoke filtration devices to be installed."

Ask students these questions:

1. What, if anything, would you say to the person you overheard spreading the rumor?

2. You complained privately to the manager, who obviously did not keep it private. Would you mention this to the manager? If so, what would you say?

3. How might you persuade coworkers to see your viewpoint?

Here are four steps that can help you respond effectively to criticism:

1. Listen to the criticism.

2. Make sure you understand the criticism. If the speaker does not specify the problem, ask him or her to do so.

3. Identify a solution to the problem.

4. Take action to remedy the problem. If the problem is complex, break it down into smaller bits. Then you can take action one step at a time.

 If you are closed to criticism, you may be following a downward spiral. **How can defensiveness prevent growth?**

On-the-Job Pressures and How to Handle Them

Meeting Deadlines 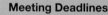	Learn to break large tasks into smaller steps. Carefully schedule when you will complete each step. If the deadline seems unrealistic, ask for help *as early as possible.*
Juggling Tasks 	A daily "to do" list, where you define and prioritize your duties, can be a lifesaver. As you complete each task, cross it off the list. For example: A. ~~Call MF and LS about the meeting Wednesday.~~ B. ~~Prepare minutes from last month's meeting.~~ C. Copy fund-raising report for GG. D. Make calls to caterers about May event.
Having More Than One Supervisor 	If two supervisors give you assignments due at the same time or if they give you conflicting instructions, speak up! Request a meeting with both supervisors so that they can sort out their priorities together.

Figure 10-3

Every job has pressure. Why is it important to have a plan for handling the different kinds of on-the-job pressure?

Extending the Illustration

Have students discuss examples of criticism that have helped them do a better job, either in school or at work.

Caption Answer: When you act defensively, you are closed to all criticism. You miss out on the valuable advice that can help you grow.

Extending Figure 10-3

Have students share their own ways of dealing with pressures, whether from part-time jobs, school, and household jobs.

Caption Answer: You can then deal with the pressure rationally and realistically. You will be better able to control your emotions.

A final word on responding to criticism: In the end, you must use your own judgment. Even if the rest of the world thinks you've made a poor decision, you may know inside that you did the right thing. This is especially true when you need to stand up for your values.

Handling Pressure

Pressure is everywhere! Supervisors set deadlines. Coworkers make demands. Difficult customers need polite attention. You wonder if you are making the right decisions. You wonder if you will ever be able to get all your work done. You wonder if you are succeeding at your job. You wonder if you are in the right job at all. ...

Sound familiar? *Figure 10-3* offers some tips that can help you handle on-the-job pressure.

Handling Gossip

Idle talk that usually consists mostly of rumors is called **gossip**. The problem with such talk is that the information it spreads is often untrue—and hurtful. According to Adele Scheele, a writer for *Working Woman* magazine, people gossip so that they can feel important. "Gossip is a bribe," she says, "a way of enhancing your status at someone else's expense."

In the end, gossip usually hurts the gossiper most. The more an employee gossips, the less coworkers will confide in that person. Eventually, the gossiper develops a reputation as someone who cannot be trusted. Before you join in gossip, ask yourself these questions:

- What is my motivation for gossiping?
- Could my comments damage someone else's reputation unfairly?

This woman has some gossip about a coworker. *Should she share it with her other coworkers? Why or why not?*

SECTION 10-2

☑ **SCANS Workplace Competencies Connection**

L1 **Serving Clients/ Customers**

Have students write how they would respond to a customer who has returned merchandise, complaining that it fell apart with its first use, and criticizing you for being too slow in completing the transaction.

L2 **Interpreting and Communicating Information**

Tell students that they are reporters assigned to write feature articles for the local newspaper. The topic of their articles is a survey of local employers on the skills that employees need to get ahead. Have students interview at least four employers about the job skills they see as most valuable. Using their interview information, have students write 200-word articles.

L3 **Using Computers to Process Information**

Have students use the desktop publishing features of their word processing programs to format and print out their articles from the preceding activity in newspaper article style. If possible, have students scan in appropriate photos.

Extending the Illustration

Have students brainstorm ways to avoid being caught in the gossip trap. (Try to change the subject quickly, avoid being around people who gossip.)

Caption Answer: No. Not only could gossiping damage the reputation of the person involved, it could damage the gossiper's own reputation by undermining her coworkers' trust in her.

Independent Practice
Research

Have students research ways to develop good human relations skills. Have students list at least five suggestions, with at least one of the suggestions relating to giving and receiving constructive criticism.

ASSESS

Assessment
Content

Divide students into groups to create a bulletin board on constructive criticism. Evaluate students' displays for creativity, and for accuracy.

Evaluation

Assign the section review.

MINI QUIZ

True-False

1. It's how well you do your work, not your attitude, that will determine future promotions. (false)

2. Positive thinkers find it easier to achieve their goals. (true)

3. Showing how you feel is better than being enthusiastic about work you'd rather not be doing. (false)

4. Criticism of your attitude is more constructive than criticism of your behavior. (false)

5. If you're defensive, you may fail to hear the constructive part of criticism. (true)

Controlling Anger

Some frustration is inevitable in any job. As you work to develop new skills and advance in your career, things will not always go well. However, you must avoid letting frustration turn to anger and your anger boil over on the job. If you do get angry, here are some tips for "damage control:"

- Count to 10. It gives you a chance to calm down and not say something you will regret later.

- Consider what you are really angry about. Are you angry about a situation at work or with friends?

- Channel your energy into problem solving. Here's a five-step model: (1) define the problem, (2) decide on possible solutions, (3) evaluate those solutions, (4) make a decision, (5) take action.

Career Do's & Don'ts

When Learning to be Positive...

Do:
- accept challenges.
- be considerate and responsive to everyone, even if it's not reciprocated.
- compliment others.
- be at peace with yourself.

Don't:
- say "It's not my job."
- allow other people to whine or complain to you unless they recommend solutions.
- put people on the defensive.
- gossip.

SECTION 10-2 *Review*

Understanding Key Concepts

Using complete sentences, answer the following questions on a separate sheet of paper.

1. Sean's supervisor wants to speak to him about some problems with the project he just completed. Sean feels that he worked hard on the project and did an excellent job. What should he do when he meets with his supervisor?

2. Jake is overwhelmed by the amount of work he must complete every day. What is one step Jake can take to reduce the pressure he feels?

3. What is the difference between sharing helpful information with your coworkers and gossiping?

4. List three tips for controlling anger on the job.

SECTION 10-2 *Review* ANSWERS

1. Possible answer: What Sean should not do is arrive with his defenses up. Instead, he should approach his supervisor with an open attitude, ready to listen to what he or she has to say.

2. Break down large tasks into smaller steps and create a daily "to do" list.

3. Helpful information involves facts that have been verified and will aid your coworkers on the job. Gossip is usually not based on facts and can damage someone's reputation, including the gossiper's.

4. Count to 10, consider what you are really angry about, and channel your energy into problem solving.

Key Terms

attitude *(p. 194)*
self-esteem *(p. 197)*
enthusiasm *(p. 198)*
assertiveness *(p. 200)*
arrogance *(p. 201)*

SECTION 10-1 Summary

- While employees cannot control everything that happens on the job, they can control how they react. A positive attitude can help workers succeed.

- A positive attitude is based on self-esteem. Self-esteem and confidence in your abilities are closely related.

- To build self-esteem, you can train your positive inner voice to "outtalk" your negative inner voice.

- Employers value an upbeat attitude. You can learn to act with enthusiasm even during your job's down moments.

- Be patient with yourself. It's OK to make mistakes as long as you try to learn from them.

- Being assertive, but not arrogant, can help you get the recognition you deserve on the job.

Key Terms

professionalism *(p. 203)*
constructive
    criticism *(p. 204)*
defensiveness *(p. 205)*
gossip *(p. 207)*

SECTION 10-2 Summary

- Employees need to handle criticism gracefully and to react maturely. These are important aspects of professionalism.

- It is best to avoid being defensive when receiving constructive criticism.

- Learning to handle pressure effectively will help you succeed at your work.

- People usually gossip to enhance their status. However, gossipers often end up damaging their own reputations.

- Things at work don't always go the way you want them to. Employees must learn to prevent frustration from becoming anger and anger from boiling over.

Chapter 10 • Developing a Positive Attitude **209**

Computer Activity

Using a word processing software package, have students write personal reference letters for another student in class. In the letters they should highlight their peer's positive traits and behaviors. The letters should not only illustrate the type of person the individual is, but also the type of worker he or she could be for an employer.

Use the Testmaker to create a customized test for Chapter 10.

Reteaching

1. Tell students that they are training new employees for their company. Have students write a training skit on professional behavior. Their skits should include examples of constructive criticism and how to respond to criticism, how to handle gossip, and how to deal with anger on the job.

2. Assign and review vocabulary terms, chapter questions, and activities from the Chapter Review.

Extending the Content

Assign the appropriate Chapter 10 activities in the *Student Activity Workbook*.

Have students interview at least three people who have full-time jobs and ask them to describe the personal traits they think are most important to career success. Tell students to list the traits and share them in class.

CLOSE

Have students complete this sentence: "The personal traits or attitudes that will help me to succeed in my chosen career are . . . ." (Students' lists will vary but could include a positive attitude, good self-esteem, ability to handle criticism, being assertive.)

Answers
Reviewing Key Terms

Short stories will vary but should include all key terms.

Recalling Key Concepts

1. True
2. True
3. False: Failure involves something you did, not who you are.
4. False: Arrogance is acting in an overbearing way and being full of self-importance.
5. True

Thinking Critically

1. It helps by getting you into the habit of thinking positively about yourself and your abilities.
2. Possible answer: It's OK to "push" it because acting with enthusiasm can help you really feel enthusiastic. It's more a helpful technique than a lie.
3. Possible answer: taking a few deep breaths, repeating a helpful phrase

SCANS Foundation Skills and Workplace Competencies

1. You can write lists of your abilities and successes. You can challenge your negative inner voice by repeating positive statements to yourself. You can listen carefully to criticism rather than react defensively.

Reviewing Key Terms

On separate paper, write a short story about a high school graduate's first week of work. Use the terms below in your story.

attitude	professionalism
self-esteem	constructive
enthusiasm	criticism
assertiveness	defensiveness
arrogance	gossip

Recalling Key Concepts

On a separate sheet of paper, tell whether each statement is true or false. Rewrite any false statements to make them true.

1. Optimists get sick less often than pessimists.
2. When you act with enthusiasm, you are more likely to start feeling enthusiastic.
3. Failure is who you are, not something you did.
4. Assertiveness is assuming you know everything and bragging about your accomplishments.
5. People usually gossip so that they will feel more important.

Thinking Critically

Using complete sentences, answer each of the questions below on a separate sheet of paper.

1. Why do you think positive "self-talk" can help you build self-esteem and confidence?
2. Do you think it's OK to "push" enthusiasm when you're feeling down on the job? Is this dishonest? Why or why not?

---

3. When you are angry, counting to 10 can help you calm down and think clearly. What other techniques might accomplish the same goal?

SCANS Foundation Skills and Workplace Competencies

Thinking Skills: *Knowing How to Learn*

1. Explain how each of the following SCANS skills can help you develop a better attitude on the job: writing, thinking, listening.

Interpersonal Skills: *Participating as a Team Member*

2. Abigail, Dara, and Thomas work as a team as cashiers and baggers at a supermarket. All of them are being considered for one new managerial position. Though the three are good friends, Thomas and Dara tell Abigail that they think she is "playing up" too much to their supervisor by always complimenting him on his supervision. How should Abigail respond to this criticism? Should she change her behavior? Why or why not?

Connecting Academics to the Workplace

Human Relations

1. Arrange to interview the human resource administrator or a manager at a company that employs many workers. What human relations problems are of particular concern at that company? Find out how the administrator works

---

2. Students should be aware that Thomas and Dara may not be objective critics. They are competing with Abigail for a position, so it might be in Thomas and Dara's interest for Abigail to look bad. Dara should continue to practice assertiveness while trying to be a good team worker.

Connecting Academics to the Workplace

1. Students should prepare their interview questions beforehand and be sure to thank the interviewee afterward for his or her time. Reports should focus on human relations issues in the workplace.

to solve those problems and improve the working environment. Report your findings to the class.

Health and Physical Education

2. Do research in the library or on the Internet to find out what long-term effects a negative job attitude and work-related stress and anger can have on a person's health. What do doctors recommend to prevent these health risks?

Music/Science

3. Many companies pipe music into certain areas of the workplace in an attempt to improve the working environment and boost worker performance. What kinds of music do employers in your area use and why? Contact such employers as supermarkets, mall stores, and doctors' offices to find out.

Developing Teamwork and Leadership Skills

In a team of five or six students, develop a one-act play about an employee struggling with a supervisor who is critical of his or her work. Two students might work as writers, one as a director, and two or three as actors. Alternatively, the team can write the play collectively. Present the play to the class. Have the class discuss the "employee's" behavior.

Real-World Workshop

As a class, simulate an office environment. Each student may choose a role to play. Roles should include executives, department directors, administrative assistants, outside clients, a receptionist, and so forth. Students should take turns playing a new employee on his or her first day at work. "New employees" should introduce themselves to people in the office, applying the skills they learned in the chapter. After each student takes a turn at role-playing, the class should discuss and evaluate his or her performance.

School-to-Work Connection

Using the Yellow Pages or the Internet, identify a local business of career interest. Arrange an informational interview to discuss what qualities that business looks for when hiring new employees.

Individual Career Plan

Write a brief report on the personal qualities you believe are most important for the career you have chosen. Base your report on the chapter you have just read and the information you collected at your informational interview in the School-to-Work Connection activity. For each quality you name, consider to what extent you already have that quality and how you might develop it further.

Real-World Workshop

Evaluations should focus on whether students present themselves positively and professionally. Specific comments might focus on speaking and listening skills, body language, friendliness and enthusiasm, appropriateness, and so on. Students should be asked to assess whether each "new employee" is assertive or arrogant.

School-to-Work Connection

Students might be asked to compare the information they gathered, determining as a class which qualities seem to be desirable for specific careers and which are desirable across the board. The qualities discussed throughout the chapter should be included.

Individual Career Plan

Reports should be filed in students' portfolios. Instruct students to update their reports as they continue to develop the personal qualities they cited.

Chapter 10 • Developing a Positive Attitude   **211**

2. Students should be able to cite up-to-date scientific sources for their findings and health recommendations.

3. Students' responses should include the kind of employer contacted, the kind of music played, and the effects of the music on the workers.

Developing Teamwork and Leadership Skills

Plays will vary. Discussion should be based on what students learned from the chapter.

···PLANNING GUIDE···
Chapter 11

SECTION 1 *Becoming a Healthy Worker*

SECTION OBJECTIVES	SECTION FEATURES	SECTION RESOURCES
• Recognize the relationship between good health and career success. • Explain the health benefits of a balanced diet, exercise, and rest. • Describe causes and effects of stress. • Develop effective strategies for coping with stress.	Personal Career Plan, p. 213 You're the Boss!, p. 215 Attitude Counts, p. 220 Exploring Careers, p. 221	Workforce 2000 Videodisc and Videotape Section 11-1 Review, p. 220 Student Activity Workbook

SECTION 2 *Safety on the Job*

SECTION OBJECTIVES	SECTION FEATURES	SECTION RESOURCES
• Identify rules and procedures for maintaining a healthy and safe work environment. • Identify workplace conservation and environmental practices and policies. • Describe American Red Cross procedures to follow when accidents occur. • Explain how to respond appropriately to fire and weather emergencies.	Excellent Business Practices, p. 225 Career Do's and Don'ts, p. 228	Workforce 2000 Videodisc and Videotape Section 11-2 Review, p. 228 Chapter 11 Review, pp. 230–231 Student Activity Workbook

CHAPTER RESOURCES

- Chapter Transparencies and Lesson Plans
- Chapter 11 Test
- Spanish Resources, Chapter 11
- School-to-Work Activity Handbook, Chapter 11 Activity
- Teacher's Lesson Plans, Chapter 11
- Implementing Block Scheduling, Chapter 11
- Print, Media, and Internet Handbook
- Strategies for Implementing Work-Based Learning
- Strategies for Implementing Connecting Activities

Career Notes

SCANS CORRELATION CHART

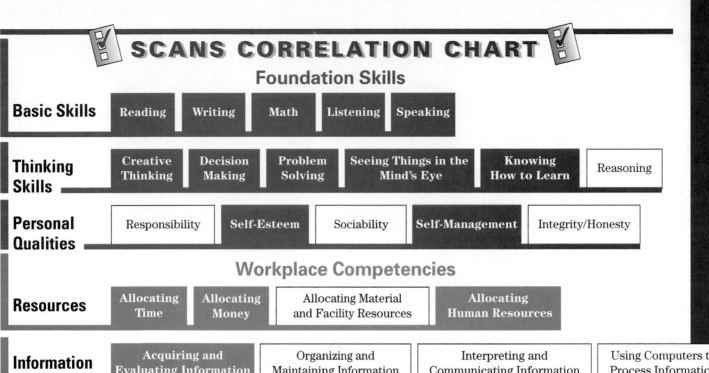

Foundation Skills

Basic Skills	Reading	Writing	Math	Listening	Speaking	

Thinking Skills	Creative Thinking	Decision Making	Problem Solving	Seeing Things in the Mind's Eye	Knowing How to Learn	Reasoning

Personal Qualities	Responsibility	Self-Esteem	Sociability	Self-Management	Integrity/Honesty

Workplace Competencies

Resources	Allocating Time	Allocating Money	Allocating Material and Facility Resources	Allocating Human Resources

Information	Acquiring and Evaluating Information	Organizing and Maintaining Information	Interpreting and Communicating Information	Using Computers to Process Information

Interpersonal Skills	Participating as a Member of a Team	Teaching Others	Serving Clients/ Customers	Exercising Leadership	Negotiating to Arrive at a Decision	Working with Cultural Diversity

Systems	Understanding Systems	Monitoring and Correcting Performance	Improving and Designing Systems

Technology	Selecting Technology	Applying Technology to Task	Maintaining and Troubleshooting Technology

Highlighted blocks indicate areas covered in the Chapter.

Additional Activities

 Internet Connection

Ask students to use the Internet to find resources on health and safety issues in the workplace, such as state and local regulations, numbers of attorneys who specialize in these cases, or information about specific health issues. Ask them to list at least 10 resource and information sites.

 Field Trip Suggestions

Arrange a tour of a local manufacturing company in which the company representative will highlight precautions taken for the sake of employees' health and safety. Ask students to look for instances in which employees are not following safety precautions. Discuss these in class.

 Guest Speaker Suggestions

Invite to class someone from OSHA, a corporate environmental-affairs office, or a related government office. Have the guest lead a discussion on environmental and workplace health and safety issues corresponding to regulation and resolution of disputes.

Key to Ability Levels

Each section gives skill-building activities. Each activity has been labeled for use with students of various learning styles and abilities.

L1 Level 1 activities are basic activities and should be within the range of all students.

L2 Level 2 activities are average activities and should be within the range of average and above average students.

L3 Level 3 activities are challenging activities designed for the ability range of above average students.

Chapter 11

Workplace Health and Safety

212

212

Chapter 11

Workplace Health and Safety

Section 11-1
Becoming a Healthy Worker

Section 11-2
Safety on the Job

In this video segment, learn how to create a safe and healthy work environment.

Journal
Personal Career Plan

How healthy are you? Write a brief journal entry, describing your own health. Then, after you have studied this chapter, reread your journal entry. Has your understanding of your own health changed? Write a second journal entry explaining your new ideas.

213

School-to-Work Connecting Activities

Have each student interview a safety administrator in a local manufacturing company. Tell students to ask about the specific workplace hazards and the safety precautions the company takes to make the work environment safe (for example, use of eye guards or other safety equipment). Have students write reports on their findings, then share their information in class.

Work-Based Learning Strategies and Activities

Arrange to have students take a tour of a local company's warehousing or manufacturing facilities. Have the tour guide explain the types of training the company provides to ensure that employees use equipment properly. Also ask the tour guide to share information about the company's training record and how often the operation has been inspected by an Occupational Safety and Health Administration (OSHA) representative.

WORKFORCE 2000 Training Video

Have students view the video and perform the interactive exercises to reinforce important chapter concepts and thinking processes.

Chapter 11

Addressing LEARNING Styles

Logical/Mathematical Learner

Have students choose careers that interest them and research each briefly using an appropriate book or resource. They should then make two lists: one of potential safety hazards on the job—such as falling—and one of potential health hazards—such as repetitive stress injury. Have them identify ways companies can protect employees from such hazards.

213

FOCUS

Bell Ringer

Draw a large pie containing four pieces on the chalkboard: nutrition, exercise, sleep, prevention. Title the chart "A Healthy Lifestyle." Have students copy it and, for each piece, write three things they do to lead healthy lives.

Introducing the Section

Ask students to share their examples from the Bell Ringer activity. Write examples on the chalkboard in the appropriate segment. Discuss some of the obstacles to staying healthy (such as lack of time to fix proper meals or to exercise). Discuss the fact that although staying healthy requires commitment, the long-term benefits are great. Being healthy and fit can also help students succeed in their careers.

Motivational Activity

Oral Presentation

Have a doctor, nurse, or other health-care professional address the class on the value of preventive health care. Ask the speaker to focus on diet, exercise, preventive checkups, long-term effects of substance abuse, and the need for emotional well-being.

Becoming a Healthy Worker

OBJECTIVES

After studying this section, you will be able to:

- **Recognize the relationship between good health and career success.**
- **Explain the health benefits of exercise, a balanced diet, and rest.**
- **Describe causes and effects of stress.**
- **Develop effective strategies for coping with stress.**

KEY TERMS

nutrients
Food Guide Pyramid
sedentary
addiction

Athletes know that good health makes success possible. Without it, there are no touchdown passes, no 20-foot jump shots. To score the kinds of goals you want in whatever career you choose, you, too, need to pay attention to your health.

What It Takes to Be Healthy

Good health means more than being free of pain and illness. It means having the mental and physical energy to do what you need and want to do. You can't have total control over your health, but you can influence these major health factors:

- diet,
- exercise, and
- rest.

You can also do one more thing—stay on guard against disease and addiction. Following this advice will help you build a solid foundation for career success.

Eating Wisely

Maria Cisneros, a telemarketer, assumed she was healthy. Yet after a busy day at work, all she wanted

214 *Unit 4 • Joining the Workforce*

Implementing Teamwork

Divide the class into teams of five or six to design a health and fitness event for a company. After each team has decided on an activity, have members design a flyer to announce the event.

to do was pick up a pizza, collapse on the couch, and watch television. "I was really tired, and I blamed my job," she recalls. "I gave it all I had." Then her doctor explained that she was tired because she wasn't getting enough **nutrients**—the substances in food that the body needs to produce energy and stay healthy.

Check for the nutrients you need in *Figure 11-1* on page 216, which shows the **Food Guide Pyramid**. This is a guideline created by the U.S. Department of Health and Human Services to help you get the nutrients you need each day.

Exercising for Fitness

Exercise takes energy, but it also gives *back* energy. Exercise helps you do the following:

Eating wisely does not necessarily mean eating less. It means eating foods that nourish you. *What foods would make up another nutritious breakfast?*

YOU'RE THE BOSS!

Solving Workplace Problems

Last week a customer suffered a heart attack in your pharmacy. You were able to administer CPR while your clerk phoned for an ambulance, and the customer is recovering well. However, you have discovered that all your employees consider phoning 9-1-1 the only response to accidents and emergencies. What will you do?

- build strength and endurance,
- feel mentally alert, and
  - reduce tension and anxiety.

Employees who exercise are productive and don't get ill as often as employees who don't exercise. Exercise is particularly important if you have a **sedentary**

SECTION 11-1
TEACH

Guided Practice
Teaching Strategies

1. Assign and review Section 11-1.
2. Use the transparency for this section.
3. Assign and review the Case Study.

Discussion Starter

Discuss with students the effect of good nutrition and exercise on energy levels and good health.

Teaching Tip

According to government statistics, many teens do not get the nutrients they need. Take a class survey and ask what students have eaten so far today. Compare their foods with those in the Food Guide Pyramid. Are they shortchanging themselves?

Critical Thinking

Ask students to think about their overall state of health. Have them list about 10 adjectives that describe them in that regard. Then ask them to complete this statement: "I generally feel . . . ." In their statements, they should include three of the adjectives they listed previously. Have them decide whether they need to improve their health habits.

Extending the Illustration

Poll students to find out how many skip a meal during the day. Discuss the importance of breakfast and eating regular meals.

Caption Answer: One possible answer is juice, a bagel, and milk.

Teaching YOU'RE THE BOSS!

Possible responses: Arrange for employees to take first aid and other safety courses; perhaps pay for those courses, or arrange a special safety training session for all employees.

L1 **Self-Management**

Have students create personal exercise plans that include at least 30 minutes of exercise three or four times a week. Then have them use a weekly planner to schedule the times they will exercise.

L2 **Math**

Tell students that they've invited three friends to dinner. They plan to serve a salad, two vegetables, and poultry. If a serving of a vegetable equals one-half cup, how many cups of vegetables should they plan to cook? If a roasted chicken has a cooked weight of one pound, five ounces, and a serving is three ounces, how many servings are in the chicken? (vegetables—4 cups total: ½ cup × 2 × 4; chicken—7 servings total: 16 ounces + 5 = 21 ÷3)

L3 **Decision Making**

Bring one or two all-purpose cookbooks to class. Have students look at the Food Guide Pyramid and think of one food in at least three of the food groups (exclude fats, oils, and sweets) that they've never eaten. Have them check a cookbook to see how the food is prepared. Then have them choose an appetizing way of preparing it.

The Food Guide Pyramid

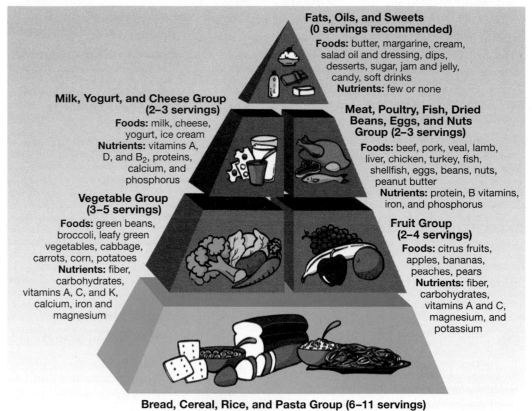

Fats, Oils, and Sweets (0 servings recommended)
Foods: butter, margarine, cream, salad oil and dressing, dips, desserts, sugar, jam and jelly, candy, soft drinks
Nutrients: few or none

Milk, Yogurt, and Cheese Group (2–3 servings)
Foods: milk, cheese, yogurt, ice cream
Nutrients: vitamins A, D, and B₂, proteins, calcium, and phosphorus

Meat, Poultry, Fish, Dried Beans, Eggs, and Nuts Group (2–3 servings)
Foods: beef, pork, veal, lamb, liver, chicken, turkey, fish, shellfish, eggs, beans, nuts, peanut butter
Nutrients: protein, B vitamins, iron, and phosphorus

Vegetable Group (3–5 servings)
Foods: green beans, broccoli, leafy green vegetables, cabbage, carrots, corn, potatoes
Nutrients: fiber, carbohydrates, vitamins A, C, and K, calcium, iron and magnesium

Fruit Group (2–4 servings)
Foods: citrus fruits, apples, bananas, peaches, pears
Nutrients: fiber, carbohydrates, vitamins A and C, magnesium, and potassium

Bread, Cereal, Rice, and Pasta Group (6–11 servings)
Foods: whole-grain or enriched breads, cereals, rice, pasta
Nutrients: carbohydrates, fiber, B vitamins, and iron

▲ **Figure 11-1** Foods are usually grouped according to the nutrients they provide. This pyramid shows you how many daily servings from each food group you need. Why doesn't the Food Guide Pyramid recommend any servings of fats, oils, and sweets?

job—one in which you spend much of your time sitting. Think you're too busy to exercise? Think again. Health professionals say you need only 20 minutes of exercise three times a week to reap the benefits. So what do you like? Aerobics? Dancing? Basketball? Go for it!

Recharging Yourself—Sleep

There's a lot happening in Laurie McBride's life. Three nights a week, she has a class at the community college. At other times, she goes out with friends. Most nights, after taking care of household

▶▶ Extending Figure 11-1 ◀◀

Have students list the foods they ate yesterday. Were they close to the recommendations of the Food Guide Pyramid?

Caption Answer: These foods provide few nutrients. Also, eating too much of any of these foods has been linked to health problems, such as obesity and heart disease.

Computer Activity

Using a spreadsheet software program and the Food Pyramid, have students create a menu for five days. Title the columns *breakfast*, *lunch*, *snack*, *dinner*, and *calories*. Title the rows *Monday* through *Friday* and *Total Calories*. Have students create a formula to total the daily caloric intake. Limit daily calories to 2,400.

The secret of a successful exercise program is doing something you enjoy. *If you exercise regularly, what are some of the health benefits you experience?*

Staying on Guard

Beyond maintaining a balanced diet and getting the right amounts of exercise and rest, you need to stay on guard to stay healthy. That means following rules of hygiene, getting regular check-ups, and guarding against drug and alcohol addiction.

Addiction is a physical or psychological need for a substance. Addictive substances can include alcohol and prescription drugs, as well as illegal substances such as marijuana and cocaine. Addiction can lead to devastating physical and mental effects, including depression, heart attack, liver disease, and even death.

Addiction can have a drastic impact on business, causing injuries, absenteeism, and poor productivity. That is why many

chores and winding down in front of the television set, she usually gets about six hours of sleep. What's the result? Laurie struggles to stay alert at work.

Almost everyone needs about eight hours of sleep a night. Too little sleep can cause difficulty concentrating and make a person more prone to accidents.

Sleep restores the body and recharges the brain. To get a good night's sleep, try to go to bed about the same time every night. Avoid caffeine-rich foods and drinks, such as chocolate and caffeinated sodas, before bed.

Eating or drinking certain foods, such as milk, before bedtime helps some people sleep well. *What other nighttime routines might help this person get a good night's rest?*

Chapter 11 • Workplace Health and Safety **217**

Extending the Illustration

Poll students to find out how many of them exercise regularly. Invite the school coach to discuss the benefits of lifelong exercise.

Caption Answer: Better circulation, lower blood pressure, increased energy and endurance, mental alertness, reduced stress, and fun.

Extending the Illustration

Sleeping disorders usually occur later in life. Have students ask their parents about what they do when they have trouble sleeping.

Caption Answer: Having a relaxing bedtime routine, such as reading or listening to music, and going to bed at a reasonable hour each night.

SCANS Workplace Competencies Connection (cont'd.)

L3 Allocating Money

Tell students that they have $50 to buy food for a week. Have them make shopping lists based on the Food Guide Pyramid. Have students take their lists to the grocery store and write the price of each item and how many servings they would get at that price. In class, have students share their findings. Were they able to buy a week of meals for $50? If not, how would they adjust their spending to buy nutritious food?

Independent Practice

Assign as homework the chapter activity in the *School-to-Work Activity Handbook.*

Research

Have students research nutrition using the Internet. Keywords to search might include *diet* and *nutrition.* Have students share their information in class.

Writing: *Persuasion*

Tell students to imagine that they have a friend with a health-endangering habit—perhaps taking drugs, smoking, or drinking. Have students write a note to the friend persuading him or her to find ways to change the behavior. Caution students not to judge the other person.

companies have established *drug-testing programs*, programs designed to detect illegal drug use. Some companies might test you when you apply for a job; others have a policy of testing employees periodically. Companies are not likely to hire job applicants who test positive for drugs. Employees with positive drug tests face possible job termination or may be referred to counseling and treatment.

Managing Stress

Another vital factor in staying healthy is learning to manage stress. Sam Burnett, a real estate agent, faced a hectic daily schedule. An economic downturn in his region made selling homes a difficult task. Although some amount of stress is natural, Sam found that the pressure gave him severe headaches. The stress—which is one's physical and emotional reaction to change or conflict—was getting to him.

In a recent survey by *U.S. News and World Report* and the advertising agency Bozell Worldwide, Inc., 7 out of 10 people said that they feel stress at least once a workweek, and 43 percent reported physical and emotional symptoms. The survey estimated that stress costs the United States $7,500 per worker per year.

Stress—Positive and Negative

Stress is a natural reaction to conflict. When you are challenged, your heart rate and breathing accelerate, your muscles tighten, and your blood pressure climbs. In the short term, these effects can be positive because they help you focus more clearly and act more decisively. When the challenge is over, your body returns to normal.

Stress becomes negative, however, when your body doesn't return to normal but stays in an unnecessary state of alertness. This state can wear you out and produce such effects as headaches, chest pain, irritability, and depression.

Coping with Stress

Health experts say that one of the most effective ways of dealing with stress is to identify the cause of the stress and then to

The major sources of stress are change, conflict, the environment, and overwork. *What could this man do to cope with the stress of his job?*

218 *Unit 4 • Joining the Workforce*

▶ Extending the Illustration

Ask students whether they feel stress when they have a deadline. What symptoms do they have? How do they deal with stress?

Caption Answer: Possible answers include deep breathing, visualization, or taking a time-out.

Figure 11-2

Coping with Stress	
Recognizing the Problem	**Finding Solutions**
Major changes, such as marriage, a new job, or the death of a family member	Try to limit changes in other areas of your life. If you've just started a new job, for example, you might want to delay other changes (such as getting married).
Conflict or uncertainty caused by disagreements with coworkers or unclear instructions about what is expected of you	Talk the problem out with a trusted coworker, human relations worker, or company counselor. If the problem persists, consider getting someone to mediate—to listen to what you both have to say—and negotiate.
Prolonged overwork or pressure when you have to pick up the work of employees who have been laid off or when you have to work additional hours during seasonal deadlines	Review your responsibilities with a coworker or mentor. Can one person do them all? Are there ways to do them more efficiently? If the workload is not doable, discuss getting help from your supervisor. Until help comes, set priorities, and take one step at a time.
Environmental stresses, such as noise, uncomfortable temperatures, crowding	Brainstorm with coworkers. Bring comforts from home, such as headphones, a small fan or heater, or a desk lamp. Use visualization to move to a calmer, quieter place.

◀ Figure 11-2

You can use your SCANS problem-solving skills to manage stress on the job. What positive aspects of a workplace might relieve stress?

address the problem directly. *Figure 11-2* identifies some problems and their possible solutions. In addition, you can develop your own relaxation techniques. Here are three widely used methods:

- *Deep breathing.* Slowly fill your lungs with air. Hold it. Release.

- *Visualization.* Close your eyes and picture yourself in a calm place—for example, resting on a beach or under a tree.

- *Taking a time-out.* Get away from a pressure-packed situation for a few minutes—for example, take a walk

Chapter 11 • Workplace Health and Safety **219**

Role-Play

Have pairs of students role-play conversations about changing unhealthful habits. Each pair will choose a habit, behavior, or unhealthy activity and spend some time discussing reasons why one of them might follow that behavior and why the other might argue against the behavior.

After conducting the role-plays, ask students which reasons for stopping unhealthy behavior seemed most valid and whether their own attitudes have been changed as a result.

Discussion Starter

Take a class poll to determine what activities are most stressful to students. List them on the chalkboard. Then ask students how they avoid or at least manage stress.

Teaching Tip

Remind students that stress is a part of everyday life. What can people do to lessen its impact? Review each of the problems listed in Figure 11-2 and ask students why they think the events described create stress. Use these events to distinguish between positive and negative stress; then discuss the techniques for managing stress.

▶▶ Extending Figure 11-2 ◀◀

Ask students who have part-time jobs to share examples of stress they've experienced. Which solutions in Figure 11-2 might help them deal with it?

Caption Answer: Possible answers include friendships, satisfaction in a job well done, and physical labor.

▶▶ Extending the Illustration

(see illustration on page 220)

Ask students to think of instances when they've been almost immobilized by stress. What could they have done to relieve the stress?

Caption Answer: Take a break; in the long run, it's more productive to rest now than break down later.

TEACH *(cont'd.)*

Teaching Tip

Remind students that a positive attitude helps people deal with stress; it helps put the causes of stress in perspective.

Ask them to think of times when they've created a lot of stress for themselves, such as worrying about a test or making a good impression at a job interview. How could a positive attitude have helped in those situations? (Students worrying about passing a test could study well before the test instead of at the last minute. Preparing for a job interview by practicing answers to questions would help lessen stress.)

ASSESS

Assessment

Content

Have students complete personal plans for a healthy lifestyle, describing their diet, exercise, and rest and sleep habits. Also have them identify effects of stress and some coping techniques they might use.

Evaluate students' plans for inclusion of proper foods from the Food Guide Pyramid, proper amounts of exercise and sleep, and recognition of the effects of stress and how to counteract it.

Evaluation

Assign the section review.

220

outside. When you return, you may see solutions you didn't see before.

The benefits of reducing stress can be increased productivity, greater job satisfaction, and better self-management (a SCANS skill). Handling stress is also a leadership skill: Only people who can manage themselves can lead others effectively.

Attitude Counts ✔

Exercise is terrific for your physical health, but its benefits go beyond fitness. Regular exercise can improve your attitude and your outlook on life. So, when the stresses of work make you feel pessimistic and exhausted, set aside a half hour in the day to exercise. Not only will this do wonders for you physically, but it will help you mentally too.

 Cathy, the character in this cartoon, is overwhelmed by her work. **What advice would you give Cathy?**

cathy®   **by Cathy Guisewite**

Source: CATHY ©1996 Cathy Guisewite. Reprinted with permission of UNIVERSAL PRESS SYNDICATE. All rights reserved.

SECTION 11-1 *Review*

Understanding Key Concepts

Using complete sentences, answer the following questions on a separate sheet of paper.

1. In what ways can being healthy help your career?

2. Name three obstacles that keep people from regularly managing their diet, exercise schedule, and rest schedule?

3. What negative effects could stress have on your work?

4. Why is it important to prepare yourself to cope effectively with stress on the job?

220   *Unit 4 • Joining the Workforce*

SECTION 11-1 *Review* ANSWERS

1. Being healthy can lead to better self-management.

2. Possible answers: too many activities, belief that their health will take care of itself, lack of knowledge

3. Stress could make you irritable and hard to get along with.

4. Experimenting with coping strategies could help you in the future.

Teaching Attitude Counts ✔

In a brief class discussion, let students share their own experiences regarding the benefits of exercise. Then ask one or two volunteers to research the psychological benefits of exercise. Have students share their findings with the class.

CASE STUDY

Exploring Careers: Communications and Media

Suzanne Wade
Trade Magazine Editor

Q: What training did you have to become an editor?

A: I received my bachelor's degree through a university co-op program. After my freshman year, I alternated spending six months in school and six months working as a reporter for a local newspaper. My co-op experience was critical in getting the job experience I needed to move into the field.

Q: What is a typical day like for a magazine editor?

A: What I love about being an editor is that there's no such thing as a typical day. I may talk to writers, edit material, or work with the production department. I have to be able to set my priorities—there are always 20 different projects clamoring for attention. I have to determine what can wait. It's stressful working with deadlines.

Q: Did you always know you wanted to work for a magazine?

A: I decided very young to be a writer. When I was deciding what I wanted to do for a living, I stumbled onto journalism. I'm a better writer than journalist—I like regular hours as opposed to the hours you keep as a reporter. I never intended to be the editor of a trade magazine. I don't know where I'm going from here.

Thinking Critically

Writing skills are critical for an editor. How might you depend on writing skills in your chosen career?

CAREER FACTS

Nature of the Work:
   Plan content of magazine; assign work to writers; edit, organize, rewrite articles; work with sales and design staff.

Training or Education Needed:
   English, journalism, or communications background preferred.

Aptitudes, Abilities, and Skills:
   Listening, speaking, and interpersonal skills; problem-solving skills; reading and writing skills; ability to allocate time, material, and human resources.

Salary Range:
   Depends on the size of the magazine's circulation; average starting salary—$25,000; average top salary—$45,000.

Career Path:
   Start as a writer, or an editorial assistant; advance to managing editor; move to other magazines or other types of publishing.

Chapter 11 • Workplace Health and Safety **221**

Reteaching

On the chalkboard, redraw and label the pie chart from the previous Bell Ringer activity. This time, have students tell you the label for each of the four segments as well as the key points for each segment.

Extending the Content

Assign the appropriate Chapter 11 activities in the *Student Activity Workbook*.

Have students investigate community programs that help people struggling with substance abuse, such as Alcoholics Anonymous, Alanon, Alateen, Adult Children of Alcoholics, Overeaters Anonymous, or Narcotics Anonymous. Have students report on how the program was formed, the population it serves, when and where it meets, and how to enroll.

CLOSE

Have students explain the meaning of the following statement: "You are what you eat." (Students' responses should recognize the role of food in providing energy and helping one to maintain a desirable weight and a healthy lifestyle.)

Extending the CASE STUDY

Answer: Writing letters, reports, ads, contracts, proposals, and requests for funding are some examples.

Further Application: Have students discuss the images that they had of their chosen careers before they began to research them. Did they think attorneys were glamorous, artists had fun, writers made lots of money, or entrepreneurs had lots of free time? Have them compare their former concepts with what they know about the careers now in terms of working conditions, salary range, job complexity, and future prospects.

SECTION 11-2
FOCUS

Bell Ringer

Have students list all of the safety precautions they can think of. Give as an example orange traffic cones that alert motorists to roadwork and help protect highway workers.

Introducing the Section

Ask students to share their lists from the Bell Ringer activity. Point out that safety is not just a matter of cost to a business. Hundreds of people are killed on the job each year.

Ask students to discuss the role government has played in making the workplace safer, primarily OSHA. Use this discussion to lead into financial protection for workers who are injured on the job (workers' compensation).

Motivational Activity
Critical Thinking

Some people criticize the role of the federal government in addressing safety issues in the workplace. Divide students into two debate teams: one to argue in support of the safety laws passed by the federal government (for example, fewer people get hurt or killed), the other to argue against (safety precautions cost business too much money). Have teams research the issue prior to the debate.

Safety on the Job

OBJECTIVES

After studying this section, you will be able to:

- Identify rules and procedures for maintaining a healthy and safe work environment.
- Identify workplace conservation and environmental practices and policies.
- Describe American Red Cross procedures.
- Explain how to respond to fire and weather emergencies.

KEY TERMS

Occupational Safety and Health Administration (OSHA)
workers' compensation
repetitive stress injuries
ergonomics
first aid

Accidents happen—but they don't have to happen regularly or to have such serious consequences. More than 6.5 million people are injured on the job every year. Part of your job is to make sure you're not one of them. Accidents cost businesses billions of dollars annually in lost wages, medical expenses, and insurance claims.

Rules and Regulations

Government, employers, and workers all have a stake in preventing accidents. Therefore, they cooperate to make workplaces safer.

The Government's Role

The federal government protects American workers by setting workplace safety standards and by making sure that accident victims receive care. The **Occupational Safety and Health Administration (OSHA)** is the branch of the U.S. Department of Labor that sets job safety standards and inspects job sites. If a company fails to meet OSHA's standards, it can face fines and other penalties. OSHA keeps pace with the world of work by revising standards when work conditions change or new technology, such as the use of lasers, is developed.

The government also makes sure that workers are compensated, or paid, if they have an accident and can't work. **Workers' compensation** laws guarantee that if you are hurt on the job, you will receive financial help to cover lost wages and medical expenses.

222　Unit 4 • Joining the Workforce

Workforce 2000 Trends

Companies of the future will be small, innovative, and knowledge-intensive. Their success will depend on the dedication, determination, and knowledge of employees. The concerns of the employees will become the concerns of the company.

Employers' Roles

Safety regulations for employers can be very complex. In a nutshell, employers must do the following:

- provide a workplace free from recognized health and accident hazards,
- provide equipment and materials needed to do the work safely and teach employees how to use them,
- inform employees when materials or conditions are hazardous, and
- keep records of job-related illnesses and injuries.

In addition, employers establish policies and procedures for conservation and environmental protection. These procedures—such as those for recycling glass and safely disposing of hazardous waste—may vary from company to company. It is everyone's responsibility, however, to see that they are carried out in line with government regulations. If you work in an office, for example, you may be asked to sort wastepaper into separate bins for recycling. If you work with chemicals, you'll have to follow strict guidelines to prevent injury to coworkers and damage to the environment.

Employers are also concerned with new risks fostered by emerging technologies. For example, each year several hundred thousand workers, from computer users to meatpacking plant workers, suffer from **repetitive stress injuries**, ailments that develop after the same motions are performed over and over. To address this problem and other similar injuries, industrial engineers are engaged in a new field of applied science called **ergonomics**, in which they redesign workstations to make them safer, more comfortable, and more efficient.

Workers' Responsibilities

Workplace safety is also the responsibility of individual employees. In addition to following regulations for environmental

Employers and employees are responsible for protecting the environment. **What is one step you can take to do this?**

Chapter 11 • Workplace Health and Safety **223**

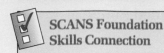
L1 **Seeing Things in the Mind's Eye**

If your school offers a shop class, arrange to have students view a demonstration of the safe way to use a piece of equipment. Have students write a paragraph describing the process.

L2 **Knowing How to Learn**

Ask students what they think about the federal government's role in protecting the environment. Have them research the issue of environmental protection, then write 200-word reports either supporting the current laws or advocating changes. Tell students to cite at least two reasons for their recommendations.

L3 **Problem Solving**

Have each student scrutinize his or her home for safety hazards, checking such things as loose wires, uncovered outlets, and loose floorboards. Have them list the things that need repair and plan how those repairs could be made. Also, have students discuss with their families whether there is a household plan for exiting the residence in the case of fire, tornado, earthquake, or other natural disaster. If not, tell students to formulate such a plan.

protection, workers must learn and follow safety regulations set down by OSHA. These include the following:

- learning to perform a job safely,

- knowing how to operate, maintain, and troubleshoot tools and equipment safely, and

- reporting unsafe conditions or practices immediately.

Responding to Emergencies

Your own safety and the safety of other employees can depend upon your awareness of what to do in an emergency. Knowing **first aid**—what to do *first*, before help arrives—may mean the difference between life and death.

Juwon Taylor, a student driving home in a heavy windstorm, watched helplessly as a giant tree limb came crashing down on the car in front of him. Stopping his own car, Juwon started toward the damaged vehicle to see if anyone was injured. Quickly taking in the scene as he approached, Juwon spotted an exposed power line draped across the car's hood. By looking around before touching the car, Juwon saved his own life and allowed himself to get help for the injured motorist.

Always survey an accident scene before you do anything. Don't make any assumptions. Quickly figure out what has already happened, and try to determine what may happen next. If someone is injured and you are nearby, follow the easy-to-remember American Red Cross guidelines in the following sections.

Provide A-I-D

The letters of the word *AID* help you remember what to do.

- **A**sk for help. If someone is seriously injured, call the Emergency Medical Service immediately.

- **I**ntervene, but ask the victim first.

- **D**o no further harm. Do not move a victim whose back or neck may be broken.

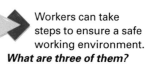
Workers can take steps to ensure a safe working environment. *What are three of them?*

224   *Unit 4 • Joining the Workforce*

Extending the Illustration

Ask students who have part-time jobs to describe the types of equipment they use and the training they received to use it safely.

Caption Answer: Learn to perform the job safely, know how to operate equipment safely, and report unsafe conditions.

Know Your ABCs

The ABCs are another easy way to remember priorities in an emergency.

- **Airway.** If necessary, clear the victim's airway (the passage that allows the person to breathe). Do this by placing one hand on the person's forehead and two fingers of the other hand under the person's chin. Tilt the head back by pushing on the forehead and lifting the chin.
- **Breathing.** Check to see if the victim is breathing.
- **Circulation.** Check to see if the victim has a pulse and whether he or she is bleeding severely. If so, press a clean cloth on the wound, and hold firmly with your palm.

Always follow the ABCs. If necessary, administer rescue breathing, shown in *Figure 11-3* on pages 226–227.

When the Elements Strike

Nature's fury can cause emergencies too. You need to know what to do to protect yourself and those you live and work with in case of fire or weather emergencies.

EXCELLENT BUSINESS PRACTICES

The Effect of Fitness Screenings

The Victorville, California, Fire Department recognizes the value of keeping firefighters physically fit, especially since their work makes them particularly prone to injury and heart attacks.

Victorville hires a firm to perform fitness screenings twice a year. These screenings include measuring cholesterol levels and blood pressure, blood profiles to screen for irregularities, treadmill tests, and nutrition profiles. Participants also are measured for such physical performance as abdominal endurance, push-ups, and vertical jump and grip strength. Individuals receive confidential consultations with a professional who makes recommendations for improving their health and fitness status.

Since the fire company initiated the program, the firefighters have shown improvements even as they get older. The average cholesterol level has dropped, and strength performance has increased. The firefighters are motivated to lower their risks for injury and illness. As a result, the department has had fewer injuries and those who have been injured have healed quickly.

Thinking Critically

In what ways does even moderate physical fitness enhance performance?

Chapter 11 • Workplace Health and Safety **225**

Extending EXCELLENT BUSINESS PRACTICES

Answer: It improves alertness.
Further Application: Have students call their local fire or police department.

Does the department have a program to help workers achieve maximum physical fitness? If so, describe it. If not, why not?

SCANS Workplace Competencies Connection

L1 Acquiring and Evaluating Information

Have students research an environmental group (for example, Greenpeace, the Sierra Club, Green Seal) and write 200–250 word articles for its newsletter. Articles should include information about the organization's goals and practices.

L2 Allocating Human Resources

Tell students that they are supervisors in charge of scheduling workers for a night shift at a local factory. The factory employs 35 people on the night shift in teams of five workers. To operate equipment safely, each team needs all five workers. The company uses a temporary agency when it needs extra employees or when someone is out sick or on vacation.

One evening, four people call in sick; four others are on vacation this week. The company does not have any rush orders and could shut one team down. Have students allocate workers to fill the remaining teams. How many temporary workers would need to be called? (To operate six teams, 30 workers are needed; three temporary workers will be needed.)

☑ **SCANS Workplace Competencies Connection (cont'd.)**

L3 Exercising Leadership
Have students assume that they work for a local company that manufactures pesticides and other chemicals. The trucking company the manufacturer uses to haul toxic wastes to an approved landfill is on strike, and storing the chemical wastes has become a problem. The supervisor has directed workers to dump the wastes in a local river. What would students do? (Answers will vary. Discuss options such as informing the EPA, a state or local government official, or a media agency.)

Independent Practice
Research
Make a list of local hospitals and other emergency facilities and divide students into small groups. Assign each group the task of visiting one of the facilities to determine the type of care provided, cost of care, hours of service, and average length of time a patient must wait before receiving medical care. Tell the groups to call for appointments to interview facility personnel. Have each group report its findings to the class.

Fire

Your best protection against fire is to be prepared. Learn the location of fire exits at your workplace, and know your escape routes. If a fire breaks out, take these precautions:

▶ **Figure 11-3**

Rescue Breathing

Rescue breathing is an important first-aid method.

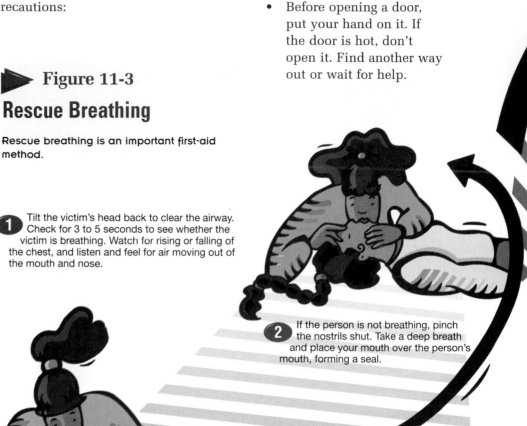

1 Tilt the victim's head back to clear the airway. Check for 3 to 5 seconds to see whether the victim is breathing. Watch for rising or falling of the chest, and listen and feel for air moving out of the mouth and nose.

2 If the person is not breathing, pinch the nostrils shut. Take a deep breath and place your mouth over the person's mouth, forming a seal.

- Leave the building immediately. Take the stairs or go out a window; do not use an elevator.
- If you cannot leave, stay close to the floor to avoid smoke.
- Before opening a door, put your hand on it. If the door is hot, don't open it. Find another way out or wait for help.

226 *Unit 4 • Joining the Workforce*

◀◀ **Extending Figure 11-3** ▶▶

Other emergency procedures students might want to learn are how to help a person who is choking and how to give CPR. Ask a local emergency rescue worker to visit your class and demonstrate techniques.

3 Give the person two full breaths that last 1 to 1½ seconds each. After two breaths, remove your mouth and allow the victim to exhale (the chest should fall).

4 Repeat steps 2 and 3, giving about one breath every 5 seconds, until the person is breathing on his or her own.

Source: American Red Cross.

- If your clothes catch fire, stop, drop to the floor, and roll to put the fire out.
- Leave fire fighting to the experts. Don't try to put out the flames yourself.

Earthquakes

The most common danger in an earthquake comes from collapsing structures, falling objects, and glass. When an earthquake strikes, follow these precautions:

- If you are inside, stay inside. Move to a doorway or under a table or desk.
- If you are outdoors, stand in the open, away from tumbling trees, utility poles, and buildings.

Hurricanes

These powerful storms can pack raging winds and driving rains. When a hurricane threatens, take these precautions:

- Listen to bulletins from the National Weather Service. Be prepared with candles and matches, a flashlight, and a battery-operated radio.

Chapter 11 • Workplace Health and Safety **227**

Addressing Workplace Diversity

Native speakers of English should be sure they listen carefully to coworkers who have trouble speaking English, especially when responding to emergencies. They should use standard English and speak clearly. They should take all opportunities to help non-native coworkers learn vocabulary commonly used in the workplace.

Skills Practice

Have students list people who deal with accident victims, such as police officers or paramedics. What human-relations skills would these people need to do their jobs?

Discussion Starter

Tell students that they and a friend are working alone at a workshop and the friend suffers an electrical shock and stops breathing. What would they do?

Teaching Tip

Ask students how many of them know CPR or have seen it demonstrated. Arrange for a paramedic to give a demonstration to your class.

Ask a safety officer of a local manufacturing company to give students a tour of the plant. Have him or her describe both the hazards in a manufacturing environment and the company's systems for protecting employees.

Skills Practice

Lincoln's Lumberyard has had a total of 43 employee and customer accidents this year. Last year, the company had only 26 such accidents. Have students calculate how many more accidents the company has had this year and the percentage increase. ($43 - 26 = 17$, an increase of 65 percent)

Last year, 15 percent of the Madison Company's employees called in sick. If the company has 2,658 employees, how many people called in sick? (399 people: $2,658 \times .15 = 398.7$ or 399)

MINI QUIZ

Short Answer

1. _____ give you the energy you need to stay active. (Nutrients)

2. Exercise is especially important for people who have _____ jobs. (sedentary)

3. Jobs cause _____ for a majority of workers. (stress)

4. If you are hurt on the job, your lost wages and medical expenses will be paid by _____ insurance. (workers' compensation)

5. Checking the ABCs in an emergency stands for checking _____, _____, and _____. (airways, breathing, circulation)

 Use the Testmaker to create a customized test for Chapter 11.

Be prepared to handle emergency situations. **What should you do if a fire breaks out at work?**

- At home, board up windows and doors. Tie down or remove loose objects or furniture.

- If evacuation is ordered, follow police instructions.

Tornadoes

These unpredictable funnel-shaped windstorms have enough power to pick up entire buildings and smash them down miles away. If a tornado threatens, take these precautions:

- Go indoors and stay away from windows. (Hallways and basements are

safest.) Cover yourself with a mattress or blanket.

- If you cannot get inside, dive into a ditch or another low ground area, and stay down.

Career Do's & Don'ts

When Ensuring Your Health and Safety...

Do:

- make your health and safety your highest priority.
- clean your own workplace and move any obstructions you see elsewhere.
- follow all safety regulations you are taught at work.
- offer suggestions for making a work area or work process more safe.

Don't:

- ignore potential health or safety hazards.
- fail to report an accident.
- do physical work that is too strenuous in general or if you are particularly tired.
- be pressured by coworkers into doing something that is not safe.

SECTION 11-2 *Review*

Understanding Key Concepts

Using complete sentences, answer the following questions on a separate sheet of paper.

1. What does the acronym OSHA stand for, and how does OSHA help workers?

2. How might you protect the environment at work?

3. How can clear thinking skills help you in an emergency situation?

SECTION 11-2 *Review* ANSWERS

1. OSHA is the Occupational Safety and Health Administration of the U.S. Department of Labor. OSHA protects workers by trying to make workplaces healthy and safe.

2. You might follow rules for recycling and be sure you dispose of hazardous materials in the proper way.

3. Thinking skills can help you assess a situation and decide what to do. By thinking effectively, you may save your own life and the lives of others.

Key Terms

nutrients *(p. 215)*
Food Guide Pyramid
(p. 215)
sedentary *(p. 215)*
addiction *(p. 217)*

SECTION 11-1 **Summary**

- Being healthy means having the mental and physical energy to pursue your goals.

- Nutrients are the substances in food that your body needs to produce energy and stay healthy. The Food Guide Pyramid shows how you can achieve a balanced diet.

- Everyone needs to exercise regularly and get enough rest.

- Addiction is a physical or emotional dependence on alcohol, illegal substances, or prescription drugs. It can cause devastating effects.

- Stress—a natural reaction to change or conflict—needs to be managed. People can cope with stress by identifying the causes of stress and by taking action to minimize its harmful effects.

Key Terms

Occupational Safety and
    Health Administration
    (OSHA) *(p. 222)*
workers' compensation
    (p. 222)
repetitive stress injuries
    (p. 223)
ergonomics *(p. 223)*
first aid *(p. 224)*

SECTION 11-2 **Summary**

- Government, employers, and employees share responsibility for creating and maintaining safe workplaces.

- The government sets and enforces safety standards.

- Employers must provide hazard-free workplaces, safe equipment, and health and safety information.

- Employees should know and follow safety rules.

- When an emergency occurs, you should follow American Red Cross guidelines: first survey the scene, then follow AID and ABC guidelines.

- To respond safely to fire and weather emergencies, be prepared and know what to do in each emergency.

Chapter 11 • Workplace Health and Safety   **229**

▶ Extending the Illustration

Ask students to describe school safety rules. For example, what is the first thing they should do if the fire alarm goes off? (If you have written safety rules, share a copy with students.)

Caption Answer: Students should list the steps outlined in the bulleted list.

Reteaching

1. Have students work individually or in groups to create accident prevention posters for the workplace (for example, using safety equipment; knowing the equipment and materials to use; knowing physical limitations). Have them obtain safety materials from local companies or use pictures from newspapers, magazines, catalogs, or other sources.

2. Assign and review vocabulary terms, chapter questions, and activities from the Chapter Review.

Extending the Content

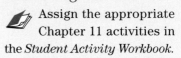 Assign the appropriate Chapter 11 activities in the *Student Activity Workbook*.

Tell students to imagine that they are watching a nine-year-old who falls and hits her head. After a brief period of unconsciousness, she revives, saying she feels dizzy. Have students call their local Red Cross or head injury center for information on how to handle such a situation. Tell them to write 50–100 word reports describing the steps, in order, they would follow to take care of the child.

CLOSE

Have students complete the following statement: "The best thing I can do in an emergency is to . . . ." (Keep your head; follow learned safety procedures.)

Answers

Reviewing Key Terms

Newsletters will vary but should use and show an understanding of all terms listed.

Recalling Key Concepts

1. c
2. c
3. b
4. c
5. a

Thinking Critically

1. Healthy employees ensure lower health-care costs, higher productivity, and fewer accidents.

2. In situations of positive stress, heart rate and breathing accelerate, muscles tighten, and blood pressure climbs, enabling you to focus more clearly and act more decisively. In situations of negative stress, the body remains in an unnecessary state of alertness that can cause headaches, chest pain, irritability, and depression. Positive stress actually makes you more productive; negative stress can be self-defeating.

3. Possible answer: OSHA sets and enforces standards; employers oversee on-site safety and training; employees must know and follow safety rules. The system enforces rules and encourages individuals

Reviewing Key Terms

On separate paper, write a company newsletter describing proper health and safety practices to be used on the job. Use the terms below in your newsletter.

nutrients

Food Guide
   Pyramid

sedentary

addiction

first aid

OSHA

workers'
   compensation

ergonomics

repetitive stress
   injuries

Recalling Key Concepts

Choose the correct answer for each item below. Write your answers on a separate sheet of paper.

1. The main purpose of following the Food Guide Pyramid is to ____.
   (a) lose weight (b) save money
   (c) get the nutrients your body needs

2. In order to cope with stress, ____.
   (a) take a deep breath
   (b) take a brief break
   (c) do both a and b

3. Workers' compensation is ____.
   (a) pay for working overtime
   (b) medical coverage and partial pay for an injury
   (c) time off without pay

4. In order to help protect the environment, businesses often ask employees to ____.
   (a) wash their hands
   (b) avoid repetitive stress
   (c) recycle paper

230   *Unit 4 • Joining the Workforce*

5. The first thing you should do in an emergency is ____.
   (a) survey the scene
   (b) check the victim's breathing
   (c) call for help

Thinking Critically

Using complete sentences, answer each of the questions below on a separate sheet of paper.

1. Why would a prospective employer be interested in your health?

2. Compare the effects of positive and negative stress.

3. Describe how government, employers, and employees—working together—create a comprehensive system to ensure workplace safety.

4. Explain how the ABCs of first aid help you deal with emergencies effectively.

5. What are the advantages and disadvantages of workplace fire drills? What would you do to make them more useful?

SCANS Foundation Skills and Workplace Competencies

Thinking Skills: *Problem Solving*

1. Mark and Keisha work on an assembly line in a toy factory. Lately, they are both feeling negative stress because their workload has increased and their boss is pressuring them to perform more efficiently. Describe in writing a strategy for solving their problem and reducing their symptoms of stress.

to be responsible. Each part of the system acts as a check on the others.

4. They deal with life-threatening situations: a blocked airway, stopped breathing, or severe bleeding.

5. Possible answer: Fire drills prepare people to act quickly and calmly. However, if fire drills are too frequent, employees may not take them seriously. Answers

may vary but might include having them at reasonable intervals and making sure each employee practices taking charge.

SCANS Foundation Skills and Workplace Competencies

1. Descriptions will vary, but a strategy for solving Mark and Keisha's problem and

Explain the benefits of learning to handle stress effectively.

Technology Skills: *Maintaining and Troubleshooting Technology*

2. Research employee manuals or interview a supervisor in a company to find out how one company ensures safe operation and maintenance of its equipment. Prepare a report that identifies three pieces of equipment and the training and maintenance procedures that lead to a safe workplace.

Connecting Academics to the Workplace

Art

Tom, a teacher's aide at your school, says he doesn't have time to do the shopping and cooking it takes to eat wisely. Design a Food Guide Pyramid poster for people such as Tom, including foods that are easy to buy and prepare. Use paints or a collage to make the poster as appealing as possible.

Developing Teamwork and Leadership Skills

Working in a small group, create a weather emergency plan for a new office building in your town or city. Choose a specific weather emergency that could occur in your area: hurricane, flood, tornado, earthquake, blizzard, or other severe condition. Identify the specific procedures for workers to follow in an emergency. Include as many details as you can, and present your plan to the class.

Real-World Workshop

With a partner, create and role-play a situation in which an employee reports an unsafe or unhealthy condition to an employer. Identify the type of workplace and have the employee describe the health or safety hazard in detail. The employer should describe what he or she is going to do to solve the problem.

School-to-Work Connection

Interview someone in an industry you are interested in to learn about conservation and environmental practices followed in his or her workplace. Find out how the company works with local government to conserve resources and how the company attempts to protect the environment. Prepare a report that describes the findings from your interview, as well as any additional recommendations you might have for the company.

Individual Career Plan

Write a profile of how one particular career area of interest to you matches your personal outlook on health and fitness. What aspects of the career seem to fit well with your health and fitness habits? What aspects of this career area might be challenging for you? What changes might you make in your health habits if you decide to pursue a career in this particular field?

Chapter 11 • Workplace Health and Safety **231**

Developing Teamwork and Leadership Skills

Answers will vary, depending on the weather emergency chosen, but students should do adequate research, identify specific emergency preparations, and present clear instructions for protection and evacuation.

Real-World Workshop

The situations and conditions will vary with the workplace. The employee should identify the source of the hazard and its possible short- and long-term effects. The employer should identify immediate actions to be taken to ensure that the condition does not recur.

School-to-Work Connection

Answers will vary according to the industry, the specific company, and the company's environmental policies. Briefly discuss students' reports in class and comment on any additional recommendations students suggest.

Individual Career Plan

Students should seek a balance between the demands of their career and their attitude toward health and fitness. Answers will vary regarding possible future changes in health habits.

reducing their symptoms may be to bring the problem to their boss's attention, practice deep breathing and visualization, and take regular breaks.

2. Reports will vary but should give a clear indication of how the company attempts to ensure the safe operation and maintenance of equipment.

Connecting Academics to the Workplace

Posters will vary but should include the food groups and suggested number of servings from the Food Guide Pyramid, along with specific foods from each group that are easy to buy and prepare.

···PLANNING GUIDE···
Chapter 12

SECTION 1 · *Laws About the Workplace*

SECTION OBJECTIVES	SECTION FEATURES	SECTION RESOURCES
• Identify laws that affect the workplace. • Describe discrimination in the workplace and identify some of the laws that fight it. • Recognize sexual harassment and identify actions to take against it.	Personal Career Plan, p. 233 Excellent Business Practices, p. 237 Career Do's and Don'ts, p. 240 Exploring Careers, p. 241	⊙ Workforce 2000 Videodisc and Videotape 📁 Section 12-1 Review, p. 240 📖 Student Activity Workbook

SECTION 2 · *You and the Legal System*

SECTION OBJECTIVES	SECTION FEATURES	SECTION RESOURCES
• Identify types of civil law cases and explain how they get resolved. • Understand the difference between civil and criminal law. • Identify and evaluate legal services that can help you solve problems.	Ethics in Action, p. 247 You're the Boss!, p. 248	⊙ Workforce 2000 Videodisc and Videotape 📁 Section 12-2 Review, p. 248 📁 Chapter 12 Review, pp. 250–251 📖 Student Activity Workbook

CHAPTER 12

CHAPTER RESOURCES

- Chapter Transparencies and Lesson Plans
- Chapter 12 Test
- Spanish Resources, Chapter 12
- School-to-Work Activity Handbook, Chapter 12 Activity
- Teacher's Lesson Plans, Chapter 12
- Implementing Block Scheduling, Chapter 12
- Print, Media, and Internet Handbook
- Strategies for Implementing Work-Based Learning
- Strategies for Implementing Connecting Activities

Career Notes

SCANS CORRELATION CHART

Foundation Skills

Basic Skills	Reading	Writing	Math	Listening	Speaking

Thinking Skills	Creative Thinking	Decision Making	Problem Solving	Seeing Things in the Mind's Eye	Knowing How to Learn	Reasoning

Personal Qualities	Responsibility	Self-Esteem	Sociability	Self-Management	Integrity/Honesty

Workplace Competencies

Resources	Allocating Time	Allocating Money	Allocating Material and Facility Resources	Allocating Human Resources

Information	Acquiring and Evaluating Information	Organizing and Maintaining Information	Interpreting and Communicating Information	Using Computers to Process Information

Interpersonal Skills	Participating as a Member of a Team	Teaching Others	Serving Clients/ Customers	Exercising Leadership	Negotiating to Arrive at a Decision	Working with Cultural Diversity

Systems	Understanding Systems	Monitoring and Correcting Performance	Improving and Designing Systems

Technology	Selecting Technology	Applying Technology to Task	Maintaining and Troubleshooting Technology

Highlighted blocks indicate areas covered in the Chapter.

Additional Activities

Internet Connection

Ask students to use the Internet to find out what information is available on workplace discrimination and/or sexual harassment. Ask them to write a paragraph on one or two sites they find interesting.

Field Trip Suggestions

Contact the municipal court and find out when a workers' compensation or bankruptcy case is coming up. Take students to listen to at least part of the proceedings. Afterward, talk to students about the case and how the suit might have been avoided.

Guest Speaker Suggestions

Invite to class a labor arbitrator or mediator. Ask the guest to discuss the most common problems employers and employees have, to advise students how to avoid conflicts and how to resolve those that arise, and to discuss the kinds or resources available.

Key to Ability Levels

Each section gives skill-building activities. Each activity has been labeled for use with students of various learning styles and abilities.

L1 Level 1 activities are basic activities and should be within the range of all students.

L2 Level 2 activities are average activities and should be within the range of average and above average students.

L3 Level 3 activities are challenging activities designed for the ability range of above average students.

Chapter 12

Workplace Legal Matters

School-Based Learning

Chapter Overview

Chapter 12 familiarizes students with laws that affect employment.

Section 12-1 introduces the labor laws that guide work and pay. This section describes laws against discrimination and outlines an employee's rights on the job.

Section 12-2 introduces civil law and guides students through the steps that might be followed to settle a workplace issue in our legal system.

Background Information

Write chapter objectives (Sections 12-1 and 12-2) on the chalkboard or use the chapter objective transparency for class discussion.

Choose assignments from the *Student Activity Workbook* and write them on the chalkboard.

Have students preview the chapter, looking at pictures, reading captions, and noting content headings. Ask students to describe what they expect to learn in this chapter.

Preteaching Vocabulary

Write the Key Terms from Sections 12-1 and 12-2 on the chalkboard. Have students describe how each term relates to legal issues in the workplace.

232

Meeting SPECIAL Needs

Limited Proficiency in English

Encourage all students to participate in class. Fluency and accuracy in English increase with use. Foreign students may not be familiar with the participatory nature of most U.S. classrooms and may need encouragment to share their comments. Active participation also lets you assess students' understanding of the subject.

Chapter 12

Workplace Legal Matters

Section 12-1
Laws About the Workplace

Section 12-2
You and the Legal System

In this video segment, find out about legal issues that affect the workplace.

Journal
Personal Career Plan

In your journal, list five words or phrases that each of these terms brings to mind:

- police officer
- lawyer
- judge

What do you think your responses say about your understanding of—and attitude toward—our legal system?

Have each student visit a legal aid office and an attorney's office. At each site, have students ask questions about the types of cases handled and the job activities of the people who work there. Tell students to describe the various types of job skills required for each type of legal service.

Work-Based Learning Strategies and Activities

Arrange opportunities for your students to observe a variety of people who work in the legal profession or law enforcement. People you may want to contact include judges, the district or assistant district attorney, civil and criminal attorneys, paralegals, court reporters, police officers, or legal assistants.

Have students write about their observations and decide whether a legal career appeals to them.

WORKFORCE 2000 Training Video

Have students view the video and perform the interactive exercises to reinforce important chapter concepts and thinking processes.

Chapter 12

Addressing LEARNING Styles

Interpersonal Learner

Ask students to review last year's local newspapers to find examples of sexual harassment in the workplace or discrimination due to gender, age, disability or race. Break the class into groups with each group taking one issue. Ask the groups to discuss whether the charges and resolution to the problem were fair. They should also discuss ways they would have handled each situation. Afterward, have one member of each group summarize the group's discussion for the class.

FOCUS

Bell Ringer

Write this situation on the chalkboard: You agree to work for a company that offers to pay you $5.25 an hour. When you get your first paycheck, you find that you were paid only $4.50 an hour. What could you do?

Introducing the Section

Have students share their ideas from the Bell Ringer activity. Discuss the Fair Labor Standards Act and the role it plays in guaranteeing a minimum wage for most workers. Ask students how the amount of the hourly minimum wage is established (by the U.S. Congress). Also identify the amount of the current minimum wage.

Motivational Activity

Reading

Have students obtain a copy of your state's laws regarding the employment of minors (or order a copy from your state's attorney general) and read the section that outlines work restrictions for employers who hire minors. Hold a class discussion about employment laws affecting teens, especially teens who work during the school year. Ask students whether they agree or disagree with all the requirements. Do their employers always follow the requirements?

Laws About the Workplace

OBJECTIVES

After studying this section, you will be able to:

- Identify laws that affect the workplace.
- Describe discrimination in the workplace and identify some of the laws that fight it.
- Recognize sexual harassment and identify actions to take against it.

KEY TERMS

minimum wage
compensatory time
collective bargaining
discrimination
affirmative action
sexual harassment

You're standing at a major intersection, and cars are whizzing by as you wait to cross. Then the light facing you turns green. Sure, you take a quick glance to either side before you step into the street. Still, you assume that drivers will obey the law and stop so that you can cross. This everyday event reminds us that the life of our society—from crossing the street to electing a leader—depends on laws.

Labor Laws

Just like traffic laws, labor laws set some ground rules. The difference is these laws are designed to protect you from unfair treatment on the job. They strive to ensure that all Americans have an equal opportunity to get and to keep a job, to be paid a just wage, to be considered fairly for promotion, and to be protected in times of personal and economic change. It is important that you understand your rights and responsibilities concerning labor laws.

Laws About Work and Pay

In 1938, the federal government passed the Fair Labor Standards Act (FLSA). This important law requires employers to pay a **minimum wage**—the lowest hourly wage that an employer can legally pay for

Implementing Teamwork

Organize your class into groups of four and ask each group to research a local company's compliance procedures with the 1990 ADA law. Have students ask the company if they had to make any facility adjustments; if yes, ask them to list the specific changes. Have each group present their findings to the class.

 This photo, taken in the early 1900s, shows the inside of a cotton mill factory. *How would you describe this work environment? Does it strike you as unfair?*

a worker's services. Believe it or not, the first minimum wage was set at 40¢ per hour, although it has risen to more than $5 over the years. The FLSA also set the 40-hour workweek and created the practice of *overtime* for hourly workers who work more than 40 hours a week. You read about this practice in Chapter 8. In addition, employees may receive **compensatory time,** paid time off from work rather than cash in exchange for working overtime. Employees, however, must agree in advance to this arrangement.

Child labor laws are another product of the FLSA. Imagine a 10-year-old working 60 hours a week in a factory! Sad to say, children worked under terrible conditions in this country less than 100 years ago. To put an end to a practice that robbed children of their childhood—and often of their good health as well—the FLSA set the minimum age for factory jobs at 16.

The Organization of Labor Unions

In another effort to protect people who work, the Wagner Act of 1935 (also called the National Labor Relations Act) made it legal to organize labor unions and engage

Chapter 12 • Workplace Legal Matters **235**

Discussion Starter

Tell students to close their eyes. Then have one row of students stand and walk to a corner of the room without opening their eyes. For the next row, have one student with eyes open assist a "blind" student to the corner. Alternate these actions until all students are in the corners of the room.

After students have returned to their desks, have them discuss how much easier it was to reach their destinations with help. Ask students how much the government should do to help people with disabilities gain employment and become self-supporting.

Teaching Tip

Ask students to name examples of local public facilities that help people with disabilities gain mobility (street curbs and building ramps that allow wheelchair access, elevators with panels in Braille). Can they think of other things that might be done to assist those with disabilities?

SCANS Foundation Skills Connection

L1 **Reading**

Have students read an article about work conditions in another country, preferably a developing country. Ask them to compare the conditions in that country with those in the United States.

in union activities. Labor unions represent workers in their dealings with employers. The workers elect union leaders, who establish and extend employee rights through **collective bargaining.** In other words, unions use the power of their numbers (the workers in the union) to bargain for better wages, increased benefits, better safety rules, and other job improvements. Today, about 15 percent of all American workers belong to a union.

Providing a Safety Net

State laws provide for unemployment insurance to help workers cope with the loss of a job. For example, Ben Dyal worked for five years selling athletic gear to department stores. The competition was fierce, and when his company suddenly went out of business, Ben had trouble landing a new job right away. "I had to eat," he said. "I had to pay the rent. So I went down to the local government office and filed for unemployment." Soon he received an unemployment check each week. "It allowed me to pay my basic living expenses until I found a new job. The temporary funds gave me a chance to get back on my feet."

Many workplaces include individuals from a variety of racial and ethnic backgrounds. *What advantages could this bring to business?*

Extending the Illustration

Have students read an article from a magazine that focuses on a culture different from their own (for example, *Hispanic, Ebony, Emerge*). Ask students to share their impressions.

Caption Answer: Students may suggest that it makes a workplace more interesting, exposes workers to a greater variety of perspectives, or helps individuals get to know a variety of people.

Sometimes accidents and illness throw lives out of balance as well. Workers need to know that if they get sick, their jobs won't be given away to other workers. Some people need to take time off from work to care for relatives. To meet these needs, Congress passed the Family and Medical Leave Act in 1993. This law guarantees employees (at companies with more than 50 employees) up to 12 weeks' leave for family or personal medical care or for the birth or adoption of a child.

Drawing the Line

Law goes a long way toward protecting workers, but it draws the line at people who are working illegally. The Immigration Reform and Control Act of 1990 makes it very difficult for illegal immigrants (noncitizens living in our country without authorization from our government) to find work. Employers should make sure that *all* new employees have proper working papers and identification. Businesses can face huge fines if they break this law.

Discrimination

Under laws passed by Congress, it is illegal for employers to engage in **discrimination**—unequal treatment based on such factors as race, religion, nationality, *gender* (being male or female), age, or physical appearance.

EXCELLENT BUSINESS PRACTICES

Resolving Conflicts

Brown & Root Inc., a Houston-based engineering, construction, and maintenance company of 35,000 employees, has a dispute-resolution program. The program allows workers to voice their complaints. Through the company's employee hot line and legal consultation program, employees may receive free and confidential advice from professional advisers.

Employees may take complaints to any level of management in the organization, individually or in conference, through the company's open-door policy.

More than 500 employees have used the program since it was implemented, and about 80 percent of disputes have been resolved in fewer than four weeks.

Thinking Critically

How can a legal counselor save you time and help you avoid worrying about what to do? Why would the advice have to be confidential?

Chapter 12 • Workplace Legal Matters 237

Extending EXCELLENT BUSINESS PRACTICES

Answer: Having a legal counselor readily available allows you to resolve conflicts before they can escalate. The professional advice helps you avoid worrying about the proper course of action.

Confidential advice permits you to discuss issues that might involve coworkers and thus avoid any misinterpretation. Confidentiality protects you from unwarranted retaliation.

Further Application: Have students find organizations in their community that offer free legal advice. Who do they offer the advice to? Is the advice based on specific legal issues?

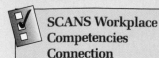 SCANS Workplace Competencies Connection

L1 Working with Cultural Diversity

Have students go to the local public library and listen to at least three CDs they would normally never listen to. Have them list each type of music and then write at least five words or phrases describing the type of person they think listens to that music. What stereotypes did they use in describing each person?

L2 Acquiring and Evaluating Information

Have students visit at least five businesses in your area that employ minors in part-time jobs to obtain information about hiring policies. Have students compile a list of jobs that are available for minors at different ages (for example, minors 14–16 may be hired with a work permit). Have them identify work restrictions for each age group (for example, number of hours of work or type of work).

L3 Understanding Systems

Have students write 200-word papers describing how laws are enacted and enforced in the U.S. legal system. Also have them indicate steps citizens may take when they believe they have been treated unfairly or have a financial claim against another person.

238

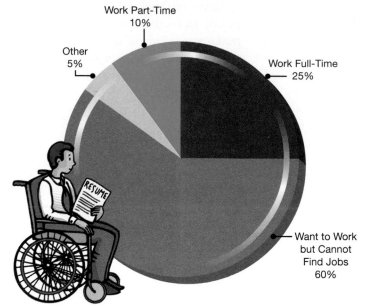

People with Disabilities in the Workforce

Work Part-Time 10%

Other 5%

Work Full-Time 25%

Want to Work but Cannot Find Jobs 60%

Estimated number of people with disabilities in America aged 16–64: 27 million

Source: Carol Kleiman, *The 100 Best Jobs for the 1990s and Beyond*, Berkley Books, New York, 1992, p.10.

Figure 12-1

Entering the world of work can be a challenge for Americans with disabilities. Use your basic math skills to figure out the total number of people with disabilities who would like to work but are unable to find jobs.

Major Antidiscrimination Laws

Every employee has a legal right to fair treatment under one of a number of state and federal laws.

- The **Civil Rights Act of 1964** bans discrimination in employment based on race, color, religion, or gender.

- The **Age Discrimination Act of 1967** makes it illegal to discriminate against people over 40 in hiring, promoting, or discharging employees.

- The **Rehabilitation Act of 1973** and the **Americans with Disabilities Act of 1990** protect the rights of individuals with *disabilities*—conditions that include blindness, visual or hearing impairment, mental illness,

or paralysis. For example, the law requires businesses to provide aids such as wheelchair ramps and other special equipment for disabled workers. *Figure 12-1* shows statistics on people with disabilities in the workforce.

Courts have recognized some exceptions to the fundamental discrimination laws. Some employers are allowed to hire only people with certain qualifications if those qualifications are necessary to do a particular job. Models and actors, for example, may need to be a particular age or gender to do a particular job.

The government also created **affirmative action** plans that aim to provide

Extending Figure 12-1

Invite a disabled worker to speak to your class about the challenges of finding job opportunities and getting to and from work. Ask the person to discuss government and community organizations that help disabled workers.

Caption Answer: 16.2 million people

access to jobs for those who suffered discrimination in the past and to give everyone a fair chance to compete in the working world. These plans, which continue to be the subject of intense debate, sometimes set numerical goals for the hiring of groups such as ethnic minorities, females, or people with disabilities.

Equal Rights on the Job

Look at *Figure 12-2,* which shows how the percentage of women in the workforce has grown. Before 1960, few women worked full-time, and those who did worked in positions not usually held by men. Now men and women often compete for the same jobs and aim for the same raises and promotions. Have you ever wondered how being a male or a female might affect your career?

Hilary Frye worked as a laborer with a landscaping company. One day she had lunch with a male coworker who casually mentioned his salary. Hilary was surprised to find that he was getting paid $3 an hour more than she was—for doing the same job with the same amount of experience for the same amount of time. Hilary was a victim of discrimination. **The Equal Pay Act of 1963** requires equal pay for equal work.

Sexual Harassment

Another gender-related problem in the workplace is **sexual harassment**—any unwelcome behavior of a sexual nature. Such behavior may include jokes, gestures,

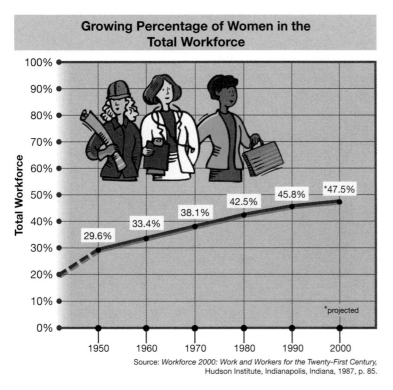

Growing Percentage of Women in the Total Workforce

29.6% (1950)
33.4% (1960)
38.1% (1970)
42.5% (1980)
45.8% (1990)
*47.5% (2000)

*projected

Source: *Workforce 2000: Work and Workers for the Twenty-First Century,* Hudson Institute, Indianapolis, Indiana, 1987, p. 85.

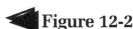 **Figure 12-2**

Women have steadily taken their places in the world of work since World War II. What do you predict will happen in terms of the percentage of women in the total workforce in the 21st century? Base your prediction on the pattern shown in this graph.

Chapter 12 • Workplace Legal Matters **239**

Extending Figure 12-2

Have students brainstorm reasons why so many women are in the workforce today. (Reasons might include the need for a second family income, delayed age of marriage, personal career goals, and fewer barriers to working in a desirable career.)

Caption Answer: It will probably keep growing slowly until it equals the percentage of women in the general population.

Independent Practice

Assign as homework the chapter activity in the *School-to-Work Activity Handbook.*

Reading

Have students look through the "Government Offices" listings of your local telephone directory. How is the information organized? (Listings are by city, state, and federal government agencies.) What legal organizations appear in this section? (Examples might include a city police department, a state attorney general, or the Federal Bureau of Investigation.)

Writing: *Journal*

Have students write a 50–100 word entry for their career journals describing the state and federal laws that guarantee job rights and equal opportunities.

Teaching Tip

Ask students to describe an example of an affirmative action plan. Then have them discuss the pros and cons of affirmative action.

Interview

Invite a local person who worked before the Civil Rights Act was passed to speak to your class. Ask the person to discuss the effect of the act on opportunities for women and minorities. Have students prepare questions to ask the speaker.

Skills Practice

Tell students that they have a friend who has an after-school job. The friend has been leaving school an hour early two days a week to meet the employer's scheduling demands. Ask students what advice they would give their friend in this situation. (The employer is breaking the law and should be reported to the proper authorities.)

Discussion Starter

Ask students whether any of them know someone who has been the subject of sexual harassment. What did the person do to solve the problem?

Teaching Tip

Bring to class copies of several articles describing different types of incidents of sexual harassment in work situations. Have students discuss the issues involved and how the victims could respond in each situation.

Critical Thinking

Have students write 50-word paragraphs describing what they would do if a supervisor made sexual comments about their appearance. Ask them how they could protect themselves while getting the supervisor to stop making the unwanted remarks.

repeated or threatening requests for dates, and unwanted touching. Although most reported victims are female, males have also been the victims of sexual harassment.

Would you consider the following two examples cases of sexual harassment? Courts have declared that they are.

- A male worker's female boss told him that he could keep his job only if he started to date her.

- Female employees were "rated" by male employees, who also made comments about their physical appearance, as the women walked past the male employees' desks.

What if you feel you are the victim of sexual harassment? Here are some practical suggestions:

- Immediately tell the person to stop. Be clear and direct; don't assume the harassment will stop if you ignore it.

- Write down what happened, noting the date, time, and place. Include the names of any witnesses and your own comments about how the harassment directly affected your work.

- Inform a trusted supervisor or human resource officer of the incident.

Career Do's & Don'ts

When Protecting Your Legal Interests...

Do:
- be honest.
- voice any legal concerns as soon as possible.
- use company channels.
- deliver your company's part of any contract if it's part of your job.

Don't:
- be afraid of confrontation.
- take on someone else's battle.
- deny or cover up a potential legal problem.
- threaten legal action without first investigating all other options.

- If the issue is not resolved within your company, you can get help from your local human rights office or the office of the U.S. Equal Employment Opportunity Commission.

SECTION 12-1 *Review*

Understanding Key Concepts

Using complete sentences, answer the following questions on a separate sheet of paper.

1. Describe one law that is designed to establish and maintain fairness in the workplace.

2. How do employers benefit from hiring people over 40?

3. How does sexual harassment create problems in the workplace?

SECTION 12-1 *Review* ANSWERS

1. Answers will vary, depending on the law chosen.

2. Employers benefit from the maturity and experience of older employees.

3. Sexual harassment may create problems in the workplace by making employees uncomfortable or afraid. It can negatively affect their productivity, and damage relationships between workers.

CASE STUDY

Exploring Careers: Construction

Dave Hiebert
Plumber

Q: Why did you choose plumbing as a career?

A: I actually got into it by accident. I answered an ad for a delivery person. That's how most people start out in the trade—driving a truck or working as a helper. They eventually work into the apprenticeship program.

Q: Why did you stay in the field?

A: It was the opportunity to do something mechanically minded. The second reason is that, as a plumber, I could go anywhere in the world and have a job.

Q: What do you like about plumbing?

A: Actually, there isn't a whole lot I don't like about it. I'm one of the few who absolutely love plumbing. I like the mechanical side of it. I love the problem solving. Additionally, by being a service plumber, I get to meet people.

Q: What advice would you give someone who wanted to become a plumber?

A: Be very attentive and be aggressive. By that, I mean always find something to do. Do not ever stand around. There are work ethics to our trade, which have been handed down from the older generation. If an experienced plumber happens to see you standing around, you won't go very far.

Thinking Critically ─────────

Why is problem-solving ability so critical to a plumber?

CAREER FACTS

Nature of the Work:
Solve plumbing problems; make repairs, often in small, cramped areas.

Training or Education Needed:
A four- to five-year apprenticeship; state licensing to become an experienced plumber; continuing education to maintain your license.

Aptitudes, Abilities, and Skills:
Math and listening skills; problem-solving skills; self-management skills;

ability to work with your hands; physical stamina; mechanical aptitude; patience; ability to concentrate; communication skills.

Salary Range:
Experienced plumbers earn approximately $20 to $35 an hour, depending on the location.

Career Path:
Work as an apprentice; work for a plumbing firm; possibly start own business.

Chapter 12 • Workplace Legal Matters **241**

Extending the CASE STUDY

Answer: Plumbing runs in hidden places; plumbers must know how the lines run, be able to determine the possible causes of the problem, and be able to use the proper techniques to solve the problem.

Further Application: Have students discuss their work ethics, including what they expect to give and what they expect to

get from a working situation. Student responses should include expected salary and benefits, along with what they expect to give to their work in terms of time, quality, and enthusiasm. Emphasize that working comes with employee responsibilities as well as expectations of what employers should provide.

Assessment

Content

List the following labor laws on the chalkboard: Fair Labor Standards Act, Wagner Act, Family and Medical Leave Act, Immigration Reform and Control Act, Antidiscrimination Laws. Have students write two or three sentences about each law, describing its purpose and how it protects employees.

Evaluate students' sentences for grammatical accuracy and for completeness.

Evaluation

Assign the section review.

Reteaching

Have groups of students choose one of the laws discussed in this section and create posters, providing examples of how the law is applied, and illustrating the law with cut-outs from magazines.

Extending the Content

Assign the appropriate Chapter 12 activities in the *Student Activity Workbook*.

Have students write 100-word reports about whether the information in this section changed their concepts of their legal rights as employees.

CLOSE

Have students write a paragraph about why they think labor laws are needed, giving the most important benefits of those laws.

FOCUS

Bell Ringer

Have students respond to this situation: You and a friend agree to trim a neighbor's tree, rake the leaves, sow grass seed, and fertilize the lawn for $50. When you complete the job, the neighbor claims that you did not spend enough time on the yard and pays you only $40. How could you settle this dispute?

Introducing the Section

Review students' answers from the Bell Ringer activity. The neighbor is legally bound to pay the full amount because the work contract was an oral contract. Discuss the points in Figure 12-3 on pages 244–245, and ask students which of these methods might be used to settle this dispute (small claims court or mediation).

Motivational Activity
Writing

Have students research legal jobs; then arrange for them to observe a civil trial. As they observe the trial, have them take notes about the various people in the court who are employees of the legal system. Have them write a paragraph describing each job. (Jobs will most likely include judge, lawyer, bailiff, and court reporter.)

You and the Legal System

OBJECTIVES

After studying this section, you will be able to:

- Identify types of civil law cases and explain how they get resolved.
- Understand the difference between civil and criminal law.
- Identify and evaluate legal services that can help you solve problems.

KEY TERMS

civil law
summons
criminal law
felony
misdemeanor
contingency fee

Most of us have recited the Pledge of Allegiance, which ends: "with liberty and justice for all." You have seen how labor laws strive to make these noble words a reality in the workplace, protecting workers and serving as a ballast in times of personal and social change. Many job-related situations, however, are not clear-cut or easily resolved. Therefore, one responsibility of the legal system is to provide a set of procedures for resolving conflicts. In court, lawyers, judges, and sometimes jurors make decisions about *disputes,* or disagreements, between employers and employees. It is important that you learn some basic facts about the law and how it affects you. As you become more responsible for your own actions, you will have more dealings with the law.

The Legal Battlefield

Many court cases involve **civil law,** which applies to conflicts between private parties, concerning rights and obligations. Divorce, custody battles, and personal injury cases all fall into this category. Companies may also become involved in civil law disputes. Here are a few examples of civil law cases:

- Tracy worked as a bank teller, and her employment contract stated that the company provided paid maternity leave. When she became pregnant, the bank fired her, claiming that it couldn't

242   *Unit 4 • Joining the Workforce*

Addressing Workplace Diversity

United Technologies, Inc., an aerospace corporation, formed a task force in 1988 whose goal was to ensure that 4 percent of its executive positions were filled by minorities by 1993, a goal they exceeded. By 1993, 5.9 percent of the corporate executives were minorities.

 When a high court makes a decision about a labor law, it sets the standard for future cases. **How do you think this process helps laws keep up with changes in society?**

afford to pay for her benefits. According to civil law, the bank broke the contract and was *liable,* or responsible, for doing what it had originally promised.

- John, an accountant, sued his employer because he developed chronic bronchitis as a result of being placed in an office with several heavy smokers. The employer was found guilty of *negligence,* or disregard, of John's right to a smoke-free environment.

- Michael, an autoworker, was physically searched by his company's security guards, who suspected him of stealing. The guards found no stolen goods, and Michael's shoulder was bruised during the search, when he was shoved against a wall. A court found the company guilty of *deliberate* (purposeful) injury.

How do cases such as these move from the workplace to the courtroom? The process starts when a person files an official complaint with the court. The

Chapter 12 • Workplace Legal Matters **243**

243

TEACH (cont'd.)

Teaching Tip

Ask students if they have ever been involved in mediation. Remind them that if a parent has had to step in and settle a problem between siblings, that is a form of mediation.

Critical Thinking

Ask students to think about famous court cases that have received a lot of media attention. Ask students to write 100–150 word papers describing the pros and cons of allowing TV cameras to broadcast court procedures.

SCANS Foundation Skills Connection

L1 **Listening**

Invite a person who handles both mediation and arbitration to speak to your class. Have students listen to the person's descriptions of both processes, then write a paragraph or two explaining each process and how the two differ.

L2 **Creative Thinking**

Tell students that they are running for election to their state's House of Representatives. Have them create campaign slogans dealing with a law-and-order issue. Then have them write their campaign platforms, including at least three major legal programs or work-related issues they would attend to if elected.

court clerk delivers a **summons,** or an order to appear in court, to the accused party. This person (or company) then files an answer.

For some business problems, small-claims court is an effective low-cost solution. *Small-claims court* is designed to handle minor disputes and small claims on debts. It does not require lawyers. Rules vary from state to state, but in general, small-claims court procedures and paperwork are less complicated than those in other courts.

Most people resolve their civil cases before they get to court. Opponents often come to a mutual agreement, or *settlement,* that does not state that either party is right or wrong. A settlement often takes

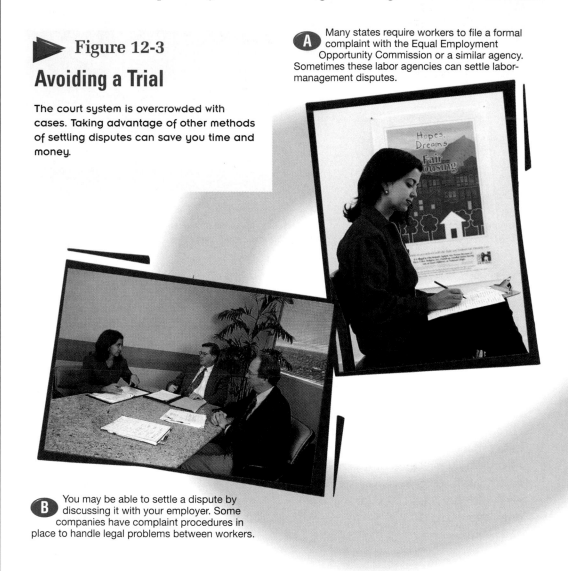

▶ **Figure 12-3**

Avoiding a Trial

The court system is overcrowded with cases. Taking advantage of other methods of settling disputes can save you time and money.

A Many states require workers to file a formal complaint with the Equal Employment Opportunity Commission or a similar agency. Sometimes these labor agencies can settle labor-management disputes.

B You may be able to settle a dispute by discussing it with your employer. Some companies have complaint procedures in place to handle legal problems between workers.

244 *Unit 4 • Joining the Workforce*

▶▶ **Extending Figure 12-3** ◀◀

Have students research the Equal Employment Opportunity Commission and write two or three paragraphs describing when it was formed, its purpose, and the effect it has had on labor practices. (The EEOC was created as part of the Civil Rights Act of 1964 to give employees who believe they've suffered discrimination a forum for complaint. The EEOC helps to enforce equal employment opportunities and has helped make the workplace more open to women and minorities.)

the form of a cash award or a correction of the situation that caused the complaint. Many states require that both sides in a civil case first try to settle out of court, thus avoiding trial. *Figure 12-3* explains still other ways to resolve civil disputes and avoid trials.

D *Mediation* is a process in which you and your opponent present the case to a neutral third person, who helps you both talk to each other and reach a compromise, or a settlement.

E Union disputes are often resolved through *arbitration*. Both sides present evidence and witnesses to an arbitrator, who issues a written decision, just as a judge or a jury would do.

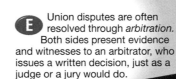

C If your dispute involves less than $5,000, you may be able to go to small-claims court and argue your own case for a fee as low as $25. The judge's decision carries just as much weight as a state or federal court decision.

Chapter 12 • Workplace Legal Matters **245**

L3 **Knowing How to Learn**

Have students read at least two weeks of issues of the local newspaper and make a list of the crimes or legal matters reported. Have them identify civil actions and criminal actions, and discuss their findings. What type of crime is most common in your community? What type of civil action is most common?

SCANS Workplace Competencies Connection

L1 **Acquiring and Evaluating Information**

Arrange for a union leader to visit your classroom to discuss the role that unions play in your state. Have students prepare questions beforehand, and set aside time for a question-and-answer session. Have students write two or three paragraphs about their impressions.

L2 **Interpreting and Communicating Information**

Have students research the issue of collective bargaining. What do they think are its advantages and disadvantages? When might it benefit them as employees? Have students share their research and conclusions in class.

Workforce 2000 Trends

In the mid-1990s, the federal administration advocated "tech-prep" programs and apprenticeships to help train and prepare students not on the college track. A national standards board would help establish industry standards, and certify those who met those standards.

**SCANS Workplace
Competencies
Connection (cont'd.)**

L3 **Maintaining and
Troubleshooting
Technology**

Have students research
the legal databases that are
available to attorneys and
law enforcement personnel.
(For example, what data-
bases might a police officer
use when investigating a
scam?) Tell students to interview legal representa-
tives and find out who
maintains the databases,
how often they are updated,
and who has access to
them. Have students share
their findings in class.

Independent Practice
Role-Play

Have pairs of students role-
play a discussion they might
have with an employer who
may be in violation of child
labor laws. Tell students to approach the role-plays from two
standpoints: the employer who
regularly violates child labor
laws and the employer who is
perhaps unaware of the requirements of the laws. After
the role-plays, discuss how one
might approach each employer.

Research

Have students research the
civil court system in your state,
from local courts, city and
county courts, to the state's
highest court. Have students
create charts showing each
level of court and the types of
cases they handle.

 The employer and employee shown here with the employee's lawyer
have just settled a dispute out of court. *Why might a company agree
to pay an employee for damages rather than take the dispute before
a judge and jury?*

Civil laws cover most workplace disputes, but sometimes incidents will occur
on the job site that fall under criminal law.
Under **criminal law,** the government
brings an *indictment,* or list of charges,
against a person or a business. The charges
state that a crime, such as assault or fraud,
has been committed. A serious crime pun-
ishable by imprisonment or death, such as
murder or rape, is called a **felony.** A less
serious crime is called a **misdemeanor** and
could be anything from shoplifting to strik-
ing another worker during a dispute.

Using Legal Services

If you have tried to solve a problem too
big for small-claims court and feel that
other legal action is the only answer, then
your best bet is to contact a lawyer. Laws
are very complex, and legal procedures are
often confusing. It usually takes an expert
to argue a case in court.

Finding a Lawyer

If you had a cavity, you wouldn't
dream of going to an eye doctor to get it

246 *Unit 4 • Joining the Workforce*

Extending the Illustration

Ask students what steps they would
take if they had a dispute with an employer
involving unfair treatment or discrimination. (Answers will vary but could include
first talking with the employer, taking the
dispute to your state's equal employment
commission, or hiring an attorney specializing in labor issues.)

Caption Answer: One possible answer
is that the company might think it has no
case or it might save money in lawyers' fees.
Another is that the company might also
want to avoid bad publicity.

taken care of. One doctor isn't the same as another. Similarly, you'll want to take your legal problem to a lawyer with just the right specialty. To start your search, try the following:

- Use your phone book to find legal referral services. The local bar association and your state's chapter of the Association of Trial Lawyers of America are possible sources of help.

- Ask friends and family members if they know any lawyers. These contacts may lead you to others.

Many lawyers will have an initial meeting with you before charging you a

ETHICS in Action

Although you are a minor, you and a neighbor have entered into an oral work contract. You have agreed to do certain repair work, and the neighbor has agreed to pay you a set amount. However, after you've done the work, your neighbor refuses to pay you. What steps are you willing to take toward your neighbor?

The media often cover exciting criminal court cases. *Why do you think people are often so interested in criminal cases?*

Chapter 12 • Workplace Legal Matters   **247**

Discussion Starter

Ask students to brainstorm situations in which they might need the services of an attorney. (Situations might include an auto accident, or a case of sexual harassment, or discrimination at work.)

Teaching Tip

Ask students how they would go about finding an attorney if they needed one. Discuss how to research an attorney through references and local legal groups. Also, have students write to the American Bar Association asking for guidelines for evaluating attorneys.

ASSESS

Assessment
Content

Have students develop civil dispute scenarios. Then have them describe the possible ways the dispute might be resolved, recommend one resolution method, and explain the reason for the recommendation.

Evaluate students' cases to determine whether they are civil or criminal issues. They should list the resolution methods described in Figure 12-3. Determine whether the student's recommended method of resolution is appropriate for the case presented and whether the student offers reasons that support his or her choice.

Extending the Illustration

Ask an attorney to speak to your class and explain differences in the handling of civil and criminal cases.

Caption Answer: Because of the celebrity of the accused, the debate over whether the accused is guilty, the nature of the crime, or the potential severity of the sentence.

Teaching ETHICS in Action

Have students follow these steps to help them make a decision.

1. What are the ethical issues?
2. What are the alternatives?
3. Who are the affected parties?
4. How do the alternatives affect the parties?
5. What is your decision?

Evaluation

Assign the section review.

MINI QUIZ

True-False

1. Labor laws set standards for what an employer must pay workers in all types of jobs. (false)

2. Labor unions negotiate work conditions and pay with employers through collective bargaining. (true)

3. The Americans with Disabilities Act is an example of an antidiscrimination law. (true)

4. Disputes between employers and employees are governed by civil law. (true)

5. If you have a legal dispute, your first step should always be to hire a lawyer. (false)

Use the Testmaker to create a customized test for Chapter 12.

---

fee. Use this opportunity to interview a lawyer carefully. Is the lawyer efficient and organized? Does he or she have the kind of experience you need? Do you feel you can trust this person?

Lawyers' Fees

Lawyers generally charge an hourly rate or set a flat fee based on how much work they expect to do for you. Some lawyers work for a **contingency fee**. This means that they take as payment a percentage of any money that you win in the lawsuit. Make sure you understand the fee system and projected costs before you agree to anything. Legal advice can be expensive.

Low-cost legal assistance in civil cases may be available from the Legal Aid Society. In criminal cases, the office of the public defender can provide free legal representation.

No matter where you go for legal advice, be prepared for the meeting:

YOU'RE THE BOSS!

✓ *Solving Workplace Problems*

You are the owner of a busy convenience store. When you witness one of your part-time employees, a high school student, taking money from the cash register, you fire him but agree not to file criminal charges. Then the student's father calls. He's irate that his son has been fired, and threatens to sue you. What will you do?

---

bring documents, records, and names of witnesses. Remember, too, that legal proceedings can take a very long time—months or even years.

SECTION 12-2 *Review*

Understanding Key Concepts

Using complete sentences, answer the following questions on a separate sheet of paper.

1. Why might you want to resolve a civil case out of court rather than through a trial?

2. Describe a workplace situation that could lead to a civil case and one that could lead to a criminal case.

3. Do you think it is a good idea to defend your own case in court? Why or why not?

SECTION 12-2 *Review* ANSWERS

1. Going to court can be expensive and time-consuming.

2. Possible answer: A dispute over age discrimination might lead to a civil case; a disagreement that ended in a physical fight in which a worker was injured might lead to a criminal case.

3. Possible answers: yes, if the case is appropriate for small-claims court; or no, because laws, legal language, and court procedures can be complex and require training and expertise.

SECTION 12-1 Summary

- Labor laws set basic rules for fair treatment in the workplace.
- Labor unions organize workers and bargain with employers to protect workers' rights.
- Labor and employment laws help employees deal with medical and financial emergencies.
- Antidiscrimination laws protect workers from job discrimination based on factors such as race, religion, age, gender, and disability.
- The government creates programs to help employers put antidiscrimination laws into action.
- Sexual harassment is unwelcome behavior of a sexual nature. If you experience harassment, you should take immediate steps to deal with it.

Key Terms

minimum wage *(p. 234)*
compensatory time *(p. 235)*
collective bargaining
 (p. 236)
discrimination *(p. 237)*
affirmative action *(p. 238)*
sexual harassment *(p. 239)*

SECTION 12-2 Summary

- The legal system—with its courts, judges, and lawyers—provides a set of procedures for resolving conflicts.
- Civil law applies to conflicts between private parties, such as an employee and a company, concerning rights and obligations.
- There are several ways to resolve a civil dispute without going to trial, including mediation and arbitration.
- Criminal law involves cases in which the government charges a person or a business with committing a crime. More serious offenses are called felonies, and less serious offenses are called misdemeanors.
- If you need to take legal action, consider going to small-claims court or hire a lawyer. Before you hire a lawyer, search carefully for the best person, make sure you understand what the fees will be, and provide all pertinent information to the lawyer you choose.

Key Terms

civil law *(p. 242)*
summons *(p. 244)*
criminal law *(p. 246)*
felony *(p. 246)*
misdemeanor *(p. 246)*
contingency fee *(p. 248)*

Chapter 12 • Workplace Legal Matters **249**

Reteaching

1. Have students identify the major legislation defining employer-employee relations. For each law, have students describe how it protects employees. Then have students describe the legal system that is used if there is a dispute between an employer and employee. Ask them to describe methods of resolving disputes before seeking a court trial.

2. Assign and review vocabulary terms, chapter questions, and activities from the Chapter Review.

3. Assign and review the Unit Project on the unit opener pages.

Extending the Content

Assign the appropriate Chapter 12 activities in the *Student Activity Workbook*.
 Now that students have learned about civil law, have them research the criminal system in your state. Tell students to write a step-by-step description of what happens from the time a person is arrested and charged with a crime to the resolution of the case, including descriptions of the courts involved—from the local level to the top state criminal court.

Teaching **YOU'RE THE BOSS!**

✓ Possible responses: Explain the situation to the father, being sure he understands that you saw his son stealing from the store; suggest a meeting with both father and son.

Computer Activity

Using the phone book, have students locate attorneys' names, addresses, and phone numbers and create a database for referrals. Students should locate an attorney or a legal firm for each of these categories: civil, criminal, estate planning, family law, and labor relations. Have students create a list of their referrals by the type of law practiced.

CLOSE

Have students complete this sentence: "As an employee, I am protected by law in these ways . . . ."

See the Unit Closure and Unit Evaluation located on page 153.

Answers

Reviewing Key Terms

Interview questions will vary, but they should reflect an understanding of the legal application of each term.

Recalling Key Concepts

1. False: The minimum wage has been adjusted to keep pace with inflation and other economic factors.
2. True
3. True
4. False: Criminal law refers to charges the government brings against individuals or companies.
5. False: Because laws and courtroom procedures are complex, it is best to consult a lawyer.

Thinking Critically

1. Antidiscrimination laws protect people from unfair treatment based on race, religion, gender, age, or disability.
2. Possible answer: Strong speaking skills could help you discuss your grievance with your employer; good writing skills could help you write an effective letter to a government agency.
3. Possible answers: Sexual harassment might hinder the victim's job performance. It might result in the harasser's being fired.

Reviewing Key Terms

You are interviewing a lawyer who specializes in labor and employment law. On a separate sheet of paper, write out a list of questions, using each of the following terms.

minimum wage
compensatory time
collective bargaining
discrimination
affirmative action
sexual harassment
civil law
criminal law
summons
felony
misdemeanor
contingency fee

Recalling Key Concepts

On a separate sheet of paper, tell whether each statement is true or false. Rewrite any false statements to make them true.

1. The minimum wage has remained the same since it was first created.
2. Antidiscrimination laws protect certain groups of citizens from unfair employment practices.
3. Sexual harassment is any unwelcome behavior of a sexual nature.
4. Civil law refers to charges the government brings against a person.
5. You do not need to hire a lawyer if you are taking a case to a court other than small-claims court.

Thinking Critically

Using complete sentences, answer each of the following questions on a separate sheet of paper.

1. Why are antidiscrimination laws important?
2. How could effective communication skills help you defend yourself against an unfair situation at work?
3. How might sexual harassment interfere with a person's career advancement?
4. Explain the difference between criminal law and civil law.
5. Give an example of a case that you might take to small-claims court.

 ### SCANS Foundation Skills and Workplace Competencies

Basic Skills: *Reading and Writing*

1. Working in a team of three, locate and read several articles on sexual harassment in the workplace. Together, create a list of do's and don'ts for a fair and comfortable business environment.

Thinking Skills: *Problem Solving*

2. Working in a group of three, come up with an imaginary dispute that requires arbitration. Decide who will be the arbitrator, and have the other two group members defend their side of the dispute. After listening to both arguments, the arbitrator should make a judgment in favor of one side, explaining his or her reasons. Then switch roles until all group members have had a chance to play arbitrator.

4. Civil law deals with disputes about rights and responsibilities between people or companies. Criminal law involves charges by the government against people or companies.
5. Answers will vary.

 ### SCANS Foundation Skills and Workplace Competencies

1. Lists will vary, depending on the articles read, but they should display sensitivity and respect.
2. Make sure that each student gets to role-play both a disputing party and the arbitrator. Have students discuss whether they found it difficult to listen to both

Connecting Academics to the Workplace

Language Arts

1. Tamika is applying for a job. On the application form, she is asked the following questions:
   - Where were you born?
   - How much do you weigh?
   - Do you plan to have children?

   Explain why it would be a violation of antidiscrimination laws for the employer to base an employment decision on Tamika's answers to these questions.

Social Studies

2. Labor laws have played a major role in American history and culture. Choose one aspect of the world of work—such as hours, wages, child labor, minorities, unions, safety, benefits, or pollution—and research one federal or state law that has affected that aspect. Report to the class on what conditions were like before the law existed and how conditions changed after the law was passed.

Developing Teamwork and Leadership Skills

Working with a small group, develop a short handbook for employers that will show their legal responsibilities in terms of hiring and promotion practices as well as labor issues. Conduct research as needed to find additional facts about an employer's legal responsibilities. Present the handbook in an easy-to-use format.

Real-World Workshop

Using the phone book or the Internet, locate the local branch of a state or federal labor organization such as the Department of Labor or the Equal Employment Opportunity Commission. Research the procedures for filing a claim by either visiting the appropriate office or requesting information over the telephone. Report your findings to the class.

School-to-Work Connection

Arrange a visit to a state or federal courthouse, and sit in on a trial. You can do this by writing a letter to the court clerk or by calling the courthouse. (Check the telephone book's government pages under "Courts.") Take notes on the court process, indicating at least four career opportunities in the court system.

Individual Career Plan

The law states that all new employees must fill out an I-9 form to prove their eligibility to work. When you fill out this form, you will be asked for three forms of identification. Conduct research to find out what identification is required, and gather the various cards and papers you could present. The Immigration and Naturalization Service, part of the Justice Department, can provide information.

Chapter 12 • Workplace Legal Matters **251**

Developing Teamwork and Leadership Skills

Students should present accurate information in a format that would be useful to an employer.

Real-World Workshop

After students have reported their findings, have them combine the results of their research to create a resource manual with telephone numbers and addresses of local agencies and offices.

School-to-Work Connection

Have students compare their notes and make a class list of law-related career opportunities, such as court stenographer, lawyer, court clerk, bailiff, and judge.

Individual Career Plan

Form I-9 designates three categories of identification. Either one document from List A or a document each from List B and List C must be shown. List A documents, such as a passport or certificate of naturalization, prove both identity and employment eligibility. List B documents, such as a driver's license or U.S. military card, prove identity only. List C documents, such as a Social Security card or birth certificate, prove employment eligibility only.

sides impartially and whether they found it difficult to make a decision.

Connecting Academics to the Workplace

1. These questions could lead to discrimination based on race or national origin, physical appearance, or gender, all of which are prohibited by law.

2. Answers will vary. (For example, the Social Security Act of 1935 established an old-age insurance system for American workers. Previously, retired workers had to rely entirely on their own savings. After the law was passed, a system was established that uses taxes on employers and employees to build funds for workers' old-age security.)

Aspects of Industry: Health, Safety, and Environmental Issues

Students who are fairly sure of their future careers may use the Labs to investigate all the aspects of industry for one career. Other students may want to investigate a different job cluster with each Lab.

STEP A

To select a job, students may brainstorm with other students or research the possibilities in the *Occupational Outlook Handbook (OOH)* or other career references.

To help students prepare for this exercise, you might review the different types of resources available at the library. Encourage students to make a bibliography of their sources. All references should include the name and date of publication.

Discuss in class some of the potential health risks that workers face (carpal tunnel syndrome, exposure to electromagnetic radiation, exposure to toxins); safety risks they face (working high above the ground, with heavy equipment, driving vehicles); and risks in their working environment (working in a smoking environment, exposure to the elements).

Then discuss what kinds of health, safety, and environmental issues may affect the community at large (unsafe dumping of toxic or contaminated materials, chemical

ASPECTS OF INDUSTRY: *Health, Safety, and Environmental Issues*

Overview

In Unit Four, you read about starting a new job and the ethics and proper attitude that will sustain you throughout your working career. You also began to look into some of the health, safety, and legal issues that arise in the workplace. In this Unit Lab, you will use what you have learned while exploring another aspect of industry: **Health, Safety, and Environmental Issues.**

The Health, Safety, and Environmental Issues aspect of industry covers an employee's health, safety, and environment while at work. It also covers how businesses affect the health, safety, and environment of the community at large.

252

Tools

1. Internet
2. Trade, health, environmental, and business magazines
3. Newspapers

Procedures

STEP A

Choose one of the 15 job clusters shown in Figure 3-1 in Chapter 3. You may choose the same cluster you explored in the previous Lab, or a different one.

Choose one job in the job cluster that you would seriously think about pursuing. Use trade, health and environmental magazines, newspapers, and the Internet to pinpoint a health, safety, or environmental issue that affects workers in that industry. Examples of some issues might be the use of chemicals, working high above the ground, or working with computers.

Next, pinpoint a health, safety, or environmental issue in the industry you have chosen that affects the community at large. Some issues might be hazardous waste disposal policies, building standards, or air pollution.

Keep copies of the articles you find. You may want to refer to them later when you write your Report.

runoff in water, proper use of building materials or structural safety, non-earthquake proof buildings, water and air pollution, overuse of resources, and so on).

STEP B

Because health, safety, and environmental issues can be controversial, students should try to choose companies with a positive track

STEP B

Find and research two local companies that employ people in the job you've chosen. Choose companies that have a positive record in dealing with health, safety, and environmental issues.

Contact the person at each company who is in charge of worker safety or community relations, probably someone in the personnel department for employee issues. Ask permission to do a 20- to 30-minute interview for a class project.

Some of the questions you might ask about employee working conditions are:

1. What situations on the job might affect a worker's health or safety?

2. What steps does the company take to ensure employees' health and safety? (Thorough training? Safety equipment?)

Some questions you might ask about the affect of the industry on the community are:

1. How might the work of the industry affect the health, safety, and environment of the community?

2. What steps does the company take to minimize risk to the community?

Use the same interview etiquette in this Lab as in the previous Labs. Be prompt, courteous, and send a thank-you letter.

REPORT

Write a one-page, word-processed report using the information you gathered in your research, interview, and team discussion.

- Does the attitude of the industry you've chosen toward worker health and safety correspond to the conditions under which you want to work? Is this an industry-wide attitude? How would you feel about working for the company you interviewed, or the industry in general?

- Does the industry's attitude toward public safety correspond to your values? Explain.

Keep your research, interview notes, and report in a folder entitled "Career Exploration."

the student toward another company.

Have students write out all questions in advance. Make sure they are phrased in a positive manner.

You might want to work on brushing up interpersonal skills, teaching students how to deal with a potentially hostile interviewee. This is a life skill they will need regardless of the work they pursue. You might want to do this through role-playing, or through a discussion of unpleasant confrontations students have had with classmates, teachers, parents, salespeople, or strangers. Have the class brainstorm ways a student might have handled the situation more positively.

Report

You might want to have students look at the ethics of the workplace regarding worker safety, health, and environment. Have them look at how they can respond if they find themselves in a work situation that conflicts with their personal ethics. Have them address these issues in their report, or in a classroom discussion.

record. If the company's record is unknown, or if the company is of great appeal to the student despite some bad publicity, caution the student not to be confrontational in the interview. Urge students to be polite at all times. Explain that they should not argue with their interviewees, even if the two of them appear to approach the issues from different points of view. If the company in question has been or is involved in a lawsuit involving any of these issues, steer the

253

Unit Overview

In this unit, students will look at the importance of developing good interpersonal skills, working as a team member or leader, and communicating effectively. This unit also helps students develop their decision-making and problem-solving skills. Learning about technology skills and how to manage time and materials effectively close the unit.

Introducing the Unit

Turn to the table of contents and read aloud the title of each chapter in this unit. For each chapter, have students brainstorm a list of skills that might be covered. Ask students to describe how those skills would be used on the job.

Unit Project

Before beginning this unit, have students start a notebook entitled "Skills and Knowledge I Need for My Chosen Career." Allow each student to choose one business that he or she might like to work for or even to start as an entrepreneur. After you complete each chapter, have students think about the skills and/or knowledge outlined in that chapter and write in their notebooks how it applies to the career they have chosen, and how they will gain those skills. Have students hand in their notebooks at the end of this unit, after they have completed the Unit Closure activity.

254

UNIT 5

Professional Development

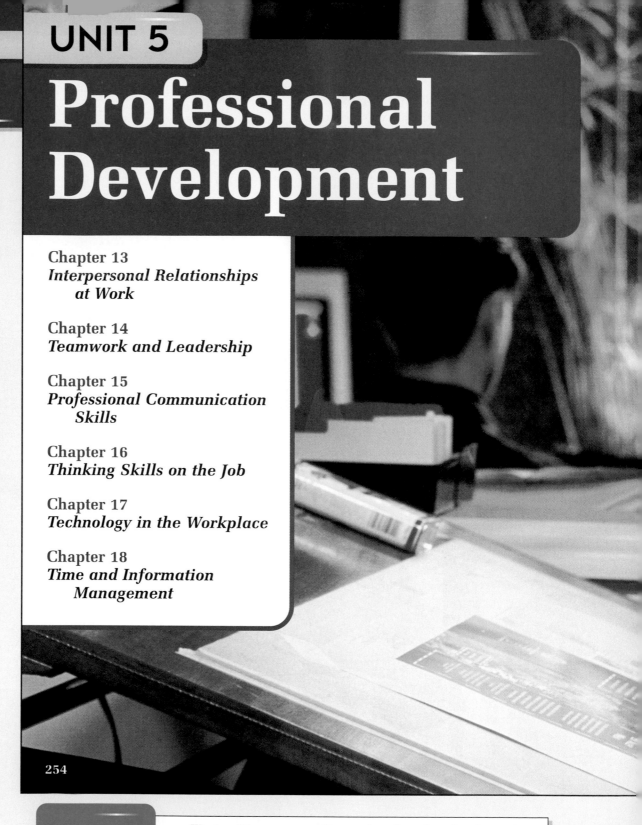

Chapter 13
*Interpersonal Relationships
at Work*

Chapter 14
Teamwork and Leadership

Chapter 15
*Professional Communication
Skills*

Chapter 16
Thinking Skills on the Job

Chapter 17
Technology in the Workplace

Chapter 18
*Time and Information
Management*

254

**Developing
Community
Involvement**

Work with a community newspaper or other organization to sponsor a teen issues night. Solicit topics of concern from area high school students through the Internet, newspaper or school surveys. Find a place to hold the event. Provide food and music through donations from local organizations and businesses. Invite an improvisation group to act out situations—such as the wrong way to deal with a suicidal friend—and ask speakers specializing on the topic to comment.

Resources for Enrichment

Books

- *The Quality Imperative* by editors of *Business Week*
- *The Road to the Baldrige Award* by Haavind
- *The Time Trap* by Mackenzie
- *Ready, Set, Organize!* by Peterson

Magazines

Business Week, Forbes, Fortune, Nation's Business, PC Magazine, MACWorld

Organizations

- National Association of Colleges and Employers
- National Institute of Standards and Technology (for information on Baldrige Award)

Internet

Career Mosaic—On-line job fairs, jobs and internships for college students: http://www.careermosaic.com/cm

Occupational Outlook Handbook—On-line version of Labor Dept. information on careers: http://www.espan.com/docs/oohand.html

Unit Closure

Have students use the notebook they developed for the Unit Project to write a brief summary of the skills and knowledge they will need for their chosen career.

Unit Evaluation

Administer the reproducible test for Unit 5, which you will find in your Performance Assessment Binder, or construct your own test using the IBM Testmaker Software.

UNIT 5 QUIZ:
What Do You Know About Professional Development?

- What does it take to get along with coworkers?
- How do you create an effective team?
- What makes a great leader?
- How are communication skills used in the workplace?
- How would you handle decisions and problems people face every day in the workplace?
- How is technology used in the workplace?
- What is the secret to managing your time and information?

255

Building Partners in Industry

How can a service learning program help your students? Once your students begin participating in community-service volunteer programs, you'll recognize many special benefits. These programs help students learn appropriate work attitudes and practices. They also encourage self-esteem as students recognize their own ability to make meaningful contributions to others. Further, these programs help students see themselves—now and in the future—as participating members of the community.

SECTION 1 *Your Personal Traits at Work*

SECTION OBJECTIVES	SECTION FEATURES	SECTION RESOURCES
• Recognize and develop personal traits for getting along with others in the workplace. • Develop behaviors for being a successful and effective coworker.	Personal Career Plan, p. 257 Career Do's and Don'ts, p. 262 You're the Boss!, p. 263 Excellent Business Practices, p. 263 Attitude Counts, p. 264 Exploring Careers, p. 265	Workforce 2000 Videodisc and Videotape Section 13-1 Review, p. 264 Student Activity Workbook

SECTION 2 *Applying Interpersonal Skills*

SECTION OBJECTIVES	SECTION FEATURES	SECTION RESOURCES
• Understand and practice proper workplace etiquette. • Understand and practice effective methods of conflict resolution. • Appreciate and increase sensitivity to diversity in the workplace.		Workforce 2000 Videodisc and Videotape Section 13-2 Review, p. 270 Chapter 13 Review, pp. 272–273 Student Activity Workbook

CHAPTER 13

CHAPTER RESOURCES

- Chapter Transparencies and Lesson Plans
- Chapter 13 Test
- Spanish Resources, Chapter 13
- School-to-Work Activity Handbook, Chapter 13 Activity
- Teacher's Lesson Plans, Chapter 13
- Implementing Block Scheduling, Chapter 13
- Print, Media, and Internet Handbook
- Strategies for Implementing Work-Based Learning
- Strategies for Implementing Connecting Activities

Career Notes

SCANS CORRELATION CHART

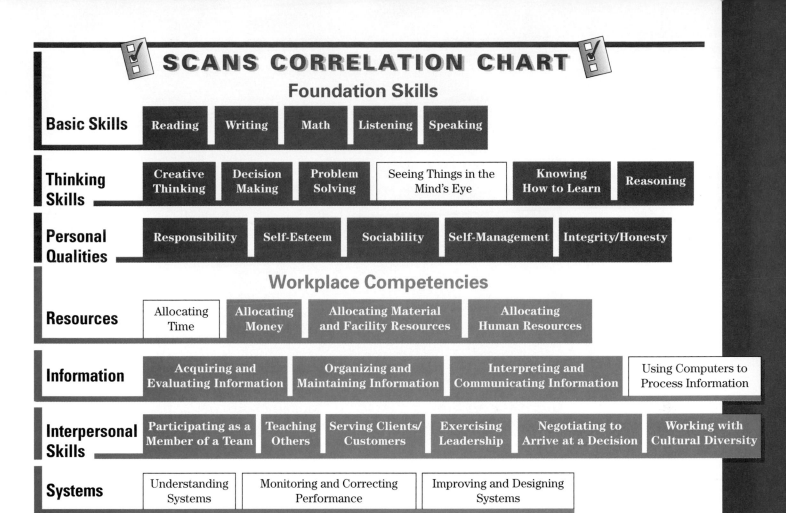

Foundation Skills

Basic Skills	Reading	Writing	Math	Listening	Speaking	
Thinking Skills	Creative Thinking	Decision Making	Problem Solving	Seeing Things in the Mind's Eye	Knowing How to Learn	Reasoning
Personal Qualities	Responsibility	Self-Esteem	Sociability	Self-Management	Integrity/Honesty	

Workplace Competencies

Resources	Allocating Time	Allocating Money	Allocating Material and Facility Resources	Allocating Human Resources	
Information	Acquiring and Evaluating Information	Organizing and Maintaining Information	Interpreting and Communicating Information	Using Computers to Process Information	
Interpersonal Skills	Participating as a Member of a Team	Teaching Others	Serving Clients/ Customers	Exercising Leadership	Negotiating to Arrive at a Decision	Working with Cultural Diversity
Systems	Understanding Systems	Monitoring and Correcting Performance	Improving and Designing Systems		
Technology	Selecting Technology	Applying Technology to Task	Maintaining and Troubleshooting Technology		

Highlighted blocks indicate areas covered in the Chapter.

Additional Activities

Internet Connection

Stereotypes provide barriers to communication and work relationships. Ask students to look at what sites on the Internet reinforce stereotypes and promote prejudice. What sites provide information and names of organizations that seek to break down stereotypes? Discuss findings in class.

Field Trip Suggestions

Arrange to visit an organization that hires and trains the handicapped. Ask for a tour of the facility, a discussion of the organization's philosophy, and perhaps presentations by workers. Ask students to write in their journals about how the visit might affect their views of diversity.

Guest Speaker Suggestions

Invite to class a counselor or workshop leader who works with businesses to improve the communication skills and the efficiency of a diverse workforce. Ask the guest to discuss resistance to diversity and how it is overcome.

Key to Ability Levels

Each section gives skill-building activities. Each activity has been labeled for use with students of various learning styles and abilities.

L1 Level 1 activities are basic activities and should be within the range of all students.

L2 Level 2 activities are average activities and should be within the range of average and above average students.

L3 Level 3 activities are challenging activities designed for the ability range of above average students.

Chapter 13

Interpersonal Relationships at Work

Chapter Overview

The goal of this chapter is to help students improve their relationships with others.

Section 13-1 examines personal traits and qualities and provides students with a four-step plan for improving their own personal traits.

Section 13-2 looks at workplace etiquette and provides suggestions for resolving conflict.

Background Information

Write chapter objectives (Sections 13-1 and 13-2) on the chalkboard or use the chapter objective transparency for class discussion.

Choose assignments from the *Student Activity Workbook* and write them on the chalkboard.

Have students preview the chapter, looking at pictures, reading captions, and noting content headings. Ask students to describe what they expect to learn in this chapter.

Preteaching Vocabulary

Write the Key Terms from Sections 13-1 and 13-2 on the chalkboard. Have students describe how each term relates personality traits and relationships with others.

256

Meeting SPECIAL Needs

Limited Proficiency in English

To make studying easier for students with limited proficiency in English, ask other students to help tape the chapter for home study. Have students divide the chapter, with each student taping one section. Ask students who use the tapes to orally summarize the ideas in each section. Students could also develop questions for quizzes.

Interpersonal Relationships at Work

Section 13-1
Your Personal Traits at Work

Section 13-2
Applying Interpersonal Skills

In this video segment, learn how to get along with others in the workplace.

Journal
Personal Career Plan

Imagine yourself working full-time in the career of your choice, and consider the people with whom you'll come in contact. In your journal, write a list of the traits you hope to find in those people. Then respond to these questions: Which of those listed traits do you have? Which should you try to develop?

257

School-to-Work Connecting Activities

Have students interview older brothers and sisters or friends who have been in full-time jobs for a couple of years, asking each person what they know now that they wish they had known when they began their first jobs. Also have students ask what techniques the workers use in getting along with others on the job. Tell students to share their questions and responses in class.

Work-Based Learning Strategies and Activities

Find a local employer that provides work-based interpersonal skills training for new supervisors or other employees. Arrange to have students attend such a training session. Have them take notes and then write summaries of what they learned. Discuss in class.

WORKFORCE 2000 Training Video

Have students view the video and perform the interactive exercises to reinforce important chapter concepts and thinking processes.

Chapter 13

Addressing **LEARNING** Styles

Kinesthetic Learner

Have students work in groups of three or four to create and present skits on dealing with diversity in the workplace. They can deal with racial issues, physical disability issues (such as access), disparity between women and men, and so on. The skits should incorporate a possible solution to the situation they present. After the presentations, have the class discuss the situation and the solution.

FOCUS

Bell Ringer

Ask students to write the name of one person they enjoy being with or working for. Then ask them to write a list of at least 10 adjectives to describe him or her.

Introducing the Section

As students share their lists from the Bell Ringer activity, write the adjectives on the chalkboard. Then categorize the words according to whether they describe responsibility, self-esteem, sociability, self-management, or integrity/honesty. Students can improve themselves in these areas by concentrating on their actions, and interactions with others. Stress the importance of these traits in helping people to be more effective in their careers.

Motivational Activity
Critical Thinking

Have students list each of the five personal traits on this page. Tell students to write a sentence or two describing how they demonstrate each trait in their personal lives. For example, what actions does the student take to demonstrate responsibility or to build self-esteem?

Your Personal Traits at Work

OBJECTIVES

After studying this section, you will be able to:

- **Recognize and develop personal traits for getting along with others in the workplace.**
- **Develop behaviors for being a successful and effective coworker.**

KEY TERMS

tact
empathize

What do you think is the most important workplace skill? According to a recent survey, many employees believe it is "getting along with others at work." Whether you're working already or beginning to plan your career, you need to think about your relationships with coworkers.

If you develop good interpersonal relationships with your coworkers, you'll enjoy your time at work more. After all, think of all the hours you'll be spending together. In addition, you'll be able to do your job more successfully. By showing a willingness to cooperate with your coworkers, you'll probably receive their cooperation in return.

What can you do to develop good relationships with your coworkers? Begin by assessing your own traits. (Look back at the work you did in Chapter 2 on getting to know yourself.) What traits do you already have that help you work well with other people? What traits do you need to develop?

Important Personal Traits

The personal traits that help you get along with others at your job are the same ones that help you at school or in social situations. As you learned in Chapters 9 and 10, the following SCANS skills are important personal qualities for the workplace:

- *Responsibility*, including dependability and positive motivation;
- *Self-esteem*, including confidence;

258   *Unit 5 • Professional Development*

> ## ▶ Extending the Illustration

(see illustration on top of page 259)

Have students list the human relations skills they practice in cooperating with others. (Listening, communicating, considering others' viewpoints or feelings, being willing to share both work and rewards.)

Caption Answer: Working well with others can enable you to get jobs done more efficiently. By cooperating with others and doing your job well, you increase your opportunities to advance in your career.

By cooperating with one another, these employees get their job done efficiently. **How can working well with others help you in your career?**

- *Sociability*, including friendliness, enthusiasm, adaptability, and respect for other workers;
- *Self-management*, including self-control and **tact**, the ability to say and do things in a way that will not offend other people; and
- *Integrity/Honesty*, including loyalty and trustworthiness.

Self-Awareness on the Job

Understanding your own unique blend of qualities can help you adjust to new work situations. If you are self-aware, you know not only your strengths but also the traits you need to improve.

Tracy Kagan of Miami, Florida, learned a great deal about her personal traits when she changed jobs at the same restaurant. After working for two years as a server, Tracy was

promoted to assistant manager. While she had been well liked as a server, Tracy was not popular when she first became an assistant manager.

"I wasn't confident that I could handle my responsibilities," she explains. In her nervousness, she yelled at the cooks and criticized servers in front of customers. Fortunately, Tracy's supervisor recognized the problem. She spoke with Tracy about her need to control her emotions and to be tactful. Still, changing was not easy.

"Whenever I felt pressured, I had to remind myself to be polite," Tracy says.

Tracy needed help from her supervisor to improve her personal traits at work. **Why is it important to be able to listen to constructive criticism?**

Chapter 13 • *Interpersonal Relationships at Work* **259**

Extending the Illustration

Ask students to review what they learned in Chapter 10 about constructive criticism. Have students describe the difference between criticism and constructive criticism.

Caption Answer: More experienced workers or a supervisor can give you helpful suggestions for improvement, and you need to be open to trying them out.

Guided Practice
Teaching Strategies
1. Assign and review Section 13-1.
2. Use the transparency for this section.
3. Assign and review the Case Study.

Discussion Starter

Tell students that a co-worker has just said something that made them angry. How would they react? How would their reactions demonstrate responsibility, self-esteem, sociability, self-management, and integrity/honesty? Encourage students to stop and think about these traits *before* they react.

Teaching Tip

Ask students to brainstorm ways to develop self-awareness. Suggest to students that one way to develop self-awareness is to ask close friends or people who work with them to give suggestions about how they could improve their skills.

Critical Thinking

Have students write 50-word descriptions of a personal or job-related experience in which they were personally effective. How many of the personal traits discussed here contributed to their success?

SCANS Foundation Skills Connection

L1 **Self-Esteem**

Have students choose local volunteer organizations and donate at least one hour of their time helping out. (Examples might include working on a Saturday morning at a shelter helping to sort clothing donated for the homeless or spending a couple of hours reading to the elderly in a nursing care facility.) After students complete their volunteer work, have them write 50-word paragraphs describing how they felt about the experience.

L2 **Self-Management**

One important aspect of self-management is realizing when you need to learn new work skills. Have students learn the basics of a word-processing software program and use it to write and create one- or two-page documents to be given to their parents. Students are to write about their career goals, how they plan to meet their goals, and the help they will need along the way. Tell students to format their documents attractively, proofread them, and then print two copies. Have students turn in one copy and share the other with their parents.

"I made it a habit to take a deep breath when I felt myself getting upset. Then I'd smile."

In time, Tracy developed her self-management skills. Now she enjoys her job and has won back the respect of her coworkers.

 Figure 13-1

Four Steps to Self-Improvement

Self-improvement takes time and effort. The process involves a series of clearly defined steps.

Step 1 **Zero in on one trait at a time.** Kylor is confident that he is sociable and honest. He's decided that he needs to focus on becoming more responsible, however.

Step 2 **Draw up a plan and stick to it.** Kylor makes a list of several things he can do on a regular basis to help out around the house. He makes sure he takes responsibility for at least one chore each day.

Improving Your Personal Traits

Can you improve yourself? Of course you can. One of the most successful people in American history—Benjamin Franklin—used a notebook to keep track of how effectively he practiced the personal qualities he wanted to improve. Each day he'd write notes for himself about such traits as justice, diligence, and sincerity.

▶▶ Extending Figure 13-1 ◀◀

Have students list the personal traits they would like to improve. Using the steps in the figure as a guide, have them create plans for which trait they will improve first and how they will track their progress and know when they have met their goal.

Look back at the list of important personal traits on pages 258–259. In your journal, write down which traits you think are your strong points and which you would like to improve. *Figure 13-1* shows four steps to self-improvement and how one person put them into action.

Becoming an Effective Coworker

Remember the "upward spirals" you read about in Chapter 10? Here's another one: By developing your positive traits, you will be better able to get along with your coworkers. By getting along with your coworkers, you will be more effective at your job. By being more effective at your job, you will be more likely to advance in your career.

Being effective—that is, getting a job done quickly and well—seldom happens in isolation. Within the workplace, you'll find that effectiveness comes about when workers cooperate with one another. Four interpersonal behaviors are essential for being an effective coworker: respect, understanding, communication, and good humor.

Step 3 Keep track of your progress. Kylor checks his progress each night by keeping a record of every responsibility he's fulfilled that day. He also writes notes to himself about areas in which he might do better. Once a week he asks his family, "How am I doing?"

Step 4 Move on. Once Kylor feels that he has made progress in becoming more responsible, he starts to work on improving another trait. He has decided to work on boosting his self-esteem by reading to students in a local elementary school.

Workforce 2000 Trends

Family problems are a major cause of work missed by women. In the future, 4 out of 10 working women will have children. A quarter of those women will be single, widowed, divorced or separated, raising their children alone. Successful companies will have to pay close attention to the concerns of working mothers.

L3 Responsibility

Have students bring in items such as a grapefruit or a box of cereal. Tell them that these items are their "babies" and they are to be responsible for them for the week, guarding and caring for them at all times. Have them think of them as they would children. At the end of the week, have students discuss their experiences. Did any of them lose their "baby" or forget to bring it along? Discuss how their actions demonstrated their sense of responsibility.

 SCANS Workplace Competencies Connection

L1 Allocating Money

Have students identify possessions that they no longer need or want. (For example, clothing that is too small or music tapes or CDs they no longer listen to.) Tell them to list the items and assign a price they would charge for each in a yard sale. Have students ask a relative or a family friend, who has experience with yard sales, to evaluate their prices and decide whether they would pay that amount for each item. Have students discuss whether their prices were too high and how they might use this information in the future.

SCANS Workplace Competencies Connection (cont'd.)

L2 **Negotiating to Arrive at a Decision**

Tell students to go to a local flea market and identify an item they like. Have students determine the asking price, then make an offer at a lower price, negotiating until they reach an agreement with the seller. Have students share their negotiating experiences in class. Was the result a win-win situation for both buyer and seller?

L3 **Exercising Leadership**

Have students choose one thing that they do well, such as math or writing, playing a musical instrument, or playing a sport. Help them find opportunities to use that skill or knowledge to tutor a classmate or a younger child. Have students report on their tutoring activities once a week.

Independent Practice

Assign as homework the chapter activity in the *School-to-Work Activity Handbook.*

Reading

Have students read an article on self-improvement from magazines like *Psychology Today.* Ask students to share at least three suggestions made in the article with the class.

262

Respecting Others

Without mutual respect, there can be little cooperation in the workplace. Which two negative traits do you think do the most to prevent respect? One is an "I'm-better-than-you" attitude. The other negative trait is jealousy.

An "I'm-better-than-you" attitude is simply the idea that you are superior to someone else. Remember that each worker—no matter what his or her job may be—has something important to contribute. Any job well done grants dignity to the worker who performs it.

Jealousy can act like a poison in the workplace. Workers who become jealous of their coworkers view them as rivals. They withhold respect, and cooperation becomes more difficult—a downward spiral. A jealous worker refuses to admit that coworkers may have worked more effectively and deserve raises or promotions.

Remember that respect is a two-way street. In most cases, the more you give, the more you'll gain in return.

Understanding Others

You don't have to have a deep understanding of your coworkers in order to work well together. Instead, you can develop understanding by being an interested observer.

Career Do's & Don'ts

To Delegate Effectively...
Do:
- assign tasks you've already mastered.
- pick associates with the skills for the job.
- make sure delegated assignments benefit the organization.
- specify what you want done, in writing if necessary.

Don't:
- give others work just to keep them busy.
- hover over their shoulders, watching every move.
- wait until the deadline to follow up.
- dwell on mistakes without offering positive guidance for the future.

262 *Unit 5 • Professional Development*

People show their feelings through body language, whether they mean to or not. *What kind of message is the woman on the right conveying? What leads you to this conclusion?*

Extending the Illustration

Bring to class several examples of people showing a variety of facial expressions and body language. Have students decide what emotion or attitude each person is projecting.

Caption Answer: The woman seems tense and angry because of her facial expression.

Teaching YOU'RE THE BOSS!

✓ Possible responses: Discuss the problem with the employees individually and together; emphasize the importance of their getting along and of modeling friendly relationships for the children.

- Notice the personal traits of your coworkers.
- Ask your coworkers about their short-term and long-term career goals.
- Try to **empathize** with your coworkers—that is, try to see things from their point of view and to gain an understanding of their situation.
- Pay attention to your coworkers' body language—how their physical actions express emotions. Be alert to facial expressions, which very often give clues to a person's inner feelings.

YOU'RE THE BOSS!

Solving Workplace Problems

You own a small day-care center, where you employ two caregivers. Both of your employees are excellent with the children, and communicate effectively with the children's parents. However, they have been unable to establish a friendly, cooperative relationship with each other. What will you do to help improve their relationship?

EXCELLENT BUSINESS PRACTICES

Networking

American Express Financial Advisors, of Minneapolis, Minnesota, sees so much value in networking that it has developed official employee networks. The groups represent the diversity of the company of 650 employees.

To receive official status, the networks present a formal mission statement to the company. The company provides each network with $5,000 to create relationships with nonprofit organizations that represent the network's mission. These may include a partnership with a museum, a special health-care interest, or other community services.

The program enhances awareness of different cultures and promotes diversity. It supports the special interests of employees and is an opportunity for the company to serve the community directly. Networking also is a means of making contacts, learning about an industry, and cultivating relationships with other people in the community who have similar interests and values.

Thinking Critically

How can participating in the same special-interest group help develop a relationship with a coworker?

Extending EXCELLENT BUSINESS PRACTICES

Answer: Discovering a shared interest gives you a chance to see a side of a coworker that you might not be aware of in the work environment. Learning more about a coworker can enhance the relationship.

Further Application: Have students attend a meeting of a club or association. Ask them: Would you join? If not, what would you like to change—the type of interest, the format of the meeting, the meeting place?

Writing: *Directions*

Have students write letters to pen pals describing what they are learning about self-improvement and the steps they can follow to improve their own personal traits.

Discussion Starter

Ask students what mental images they form when a friend describes another person as someone with a major attitude problem.

Teaching Tip

Have students share their mental images from the Discussion Starter. Then tell them they are supervisors who have an employee with that problem. What would they do to try to help the person become a more effective employee?

Discuss with students the need to respect other people's beliefs and ideas. Also discuss the idea that others' respect for your work is earned by doing good work; just showing up in the morning doesn't mean that you've earned job respect.

Research

If your school has access to the Internet, have students do on-line searches for articles and other information on self-improvement. Have students share their findings in class and discuss which of the Internet sites provided the most useful information.

Role-Play

Ask for three pairs of students to volunteer to role-play a work situation in which a supervisor is reprimanding an employee for consistently being late. Have each supervisor take a different approach (for example, one supervisor might be angry; another, empathetic and helpful).

Conduct the role-plays and have the class take notes about which attitude and approach seems to be most effective in getting the employee to improve the behavior.

Skills Practice

Tell students that they work as customer service representatives. Have students write 100-word reports describing the personal skills that would be most important in this job.

ASSESS

Assessment
Process

Have students choose one personal trait they want to improve and apply the four-step method. Have students write how they plan to apply each step. Evaluate students' plans for inclusion of all the steps and for the appropriateness of the plans.

Attitude Counts ✔

The Golden Rule may sound trite, but it's still true—you <u>do</u> benefit when you treat other people just the way you'd like to be treated. That goes for your attitude, too. Your positive attitude should extend to your family and friends, as well as to the people with whom you come into passing contact. Expect the best from them— and for them.

Communicating with Others

Communication, like respect, is a two-way street. How you listen is as important as what you say. Both listening and speaking well are especially important when you are working as part of a team. If you don't listen well, you won't benefit from being part of the team. Failure to convey information promptly and clearly can disrupt a project. It can make everyone on the team look bad.

Don't be reluctant to speak up and ask a coworker or supervisor for help if you need it. Remember that being effective means producing results. A coworker can often provide the guidance you'll need to overcome problems and get the job done.

Communicating, however, does not mean talking about your private life. You can be warm and friendly without revealing personal secrets. In the workplace, it's better to spend time discussing work-related matters.

Keep Smiling!

Your sense of humor can carry you— and your coworkers—through times of stress. It can also help unite a team and make people feel better about themselves. You don't have to be a comedian. Just try to find ways to see the light side of a situation.

SECTION 13-1 *Review*
Understanding Key Concepts

Using complete sentences, answer the following questions on a separate sheet of paper.

1. Describe a situation in which you effectively applied one of the SCANS skills listed on page 258–259. What did you learn from this experience?

2. Which of the four interpersonal behaviors discussed in this section do you think is the most important? Why?

SECTION 13-1 *Review* ANSWERS

1. Answers will vary. Students may, for example, describe taking on a new responsibility that helped them learn new skills.

2. Possible answer: Respect is the most important quality. Without it, communication, understanding, and humor will not yield positive results.

Teaching Attitude Counts ✔

Let students meet in small groups to discuss the Golden Rule. Then have group members work cooperatively to plan short skits illustrating the importance of seeing the best in others. Provide time for each group to present its skit to the class.

CASE STUDY

Exploring Careers: Family and Consumer Services

Rose Johnson
Automotive Customer Service
Adviser

Q: How did you become a service adviser?

A: I had a broken-down car and no money to fix it. I'm good with my hands, so I figured out how to fix my car myself. When I went to the community college, I trained to be an automotive technician. However, I realized I would be physically unable to do that kind of work for a long time.

Q: So you switched to service advising?

A: Dealerships are reluctant to give that kind of position to someone just out of college. So I started out washing cars and moving them around the lot. As a cashier, I learned computer skills. Later, as a dispatcher, I scheduled up to 100 cars a day, making sure they were done on time. From there, I moved to the position of service adviser.

Q: What skills are most important in your work?

A: It's necessary to know about cars. That's the most helpful skill in giving advice to customers. If customers hear doubt in your voice, they are doubtful about your advice. Computer skills, math skills, and good phone etiquette are also important. You have to be able to work long hours—up to 11 hours a day, 5 days a week. You have to be very detail-oriented. There's no room for mistakes. You have to be able to deal with people. It's a big race every day to get everything done.

Thinking Critically

What would make an automotive service adviser's work stressful?

CAREER FACTS

Nature of the Work:
Write up estimates for car repairs; handle customer complaints and problems.

Training or Education Needed:
Training on the job or through a community college.

Aptitudes, Abilities, and Skills:
Math, listening, speaking, and interpersonal skills; reading and writing skills;

problem-solving skills; self-management skills; ability to manage people.

Salary Range:
Combination of base pay and commission; average starting earnings—$18,000; with experience, average top earnings—$50,000.

Career Path:
Work your way up through the industry from car washing to advising about auto service; move up to service manager.

Chapter 13 • Interpersonal Relationships at Work **265**

Extending the CASE STUDY

Answer: Dealing with customer complaints; ensuring that cars get done on time; coping with customer pressure when parts don't come in on time; handling unexpected problems.

Further Application: Stress is a part of every job. Have students discuss the possible stressful areas in their chosen career. (For example, tax time is stressful for accountants; writers face deadlines; people who work with the environment are under pressure from a variety of conservation, governmental, and business groups.)

Evaluation

Assign the section review.

Reteaching

Divide students into five groups. Assign each group one of the personal traits described at the beginning of this section. Have students create flip charts explaining the trait, giving examples of actions that demonstrate the trait, and providing three suggestions for actions one could take to improve the trait. Have each group incorporate the four-step method to self-improvement in their presentations. Have each group explain how that particular trait helps people perform better on the job.

Extending the Content

Assign the appropriate Chapter 13 activities in the *Student Activity Workbook*.

Divide students into groups and have each group brainstorm ways to deal with emotions, such as anger or jealousy on the job. Have each group present its list to the class and discuss how the suggestions can be used for self-improvement.

CLOSE

Have students complete these sentences: "My strongest personal trait is . . . . My weakest personal trait is . . . ." Tell students to give reasons for each of their answers and indicate how they plan to improve their weakest trait.

FOCUS

Bell Ringer

Have students list at least 10 words that come to mind when they think of the word "etiquette."

Introducing the Section

Have students share their lists from the Bell Ringer activity. Write the words on the chalkboard. Tell students that etiquette applies to personal manners and eating habits, but it also applies to personal behavior in the workplace. Use this discussion to help students see that *how they behave on the job*—aside from actual *job performance*—can attribute to their success.

Ask students if they've ever had conflicts with a coworker. Chances are most of them have. Discuss conflict resolution and how it is used to help people work through their problems.

Motivational Activity

Oral Presentation

Have students work in groups and prepare two-minute presentations demonstrating some form of workplace etiquette. For example, one group may want to demonstrate how to introduce two or three people to a company manager. Another might want to demonstrate how to bring a meeting to order.

Applying Interpersonal Skills

OBJECTIVES

After studying this section, you will be able to:

- **Understand and practice proper workplace etiquette.**
- **Understand and practice effective methods of conflict resolution.**
- **Appreciate and increase sensitivity to diversity in the workplace.**

KEY TERMS

etiquette
conflict resolution
diversity
stereotype

Etiquette may sound more like something you need to have at a wedding than at the workplace. However, **etiquette** really just means having good manners in your dealings with people.

How do you identify the right behavior for your workplace? First, use common sense. Treat people as you would want them to treat you. When in doubt, observe experienced and well-liked workers who are successful in their jobs. How do they conduct themselves at work? What do they do to get along with other people? What kinds of actions or responses do they avoid?

Workplace Etiquette

Here are a few basic do's and don'ts of etiquette that apply to all workplaces:

- *Be courteous.* Greet your coworkers when you come to work, and address people by name whenever you can. Don't interrupt private conversations, and don't talk so loudly that you disturb other people, especially those working near you. Avoid tying up equipment that other people may need to use.

- *Dress appropriately.* Whether your job has a dress code or not, you should wear neat, clean clothes. As a new employee, don't use your wardrobe or hairstyle to attract attention. Let your on-the-job performance speak for itself.

- *Be punctual.* Be at work on time, arrive at meetings promptly, and meet your deadlines. If you

266   *Unit 5 • Professional Development*

Implementing Teamwork

Group students in teams of four. Ask each group to research a recent court case related to the electronic invasion of privacy (for example, computers, E-mail, videotaping). Each group should write a one-page summary of the case. Use this information to discuss about the use of technology and the invasion of privacy.

promise someone that you'll call at a certain time, be sure to keep your word.

- *Avoid workplace gossip.* Gossiping wastes valuable work time and can result in the spread of false or hurtful rumors. Gossiping is just plain unprofessional.

Respecting Privacy

Workplace etiquette also involves respecting your coworkers' privacy. This concerns more than not listening in on telephone calls and private conversations.

- *Faxes, E-mail, and voice mail.* Treat these means of electronic communication as you would treat private mail. Don't read or listen to them unless they are addressed to you.

- *Computers.* Sharing a computer with a coworker does not give you the right to examine or alter files that

you have not created—unless you have permission.

- *Shared office space.* Respect your coworkers' private spaces. Never look in a locker, file cabinet, or desk that is not your own.

Working with Your Supervisor

If you treat your supervisor with the same proper respect and courtesy that you do your coworkers, you should get along well. Naturally, however, you face the added element of wanting—and needing—your supervisor's approval. Here are some things you can do to develop and maintain a good working relationship with your supervisor:

- Deal with any criticism from your supervisor in an objective and professional manner. Do not get defensive.

- Practice initiative instead of bothering your supervisor with details that do not need his or her approval.

- Whenever you can, offer to help your supervisor.

- If you have a work-related complaint, discuss it with your supervisor. Be prepared, however, to suggest your own solution.

Conflict Resolution

Even when coworkers practice mutual courtesy and respect, it is a rare workplace that does not experience tension from time to time. When conflicts arise in the workplace, you will have to decide how to deal with them.

Fax machines allow people in offices to send and receive large amounts of written communication every day. *Why is it an example of improper etiquette to send a lengthy fax without first telephoning the receiver?*

Chapter 13 • Interpersonal Relationships at Work **267**

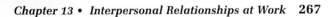

Extending the Illustration

Since many office fax machines are located in a central area, ask students how they can help maintain privacy for the faxes addressed to an individual. (By assigning one person to distribute faxes regularly, or by having people call first so the recipient can be near the fax machine.)

Caption Answer: A long fax can tie up the office fax machine. If the fax does not need an immediate response, a better method might be to send the information by mail.

Guided Practice

Teaching Strategies

1. Assign and review Section 13-2.
2. Use the transparency for this section.

Discussion Starter

Ask students how they would react if someone found a personal letter that had fallen from their book bags and shared it with others in the school.

Teaching Tip

Use the previous Discussion Starter to introduce the issue of privacy. Since so many offices today have cubicles, there is often little privacy at work. Tell students that respecting others' privacy can be considered a desirable trait.

Critical Thinking

Ask students what they would do if they overheard a coworker's conversation in which the person discussed the probability that several people would be laid off in the future.

SCANS Foundation Skills Connection

L1 **Problem Solving**

Have students comment on this scenario. "Derek often gets to work early and leaves after everyone else. His supervisor seems only to criticize his work. What should Derek do to find out what is wrong?"

SCANS Foundation
Skills Connection
(cont'd.)

L2 **Responsibility**

Have students write 75–100 word responses describing what they would do in this situation. "Jackson wants to earn extra money and has agreed to do household chores. Last week he didn't finish all the chores because he took time to be with friends.

"This week, Jackson plans to go away for the weekend and won't have time to do all the chores. He still wants to be paid for the work because he says he'll do it eventually." What kind of responsibility is Jackson demonstrating? How would students respond if they employed Jackson?

L3 **Knowing How to Learn**

Have students research companies that are considered socially responsible. One good source is *The Job Seeker's Guide to Socially Responsible Companies* by Jankowski.

Have students choose one company that appeals to them. Tell them to write a profile of the company, giving its name, what it does, and its socially responsible activities. Also have them describe unusual employee benefits (such as exercise facilities or day care). Have students discuss their research in class.

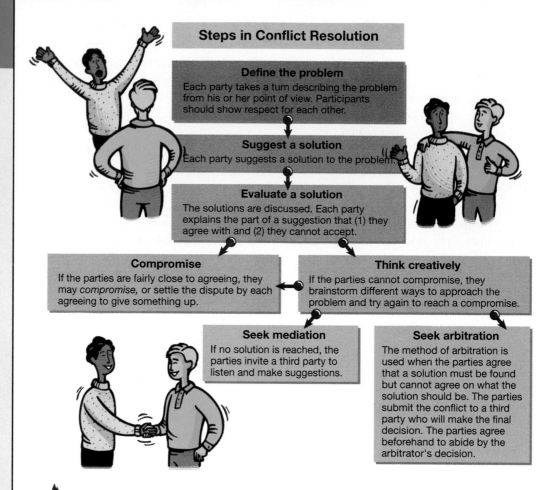

Steps in Conflict Resolution

Define the problem
Each party takes a turn describing the problem from his or her point of view. Participants should show respect for each other.

Suggest a solution
Each party suggests a solution to the problem.

Evaluate a solution
The solutions are discussed. Each party explains the part of a suggestion that (1) they agree with and (2) they cannot accept.

Compromise
If the parties are fairly close to agreeing, they may *compromise,* or settle the dispute by each agreeing to give something up.

Think creatively
If the parties cannot compromise, they brainstorm different ways to approach the problem and try again to reach a compromise.

Seek mediation
If no solution is reached, the parties invite a third party to listen and make suggestions.

Seek arbitration
The method of arbitration is used when the parties agree that a solution must be found but cannot agree on what the solution should be. The parties submit the conflict to a third party who will make the final decision. The parties agree beforehand to abide by the arbitrator's decision.

▲ **Figure 13-2** Conflict resolution is a way for the people involved in a dispute to work out a solution to their problem. They try to work together to bring the conflict to an end. Why do you think this diagram shows a choice of steps for finding a resolution?

As a worker, you may find yourself involved in a process called **conflict resolution.** This is a problem-solving strategy for settling disputes. Its aim is to find a solution that will allow each side to "save face" and leave the least amount of ill-feeling. *Figure 13-2* shows the steps in this strategy.

Remember that conflict resolution focuses on the issues, not on the personalities of the people involved. How can you best prepare yourself for conflict resolution in the workplace? You can do so by practicing your communication and problem-solving skills in school and in the minor disputes you may have with friends.

► **Extending Figure 13-2** ◄

Ask students to give examples of conflicts they've experienced. List several on the chalkboard, then have students decide which of the methods might be used to resolve each one.

Caption Answer: It may take more than one approach for parties to resolve their conflict.

Addressing Workplace Diversity

As American companies expand globally, overseas offices will be staffed with non-Americans. Americans working with these companies will interact with large numbers of people from different backgrounds in training classes and work situations.

Diversity in the Workplace

The United States has always been a nation of **diversity**, or variety, where each group contributes something special. In most workplaces in this country, many different kinds of people come together for a common purpose—to get a job done and to earn a living. *Figure 13-3* shows how the U.S. population is expected to continue to become more diverse.

Embracing this diversity is one way to discourage conflict at work. How can you accomplish this? Begin by showing respect for cultural differences as well as for differences in religion, age, gender, and viewpoint. Embracing diversity in the workplace is a way of acknowledging that you are part of a community of workers with common needs and goals. It's also a way to broaden your understanding—and perhaps make some exciting discoveries as well.

Overcoming Stereotypes

To succeed in a diverse workplace, workers need to look beyond stereotypes of groups of people. A **stereotype** is an oversimplified and distorted belief about a person or group. The danger of thinking in stereotypes is that it does not allow for individuality. In addition, it encourages an "us versus them" mentality.

How can you get along with a diverse group of people? As in any group situation, respect, understanding, and communication are important. In addition, you'll need to develop a sensitivity to your coworkers' different situations. Many businesses

L1 Acquiring and Evaluating Information

Have half the class research techniques of mediation and the other half research arbitration. Each group will collect examples from newspaper or magazines of cases where either mediation or arbitration has been used to settle disputes. Discuss findings in class.

L2 Allocating Material and Facility Resources

Give students the dimensions of a room 44 feet long by 23 feet wide. There are two doors to the room, one at either end. One long side of the room has windows; the other is a solid wall. The doors to the room are next to the solid wall. Have students allocate space to create at least two private offices that are each 10 by 12 feet and seven cubicles that are 8 feet square. Remind students to allow for aisles, which are usually 3 feet wide, and clear space in front of the doors.

L3 Applying Technology to Task

Have students use the Internet to research federal job openings. Tell students to do keyword research using *careers* and *federal government employment opportunities*.

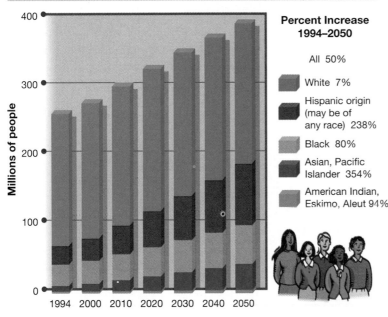

U.S. Population Projections, 1994–2050

Percent Increase 1994–2050

All 50%

White 7%

Hispanic origin (may be of any race) 238%

Black 80%

Asian, Pacific Islander 354%

American Indian, Eskimo, Aleut 94%

Millions of people — 400, 300, 200, 100, 0

1994 2000 2010 2020 2030 2040 2050

Figure 13-3

Whites accounted for 74% of the U.S. population in 1994. By 2050, that percentage is expected to be 52.5%. According to the graph, which ethnic group will account for the second largest segment of the population? Which will increase by the largest percentage?

Computer Activity

Using a spreadsheet software package, have students create a table illustrating employee diversity at a large employer in your community. Ask students to gather numerical data related to gender and cultural diversity. Display that information in a spreadsheet; then, have students create a chart from that data.

Extending Figure 13-3

Have students brainstorm about how changing population trends will affect the workplace. (For example, more women and minorities will be in leadership positions.)

Caption Answer: Hispanics, with 22.5 percent of the population; the Asian and Pacific Islander group will show the largest increase, 354 percent

Independent Practice
Reading

Have students read an article about a person who has been successful in business. Have them identify his or her personal skills. How did those skills contribute to the individual's success? Discuss in class.

ASSESS

Assessment
Oral

Have students explain workplace etiquette. Then evaluate students' answers for an understanding of appropriate behavior on the job.

Evaluation

Assign the section review.

MINI QUIZ

True-False

1. Self-awareness means understanding your strengths and weaknesses. (true)

2. Having empathy means that you see things from your own perspective. (false)

3. Conflict resolution is a process of solving problems. (true)

4. Workplace diversity refers to the variety of jobs available in our economy. (false)

5. Stereotyping can cause difficulties in getting along with people from different cultural groups. (true)

---

today sponsor diversity training programs to help employees overcome stereotyping in the following areas.

- *Cultural distinctions.* People from different ethnic backgrounds have different customs. What's polite in one society may be rude in another, such as certain gestures or forms of address. It's important to remember, however, that cultural blunders happen even among the best-intentioned people. Learn by reading and observing, and apologize if you are unintentionally impolite.

- *Gender distinctions.* Effective coworkers have mutual respect for members of the other sex. It is not sexist to acknowledge that women and men may have different styles of working and interacting. It is wrong—and illegal—however, to harass anyone because of his or her gender.

- *Generational distinctions.* People of one age group sometimes feel they have little in common with other age groups. As a young person, you may have a different point of view from someone several years older than you. You can bridge the difference by listening carefully to the other person's point of view and finding ideas on which you can agree.

Overcoming stereotypes can lead to good working relationships. *How can getting along with different people at work affect other aspects of your life?*

SECTION 13-2 *Review*

Understanding Key Concepts

Using complete sentences, answer the following questions on a separate sheet of paper.

1. How does technology affect etiquette in the workplace? Give an example.

2. Why is creative thinking an important part of conflict resolution?

3. Why are respect, understanding, and communication especially important in a diverse workplace?

SECTION 13-2 *Review* ANSWERS

1. Technology creates the need for new rules in the workplace. Students may give the example of faxes and E-mail, which could easily be read by other workers but which should be treated as private.

2. Creative thinking allows people to see solutions that may not have occurred to them at first.

3. Respect allows you to be positive about someone else despite differences. Understanding helps you perceive those differences. Good communication skills are especially important when different languages or cultures come together.

Key Terms

tact *(p. 259)*
empathize *(p. 263)*

SECTION 13-1 Summary

- Getting along with your coworkers means you will have greater job satisfaction and enjoy your time at work more.

- Personal traits you need to develop to get along with your coworkers include responsibility, self-esteem, sociability, self-management, and integrity/honesty.

- To improve your personal qualities, work on one trait at a time, devise a plan for working on the trait, check your progress, and then proceed to work on other traits.

- To be an effective coworker, you need to respect others, try to understand them, communicate well, and maintain a sense of humor.

Key Terms

etiquette *(p. 266)*
conflict resolution *(p. 268)*
diversity *(p. 269)*
stereotype *(p. 269)*

SECTION 13-2 Summary

- Basic etiquette in the workplace includes being courteous, dressing appropriately, being punctual, and avoiding gossip. Etiquette also includes respecting your coworkers' privacy.

- You can develop and maintain a good working relationship with your supervisor by dealing with criticism objectively, practicing initiative, offering your help, and suggesting solutions to problems.

- When trying to resolve a conflict, discuss issues, not people. When compromise is not possible, creative thinking may lead to a solution. Mediation and arbitration are other possible ways to arrive at solutions.

- The U.S. workplace is diverse, and workers need to be sensitive to cultural, gender, and generational differences.

Chapter 13 • Interpersonal Relationships at Work **271**

SECTION 13-2

Use the Testmaker to create a customized test for Chapter 13.

Reteaching

1. Tell students to imagine that one of their coworkers had an argument with a supervisor (who hates to be wrong about anything) about a recent news event. The next day, the coworker brings in an article to prove that the supervisor was wrong. What effect will this action have on the supervisor? (The coworker should have been courteous, avoided the argument, allowed the supervisor his or her viewpoint, and let the supervisor save face by ignoring the article.)

2. Assign and review vocabulary terms, chapter questions, and activities from the Chapter Review.

Extending the Content

Assign the appropriate Chapter 13 activities in the *Student Activity Workbook*.

Have students choose a cultural group different from their own and research its cultural distinctions. Have students share their findings in class.

CLOSE

Have students complete this sentence: "In my career, interpersonal skills will be important because . . . ."

> ### Extending the Illustration

Tell students that you have arranged for them to attend a classical music concert. Ask them to describe what they think the audience will be like. List their descriptions on the chalkboard. Ask students to identify stereotypes.

Caption Answer: By learning to get along with a diverse group of people at work, you are less likely to be prejudiced in other areas of your life.

Answers
Reviewing Key Terms

Paragraphs will vary but should show an understanding of the terms listed.

Recalling Key Concepts

1. False: The personal traits that help you get along with others at your job are the same ones that help you in school and in social situations.
2. True
3. False: It is not acceptable to read a coworker's fax because a fax is a private communication, like private mail.
4. False: When you compromise to resolve a conflict, each person gives up a part of what he or she wants.
5. True

Thinking Critically

1. Both traits involve working on one's own, initiative, and the ability to see a task through to the end.
2. Sources of praise or criticism can be supervisors, coworkers, customers, and clients. Students' responses should demonstrate effective interpersonal skills.
3. Working on one trait at a time allows you to concentrate all your efforts on just one goal, increasing the likelihood of success.
4. Possible answer: Separating the problem from

Reviewing Key Terms

On a separate sheet of paper, write one or two paragraphs on getting along with coworkers. Use the terms below in your paragraph(s).

tact	conflict resolution
empathize	diversity
etiquette	stereotype

Recalling Key Concepts

On a separate sheet of paper, tell whether each statement is true or false. Rewrite any false statements to make them true.

1. The personal traits that help you get along with others at your job are different from the ones that help you in school or in social situations.
2. Effective coworkers display respect, understanding, and good communication skills.
3. It is acceptable to read a fax that arrives for a coworker because the fax machine is there for everyone to use.
4. When you compromise to resolve a conflict, you let the other person have his or her way.
5. Being sensitive to diversity helps overcome stereotyping.

Thinking Critically

Using complete sentences, answer each of the questions below on a separate sheet of paper.

1. How are the personal traits of responsibility and self-management related to each other?

2. Identify two sources of praise you might receive in the workplace and two sources of criticism. Tell how you would respond to each.
3. When trying to improve yourself, why should you work on one trait at a time?
4. Why does conflict resolution focus on the problem rather than the personality of the opposing person?
5. Describe how you might broaden your perspectives by communicating with others in a diverse workplace.

SCANS Foundation Skills and Workplace Competencies

Personal Qualities: *Self-Management*

1. Write a one-page paper on why it is important to control emotions in the workplace. Discuss ways that emotions can be channeled properly to allow people to work together effectively. Within the paper, note possible consequences of lack of emotional control.

Interpersonal Skills: *Working with Diversity*

2. Research some of the cultural differences between your culture and that of another country. Focus on differences that affect the workplace. Summarize your findings for the class.

Connecting Academics to the Workplace

Computer Science

1. Imagine that you are an employee in an office that has just acquired new

the personality helps one deal with the conflict as something that can be resolved reasonably. Also, it allows people to work together more effectively.

5. By getting to know different people, you may learn about interesting customs, food, or ways of relating. You may also learn about new ways to solve problems.

SCANS Foundation Skills and Workplace Competencies

1. Students' papers will vary, but students should note that lack of emotional control could lead to hurt feelings, poor working relationships, and even violence. Workers can channel their emotions by learning techniques such as taking a break or deep breathing when

word-processing software. Luckily for you, it's a program you are familiar with. Describe steps you would take to teach a coworker to use it. Keep in mind that this coworker is much older than you and has limited knowledge of computers.

Human Relations

2. Brittany is an administrative assistant in a human resources department. Her supervisor wants to develop a checklist of positive attitudes for the workplace. He has asked Brittany to submit a list of her own. Draw up a list that Brittany could submit to her supervisor. In addition, make a list of attitudes to avoid.

Math

3. Stephen works in a busy music store at a mall. Part of his job is to check the addition on purchase orders before they are sent to the distributor. Stephen's coworker, Max, suggests that he make a rough estimate before adding the prices on a calculator. Stephen thinks estimating is a waste of time. Imagine that you are Max, and explain to Stephen why estimating helps accuracy.

Developing Teamwork and Leadership Skills

To gain insight into interpersonal relationships, observe how you work with your fellow students. With a small group of students, plan and make a pamphlet or other visual presentation that describes personal qualities people need to be part of a successful team. Examine your own teamwork

on this project, and include that information in your presentation.

Real-World Workshop

Working in a group of three, find and read one article or book chapter on conflict resolution. Then, with other group members, create a realistic workplace conflict situation. Role-play how this conflict might be resolved successfully, using information from your textbook and the outside resource that you found. Present your role-play to the class.

School-to-Work Connection

Set up an informational interview with a manager working in a career field that interests you. Choose a workplace that employs 25 or more people. Ask the manager to explain the diversity of his or her workplace and provide details about how that diversity benefits workers and the business. Question the supervisor about ways this particular workplace has encouraged diversity and what procedures are in place for handling problems that may arise. Present a report on your interview to the class.

Individual Career Plan

Write a thank-you letter to the manager you interviewed for the School-to-Work Connection activity. Describe the positive things you learned during the interview, and express your appreciation of the way the workplace is working to encourage diversity.

mistakes, aim to do the best job you can. Negative attitudes may include trying to get away with doing as little as possible, and assuming that you are always right.

3. Max could politely explain that making a rough estimate would allow Stephen to check to see that his calculated sum is reasonable.

Developing Teamwork and Leadership Skills

The pamphlet or presentation should include helpful tips on personal qualities that promote teamwork. Students should demonstrate an ability to assess their own teamwork as they complete this project.

Real-World Workshop

If necessary, direct students to sources for articles or books on conflict resolution. The conflicts they present should be realistic, and their solutions should demonstrate an understanding of conflict-resolution procedures.

School-to-Work Connection

As a class, students should discuss the benefits of a diverse workplace as well as its potential problems.

Individual Career Plan

The letters should follow standard business format. They should also be free of spelling, capitalization, and punctuation errors.

emotions run strong. Students may also suggest the advantage of having someone outside the workplace to talk to about problems.

2. Summaries and presentations will vary, depending on the countries chosen, but students should demonstrate respect for the differences in culture.

Connecting Academics to the Workplace

1. Students should include, in clear order, the details of how to use the software. They should mention that they need to be courteous and patient when teaching.

2. Brittany's list may include the following: look for the best in people and situations, realize that you can make

···PLANNING GUIDE···
Chapter 14

SECTION 1 *Teamwork*

SECTION OBJECTIVES	SECTION FEATURES	SECTION RESOURCES
• Explain how team-work benefits both team members and businesses. • Describe the steps involved in team planning. • Identify common obstacles to team success. • Define *total quality management* and discuss its effect on workers.	Personal Career Plan, p. 275 Career Do's and Don'ts, p. 277 Excellent Business Practices, p. 281 You're the Boss!, p. 282 Exploring Careers, p. 284	Workforce 2000 Videodisc and Videotape Section 14-1 Review, p. 283 Student Activity Workbook

CHAPTER RESOURCES

• Chapter Transparencies and Lesson Plans
• Chapter 14 Test
• Spanish Resources, Chapter 14
• School-to-Work Activity Handbook, Chapter 14 Activity
• Teacher's Lesson Plans, Chapter 14
• Implementing Block Scheduling, Chapter 14
• Print, Media, and Internet Handbook
• Strategies for Implementing Work-Based Learning
• Strategies for Implementing Connecting Activities

SECTION 2 *Leadership*

SECTION OBJECTIVES	SECTION FEATURES	SECTION RESOURCES
• List the qualities of a good leader and compare leadership styles. • Describe the charac-teristics of an effec-tive supervisor. • Describe procedures commonly used in leading formal meetings.	Ethics in Action, p. 290	Workforce 2000 Videodisc and Videotape Section 14-2 Review, p. 290 Chapter 14 Review, pp. 292–293 Student Activity Workbook

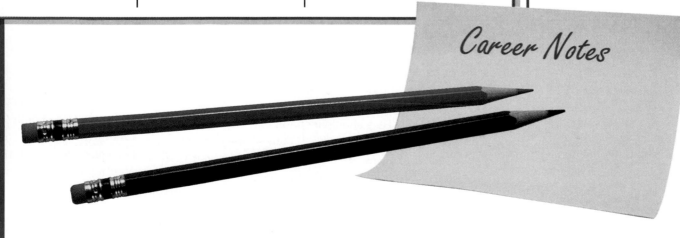

Career Notes

SCANS CORRELATION CHART
Foundation Skills

Basic Skills	Reading	Writing	Math	Listening	Speaking

Thinking Skills	Creative Thinking	Decision Making	Problem Solving	Seeing Things in the Mind's Eye	Knowing How to Learn	Reasoning

Personal Qualities	Responsibility	Self-Esteem	Sociability	Self-Management	Integrity/Honesty

Workplace Competencies

Resources	Allocating Time	Allocating Money	Allocating Material and Facility Resources	Allocating Human Resources

Information	Acquiring and Evaluating Information	Organizing and Maintaining Information	Interpreting and Communicating Information	Using Computers to Process Information

Interpersonal Skills	Participating as a Member of a Team	Teaching Others	Serving Clients/ Customers	Exercising Leadership	Negotiating to Arrive at a Decision	Working with Cultural Diversity

Systems	Understanding Systems	Monitoring and Correcting Performance	Improving and Designing Systems

Technology	Selecting Technology	Applying Technology to Task	Maintaining and Troubleshooting Technology

Highlighted blocks indicate areas covered in the Chapter.

Additional Activities

Internet Connection

Businesses rely more and more on employee teamwork to get jobs done. Have students use the Internet to find current articles on teamwork used by specific businesses. What kinds of businesses require teamwork? How do they use teams? Have the teams helped the company improve its profitability?

Field Trip Suggestions

Arrange to take students to a city council meeting. Have your local representative explain to students how city council members debate issues, and how the organization works together to achieve its ends. Discuss with students what they learned about achieving common goals.

Guest Speaker Suggestions

Invite to class a teacher of leadership skills, someone from Toastmasters or Junior Achievement, perhaps. Ask the guest to discuss how students can hone and develop leadership skills in the workplace and in the community, especially communication skills.

Key to Ability Levels

Each section gives skill-building activities. Each activity has been labeled for use with students of various learning styles and abilities.

L1 Level 1 activities are basic activities and should be within the range of all students.

L2 Level 2 activities are average activities and should be within the range of average and above average students.

L3 Level 3 activities are challenging activities designed for the ability range of above average students.

Teamwork and Leadership

School-Based Learning

Chapter Overview

This chapter highlights the role of teamwork in the workplace and instructs students how to be effective team members or leaders.

Section 14-1 describes types of business teams and the roles that individuals play as team members.

Section 14-2 introduces the qualities that leaders possess and discusses how leadership skills are used in the workplace.

Background Information

Write chapter objectives (Sections 14-1 and 14-2) on the chalkboard or use the chapter objective transparency for class discussion.

Choose assignments from the *Student Activity Workbook* and write them on the chalkboard.

Have students preview the chapter, looking at pictures, reading captions, and noting content headings. Ask students to describe what they expect to learn in this chapter.

Preteaching Vocabulary

Write the Key Terms from Sections 14-1 and 14-2 on the chalkboard. Have students describe how each term relates to teamwork and leadership skills.

274

Meeting SPECIAL Needs

Learning Disabled

Students with attention difficulties may find it easier to concentrate if actively involved in learning. Have students take a section of this chapter such as team goal-setting or TQM and teach it to another student. Afterward, discuss whether students learned better as the teacher or the student.

Chapter 14

Teamwork and Leadership

Section 14-1
Teamwork

Section 14-2
Leadership

In this video segment, discover how teamwork benefits everyone in the workplace.

Journal
Personal Career Plan

Think about your recent group activities in school or at work. In most situations, are you more comfortable as a group leader or as a cooperative group member? Why? Record your ideas in your journal.

Addressing LEARNING Styles

Intrapersonal and Interpersonal Learners

Ask the class to choose four or five work topics of concern to them—pay, child care, or discrimination, for example. Have each student choose one topic and research. Break the class into groups by topic. Have each team choose a facilitator, then discuss their individual findings and opinions. The group should then choose another member to present a summary of the discussion to the class.

FOCUS

Bell Ringer

Ask students to list at least three ways their families practice teamwork. Give the example of a parent preparing a meal while another family member sets the table.

Introducing the Section

Have students share their lists from the Bell Ringer activity. Ask students to describe the advantages of teamwork (work is done faster, people can specialize in activities that interest them or that use their specific skills, more creative solutions result, people are more motivated to work).

Discuss how businesses benefit from employee teamwork. Then discuss the types of teams (Figure 14-1) and how teams set goals to accomplish their work.

Motivational Activity

Discussion

Ask students who play on sports teams to share their thoughts about how teamwork helps them perform better. Discuss reliance on others and how team membership influences their attitude or performance. Then, have students with part-time jobs share their teamwork experiences. Ask students to compare the two situations.

Teamwork

OBJECTIVES

After studying this section, you will be able to:

- **Explain how teamwork benefits both team members and businesses.**
- **Describe the steps involved in team planning.**
- **Identify common obstacles to team success.**
- **Define *total quality management* and discuss its effect on workers.**

KEY TERMS

self-directed
functional team
cross-functional
   team
team planning
facilitator
total quality
   management
   (TQM)

Have you ever worked in a cooperative learning group at school? A learning group is one type of team. This is a group of people who work together to reach a common goal. Working as a team member in school will prepare you for today's business world.

Teamwork in Business

Today, businesses rely more and more on teams of workers to get jobs done. Once, such teamwork was rare. For example, in the past, automobile assembly-line workers did just one task. They might attach a radiator or put on a door. They would perform the same job over and over again. Today, workers are more likely to be part of a team. Teams work together to complete an entire phase of production. Members of such teams share the responsibilities and the rewards of their efforts.

Some teams are supervised by managers. Others are **self-directed,** or responsible for choosing their own methods for reaching their goals. Self-directed teams work without supervision. If you were a member of such a team, you might work without a manager from the start to the finish of a lengthy project.

Why Businesses Encourage Teamwork

Companies have found that teamwork pays off. It's good for team members and for businesses. Why? Teams tend to be more productive than the same number of employees working separately. Greater

Addressing Workplace Diversity

Many companies have discovered that working in teams promotes the goals of diversity. Because team members don't have a manager to take complaints to, they have to deal personally with their difficulties among them.

Implementing Teamwork

Divide your class into "quality circle" groups of five to six students. Each group should choose the type of products their company manufactures. Ask the group to brainstorm an improvement needed in their company's product line.

productivity means greater profits. Other business benefits include:

- improved quality and customer service,
- increased employee morale, and
- fewer layers of management.

Individual workers also benefit from being part of a team. Workers report the following rewards:

- *Greater job satisfaction.* Teams often rotate tasks among members. This variety reduces boredom and allows each team member to develop an array of skills.

- *Improved self-esteem.* As a rule, each team member is given the authority to help make and carry out decisions. Many team members report that the most satisfying part of their jobs is feeling in charge of their own work. Of course, team members must be *self-starters.* They have to work without always being told what to do.

- *Better communication.* Here's an extra bonus. When people work in a team, they've got to talk. As a result, they get to know each other better.

Career Do's & Don'ts

To Become a Leader...

Do:
- get involved.
- expand your boundaries beyond your job description.
- cultivate your intuition.
- earn the respect of your peers first; respect from higher-ups will follow.

Don't:
- be controlling.
- be afraid of taking risks.
- be a perfectionist.
- discard established practices— work within the system.

Workers learn about each other's behavior, attitudes, and ways of thinking. They get along better and are not so quick to judge one another. Tension and conflict among workers are reduced.

These students are working on a science project. *Why do you think their teacher requires them to work in teams?*

Chapter 14 • Teamwork and Leadership **277**

SECTION 14-1

TEACH

Guided Practice
Teaching Strategies

1. Assign and review Section 14-1.

2. Use the transparency for this section.

3. Assign and review the Case Study.

Teaching Tip

Obtain a jigsaw puzzle with about 50 pieces. Give each student two pieces; keep any leftover pieces. Have students discuss how they will put the puzzle together. Who will start? Will those with outside pieces put them together first? Point out that they are working as a self-directed team.

When all puzzle pieces are in place, minus the pieces you hold, ask students how the puzzle relates to work projects that cannot be completed because one team member withholds information (in this case, certain puzzle pieces) or does not cooperate.

Critical Thinking

Have students write 100-word papers describing the interpersonal skills team members need. (Students' answers will vary but might include cooperativeness, responsibility, initiative, consideration of others' ideas, willingness to share tasks and responsibility, or the ability to accept constructive criticism.)

Extending the Illustration

Have students brainstorm ways teams might be used in the workplace. (Examples might include manufacturing cars, sharing ideas for new product development, or construction teams.)

Caption Answer: Teamwork is an efficient way to accomplish complex projects. Team members learn from one another. Learning how to work in teams at school will prepare students for the world of work.

SCANS Foundation Skills Connection

L1 **Math**

Tell students to imagine that they work for a company that manufactures computers. They work in self-directed teams and are paid for the number of machines completed by the team. If they earn $90 per computer and their team of three can finish four computers in a day, how much would each person earn a day? ($120: 4 × $90 = $360 ÷ 3)

L2 **Problem Solving**

Tell students they are members of a work team that packages gift baskets of food. Each member adds different products. One person consistently puts products in the wrong place and the next team member has to rearrange the products to fit others in the basket. This causes their team to finish fewer baskets than other teams. Ask students how they would deal with this issue.

L3 **Reading and Writing**

Have each student find and read a current article on teamwork used by a specific business. Tell students to write 100-word summaries describing the business, how it uses teams, and how the teams have helped the company improve its work or profitability.

 The members of this team are from a variety of national and ethnic backgrounds. *How might their working on a team benefit their company?*

Types of Teams

On a business team, you may work with as many as 9 or 10 other people. As *Figure 14-1* shows, your team will be either a **cross-functional team** or a **functional team.**

Team Planning

Imagine that you and your friends have decided to throw a surprise birthday party. If each of you goes ahead and does what you think should be done, the result may be chaos. If, however, you plan who will send invitations, set up decorations, be in charge of music, and buy the food, the result will probably be a great party.

The same goes for running a successful team project at work. Before you start, make a plan. Since you will be working as a team, plan as a team. **Team planning** involves setting goals, assigning roles, and communicating regularly.

Setting Goals

Do you remember the personal career goals you set in Chapter 5? When you work in a team, think about group goals. Your company's overall goal, or *mission,* is a place to start.

 Extending the Illustration

Ask students to discuss how teamwork helps people reject stereotyping.

Caption Answer: Teamwork helps break down cultural barriers by encouraging communication. The result is a more unified workforce and greater productivity.

Extending the Illustration

Show students examples of business mission statements and have them review business annual reports.

Caption Answer: Keeping a larger goal in mind helps workers focus on the overall purpose of every task, which leads to a higher-quality output and greater unity among employees.

Two Types of Business Teams

	Definition	Examples
Functional Team	A group of people from one company department or area of expertise, working together to reach a common business goal	• Six architects designing a building complex for an architectural firm • Seven chemists developing a cold medicine for a medical laboratory
Cross-Functional Team	A group of people from two or more departments or areas of expertise, working together to reach a common business goal	• A building maintenance supervisor, two bricklayers, a landscaper, and a financial officer planning the gardens around a company's new headquarters

Figure 14-1

Cross-functional teams are becoming more and more common in the business world. What is an advantage of a cross-functional team?

A company's mission includes its purpose and values. It can often be stated in one sentence. For example, Volkswagen's mission statement is "to provide an economical means of private transportation."

Keep your company's mission in mind. Then set short-, medium-, and long-term project goals. Imagine that you are working on a team for a sportswear company. Your goals might include the following:

- **Short-term goal:** Analyze the team's procedure for assembling jackets.
- **Medium-term goal:** Figure out more efficient procedures.
- **Long-term goal:** Produce more jackets in less time.

As you know from reading Chapter 5, the best way to approach a large project is to use "stepping-stone goals." First, break

 One of the U.S. space program's current missions is to land exploratory probes on Mars. *Why should all team members keep their company's mission in mind when working on daily tasks?*

Chapter 14 • Teamwork and Leadership **279**

▶▶ Extending Figure 14-1 ◀◀

Ask students how a sports team is a cross-functional team. (In basketball, the center, forward, and guards specialize in different types of play. Likewise in football, the quarterback, receivers, and defensive linemen all specialize in different activities.)

Caption Answer: People with different professional backgrounds bring a variety of abilities and experiences to a team, enriching and improving its work.

the project into smaller tasks. Then assign a start date and an end date for each task. A useful tool for teams is a *tracking schedule.* Such a schedule identifies the people who will be working on each part of a project. It tells when they will start and when they will finish.

Assigning Roles and Duties

Remember the party you planned? You could have chosen one friend to oversee the process. Then the tasks might have been done even more efficiently. Likewise, team projects often work more smoothly if the team appoints a **facilitator,** or leader. This is especially true for self-directed teams. The facilitator coordinates the tasks so that the team works efficiently.

When assigning roles in the workplace, it is important to match tasks to abilities. For example, Jason Sedrick works on the landscaping crew at a community zoo. Recently, he was assigned to a self-directed functional team to work on a new zoo entrance. The team chose a facilitator who had experience in landscape design. Jason knew about stonework. He agreed to handle this part of the job. Other members were assigned roles based on their skills.

Jason explains: "I felt uncomfortable at first. I wasn't used to working without a supervisor to report to. I thought, 'What if we do something wrong? What if no one finds out until it's too late?' I got used to taking responsibility, though. Now it feels good to be trusted. I like relying on the team and making our own decisions."

 When you are part of a team, you need to take time-outs occasionally to communicate about strategy. *How can asking and answering questions help a team succeed?*

Regular Assessment

If a project doesn't get assessed regularly, small problems can become major obstacles. Communication is the key to assessment. Jason's team, for example, meets daily for quick updates. They meet weekly to evaluate overall progress. Sometimes the team has to rethink its goals.

Potential Obstacles

Can there be trouble in "team paradise"? Of course. These are some common team problems:

- unclear goals,
- misunderstandings about how much authority the team has and how much authority individuals have.
- confusion about how to assess the performance of individuals,
- competitiveness among various team members,
- resentment at lack of individual recognition, and
- reduced effort by individuals on the team, especially as the size of the team increases.

EXCELLENT BUSINESS PRACTICES

Building Teamwork Through Experiential Training

To improve teamwork skills, Evart Glass Plant, a division of Chrysler Corporation, sent all 257 plant employees on a high-adventure training program at Eagle Village. Eagle Village is an experiential-based adventure center near the automobile plant. All employees were well-briefed about the program beforehand and the training took place during regular shift work hours.

Employees participated in a number of activities, such as juggling as a team, going through a maze, solving puzzles blindfolded, or lifting someone through an "electric fence." During the process they learned that all members affect the outcome and each individual has strengths. They also learned that a team can achieve something an individual can't, and some people are natural leaders. The activities helped them support

and trust each other, go past their personal comfort zones, and value emotional and verbal support in pushing boundaries.

Employee attitudes became more positive as a result of the training. Employees were more likely to help others and to include everyone's opinion in discussions. Employees experienced higher overall motivation, increased abilities to work within a team, and more personal confidence.

Thinking Critically

Why is trusting each other important when individuals work as a team?

Writing: *Directions*

Working in teams of four or five, have students imagine that they have been assigned to teams that will work together over the next several months. Have them list rules for how the team members are to work together. For example, one rule might be that all team members must participate. Have teams share their rules, then discuss how cooperation helps teams accomplish goals.

(Students' rules will vary but might include: members must attend and arrive at all meetings on time, avoid negative criticism, acknowledge all members' ideas, and avoid distracting team members from their tasks.)

Teaching Tip

Tell students that team members must sometimes take a stand on an issue that may be unpopular with coworkers. Write these issues on the chalkboard: regular drug testing of employees, national health insurance, mandatory child day care provided by employers, termination of the Social Security system. Add other topics that may be of interest to your students.

Have each student choose one of the topics, then take either a pro or con position. Group all students choosing the same stance together. Have each team discuss the reasons for supporting their issue, then describe those reasons to the class.

Extending EXCELLENT BUSINESS PRACTICES

Answer: It is important to be able to trust in the abilities of others so that you can count on them to help get a project done.

Further Application: Have one group of students create an activity that requires several people to accomplish the goal. Have them enlist other students to participate in

the activity. Listen carefully to the comments and suggestions during the activity. Ask students what they can learn about other people through this type of group cooperative effort. How can they improve their teamwork skills?

Interview

Explain to students that leaders of volunteer organizations must motivate people to work without using money as a reward. Have each student interview the leader of a local volunteer group to find out how that person motivates teams of volunteers. Have students discuss whether the interpersonal skills needed by the volunteer leader might differ from those needed for a business team leader. Have students share their findings in class.

Critical Thinking

Tell students that the TQM theory was created by W. Edwards Demming, an American who worked with Japanese companies. Only after they saw the successful results of TQM in Japan did U.S. business managers show interest in it. Ask students to discuss the role that global business plays in helping workers and managers improve the way they work. (A possible answer is that not all the best ideas are developed in one country. Using ideas from other cultures helps broaden perspectives.)

Research

The Baldrige Award was developed to reward U.S. companies that show significant quality improvement. Have students research the award and write 150-word papers about it, mentioning past winners, and how winners are chosen.

282

YOU'RE THE BOSS!

Solving Workplace Problems

You have encouraged the employees at your public relations agency to become active in various civic organizations. One of your most successful managers is now so involved with community activities that her work is suffering. What will you say to this employee? What action might you take?

Most obstacles can be overcome if teams define goals clearly, take action promptly, and—above all—keep communicating. Poor communication can create serious obstacles to success—from a single missed deadline to repeated personality clashes. Talking with the team leader or calling a team meeting is a good way to start to solve problems.

Being a Valuable Team Member

What makes a person a good team player? The following list describes valuable attitudes and actions. How can these help you overcome the obstacles you just read about?

- Make the team's goals your top priority.
- In meetings, listen actively and offer suggestions. Continue to

communicate with team members outside meetings.

- Follow up on what you've been assigned to do.
- Work to resolve conflicts among team members. Respect the other members of your team.
- Try to inspire other employees to get involved.

Total Quality Management

Total quality management (TQM) is a theory of management that seeks to continually improve product quality and *customer satisfaction*. TQM is sometimes referred to as the "quality movement."

According to TQM, quality comes first at every stage of the business process. It begins with planning and design and carries through to production and distribution. Every worker at every stage is challenged to find ways to improve the quality of the product. The goal? To maximize customer satisfaction.

Here's a twist, however: TQM defines a *customer* as anyone who receives the results of your work. That can mean either a coworker within the company or an outside consumer. This way of defining customers means that the responsibility for providing quality isn't limited to the salespeople. It involves each employee all the way down the line. Each person, in fact, is encouraged to determine how his or her own job might be done better. *Figure 14-2* shows the upward spiral that can result when TQM is put to work.

Teaching YOU'RE THE BOSS!

Possible responses: Discuss with the employee your concerns about her work and suggest that she might cut back on community activities, or if appropriate, discuss with the employee the possibility of her being a representative of your agency in community activities.

Extending Figure 14-2

W. Edwards Demming is credited with the idea of TQM. Have students research Demming and write a short report.

Caption Answer: A possible answer is that a low-quality product might be profitable in the short term, but by continually making quality improvements, workers ensure that long-term profits increase.

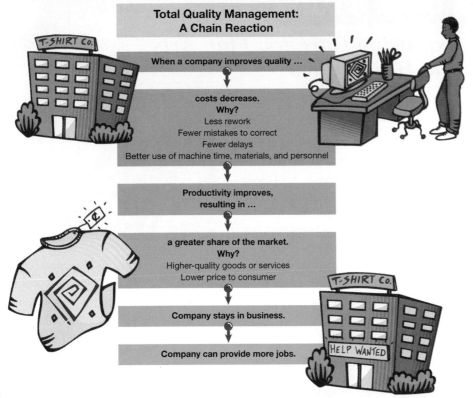

**Total Quality Management:
A Chain Reaction**

When a company improves quality ...

costs decrease.
Why?
Less rework
Fewer mistakes to correct
Fewer delays
Better use of machine time, materials, and personnel

Productivity improves,
resulting in ...

a greater share of the market.
Why?
Higher-quality goods or services
Lower price to consumer

Company stays in business.

Company can provide more jobs.

T-SHIRT CO.

HELP WANTED

▲ **Figure 14-2** An important part of the TQM philosophy is that providing high-quality goods or services actually costs less than providing low-quality ones. Why do you suppose this is true?

SECTION 14-1 *Review*

Understanding Key Concepts

Using complete sentences, answer the following questions on a separate sheet of paper.

1. What might be the consequences of employees not working as a team?

2. The salespeople in an appliance store are planning a campaign to improve sales. Identify a short-, a medium-, and a long-range team goal.

3. Choose two obstacles to team success, and provide suggestions for dealing with them.

4. Your company has decided to change to a TQM style of management. Describe two ways that this might affect you as an employee.

Chapter 14 • Teamwork and Leadership **283**

Skills Practice

Tell students that they are employed by the Collins Moving Company, which uses teams to handle different parts of the move; for example, packing, loading, driving, and unloading. Collins has given an estimate to one client that it will take a team of four people nine hours to move her belongings. What is the total of hours required? If each packer is paid $12.50 per hour, how much will each person earn for this job? (36 hours; earnings, $9 \times \$12.50 = \$112.50$ each)

ASSESS

Assessment
Performance

Cut up slips of paper to give to each student. Write one of the following words on each: plumber, electrician, carpenter, painter, bricklayer, roofer. Then have each student choose a slip. Tell students first to form functional groups, according to occupation. Have each group read the word on its slips of paper. Next, tell students to form cross-functional groups. Ask groups to read its occupations to the class.

Evaluate students for understanding of how the concepts of functional and cross-functional apply to skills of individuals within a group.

Evaluation

Assign the section review.

Reteaching

Divide students into three teams. Assign each team one of the following topics from this section:

- Teamwork in Business
- Team Planning
- Being a Valuable Team Member/Total Quality Management

Have each team prepare flip charts with key points made in their assigned topic and teach the content to the remainder of the class.

Extending the Content

Assign the appropriate Chapter 14 activities in the *Student Activity Workbook*.

Have students research total quality management as it is used by U.S. businesses, and then write 150–200 word papers describing its benefits and drawbacks. Tell them to find examples of companies that have implemented TQM and state the results. Have students discuss their findings in class.

CLOSE

Have students complete this sentence: "When I work as a team member in a future job, I will remember to . . . ."

CASE STUDY

Exploring Careers: Fine Arts and Humanities

Thomas R. McPhee
Sculptor

Q: Did you have formal fine arts training?

A: I went to art school for a while, but I never graduated. The instructors taught abstract art. I wanted to do small realistic stuff. Mostly I learned on my own. I drew for hours each day.

There's a lot of informal education possible. You can search out artists whose work you admire and see if you can study with them.

Q: Why do you specialize in gemstone sculpture?

A: Gemstone material fascinates me. It has everything I want in a medium. It holds any image I put into it. It has a hardness and a durability that no other medium has. I like that a lot. I like to think that some of my work will last a long time.

Q: Can someone make a living as a sculptor?

A: Anyone who wants to work with realistic, figurative sculpture, either of animals or humans, is practically guaranteed work, but the pieces have to be very accurate.

You can work for the film industry, design gift items, work in advertising, make architectural sculptures, or make models for the pewter, porcelain, or glass industries. There is no end of work you can get. The key is to work in whatever field interests you.

Thinking Critically

What problems or conflicts might an artist face while working in a mass-market business such as the manufacture of gift items?

CAREER FACTS

Nature of the Work:
Work in a variety of media to express an artistic idea.

Training or Education Needed:
Bachelor's degree in fine arts or independent art study.

Aptitudes, Abilities, and Skills:
Ability to work with tools and equipment; good hand-eye coordination; ability to concentrate for extended periods of time; an eye for color, form, and composition.

Salary Range:
$40,000 to $45,000 once established; much higher as reputation grows.

Career Path:
Work as an apprentice for a sculptor; work in a business using your specialty; work independently as a freelance artist.

Extending the CASE STUDY

Answer: The artist's idea of how the product is to look may be different from the manufacturer's; creative people may have trouble meeting deadlines; the artist may have to take criticism from nonartists.

Further Application: Creativity is not restricted to artists. Have students discuss the ways that they could be creative in their career searches as well as in their chosen careers. Creative approaches could be used in problem-solving situations. (For example, working out conflicts with parents about career choices; deciding how to obtain job interviews; or, after securing a job, planning presentations to prospective customers.)

Leadership

OBJECTIVES

After studying this section, you will be able to:

- List the qualities of a good leader and compare leadership styles.
- Describe the charac- teristics of an effec- tive supervisor.
- Describe procedures commonly used in leading formal meetings.

KEY TERMS

leadership style
parliamentary procedure

What do your favorite teacher, a coach, and the president of the United States have in common? All are leaders. Consider what it takes to be a leader. Then write a list of qualities in your journal. As you read this section, revise and add to your list.

What Makes a Leader?

Whether you are a supervisor, a team facilitator, or simply the person in charge of training a new intern, you are a leader. Leaders are necessary if work- ers are to achieve their maximum potential. People have different ideas about what makes a good leader, but most agree on certain qualities.

Personal Qualities: A Leadership Checklist

Look back at the list you wrote in your journal. Now compare the items on your list to the leadership qualities defined in *Figure 14-3* on page 286.

Of course, no one is born with every quality. If you want to be a leader, you must work at developing those qualities that are most useful to you. How do you know which ones those are? Both your career choices and your personal values will be a guide.

Chapter 14 • Teamwork and Leadership **285**

Bell Ringer

Ask students to think about group situations in which one person has emerged as the leader even though he or she was not elected or chosen as such. Have students list this person's skills.

Introducing the Section

As students share their lists from the Bell Ringer activity, write the descriptions on the chalkboard. Have students ex- plain why they think the per- sonal qualities they mentioned are important in good leaders. Then discuss the list of leader- ship qualities in Figure 14-3 on the next page.

Have students name fa- mous people who are leaders. List the four leadership styles on the chalkboard and ask stu- dents which style might fit each person.

Motivational Activity
Critical Thinking

Ask students to respond to this sentence: "Good leaders are born, not made." Have stu- dents write 100-word papers telling whether they agree or disagree with the statement, explaining the reasons for their positions, and giving examples.

Workforce 2000 Trends

Working for a large corporation with diverse subsidiaries can offer lots of op- portunity for advancement. Take charge of your career; have a plan for your growth with the company that you can discuss with your supervisor during per- formance reviews.

Teaching Strategies

1. Assign and review Section 14-2.

2. Use the transparency for this section.

Discussion Starter

Ask students to name people they consider leaders. Write the names on the chalkboard.

Teaching Tip

Ask students what the people mentioned have in common. Write the qualities on the chalkboard. Then review the list of leadership qualities listed in Figure 14-3. What qualities in the list did students not mention?

Critical Thinking

Tell students that their boss wants to promote them to a supervisory position. They will be training new employees and directing their work. Students are apprehensive and feel that they need additional job training before they will feel confident enough to become a supervisor. Ask students how fear might stand in the way of a promotion and how they could decide what to do.

(One way to overcome fear is to simply face it; in this case, accept the promotion. The boss probably would not have suggested the promotion unless he or she felt a person could handle the job.)

286

Leadership Styles

How you behave when you are in charge of other employees is called your **leadership style.** Here are the four basic styles:

1. *directing,* or giving others specific instructions and closely supervising tasks;

2. *coaching,* or closely supervising but also explaining decisions and asking for suggestions;

3. *supporting,* or sharing decision-making responsibility and encouraging independent completion of tasks; and

4. *delegating,* or turning over responsibility for decision making and completion of tasks.

The most effective leaders combine these styles. The challenge is to decide which style will work best in a given situation. Whatever style you use, your

Leadership Qualities	
Quality	**Definition**
Accountability	Willingness to take both the credit and the blame for one's actions
Anticipation	Ability to predict, on the basis of experience, what is likely to happen
Competitiveness	Drive to succeed or to be the best
Courage	Ability and willingness to face difficulties and take risks
Credibility	Trustworthiness
Decisiveness	Clarity of purpose, determination
Dependability	Stability, constancy
Emotional strength	Mental alertness, evenness of temper, ability to recover from disappointment
Empathy	Identification with and understanding of others
Enthusiasm	Eagerness, passion, excitement
Honesty	Truthfulness, sincerity
Imagination	Creativity, ingenuity, resourcefulness
Integrity	Soundness of moral character, sticking to one's values
Loyalty	Faithful commitment, fidelity
Physical strength	Good health, vigor, energy
Positive attitude	Optimistic outlook on life
Responsibility	Reliability, accountability
Self-confidence	Belief in oneself and one's ability to succeed
Sense of humor	Ability and readiness to see the comic side of things
Stewardship	Ability to take care of resources, including human resources
Tenacity	Unyielding drive to accomplish one's goals
Timing	Ability to judge the best moment for action
Vision	Clear idea of where one wants to go

◀ Figure 14-3

No one could be expected to have <u>all</u> these leadership qualities! Which ones do you strive to develop? Why?

286 *Unit 5 • Professional Development*

▶▶ Extending Figure 14-3 ◀◀

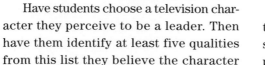

Have students choose a television character they perceive to be a leader. Then have them identify at least five qualities from this list they believe the character demonstrates.

Caption Answer: Answers will vary on the basis of students' career goals and personal values. Students should be able to explain why they have chosen particular qualities.

success as a leader will depend on your ability to communicate well.

Leading a Meeting: Parliamentary Procedure

As a team leader or supervisor, you will probably find yourself leading meetings. Most business meetings are casual. However, some are formal, especially when many people are involved. To keep meetings running smoothly, many companies follow a formal process with strict rules of order. It is known as **parliamentary procedure.** This way of running meetings was developed in 16th-century England to keep order in Parliament, England's governing body.

The best way to learn parliamentary procedure is to observe it in action. You might try, for example, sitting in on meetings of your school board or community government. *Figure 14-4* lists some of the parliamentary terminology that you'll hear

Parliamentary Terminology

adjourn motion to close a meeting	**majority** number greater than one-half of the voting members at a meeting
agenda list of items to be adressed at a meeting	**minority** number less than one-half of the voting members at a meeting
amend change a motion	
aye formal way of saying yes (pronounced *eye*)	**minutes** written record of what is said and done during a meeting; kept by the secretary
bylaws rules and regulations that govern an organization's operation, including such matters as the election of officers, membership qualifications, and meeting times	**motion** official request for a group to take action or reach a decision
	nay formal way of saying no
call to question statement made by a member when he or she believes it is time to vote on a motion	**new business** topic brought before the group for the first time
chair chairperson; one who is in charge of a meeting	**quorum** minimum number of members who must be present at a meeting for the group to conduct official business
constitution document stating an organization's official name, objectives, and purposes and describing how it is organized	**second** statement made to show approval of a motion made by another member of the group; at least one member must second a motion before it can be discussed
convene gather for a meeting; call a meeting to order	**table** postpone making a decision on an issue under discussion
gavel mallet used by the chair to bring a meeting to order	**unfinished business** topic brought before the members for at least the second time

Figure 14-4 The terms used in parliamentary procedure have evolved over several centuries. How do you think formal terminology and an established procedure help large meetings?

SCANS Foundation Skills Connection

L1 **Problem Solving**

Have students imagine they have been promoted to new jobs in which they feel comfortable about their leadership skills. However, one of their new subordinates resents their promotion and resists following their direction. Have students write 50-word paragraphs describing how they will resolve this issue.

L2 **Creative Thinking**

Tell students to imagine that they lead a school club. At the time a club meeting is scheduled to begin, several members keep talking instead of paying attention. Ask students how they, as group leaders, would deal with the problem of getting the meeting started. Call on students to role-play possible solutions.

L3 **Responsibility**

Tell students that they were recently elected to the position of president of a school club that does volunteer work for local charitable organizations. As president, it is their job to schedule volunteers when and where they are needed. At a recent meeting, only two people volunteered to work at a local soup kitchen. Ask students how they would get other members to participate.

▶▶ Extending Figure 14-4 ◀◀

Obtain a videotape demonstrating parliamentary procedure and have students view it. Have them discuss how parliamentary procedure is used in their school club meetings.

Caption Answer: In large meetings, a formal structure allows the meetings to run in an orderly manner.

SCANS Workplace Competencies Connection

L1 **Participating as a Member of a Team**

Divide students into groups of four or five. Give each group a list of these leadership traits: intelligence, imagination, honesty, integrity, knowledge, energy, enthusiasm, decision-making ability, and good health. Then give each group a list of leadership roles: vice-president of a national bank, president of a local entrepreneurial business, and chief executive officer of a major multinational corporation. For each role, have groups rank the leadership traits in the order of their importance to carrying out the job.

L2 **Acquiring and Evaluating Information**

Have students interview the president of one of your school's vocational organizations. Tell students to find out how long the president has been a member of the organization, whether he or she has held other positions within the organization, and what skills the person needs to function as president of the group. Have students ask how the person prepared for a leadership position. Tell students to write 100-word summaries of their findings and share their information.

used at such meetings. You can further develop your skills with the help of groups such as the Future Business Leaders of America, who hold conferences and competitions on a range of leadership skills.

When you attend a formal meeting, you'll find that it follows an *agenda*. This is a list of topics drawn up beforehand that will be discussed at the meeting. An agenda usually includes a reading of the minutes. The *minutes* are a written

 Figure 14-5

Parliamentary Procedure

Following parliamentary procedure can be an effective way for leaders to make sure meetings are orderly and productive. A quick formal meeting might look something like this. (Refer to Figure 14-4 for definitions of any terms you do not understand.)

A The chair taps her gavel to convene the meeting. She announces: "The meeting will now come to order." The first item on the agenda is for the secretary to read the minutes of the last meeting. Then two individuals give brief reports—the treasurer and the chair of the committee on business operations.

B Now the chair asks if there is any unfinished business. There is not, so topics in the category of new business may be introduced. A member makes a motion to create a trial cross-functional team. Another member seconds the motion.

Extending Figure 14-5

Have students attend a local government meeting and observe how parliamentary procedure is used. How was the process different from that described in this figure? Ask students to write a paragraph describing their observations.

summary of the last meeting. The agenda will usually include *unfinished business,* or topics from the last meeting that need more discussion. It will also include *new business.* **Figure 14-5** shows parliamentary procedure being followed in a sample meeting.

Parliamentary procedure may seem complicated. Remember, however, that it has a simple aim: to make sure that meetings are run efficiently and fairly. Using parliamentary procedure to run a meeting is a skill every business leader should master.

C Discussion of the motion may now occur. The chair recognizes each member who wishes to comment on the trial team motion. After all have spoken, she calls for a vote: "All in favor of forming a trial cross-functional team signify by raising their hands and saying aye." In this case, a clear majority has voted aye, and the motion is carried, or approved.

D Because there is no additional business, a member moves to adjourn. The motion is seconded, voted on, and passed. The meeting is now over.

Chapter 14 • Teamwork and Leadership **289**

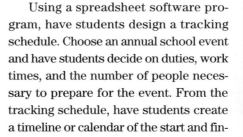

Computer Activity

Using a spreadsheet software program, have students design a tracking schedule. Choose an annual school event and have students decide on duties, work times, and the number of people necessary to prepare for the event. From the tracking schedule, have students create a timeline or calendar of the start and finish dates of each identified duty.

L3 Exercising Leadership

Have students choose a cause for which they would like to raise money; for example, medical research or an environmental issue. Have them create plans for organizing a group to work for their cause. Tell students to write descriptions of the purpose of their group, the specific means they would use to publicize its goals, and the activities they would sponsor to raise money for the cause.

Independent Practice
Skills Practice

Tell students that they are chairpersons of a school committee to organize an event to be held at a local community center. They estimate 180–200 people will attend. Food and beverages will cost an average of $2.80 per person, supplies will cost 70 cents per person, and decorations will cost $75. How much money will they need to pay for the event? ($775 for 200 people: 200 × $2.80 = $560; 200 × .70 = $140; $560 + $140 + $75)

Writing: *Memo*

Using the preceding Skills Practice, have students write memos to their committee members telling them the number of people expected to attend, the estimated costs per person, and the total cost. Have students develop an agenda for the next committee meeting and include a date and time.

Assessment

Oral

Divide students into small groups to plan and conduct a meeting for the class, using parliamentary procedure. As groups discuss their meetings, observe whether they choose a leader, or one emerges naturally. Evaluate meetings for appropriate use of parliamentary terminology.

Evaluation

Assign the section review.

MINI QUIZ

Short Answer

1. A ____ team is made up of people from one department or one area of expertise. (functional)

2. A ____ team is made up of people from two or more departments or areas of expertise. (cross-functional)

3. A team leader may also be called a ____. (facilitator)

4. A ____ leader is one who shares decision-making responsibility and encourages independent work. (supporting)

5. Formal business meetings often follow rules of order called ____. (parliamentary procedure)

Use the Testmaker to create a customized test for Chapter 14.

290

Communicating as a Leader

You already know how important communication is for team members. It's twice as important for a team leader. No matter how clear your vision of a business goal, if you cannot communicate it, your team will never reach it. Effective communication requires the SCANS skills of speaking and writing. In Chapter 15, you'll read more about how to develop these skills.

Some Tips for Supervisors

In Chapter 13, you learned some tips for working with your supervisor. Now consider the other side of the coin. How can *you* be a good supervisor? Here are some do's and don'ts for being in charge:

- Provide enough training, and be a patient teacher.
- Give clear direction.
- Know when to intervene.
- Don't be afraid to admit when you have made a mistake.
- Be consistent in what you say and do.
- Treat workers fairly and equally.
- Be firm when necessary.

ETHICS in Action

You work in a manufacturing plant and are required to punch in and out on a time clock. Your supervisor tells the members of your production group, "Don't worry about the time clock. I'll take care of it for everyone. That way our group won't have any problems." Will you follow the supervisor's instructions? If not, what will you do?

SECTION 14-2 *Review*

Understanding Key Concepts

Using complete sentences, answer the following questions on a separate sheet of paper.

1. Name a leadership quality that is important for each of the four leadership styles.

2. Which elements of a formal meeting might also help an informal meeting run more smoothly?

3. Why do supervisors need good communication skills?

290 *Unit 5 • Professional Development*

SECTION 14-2 *Review* ANSWERS

1. Possible answers: directing—decisiveness; coaching—vision; supporting—empathy; delegating—positive attitude

2. an agenda, a chairperson

3. Supervisors must provide training and give clear direction. Both involve communication skills. If supervisors cannot convey their vision of a business goal, their workers will not reach it.

Key Terms

self-directed *(p. 276)*
cross-functional
   team *(p. 278)*
functional team *(p. 278)*
team planning *(p. 278)*
facilitator *(p. 280)*
total quality management
   (TQM) *(p. 282)*

SECTION 14-1 Summary

- A team is a group of people who work together to reach a common goal. Businesses today rely more and more on teamwork.

- Teamwork benefits both team members and the companies they work for. Companies find that teams are more productive than individuals working alone. Team members experience greater job satisfaction and improved self-esteem.

- The two basic types of teams are cross-functional and functional.

- Team planning involves setting goals, assigning roles, and conducting regular assessment.

- Obstacles to teamwork include unclear goals, competitiveness among team members, and teams that are too large. Most obstacles can be overcome by clear goal definition, prompt action, and good communication.

- Total quality management (TQM) is a management process that tries to continually improve product quality and maximize customer satisfaction at every stage of the process.

Key Terms

leadership style *(p. 286)*
parliamentary
   procedure *(p. 287)*

SECTION 14-2 Summary

- To act effectively as a leader, you must develop qualities such as decisiveness, enthusiasm, and vision.

- Leadership styles include directing, coaching, supporting, and delegating. Most leaders use a combination of these styles.

- Strong communication skills are essential for a leader.

- To lead or participate in a formal meeting, you need to know the basics of parliamentary procedure. This procedure is a process that helps meetings run smoothly.

- When following parliamentary procedure, a meeting begins with the reading of the minutes. It continues with unfinished business and then with new business. Motions are made, seconded, discussed, and then voted on. The meeting ends with adjournment.

Chapter 14 • Teamwork and Leadership **291**

Teaching ETHICS in Action

Have students follow these steps to help them make a decision.

1. What are the ethical issues?
2. What are the alternatives?
3. Who are the affected parties?
4. How do the alternatives affect the parties?
5. What is your decision?

Reteaching

1. Have students create a bulletin board display on leadership. Have students choose photos of people they consider to be good leaders to illustrate each of the leadership styles. (For example, students might consider the Reverend Jesse Jackson, a leader whose primary style of leadership is supporting or coaching.)

2. Assign and review vocabulary terms, chapter questions, and activities from the Chapter Review.

3. Assign and review the Unit Project on the unit opener pages.

Extending the Content

Assign the appropriate Chapter 14 activities in the *Student Activity Workbook*.

Have each student find a picture of a contemporary political or social leader and paste the picture to a chart with these headings: *Name, Country, Significant Contributions, Significant Mistakes,* and *Significant Personal Qualities*. In class, discuss what makes each person featured a good leader.

CLOSE

Have students complete this statement: "Even if you don't aspire to become a leader, it is good to learn about leadership in the world of work because . . . ."

Answers

Reviewing Key Terms

Paragraphs will vary but should correctly use all terms listed.

Recalling Key Concepts

1. b
2. a
3. b
4. c
5. a

Thinking Critically

1. The more people there are on a team, the greater the chance for confusion and miscommunication—and the less responsible each member is likely to feel for the work of the team as a whole.

2. Students will probably choose directing or coaching because new employees need specific instructions and have not yet proved that they can work autonomously.

3. Possible answer: Yes. Teamwork leads to improved quality and customer service, which are at the heart of TQM. Teamwork also allows people at all levels of the company to contribute to planning and achieving quality.

Reviewing Key Terms

On separate paper, write several paragraphs telling what you might learn at a teamwork and leadership seminar. Use the following key terms in your description.

self-directed
cross-functional
  team
functional team
team planning
facilitator
total quality
  management
  (TQM)
leadership style
parliamentary
  procedure

Recalling Key Concepts

Choose the correct answer for each item below. Write your answers on a separate sheet of paper.

1. Which of the following is *not* a benefit of teamwork?
   (a) improved worker self-esteem
   (b) TQM (c) improved productivity

2. Potential obstacles to team success include ____.
   (a) unclear goals (b) regular assessment
   (c) conflict resolution

3. Maximizing customer satisfaction through constant quality improvement is the goal of ____.
   (a) every leadership style (b) TQM
   (c) parliamentary procedure

4. The four leadership styles are directing, coaching, supporting, and ____.
   (a) convening (b) tracking
   (c) delegating

5. A(n) ____ is a request at a formal meeting.
   (a) motion (b) agenda (c) gavel

Thinking Critically

Using complete sentences, answer each of the questions below on a separate sheet of paper.

1. Why do you think teams that are too large run into problems?

2. You've been asked to train a new intern in sales at your office. Which leadership style will you use? Why?

3. Imagine that you are running a company according to the principles of total quality management. Will you use teams? Why or why not?

SCANS Foundation Skills and Workplace Competencies

Basic Skills: *Writing*

1. Write a paper that compares the four leadership styles. Discuss at least two advantages and two disadvantages of each style.

Interpersonal Skills: *Exercising Leadership*

2. Valia is a department manager. She is concerned about the attitude of her staff. Employees are often late, show little enthusiasm, and rarely make suggestions or show initiative. What questions should she ask herself as a leader about her own role in her department's problems?

SCANS Foundation Skills and Workplace Competencies

1. Papers will vary. Students should list at least two advantages and two disadvantages for each leadership style.

2. Questions may include the following: Have I successfully communicated what I expect of my staff? Am I setting a good

example with my own behavior? Should I be delegating more responsibility?

Connecting Academics to the Workplace

1. five trucks (five drivers); five additional crates (80 × 275% = 220 crates to be delivered, and five trucks can deliver 225 crates)

Connecting Academics to the Workplace

Math

1. Imagine that you are the coordinating supervisor for the delivery team at a dairy. The dairy owns two trucks and employs two drivers. Each truck can deliver up to 45 crates of milk a day. Right now, the dairy delivers 80 crates a day. As the result of a successful advertising campaign, however, orders for the next month are 275 percent of what they were before. How many trucks (and drivers) will you need to make your new deliveries? How many additional crates will you then be able to carry before needing another new truck?

Social Studies

2. Your company is preparing a report on total quality management throughout the world. Your assignment is to research Japan's use of TQM. Use the library or Internet to learn how TQM has been applied in Japan.

Human Relations

3. Suppose you are on a personnel development team at a computer software company. Your company wants to increase its staff. It plans to hire 20 men and women with programming skills. You have been given the job of creating a list of five schools or training programs that could be sources of new talent. Make up such a list for your own community or region.

Developing Teamwork and Leadership Skills

With a team of five to seven students, plan an end-of-semester party for the class. Begin by choosing a facilitator and assigning roles. Then decide what tasks need to be completed and by what dates. Draw up a tracking schedule to lay out the entire project. Present your plan to the class, and compare it to those of the other teams. Which plan does the class think is the most workable? Why?

Real-World Workshop

Hold a class meeting to decide on and to arrange a field trip. Start by creating an agenda and selecting a chairperson. Run the meeting according to parliamentary procedure. (You may want to do additional reading on parliamentary procedure.) Final decisions should be reached by a majority vote.

School-to-Work Connection

Identify local groups that use parliamentary procedure. Arrange to sit in on a meeting either individually, in small groups, or as a class. Take notes, then prepare a brief report on the meeting.

Individual Career Plan

Research the use of teams in the career you have chosen to pursue. This may involve library and Internet research, letters of inquiry, or direct interviews either in person or by telephone. Write an article of no more than a page analyzing your findings.

Chapter 14 • Teamwork and Leadership **293**

Real-World Workshop

Meetings will vary. Field trips can either be business-related—for example, a guided tour of a local company—or simply recreational.

School-to-Work Connection

Local groups might include government bodies, businesses, community organizations, and clubs. Students' reports should describe the meeting in terms of parliamentary procedure. Discuss their reports in class.

Individual Career Plan

The articles should be clear and concise and should display an understanding of how teams are used in a particular career area.

2. Students will discover that Japan is a world leader in TQM, providing high quality with minimal waste and high consumer satisfaction.

3. Answers will vary but should include local universities or colleges, vocational-technical programs, and private trade schools.

Developing Teamwork and Leadership Skills

Students should apply the material taught in the chapter to their team planning, especially in assigning roles and devising a tracking schedule. The class should identify and explain strengths and possible weaknesses in each plan before deciding which plan is the most workable.

··· PLANNING GUIDE ···
Chapter 15

SECTION 1 *Speaking and Listening*

SECTION OBJECTIVES	SECTION FEATURES	SECTION RESOURCES
• Explain the importance of knowing purpose, audience, and subject before speaking. • Identify ways of planning and organizing oral messages. • Describe and demonstrate active listening, including taking notes. • Describe the importance of effective speaking and listening skills in customer relations.	Personal Career Plan, p. 295 Attitude Counts, p. 298 Career Do's and Don'ts, p. 301 Exploring Careers, p. 304	Workforce 2000 Videodisc and Videotape Section 15-1 Review, p. 303 Student Activity Workbook

CHAPTER RESOURCES

- Chapter Transparencies and Lesson Plans
- Chapter 15 Test
- Spanish Resources, Chapter 15
- School-to-Work Activity Handbook, Chapter 15 Activity
- Teacher's Lesson Plans, Chapter 15
- Implementing Block Scheduling, Chapter 15
- Print, Media, and Internet Handbook
- Strategies for Implementing Work-Based Learning
- Strategies for Implementing Connecting Activities

SECTION 2 *Writing and Reading*

SECTION OBJECTIVES	SECTION FEATURES	SECTION RESOURCES
• Identify and describe basic writing skills. • Describe common forms of business writing, including E-mail. • Explain how to preview and skim for main ideas when reading. • Explain the importance of writing and reading skills in customer relations.	Excellent Business Practices, p. 309 You're the Boss!, p. 310	Workforce 2000 Videodisc and Videotape Section 15-2 Review, p. 310 Chapter 15 Review, pp. 312–313 Student Activity Workbook

Career Notes

SCANS CORRELATION CHART

Foundation Skills

Basic Skills	Reading	Writing	Math	Listening	Speaking

Thinking Skills	Creative Thinking	Decision Making	Problem Solving	Seeing Things in the Mind's Eye	Knowing How to Learn	Reasoning

Personal Qualities	Responsibility	Self-Esteem	Sociability	Self-Management	Integrity/Honesty

Workplace Competencies

Resources	Allocating Time	Allocating Money	Allocating Material and Facility Resources	Allocating Human Resources

Information	Acquiring and Evaluating Information	Organizing and Maintaining Information	Interpreting and Communicating Information	Using Computers to Process Information

Interpersonal Skills	Participating as a Member of a Team	Teaching Others	Serving Clients/ Customers	Exercising Leadership	Negotiating to Arrive at a Decision	Working with Cultural Diversity

Systems	Understanding Systems	Monitoring and Correcting Performance	Improving and Designing Systems

Technology	Selecting Technology	Applying Technology to Task	Maintaining and Troubleshooting Technology

Highlighted blocks indicate areas covered in the Chapter.

Additional Activities

Internet Connection

Employees spend much of their time communicating on the job: speaking, listening, writing, and reading. Ask students to use the Internet to find examples of some common forms of business writing. Have students make note of appropriate Web sites.

Field Trip Suggestions

Arrange to take students to a presentation by a local business leader known for his or her speaking ability. Ask students to listen to how the presentation is made—repetition of ideas, gestures, tone of voice, humor. Discuss their impressions of the presentation's effectiveness.

Guest Speaker Suggestions

Invite to class a communications consultant, specializing in issues of ethnic diversity. Ask the guest to give a short demonstration of how communication can break down between people of different cultures. Ask the guest to involve the students in the demonstration.

Key to Ability Levels

Each section gives skill-building activities. Each activity has been labeled for use with students of various learning styles and abilities.

L1 Level 1 activities are basic activities and should be within the range of all students.

L2 Level 2 activities are average activities and should be within the range of average and above average students.

L3 Level 3 activities are challenging activities designed for the ability range of above average students.

School-Based Learning

Chapter Overview

Chapter 15 explores the important roles that speaking, listening, writing, and reading play in career success.

Section 15-1 examines good speaking habits.

Section 15-2 explores the elements of writing and presents some common forms of business writing. The section emphasizes good reading skills and offers techniques for improving those skills.

Background Information

Write chapter objectives (Sections 15-1 and 15-2) on the chalkboard or use the chapter objective transparency for class discussion.

Choose assignments from the *Student Activity Workbook* and write them on the chalkboard.

Have students preview the chapter, looking at pictures, reading captions, and noting content headings. Ask students to describe what they expect to learn in this chapter.

Preteaching Vocabulary

Write the Key Terms from Sections 15-1 and 15-2 on the chalkboard. Have students describe how each term relates to speaking and listening effectively and how to improve those skills.

294

Meeting SPECIAL Needs

Hearing Impaired

When speaking to students with hearing aids, be sure to stand close to them; hearing aids have a limited range. Most of them also amplify all sounds, so try to restrict background noise as much as possible by keeping the classroom quiet or speaking to the student in a quiet office. Speak in a normal tone of voice. Shouting is not necessary, but speaking clearly is. Try not to let your voice trail off at the ends of sentences. In class, repeat the questions of other students.

Chapter 15

Professional Communication Skills

Section 15-1
Speaking and Listening

Section 15-2
Writing and Reading

In this video segment, find out why effective communication skills are vital to your job success.

Journal
Personal Career Plan

At a large state convention, your vocational education club is unexpectedly invited to present a five-minute speech. You and the other club members will have only half an hour to prepare. Which do you choose to do—write the speech, deliver the speech, or both write and deliver it? Why? Write a journal entry describing your responses.

School-to-Work Connecting Activities

Have students write two- or three-page reports on the local business environment. For example, they might include information about the number of employers, the types of jobs offered, the industries represented, and the economic and employment outlooks for the next five years. Sources of information are your local Chamber of Commerce and economic publications in the public library.

Work-Based Learning Strategies and Activities

Discuss the writing skills needed by employees of a local employer and ask for samples of the types of documents the employees write. Share these documents with your students, then arrange for students to visit the company and interview the writers of the documents. Have students prepare a list of questions beforehand, then have them write 100–150 word summaries of their interviews.

WORKFORCE 2000 Training Video

Have students view the video and perform the interactive exercises to reinforce important chapter concepts and thinking processes.

Chapter 15

Addressing LEARNING Styles

Musical Learner

Words are only one method of communication. Music produces emotions and conveys messages. Choose a variety of music styles: marches, rap, classical, pop, and folk. Play short passages for students. As they listen, have them write down words, images, and emotions that the music inspires. Ask them to describe which music suits what kinds of careers—soothing music for detail work or marches for physical work? How could they use music to add to a professional presentation in their field?

FOCUS

Bell Ringer

Have students list at least three different reasons why it is important to speak well for both personal and professional purposes.

Introducing the Section

Have students share their lists from the Bell Ringer activity. Then ask students to think of someone they view as a good public speaker. What skills does that person demonstrate in speaking? (Likely skills include a good command of language, a purpose for each speech, genuine feelings about the topic, a presence that makes the speaker believable.)

Use this discussion to lead into the techniques of organizing a speech (the purpose and plan for writing and delivering your message).

Motivational Activity
Oral Presentation

Have students research a local or national issue and write a three-minute speech about it to an audience of their choice. As each student speaks, have the class take notes about the purpose of the speech, the intended audience, and the student's speaking habits. Avoid criticism of individual speaking habits, but make suggestions for how a speech might be made more effective.

Speaking and Listening

OBJECTIVES

After studying this section, you will be able to:

- **Explain the importance of knowing purpose, audience, and subject before speaking.**
- **Identify ways of planning and organizing oral messages.**
- **Describe and demonstrate active listening, including taking notes.**
- **Describe the importance of effective speaking and listening skills in customer relations.**

KEY TERMS

communication
customer relations
purpose
audience
subject
inflection
pronunciation
enunciation
active listening

If a tree falls in a forest and no one is there, does it make a sound? If you have a great idea at work but don't share it with others, does it have an effect? What's missing in both cases?

For a sound or an idea to have an effect, it needs a receiver as well as a sender. The exchange of information between senders and receivers is called **communication.** Regardless of your task at work, you'll spend much of your time communicating: speaking, listening, writing, and reading. *Figure 15-1* shows percentages of time spent speaking and listening on the job.

Speaking, listening, writing, and reading are important basic SCANS skills. You'll use them as tools to gain information, solve problems, and share ideas. Most important of all, you'll use them in customer relations. **Customer relations** is the use of communication skills to meet the needs of customers.

Consumers are more sophisticated and demanding than ever. Your success on the job will depend a great deal upon your ability to communicate effectively with customers.

Speaking: What's Your Point?

Whether you're speaking to an audience of one or one hundred, you'll want to make sure that your listeners get your point. This means that you'll need to be clear about your purpose, your audience, and your subject.

296 *Unit 5 • Professional Development*

Workforce 2000 Trends

As growing numbers of businesses work internationally, employees with competent second language skills (listening, reading, speaking and writing) will be in great demand. However, skills will need to be in standard, not colloquial, versions of the languages.

Implementing Teamwork

Divide your class into groups of three. Have students practice their listening and note-taking skills. Ask one student to take notes; one, to lead; one, to listen. The leader should give directions from his or her home to school. When finished, the listener should repeat the directions. The note-taker should correct as needed.

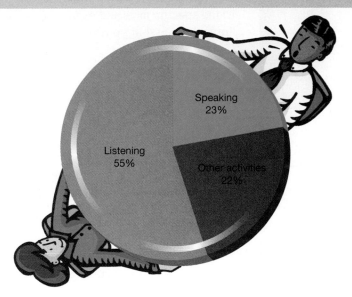

Time Spent Speaking and Listening on the Job

Speaking 23%

Listening 55%

Other activities 22%

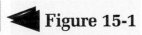 **Figure 15-1**

Statistics show that the average employee spends more than half the workday listening. Why do you think this is so?

Know Your Purpose

Who was the last person you spoke to? What was your reason for speaking? A speaker's **purpose** is his or her overall goal or reason for speaking. Purposes for speaking may include the following:

- greeting clients or customers,
- informing employees of a new policy,
- giving directions to a coworker,
- requesting help or information,
- persuading a supervisor to make a change, and
- proposing a new idea.

Sometimes you may have overlapping purposes. What examples can you give?

Know Your Audience

When you think of an audience, do you imagine people seated at a theater or a stadium? In fact, an **audience** is anyone who receives information. Once you know your purpose in speaking, you need to know your audience. You might ask yourself questions such as these:

- Who are my listeners? What are their beliefs, values, and interests?
- What do they already know about my subject? What do they need to know?
- What do they expect to learn from me? Do they expect to be entertained, informed, or persuaded?

Chapter 15 • Professional Communication Skills **297**

▶▶ Extending Figure 15-1 ◀◀

As you walk around the classroom, drop a book or pen, move a desk or chair slightly, and tap on the wall or a window. Move back to the front of the room, then ask students what they just heard during the previous minute. Did any of them hear or note your actions?

Caption Answer: In the business world, learning takes place when you are listening. You need to listen to instructions from your supervisor or manager, questions from coworkers, and requests from customers. At meetings, most of your time is spent listening. Even casual conversations require listening skills.

Guided Practice

Teaching Strategies

1. Assign and review Section 15-1.
2. Use the transparency for this section.
3. Assign and review the Case Study.

Teaching Tip

Ask students what types of speeches are boring to them or cause their minds to wander. One likely response will be class lectures or political speeches. Next, ask students what speeches hold their attention. Examples might be information on teen activities or the play-by-play commentary of a school sporting event. Why do these speeches hold interest?

Explore the purpose of speech and why good speakers consider both purpose and audience in planning speeches.

Critical Thinking

Have students imagine that they are new workers being trained to operate equipment. How would their trainer's speaking skills and knowledge of what to communicate affect them as trainees? How might such skills, or the lack of them, affect costs to the business? (A trainer with good skills can communicate needed information clearly and succinctly.)

**SCANS Foundation
Skills Connection**

L1 **Listening**

Invite a speaker to your class to talk on any topic of interest to your students. Ask the speaker to deliberately change the pace of the speech, talking fast at times and slowly at other times, or talking animatedly at times and in a monotone at other times. Tell students to take notes during the talk. Afterwards, have students share their impressions.

L2 **Speaking**

Have students write and deliver three-minute speeches on topics of their choice. Tell students to write their purpose, a brief description of their audience, and an outline of what they plan to say. After students deliver their speeches, ask them what they learned from the experience.

L3 **Self-Management**

Have each student write a paragraph describing his or her own attitude toward speaking in public. Have those who are shy about speaking make a plan to gradually force themselves to speak more; for example, volunteering to speak in class or taking a part-time job where they will have to speak with the general public. Have students set goals for improving their speaking skills.

Elicia is explaining a new company insurance program to her coworkers. **Why is it important for her to know her audience?**

Your answers to these questions can help you develop a clear idea of your subject and purpose. In addition, when you know your listeners, you're better able to reach them with your words and ideas.

Know Your Subject

The **subject** in speaking is the main topic or key idea. Which of these statements makes you stop and think: "Rain forests are important," or "Rain forests house three-fourths of the plant and animal species found on Earth"? The first statement is a *generality*, or broad statement. The second is a specific fact. Generalities are easy to make, but most people are convinced by hard facts.

Knowing your subject may require research. It's well worth the time, though. Using specific facts and examples will give "muscle" to what you say.

Speaking: What's Your Plan?

Now you know your purpose, your audience, and your subject. What more do you need? Whether you're giving a simple phone message or a formal speech, you'll need a plan.

Organizing What You Want to Say

As you plan your message, ask yourself questions such as these:

- How does my subject relate to my listeners' needs?
- What's my most important point?
- How can I make this point clearly?
- What facts and examples can I use?

No matter what technique you use, the best approach is to be clear, brief, and direct.

Attitude Counts

Everyone feels nervous about presenting a speech. Make your nervousness work for you by spending more time preparing and organizing your ideas. Plan carefully and practice, practice, practice! By the time you've started delivering your speech, you'll forget all about being nervous.

Extending the Illustration

Ask students to brainstorm ways of getting to know your audience. (Examples include knowledge of people with the same interests or asking people who plan the meeting what to expect.)

Caption Answer: Knowing her audience will help Elicia focus on the topics of interest to them and explain the subject in relevant terms.

Teaching Attitude Counts ✓

Have students meet in small groups to discuss speeches they have heard and speeches they have given. What makes a speech interesting to the listeners? What are some specific techniques for preparing an interesting speech?

Move logically from point to point as you speak. Reinforce main ideas. Look for signs from your listeners that your message is getting through. *Figure 15-2* shows various techniques for organizing your message.

Using Good Speaking Habits

Which is more important: *what* you say or *how* you say it? Your delivery, style, and attitude are as important as your message.

Say this sentence aloud: "I didn't say you were late for work." Now say it a different way, emphasizing a different word.

How many different messages can you send by changing the **inflection**, or the pitch or loudness of your voice?

Keep these suggestions in mind as you think about your spoken messages:

- Make emotional contact with listeners. "Communicating is a contact sport," advises communications consultant Bert Decker. Address people by name. Make eye contact with your listeners.

- Use posture and body language that match your message.

- Avoid nonwords such as *uh* and *um* and "empty" words such as *sort of*,

Techniques for Organizing Spoken Messages

Technique	Description	Example
Enumeration	Listing key points	"As part of our lawn service contract, we'll cut your grass, weed your flower beds, and trim your shrubs once every week."
Generalization, followed by examples	Stating a general law, condition, or principle, backed up by specific facts or examples	"The parking situation at work is getting worse. Last week, my car was blocked by another car in the parking lot. Yesterday, I couldn't even find a parking space."
Cause and Effect	Telling what happened and why it happened	"Ladies and gentlemen, Flight 473 will be delayed. The airport in Chicago is experiencing ice on the runways, and planes are unable to leave the ground."
Comparison and Contrast	Pointing out similarities and differences	"Our cheesecakes contain fresh ingredients, as do our competitor's. However, ours are much lower in fat."

 Figure 15-2 Successful speaking means being organized. Could you use more than one of these organizing techniques in the same message? If so, give an example.

Chapter 15 • Professional Communication Skills **299**

 Extending Figure 15-2

Ask students to give a different example of each technique in the figure. (For example, enumeration: five reasons to buy a new car; generalization: our new product is sweeping the country; cause and effect: school will be closed tomorrow for a teacher's training day; comparison and contrast: all roses smell sweet, but ours are the sweetest ever.)

Caption Answer: Yes, a speaker could introduce a new company product by enumerating its features and benefits and by comparing and contrasting it to an earlier product or a competitor's product.

SCANS Workplace Competencies Connection

L1 **Serving Clients/ Customers**

Tell students that they work for Tickets & More, a booking service that sells tickets to rock concerts. Have them write scripts of a telephone conversation in which they sell two concert tickets. Have students share their scripts in class.

L2 **Acquiring and Evaluating Information**

Have students research three career areas of interest to them regarding requirements for public speaking. (For example, a sales representative would be speaking to customers frequently.) Have students prepare a table listing the three career options, comparing the types of speaking required for each.

L3 **Interpreting and Communicating Information**

Many people are shy or fearful about speaking in public. Have students research books and magazine articles on this topic and write 150-word advice columns for the school newspaper describing techniques to overcome fear of speaking in public.

Independent Practice

Assign as homework the chapter activity in the *School-to-Work Activity Handbook.*

Role-Play

Divide students into teams of three or four. Have team members take turns demonstrating the correct way to answer a telephone at work, take a telephone message, and respond to a customer inquiry. After discussing and practicing these protocols, have the teams take turns demonstrating one type of speaking activity.

Writing: *Preparation for Oral Presentation*

Have students prepare speeches to give to your school's PTA about the need for the school to be connected to the Internet. (If your school is already connected, use another technology topic, such as a new computer lab or updated software.)

Discuss with students the purpose of their speeches (to persuade), ways to plan their message, and the techniques they might use to organize their speech (see Figure 15-2). Tell students to plan speeches of three to five minutes. Have students deliver their speeches to the class for practice. Also consider having students volunteer to speak to the PTA.

well, and *OK* that clutter your message and make you seem uncertain.

- Use inflection to stress key ideas.
- Pay attention to volume and speed.
- Pronounce words correctly and enunciate clearly. **Pronunciation** is how you say the sounds and stresses of a word. **Enunciation** is the speaking of each syllable clearly and separately.
- Project enthusiasm and a positive attitude, or outlook. Be courteous and attentive when speaking to customers. If you show that you really care, customers are more likely to do business with your company. When speaking in a group, be responsive to others and avoid interrupting them.

Telephone Tips

When you place calls in today's world, you may find yourself speaking to machines as often as to people. Either way, good speaking habits still apply. Keep these additional tips in mind when placing calls and leaving voice mail or answering machine messages:

- Be aware of differences in time zones when placing calls.
- Always identify yourself. Give your first and last name.
- Speak clearly and directly into the mouthpiece.
- "Smile" with your voice by using a pleasant tone.

Sometimes you'll need to take or leave a message. If you answer a call for another person, ask, "May I take a message?" Then write a brief, clear message with the date

Michael answers the phone for his department. *Why is effective speaking especially important when answering the phone?*

and time, the full name of the caller, his or her phone number, and the purpose of the call. When you leave a message, the same rules apply. Briefly and clearly state the key information as to why you are calling.

Active Listening

Is there a difference between hearing and listening? Suppose a friend is talking to you in a noisy hallway. You may hear the noise, but you're listening to your friend. Hearing is an automatic response. Listening is a conscious action. You use your brain to *interpret*, or make sense of, what you hear.

Active listening is listening and responding with full attention to what's being said.

300   *Unit 5 • Professional Development*

▶ Extending the Illustration

Tape record students giving a brief telephone message. Then have students listen to themselves and critique their telephone voices.

Caption Answer: Your listeners on the telephone can't see your facial expressions and body language. Therefore, your inflection, pronunciation, enunciation, and other voice qualities must share in the work of delivering your message.

In the world of work, active listening can be your most powerful communication tool. It involves the following steps:

- identifying the speaker's purpose;
- listening for main ideas;
- distinguishing between fact and opinion;
- noting the speaker's inflection, speed, and volume, as well as body language;
- using your own body language and facial expressions to respond to the speaker—for example, sitting up straight or leaning toward the speaker to show that you're interested; and
- reacting to the speaker with comments or questions.

Active listening can help others communicate better. "As you learn to listen," says management consultant Nancy Austin, "people will get better at telling you things."

Career Do's & Don'ts

To Be a Professional...
Do:
- listen attentively.
- treat coworkers as skilled, competent associates.
- exude confidence.
- make decisions.

Don't:
- expect that someone understands you without asking for feedback.
- fail to deliver what you promise.
- be afraid of admitting mistakes.
- blame someone else.

Taking Notes

What are some ways that taking notes in class helps you succeed in school? Note taking can help you succeed in the world of work too. It helps you remember facts and keeps your attention focused. When you take notes, both your mind and your hands are involved in listening.

"I always take notes when a client makes a special request," says caterer Janna Hyde. "That way, I always get the order right." Practice these skills as you take notes in class or on the job:

- Don't try to write down everything a speaker says. Instead, focus on key words and main ideas. Jot down summaries in your own words.

 Sonia takes notes on the teacher's main points. Later she'll review her notes before the weekly quiz. **Why is taking notes in your own words better than copying someone else's words?**

Chapter 15 • *Professional Communication Skills* **301**

Discussion Starter

Ask students if they think it's possible to talk to someone without really communicating with him or her.

Teaching Tip

Ask students to explain the difference between listening and hearing. Communication cannot take place without both hearing and listening.

Skills Practice

For her speech class, Melissa must attend three 45-minute lectures. What total amount of time must Melissa spend in lectures? (2 hours and 15 minutes: $135 \div 60 = 2.25$)

Emmanuel must give a presentation to his social studies class. He must speak for 15 minutes and answer questions for five minutes. What percentage of this entire presentation will Emmanuel spend answering questions? (25%: $5 \div 20 = .25$)

 Extending the Illustration

Have students describe how they currently take notes. Then ask whether their notes are helpful to them or too disorganized to read.

Caption Answer: Writing notes in your own words helps you "translate" what someone says in a way that is clear to you.

Addressing Workplace Diversity

Although the numbers of minorities and women in the workforce increased in the 1980s, by the late 1990s, these groups were still underrepresented in management positions. Many companies hold workshops to help managers to erradicate stereotypical attitudes toward women and ethnic groups.

Discussion Starter

Ask students why a person needs to be a good listener to be a good speaker. (Speakers who do not listen to the needs of their audiences quickly lose its interest.)

Teaching Tip

Have students list examples of body language that indicate someone is listening carefully to another. (Examples might include making direct eye contact, leaning in toward the person, or nodding the head). Ask students how they could use positive body language at work when dealing with supervisors and coworkers.

Skills Practice

Change of inflection can create different meanings for the same sentence. For example: "You did a great job." Each time you say the sentence, express a different emotion: enthusiasm, disbelief, anger, sarcasm. Have students determine the meaning based on the emotion projected.

Divide students into pairs, and have each person interview the other and find out as much as possible about his or her past. Tell students to take notes. Then have students introduce each other to the class. Ask how well each person listened, and thus conveyed information accurately.

▶ **Figure 15-3**

Handling Customer Complaints

Handling customer complaints skillfully is important to a company's success. People don't always remember when things go right, but they do remember when things go wrong. Make sure to follow your company's established policies and procedures for handling customer complaints.

- Note actions you need to take.
- Use bulleted lists, asterisks, and arrows to show relationships among ideas.
- Review your notes to make sure you understand concepts and instructions.
- If you can't take written notes, make mental notes of main points.

Figure 15-3 shows how speaking and listening skills can be used when you handle customer complaints.

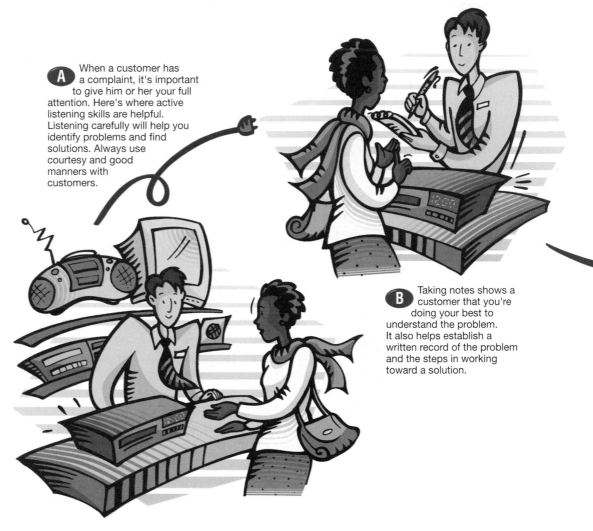

A When a customer has a complaint, it's important to give him or her your full attention. Here's where active listening skills are helpful. Listening carefully will help you identify problems and find solutions. Always use courtesy and good manners with customers.

B Taking notes shows a customer that you're doing your best to understand the problem. It also helps establish a written record of the problem and the steps in working toward a solution.

302 *Unit 5 • Professional Development*

◀◀ Extending Figure 15-3 ▶▶

Ask students who have part-time jobs to share the training they have received in handling customer complaints or experiences they have had on the job. Have them tell what actions are most effective in keeping customers satisfied. What actions don't seem to work as well?

C When speaking to a customer who has a complaint, be polite, clear, and brief. Let the customer know that you understand the problem and will do all you can to solve it.

D Your skill in handling complaints can make the difference between losing existing customers and gaining new ones.

Critical Thinking

Ask students to write 50-word responses to this question: When we're listening to someone whose body language contradicts his or her words, why are we more inclined to believe the body language? (A speaker can choose words to deliver any type of message the speaker wants the other person to hear, but emotions and attitudes tend to reflect the speaker's true feelings toward a subject.)

Research

Have students view a video from your school or public library on telephone techniques. Have students take notes as they view, then list at least 10 techniques for improving their telephone communication skills.

ASSESS

Assessment
Oral

Have each student give two- to three-minute presentations describing techniques for preparing for a speech, ways to plan and organize a speech, and the importance of good speaking habits.

Evaluate students to see if they exhibited good speaking habits in their presentations. They should have included information about purpose, audience, and organizing techniques; and demonstrated good speaking habits. Provide suggestions for improvement.

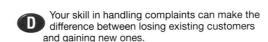

SECTION 15-1 *Review*

Understanding Key Concepts

Using complete sentences, answer the following questions on a separate sheet of paper.

1. Your supervisor wants you to give your division's progress report to company executives at their fall meeting. Should you use the opportunity to complain about the company vacation policy? Explain.

2. Why might you choose to vary your speed when making a long speech?

3. Why do people "get better at telling you things" when you listen well?

4. Why is note taking a good idea when a customer is making a complaint?

Chapter 15 • Professional Communication Skills **303**

SECTION 15-1 *Review* ANSWERS

1. No; this is neither the time nor the place to mention a complaint because it has nothing to do with a progress report.

2. Possible answer: to add variety and avoid boring the audience

3. When people perceive that you care about what they have to say, they feel comfortable and are willing to trust you with meaningful information.

4. Possible answers: It shows the customer that you're listening, it ensures that you get the correct information, and it becomes part of an official record.

Evaluation

Assign the section review.

Reteaching

Write these sentences on the chalkboard, underlining words as shown:

I <u>didn't</u> say he stole the notes.

I didn't <u>say</u> he stole the notes.

I didn't say <u>he</u> stole the notes.

I didn't say he <u>stole</u> the notes.

I didn't say he stole the <u>notes.</u>

Read each of these sentences, emphasizing the underlined word. Then ask students what meaning is conveyed in each case. Ask students to explain what this says about first understanding a sender's message before being able to interpret it.

Extending the Content

Assign the appropriate Chapter 15 activities in the *Student Activity Workbook*.

Have students listen to one TV news story and write how the reporter uses any of these organizing patterns: enumeration, generalization with example, cause and effect, comparison and contrast.

CLOSE

Have students complete the following statement: "Being able to express myself clearly at work is important because . . . ." (Your listeners and coworkers will both hear and understand the messages you are communicating.)

CASE STUDY

Exploring Careers: Public Service

Helen Jun
Elementary Schoolteacher

Q: How did you choose teaching?

A: I wanted to do something that involved working with people. I couldn't handle working in an office. I have always loved kids and worked with kids, tutoring and camp counseling. I like the feeling that I'm making a difference somehow.

Q: What is teaching like?

A: It's so much hard work. I tell friends who are thinking about teaching, "Don't think teaching is easy. You need determination and perseverance, or you're not going to make it."

Everything in the lower grades now is hands-on. This approach requires a lot more preparation for the teacher than does a traditional teaching method. The paperwork is overwhelming. There are always surveys to fill out, and grading papers takes up more hours.

Q: What sort of working relationship do you have with other teachers?

A: I really enjoy the camaraderie with the other teachers. I would never have gotten through my first year if another teacher, acting as my mentor, hadn't guided me step by step.

Thinking Critically

In your working career, you will teach and be taught. What are the attributes of a skilled teacher?

CAREER FACTS

Nature of the Work:
Prepare lessons; work with students, teachers, and parents.

Training or Education Needed:
Bachelor's degree; may require teaching credentials.

Aptitudes, Abilities, and Skills:
Math, listening, speaking, and interpersonal skills; problem-solving skills, self-management skills; reading and writing skills; ability to instruct and motivate people; patience; the flexibility to adapt to students' levels of learning.

Salary Range:
Depends on the state or district and the college degree; average starting salary—$27,000 to $31,000.

Career Path:
Most teachers continue as classroom teachers; may move into administration.

Extending the CASE STUDY

Answer: ability to listen; ability to explain clearly; patience; knowledge of the subject; respect for the students; dedication to the subject, whether it be welding, house painting, accounting, or helicopter navigation

Further Application: Have students discuss the passions they have for their chosen careers. (Some examples are the desire to help the ill and injured; to create something beautiful; to be able to repair something; to solve problems; to teach others.)

Writing and Reading

OBJECTIVES

After studying this section, you will be able to:

- Identify and describe basic writing skills.
- Describe common forms of business writing, including E-mail.
- Explain how to preview and skim for main ideas when reading.
- Explain the importance of writing and reading skills in customer relations.

KEY TERMS
E-mail
modem
previewing
skimming

Can you name a job that doesn't involve writing and reading? Vast amounts of written information are exchanged every business day. Increasingly, a company's success depends on employees who have strong skills in writing and reading.

Basic Writing Skills

Suppose you receive a customer bulletin from a local company. The bulletin begins: "Companies are increasingly turning to capacity planning techniques to determine when future processing loads will exceed processing capabilities." What does this sentence mean? It might as well be written in an unfamiliar foreign language. No customer wants to work this hard to understand a company's message.

Much of the advice for speaking well applies to writing well: define your audience, purpose, and subject; be clear, direct, and organized. Here are some additional tips to keep in mind:

- Organize your writing. Use a logical order, such as chronological, or time order, or order of importance. Use headings and subheadings when writing reports.

- Pay close attention to spelling and grammar. Use a dictionary and style book to check words and rules you are unsure of.

- Be aware of your *tone*, or manner, when you write. In a letter responding to a customer's request, you would write in a tone that is respectful and polite.

Chapter 15 • Professional Communication Skills **305**

Computer Activity

Using a database software package, ask students to create their personal address books. They should include the following information: name, address, ZIP code, phone number, E-mail address. Once complete, have them print out a copy of their addresses in a database report or listing.

Guided Practice

Teaching Strategies

1. Assign and review Section 15-2.

2. Use the transparency for this section.

Discussion Starter

Ask students how written messages differ from spoken ones. How can a writer convey emotion and establish tone the way a speaker does with voice inflection?

Teaching Tip

Point out to students that writing is a process that requires several steps. The first is to generate ideas. Then one does the actual writing. After writing one's initial thoughts, the next step is to read and revise to improve the wording or the tone. Finally, one reviews the writing for spelling, punctuation, grammatical, or formatting errors.

Critical Thinking

Have students choose local issues that are important to them and write letters to their state representative expressing their feelings about the issue. Have students research the format for letters sent to elected officials. Suggest that students mail their letters, then share the responses with their classmates.

Style Do's and Don'ts

Do...	Don't...	Examples
use language everyone can understand.	use *jargon*, or vocabulary specific to your area of work.	Instead of "Let's interface on that," write: "Let's meet to talk about that."
use your own language	use clichés, or overused phrases and expressions.	Instead of "It's raining cats and dogs," write: "It's raining hard."
use gender-neutral language.	use sexist language.	Instead of "Each man will make his own choice," write: "Each person will make his or her own choice."
use the active voice.	use the passive voice.	Instead of "The report was written by Zach," write: "Zach wrote the report."
use simple, natural words and phrases.	use complicated words or phrases.	Instead of "My home is in proximity to hers," write: "My home is near hers."
use short, simple sentences.	use long, complicated sentences.	Instead of "I am requesting that you write to the client, after which you should contact her by telephone," write: "Please write to the client. Then call her."

Figure 15-4 This chart shows ways to develop your own style. Why is developing your own style important in writing?

 Writing and reading skills are increasingly important in the world of work. **What are some tasks that depend on strong writing and reading skills?**

- When you think you are done, go back one more time and edit your work. Keep revising until your message is clear.

- Carefully proofread your work before sending it out.

Writing Style

Writer E. B. White defined *style* as "the sound [a writer's] words make on paper." Style isn't something you "add" to your writing, as a top hat or glittery necklace; it's what shines through when you write in a clear and straightforward way. See ***Figure 15-4*** for some basics on developing style.

306   *Unit 5 • Professional Development*

Extending the Illustration

Ask students to list the activities they do outside of school that require reading and writing. (Students' lists will vary but might include writing shopping lists, reading the newspaper or a magazine, and writing notes to friends or writing E-mail messages to digital pen pals.)

Caption Answer: Possible answers include taking and filling food orders, using maps in making deliveries, understanding and following company policies.

Common Forms of Business Writing

At some point in your job, you may need to write a memo, a business letter, or a report. *Figures 15-5* below and *15-6* on page 308 show standard forms for business memos and letters. *Figure 15-7* on the next page compares the purposes of memos, letters, and reports.

Using E-Mail and Fax Machines

E-mail, or electronic mail, is a fast, efficient way to communicate. E-mail is sent by modem. A **modem** translates signals from your computer into sounds that travel over an ordinary telephone line. With the push of a button or the click of a mouse, you can send a message from one computer to another in seconds.

Many companies communicate by *fax*, short for *facsimile*, which means a copy or a replica. A fax machine is much like a copy machine. It is also like a computer in that it can send written messages via telephone lines.

When sending business E-mail and faxes, many of the same tips apply: keep messages short, make sure the recipient's name is clearly stated, and don't use E-mail or faxes for personal messages at work.

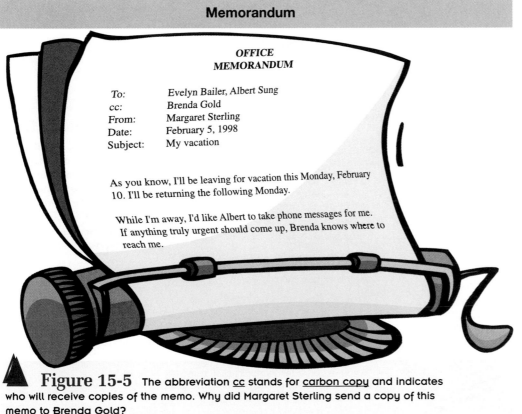

Memorandum

OFFICE
MEMORANDUM

To: Evelyn Bailer, Albert Sung
cc: Brenda Gold
From: Margaret Sterling
Date: February 5, 1998
Subject: My vacation

As you know, I'll be leaving for vacation this Monday, February 10. I'll be returning the following Monday.

While I'm away, I'd like Albert to take phone messages for me. If anything truly urgent should come up, Brenda knows where to reach me.

Figure 15-5 The abbreviation <u>cc</u> stands for <u>carbon copy</u> and indicates who will receive copies of the memo. Why did Margaret Sterling send a copy of this memo to Brenda Gold?

Chapter 15 • Professional Communication Skills **307**

SCANS Foundation Skills Connection

L1 **Listening**
Have students practice listening skills by listening to two or more cassette tapes in which narrators use inflection to express different emotions. Ask students to describe what they heard in terms of ideas and the emotions conveyed.

L2 **Reading**
Have students choose articles from current business magazines. Tell students to preview the articles by looking at photos and headings. Then have them skim through the articles focusing on key points. Tell them to close the magazines, then write summaries of the articles. Next, have students read the articles in full and take notes about any changes they would make in their original summaries. Discuss when skimming an article may be enough and when a full reading may be needed.

L3 **Knowing How to Learn**
Have students locate books in your school or public library on improving writing skills. Tell each student to skim the book and make a list of at least ten recommendations for how to improve one's writing. Have students practice the recommendations by writing a memo to you describing their findings.

▶▶ **Extending Figure 15-4** ◀◀

Bring in three samples of columns that are regularly published in your local paper. Have students read each sample and try to identify the differences in writing style.

Caption Answer: Using your own style reveals your unique personality and way of viewing the world, not someone else's.

▶▶ **Extending Figure 15-5** ◀◀

Have each student write a memo to a friend informing him or her of an upcoming social event.

Caption Answer: Brenda is mentioned in the memo. Also, it will be helpful for Brenda to know who received the memo about the upcoming vacation.

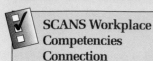

TEACH *(cont'd.)*

☑ **SCANS Workplace Competencies Connection**

L1 **Allocating Time**

Have each student write a memo informing coworkers of a half-day meeting that will begin at 8 A.M. The meeting will begin with a half-hour continental breakfast, followed by three hours of presentations, and have a 15-minute break. Tell students to attach an agenda for the meeting.

L2 **Serving Clients/ Customers**

Have students imagine that they work in the customer service department of a store. A customer writes a nasty letter to the store, angrily claiming that the refrigerator he purchased was damaged. He says he will never shop at the store again.

Have each student write a letter responding to the customer's charges, expressing empathy, and trying to retain him as a customer. Have students share their letters in class.

L3 **Using Computers to Process Information**

Tell students that they work in the supply room of their office. They notice that the supply of paper for the fax machine is low. Have them use a computer software program to write a memo to Mr. Martinez, who is in charge of ordering supplies.

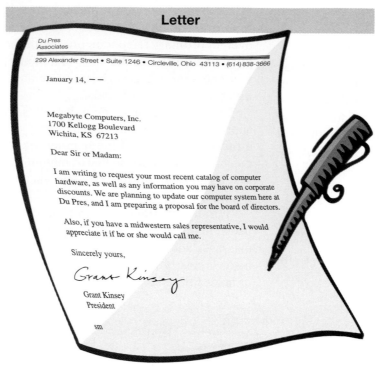

Letter

> **Du Pres Associates**
> 299 Alexander Street • Suite 1246 • Circleville, Ohio 43113 • (614) 838-3666
>
> January 14, — —
>
> Megabyte Computers, Inc.
> 1700 Kellogg Boulevard
> Wichita, KS 67213
>
> Dear Sir or Madam:
>
> I am writing to request your most recent catalog of computer hardware, as well as any information you may have on corporate discounts. We are planning to update our computer system here at Du Pres, and I am preparing a proposal for the board of directors.
>
> Also, if you have a midwestern sales representative, I would appreciate it if he or she would call me.
>
> Sincerely yours,
>
> *Grant Kinsey*
>
> Grant Kinsey
> President
>
> sm

Figure 15-6

This letter was printed in <u>block style,</u> which means that all lines begin at the left margin and a line of space separates paragraphs. How would you respond to this letter if you were an employee of Megabyte Computers?

Common Business Forms

Form	Purpose
Memo	• To communicate with others in your office • To communicate informally with people outside your office who work closely with your business • To address a limited topic
Letter	• To communicate with most people outside your office, including representatives of other businesses and clients
Report	• To communicate with people, both within and outside your office, who need extensive information about your business • To address an extended topic, such as a proposal for a new project, the progress of an existing project, or the results of research

Figure 15-7

Today, most written business communication is composed on computers instead of typewriters. What are the advantages of computers over typewriters?

▶▶ Extending Figure 15-6 ◀◀

Have students research other styles of business letters (for example, modified block with open punctuation).

Caption Answer: Answers may include writing a letter to Grant Kinsey, informing him that a catalog is on the way and that a sales representative will be calling him soon.

▶▶ Extending Figure 15-7 ◀◀

Take a poll of your students to find out their computer skills. Remind students that more and more people will use computers in their future careers.

Caption Answer: Composing and rewriting are done more efficiently on computers; and correcting errors is faster on computers.

Reading Skills

You're likely to spend as much time reading as writing on the job. Name or list in your journal some of the reading skills you've used in social studies, science, and English classes. You'll find yourself using many of these skills in your job as you acquire, evaluate, and interpret information, all of which are important SCANS skills.

You'll use them to get a job: reading help-wanted ads and job applications. You'll use them on the job: reading memos, bulletins, letters, directions, and reports. You may need them to find information or to do research for a project. Sometimes you'll want to read quickly for general information. At other times, you'll want to read carefully for specific facts.

Previewing

Do you enjoy movie previews? What information can you get from them? When you're **previewing**, you read only those parts of a written work that outline or summarize its content. These parts may include book titles, chapter titles, or headings. Previewing saves time when you need a general idea of what is in a work.

EXCELLENT BUSINESS PRACTICES

Working with Visual Impairments

Telesensory Inc., of Mountain View, California, designs, develops, and manufactures high-tech devices to serve the needs of visually impaired individuals. These devices give employers the equipment they need to set up workstations that accommodate special needs. Such devices can also help students at school and at work.

The company's products for computers include hardware and software applications that magnify images on a computer screen. The company also offers software that converts text into synthesized speech.

One innovative product is a small portable electronic device for the visually impaired to use to take notes in braille and to calculate numbers. It can also be used as an address and appointment book. The device converts the braille input to standard text for speech or print.

Through these devices, individuals gain access to and interact with print and electronic information. Employees with visual impairments can be given the same opportunities as sighted workers.

Thinking Critically

Name three types of technology equipment commonly used to communicate on the job. How could these forms of technology be modified to accommodate people with hearing and visual impairments?

Extending EXCELLENT BUSINESS PRACTICES

Answer: Possible answers include fax machines, telephones, overhead projectors, charts, graphs, and computers. Fax machines could have braille buttons, phones can have visual monitors that display typed messages, and charts could be made three-dimensional.

Further Application: Have students identify any devices or programs their school has provided to accommodate individuals with impairments. Where could more accommodation be made?

Independent Practice
Reading

Have each student read a magazine advertisement, a newspaper editorial, and an article from a technical journal such as a computer magazine. Ask them to bring their examples to class, then discuss how the writing style differs in each document. Have students decide who the audience is in each case and how that audience affects writing style.

Skills Practice

Tell students to imagine that they have to write a business memo. Tell them to write these headings on a sheet of paper: business audience, purpose, and subject. Then have them write information under each heading.

Next, have students exchange their papers with a classmate. From the information each student receives, have them write the memo. Tell students that they may modify and/or add to the information already given on the paper. Have students share their memos in class and discuss whether the information they received was clear enough for them to complete the given assignment.

Interview

Have students interview two or three people who have full-time jobs. Tell them to ask each person how they use writing and reading skills in their work. Have students make a list of the ways both writing and reading are used and share their lists in class.

Assessment

Performance

Have each student choose a local business and write a letter requesting an interview to learn about the company.

Then have each student (who has a job) write a memo to a coworker asking whether he or she would agree to being a work reference.

Evaluate students' letters and memos for appropriate style, language, and format, as well as correct grammar and punctuation.

Evaluation

Assign the section review.

MINI QUIZ

True-False

1. The exchange of information between senders and receivers is called speaking. (false)

2. Anyone who receives information from a speaker is an audience. (true)

3. The subject of a speech is the same as its purpose. (false)

4. Tone can be indicated by writing as well as by speaking. (true)

5. You might use previewing and skimming when you need to learn the details of a passage you are reading. (false)

💾 Use the Testmaker to create a customized test for Chapter 15.

310

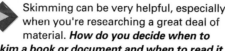

Skimming can be very helpful, especially when you're researching a great deal of material. **How do you decide when to skim a book or document and when to read it more carefully?**

Skimming

Another timesaving reading skill is skimming. In **skimming**, you read through a book or a document quickly, picking out key points. To skim, you look at the first sentences of paragraphs, as well as key words and phrases.

YOU'RE THE BOSS!

✓ *Solving Workplace Problems*

As a busy accountant, you're accustomed to checking and rechecking numbers, but you don't usually read your correspondence very carefully. Today, however, you've noticed errors in grammar, spelling, and punctuation in the letters your assistant has left for your signature. What will you do?

Taking Notes

Taking notes is important as a reading skill as well as a listening skill. Jotting down main ideas, useful quotes, new vocabulary, and your own summaries of information helps you understand and recall what you read. Note taking can be especially helpful when you're reading technical information.

SECTION 15-2 *Review*

Understanding Key Concepts

Using complete sentences, answer the following questions on a separate sheet of paper.

1. What are some ways in which you might organize the information in a report that describes your company's activities this past year?

2. Which of these business forms would you use to respond to a customer complaint: memo, business letter, E-mail, fax? Explain why.

3. Which skill—previewing or skimming—would you use to find your weekly schedule in a company memo that shows all employee schedules? Explain your answer.

4. Give a specific example of the usefulness of good reading skills in customer relations.

310 *Unit 5 • Professional Development*

SECTION 15-2 *Review* ANSWERS

1. Possible answers: in order of when the activities occurred, how long they lasted, how important they were to the company, or how successful they were

2. A business letter is most appropriate; the other forms might seem less personal.

3. skimming; because you're looking only for specific information

4. Possible answers: when filling an order on a form completed by a customer; when reading the customer relations section of a company policy manual; answers should be directed toward meeting customers' needs

Highlights

SECTION 15-1 Summary

- Communication is the process of exchanging information.
- Communication skills include speaking, listening, writing, and reading.
- Before you speak, you need to consider your purpose, audience, and subject. You also need to organize what you plan to say.
- There is more to speaking than what you say. How you say things matters too, whether in person or on the telephone.
- Active listening is especially important in customer relations. It involves body language and verbal responses.
- Taking notes can help you remember what you hear.

Key Terms

communication *(p. 296)*
customer relations *(p. 296)*
purpose *(p. 297)*
audience *(p. 297)*
subject *(p. 298)*
inflection *(p. 299)*
pronunciation *(p. 300)*
enunciation *(p. 300)*
active listening *(p. 300)*

SECTION 15-2 Summary

- Writing requires some of the same skills as speaking. You need to know your audience, purpose, and subject. You must also be clear, direct, and organized.
- When you write, you must consider your style, tone, spelling, and grammar. You must also remember to revise and proofread.
- The most common business forms are messages, memos, letters, and reports.
- In today's business world, E-mail and faxes are important communication tools.
- Good reading skills, including previewing, skimming, and note taking, are necessary for any type of job.

Key Terms

E-mail *(p. 307)*
modem *(p. 307)*
previewing *(p. 309)*
skimming *(p. 310)*

Chapter 15 • Professional Communication Skills **311**

Extending the Illustration

Have students skim the next chapter for three minutes. Contrast that kind of learning to an in-depth study.

Caption Answer: When you already know a subject and are looking for specific information, skimming is a good way to read. When you want to learn a new subject in detail, you need to read more carefully.

Teaching **YOU'RE THE BOSS!**

✓ Possible responses: Have the assistant correct those letters, and emphasize the importance of correct usage, spelling, and punctuation; consider asking the assistant to get additional training.

Reteaching

1. Have students decide whether they would write a letter or a memo in these situations: telling coworkers that the office will be painted next month (memo); informing customers about a minor change in the company's billing policy (letter).

2. Assign and review vocabulary terms, chapter questions, and activities from the Chapter Review.

3. Assign the Unit Project on the unit opener pages.

Extending the Content

Assign the appropriate Chapter 15 activities in the *Student Activity Workbook.*

Have students imagine that they are applying for work at an advertising firm with a reputation for having a casual style and at a conservative bank. Have them write a cover letter to each business. Have students read and discuss their finished letters. How well does each letter appeal to its audience? Does each letter use language appropriate to its audience? What changes might improve letters?

CLOSE

Have students complete the following statement: "Being able to write a variety of business documents is important because . . . ." (businesses need to use differing means of communicating with customers, employees, shareholders, and others)

Answers
Reviewing Key Terms
Paragraphs will vary but should show an understanding of the terms included in them.

Recalling Key Concepts
1. b
2. c
3. c
4. a
5. c

Thinking Critically
1. When you know an audience's values and expectations, you can focus on points and details that are likely to interest or matter to them.

2. Possible answers: Sit up straight, lean toward the customer, use facial expressions to show interest, and avoid distracting habits.

3. Much of the jargon specific to your field is only understood by others in that field. When you use jargon with people outside your field, you may alienate or confuse them.

4. Answers will vary. Some students may say that they would conduct workshops or have more skilled employees tutor less skilled ones.

Reviewing Key Terms

On a separate sheet of paper, write one or two paragraphs about the importance of communication skills in the world of work. Use the terms below.

communication	enunciation
customer relations	active listening
purpose	E-mail
audience	modem
subject	previewing
inflection	skimming
pronunciation	

Recalling Key Concepts

Choose the correct answer for each item below. Write your answers on a separate sheet of paper.

1. Before speaking to an audience, you should ____.
   (a) speak clearly
   (b) know who your audience is
   (c) use eye contact

2. "Our cleaning service costs less than others in town" is an example of ____.
   (a) enumeration
   (b) cause and effect
   (c) comparison and contrast

3. Taking notes when customers place orders is a type of ____ skill.
   (a) speaking (b) reading (c) listening

4. After writing a business letter to a customer, you should ____.
   (a) proofread it for errors
   (b) send it via E-mail
   (c) send it as a fax

5. To determine whether or not to buy a book for one of your projects, you should ____.
   (a) read the book carefully
   (b) skim it for the main ideas
   (c) preview it by looking at the table of contents, headings, and illustrations

Thinking Critically

Using complete sentences, answer each of the questions below on a separate sheet of paper.

1. Why is knowing your audience's values and expectations important in speaking?

2. When listening to a customer, what are some ways to show that your attention is focused on the customer?

3. Why would you want to avoid jargon when talking to people outside your department or company?

4. As an employer, how would you help employees strengthen communication skills in the workplace?

SCANS Foundation Skills and Workplace Competencies

Basic Skills: *Writing*

1. As the office manager of an accounting firm, you need to inform staff members that the office will close at 2:00 P.M. on the Wednesday before Thanksgiving. You also need to remind supervisors to submit weekly reports before the holiday closing. Use the form you learned in this chapter to write a memo that provides this information.

SCANS Foundation Skills and Workplace Competencies

1. Memos should be direct and professional, with correct grammar and spelling. The memo form used should be similar to the one presented in this chapter.

2. Possible answer: Place the letter face up on your desk. Lift the bottom of the letter and fold it so that only the top one-third of the letter shows. Now fold the top of the letter down to the new bottom edge of the page. Smooth the folded letter until it is flat.

Interpersonal Skills: *Teaching Others*

2. Using only your voice, explain to classmates how to fold a letter on paper that measures 8½ x 11 inches so that it will fit into an envelope that measures 4¼ x 9½ inches. Use the speaking skills you learned in this chapter.

Connecting Academics to the Workplace

Social Studies

1. Aaron is a truck driver for a moving company in your state. As Aaron's supervisor, you need to give him written directions for his next assignment. Using your state map, plan a route that begins at one point in the state and ends at another point. Write the directions on a sheet of paper. Provide at least three steps in the directions. Then exchange your written directions with another student. Use a pencil to map Aaron's route on a road map of your state.

Language Arts

2. Toni is checking her supervisor's voice-mail messages. There is one call, recorded at 2:10 P.M. on February 7: "Hi, John. Sam Jennings here. I need to know if you want me to order that special card stock we talked about. If you let me know by the end of the day, I can still get you the discount rate. I'll be here till six o'clock. I'm at 555-6636. Thanks. So long." Using this information, write a professional phone message for Toni's supervisor.

Developing Teamwork and Leadership Skills

Collaborate with five or six other students to prepare a newscast. Cover recent events, including sports and weather in your community and school. Choose a director, writers, researchers, reporters, and an anchorperson. Take some time to rehearse. Then present your newscast to the class.

Real-World Workshop

Prepare a brief speech on an issue in the world of work that interests you. Issues might include women in the workplace, the effects of new technology, or using the Internet at work. Present your speech to the class. You may want to have a classmate videotape your speech so that you can review and evaluate it.

School-to-Work Connection

Arrange to spend a day observing a job that interests you. For example, if you are interested in the visual arts, you might "shadow" a museum curator. Throughout the day, take notes on aspects of the job that most interest you and aspects you would like to learn more about. Save time at the end of the day to ask questions of the person you observed. Record his or her answers.

Individual Career Plan

Using the answers to your questions in the School-to-Work Connection, write a brief report about the job you observed.

Chapter 15 • Professional Communication Skills **313**

Developing Teamwork and Leadership Skills

This project offers students a good opportunity to work on the communication skills they learned in this chapter. The role of the director might include coaching the reporters and anchorperson on speaking style.

Real-World Workshop

Have classmates evaluate one another's speeches and speaking styles by citing strengths in the areas of emotional contact, posture and body language, inflection, speaking speed, pronunciation, enunciation, and attitude.

School-to-Work Connection

Notes will vary but should contain key information about the job observed.

Individual Career Plan

Students' reports should reflect an understanding of key writing skills such as organization, use of correct spelling and grammar, proofreading, and revising for clarity.

Connecting Academics to the Workplace

1. Before students exchange written routes, have them read through their directions to ensure that they are clear and that highway numbers, landmark names, and compass directions are correct.

2. Messages should include the name of the recipient (John), the name of the caller (Sam Jennings), the time of the call (2:10 P.M.), the date (February 7), the caller's phone number (555-6636), and the name of the person taking the message (Toni). Messages should emphasize that John should return the call by 6:00 P.M. to get a discount rate on the card stock.

SECTION 1 *Making Decisions on the Job*

SECTION OBJECTIVES	SECTION FEATURES	SECTION RESOURCES
• Recall the seven steps in the decision-making process. • Clarify your purposes and values in order to make decisions. • Make appropriate decisions following a chain of command. • Evaluate alternatives and the consequences of decisions. • List your work responsibilities in order of priority.	Personal Career Plan, p. 315 Excellent Business Practices, p. 318 Ethics in Action, p. 322 Exploring Careers, p. 323	◉ Workforce 2000 Videodisc and Videotape 📁 Section 16-1 Review, p. 322 📖 Student Activity Workbook

SECTION 2 *Solving Workplace Problems*

SECTION OBJECTIVES	SECTION FEATURES	SECTION RESOURCES
• Describe the six basic steps in the problem-solving process. • Identify and clarify workplace problems. • Generate alternative solutions to problems and compare their consequences. • Implement solutions and evaluate results.	Career Do's and Don'ts, p. 328 You're the Boss!, p. 330	◉ Workforce 2000 Videodisc and Videotape 📁 Section 16-2 Review, p. 330 📁 Chapter 16 Review, pp. 332–333 📖 Student Activity Workbook

CHAPTER 16

CHAPTER RESOURCES

• Chapter Transparencies and Lesson Plans
• Chapter 16 Test
• Spanish Resources, Chapter 16
• School-to-Work Activity Handbook, Chapter 16 Activity
• Teacher's Lesson Plans, Chapter 16
• Implementing Block Scheduling, Chapter 16
• Print, Media, and Internet Handbook
• Strategies for Implementing Work-Based Learning
• Strategies for Implementing Connecting Activities

Career Notes

SCANS CORRELATION CHART

Foundation Skills

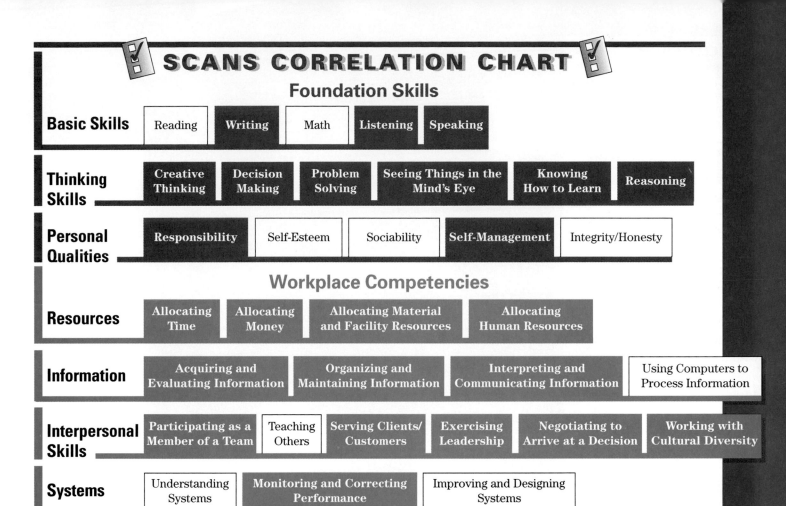

Basic Skills	Reading	Writing	Math	Listening	Speaking	

Thinking Skills	Creative Thinking	Decision Making	Problem Solving	Seeing Things in the Mind's Eye	Knowing How to Learn	Reasoning

Personal Qualities	Responsibility	Self-Esteem	Sociability	Self-Management	Integrity/Honesty

Workplace Competencies

Resources	Allocating Time	Allocating Money	Allocating Material and Facility Resources	Allocating Human Resources

Information	Acquiring and Evaluating Information	Organizing and Maintaining Information	Interpreting and Communicating Information	Using Computers to Process Information

Interpersonal Skills	Participating as a Member of a Team	Teaching Others	Serving Clients/ Customers	Exercising Leadership	Negotiating to Arrive at a Decision	Working with Cultural Diversity

Systems	Understanding Systems	Monitoring and Correcting Performance	Improving and Designing Systems

Technology	Selecting Technology	Applying Technology to Task	Maintaining and Troubleshooting Technology

Highlighted blocks indicate areas covered in the Chapter.

Additional Activities

Internet Connection

Ask students to use the Internet to find out how people approach problems in the workplace. What steps are involved to solve a problem? How do they make a decision? Students can look up articles or use chat rooms to find their information.

Field Trip Suggestions

Ask a local business that does in-house sales training if it would conduct a sales training session at the company's training center that your students could observe and/or participate in. Sales is a growing field. Discuss how selling one's skills as an independent contractor is similar to selling any other product.

Guest Speaker Suggestions

Invite to class a representative of Toastmasters or another organization that teaches public speaking. Ask your guest to involve students in giving a quick run-down of the importance of speaking skills and a demonstration of simple ways to improve speaking habits.

Key to Ability Levels

Each section gives skill-building activities. Each activity has been labeled for use with students of various learning styles and abilities.

L1 Level 1 activities are basic activities and should be within the range of all students.

L2 Level 2 activities are average activities and should be within the range of average and above average students.

L3 Level 3 activities are challenging activities designed for the ability range of above average students.

Chapter 16

Thinking Skills on the Job

School-Based Learning

Chapter Overview

The ability to think clearly is a skill prized by employers; this chapter helps students develop their thinking skills.

Section 16-1 focuses on the decision-making process and ways to use it to clarify thoughts and evaluate possible solutions.

Section 16-2 describes the problem-solving process and ways to use creative thinking and reasoning to solve workplace problems.

Background Information

Write chapter objectives (Sections 16-1 and 16-2) on the chalkboard or use the chapter objective transparency for discussion.

Choose assignments from the *Student Activity Workbook* and write them on the chalkboard.

Have students preview the chapter, looking at pictures, reading captions, and noting content headings. Ask students to describe what they expect to learn in this chapter.

Preteaching Vocabulary

Write the Key Terms from Sections 16-1 and 16-2 on the chalkboard. Have students describe how each term relates to thinking skills and learning how to make decisions and solve workplace problems.

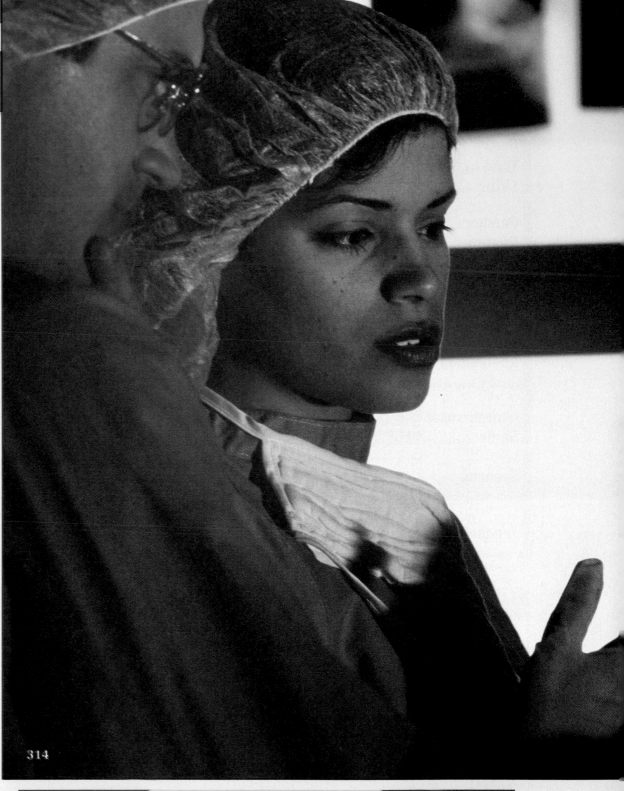

314

Meeting SPECIAL Needs

Learning Disabled

Students with learning disabilities may have trouble acquiring information from the written word. One way to help them overcome this shortcoming is to make tapes of the chapter so they can listen and read along. You can also show them how to get information focusing on learning objectives, highlighted vocabulary, text headings, illustrations, notes, and chapter summaries.

Thinking Skills on the Job

Section 16-1
Making Decisions on the Job

Section 16-2
Solving Workplace Problems

In this video segment, learn how to use thinking skills to make decisions and solve workplace problems.

Journal
Personal Career Plan

Think of a difficult situation you faced recently, either at school or at work. What was the problem? How did you try to solve it? If you could go back now and deal with the situation again, what would you do this time? Why? Discuss your experiences and ideas by writing them down in a journal.

315

Addressing **LEARNING** Styles

Visual Learner

Have visual learners prepare a bulletin board display with illustrations of thinking skills. You may want students to highlight the seven steps in the decision-making process, or the six steps in the problem-solving process. They might show a problematic work situation, the alternatives to solving that situation, and the consequences of each alternative solution.

SECTION 16-1

FOCUS

Bell Ringer

Write the following on the chalkboard:

1. Write two activities you would like to do this weekend.

2. Circle the activity you would most like to do.

3. Write the factors that influenced your choice (for example, money, family responsibilities, other commitments).

Introducing the Section

Have students share their lists from the Bell Ringer activity. Ask students whether they made their decisions abruptly or methodically. Discuss what happens when one makes a major decision without fully weighing the consequences.

Motivational Activity

Critical Thinking

Tell students that they are planning to buy used cars. Have them bring in newspaper ads and ads from other local publications and find at least three ads offering cars that appeal to them. Ask students what step this represents in the decision-making process. Then have them write the criteria they would use in deciding whether to buy one of the cars.

316

Making Decisions on the Job

OBJECTIVES

After studying this section, you will be able to:

- **Recall the seven steps in the decision-making process.**
- **Clarify your purposes and values in order to make decisions.**
- **Make appropriate decisions following a chain of command.**
- **Evaluate alternatives and the consequences of decisions.**
- **List your work responsibilities in order of priority.**

KEY TERMS

resources
criteria
consequence
procrastinate
prioritize

You make hundreds of decisions every day, some trivial, some important. Do you turn left here? What do you want for lunch? What career do you choose? In the world of work, you will want to make the best decisions possible, both everyday decisions and significant long-term ones.

Reviewing the Decision-Making Process

As you learned in Chapter 2, decision making is following a logical series of steps to identify and evaluate possibilities and arrive at a workable choice. Whether you're buying new shoes or facing a big on-the-job decision, the steps are basically the same. What decisions have you made lately that followed this process?

1. Define your needs or wants.

2. Analyze your resources.

3. Identify your choices.

4. Gather information.

5. Evaluate your choices.

6. Make a decision.

7. Plan how to reach your goal.

Implementing Teamwork

Organize your class into groups of five to six students. Ask each group to contact a non-profit organization in your community and find out its financial or manpower needs. Each group should brainstorm a fundraising or volunteer recruiting program. Have each group write up its recommendations for that organization.

 The second step of the decision-making process involves analyzing your resources. *What resources are being used here to make a decision?*

Step 1. Figuring Out What You Need and Want

Once you know what you need or want in order to meet your job responsibilities, you have completed the first step of the decision-making process. Having a strong grasp of your purpose will help you clarify the decision you need to make.

When Maria Delfino starts her new job at SuperSounds, a large music store, her duties include making sure that the display racks are kept filled with the latest CDs. When she discovers an empty rack,

she faces a decision. She needs to keep the rack filled, and she needs a new supply of CDs. She wants to fulfill her responsibility and to do a good job too.

Step 2. Checking Out Resources

Can you make something out of nothing? Of course not—you need resources. In the world of work, the most basic **resources** are time, money, material, information, facilities, and people.

At SuperSounds, Maria moves to the second step of the decision-making process

Guided Practice
Teaching Strategies
1. Assign and review Section 16-1.
2. Use the transparency for this section.
3. Assign and review the Case Study.

Discussion Starter

Ask students to list the major decisions they'll be making over the next couple of years (buying a car, renting an apartment, choosing a college, deciding on a job).

Teaching Tip

Discuss each step in the decision-making process by having students decide what they will do after high school. Have students suppose that they are considering continuing their education. Giving examples of each step, guide students through the decision-making process. Have students write answers to each of the steps.

Critical Thinking

Ask students to write 100-word paragraphs describing why making a career decision is difficult and how a formal process can help them make well-informed decisions. (Career decisions are difficult because they can affect how you live. A formal decision-making process helps you consider alternatives and consequences.)

Extending the Illustration

Ask students to share their experiences from their part-time jobs when they had to pull additional resources to finish a task.

Caption Answer: time, money, material, information, facilities, and people

317

SCANS Foundation Skills Connection

L1 Seeing Things in the Mind's Eye

Tell students to think about a time when they needed to make a decision about school or work. Did they follow the seven steps in the decision-making process outlined in the text? If not, what steps did they omit? How might their decisions have differed if they had followed this approach?

L2 Decision Making

Ask students what advice they would give in this situation: "Anne has a part-time job. Her employer has just told her that she would need to work every weeknight from now on. Anne is worried that she will not have time to study." Should she look for another job? What should she take into consideration as she makes her decision?

L3 Problem Solving

Have pairs of students discuss how to handle the following scenario. "Bradley's boss has told him to watch for an important UPS package containing material needed for a client presentation the next day. At 2:00 P.M., the package has not arrived." What should Bradley do? How can he show his boss that he is a good problem-solver?

by finding out what resources she has. She checks back in the stockroom, and she finds that the CD she needs is out of stock. She knows, however, that new supplies—additional resources—are available from a distributor.

Step 3. Identifying the Best and the Rest

What do you do when different choices all seem like good ones? Smart decision makers use **criteria**—standards of judgment—for comparing and evaluating choices.

Criteria for decision making will often be provided by your employer or other experienced coworkers. As you learn more about a workplace, you'll learn not only *how* but also *why* certain decisions are made—in other words, what criteria are important, including product quality, customer satisfaction, safety, efficiency, and economic factors known as "the bottom line."

Maria knows that SuperSounds values keeping its display racks filled. However, another criterion—the chain of command—is also important. Maria identifies her three choices. She can (a) order the CDs immediately, (b) inform her supervisor of the situation, or (c) do nothing about the CDs and wait for someone else to notice the situation.

EXCELLENT BUSINESS PRACTICES

Total Quality Management

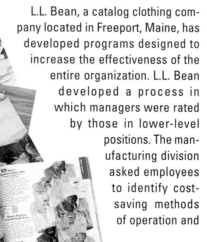

L.L. Bean, a catalog clothing company located in Freeport, Maine, has developed programs designed to increase the effectiveness of the entire organization. L.L. Bean developed a process in which managers were rated by those in lower-level positions. The manufacturing division asked employees to identify cost-saving methods of operation and made changes. Workers in the retail store traded jobs with workers in the distribution centers. As a result of the job-swap experience, workers simplified processes that previously had not been questioned.

The various programs put people before processes. The programs saved the company money, and solved potential problems at early stages.

Thinking Critically

What would be the benefit of a job-swap experience?

Extending EXCELLENT BUSINESS PRACTICES

Answer: Employees from different areas may gain additional respect for the jobs of others and may be able to provide valuable insight from another perspective.

Further Application: Arrange for students to visit an enterprise that uses a process to provide a service, such as a restaurant, dry-cleaning store, or print shop. Ask to see how the establishment operates. Have employees identify processes that have saved time and money. Can students identify any other methods of increasing the business's effectiveness?

 No one knows everything. If you have a question, ask it. *What might a supervisor think of a worker who never asks questions?*

Step 4. Collecting More Info

Sometimes you simply don't have enough information to make a good decision. What's the solution? Don't act in the dark—ask questions. Get the information you need. If you don't ask, no one will know you need information.

Maria has taken a SuperSounds training program in how to place orders. However, she does not have the authority to do so or even know the number of new CDs to order. Her next move is to ask a coworker for more *information*. Steven, an assistant who has been on the job for about six months, recommends that Maria inform the supervisor of the situation.

Step 5. Assuming the Role of Judge

Every decision you make will have a **consequence**—an effect or outcome. Evaluating alternatives usually means understanding and predicting possible consequences. These questions may help as you consider an on-the-job decision:

- What are the risks involved in this decision? Are the rewards worth it?

Chapter 16 • Thinking Skills on the Job **319**

SCANS Workplace Competencies Connection

L1 **Allocating Time**
Tell students that they have a project that will take six hours, to be completed one week from today. Working within the confines of their current schedules—including school and work activities—have them write specific days and times to tell how they will complete their projects.

L2 **Acquiring and Evaluating Information**
Have students skim the local newspaper and magazines and find at least 12 businesses that list Internet addresses. Have students call at least three of these businesses to find out why they created sites and whether they think the sites have brought them new customers.

L3 **Serving Clients/Customers**
Have students compare two of their favorite places, such as restaurants, clothing stores or music stores. Ask students what they like and dislike about the treatment they receive in these places. What do they think the managers and employees could do to improve customer service? Have students write 100-word papers.

 Extending the Illustration

Have students brainstorm reasons why people are hesitant to ask questions. (Possible answers are that they think they should already know the answer, are embarrassed or too shy to ask, or want to appear more knowledgeable than they are.)

Caption Answer: The supervisor might think that the worker doesn't care about doing the best job or that he or she doesn't understand the job well enough to know what questions to ask or when to ask them.

Independent Practice

Assign as homework the chapter activity in the *School-to-Work Activity Handbook.*

Reading

Have each student read a selection from a college reference book (available in school and public libraries) describing an institution he or she is interested in attending. Have students list at least five facts they learned from the references.

Skills Practice

Have students ask members of your school's track team to give the three fastest times in a favorite event and their three slowest times in the same event. Have students calculate an average time for the event. Then have students work together to create a chart showing the average speeds of all members of the team for one event. If possible, have students create their chart using a computer.

Figure 16-1

Prioritizing

On any job, a worker must often decide what to do first, second, third, and so on. For example, a housepainter must decide in what order to paint the surfaces of a room so as to avoid doing extra work. Various factors may influence prioritizing a sequence of decisions or actions.

A Since the moldings are to remain a natural wood color, the painter has decided to place tape over them before painting the other surfaces.

B Since the floor is not going to be refinished, the painter has decided to cover it.

320   *Unit 5 • Professional Development*

- How does this decision directly affect me? How will I be judged?
- What effect will this decision have on my team or department?
- What effect will this decision have on my company?

Maria thinks about the consequences of the three choices she faces. If she orders the CDs herself, she may be praised for her initiative. However, she may also be

▶▶ Extending Figure 16-1 ◀◀

Ask students what priorities they follow when they get up and get dressed for school in the morning. Do they follow those same priorities on weekend mornings?

reprimanded for breaking the chain of command. If she informs the supervisor, she will be following the store's standard procedure. If she waits and does nothing, she may be accused of not doing her job properly.

Step 6. Making Up Your Mind

After you've considered your options and evaluated the possible consequences, there's no need to **procrastinate**, or put off deciding, unless you still need more information. Have you ever decided not to decide? That's a decision too. Just don't procrastinate out of fear.

Maria doesn't procrastinate. She decides to follow the store's standard procedure—to inform her supervisor.

Step 7. Drawing Up Your Plan of Action

Once you've made a decision, put it into action. **Prioritize** the tasks to be done; that is, order them from first to last or from most to least important. *Figure 16-1* shows how a worker prioritizes his tasks.

C The painter has decided to start with the ceiling because any paint splatters that get on the walls will be covered when the walls are painted.

D The painter paints the walls last, covering up any splattering.

Chapter 16 • Thinking Skills on the Job **321**

Teaching ETHICS in Action

(see feature on page 322)

Have students follow these steps to help them make a decision.

1. What are the ethical issues?
2. What are the alternatives?
3. Who are the affected parties?
4. How do the alternatives affect them?
5. What is your decision?

Extending the Illustration

(see illustration on page 322)

Tell students that it is Wednesday. They have band practice on Thursday, a math test on Friday, and their parents want them to do yard work this week. Have students prioritize their activities for the next three days.

Caption Answer: To accomplish them in order of importance.

Writing: *Journal*

Have students write entries for their career journals describing the decision-making process and how they will use it.

Discussion Starter

Ask students to list all the things they had planned to do last weekend but didn't have time or forgot to do.

Teaching Tip

Point out that setting priorities is a major element in helping people meet their goals. Tell students that setting priorities means that the items that are last on the list may not get done or may be done much later. In deciding priorities, students should think about the consequences of each item and decide what would happen if it didn't get done. If the answer is "not much," that item probably has a low priority.

Skills Practice

Terry is about to buy a used car. The owner is selling it for $5,000. Terry has saved $1,500 for a down payment. The owner has offered to finance the amount owed at a simple 10 percent interest rate. How much interest will Terry pay on the balance for a year? ($350: $5,000 − $1,500 = $3,500; 0.10 × $3,500)

Critical Thinking

Describe this scenario for students. "Laura works as a medical transcriptionist. Her supervisor hands her four patient records that need to be ready for a meeting in two hours. She also asks Laura to arrange with the file clerk to retrieve three other patient folders that will be needed for the meeting.

"After her supervisor leaves, Laura glances at the records to be transcribed and decides she has time for a quick phone call to arrange a movie date with a friend. Laura talks nearly half an hour before she realizes she needs to get busy. In her haste to get the records transcribed, she forgets to call the file clerk.

"When the supervisor returns a few minutes before the meeting, Laura has to tell her that she has finished only three of the patient records and does not have the other three from filing." Ask students how setting priorities could have helped Laura.

ASSESS

Assessment
Process

Tell students that they have completed either college or a training program and have been offered jobs by two employers. Have students use the decision-making process to write each step and the actions they would take at that step.

Evaluate students' papers for inclusion of all steps and for evidence that they understand how to apply each step appropriately.

ETHICS in Action

Jake, one of your coworkers, has confided in you that he has serious problems at home, involving both his daughter's drug abuse and his mother's terminal illness. He is having a hard time keeping his mind on his work. You have promised not to tell anyone. Then your boss complains to you about Jake's work, saying that Jake might be demoted or fired. What will you do?

Maria prioritizes her tasks. She first informs her supervisor, who praises her attentiveness and places the order. Second, she rearranges the display to make it look appealing until the new supply arrives. Third, she checks the other new titles to make sure the situation doesn't happen again. Maria will reach both her short-term goal (to fill the display) and her long-term goal (to be responsible).

 Maria completes her work by prioritizing. *Why is it important to prioritize tasks?*

SECTION 16-1 *Review*

Understanding Key Concepts

Using complete sentences, answer the following questions on a separate sheet of paper.

1. In your own words, describe the seven steps of the decision-making process.

2. Why do you think having a clear purpose can make a decision easier?

3. What do you predict will happen to a business that does not have a strong chain of command?

4. In what way is customer satisfaction a criterion for decision making?

5. What do you think is the value of prioritizing your job responsibilities?

SECTION 16-1 *Review* ANSWERS

1. Decision making involves figuring out what you want to accomplish, gathering information about your possible choices and their consequences, making the best decision you can, and putting a plan into action.

2. By having a clear purpose, you can easily decide on the specific actions that will lead you to your goal.

3. Employees will lack a sense of personal responsibility, and their business will probably not function well.

4. The most important criterion is whether the end result will satisfy the customer.

5. Prioritizing job responsibilities results in a clear and practical plan of action.

CASE STUDY

Exploring Careers: Transportation

Ricky Bachan
Driver

Q: What do you do for the transit company?

A: I drive a small bus for Dial-a-Ride, a service that takes the elderly, people in wheelchairs, or people who have medical problems to the hospital or to the doctors' offices. It's a curb-to-curb service. I pick the passengers up, help them into the bus, and make sure they're seated or that their wheelchairs are secure.

Q: How did you get your job?

A: I started doing this kind of work in New York. I think my driving experience is why the company here hired me so quickly. After driving in New York, driving in Santa Clarita Valley is a cinch.

Q: What skills did you need?

A: In California, you have to have a Class B driver's license, a commercial license that allows you to carry passengers. The company trains you in assisting passengers, including how to strap down the wheelchairs. We also learn CPR and other emergency procedures.

Q: What are your days like?

A: I spend about eight hours a day on the road and cover more than a hundred miles a day. I get to meet a lot of people and I like that. I like driving, too, although sometimes it can get to you.

Thinking Critically

Why do you think there will be a growing need for drivers who provide transportation services to the elderly?

CAREER FACTS

Nature of the Work:
Pick up clients at home; take them to appointments; return to pick them up.

Training or Education Needed:
Strong driving experience; appropriate driver's license.

Aptitudes, Abilities, and Skills:
Listening, speaking, and interpersonal skills; reading and writing skills; ability to use maps; physical stamina; safe driving skills; decision-making skills.

Salary Range:
Depends on location and experience; average starting wage—$8.00 an hour.

Career Path:
Start by driving small buses or vans; qualify for the appropriate driver's license; work for a large or private transportation company.

Chapter 16 • Thinking Skills on the Job **323**

Extending the CASE STUDY

Answer: There will be a growing number of elderly as baby-boomers become senior citizens.

Further Application: Have students discuss how the growing population of elderly will or will not affect their choices of careers. Jobs in service areas, for example, might expand as people have more money and less ability to do things for themselves; health fields will expand; hospitality and recreation might expand as more people retire; office and business fields will probably expand to meet the growing demands of the retired.

Evaluation
Assign the section review.

Reteaching
Divide the class into seven groups. Assign each group one of the steps in the decision-making process. Tell groups that they are to present their steps to the rest of the class. Ask students to create posters or flip charts or use transparencies or other tools. Have them give examples illustrating the actions a person making a decision might take at that step in the process.

Extending the Content
Assign the appropriate Chapter 16 activities in the *Student Activity Workbook*.

Have students research the topic of procrastination and write 200-word articles for a career newsletter giving advice about ways to stop putting off actions or making decisions. Have students use a computer to format the articles attractively.

CLOSE
Have students complete this statement: "One major decision I have made with respect to my future career is . . . ." (Answers will vary but might include going to college, going to work, moving into an apartment, and so on.)

FOCUS

Bell Ringer

Ask students to mention instances when they've complained about items they purchased. What was the problem? How would they improve the products?

Introducing the Section

Have students share their thoughts from the Bell Ringer activity. Tell them that problem solving in the workplace frequently involves identifying the weakness and coming up with solutions for improvement. Solving problems is similar to making decisions: both processes can be used to help identify issues and options.

As you introduce each step in the problem-solving process, use one of the products and ideas from the Bell Ringer activity to illustrate each step.

Motivational Activity
Critical Thinking

Have students identify a problem in your school, perhaps overcrowding or the need for additional computer labs. Tell students to use the problem-solving process and write their answers to each step. Have students share their problems and solutions in class.

Solving Workplace Problems

OBJECTIVES

After studying this section, you will be able to:
- Describe the six basic steps in the problem-solving process.
- Identify and clarify workplace problems.
- Generate alternative solutions to problems and compare their consequences.
- Implement solutions and evaluate results.

KEY TERMS

brainstorm
analogy
assumptions

"Houston, we have a problem," crackled the voice of astronaut Jim Lovell as the damaged *Apollo 13* capsule hurtled through space. That statement set in motion a heroic group effort in problem solving—resolving a difficulty through creative thinking and reasoning.

Understanding the Problem-Solving Process

Your workplace problems may not be as dramatic as those of *Apollo 13,* but your approach to solving them should be the same. Follow these six steps:

1. Identify and clarify the problem.
2. Generate alternative solutions, using creative thinking and logical reasoning.
3. Evaluate the probable consequences of the solutions.
4. Decide on the best solution.
5. Implement the solution.
6. Evaluate the results.

Step 1. Identify and Clarify the Problem

When an obstacle stands between you and something you need or want, you've got a problem. You

324   *Unit 5 • Professional Development*

 Whether problems are simple or complex, they can usually be solved with creative thinking and logical reasoning. *What kinds of problems have you already solved during your life as a student?*

could try the ostrich approach: Stick your head in the sand and hope the problem goes away. Chances are, it won't. The wise move is to see the problem clearly for what it is—not a mystery, not a catastrophe, but just a situation that needs a solution.

First things first. Gather the facts—assemble all the information you can about the problem. Ask specific questions, and stay as objective as possible. Think about your sources too. Are they reliable? Are they giving you facts or opinions?

Lewis Iverson is a part-time assistant at Avery's, a small local hardware store. One day, Mr. Avery, the owner, tells Lewis that business has been very slow lately. He asks Lewis to think about possible solutions to the problem of the sales slump. To clarify the problem, Lewis makes this list of questions:

- Are fewer people coming in?
- Are customers spending less money?
- Do people want a different selection of goods?

Chapter 16 • Thinking Skills on the Job **325**

Guided Practice
Teaching Strategies

1. Assign and review Section 16-2.
2. Use the transparency for this section.

Discussion Starter

Ask students if they've ever thought they solved a problem only to find that it wasn't the one they started out to solve.

Teaching Tip

Explain to students that identifying the real source of a problem can sometimes be troublesome. Writing a statement describing the problem can help, as can discussing the problem with others. For example, tell students that the school's band needs new uniforms. Ask them to describe the problem. Write their descriptions on the chalkboard. (Some students may say the need for new uniforms is the problem. The real problem is how to raise the money to pay for the uniforms.)

Critical Thinking

Ask students to write 100-word paragraphs about why they think some people seem to accomplish so much more than others. Have them also include ways that show how creative decision-making and problem-solving skills help people be more productive.

Extending the Illustration

Ask students if they've ever suffered anxiety over deciding how to handle a problem. How could following a problem-solving process help them relieve anxiety?

Caption Answer: Students may cite a variety of academic and social problems, including meeting deadlines, and juggling social events.

TEACH *(cont'd.)*

L1 Responsibility

Tell students that knowing how to get along with others is very important to career success. Such skills are especially important in teamwork. Have students list instances when they've worked in teams at school. What were their individual responsibilities? What were the team's commitments to them? Have students discuss answers in class.

L2 Speaking

Working in pairs, have each student take turns explaining his or her part-time job or household jobs to the partner. Tell students to describe how they spend their time, what materials they use, what they like and dislike about the job, and what they hope to gain from their experiences.

L3 Listening

Have students listen to the local or national news at least twice over the next week. Tell them to notice how often newsmakers report decision-making activities. (For example, the local city council may be making a decision about placing a traffic light at a major intersection.) Ask students whether they think good decision-making skills are tied to leadership skills. Have them share their observations in class.

- Do people expect lower prices?
- What products do other local hardware stores offer?

By asking their regular customers these questions, Lewis and Mr. Avery clarify the problem: People are buying less of certain kinds of items, especially tools, because the selection is better at a big new home supply store.

Step 2. Generate Alternative Solutions

One of the world's great problem solvers, physicist Albert Einstein, once said, "Imagination is more important than knowledge." Do you agree? Think of the problems you've solved by changing your way of thinking, by looking at something from a new angle, by being creative.

 Group brainstorming can result in a variety of creative solutions to a problem. *Why do you think the word* brainstorm *is a good one to describe this problem-solving strategy?*

326   *Unit 5 • Professional Development*

Extending the Illustration

Have students research the techniques of brainstorming and list at least three behaviors that aid brainstorming. (Possible answers might include open communication, saying words or thoughts quickly, avoiding prejudging an idea, using word association.)

Caption Answer: Brainstorming entails having sudden, unexpected ideas that may not have occurred to you before, just as real storms can bring on sudden rain or wind.

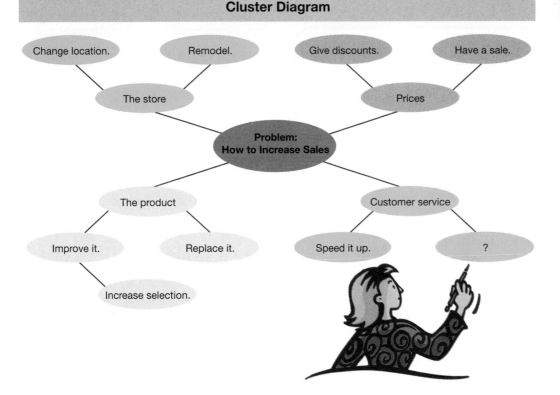

Cluster Diagram

Change location.

Remodel.

Give discounts.

Have a sale.

The store

Prices

Problem:
How to Increase Sales

The product

Customer service

Improve it.

Replace it.

Speed it up.

?

Increase selection.

▲ **Figure 16-2** A cluster diagram can help you associate a variety of ideas and see new connections. If you were using this cluster, what might you put in the oval with a question mark?

To attack a problem, come up with as many solutions as possible, no matter how "crazy" some of them might seem. **Brainstorm** alone or with a group, coming up with as many ideas as you can but not evaluating or judging those ideas right away. After all, multiple solutions increase your chances of success. Change your point of view. Putting yourself in someone else's shoes can make a problem look quite different.

Here are a few strategies for creative thinking that you can try:

- Use spider maps and clustering (techniques you've probably already used in school) to associate groups of ideas, such as the one shown in **Figure 16-2.**

- Invent a model, picture, or symbol to represent the problem. Revealing the "shape" of a problem can open a solution.

Chapter 16 • Thinking Skills on the Job **327**

☑ **SCANS Workplace Competencies Connection**

L1 **Working with Cultural Diversity**

Have students watch two or three episodes of TV shows showing people of different ethnic backgrounds in work situations. Tell students to note how the different characters behaved. Did their actions support an ethnic stereotype? What interpersonal and communication skills were demonstrated? Which skills seemed most effective in helping people work together?

L2 **Monitoring and Correcting Performance**

Have students write a paragraph about how the courses they've taken so far relate to job trends in their chosen careers. Also have them write about the courses they plan to take during the next year to help prepare for their careers.

L3 **Exercising Leadership**

Tell students to think about their experiences at home, on the job, or in extracurricular activities. Discuss responses in class. When is it appropriate for them to take action on their own? When should they seek the opinions of one or two others? When should they take matters to the entire group?

▶ **Extending Figure 16-2** ◀

Have students choose school- or work-related problems and create their own cluster diagram with ideas for solutions for each problem. (Possible problems might include how to fund new band uniforms or, for a new business, how to advertise its grand opening.)

Caption Answer: A possible answer is "Make it friendlier."

TEACH *(cont'd.)*

Independent Practice

Reading

Have each student find and read an article on creative problem-solving techniques. Have students take notes on at least three strategies suggested, then write a sentence or two about how they might apply that strategy to solving one of their own problems.

Skills Practice

To attract more customers, The Bistro restaurant began offering theme menus during the week. As a result, the restaurant has increased sales by an average of 15 percent over the past two months. If average monthly sales had been $21,600 a month before, by how much have sales increased? What is the new monthly sales average? ($3,240, $24,840: 0.15 × $21,600 = $3,240)

Interview

Many local television stations or newspapers have consumer affairs reporters who help consumers. Ask such a person from your community to visit your class to discuss how he or she hears about problems and goes about solving them. Set aside time for students to ask questions. After the interview, have each student write a paragraph describing what he or she learned.

Career Do's & Don'ts

To Be Effective in the Workplace...

Do:
- carry out procedures and get things done.
- be innovative and creative.
- find out what you don't know.
- work with associates to solve problems together.

Don't:
- argue.
- overlook details.
- be secretive.
- try to do everything yourself.

- Use an **analogy**—a seeming similarity between one thing and another thing that are otherwise dissimilar—to suggest a solution. For example: This problem is like a game of basketball. We need to pass our product from one member of the team to another more quickly.

- Question **assumptions**—beliefs you take for granted—and beware of unspoken assumptions. For example: Are we assuming that all our customers are men? What about advertising aimed at women?

Remember that, in problem solving, more heads are often better than one simply because different people bring different experiences to the table. Participate as a team member to help identify alternative solutions (a SCANS skill), and ask other

Workforce 2000 Trends

CEO George David, of United Technologies, Inc., advises workers of the future to have a long-term view of their careers. "You build the really important things in life by virtue of care and nurturing and paying attention to them over a period of years."

---

people for help when you can. Involving others—making your boss aware of a problem, for example—is often the right move.

Mr. Avery, Lewis, and Kim, another assistant, brainstorm one afternoon. Each proposes ideas, such as having a sale, lowering prices, putting up a new sign, and expanding the selection. In the spirit of imaginative brainstorming, Lewis says, "How about hiring someone to dress up in a huge hammer costume and stand outside the store?" Kim chimes in, "How about several people in costumes to show different kinds of hammers?"

Step 3. Evaluate the Probable Consequences of the Solutions

Not all solutions are created equal. After you've come up with some possible solutions, you need to evaluate how well each one will actually solve the problem.

List the specific consequences—both positive and negative—that may follow each possible solution. Which one best meets your short-term and long-term goals? What impact will the solutions have on you, on your team or department, and on your customers or clients? When you've answered these questions, you're ready to decide on one solution.

The problem-solving team at Avery's now looks at *consequences*. Mr. Avery can't afford to lower prices or to put up a big sign. Expanding the selection of all the items in the store is impractical because Avery's just doesn't have the space. The hammer-costume idea would get people's attention—a short-term goal—but it might also make people think the store was silly—missing a long-term goal of maintaining customers' respect.

Step 4. Decide on the Best Solution

When you choose a solution, remember that you're choosing the best one under the circumstances. Few solutions are perfect, and occasionally time forces you to choose when you're not quite ready. Time pressure is a reality that everyone has to deal with. Just stay calm, focus on the problem, and decide.

Lewis, Kim, and Mr. Avery decide that the best solution is a variation of what Kim said about "different kinds of hammers." They'll increase the selection of certain items—such as hammers—and specialize in tools.

Step 5. Implement the Solution

You may need to explain your solution to coworkers in order to put it into action. Identify the exact steps you need to follow and prioritize them. Following the chain of command, obtain the necessary permission and move ahead.

Mr. Avery takes action. He stops carrying certain items, such as house paint, to

 Prioritizing your steps and communicating your plan to others are keys to making a solution work. *What do you think are the advantages of presenting all the steps of a plan at a group meeting?*

Chapter 16 • *Thinking Skills on the Job* **329**

True-False

1. Figuring out your needs or wants is the first step in the decision-making process. (true)

2. Criteria in making a decision are the time, money, material, information, facilities, and people involved. (false)

3. Setting priorities helps you get the least important things done first. (false)

4. Brainstorming can only be done in a group. (false)

5. Spider maps and clustering are techniques that help people think creatively. (true)

💾 Use the Testmaker to create a customized test for Chapter 16.

Reteaching

1. Tell students that the school band has been chosen to march in Macy's Thanksgiving Day Parade in New York City. Have students, working in five teams, identify and analyze the problems to be solved, using the problem-solving process. Then have teams present their problems and solutions to the class, including their reasoning at each step in the process.

make room for a greater selection of tools. He orders and stocks the new items, sets up new displays, and advertises in the local newspaper.

Step 6. Evaluate the Results

To evaluate a solution, look at both its benefits and its drawbacks. Be as objective in evaluating a solution as you were in identifying the problem. If your solution is working, you should be able to cite benefits for yourself, your team or department, and your customers or clients.

If the solution has drawbacks or if it creates new problems, identify them and correct them as well. On-the-job problem solving is a continuous process.

Finally, ask yourself what you learned. An old saying holds true: "The only really bad decisions are the ones you don't learn from." Apply what you learn to new situations to prevent similar problems from happening again.

YOU'RE THE BOSS!

Solving Workplace Problems

You ask a cashier/clerk in your hardware store to organize a display of tools. Half an hour later, you see long lines of customers waiting for cashier service. You point the customers out to this employee, who says, "I know, but you told me to work on the display." How will you respond?

At Avery's, the greatest drawback is eliminating house paint—a moneymaker—to make room for new tools. However, tool sales are increasing dramatically, so the benefits outweigh the drawbacks, as customers are impressed with the new selection and spend more money.

SECTION 16-2 *Review*

Understanding Key Concepts

Using complete sentences, answer the following questions on a separate sheet of paper.

1. In your own words, describe the six basic steps of problem solving.

2. In an on-the-job situation, how can you identify good sources of information?

3. Why is creating alternative solutions better than relying on only one solution?

4. What do you think are the advantages of group problem solving?

5. Describe how you and another person solved a similar problem, and compare the consequences of each solution.

SECTION 16-2 *Review* ANSWERS

1. In problem solving, you clearly identify the problem, come up with possible solutions, evaluate the consequences, choose the solution that seems best, put that solution into effect, and judge the results.

2. Possible answers: by asking questions, remaining objective, and evaluating the sources for reliability

3. Creating multiple alternative solutions increases your chances of success.

4. Each member brings different perspectives and experiences to bear on the problem.

5. Problems and solutions will vary, but consequences should be compared in terms of their practical short-term and long-term effects.

SECTION 16-1 Summary

- The seven steps in the decision-making process are to define your needs or wants, analyze your resources, identify your choices, gather information, evaluate your choices, make a decision, and plan how to reach your goal.

- To determine which decisions are yours to make, follow the chain of command, and know your responsibilities.

- Use criteria for comparing and evaluating possible choices.

- If you need additional information, be sure to get it.

- Evaluate the possible consequences of alternative decisions.

- When you're ready to decide, don't procrastinate.

- Prioritize tasks to be performed in order to create a plan of action.

Key Terms

resources *(p. 317)*
criteria *(p. 318)*
consequence *(p. 319)*
procrastinate *(p. 321)*
prioritize *(p. 321)*

SECTION 16-2 Summary

- The six basic steps in problem solving are to identify and clarify the problem, generate alternative solutions, evaluate probable consequences, decide on the best solution, implement the solution, and evaluate the results.

- Gather and evaluate information, distinguishing between reliable and unreliable sources.

- Generate alternative solutions with creative thinking strategies such as brainstorming, clustering, modeling, and using analogies.

- Evaluate consequences of solutions by judging how well they meet long-term and short-term goals.

- Choose the best solution under the circumstances, and prioritize the steps needed to implement it.

- Be objective in evaluating benefits and drawbacks of a solution.

Key Terms

brainstorm *(p. 327)*
analogy *(p. 328)*
assumptions *(p. 328)*

Chapter 16 • Thinking Skills on the Job **331**

2. Assign and review vocabulary terms, chapter questions, and activities from the Chapter Review.

Extending the Content

 Assign the appropriate Chapter 16 activities in the *Student Activity Workbook.*

Have students interview at least three local entrepreneurs or small-businesses managers. One business should produce a product and another should offer a service, such as consulting. The third business might be a professional practice, such as a dental, medical, or legal practice.

Tell students to ask each person about the types of problems that occur in the business and how he or she goes about solving them. Do the types of problems differ? What are the similarities? Have students discuss in class.

CLOSE

Ask each student to write a short paragraph describing how being able to apply the problem-solving process will be useful in his or her career. (Answers will vary but might include that employers look for people who can solve a problem rather than waiting for someone else to do it.)

Teaching YOU'RE THE BOSS!

✓ Possible responses: Have the employee open another cash register right away; later, discuss priorities in the store and emphasize the importance of evaluating situations and making independent decisions.

Computer Activity

Have students use a word processing software package to design a chain-of-command chart for a small to medium-sized company. Either by hand or by using the software package, have students draw lines between the job titles to indicate the appropriate flow of work.

Answers
Reviewing Key Terms

Descriptions will vary, but students should demonstrate their understanding of the definitions of the key terms.

Recalling Key Concepts

1. False: The final step in the decision-making process is to plan how to reach your goal.

2. True

3. False: The first step is to gather the facts.

4. False: Brainstorming can be done alone or with a group.

5. False: Evaluating a solution objectively means judging its effects apart from your personal feelings.

Thinking Critically

1. Possible answer (in ascending order of responsibility): teacher, assistant principal, principal, superintendent of schools

2. Possible answer: If you are ready to put a decision into action, do so now.

3. Possible answer for cooking a meal: assembling all the ingredients, cutting, mixing, seasoning, baking

4. Possible answer: I would consider the reliability of my sources and evaluate information according to how directly it could lead to a solution.

Reviewing Key Terms

On a separate sheet of paper, write a description of one typical day at a job of your choice. Use the following key terms in your description.

resources	brainstorm
criteria	analogy
consequence	assumptions
procrastinate	prioritize

Recalling Key Concepts

On a separate sheet of paper, tell whether each statement is true or false. Rewrite any false statements to make them true.

1. The final step in the decision-making process is to evaluate your choices.

2. A criterion is a standard of judgment.

3. The first step to solving a problem is to consider analogies.

4. Brainstorming to generate alternative solutions can only be done alone.

5. Evaluating a solution objectively means taking your personal feelings into consideration.

Thinking Critically

Using complete sentences, answer each of the questions below on a separate sheet of paper.

1. Most organizations have a chain of command—a system of authority and responsibility. Describe the chain of command in one of the following: your school system, a professional sports team, your state government.

2. Explain in your own words what the following saying tells about procrastination: Don't put off until tomorrow what you can do today.

3. Identify a job or work-related goal, such as repairing a bicycle, or building a house. Prioritize at least five tasks that would lead to that goal.

4. If you were trying to solve a problem, how would you separate useful, relevant information from distracting, irrelevant information?

5. Identify a serious world problem, such as poverty or war. Brainstorm at least three creative solutions to the problem—no matter how unusual or "crazy."

SCANS Foundation Skills and Workplace Competencies

Basic Skills: *Writing/Speaking*

1. Choose a problem facing your school or community, and present a solution to the class. Use a written form—such as an advertisement, poster, or song lyric—to accompany your spoken presentation.

Information: *Acquire and Evaluate Information*

2. Imagine that you plan to open an ice-cream shop, video arcade, or other business in your community. Create a questionnaire designed to gather the information you need about the qualities and features that would attract your classmates. Make your questions as specific as possible, and distribute the questionnaire to as many students

5. Solutions and evaluations will vary, depending on the problem chosen.

SCANS Foundation Skills and Workplace Competencies

1. Presentations will vary, but students should clearly outline the solution, including as many details as possible.

2. Questionnaires will vary. Reports should demonstrate a direct connection between shop features and data supplied.

Connecting Academics to the Workplace

1. Suggestions should demonstrate a group effort to come up with novel solutions.

as you can. Evaluate the responses, and write a report describing how your shop will meet customers' demands.

Connecting Academics to the Workplace

Human Relations

1. In most jobs, productivity increases when morale is high. Workers who feel good about themselves and their work usually perform well. In a group of three, choose a type of company, identify a morale problem, and brainstorm at least five possible solutions to present to management. Then evaluate the possible solutions by asking yourself what their practical consequences are. Finally, decide on one solution, and create a presentation in which you cite the benefits of that solution.

Language Arts

2. Choose a short story or novel that you have read or a movie or television show that you have seen in which a character makes a job-related decision or solves a problem at work. Apply the steps of decision making or problem solving to the character's actions. Then explain whether you think the character should have arrived at a different decision or solution and why you think so.

Developing Teamwork and Leadership Skills

In a team of five or six, brainstorm a solution to the following problem: You are the owners and employees of a small successful restaurant; however, a large national chain is opening a fast-food restaurant next door. Conduct a meeting at which you explore multiple solutions to the situation. Listen to everyone's suggestions, and question everyone's assumptions. Then, as a group, decide on the best strategy for continuing success.

Real-World Workshop

With a partner, present a mock telephone conversation in which an employee who is a service worker (plumber, appliance repairer, delivery person) faces a problem in the field and calls the supervisor in the office. The employee may face lack of materials, lack of time, or lack of information. What questions does the employee ask? What advice does the supervisor give? What decisions are reached?

School-to-Work Connection

Interview someone who works in a career area that interests you. Ask about the usual methods for solving problems in that career area. If possible, obtain a specific example of a successful solution to a problem. Present your findings to the class.

Individual Career Plan

Different careers present different decisions to be made and different problems to be solved. For the career area that is most appealing to you, list the kinds of decisions you think you would have to make and the kinds of problems you would have to solve on a daily basis.

Chapter 16 • Thinking Skills on the Job **333**

g. He climbs a ladder, stands on the roof—and falls through. Obviously, Tim should have arrived at a different decision so he would not have fallen through the roof.

Developing Teamwork and Leadership Skills

Proposed solutions will vary. Team members should consider each other's ideas with open minds and decide objectively on the best strategy.

Real-World Workshop

Scenarios will vary. The employee may suggest possible solutions but should request help and make suggestions with the appropriate tone. The supervisor's advice should be based on a careful consideration of the information supplied by the employee.

School-to-Work Connection

Methods cited will vary, but should include group problem solving, brainstorming alternative solutions, and using logical reasoning. Examples provided will also vary.

Individual Career Plan

Students' lists of decisions and problems should reflect an awareness of each career area, and its responsibilities. Tell students that eventually they will have to match the decision-making and problem-solving characteristics of a career to their own values and goals.

Possible solutions should be evaluated according to their feasibility and their short-term and long-term consequences. The presentation should identify several practical benefits of the chosen solution.

2. Possible answer: In an episode of the TV show "Home Improvement," Tim decides to walk on the roof of an old house.

a. He wants to impress his new boss.

b. His material is the house itself.

c. He can walk on the roof or choose to stay on the ground.

d. He fails to gather adequate information about the roof's condition.

e. He does not consider the consequences of walking on the roof.

f. He doesn't heed a coworker's warning.

SECTION 1 — *Changing Technology in Everyday Living*

SECTION OBJECTIVES	SECTION FEATURES	SECTION RESOURCES
• Explain how changing technology affects the workplace. • Describe ways workers can become technologically literate.	Personal Career Plan, p. 335 Attitude Counts, p. 338 Career Do's and Don'ts, p. 342 Exploring Careers, p. 343	⊙ Workforce 2000 Videodisc and Videotape 📁 Section 17-1 Review, p. 342 📖 Student Activity Workbook

SECTION 2 — *Computer Software and Its Applications*

SECTION OBJECTIVES	SECTION FEATURES	SECTION RESOURCES
• Discuss the uses of word-processing, database, spreadsheet, and desktop-publishing programs. • Explain business uses of the Internet. • Explain basic copyright law protections.	You're the Boss!, p. 346 Excellent Business Practices, p. 347	⊙ Workforce 2000 Videodisc and Videotape 📁 Section 17-2 Review, p. 350 📁 Chapter 17 Review, pp. 352–353 📖 Student Activity Workbook

CHAPTER 17

CHAPTER RESOURCES

- Chapter Transparencies and Lesson Plans
- Chapter 17 Test
- Spanish Resources, Chapter 17
- School-to-Work Activity Handbook, Chapter 17 Activity
- Teacher's Lesson Plans, Chapter 17
- Implementing Block Scheduling, Chapter 17
- Print, Media, and Internet Handbook
- Strategies for Implementing Work-Based Learning
- Strategies for Implementing Connecting Activities

Career Notes

SCANS CORRELATION CHART

Foundation Skills

Basic Skills	Reading	Writing	Math	Listening	Speaking

Thinking Skills	Creative Thinking	Decision Making	Problem Solving	Seeing Things in the Mind's Eye	Knowing How to Learn	Reasoning

Personal Qualities	Responsibility	Self-Esteem	Sociability	Self-Management	Integrity/Honesty

Workplace Competencies

Resources	Allocating Time	Allocating Money	Allocating Material and Facility Resources	Allocating Human Resources

Information	Acquiring and Evaluating Information	Organizing and Maintaining Information	Interpreting and Communicating Information	Using Computers to Process Information

Interpersonal Skills	Participating as a Member of a Team	Teaching Others	Serving Clients/ Customers	Exercising Leadership	Negotiating to Arrive at a Decision	Working with Cultural Diversity

Systems	Understanding Systems	Monitoring and Correcting Performance	Improving and Designing Systems

Technology	Selecting Technology	Applying Technology to Task	Maintaining and Troubleshooting Technology

Highlighted blocks indicate areas covered in the Chapter.

Additional Activities

 ### Internet Connection

Changing technology has provided alternatives to even how people apply for jobs. Ask students to scan the Internet to find out how to apply for a job on-line. How does the on-line process differ from standard procedures? How successful is the process? Discuss results in class.

 ### Field Trip Suggestions

Arrange a trip to a local company that uses computers in a variety of ways. Ask an employee who is knowledgeable about all the computer systems to give students an idea of how the systems interconnect, and perhaps how they have changed the way this company does business.

 ### Guest Speaker Suggestions

Invite someone skilled in the use of the Internet to explain ways the Internet has changed how businesses and job seekers gather information. The guest may also want to discuss issues of privacy as it relates to the Internet.

Key to Ability Levels

Each section gives skill-building activities. Each activity has been labeled for use with students of various learning styles and abilities.

L1 Level 1 activities are basic activities and should be within the range of all students.

L2 Level 2 activities are average activities and should be within the range of average and above average students.

L3 Level 3 activities are challenging activities designed for the ability range of above average students.

Technology in the Workplace

Chapter Overview

Chapter 17 discusses the effects of technology in the workplace and describes the skills needed for technological literacy.

Section 17-1 describes personal computers and how their use is changing the way people work.

Section 17-2 focuses on various types of software and the use of the Internet as a business tool.

Background Information

Write chapter objectives (Sections 17-1 and 17-2) on the chalkboard or use the chapter objective transparency for class discussion.

Choose assignments from the *Student Activity Workbook* and write them on the chalkboard.

Have students preview the chapter, looking at pictures, reading captions, and noting content headings. Ask students to describe what they expect to learn in this chapter.

Preteaching Vocabulary

Write the Key Terms from Sections 17-1 and 17-2 on the chalkboard. Have students describe how each term relates to computer technology and technological skills needed in the workplace.

334

Gifted

Gifted students may find that the material in the the text gives them their first look into the real world of work. Encourage students to take on a wide variety of enrichment and independant practice activities that put them in contact with people in the business world and allow them to observe the daily practices that lead to success. Be sure they have the opportunity to present written summaries of their findings. Explore with them them what they have observed.

Chapter 17

Technology in the Workplace

Section 17-1
Changing Technology in Everyday Living

Section 17-2
Computer Software and Its Applications

In this video segment, learn how to use thinking skills to make decisions and solve workplace problems.

Journal
Personal Career Plan

Talk with an older adult about how computers and their uses have changed during that person's lifetime. Then think about further changes that may occur during your lifetime. Write a journal entry discussing your findings and ideas.

335

School-to-Work Connecting Activities

Have students research a form of technology related to their career interests. (For example, a student interested in meteorology might research how computers are used in forecasting weather; a future accountant might research accounting software and the technological skills one needs to use it.) When students complete their research, have them write an entry for their career journals describing the career area, how technology is used in that career, and the skills they will need to learn to use technology in the career.

Work-Based Learning Strategies and Activities

Arrange to have students visit a local employer that uses computers either as a part of its manufacturing process or for handling administrative or accounting tasks. Preferably, find a business that uses computers in several different ways. Have students observe each department. Then have them return to class and share their observations.

WORKFORCE 2000 Training Video

Have students view the video and perform the interactive exercises to reinforce important chapter concepts and thinking processes.

Chapter 17

Addressing **LEARNING** Styles

Kinesthetic Learner

Have students demonstrate physical skills they possess that will aid them in their chosen careers. (For example, a data entry job calls for quick computer/keyboard skills. A future paramedic may demonstrate bandaging skills learned in a first-aid class.) Have each student explain the skill as he or she is demonstrating it, explain why it is important to his or her future career, and tell the class how it was acquired. Involve as many students as possible.

FOCUS

Bell Ringer

Have students list things they've done today that are affected by technology. (For example, if they drove to school, their cars make use of microcomputer chips; or perhaps they stopped to get cash at an ATM.)

Introducing the Section

Have students share their lists from the Bell Ringer activity. Then discuss how manufacturing jobs are increasingly being replaced by technology-based service jobs. Future workers will need technology skills to be successful in finding jobs that pay well and offer opportunities for advancement.

Emphasize that the economy also has changed because of globalization. Technology allows even small businesses to sell their products or services world-wide.

Motivational Activity
Demonstration

Have students choose a computer software program they want to know more about. Then ask your computer lab director or a lab assistant to demonstrate this software and describe some of the ways a business might use that type of program.

Changing Technology in Everyday Living

OBJECTIVES

After studying this section, you will be able to:

- Explain how changing technology affects the workplace.
- Describe ways workers can become technologically literate.

KEY TERMS

globalization
teleconferencing
laptop

Can you imagine a world not linked by telephone lines and satellite communications? Can you picture schools without computers or business offices without fax machines? You probably can't. Computer technology has become a part of everyday life.

People use a computer when they get money from an automated teller machine (ATM). At the supermarket and the department store, bar codes on purchases are computer-scanned. At school, you may use computers for doing research or writing and revising paragraphs. You can count on the fact that no matter where you choose to work, you will use some type of computer technology in your job.

Technological Change and the Workplace

Technological change isn't new. Technology has been advancing for thousands of years, from simple stone tools to the waterwheel, to the printing press, and to the automobile. The difference today is in the pace of change. Technology seems to be advancing at ever greater speed.

In just a couple of decades, businesses, large and small, have come to depend on computers and fax machines. Today more and more companies are using devices such as cellular phones, voice mail, electronic schedules, and document scanners. Many experts

336   *Unit 5 • Professional Development*

Addressing Workplace Diversity

Businesses that use self-directed teams to manage projects find that team members derive a sense of community that crosses cultural, gender, and physical differences. Working in teams often results in new after-work friendships.

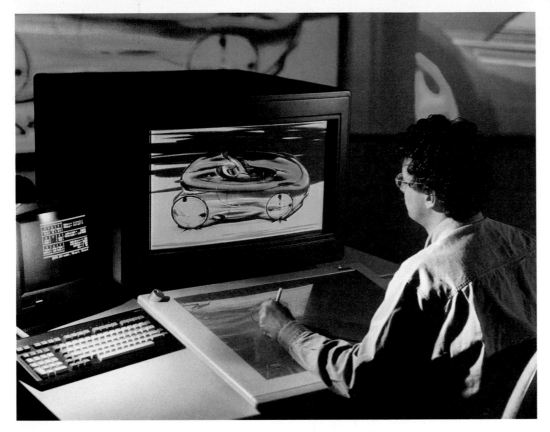

 Computers are used extensively in engineering. **How might computer simulations be used in designing new automobiles or aircraft?**

expect this trend toward greater use of technology to continue into the foreseeable future. How will this trend affect the workplace—and you?

A High-Tech Global Village

One effect of changing technology is the globalization of the workplace. **Globalization** refers to the establishment of worldwide communication links between people and groups. These links are made possible through modern technology.

Globalization is at work when a business owner in Chicago, Illinois, instantly communicates an investment decision to her partner in Sydney, Australia.

Globalization is at work when the two individuals meet through teleconferencing to discuss that decision. **Teleconferencing** involves simultaneous discussion among people in different locations, using electronic means. Teleconferencing is faster and less expensive than setting up a face-to-face meeting.

 Extending the Illustration

Have students visit your local science museum and find out how computers are used in simulations for museum exhibits.

Caption Answer: Designers might construct prototypes on screen and run them through various types of simulated tests, saving time and money.

Guided Practice
Teaching Strategies

1. Assign and review Section 17-1.
2. Use the transparency for this section.
3. Assign and review the Case Study.

Discussion Starter

Ask students if they would like to be able to talk with three or four friends on the telephone at the same time—and also be able to see them. How could they do this? (with a teleconference)

Teaching Tip

Invite a local business person who has teleconferencing facilities to speak to your class, or ask if your class can visit the business and observe a part of a teleconference in action. When back in class, discuss how businesses might use teleconferencing to save money and to communicate better with its customers and/or suppliers.

Critical Thinking

Have students research the use of debit and credit cards, explaining the difference between them, and the advantages or disadvantages each offers both to the store accepting them and to the customer using them. Have students write 150-word summaries. Discuss in class how technology makes the use of these cards possible.

SCANS Foundation Skills Connection

L1 **Reading**

Have students search several news magazines *(Time, Newsweek, U.S. News & World Report)* or business magazines *(Forbes, Fortune, Business Week)* for articles about companies that are adapting to competition in a world market. Ask students if they think globalization of business will mean more opportunities for them. Why?

L2 **Reasoning**

Explain that more companies are instituting policies such as flex time and telecommuting to allow employees to lead balanced lives. Discuss what flex time might mean for students. How does flex time affect the company? Encourage students to see both pros and cons.

L3 **Writing**

Many businesses announce the hiring of a new person through an inter-office memo, which welcomes the new hire and outlines the skills and qualifications the individual brings to the job. Ask each student to write a memo introducing himself or herself. Suggest that they highlight their technical skills in the memo.

Attitude Counts ✓

Do you find that some tasks make you feel uncertain or even nervous? Those aren't the jobs to avoid—they're the ones to tackle right away. Putting a difficult task off will only make you feel less confident. So, get that difficult job out of the way. You'll boost your confidence and make time for the tasks you find more enjoyable.

Through technology, the world becomes smaller—a global village. In the workplace, globalization means that you will have contact with people who are living in other cultures. You will need to know and understand what happens in other parts of the world. Those events may directly affect you and your workplace.

New Ways to Work

Technology has also brought about other types of changes in the workplace. Some examples follow.

 Business travelers often use laptop computers to make the most of their travel time. *How else might laptops be used in today's workplace?*

Extending the Illustration

Have students visit a local computer store or view the ads in a computer magazine such as *PC World, MACWorld,* or *PC Magazine.* Have them find out differences between laptop computers and desktop computers.

Caption Answer: Possible answers are that they might be used by employees working at home on some days, taken home over the weekend so workers could catch up, or taken to a presentation or business conference.

- *Businesses are moving toward a "distributed" workforce.* In other words, employees no longer work just at a company's place of business. Instead, they are distributed, or spread about, in many places. Many employees, for example, work at home.

  Chapter 1 introduced you to the concept of telecommuting. Thanks to personal computers, an employee can be on the job without leaving home. The New York-based research firm Link Resources, Inc., predicts that as many as 13 million people will soon be telecommuting.

  Another device that is distributing the workforce is the laptop computer. **Laptop** computers are small, portable computers with a screen and a keyboard. They make working outside the office easier. Many businesspeople travel. By taking their laptop computer along, their office goes with them.

- *Companies will need more "knowledge workers."* In the next decade, an emerging group of workers will be "knowledge workers." These workers will not produce products but will manage information. They will be responsible for finding, organizing, and delivering data. Today's medical technologists and computer installers are knowledge workers.

 Laboratory technicians are knowledge workers. *What SCANS skills and competencies would be especially valuable for someone who wants to be a lab technician?*

What about tomorrow's knowledge workers? Consider a job in which a person navigates through the Internet, locates and packages valuable information, and delivers it to subscribers. This position, called "Internet surfer," has been predicted as one of the "hot" jobs of the 21st century.

Chapter 17 • Technology in the Workplace **339**

Independent Practice

 Assign as homework the chapter activity in the *School-to-Work Activity Handbook.*

Reading

Have students read the help-wanted ads in your local newspaper to determine how many of them specify knowledge of computers or a specific software program. Have students share their findings.

Writing: *Preparation for Oral Presentation*

Have students make five-minute presentations to a PTA group describing the use of technology in your school and the skills students are learning. If you have access to a presentation program, have students use it to create electronic presentations. (Examples of presentation programs include *Powerpoint, Harvard Graphics,* and *Persuasion.*)

Discussion Starter

Ask students what skills they will need to use computers in their future careers.

Teaching Tip

Take students to a local bank and have an official there explain how computers are used. Have the official describe the technological skills its employees are expected to have and how they use these skills on the job.

Technological Literacy

How can you prepare for the technological workplace? First, you need to be comfortable with computer technology. Important SCANS skills to master include the following:

- using computers to process information,
- selecting technology,
- applying technology to task, and
- maintaining and troubleshooting technology.

 Figure 17-1

Skills for a Technological Workplace

Changes in technology often require new workplace skills. The following skills will be especially valuable in the workplace of the future.

A All workers, but especially managers, will need specialized communication skills. Communicating by electronic means does not provide the same type of feedback that is available in face-to-face meetings. New skills will be needed to make communication effective.

Extending Figure 17-1

Have students brainstorm the number of jobs that use computers today. For example, many police officers have computers in their cars. Grocery stores use computers to scan bar codes at checkout stations. What other examples can students supply? (Others might include shipping services that track parcels by computer, doctors who use computers in medical diagnoses.)

All of these skills are a part of *technological literacy*, which is knowing about and being able to use technology effectively. What else will you need in a high-tech workplace? *Figure 17-1* gives a few suggestions.

Tech for Success

Technological literacy is basic to workplace success. Fortunately, you probably already know quite a lot about computers. Continue to build your skills, however. At your job, don't just learn enough of a

B Because electronic communication is so rapid, people may need to respond more swiftly to decisions and events. The SCANS skills of reasoning and creative thinking will be increasingly important.

C The 21st century workplace may require new decision-making skills as well. The good news is that more people will be able to participate in decision making through such devices as electronic bulletin boards and E-mail. Decision makers, however, will need to discover ways to control the process and make it work smoothly.

Chapter 17 • Technology in the Workplace **341**

Workforce 2000 Trends

Technology not only changes jobs, it can eliminate them by changing the way that work is done. Mazda Motors' accounts payable system, for example, took only five people using computers to do what it took Ford Motor Co. 400 people to do using old filing systems.

SECTION 17-1

Discussion Starter

Poll students to see how many of them believe they are technologically literate.

Teaching Tip

Use the poll from the Discussion Starter to discuss what it means to be technologically literate. For example, how many of your students can use word processing, spreadsheet, and database programs, or have surfed the Internet? Also discuss the speed of technological change and the need for continuous learning.

Research

Have each student find and read an article about telecommuting and/or home-based businesses that rely on the computer. Discuss how people who work in careers which students are thinking about might be affected by telecommuting or home-based businesses.

Skills Practice

Darron wants to use his family's home computer to surf the Internet, but his parents object to his tying up their only telephone line. Darron has found that he can have a second line installed for $81, with a monthly charge of $14.95. An Internet service provider will charge $19.95 a month for the connection. How much would Darron spend in a year? ($499.80: $14.95 + $19.95 = $34.90 × 12 = $418.80 + $81)

Teaching Tip

Ask students to think about different types of technology; for example, ask what types of technology are used at an ATM. Write responses on the chalkboard. (In addition to checking a user's account to see if money is available and counting out the amount requested, other types of technology are used: cameras to record images, 911 buttons for emergencies, etc.)

Research

Have students research job opportunities in the technology industry, creating charts that show types of jobs and estimated percentage of growth for each over the next several years.

Assessment

Oral

Working in groups of four or five, have each group choose a career that uses computer technology and prepare a presentation describing how technology is used in this career, the impact of globalization, where people work in this career, the type of equipment used, and the computer literacy skills required.

Evaluate presentations on content as well as inclusion of work from all team members.

---

program to get by. Read books or take courses. Ask questions to learn more about equipment you are using. Keep up-to-date with the latest workplace technology. The more you know, the more valuable you will be to your company.

Marissa Kovak, an office manager for a construction company, was asked to provide monthly project status reports in memo form. She took the assignment a step further and learned how to link her memos to detailed budget tables kept for all projects. Her method saved a time-consuming updating step. When Marissa showed her discovery to her boss, he was grateful enough to offer Marissa a bonus—and eventually a promotion.

New Skills for a New Workplace

What's the bottom line? Stay alert, be flexible, and sharpen your information-handling skills. Workers who can locate information quickly and present it in a clear and logical way will be valuable in tomorrow's workforce.

Career Do's & Don'ts

When Using Technology...

Do:

- stay current with the latest technological equipment in your workplace.
- ask for training and help when needed.
- constantly improve your technology skills.
- share your knowledge.

Don't:

- be resistant to learning new technology skills.
- try to learn everything by yourself.
- make changes without appropriate approvals.
- try to fix equipment with which you are not familiar.

SECTION 17-1 *Review*

Understanding Key Concepts

Using complete sentences, answer the following questions on a separate sheet of paper.

1. How could globalization create a more diverse workplace?

2. What can you do now while in school to increase your technological literacy?

SECTION 17-1 *Review* ANSWERS

1. Because businesses are making connections all over the world, workers have contact with people from many cultures. This makes the workplace more diverse.

2. Possible answers: take courses in school or outside school, read magazines and books, practice on school or home computers

CASE STUDY

Exploring Careers: Business and Office

**Karlene Westerlund
Certified Insurance Claims
Assistant**

Q: How did you become a claims assistant?

A: I did a lot of career exploration at the community college and found I liked office work. I took office administration at the college which gave me the basics of working on the computer and an overview of all other office skills. The last six months, I worked in a cooperative work experience program with a large insurance company. That was the best hands-on experience.

Q: Why did you stay with the insurance company?

A: I had a friend there who had moved up quickly. It's such a large corporation, so it has many different departments: legal, claims, and medical. It seemed like the company had a lot to offer.

I was also attracted by the ongoing education programs. Some people don't think of training as a benefit. However, education is so expensive that if you have to take money out of your own pocket to pay for skills required to advance in your job, it could be hard.

Q: What would you tell people who are just entering the workforce?

A: When I went for my interview, my attitude was that the company needed me. I let the interviewer know that by the way I responded to questions. Treat yourself as the best product on the market.

Thinking Critically

Why is the ability to work with people necessary for an insurance claims assistant?

CAREER FACTS

Nature of the Work:
Provide support for insurance claims adjusters; make phone calls and appointments for clients and adjusters; write letters; work with attorneys.

Training or Education Needed:
Strong office experience or training in office administration; may require state certification.

Aptitudes, Abilities, and Skills:
Math, listening, speaking, and interpersonal skills; reading and writing skills.

Salary Range:
Average salary—$1,600 to $2,200 a month.

Career Path:
Work in other offices; train on the job; move into other insurance specialties.

Chapter 17 • Technology in the Workplace **343**

Extending the CASE STUDY

Answer: People making insurance claims have suffered a loss—of time, money, or the ability to work. They want claims settled quickly and in their favor. The process may be slow, and the outcome may not be completely favorable. Those with worker's compensation claims may be in pain, out of work, and losing income. They may see the insurance company as an adversary, not a helper.

Further Application: Have students discuss ways they can present themselves in interviews as the "best product on the market." (For example, they can dress properly; stress their skills, their experience, and their education; and use proper English.)

Evaluation
Assign the section review.

Reteaching
Have students who use computers on the job discuss the following with the class:
- How do they use computers?
- How does the computer make their job easier/more difficult?
- How easy or difficult was it to learn to use the computer?
- What type of training was provided?
- What courses should they have taken to improve their skills?

Extending the Content
Assign the appropriate Chapter 17 activities in the *Student Activity Workbook*.

Have students research the impact of globalization on businesses in your area by contacting the Chamber of Commerce or other local business organizations. Have students ask about companies that export goods or import parts from another country; they should share their information in class.

CLOSE
Have students complete this sentence: "The technological skills I will need for my future career are . . . ."

FOCUS

Bell Ringer

Ask students to list the different types of software programs they have used or have read about.

Introducing the Section

Have students share their lists from the Bell Ringer activity. Write their responses on the chalkboard. Then discuss the function of software (basically, a set of instructions telling the computer what to do).

As use of computers has spread, the number of software programs has grown tremendously. Nonetheless, the basic programs remain word-processing, spreadsheet, and database activities. Knowledge of these three types of programs must be a part of students' technological skills.

Motivational Activity
Critical Thinking

Have students skim through ads in current issues of several computer magazines, listing the different types of software described. Then have them brainstorm jobs where each type of software might be used. (For example, graphics or illustration software might be used by a magazine's art director.)

Computer Software and Its Applications

OBJECTIVES

After studying this section, you will be able to:

- **Discuss the uses of word-processing, database, spreadsheet, and desktop-publishing programs.**
- **Explain business uses of the Internet.**
- **Explain basic copyright law protections.**

KEY TERMS

word processing
database
spreadsheet
desktop publishing
copyright

Computers sometimes seem to have minds of their own, especially when errors crop up or viruses creep in. *Viruses* are programs that can damage computer files and even hard drives. Basically, however, computers do what they are instructed to do by their software. Selecting technology such as the most appropriate software and applying it to your task are valuable SCANS skills.

Using Computer Software

There are many different types of business software. Some of the simplest programs allow workers to produce text documents efficiently. More complex software, on the other hand, may permit architects to plan "virtual buildings" that can be navigated electronically. The types of software used most commonly in business include word-processing programs, databases, spreadsheets, and desktop publishing.

Word Processing

Using any software program that creates text-based documents is called **word processing**. Word processing allows you to create, edit, and format text. The difference between word processing and typing is that word processing allows you to add, move, and delete material (from letters to whole paragraphs or series of pages) with a couple of keyboard strokes. Most word-processing programs also include additional aids that check spelling and provide definitions and synonyms for words.

344 *Unit 5 • Professional Development*

Implementing Teamwork

Organize students into five groups. Have each group choose a course at their school that could be taught through the Internet. Each group should write a course description that explains how the Internet will be used and name/rename the course to showcase the technology involved.

Spreadsheets are useful for accounting, budgeting, and scheduling. Each box on the spreadsheet is called a cell. Changing a number in one cell automatically causes adjustments in all the other cells. *How might this be used for making up or changing a schedule?*

Database Programs

Organizing business records is made easy with database programs. In a **database**, information is stored in a number of different formats, or tables. The program allows you to search through, sort, and recombine the stored data. A retail store owner, for example, may use a database program to record day-to-day inventory and sales information. Data can be recombined, however, to produce a sales report. Data might also be sorted to show fastest- or slowest-selling items.

Spreadsheet Programs

Data can be viewed and manipulated with a **spreadsheet**. This is a computer program that arranges or "spreads" data, usually numbers, into rows and columns. Spreadsheet programs also perform calculations. Businesspeople can try various calculations to see what would happen if different business decisions were made. These calculations help them make decisions. Spreadsheets are popular for such tasks as keeping accounts payable records and projecting sales and expenses.

Chapter 17 • Technology in the Workplace **345**

Extending the Illustration

Obtain a spreadsheet program and demonstrate its use to students.

Caption Answer: If the start date of a project is delayed one week, all the other dates on the spreadsheet will be changed accordingly.

Guided Practice

Teaching Strategies

1. Assign and review Section 17-3.
2. Use the transparency for this section.

Discussion Starter

Ask how many students have ordered clothing from a mail-order catalog (for example, LL Bean or Land's End).

Teaching Tip

Explain to students that mail-order companies put their merchandise in a computerized database. Each order-taker works at a computer terminal and has instant access to product information. Ask students what information might be included in a database for a mail-order clothing company. (Product stock numbers, colors, sizes, availability, shipping and weight.)

Interview

Have each student interview a person who uses a computer on the job. Tell students to ask questions about how much time the person spends at the computer, the job tasks completed with a computer, and how he or she learned computer skills. Have students share their findings in class.

SCANS Foundation Skills Connection

L1 Integrity/Honesty

Lead a class discussion about software piracy. Ask questions such as these: How does copying a friend's software hurt the software company? Is it different from copying pages from a book in the library? Have your school's network administrator explain the policy for using software.

L2 Creative Thinking

Tell students to imagine they have a chance to design personal home pages on the Internet. What would their topics be? What information would they include? Would it be humorous or serious? Have students draft ideas and share them with classmates. If possible, have students view a few home pages before they begin this activity.

L3 Writing

Desktop publishing has made it possible for thousands of business owners to produce newsletters advertising their businesses. Divide students into two groups. Have each group select a business (or a hobby or school activity) and write a two-page newsletter for the school. Since the goal is to attract interest, they should make the writing interesting and use an attractive page layout.

346

Desktop Publishing

Many people now have their own publishing facilities—on their desks. This is the origin of the term *desktop publishing*. **Desktop publishing** involves using computers and special software to create documents that look as if they were printed by professional printers. You can produce just about anything this way, including reports, brochures, newsletters, invitations, greeting cards, and calendars. Desktop-publishing methods save businesses and individuals both time and money. They also provide greater control over the printed product.

Maintenance and Troubleshooting

Have you ever heard of Murphy's Law? Basically, it says that if something can go wrong, it will go wrong.

Here's a positive twist to Murphy's Law: If you are prepared for something to go wrong, you may be able to prevent it.

Fortunately, you won't have to be a technical wizard to help prevent software problems. The following

Desktop publishing is especially useful for people who are in business for themselves. **Why do you think this is true?**

▶ Extending the Illustration

Have students visit a local office supply store and view the products designed for use with desktop publishing programs. (Products include envelopes and stationery designs on which a business can print its letterhead or address.)

Caption Answer: Business owners can customize brochures or flyers while saving both time and money.

Teaching YOU'RE THE BOSS!

✓ Possible responses: Instruct clerks to write each sale down on a tablet, using calculators to figure totals and sales tax. Help the clerks and/or talk with the customers; be sure someone is working on getting the computer system back in order.

tips will help you maintain and troubleshoot software at work.

- Attend training sessions and workshops whenever possible.
- Read operating manuals. Use your SCANS reading skills to improve your ability to understand technical material.
- Use the program's "Help" feature.
- Pay attention to what the machine is telling you. Copiers and fax machines, for example, often have a display that flashes a numerical code to indicate a specific problem.
- Know whom to call for help. Most commercial software programs have 800 or 888 help lines.
- Save your work frequently. Use the computer's autosave features, but don't rely on them. Save every half hour or so. At the end of the day, make disk copies and keep hard copy if you need to do so.

The Internet

You can hardly turn on the television set or look through a magazine today without encountering a reference to the Internet. The Internet, which millions of people navigate, is a vast network of computer

SCANS Workplace Competencies Connection

L1 Using Computers to Process Information

Have students explore the Internet, either at home, school, or the public library. Instruct them to use the Search feature to find information about a local college or university (admissions policy, fees, registration, and classes). Encourage students to follow the hypertext links they may find at a particular Web site.

L2 Selecting Technology

Have students imagine an "ideal" setup where they could study, pursue an extracurricular interest, or play computer games. Have them list the equipment and technology they need to do the tasks related to each activity.

L3 Interpreting and Communicating Information

Ask each student to give a three- to five-minute oral presentation that outlines the features of his or her favorite computer software (including games). Tell students to prepare either a handout that demonstrates the software's capability or present information on an overhead transparency. If you have computers in your classroom, students might give a brief demonstration of the chosen software.

EXCELLENT BUSINESS PRACTICES

Preparing Students for Working with Technology

Intel Corporation, a semiconductor manufacturer, has responded to the need to help prepare students for the workplace. The company has created partnerships with schools and colleges to enhance their math, science, and technology programs.

Intel has developed a curriculum and donated millions of dollars to educational institutions in New Mexico and Arizona, where it has large manufacturing plants. The company encourages schools to teach students about skills needed in the business environment, such as technology. Instructors of community colleges are invited to Intel for the summer and paid salaries. There they gain valuable experience for themselves and bring the practical applications back to the classroom.

Intel also supports the future technology workforce by establishing a variety of work-study programs, by offering scholarships, and by donating equipment. The more education and training employees bring into the company, the less on-the-job training the company needs to provide.

Thinking Critically

Why is it important for companies, like Intel, to create technology partnerships with schools?

Extending EXCELLENT BUSINESS PRACTICES

Answer: These partnerships teach students about skills needed in business. Companies like Intel benefit by identifying potential employees who are aware of current technology.

Further Application: Ask students to write to computer hardware and software manufacturers, asking about policies the companies have with regard to providing products or training to schools. If your school is eligible, initiate the process of forming a partnership with a company.

TEACH *(cont'd.)*

Independent Practice

Reading

Have each student find and read an article on a new technology that is being developed. Have students share their findings in class.

Skills Practice

Latiya has found that she can purchase one computer model for $1,499, including all the software she needs. Another model costs only $999, but she will need to buy two software packages costing $249 and $289. Which is the better deal? ($1,499; the other totals $1,537)

Taylor is buying a software program priced at $149 with 40 percent off, a new printer priced at $389 with a 30 percent discount, and speakers priced at $199 with a 25 percent discount. How much will these items cost? ($510.95: $149 − (0.40 × $149) = $89.40; $389 − (0.30 × $389) = $272.30; $199 − (0.25 × $199) = $149.25; $89.40 + $272.30 + $149.25)

Writing: *Journal*

Have students use a word processing program to write an assessment of their current technological skills, an analysis of the skills needed, and a plan for acquiring needed skills. Have them include this assessment in their career journals.

Internet Terminology

Term	Definition
Browser	A program you can use to visit sites on the Internet
Download	Transfer a file from an Internet site to your computer's hard drive
E-mail	A message composed on one computer to be received by another computer
FAQ	Abbreviation for frequently asked questions; a document that displays answers to common questions about particular sites on the internet
Freeware	Software provided by its creator at no charge
Home page	The name for the screen you see when you go to a site on the World Wide Web; also refers to the site itself
Hyperlink	A highlighted word, phrase, or image in a Web document; by clicking on it you can jump to a document about that subject
Log in, log on	Terms used to describe the process of connecting with a remote computer
Net	Nickname for the Internet
Search engine	Software that finds and retrieves data on the Internet
Shareware	Software you may download free to test; if you decide to use it, you should send the requested payment to the creator
Site	A location on the Internet
URL	Abbreviation for uniform resource locator; an Internet address
Web browser	See **browser**
Web site	See **site**

 **Figure 17-2** This Internet terminology is important for a "newbie" (newcomer) to know. Why would it be a good idea to look over FAQ files before you visit a site?

networks. In plain language, however, the Internet is people, their computers, the connections between them, and the software used to run the computers.

Figure 17-2 provides a list of Internet terms and their definitions. Look through the list. How many terms do you already know?

348 *Unit 5 • Professional Development*

► **Extending Figure 17-2** ◄

If your school has access to the Internet, arrange to demonstrate it to your students.

Caption Answer: Many of the questions you are likely to have will be answered there, and you will not need to waste any time finding answers.

Uses of the Internet

Through the Internet, you can communicate with people all over the world. You also have access to vast amounts of information, including text, graphics, sound, and video. Businesses use the Internet in a variety of ways, some of which are indicated here:

- for low-cost, speedy communication and as an alternative to faxing for long documents;
- to advertise and sell products;
- to provide consumer information and assistance;
- to find information; and
- to advertise job openings and locate potential applicants.

Netiquette

Netiquette is a term referring to accepted rules of conduct when using the Internet. When you use the Internet at work, you need to be especially careful to use good manners. The following list gives a summary of netiquette principles.

- When sending a message, always include a clear subject line to help readers identify your subject.
- When responding, state to what you are responding. Never just say yes or no.
- Don't type in all caps.
- Don't ramble. Internet users appreciate specific, focused communications.
- Use a definite closing. Sign your name or write "the end."
- Don't publish other people's messages without their permission.
- Avoid personal or sensitive issues. Never use obscenity or make racial or ethnic slurs.
- Use *emoticons*, groups of keyboard symbols designed to show the writer's feelings. See *Figure 17-3* for examples.

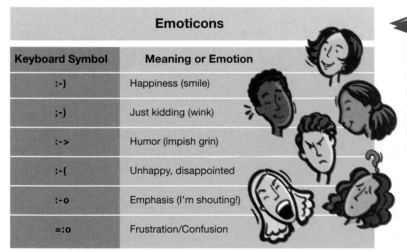

Emoticons

Keyboard Symbol	Meaning or Emotion
:-)	Happiness (smile)
;-)	Just kidding (wink)
:->	Humor (impish grin)
:-(	Unhappy, disappointed
:-o	Emphasis (I'm shouting!)
=:o	Frustration/Confusion

Figure 17-3

Emoticons are also called smileys. When turned sideways, they look like a face displaying an emotion. Why do you think they are used on the Internet?

Discussion Starter

Ask students to share what they know about the Internet. How does it work? Who uses it, and why?

Teaching Tip

If your school does not have access to the Internet, arrange for a demonstration from a local business or organization that does. During the demonstration, discuss how students might use the Internet to research companies, colleges, and career opportunities.

Research

Have students research a key figure in computer technology, such as Bill Gates or Steve Jobs. Tell them to write 200-word papers describing the person's background and his or her contribution to the development of computer technology. Have students discuss their research in class.

Critical Thinking

Knowing how to learn is an important SCANS skill. The Internet is a resource that offers a great deal of information. Discuss with students the content of the Internet. For example, people are free to put anything they want on the Internet. Then ask students how they know whether the information they find on the Internet is accurate. (One way to verify accuracy is to check information through other means, such as books and magazines.)

►► Extending Figure 17-3 ◄◄

Have students visit an on-line chat group on the Internet to observe the use of emoticons.

Caption Answer: Because communication is not face-to-face, it may be hard to know what feeling the writer is trying to convey.

349

ASSESS

Assessment

Performance

Divide students into five groups. Assign each group one of the following: *word processing, spreadsheet, database, desktop publishing, the Internet.* Have each group prepare a poster, flip chart, or transparency describing the purpose of the software, some common features, and the types of documents created by using the software. Then have groups present their information.

Evaluate students' presentation for accuracy.

Evaluation

Assign the section review.

MINI QUIZ

Short Answer

1. Technology has made it possible for people in different locations to have a discussion. This is called ____. (teleconferencing)

2. People who manage information are called ____. (knowledge workers)

3. Being able to use technology effectively is called ____ literacy. (technological)

4. Rules of conduct that guide the use of the Internet are called ____. (netiquette)

5. A smiling face is used on the Internet to show feelings and is called a/an ____. (emoticon)

Legal and Ethical Technology Issues

In earlier chapters, you learned about ethical issues such as honesty and confidentiality. In business, one form of honesty involves giving credit to others when you make use of something they have created. This applies whether you are using an article from a magazine or a file you've downloaded from the Internet. Newer forms of technology don't change basic ethics.

Copyright law has been developed to help people protect what they create. **Copyright** is the legal right of authors or other creators of works to control the reproduction and use of their works. Permission is usually required to use copyrighted material. Works covered by copyright law include the following types:

- literary and dramatic works, such as poetry;
- computer software and databases;
- photographs, videos, and film;
- musical and artistic works; and
- recordings.

Copyright protection means that the copyright owner has the sole right to do the following, or to authorize others to do so:

- make copies,
- distribute copies for sale or lease,
- perform (play) or display (movie, photo), and
- prepare translations or adaptations.

Copyright law protects all written works, whether or not they have been formally published. A file from the Internet and even information you've created on your computer is protected. It is ethical to give credit to the source of any facts you use.

Get to know enough about copyright laws to protect yourself. There are many books and courses available on copyright protection. If you are not sure whether or not you need to ask permission, always do so—just to be safe.

SECTION 17-2 *Review*

Understanding Key Concepts

Using complete sentences, answer the following questions on a separate sheet of paper.

1. Why do you think word processing has replaced typewriting in the workplace?

2. What do you think is one of the most important uses of the Internet for businesses? Explain your answer.

3. Why do you think having copyright laws is important?

SECTION 17-2 *Review* ANSWERS

1. Word processing allows text to be created and changed much more easily; instead of retyping a page or a document, for example, a single error can be corrected and a new copy printed out.

2. Students may mention locating up-to-date information or transmitting information quickly and relatively inexpensively.

3. Copyright laws allow people who create materials to get credit for and profit from their creations.

SECTION 17-1 Summary

- Changes in every aspect of life have resulted from computer technology. Businesses are likely to continue to increase their use of technology.

- New technology has helped bring about globalization, or worldwide communication links. Teleconferencing is one example of globalization.

- Computers and telecommuting technology are making today's workforce more distributed (rather than centralized). Knowledge workers, who find and process information, are becoming increasingly important.

- Technological literacy involves knowing about and being able to use technology effectively.

- Workers should learn as much as they can about the technology they are using. Technology requires new communication and decision-making skills as well as quicker response times.

Key Terms

globalization *(p. 337)*
teleconferencing *(p. 337)*
laptop *(p. 339)*

SECTION 17-2 Summary

- There are many different types of business software. Word processing is used for creating, editing, and formatting documents.

- Database programs store data and allow workers to sort and combine them in various forms.

- Spreadsheet programs allow data to be viewed and manipulated in a table format.

- Desktop publishing, which is the use of computers and special software for creating professional-looking documents, saves businesses and individuals time and money.

- Ways to prevent software problems include attending training sessions and workshops, reading operating manuals, and saving work frequently.

- The Internet is a network of computer networks. For business, it offers low-cost, speedy communication and access to information.

Key Terms

word processing *(p. 344)*
database *(p. 345)*
spreadsheet *(p. 345)*
desktop publishing *(p. 346)*
copyright *(p. 350)*

Chapter 17 • Technology in the Workplace **351**

SECTION 17-2

Use the Testmaker to create a customized test for Chapter 17.

Reteaching

1. Arrange for the class to meet in the computer lab, and demonstrate each of the four major types of software described in this section. As you (or a lab assistant) demonstrate each program, describe examples of how it is used in the workplace. Complete the lesson by having students produce short documents using each type of software program.

2. Assign and review vocabulary terms, chapter questions, and activities from the Chapter Review.

Extending the Content

Assign the appropriate Chapter 17 activities in the *Student Activity Workbook.*

Have students use a word processing program and create a dictionary of computer terms. Students can find terms by reviewing current issues of computer magazines. Some magazines, such as *PC Novice*, publish glossaries of computer terms and definitions.

CLOSE

Have students complete this sentence: "I am interested in computer technology because . . . ."

Computer Activity

Using a database software program, have students gather data about different brands of computer/office equipment. Have students look for information about these products: computers, scanners, printer, modems, and fax machines. Create a database of information on the brands, pricing, and features for each piece of equipment. Have students sort the database by subject, alphabetically. Ask them to present a complete consumer report on their findings.

CHAPTER 17 *REVIEW*

Answers
Reviewing Key Terms

Dialogues will vary but should show an understanding of the terms listed.

Recalling Key Concepts

1. False: Teleconferencing is a good example of globalization.
2. True
3. False: Word-processing programs are designed to create, edit, and format text.
4. False: Businesses use the Internet in many ways—for example, for speedy communication and to seek information.
5. True

Thinking Critically

1. Many businesses need computer-trained employees and may give preference to an applicant who is computer literate.
2. No. Students should point out that technology sometimes malfunctions, making jobs more difficult, and that people may use technology to physically isolate themselves from others.
3. One advantage might be greater convenience for the individual worker; one disadvantage might be inadequate communication when the workforce is decentralized.
4. Possible answers: Internet users could save

Reviewing Key Terms

On a separate sheet of paper, write a dialogue between two friends talking about technology in the workplace. Use the terms below.

globalization
teleconferencing
laptop
word processing
database

spreadsheet
desktop
  publishing
copyright

Recalling Key Concepts

On a separate sheet of paper, tell whether each item below is true or false. Rewrite any false statements to make them true.

1. Teleconferencing is not an example of globalization.
2. Technological literacy involves knowing about and using technology effectively.
3. Spreadsheet programs are designed to create, edit, and format text.
4. The Internet has very few business uses.
5. Permission is usually required to use copyrighted material.

Thinking Critically

Using complete sentences, answer each of the questions below on a separate sheet of paper.

1. Why would it be wise for you to learn computer skills before entering the workforce?
2. Does technology always make life easier and draw people together? Explain your answer.

---

3. What might be one advantage and one disadvantage of a distributed workforce?
4. Discuss at least two ways that using the Internet to locate information could save time and money.

SCANS Foundation Skills and Workplace Competencies

Personal Qualities: *Integrity/Honesty*

1. A friend and coworker in your office is preparing to use her desktop-publishing capabilities to publish and distribute an essay about environmental hazards in industry. She plans to state that the work is her own. You know, however, that the essay appeared recently in a magazine. What should you say to your friend about copyright violation? Write a paragraph explaining and justifying your advice.

Technology: *Selecting Technology*

2. Purchasing a computer can be challenging. How do you know you are buying the right model? How do you decide which features you want and need? How do you know if the price is fair? What resources would you use to answer these questions?

Connecting Academics to the Workplace

Computer Science

1. Charles has just begun working for a public relations company that does a lot of desktop publishing.

---

time by not having to go to the library, and could avoid the cost of subscribing to periodicals.

SCANS Foundation Skills and Workplace Competencies

1. Students should point out that copyright law requires the friend to ask permission to use the essay. Students should say

they would make this clear, both to help keep the friend out of legal trouble and to protect the author's rights.

2. Students should list actions such as consulting consumer periodicals (perhaps on the Internet) about brands, models, features, and prices; talking to recent purchasers of computers; and visiting stores and talking to salespeople.

His supervisor tells him that he will be expected to use a document scanner in his work. Do research to find out what a document scanner is and how it is used. Write a short report that would help Charles use this device.

Business and Office Education

2. You are employed by an advertising agency. Your firm needs to hire five temporary workers, but no office space is available. Your supervisor has asked you to research the advantages of having these workers telecommute. List the advantages to your company. Then suggest three ways to help the workers adjust to the agency.

Math

3. Ellen's supervisor is writing an article on the increased use of technology in everyday life. He has asked her to construct a graph that shows how the use of a particular type of technology, such as the personal computer, has increased. First, locate statistics about increased use of a particular type of technology. Then construct a graph. Finally, create a credit line that tells where you got the information.

Developing Teamwork and Leadership Skills

Working with a team of three people, create a chart that compares two brands of word-processing or spreadsheet software. Together, research the software by reading magazines, talking with store owners, and talking with users. Create a chart that compares the two products, showing strengths and weaknesses of each.

Real-World Workshop

Visit a company that employs telecommuters, and interview someone who works with them. Ask how the company communicates with these employees. What kind of work do they do? What are the advantages and disadvantages to the company? What is the future of telecommuting in the company? Share what you learn with your classmates.

School-to-Work Connection

Locate a business office or industry in your community that interests you. Meet with a representative to discuss the ways computers and other modern technology are used there. Ask the representative to indicate how the use of technology in that career field has changed over the last 10 years and how she or he expects it to change in the future. Prepare a brief report on your findings, identifying positive and negative effects of the changes.

Individual Career Plan

Select one work activity involving computers that appeals to you. In a career reference book, find a job related to this area of interest. Explain in a paragraph your interest and the job you have chosen, describing potential job opportunities.

the office by personal computer.

3. Students should construct accurate graphs and should give proper credit to the source of their statistics.

Developing Teamwork and Leadership Skills

Charts will vary. All charts should demonstrate sufficient research as well as an understanding of the unique aspects of each type of technology.

Real-World Workshop

Reports will vary. Students should ask the questions provided and record the individual's answers accurately. You may wish to lead a class discussion that revolves around the advantages and disadvantages of telecommuting.

School-to-Work Connection

Reports should reflect the level of technology in the office or industry chosen. All reports should be clear and well organized.

Individual Career Plan

Paragraphs will vary, but students should select one work activity involving computers, identify a career in which they might use that activity, explain their interest in the career chosen, and indicate job opportunities in that career.

Connecting Academics to the Workplace

1. Students should write clear paragraphs that convey what a document scanner is and how it can be used.

2. Possible answers: saving the cost of renting new space; saving the cost of leasing computers, furniture, and other equipment; avoiding overcrowding of existing space. Suggestions for easing the adjustment of temporary workers may include assigning each worker a mentor from the company, giving workers an abbreviated version of the company manual, and creating an orientation program geared especially to temporary workers. All of these suggestions could be fulfilled by linking the workers to

• • • PLANNING GUIDE • • •
Chapter 18

SECTION 1 *Using Time Effectively*

SECTION OBJECTIVES	SECTION FEATURES	SECTION RESOURCES
• Prepare a schedule to accomplish your most important tasks. • Employ common techniques to use time effectively.	Personal Career Plan, p. 355 You're the Boss!, p. 358 Ethics in Action, p. 362 Career Do's and Don'ts, p. 364 Exploring Careers, p. 365	💿 Workforce 2000 Videodisc and Videotape 📁 Section 18-1 Review, p. 364 📖 Student Activity Workbook

SECTION 2 *Organizing Your Work*

SECTION OBJECTIVES	SECTION FEATURES	SECTION RESOURCES
• Organize yourself and your tasks. • Develop and maintain a useful system for filing paperwork. • Create and maintain computer files.	Excellent Business Practices, p. 369	💿 Workforce 2000 Videodisc and Videotape 📁 Section 18-2 Review, p. 370 📁 Chapter 18 Review, pp. 372–373 📖 Student Activity Workbook

CHAPTER RESOURCES

- Chapter Transparencies and Lesson Plans
- Chapter 18 Test
- Spanish Resources, Chapter 18
- School-to-Work Activity Handbook, Chapter 18 Activity
- Teacher's Lesson Plans, Chapter 18
- Implementing Block Scheduling, Chapter 18
- Print, Media, and Internet Handbook
- Strategies for Implementing Work-Based Learning
- Strategies for Implementing Connecting Activities

Career Notes

SCANS CORRELATION CHART

Foundation Skills

Basic Skills	Reading	Writing	Math	Listening	Speaking

Thinking Skills	Creative Thinking	Decision Making	Problem Solving	Seeing Things in the Mind's Eye	Knowing How to Learn	Reasoning

Personal Qualities	Responsibility	Self-Esteem	Sociability	Self-Management	Integrity/Honesty

Workplace Competencies

Resources	Allocating Time	Allocating Money	Allocating Material and Facility Resources	Allocating Human Resources

Information	Acquiring and Evaluating Information	Organizing and Maintaining Information	Interpreting and Communicating Information	Using Computers to Process Information

Interpersonal Skills	Participating as a Member of a Team	Teaching Others	Serving Clients/ Customers	Exercising Leadership	Negotiating to Arrive at a Decision	Working with Cultural Diversity

Systems	Understanding Systems	Monitoring and Correcting Performance	Improving and Designing Systems

Technology	Selecting Technology	Applying Technology to Task	Maintaining and Troubleshooting Technology

Highlighted blocks indicate areas covered in the Chapter.

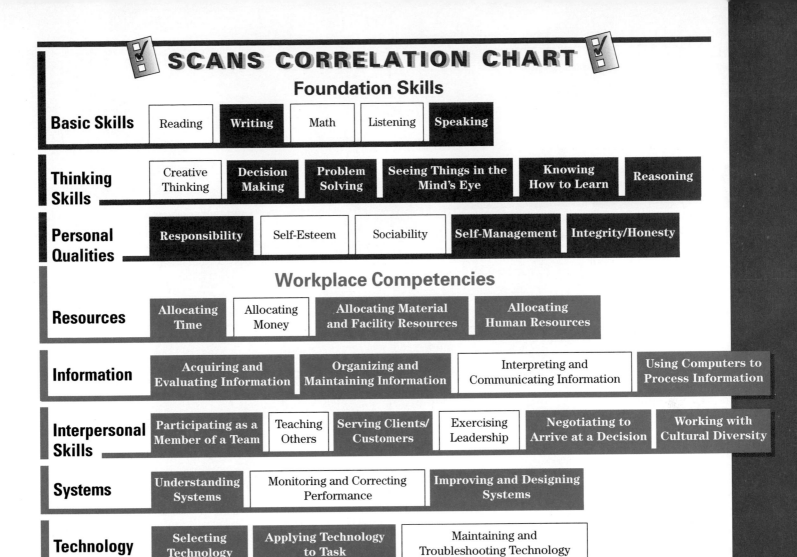

Additional Activities

Internet Connection

Ask students how many of them make a schedule of what they need to do each week. Have them use the Internet to find articles that provide tips on time management. Or, have them research scheduling software programs that might be available on-line.

Field Trip Suggestions

Arrange to visit a company that does much of its business abroad. Ask a company representative to explain how the Internet, faxes, and high-tech communication affect its business, how products are marketed in other countries, and how it meets the demands of a multi-ethnic staff.

Guest Speaker Suggestions

Invite a person who must constantly manage his or her own time, such as a freelance writer. Ask your guest to explain how to keep track of the time spent on each project, how to decide which project to work on, and how to keep all work moving smoothly.

Key to Ability Levels

Each section gives skill-building activities. Each activity has been labeled for use with students of various learning styles and abilities.

L1 Level 1 activities are basic activities and should be within the range of all students.

L2 Level 2 activities are average activities and should be within the range of average and above average students.

L3 Level 3 activities are challenging activities designed for the ability range of above average students.

School-Based Learning

Chapter Overview

Chapter 18 informs students of techniques that can help them make the best use of their time and knowledge.

Section 18-1 introduces time management skills and helps students learn to use their time wisely.

Section 18-2 focuses on how to organize information and make decisions about which documents are important to keep and for how long.

Background Information

Write chapter objectives (Sections 18-1 and 18-2) on the chalkboard or use the chapter objective transparency for class discussion.

Choose assignments from the *Student Activity Workbook* and write them on the chalkboard.

Have students preview the chapter, looking at pictures, reading captions, and noting content headings. Ask students to describe what they expect to learn in this chapter.

Preteaching Vocabulary

Write the Key Terms from Sections 18-1 and 18-2 on the chalkboard. Have students describe how each term relates to using time efficiently and managing information.

354

Meeting SPECIAL Needs

Learning Disabled

Students with learning disabilities may require additional guidelines or study aids to get the most out of text material. You may wish to make audio tapes for students who find written text difficult to use. Establish a relaxed reading pace and use a bell or clicker to signal page turns. Elicit the help of classmates who have clear voices.

Chapter 18

Time and Information Management

Section 18-1
Using Time Effectively

Section 18-2
Organizing Your Work

In this video segment, learn the importance of managing your time and organizing your work.

Journal
Personal Career Plan

Over the next two days, keep track of how you spend your time. Then consider your record. How much time—if any—is "wasted"? What do you think you should be doing with that time? Why? Write a journal entry detailing your time record and discussing your ideas.

355

School-to-Work
Connecting Activities

Tell students that they are working as counselors in a summer camp for 8- to 10-year-olds. Their job is to plan activities and make sure the kids are safe. Camp activities include swimming, tennis, nature hikes, softball games, rowing, and horseback riding. Breakfast is from 8 to 9 A.M.; lunch, from noon to 1 P.M.; and dinner, from 6 to 7 P.M. Quiet time is from 7 to 9 P.M., and lights go out at 9:30. Have students plan a week of activities for their campers.

Work-Based
Learning Strategies
and Activities

Interview several local employers whose workers must decide priorities for various work activities. Arrange for students to observe workers for half a day or so. Have students ask employees to share their time-management techniques and take notes on the systems they use to help them manage their time. Have students share their observations in class.

WORKFORCE 2000
Training Video

Have students view the video and perform the interactive exercises to reinforce important chapter concepts and thinking processes.

Chapter 18

Addressing LEARNING Styles

Logical Learner

Have students keep track of how they use their time during one week: meals, study, travel to and from school or work, errands, television watching, extracurricular activities, and so on. Have them chart their time in 15 minute increments. In what areas can they make better use of their time? How much time do they waste making unnecessary or extra trips? How can they reorganize activities to get more out of their time?

SECTION 18-1

FOCUS

Bell Ringer

Have students list at least five habits they have that prevent them from getting things done on time (for example, spending too much time on the telephone).

Introducing the Section

As students share their lists from the Bell Ringer activity, write their responses on the chalkboard. Then ask students how they could eliminate some of the things that waste their time. Use this discussion to lead into setting priorities and how doing the most important tasks first helps people accomplish their more important goals.

Motivational Activity
Critical Thinking

Write these descriptions on the chalkboard:

- work on several projects at the same time
- like to plan what to do but have trouble carrying out plans
- can't make decisions about what to do first
- everything must be perfect, even if it's late
- work on projects only at the last minute.

Have students choose one of the above types that best describes their approach to using time and write a paragraph explaining why they fit that type.

Using Time Effectively

OBJECTIVES

After studying this section, you will be able to:

- **Prepare a schedule to accomplish your most important tasks.**
- **Employ common techniques to use time effectively.**

KEY TERMS

time line
schedule
downtime
delegating

Does time sometimes get away from you? Have you found yourself staying up late to finish a report or to prepare for an exam? When you move into the work world, time can get away just as fast. The consequences, however, can be even worse. In school, it's usually just you who suffers when you don't manage your time well. On the job, other people suffer as well—your coworkers, supervisor, and employer.

So what's the solution? Stay on top of your work by using your self-management skills and learning how to manage your time.

To Do or Not to Do

Think of time management as making choices. You can spend your time doing this task or that task. You've got to decide which one to do *now*. If you have just a few choices, the decision may be easy. If you have lots of tasks, though, you may need some tools to help you make the right decisions. The following process can help you manage your time.

1. List all your projects, appointments, and other tasks.
2. Rate the tasks by their importance.
3. Break large, complex projects into small steps.
4. Estimate the time needed to complete each task.
5. Set up a schedule for your tasks.

356   *Unit 5 • Professional Development*

Implementing Teamwork

Divide your class into four groups and assign each group the task of planning a schedule for a major school event (for example, the homecoming parade). Groups must decide who will participate, when the event takes place, and how many meetings will be needed to complete plans. Ask each group to create a time line.

 In the business world, your work will always be connected to the work done by others. **What would happen to your coworkers if your assignments were always late?**

Make a List

How can you make good choices? First, you have to know what your choices are, so make a task list. Write down every project, appointment, or meeting you have. List those you must do today plus all those you must complete in the days and weeks ahead. Include the meeting next Saturday, and the training session in December. Next to each task, write the date or time by which you must complete it.

What's Most Important?

If your task list is long, you may be thinking you'll never get it all done. It's okay if you don't. Successful time management doesn't mean always finding time

to get *everything* done. It means getting the *most important things* done. You've got to prioritize, or decide the order of importance of completing all the different tasks.

Go back to your task list and analyze the tasks. Label them A, B, or C, according to order of importance. In deciding your priorities, consider the following:

- What were you hired to do? If you're a salesperson, your most important job is to sell. If you're a production worker, your most important job is to produce.

- Are you working alone or with others on a project? If you're working with others, you must coordinate your schedules to get the job done.

Chapter 18 • Time and Information Management **357**

 Extending the Illustration

Invite a local business manager who regularly evaluates employees on how they manage their time to speak to the class about employer's attitudes toward the use of time.

Caption Answer: Their work might also be late. They might not be as successful as they would otherwise be. They might not receive the raises or promotions that usually result from success at work.

SECTION 18-1

TEACH

Guided Practice

Teaching Strategies

1. Assign and review Section 18-1.

2. Use the transparency for this section.

3. Assign and review the Case Study.

Discussion Starter

Ask students how many of them make a list of what they need to do each week.

Teaching Tip

Probably few students make written lists, although most will have mental lists. The problem with a mental list is that it's easy to forget things. Have students discuss the advantages of a written list.

Critical Thinking

Have students make a list of everything they need to do at school, at work, and at home for the next week, assigning an A, B, or C to each item to rank its importance. Then have students estimate the time it will take to complete each item, including routine activities such as sleeping, eating, traveling to and from school or work. Then they should determine whether they can complete everything on their lists. If not, what would be the consequences of not doing some of the items labeled C?

L1 **Writing**

Assign students to write three goals they want to accomplish in the next week. For each goal, have them identify what they can do to accomplish it with ease, such as making a list of materials needed, delegating a task to someone, or acquiring information needed.

L2 **Knowing How to Learn**

Tell students that almost everyone who works faces the challenge of keeping to a schedule while handling day-to-day disruptions and problems that occur. Have students interview their parents, neighbors, relatives, or friends to discover what time-management skills they use in their work.

L3 **Decision Making**

Tell students that it is often easy to feel overwhelmed by everything they may need or want to do. Have students list three short-term goals (to be met within the next two to three weeks) and three long-term goals (covering the next two to three months). Have students rank their goals in order of importance. Have students analyze both sets of goals. Are any long-term goals dependent upon their meeting a short-term goal?

- What must you do to fulfill your obligations to the company? Are you expected to do paperwork or file reports? You must fulfill your obligations, even if they don't seem important to you.

Break Big Projects into Small Steps

Now take a second look at the major projects on your list. These large or long-term projects are often the most difficult to manage. People tend to focus on what has to be done today and tomorrow and to overlook things that are farther off. Moreover, long-term projects are often complex and require more work. It's hard to get a grip on what needs to be done today on a long-term project to ensure that it will be completed two months from now.

How can you deal with major projects? The best way is to break them into manageable steps. Then you can treat each part as a separate task.

358 *Unit 5 • Professional Development*

✓ *Solving Workplace Problems*

You run a successful janitorial service. One of your employees does excellent work. However, she has trouble arriving at the job on time and always seems to be in a rush by quitting time. Is it your responsibility to help this employee manage her time better? If so, how will you try to help her?

When Walter Sanchez became assistant manager in an auto parts store, he was given several new responsibilities. One task was to find three new employees. Sanchez broke the job down into the following steps:

1. Compose and place a classified ad in the newspaper.

2. Review job applications and choose candidates for interviews.

3. Schedule and conduct interviews.

4. Select the best candidates and schedule them for interviews with the store manager.

5. Meet with the manager to make hiring decisions.

This process of identifying the steps in a project is essential. You have to know what you're facing so you can know

Walter Sanchez has three weeks to hire three new employees. *Why must Walter get started right away? What will happen if he puts the search off until the last week?*

Extending the Illustration

Ask students to brainstorm ways they procrastinate in school, or on the job. Then have them think of techniques they could use to overcome such a bad habit(s).

Caption Answer: It will take time to find the best employees.

Teaching YOU'RE THE BOSS!

✓ Possible responses: Yes, so that you can keep the employee and benefit from her good work. Discuss time management directly with her; help her understand the importance of being on time; see what kinds of help—if any—she needs in organizing non-work responsibilities.

how you're going to get it done. The SCANS skill of seeing things in the mind's eye will help you figure out the steps in a complex project. This is the skill of visualization. You'll use it to envision how to break down a project into manageable parts.

Estimate Time Needed to Do Tasks

You now know what jobs you have to do. How long will it take you to do each one?

- If you've done the job before, base your estimate on past experience.
- If the job is new to you, ask someone with experience how long it took him or her.
- If you've been assigned the job, ask your supervisor how long it should take.
- Be wary of underestimating how long a job will take.
- If a job depends on other people, allow for their time.

For large projects, such as Walter Sanchez's, you'll want to set deadlines for completing each step in the project. One way to figure out a timetable for long-term projects is to create a time line. A **time line** is a type of chart that shows the order in which events occur in time. It will help you visualize an entire project so that you can see when to work on each step.

Set Up a Schedule

Now it's time to pull all the steps in this process together. How? By making a schedule. A **schedule** is a list or chart showing when tasks must be completed. If

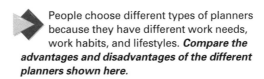

People choose different types of planners because they have different work needs, work habits, and lifestyles. *Compare the advantages and disadvantages of the different planners shown here.*

a task must be completed today and you know that it will take an hour, write the time you'll start the task on your schedule. You will then know that an hour of time is set aside for one purpose, getting that task completed. Fill in your schedule hour by hour.

You now have a daily schedule that shows everything to be done today. Your daily schedule will be part of a long-term schedule that shows tasks well into the future. Many people use a calendar or day planner for scheduling. They can enter tasks on the schedule as soon as they know about them. That way, they always know what's coming up.

Here are some more suggestions for making up your schedule:

- Think about your work habits. Are you a morning person or an afternoon person? Schedule difficult

Chapter 18 • Time and Information Management **359**

SCANS Workplace Competencies Connection

L1 Allocating Time

Have students create schedules for the weekend, including errands, recreational activities, study time, work and household responsibilities. Then have them create timelines that show when and how long they will do each item on their schedules.

L2 Serving Clients/ Customers

Certain workers, such as airline reservation agents, sometimes put customers on hold; customers usually resent being put on hold for long periods of time. Discuss how using good time-management techniques would help in a job where time is an important factor in keeping all customers happy.

L3 Working with Cultural Diversity

Working in groups of three or four, have students discuss their views of time and answer these questions: Are you punctual? Are you the last one to arrive at a party? What do you do when you're working with someone, either in school or at work, who has a different perspective about time and schedules? Tell students that different attitudes toward time may reflect a person's cultural background.

Extending the Illustration

Ask students what type of planner might be most useful for them in scheduling school-related and other activities.

Caption Answer: Some planners allow users to see a week of activities at a time, while others put a month on a page. Still others are organized by days and break time into hours or half-hours. Small planners may be disadvantageous for people who need to list a lot of tasks. Large planners may be disadvantageous for people who need something more portable.

Discussion Starter

Ask students whether they think ahead to the next few days in order to decide what they need to do, or if they wait until something demands their time and then do it.

Teaching Tip

Explain to students that many people must work around scheduled activities, such as department meetings, to get other work done. Knowing how to set up and follow a schedule is a valuable workplace skill.

Independent Practice

 Assign as homework the chapter activity in the *School-to-Work Activity Handbook.*

Skills Practice

Bruce noticed an ad in the paper for CDs on sale at a local music store. If he buys one CD at the regular price of $12, he can get the second CD for half-price. He can purchase a third CD at one-third the regular price. If Bruce purchases three CDs, how much will they cost? ($21.99: $12 + (½ × $12) + (⅓ × $12))

If the state sales tax where Bruce lives is 6 percent, what will be the total cost of the three CDs? ($23.31: 0.06 × $21.99 = $1.32 + $21.99)

tasks for times when you perform at your peak.

• Consider color coding your schedule. Use different colors for deadlines, meetings, travel, and so on.

• Transfer your priorities from your task list to your schedule. If you run out of time, you can see at a glance which tasks you can postpone.

• Check off tasks as you complete them. The accumulating check marks will give you a boost.

Building a schedule is an ongoing process. *Figure 18-1* shows the process Walter Sanchez might follow to put together his schedule. Look at his task list and time line. How do they appear on his schedule?

▶ **Figure 18-1**

Creating a Schedule

Managing time effectively is a process involving several steps.

A Making a task list is a first step in using time wisely. List everything that's coming up, such as meetings, projects, and luncheons. Include personal and business appointments. That way you won't mistakenly schedule two things for the same time. Prioritize tasks by labeling them A, B, or C.

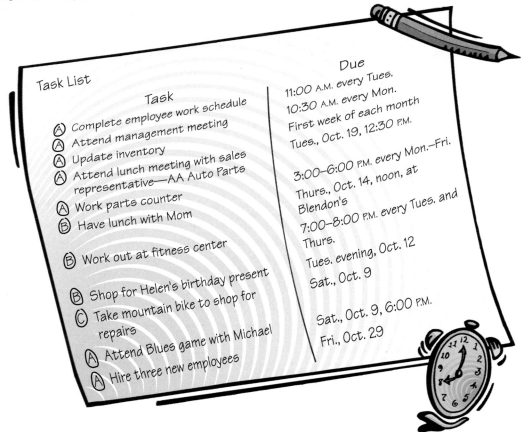

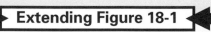

►► Extending Figure 18-1 ◄◄

Ask students how creating schedules and preparing time lines could improve their chances for success at work. (Possible answers include being better organized, being prepared for meetings, gaining a reputation for using time efficiently, and not forgetting to do some work since it will be on a task list. Employers want people who use time well and get things done.)

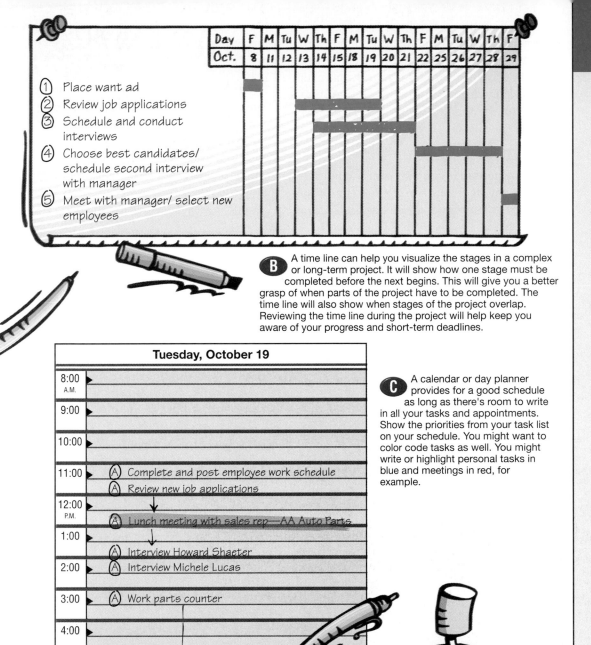

Day	F	M	Tu	W	Th	F	M	Tu	W	Th	F	M	Tu	W	Th	F
Oct.	8	11	12	13	14	15	18	19	20	21	22	25	26	27	28	29

① Place want ad
② Review job applications
③ Schedule and conduct interviews
④ Choose best candidates/ schedule second interview with manager
⑤ Meet with manager/ select new employees

B A time line can help you visualize the stages in a complex or long-term project. It will show how one stage must be completed before the next begins. This will give you a better grasp of when parts of the project have to be completed. The time line will also show when stages of the project overlap. Reviewing the time line during the project will help keep you aware of your progress and short-term deadlines.

Tuesday, October 19

8:00 A.M.

9:00

10:00

11:00 ⓐ Complete and post employee work schedule
⬆ⓐ Review new job applications

12:00 P.M. ⓐ Lunch meeting with sales rep—AA Auto Parts

1:00 ⓐ Interview Howard Shaeter

2:00 ⓐ Interview Michele Lucas

3:00 ⓐ Work parts counter

4:00

5:00

6:00

7:00 ⓔ Work out—fitness center

C A calendar or day planner provides for a good schedule as long as there's room to write in all your tasks and appointments. Show the priorities from your task list on your schedule. You might want to color code tasks as well. You might write or highlight personal tasks in blue and meetings in red, for example.

Chapter 18 • Time and Information Management **361**

Computer Activity

Have students use a spreadsheet software package to design their own time-management schedule. Ask them to choose an event that occurs annually (for example, one related to school, church or temple, or family). They should consider the tasks, steps to be completed, number of people involved, and the priority for each task.

Writing: *Journal*

Have students write in their career journals describing the time-management techniques they will use to improve their school and job performance.

Teaching Tip

Bring in a sample of a day planner, a planning calendar book divided into weeks or months, or some other time-management system. Allow students to look through each sample and review the features. (For example, some calendar books also have pages for addresses and telephone numbers, as well as expense sheets for work-related expenses.) Ask students how they might use such a device to help them use their time more efficiently.

Have students create a time-line display for the bulletin board for school activities for the remainder of the semester.

Critical Thinking

Tell students that they have been assigned a major report on any topic of their choice that is due in two weeks. Have students create a time line for the project, beginning with today's date and ending two weeks from now. Tell students that they are to desktop publish the report.

(Students should break the project into parts, such as finding ideas, reading and research, writing, revising, desktop publishing, and proofreading and finishing.)

Teaching Tip

Have students keep a time log for the next three days covering the amount of time they spend on the telephone with friends and watching television. Then discuss whether there were things they had planned to do but could not find the time for. Have students suggest other ways they waste time.

Skills Practice

Read this scenario to students. "Susan and Louann work for a video production company as office assistants. Susan plans her work assignments and almost always has them finished on time. Louann often procrastinates and has to rush to finish her work on time; her manager has had to ask her to redo some work that was incomplete.

"Both Susan and Louann speak with friends on the telephone. Susan, though, keeps her calls to under five minutes and rarely has more than a couple of calls per week. Louann speaks with three or four friends a day and sometimes spends half an hour on a call." Tell students they are managers who must give an annual review to Susan and Louann. What would they say?

Interview

Have students interview parents, friends, neighbors, or relatives and ask what types of time-management techniques they use on their jobs. Have students share their findings in class.

362

A schedule is a helpful tool for managing your time. You must keep it current, however. Take a few minutes every morning to look at it, update it, and plan. As necessary, make a new task list and go through the scheduling process again.

Timely Tips

A schedule is one part of efficient time management. There's more you can do to use your time and other people's time wisely.

Using Your Time Wisely

Everyone has occasional periods when nothing is on his or her schedule. This is called **downtime**. Don't waste it! Downtime is a good time to get ahead or to improve your skills. You might read an

equipment service manual or learn a new computer program.

Avoid procrastination. As you read in Chapter 16, procrastination is the putting off of work you should be doing. If a job has to be done, do it.

Be flexible. Everything won't work out just as you plan it. The copier may break down, or a client may postpone an appointment. Shift gears and go on to something else on your schedule.

Don't let the telephone control your time. The checklist shown in **Figure 18-2** suggests how to make better use of the telephone.

Look for ways to combine tasks. For example, if you take public transportation to work, read while you're riding. If you drive to work, consider listening to instructional tapes.

 Downtime isn't off time. These medical employees are using downtime to learn more about keeping accurate charts. *How will learning something new about your job help you better manage your time on the next project?*

362 *Unit 5 • Professional Development*

Extending the Illustration

Have students brainstorm ideas on things they could do during downtime.

Caption Answer: More knowledge will help you get work done faster, thus saving time. You won't have to look up information at some later date when you don't have as much time.

Teaching ETHICS in Action

Have students follow these steps to help them make a decision.

1. What are the ethical issues?
2. What are the alternatives?
3. Who are the affected parties?
4. How do the alternatives affect the parties?
5. What is your decision?

Always be prepared to get work done. Carry a pen and paper with you all the time. You can write notes when stuck in traffic or waiting in line somewhere.

Using Other People's Time Wisely

When you work with other people, be aware of how you use their time. When people are busy, keep your conversations focused. Give them only the important information. Don't bother them with nonessential details.

When you are assigned a task, listen carefully to the details. Ask questions if you don't understand something. Then you won't have to go back later and interrupt your supervisor or coworker with more questions.

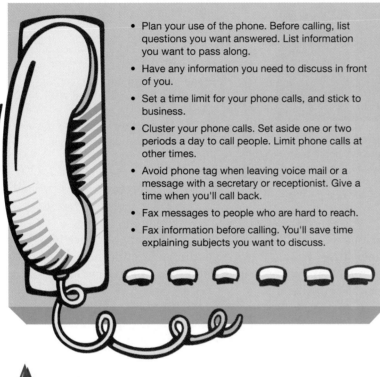
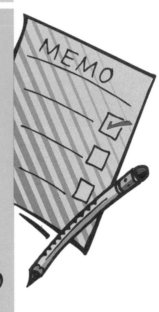

Getting the Most from Your Telephone

- Plan your use of the phone. Before calling, list questions you want answered. List information you want to pass along.
- Have any information you need to discuss in front of you.
- Set a time limit for your phone calls, and stick to business.
- Cluster your phone calls. Set aside one or two periods a day to call people. Limit phone calls at other times.
- Avoid phone tag when leaving voice mail or a message with a secretary or receptionist. Give a time when you'll call back.
- Fax messages to people who are hard to reach.
- Fax information before calling. You'll save time explaining subjects you want to discuss.

Figure 18-2 The telephone can take a great deal of your time. This checklist can help you use the phone more efficiently. How can you use the telephone to save time?

► ► Extending Figure 18-2 ◄ ◄

Have students research telephone etiquette—for example, how to answer the telephone for a business and how to communicate friendliness to customers. Have them write a list of at least five techniques that could improve their telephone communications.

Caption Answer: Call people instead of going to see them or writing to them.

Discussion Starter

Ask students why E-mail might be more efficient than a telephone call. When might a telephone call be more efficient than E-mail? (E-mail takes only a few minutes to compose and send, while a telephone call may take much longer because speakers can go off on tangents. If you need an immediate answer, though, the telephone may be more efficient.)

Teaching Tip

Ask students who have part-time service jobs what they do when they are not waiting on customers. Do they try to find other things to do to be productive? Do their supervisors suggest other things for them to do?

Role-Play

Have students role-play several telephone conversations. For example, a pair of students might role-play an irate customer and a customer service employee. Another pair could role-play a business receptionist and a person calling to learn the name of the human resources director. A third pair might role-play a business person and a job applicant calling to make an appointment. Another group might role-play a follow-up call to an interview.

Teaching Tip

Go back to the Critical Thinking activity at the beginning of this section in which students were asked to determine their styles for completing projects. Ask students what happens on the job when two people with different time-management styles must work together; for example, someone who prefers to get things done early versus someone who waits until the last minute to begin a project. What skills might be useful in working with people who have differing styles? (Students might mention good communication skills, ability to be flexible and accept other people's work styles, ability to see someone else's perspective, and skills in negotiating compromises between people with different styles.)

ASSESS

Assessment

Content

Have students write articles for the school newspaper giving time-management tips to their fellow students. Tell them to include an appropriate title.

Evaluate students' articles for correct grammar and punctuation. Articles should mention techniques such as making a list, assigning priorities to activities, breaking big jobs into small steps, creating a time line, setting up a schedule, and using their own and other peoples' time wisely.

There's no reason to just sit and wait while waiting for the bus. Get something done. The work you do may give you more time later for an activity you enjoy. **What kinds of work might you do while riding a bus or waiting in traffic?**

Give complete instructions when delegating work to others. **Delegating** means assigning tasks to other people. Make sure they understand what you're asking them to do. Take time to answer questions. How will spending more time answering questions initially save you time later?

Career Do's & Don'ts

When Managing Time Effectively...

Do:
- plan.
- focus on activities with long-term payoffs.
- complete the most important work first.
- tackle one task at a time.
- write down questions you have ahead of time, then plan a short meeting in which you can obtain answers to your questions.

Don't:
- procrastinate.
- spend your prime time cleaning your desk area or chatting with associates.
- get stuck on minor details to the extent it jeopardizes the bigger picture.

SECTION 18-1 *Review*

Understanding Key Concepts

Using complete sentences, answer the following questions on a separate sheet of paper.

1. How can a schedule help you use your time more efficiently?

2. Why is it important to use your coworkers' time wisely?

364 *Unit 5 • Professional Development*

SECTION 18-1 *Review* ANSWERS

1. A schedule forces you to think about what you must accomplish during the day and provides deadlines for doing so.

2. Their time is valuable also. The success of a business depends on everyone's using his or her time effectively.

Extending the Illustration

Have students brainstorm situations where trying to do two things at once might be dangerous. (Situations might include trying to read a newspaper while driving or operating equipment.)

Caption Answer: You could review or update your schedule, jot down notes, make a to-do list, or brainstorm solutions to a work problem.

CASE STUDY

Exploring Careers: Hospitality and Recreation

Ted Lai
School Food Service Manager

Q: Do you have a background in food service?

A: The first food service experience I had was helping feed the homeless when I was in high school. I worked in food service jobs to help put myself through college.

When I started in food service, I began by washing dishes. After a while, I began helping by making salads. Then I moved up to doing some cooking. Finally, I advanced to manager.

Q: How is school food service different from work in a restaurant?

A: The biggest difference is that schools have regular hours: 6 A.M. to 2:30 P.M., Monday through Friday, with the holidays and the weekends off. When you're working in schools, you usually have better health benefits than you do in when working in a restaurant. However, the financial reward is higher in restaurant work, and there is more chance for advancement.

Q: What do you like about food service?

A: It's not only a good industry but also one that will always be needed. I think the art of cooking at home is being lost. Instead, a lot of people are going out to dinner.

I like the cooking aspects of food service more than the management aspects. Cooking lets you explore the creativity of food. I like getting people to enjoy something I've made.

Thinking Critically

What skills do you have that would be useful in a food service career?

CAREER FACTS

Nature of the Work:
  Make sure supplies are available; oversee work crew; keep records of compliance with government regulations.

Training or Education Needed:
  Bachelor's degree in food service management; experience in the industry.

Aptitudes, Abilities, and Skills:
  Reading and writing skills; knowledge of cooking; skill in menu planning, food purchasing, and presentation; organizational skills; management skills, including the ability to supervise others.

Salary Range:
  $18,000 to $50,000.

Career Path:
  Start in the restaurant kitchen; work through different jobs to a managerial position.

Chapter 18 • Time and Information Management **365**

SECTION 18-1

Evaluation
Assign the section review.

Reteaching
Ask for volunteers to tell what tasks they have planned for the next week. Write tasks from two or three students on the chalkboard. Have students assign priorities, identify the tasks that make up larger activities, prepare a time line and a schedule, and make suggestions for downtime or the delegation of some of the tasks to others.

Extending the Content
Assign the appropriate Chapter 18 activities in the *Student Activity Workbook*.
Have students research time-management and scheduling software (personal information management software) in computer magazines. Have them write brief descriptions of the tasks each software program automates. Ask students how they might use such a program either in their school work or in their future careers.

CLOSE
Ask students to write 50-word paragraphs about one time-management technique, describing how they will practice it during the next week.

Extending the CASE STUDY

Answer: Answers will vary.

Further Application: School and restaurant food service are only two ways to be involved in the food industry. Food-service managers could also work in grocery stores, hospitals, or corporate and government cafeterias. Have students discuss the various types of jobs available in their chosen career areas. For example, a pilot could work for an airline, an overnight delivery company, or for a corporation. An environmental consultant could work for a business, government agency, or privately funded organization.

FOCUS

Bell Ringer

Have each student decide which sentence he or she agrees with.

- The employer should accommodate employees' individual working styles.
- The employee should adapt to the employer's working requirements.

Introducing the Section

Have students share their opinions from the Bell Ringer activity. Poll the class to find out student responses.

While some employers will accommodate employee individuality to some degree, most want their employees to accomplish work in accepted ways. Have students discuss how career success might depend on their ability to adapt to different working styles and expectations.

Motivational Activity

Writing

Have students create charts showing how they will organize their career-related materials. For example, students might have a folder for letters responding to job ads, and others for materials describing specific careers. Tell students to draw a folder representing each topic, then list beneath it the types of documents they will file in that folder. Have students share their charts in class.

Organizing Your Work

OBJECTIVES

After studying this section, you will be able to:

- **Organize yourself and your tasks.**
- **Develop and maintain a useful system for filing paperwork.**
- **Create and maintain computer files.**

KEY TERMS

access
directory
subdirectories

You've learned strategies for using your time more effectively. What else can you do to get your work done faster and better? First, you can organize the things around you in your work area. Second, you can organize the information you use to do your work.

Organizing Your Work Area

You may be very skilled at your job. However, if you can't quickly find the tools or materials you need to do your job, your skill won't matter. Think about your work area. Find a place for everything.

Everything in Its Place

The first rule for organizing a work area might be called the near-far rule. What things do you use most often? They should be near you. What things do you use less frequently? These things can be placed farther away.

Plumbers, for example, carry a toolbox with them when they make a house call. The toolbox contains the most frequently used tools of their trade. Plumbers keep these tools close at hand. Tools used less frequently are kept in the truck.

A second guideline is to put like things together. Files, supplies, and tools used for one project or type of job should be kept together. Those used for another project or job might be kept in a separate area.

366 *Unit 5 • Professional Development*

Workforce 2000 Trends

Employers want workers who have a firm grasp of the fundamentals of their field. However, they also want workers with a broad range of interests and skills who can easily cross-train. Take advantage of education and reading to widen your knowledge and interest bases.

Addressing Workplace Diversity

Although women will continue to be the primary child and elder caretakers, they will continue to enter the workforce in increasing numbers. The availability of company-provided child and elder care will become valued benefits for working women.

Organizing your work area only takes a little thought, but it can save you much time. Begin by listing things you use a lot, a little, and rarely. *What items does this woman use frequently?*

If you store things in boxes, drawers, or files, label them. You won't have to open every box to find the one item you need. If you have lots of boxes or files, alphabetize them, group them by content, or organize them in some other logical order.

Making Neatness Count

Did you ever hear the phrase "neatness counts"? Did you know that neatness also saves time? Take time occasionally to put your work area back in order. Return tools to their right places. Straighten and reorganize your desk. Keeping things orderly will save you time later. You'll know where everything is.

Organizing Information

Do you have to handle lots of information? Then you've got to be able to organize it. Otherwise, it loses its usefulness. Think

about a library. A good library contains vast amounts of information. It's only useful, however, if the information is organized so that you can **access**, or find and use it. Organizing and maintaining information—a SCANS competency—is one key to success.

Is It Important?

The first step in managing information is to decide whether it is important. Ask yourself whether the information is something you need to know or act on. Is it information someone else needs? Is it something you may need to refer to later? If you answer no to these questions, your best management choice may be to discard it. Information you don't need becomes clutter. It blocks access to the information you do need.

If the information is necessary, try to do something with it the first time you look at it. If you put it in a *pending*, or holding file, you'll have to look at it again later. Then you will have spent time on it

Extending the Illustration

Ask students how their study areas at home are organized. What could they do to make the space more efficient?

Caption Answer: drawing pen, colored markers, straight edge, X-ACTO knife, reference sources

SECTION 18-2

TEACH

Guided Practice

Teaching Strategies

1. Assign and review Section 18-2.

2. Use the transparency for this section.

Discussion Starter

Ask students to visualize their work or study space at home. What do they see? How many would say their study areas are neat, messy, or somewhere in between?

Teaching Tip

Have students imagine that their boss, who is on an international phone call, asks them for the plans for a new office the company is building for the client on the phone. How would neatness and knowing where everything is enable students to quickly locate the plans?

Critical Thinking

As they look for jobs, students will likely collect information about employment agencies, names of interviewers, and telephone numbers and E-mail addresses. Have students create ways to organize this information, either in physical or electronic form. (A card file with the names of agencies, businesses, and individuals with their addresses, telephone numbers, and E-mail addresses would be most efficient. For those with computers, personal information management software might be used.)

SCANS Foundation Skills Connection

L1 **Speaking**

Divide students into teams. Within the teams, have each team member speak about how he or she prepares and organizes for classes. Have students share information about processes that they use to manage their time.

L2 **Seeing Things in the Mind's Eye**

Have students think about their work spaces. Have them sketch a layout of the spaces, identifying materials that are critical for them to handle their tasks. Have them evaluate their sketches and determine whether they could organize materials differently to make them more accessible or easier to use.

L3 **Knowing How to Learn**

Have students choose a career and research how the work area in that field is usually laid out. (For example, would they be sitting at a desk? If so, would the desk be in an open space or in a cubicle? Would they need special equipment, such as a drafting table? What materials would they need to keep the work organized and accessible?) Have students describe their careers and their physical settings in class.

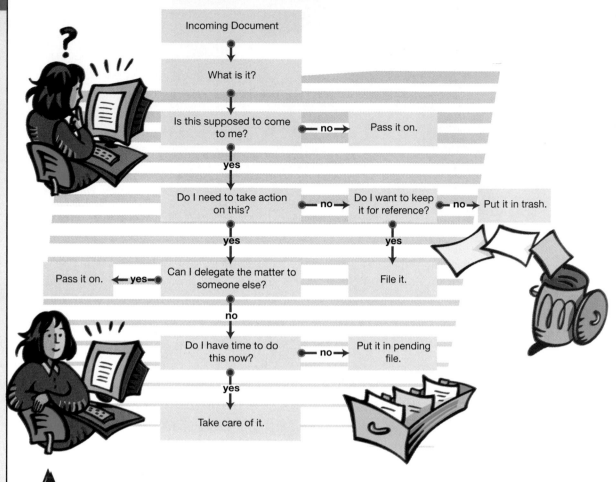

Managing Information

- Incoming Document
- What is it?
- Is this supposed to come to me? → **no** → Pass it on.
- **yes**
- Do I need to take action on this? → **no** → Do I want to keep it for reference? → **no** → Put it in trash.
- **yes** / **yes**
- Pass it on. ← **yes** ← Can I delegate the matter to someone else? / File it.
- **no**
- Do I have time to do this now? → **no** → Put it in pending file.
- **yes**
- Take care of it.

▲ **Figure 18-3** This chart shows the decision-making process used for incoming paperwork. Would this process work for information received via E-mail or other electronic means? Why or why not?

twice. **Figure 18-3** above charts the basic decision-making process for dealing with information.

Paper Chase

If you think you'll need to refer back to a paper document later, file it. Put your documents in file folders. Then group the folders in hanging files. These hints will help you set up a system:

- Categorize information. You might organize documents by customers, projects, or dates of receipt.
- Label each file and hanging folder.

► Extending Figure 18-3 ◄◄

Ask students how a process such as the one illustrated here could help them make decisions. (Evaluating data as you get it helps you avoid procrastinating.)

Caption Answer: The files used might be electronic rather than paper files, but the process used would be the same.

► Extending the Illustration

Have students ask their parents what type of filing system they use for important household papers such as product warranties, copies of repair bills, or legal documents.

Caption Answer: Students may suggest a hanging file for each class with file folders for projects, exams, writing assignments, and so on.

- Avoid putting each document in a separate file. Group documents by type.

- Avoid massive files with many documents. Divide them by subtopics.

- Color-code folders or labels to help identify categories or subcategories. For example, green folders might indicate one project, blue another, and so on.

- File on a regular basis.

 Filing systems should be organized in the most logical way possible. People using them should be able to locate needed information quickly. *How might you organize a filing system for your school classes?*

SCANS Workplace Competencies Connection

L1 Organizing and Maintaining Information

Have students set up filing systems to keep the information they gather about careers, job possibilities, specific companies, and so on as they prepare for their job searches.

L2 Allocating Material and Facility Resources

Tell students to keep track of how much time they spend looking for things for a one-week period. Have each determine a system he or she could use to be more efficient about storing and organizing books, car keys, and other possessions.

L3 Negotiating to Arrive at a Decision

Divide students into teams of four or five. Each team's goal is to identify a business that all team members would like to visit to observe how work spaces are organized. After choosing a business, teams are to put together a time-line for when the field trip could occur, list the objectives of the trip, and prepare reasons why such a business should be chosen. After each team presents its choice, negotiate a class decision of which business to visit.

EXCELLENT BUSINESS PRACTICES

On-Site Child Care

PacifiCare Health Systems is one of the nation's largest managed health-care organizations. To help serve its employees better, it has built an on-site child-care center.

Company employees working 32 or more hours a week are eligible to enroll their dependents from six weeks old to kindergarten-entry age. For working parents, the child-care center offers the convenience of bringing their children to the workplace and the comfort of having their youngsters close enough to visit during lunch. For businesses, on-site child care is proving to be a cost-effective investment that results in more loyal and productive employees, reduced absenteeism due to child-care problems, and enhanced job satisfaction. PacifiCare Health

Systems also offers employees access to child- and elder-care counselors, child-care subsidies, and parenting and elder-care workshops.

Thinking Critically

If you were a working parent with a young child or children, why would you want to work at a company that had an on-site child-care facility?

Chapter 18 • Time and Information Management **369**

Extending EXCELLENT BUSINESS PRACTICES

Answer: This benefit provides employees with a needed service. It shows that the company is concerned with helping its employees.

Further Application: Have students research the types of benefits provided by companies in your area.

Independent Practice

Writing: _Directions_

Have students draw a chart illustrating how directories and subdirectories work. Tell them to think of a directory name, then name possible topics for subdirectories.

ASSESS

Assessment

Content

Have students write about techniques for organizing both paper and electronic documents. Then evaluate their paper for accuracy of content, and understanding of the logic behind organizing information.

Evaluation

Assign the section review.

MINI QUIZ

True-False

1. Making a to-do list isn't important if you can remember most of them. (false)

2. Breaking big projects into small steps makes them more manageable. (true)

3. A time line is a list of all projects you need to complete in no particular order. (false)

4. The near-far rule means that items you use most often should be closest to you. (true)

5. For a computer file, a directory is the equivalent of a folder. (true)

Managing Computer Information

If you look around most offices, you'll see desks covered with paper. Despite appearances, more and more information is entering offices as computer files and E-mail. Managing electronic information has become as great a challenge as managing paper documents.

Many of the rules for managing paper documents also apply to managing electronic files. Don't clutter your files with information you don't need. Make a separate **directory**, or computer file, for each category of information. A directory is like a filing cabinet that contains many files on a large topic, such as a project.

Don't let directories get too full; create new **subdirectories**. These are smaller groupings of files. For example, you may have a directory for XYZ Company. As business improves, you might create subdirectories for invoices, orders, letters, and so on.

Choose names for computer files carefully. Select logical, descriptive names, ones you'll remember six months from now. It's also helpful to keep a written record of file names.

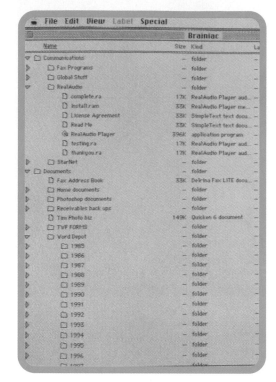

Directories and subdirectories should be given logical, brief names. Some software programs only record up to eight letters for a name. Use abbreviations that are easy to recognize. **_What might you name a directory for_ Succeeding in the World of Work?**

SECTION 18-2 _Review_

Understanding Key Concepts

Using complete sentences, answer the following questions on a separate sheet of paper.

1. How can organizing your work space make you more efficient?

2. Why should you avoid creating very large files with many documents?

3. Why is it important to choose names for computer files carefully?

SECTION 18-2 _Review_ ANSWERS

1. It can ensure that you don't waste time looking for tools, materials, or other things you need to do your job.

2. They contain too much information; it's too difficult to sort through so many documents to find what you need.

3. If the names are not obvious or if you can't remember them easily, you'll have trouble finding the files later on.

CHAPTER 18 *Highlights*

Key Terms

time line *(p. 359)*
schedule *(p. 359)*
downtime *(p. 362)*
delegating *(p. 364)*

SECTION 18-1 Summary

- The effective use of time requires knowledge of the SCANS skill of self-management and the SCANS competency in time management.
- Time management is a process of deciding how to use your time wisely. The first step is to identify all your tasks by making a task list. Then prioritize each task.
- Manage long-term projects best by breaking them into smaller, more manageable parts. Then treat the parts as separate tasks.
- Decide how long each task will take to complete. Make a time line to help you figure out how long larger projects will take.
- There are many forms for schedules. Choose the form that fits your style and individual needs.
- Keep your schedule current. Review it daily.
- Use your time wisely by making use of downtime, avoiding procrastination, and being flexible when plans don't work out. Use the telephone wisely, and combine tasks.
- Use other people's time wisely. Keep conversations brief, listen to assignments carefully, and give complete directions when delegating tasks.

Key Terms

access *(p. 367)*
directory *(p. 370)*
subdirectories *(p. 370)*

SECTION 18-2 Summary

- Organizing your work area helps you work efficiently.
- Keep your work area organized so that you can find tools and supplies when you need them.
- Organize information so that it is accessible. Discard information you do not and will not need.
- File paper documents in file folders. Place the folders in hanging files. Categorize information. Avoid creating files with either too many or too few documents. Label files, and consider using color coding to identify information.
- Many of the rules for managing paper documents also apply to managing computer information.

Chapter 18 • Time and Information Management **371**

Use the Testmaker to create a customized test for Chapter 18.

Reteaching

1. Write names of several folders (such as Letters) and document types that might fit in each folder (such as XYZ Company letter) on a sheet of paper. Copy this sheet for each student, then cut the paper into strips containing one folder or document type. Give each student a set of the paper strips and have them create a system to organize the information, applying the techniques in this section. Afterwards, have them use the folder and document names to create electronic directories and subdirectories.

2. Assign and review vocabulary terms, chapter questions, and activities from the Chapter Review.

3. Assign and review the Unit Project on page 254.

Extending the Content

Assign the appropriate Chapter 18 activities in the *Student Activity Workbook*.

CLOSE

See the Unit Closure and Unit Evaluation located on page 255.

Extending the Illustration

Have students (or a computer lab assistant) who are familiar with computers give a demonstration of how to set up directories and files electronically.
Caption Answer: The directory might be called "SWW."

Answers

Reviewing Key Terms

Paragraphs will vary but should indicate an understanding of all key terms.

Recalling Key Concepts

1. False: A schedule should include all tasks.
2. True
3. True
4. False: You should discard it.
5. True

Thinking Critically

1. If your aim is to get everything done, you may hurry through high-priority tasks and not do them as well as you should.

2. Working on the small parts of a task allows you to see more easily what has to be done. You also know when you should start and finish each task.

3. No. Time lines are not useful for small tasks that have only one or a few steps. They may not be necessary for larger tasks if the steps are obvious and the time frame is clear.

4. If the work area is disorganized, you won't know where the tools, materials, and other items you need are. Looking for them wastes time.

Reviewing Key Terms

On a separate sheet of paper, write one or two paragraphs explaining how you can better manage your time and information. Use each term below.

time line	access
schedule	directory
downtime	subdirectories
delegating	

Recalling Key Concepts

On a separate sheet of paper, tell whether each statement is true or false. Rewrite any false statements to make them true.

1. A schedule should include only tasks of the highest priority.

2. A time line helps you visualize how the parts of a large project fit together.

3. If you organize your work space by the near-far rule, the materials you use most often will be within easy reach.

4. If you don't need the information in a document and are sure you won't need it in the future, you should file it.

5. When setting up computer files, you should create subdirectories to prevent directories from becoming too full.

Thinking Critically

Using complete sentences, answer each of the questions below on a separate sheet of paper.

1. In managing your time, why should your emphasis be on getting the most important things done rather than on getting everything done?

2. How does breaking a large task into smaller parts help you manage the work?

3. Should you make a time line for every task? Why or why not?

4. How does a disorganized work area waste your time?

5. Is managing information a greater challenge if the information is on paper or in electronic files? Explain your answer.

SCANS Foundation Skills and Workplace Competencies

Thinking Skills: *Seeing Things in the Mind's Eye*

1. You've been asked to plan your company's annual employee picnic. You must take care of all details. Break down the assignment into manageable parts. List the smaller tasks.

Information: *Organizing and Maintaining Information*

2. Documents on the following topics have arrived on your desk: revised employee insurance policy, company holidays for 1998, winter hours for the child-care facility, vacation policy, flu shots covered under health plan, how to file for health insurance coverage, New Year's Day work schedule, and child-care policy for children who are ill. Make a list to show how you would organize the topics in files and folders. Name each file and folder.

5. Both forms are equally challenging. Information that is not well managed is inaccessible and therefore useless.

SCANS Foundation Skills and Workplace Competencies

1. Possible answers: decide on the date and time, choose and arrange for the location, select the menu, oversee food preparation, line up entertainment, make alternate plans for bad weather

2. Answers will vary. Students should group topics logically and avoid setting up files containing only one document.

Connecting Academics to the Workplace

Social Studies

1. Jeffrey manages a small electronics store. He has three salespeople and an office assistant. The owner has come to town unexpectedly and has called an all-afternoon meeting. Jeffrey cannot finish the following tasks that remain on his schedule. What should he do about them?

    Meet with distributor of new products—2:00 P.M.

    Complete inventory of computer software.

    Select items for next week's sale.

    Read and deal with mail, E-mail, and faxes.

    Lunch with sister at noon.

    Train new salesperson in how to demonstrate camcorders.

Computer Science

2. Do research to learn about computer software that will create personal schedules. Compare and contrast the software available, and determine the pros and cons of each. Summarize your findings in a 250-word report.

Developing Teamwork and Leadership Skills

Work with a group of classmates. Together, choose a type of business. Imagine that you are designing the work space for a specific department in that business. Investigate the kinds of work done in that department. You may want to tour a similar business in your area and talk to employees to learn what goes on in the chosen department. Then design the department work space for your company. Make the space as efficient as possible.

Real-World Workshop

Think about one of the jobs you've had. It may have been either a volunteer or for-pay job. How well did you use your time on the job? List the ways that you used time well. List the ways in which you could have improved your use of time.

School-to-Work Connection

With a partner, select a local company. Then contact the personnel director or another supervisor at that firm. Make an appointment and interview the person about ways in which the company manages work areas and employee time to improve efficiency. Report your findings to the class.

Individual Career Plan

Write a self-evaluation of how you manage your time. Do you procrastinate? Are you a morning or afternoon person? Do you meet deadlines easily, or do you scramble to get them done on time? Are you always on time, or do you often show up late? List things you might do to improve your use of time.

Developing Teamwork and Leadership Skills

Answers will vary. Student designs should use the near-far rule and put like things together.

Real-World Workshop

Answers should reflect students' knowledge of time-management.

School-to-Work Connection

Answers will vary, depending on the company and supervisor interviewed.

Individual Career Plan

Students should write honest self-appraisals of their use of time and list ways in which they can improve their management of time.

Chapter 18 • Time and Information Management **373**

Connecting Academics to the Workplace

1. He should postpone the meeting with the distributor; deal with the mail, E-mail, and faxes tomorrow; delegate authority to experienced salespeople for completing the inventory, choosing the sale items, and providing the camcorder training; and cancel lunch with his sister.

2. Reports will vary, but students should identify scheduling software programs available and learn enough about them to explain the benefits and drawbacks of each.

Aspects of Industry: Underlying Principles of Technology

Students who are fairly sure of their future careers may use the Labs to investigate all the aspects of industry for one career. Other students may want to investigate a different job cluster with each Lab.

STEP A

Because this Lab has to do with preparing for potential changes in career, and skill transferability, urge students to look at a broad spectrum of careers. It might be beneficial for them to choose one career that seems interesting but that they have never seriously considered. Remind them that this is the time to explore as many careers as possible. The career they think they want might not end up being the career they really enjoy.

To select jobs, students may brainstorm with other students, or research the possibilities in the *Occupational Outlook Handbook (OOH)* or other career references.

By doing this exercise, students should get a feel for how rapidly careers can change. To prepare them for their research, you might want to have the class discuss certain types of technology that have disappeared in the last 10 years—along with the jobs that supported them—and the technology that is here today that was in its infancy 10 years ago.

Urge students to pay special attention to the predictions trade publications made about

coming changes 10 years ago. By comparing those predictions to what is true today, they may be better able to evaluate what is being predicted today about the future.

STEP B

Students should look at publications outside the trade as well. Discuss in class how

---

ASPECTS OF INDUSTRY
Underlying Principles of Technology

Overview

In Unit Five, you read about a variety of skills you'll use in your career. In this Unit Lab, you will put into practice what you have learned about using thinking skills and technology in the workplace while exploring another aspect of industry: **Underlying Principles of Technology.**

Technology is the way in which science is applied to the practical aspects of life—in this case, work. Understanding the Underlying Principles of Technology can be vital to your career. If you can't keep pace with technological changes, you may be out of a job. By understanding how technology can affect your career, you can plan for training or even a career change.

Tools

1. Internet
2. Trade and business magazines
3. Science, general interest, and news magazines

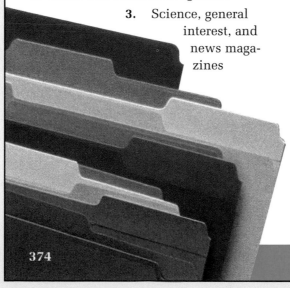

374

Procedures

STEP A

Choose three careers that interest you from the 15 job clusters shown in Figure 3-1 in Chapter 3. You may choose the careers from the same cluster, or from three different clusters. You may choose the same cluster you explored in the previous Lab, or a different one.

For each career, find at least three trade publications from 10 years ago. What technology was being used? What was new at the time? What scientific developments were affecting the career? What predictions were being made about the future of the career?

Next, find at least two science magazines (such as *Discover*), two general interest magazines (such as *Smithsonian*), and two news magazines (such as *Time*) from 10 years ago. Skim them for stories that relate to your chosen field. Note the technological, scientific, economic, and social trends of the time. What were the concerns of the public?

Keep copies of the articles you read or take notes. Refer to them when you do Step C and when you write your report.

STEP B

Fast forward to the present. Follow the procedure in Step A, using at least three

general interest, science, and news magazines may reveal trends that may affect students' careers. Social, economic, and political issues may force technological changes that affect a wide variety of careers.

This Lab requires a lot of reading; to save time and make it more interesting for students, you may want to assign the general interest, current trade publications (or two publications and an Internet source) to find out what technology is being used today. What is new? What scientific discoveries are affecting the career? What predictions are being made about the future?

Next, skim magazines published within the last year for stories that relate to each field. Note the technological, scientific, economic, and social trends, and public concerns.

STEP C

Flash 10 years into the future. You are recruiting high school and college students for a company or agency in one of the fields you previously researched. Working alone or with classmates, prepare a recruitment campaign.

In your campaign, show how the career has changed over the previous 20 years, and how it has been affected by scientific, technological, economic, and social changes. In your "trip to the future," you may discover that your chosen field has undergone considerable transformation. Show how that change took place, and why. Note the training that students of the future will need, or that your company may provide. What are the benefits of working in your career of the future?

Help students take advantage of their individual learning styles to create their campaigns. Suggest, for example, that kinesthetic learners build a diorama or display, or recommend that musical learners use music in their recruitment.

Encourage students to pool their strengths—logistic learners working with musical learners, or linguistic learners with kinesthetic learners.

Presentations should be as professional as possible. If students are performing presentations, remind them to dress the part.

Report

By this time, many students will have a fairly good idea of the career clusters, and the particular careers they are interested in. Encourage them, in their reports, to explore what the careers they've chosen will be like in the future.

REPORT

Write a one-page, word-processed report using the information you gathered in your library and Internet research.

- Describe how the predictions made 10 years ago about each career were or were not fulfilled.
- Which predictions being made now about the careers for the future seem most likely to you?
- Which of the three careers you researched seems best able to withstand current social, economic, scientific, and technological changes?

Keep your research, interview notes, and report in a folder entitled "Career Exploration."

375

science, and news readings to groups. Have each group report to the class on past and/or current trends in politics, economics, cultural, and social trends. Discuss, in general terms, how these trends might affect the 15 career clusters.

STEP C

Encourage students to think positively and creatively about the future in this assignment. You might want to work with other classes, staging a "job fair of the future."

Unit Overview

In this unit, students learn how to be wise consumers and money managers. They will explore banking services. They will examine the advantages and disadvantages of credit. Students will also learn to assess their insurance needs and, finally, the variety of taxes they must pay.

Introducing the Unit

Tell students that these chapters will help them learn how to spend their money wisely. Have students write a short explanation of:

- the term *consumer*,
- how they currently manage their money,
- the banking services they use,
- whether they've used credit and what type,
- whether they have insurance coverage and what types, and
- what taxes they pay.

Review students' answers. Then describe the chapters they will study in this unit.

Unit Project

Have students keep logs of all purchases they make during the course of this unit. The logs should include all goods and services—from clothing to entertainment to food. Tell students to include the amount of each purchase and what prompted the purchase. Have students tell how much money came in and went out each week.

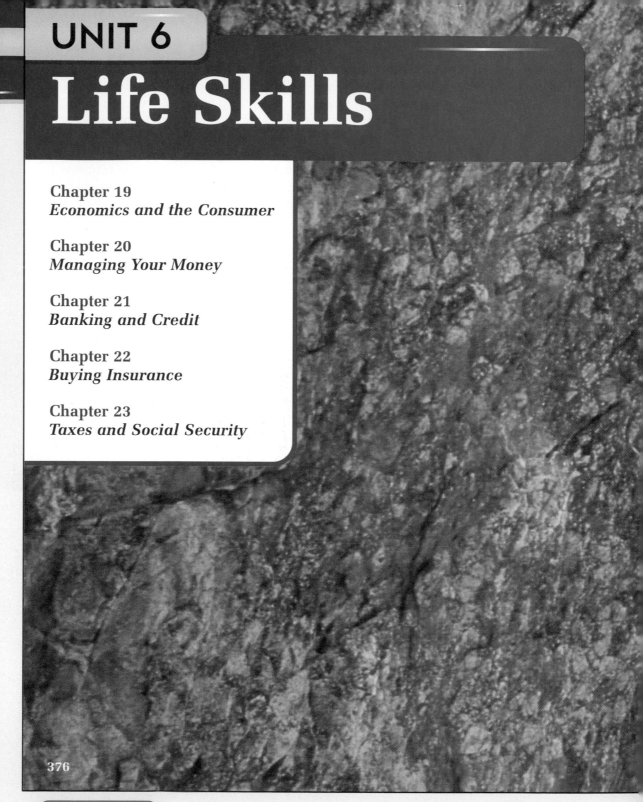

UNIT 6
Life Skills

Chapter 19
Economics and the Consumer

Chapter 20
Managing Your Money

Chapter 21
Banking and Credit

Chapter 22
Buying Insurance

Chapter 23
Taxes and Social Security

376

Developing Community Involvement

Work with a health organization in your area to develop an informational program for teens. Have students brainstorm topics they want to cover. (For example, depression, suicide, teen pregnancy, sexually transmitted diseases, or eating disorders.) Invite speakers and plan poster campaigns in local area high schools. Make the presentations fun as well as informative, perhaps involving local radio or television personalities or sports figures.

Resources for Enrichment

Books

- *Adventure Careers* by Hiam & Angle
- *The Minority Career Guide* by Kastre, Kastre, Edwards

Magazines

Best's Review (insurance), *Kiplinger's Personal Finance*, *Consumer Reports*

Organizations

- Council of Better Business Bureaus
- Small Business Administration

Internet

FedLaw—federal and government legal information: http://www.legal.gsa.gov

A Business Compass—Internet directory of business sites: http://www.abcompass.com

The Annual Report Gallery—Company annual reports: http://www.reportgallery.com

Unit Closure

Have students review their logs and calculate what they spent the most money on and who or what influenced them most. Have students decide how much money they could have spent more sensibly.

Unit Evaluation

Administer the reproducible test for Unit 6, which you will find in your Performance Assessment Binder, or construct your own test using the IBM Testmaker Software.

UNIT 6 QUIZ:

What Do You Know About Life Skills?

- How does the economy affect your life?
- How can you effectively manage your money?
- Can you name three ways to save money?
- Why is insurance important?
- Why do we pay taxes?

377

Building Partners in Industry

Does your city or town, your school, or perhaps even your school-to-work program have its own home page on the Internet? If so, you have a great opportunity to link all your program's participants—and even its potential participants—and to share your program's latest news. You can use the Internet to identify employers, to find new mentors, to share information about student-learners, and to let the rest of your community know what's going on in your school-to-work program.

• • • PLANNING GUIDE • • •
Chapter 19

SECTION 1 *Our Economic System*

SECTION OBJECTIVES	SECTION FEATURES	SECTION RESOURCES
• Define a free enterprise system and identify producers and consumers. • Describe the marketplace and explain why prices go up and down. • Explain three ways that the health of the economy can be measured.	Personal Career Plan, p. 379 Excellent Business Practices, p. 385 You're the Boss!, p. 386 Exploring Careers, p. 387	Workforce 2000 Videodisc and Videotape Section 19-1 Review, p. 386 Student Activity Workbook

CHAPTER 19

CHAPTER RESOURCES

- Chapter Transparencies and Lesson Plans
- Chapter 19 Test
- Spanish Resources, Chapter 19
- School-to-Work Activity Handbook, Chapter 19 Activity
- Teacher's Lesson Plans, Chapter 19
- Implementing Block Scheduling, Chapter 19
- Print, Media, and Internet Handbook
- Strategies for Implementing Work-Based Learning
- Strategies for Implementing Connecting Activities

SECTION 2 *You, the Consumer*

SECTION OBJECTIVES	SECTION FEATURES	SECTION RESOURCES
• Identify ways to make wise shopping decisions. • Describe common kinds of consumer fraud. • Identify ways to protect yourself as a consumer.	Attitude Counts, p. 390 Career Do's and Don'ts, p. 391	Workforce 2000 Videodisc and Videotape Section 19-2 Review, p. 392 Chapter 19 Review, pp. 394–395 Student Activity Workbook

Career Notes

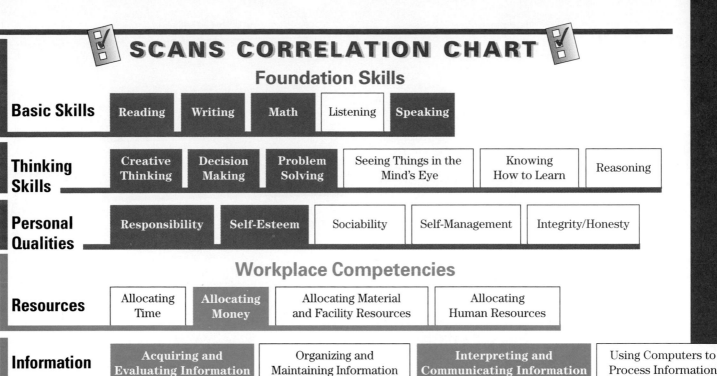

SCANS CORRELATION CHART

Foundation Skills

Basic Skills: Reading | Writing | Math | Listening | Speaking

Thinking Skills: Creative Thinking | Decision Making | Problem Solving | Seeing Things in the Mind's Eye | Knowing How to Learn | Reasoning

Personal Qualities: Responsibility | Self-Esteem | Sociability | Self-Management | Integrity/Honesty

Workplace Competencies

Resources: Allocating Time | Allocating Money | Allocating Material and Facility Resources | Allocating Human Resources

Information: Acquiring and Evaluating Information | Organizing and Maintaining Information | Interpreting and Communicating Information | Using Computers to Process Information

Interpersonal Skills: Participating as a Member of a Team | Teaching Others | Serving Clients/Customers | Exercising Leadership | Negotiating to Arrive at a Decision | Working with Cultural Diversity

Systems: Understanding Systems | Monitoring and Correcting Performance | Improving and Designing Systems

Technology: Selecting Technology | Applying Technology to Task | Maintaining and Troubleshooting Technology

Highlighted blocks indicate areas covered in the Chapter.

Additional Activities

 Internet Connection

Ask students to go on-line to discover what kinds of products are available, and how to purchase products and compare prices. Discuss their findings in class. Then ask them to discuss the advantages or disadvantages of shopping through the Internet.

 Field Trip Suggestions

Take students to a downtown shopping mall. Arrange to visit several types of retail stores, such as clothing, music, food, books, and so on. Talk to the staff briefly abut the skills needed, and the rewards of the job as well as problems. Have store managers explain buying and marketing.

 Guest Speaker Suggestions

Contact a local newspaper, or radio or television station, and invite the consumer affairs reporter to your class. Ask the guest to discuss the most common kinds of fraud and ways to avoid fraud. Have students prepare for the visit by researching consumer fraud.

Key to Ability Levels

Each section gives skill-building activities. Each activity has been labeled for use with students of various learning styles and abilities.

L1 Level 1 activities are basic activities and should be within the range of all students.

L2 Level 2 activities are average activities and should be within the range of average and above average students.

L3 Level 3 activities are challenging activities designed for the ability range of above average students.

Economics and the Consumer

Chapter Overview

Chapter 19 helps students become responsible consumers in a free enterprise economic system.

Section 19-1 describes the U.S. economic system and the roles that producers and consumers play in it.

Section 19-2 introduces factors that influence consumers, looks at ways to maximize buying power, and informs students of sources of consumer assistance and protection.

Background Information

Write chapter objectives (Sections 19-1 and 19-2) on the chalkboard or use the chapter objective transparency for class discussion.

Choose assignments from the *Student Activity Workbook* and write them on the chalkboard.

Have students preview the chapter, looking at pictures, reading captions, and noting content headings. Ask students to describe what they expect to learn in this chapter.

Preteaching Vocabulary

Write the Key Terms from Sections 19-1 and 19-2 on the chalkboard. Have students describe how each term relates to private enterprise and good consumer habits.

378

Meeting SPECIAL Needs

Behaviorally Disordered

Students with behavior disorders often must struggle to maintain the level of attention needed to deal with challenging material. To assist these students and encourage them to persist, you may wish to speak to them on an individual basis about their strengths and weaknesses. It might also be helpful to outline chapter objectives with an eye towards helping them feel successful.

Chapter 19

Economics and the Consumer

Section 19-1
Our Economic System

Section 19-2
You, the Consumer

In this video segment, find out how to become a wise consumer.

Journal
Personal Career Plan

In your journal, list the last five purchases you have made. For each purchase, record at least two factors that influenced you to buy that specific item at that specific time. On the basis of this list, how would you describe yourself as a consumer?

379

379

FOCUS

Bell Ringer

Write the word *choice* on the chalkboard. Have students write a definition of the word.

Introducing the Section

Have students share their definitions from the Bell Ringer activity. Then have them brainstorm a list of the economic choices we can make as U.S. citizens (for example, we can choose what to buy, where to buy it, where to work, where to live). Write the choices on the chalkboard.

Next, write the term *free enterprise* on the chalkboard. Ask students to define each word, then the term. Tell them that a free enterprise system is one that allows them to make economic choices.

Motivational Activity

Discussion

What factors might affect personal economic choices? (One of the key factors that affects personal economic choices is the financial ability to pay for items. Financial ability results from education or training that leads to a good-paying job; it results in career mobility and abundant work opportunities.)

Our Economic System

OBJECTIVES

After studying this section, you will be able to:

- **Define a free-enterprise system and identify producers and consumers.**
- **Describe the marketplace and explain why prices go up and down.**
- **Explain three ways that the health of the economy can be measured.**

KEY TERMS

economics
economic system
free enterprise
consumers
producers
marketplace
gross domestic
    product (GDP)
inflation

You buy goods and services all the time. It may seem like a simple process, but is it? What do you know about why businesses make and sell the goods they do? How are prices set? What causes prices to drop, or rise? How does this system of buying and selling goods and services work? How does it affect you?

You'll find answers to these questions by studying **economics**, the field of study that tries to explain how people produce, distribute, and use goods and services. The way people participate in these activities depends on the economic system of the country where they live.

An **economic system** is a country's way of using resources to provide goods and services that its people want and need. *Producing* means creating goods or services. *Distributing* means making goods and services available—through selling or delivering, for example—to the people who need them. What kind of economic system does the United States have?

As you learn about how our economic system works, you will also learn why conditions change so rapidly. With a basic understanding of the system, you will be able to prepare yourself for the challenges such a system presents.

Workforce 2000 Trends

Successful workers in the twenty-first century will continue to learn after they begin their careers by getting involved in industry organizations, reading trade and general interest magazines, and taking classes. Knowledge will give them the flexibility to take advantage of opportunities.

Addressing Workplace Diversity

Men and women are different, but talking about the differences can make people nervous. Their discomfort can manifest itself as intolerance. It is still important to talk about the differences until men and women understand the benefits that different perspectives bring to business.

The Free-Enterprise System

The economic system used in the United States is known as the free-enterprise system. **Free enterprise** means that individuals or businesses may buy and sell and set prices with little government interference. The government does have a role in our economic system, however. Laws set safety standards, regulate some prices and wages, and protect **consumers**. These are the people who buy and use goods and services.

Producers and Consumers

The companies or individuals who make or provide goods and services are known as **producers.** If you make specialty T-shirts, you are a producer of goods. If you baby-sit, you are a producer of a service. Have you ever been a producer?

What happens once goods and services are produced? People or other businesses *consume,* or buy and use, them. The people who buy your T-shirts and the people for whom you baby-sit are consumers. You become a consumer when you buy lunch, have clothes cleaned, or ride the subway.

Most people are both consumers and producers, although usually not at the same time. *Who are the consumers in this photograph? Who are the producers? How do you know?*

Guided Practice
Teaching Strategies

1. Assign and review Section 19-1.
2. Use the transparency for this section.
3. Assign and review the Case Study.

Discussion Starter

Ask students what they would do if, while shopping, they couldn't find anything they were looking for. Would they be surprised? What expectations do they have regarding product availability?

Teaching Tip

Discuss with students the huge variety of products that are available in the U.S. Who makes all these products? How does global business affect products teens can buy?

Explain to students that products may be made anywhere—in their city or another country. Local stores buy products from many different sources to meet the needs of consumers.

Critical Thinking

Tell students that they are writing to a teen living in a country that has a traditional or command economic system in which the government decides what products will be available to the public. Have students describe the U.S. free enterprise system to the teen.

▶ Extending the Illustration

Ask students how they are producers and consumers. (They are producers if they work for a company that provides goods or services; they are consumers when they buy goods or services.)

Caption Answer: Members of the audience are the consumers because they are using the services of the band. Members of the band are the producers because they are supplying the entertainment.

SCANS Foundation Skills Connection

L1 **Reading**

Have students read the business section of the local newspaper or *The Wall Street Journal*, clip at least three articles, and circle terms and concepts they studied in this section. Then have them discuss how these terms and concepts relate to a free enterprise economy.

L2 **Creative Thinking**

Have students think about a rice farmer living in southern Lousiana and a professor at a university in Chicago. Have students write about the two individuals' similarities and differences as consumers. What factors affect their decisions on which products to buy? (Factors include income, where they live, and job-related needs.)

L3 **Problem Solving**

Assign students to work in small groups to discuss whether price should be *the* major consideration when making a purchase. Tell students to consider how quality and function enter into the final decision to buy. Ask them if they have ever been disappointed with a product for which they paid a top price. How do they decide if something is a bargain? Have students share their comments in class.

Producers and consumers are like two sides of a coin. Although they're opposites, one can't exist without the other. *Figure 19-1* shows the flow of economic activity between producers and consumers. While you may be both a producer and a consumer, your goals are different in each role.

- Producers try to make goods or provide services that consumers will buy. A producer's main purpose is to make a net profit. As you know, net profit is the money left after operating costs and the cost of the goods or services have been paid.

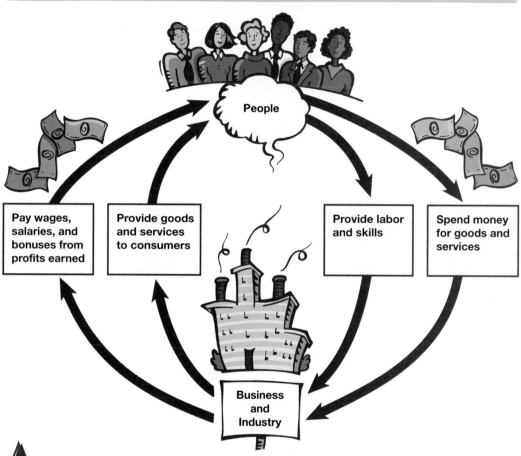

The Pattern of the Economy

People

Pay wages, salaries, and bonuses from profits earned

Provide goods and services to consumers

Provide labor and skills

Spend money for goods and services

Business and Industry

Figure 19-1 You are a participant in the free-enterprise system. You will work to help produce goods and services (if you don't already), and you consume goods and services. The outer circle of this illustration shows how consumer spending goes into businesses and comes back to you as a worker. The inner circle shows how your skills help produce goods and services, which consumers such as you need and want. How does the freedom of choice of a free-enterprise system affect these circles?

382 *Unit 6 • Life Skills*

▶▶▶ Extending Figure 19-1 ◀◀◀

Ask students what they think happens when consumers lack money to spend on the goods and services marketed by the producers. (Economic activity decreases and a recession may occur.)

Caption Answer: In our free enterprise system, you can choose where you work and what work you do. You can also choose what to consume.

- Consumers try to get what they need and want within the limits of how much money they have. Consumers influence what is made by what they buy.

How do producers and consumers accomplish their aims? They go to the marketplace!

What Is the Marketplace?

The **marketplace** is where buying and selling occur. This term really covers the whole realm of trade and business. Sometimes the producer and consumer are actually in the same place, as when you get your hair cut. Producers and consumers can also be geographically far apart. For example, you might buy a computer that was produced in another country or buy a magazine that was published in another state.

To reach consumers and to promote buying, producers practice marketing. *Marketing* is the process of getting products to consumers. It includes packaging, shipping, advertising, and selling goods and services. Because our economy is based on buying and selling, our free-enterprise system is called a market system.

Price Fluctuations

Have you noticed how the prices of CDs, jeans, haircuts, and other goods and

All of these "places" are part of the marketplace. *What are some examples of the marketplace you've "visited" recently?*

services keep changing? This is normal in a free-enterprise system. Why? Prices *fluctuate,* or go up and down, as a result of three main factors.

- *Supply and demand.* Supply is the amount of goods and services available for sale. Demand is the amount of goods and services that consumers want to buy. When supply is greater than demand, prices lower. When demand is greater than supply, prices rise.

- *Production costs.* The more it costs to make a good or provide a service, the higher its price will be. Because businesses must make a profit, they

Chapter 19 • Economics and the Consumer **383**

SCANS Workplace Competencies Connection

L1 Interpreting and Communicating Information

Have students work in small groups to investigate a particular category of consumer goods. Have them review issues of *Consumer Reports* and other periodicals that rate consumer goods. Have each group present its findings to the class and recommend a particular brand. Suggest that students use visual aids.

L2 Understanding Systems

Experts predict that the trend of people becoming entrepreneurs will continue as traditional, full-time jobs are replaced by temporary, part-time positions. Have students research which U.S. cities rank high in terms of opportunities and good business climate for entrepreneurs. What do these cities have in common? Discuss results in class.

L3 Acquiring and Evaluating Information

Divide students into teams and have them decide on a product or service to offer to classmates. Tell teams to discuss all aspects of making the product available and set a price, taking into account the costs they'll incur in getting their product to market.

Extending the Illustration

If your school has access to the Internet, have students visit some cybershopping sites. If not, obtain a magazine or a book that describes shopping on the Net and discuss in class. How might electronic shopping affect local malls and other stores? (Business could decrease as people buy through on-line shopping services.)

Caption Answer: Possible answers include a mall, video store, fast-food restaurant, radio or television commercial, advertising billboard, direct-mail letter, and so on.

Independent Practice

 Assign as homework the chapter activity in the *School-to-Work Activity Handbook.*

Reading

Have each student find and read an article describing the current state of the economy. Tell students to determine the level of unemployment, the level of inflation, and the percentage of annual growth in gross domestic product. Discuss in class how these factors affect the economy. (High unemployment means that fewer jobs are available. Inflation means that consumer products cost more. Low GDP growth may mean fewer new jobs and business opportunities. High growth may mean more jobs and opportunities.)

Skills Practice

In order to increase students' awareness of their roles as consumers, ask each of them to keep a Consumer Log for two weeks. Have them make a detailed record of each purchase and indicate whether it is a good or service, the quantity and price, and where they purchased it. Have students set up their logs in the form of a chart or a list.

After students complete their logs, hold a class discussion on how students, as consumers, are playing an active part in the free enterprise system.

must sell their goods or services for more than it costs to produce them.

- *Competition.* When two similar products are offered for sale, they are in competition. When competition is great, prices tend to be lower. When there is little or no competition, prices are higher.

In addition to prices going up and down, the economy itself fluctuates. This movement from good times to bad and back to good is known as the *business cycle.* **Figure 19-2** illustrates the four parts of this cycle.

▶ **Figure 19-2**

The Business Cycle

The economy normally goes up and down—somewhat like a roller coaster. However, no one can really be sure when each period of the business cycle will occur or how long it will last. For this reason, many economists prefer to talk about business fluctuations rather than the business cycle.

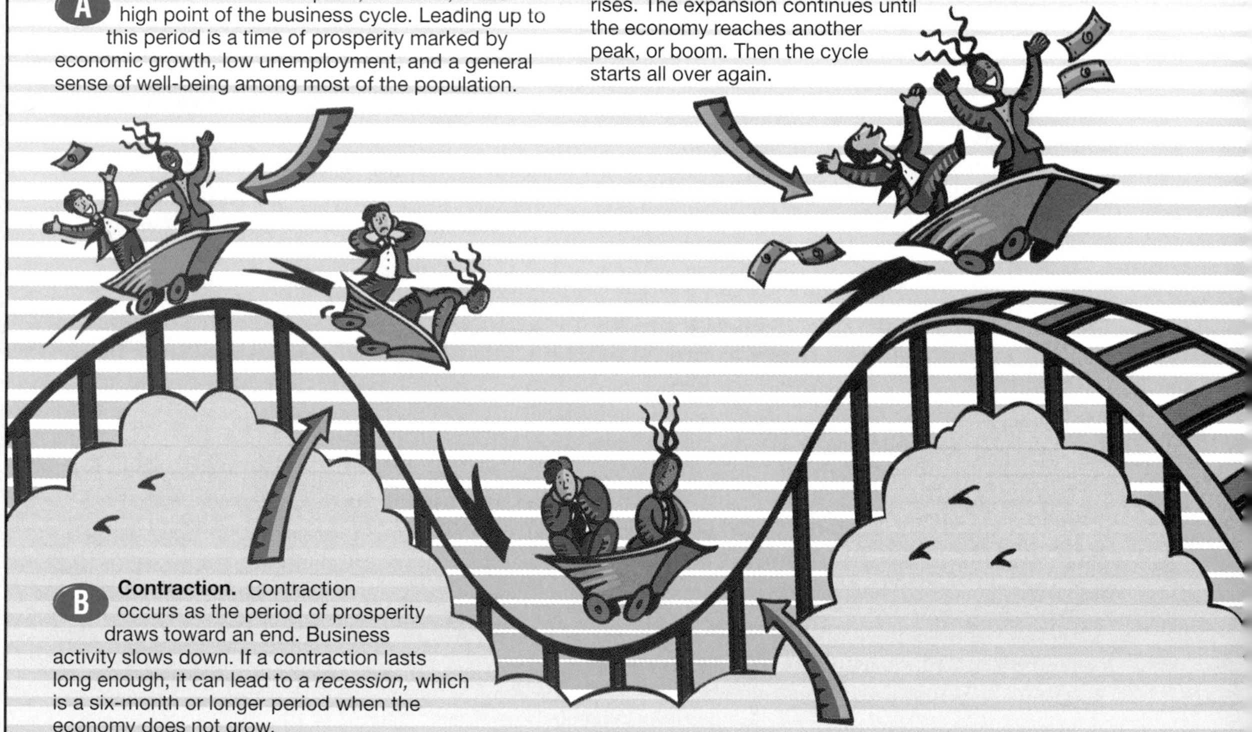

A **Peak or Boom.** The peak, or boom, is the high point of the business cycle. Leading up to this period is a time of prosperity marked by economic growth, low unemployment, and a general sense of well-being among most of the population.

B **Contraction.** Contraction occurs as the period of prosperity draws toward an end. Business activity slows down. If a contraction lasts long enough, it can lead to a *recession,* which is a six-month or longer period when the economy does not grow.

D **Expansion.** Expansion is an increase in business activity after a depression or recession. The economy starts to recover. People begin to spend money and open new businesses again, and employment rises. The expansion continues until the economy reaches another peak, or boom. Then the cycle starts all over again.

C **Depression.** If things continue to go poorly after the contraction, the economy can slide into a *depression,* which is a very serious recession. During a depression, many businesses fail, prices drop, and unemployment shoots up. Not every recession turns into a depression. In each cycle, the trough is the lowest point to which the economy falls.

384 *Unit 6 • Life Skills*

▶ Extending Figure 19-2 ◀

The U.S. government publishes data on specifics of the business cycle, including charts and graphs. Obtain some current graphs, either through the Internet or from your public library, and share them with students. Have them trace the economic cycles during their lifetime and during their parents' lifetimes.

Teaching **YOU'RE THE BOSS!**

✔ *(see feature on page 386)*

Possible responses: Talk to the customer to find out how the problems might be rectified; or observe the cashier more closely to see whether she is usually attentive to customers; or discuss with the cashier the importance of responding to any form of complaint from customers.

Measuring the Economy

Does the condition of the economy affect you? Absolutely! It can determine how much you make at a job, what you can afford to buy, and whether you can save money. Economic indicators measure the performance of the economy each year.

Gross Domestic Product

The total dollar value of all goods and services produced in the United States during a year is known as the **gross domestic product,** or **GDP.** This is the main indicator of the condition of the economy.

It enables one to compare this year's economy with last year's.

Consumer Price Index

The consumer price index, or CPI, measures changes in the prices of consumer goods and services. It is based on a monthly survey conducted by the Bureau of Labor Statistics. The survey tracks prices for a specific group of household goods and services. Among these are the costs for food, clothing, shelter, fuel, and medical services.

By showing increases or decreases in the cost of living, the CPI also measures inflation. **Inflation** occurs when the average

---

EXCELLENT BUSINESS PRACTICES

Ribs 101

Gates Bar-B-Q, a fast-food chain in Kansas City, Missouri, sends all 300 of its employees to training school. The company created seven basic classes to teach employees how to serve quality products. Each course lasts about two hours and concludes with a written test. Depending on their job, employees might learn how to cut a sandwich without leaving fingerprints, how to cut ribs, or how to brush sauce on the ribs and create an appetizing platter. All employees must attend classes, and they receive a nominal hourly raise upon completion.

Training helps solve the challenge of maintaining consistent quality in a service business with multiple locations. It creates a

pattern of teamwork and accountability and employees feel the company has a vested interest in their success.

Thinking Critically

How does consistency affect the consumer?

Extending EXCELLENT BUSINESS PRACTICES

Answer: When patronizing chain restaurants, consumers expect a certain level of quality. If service or quality of food is not the same from one restaurant to another, consumers may choose to avoid all restaurants in the chain.

Further Application: Have students visit a local franchise of a regional or national company. Ask the manager about the training program the company has established to ensure consistent quality.

Writing: *Informational*

Have students write 150-word reports describing how the business cycle might affect their future career choices. For example, what are the opportunities when business is in an expansion phase versus a contraction phase?

Discussion Starter

Ask students how the economy might affect the cost of a college education.

Teaching Tip

As students think of ways the economy might affect the future cost of higher education, write their ideas on the chalkboard. Be sure to include interest rate on student loans, tuition increases, cost of renting a dormitory room or an apartment, and cost of books and supplies.

Remind students that when interest rates are low, their college loans will cost less. Also, the overall condition of the economy will affect whether prices are increasing (as in inflationary times) or remaining steady (normal growth times).

Interview

Invite a local stockbroker to speak to your class about how the stock market operates. Ask the speaker to explain how economic activity affects stock prices and the volume of activity in the market. Set aside time for students to ask questions.

TEACH *(cont'd.)*

Research

Divide students into small groups. Tell each group to select a business they want to start; they each have $100,000. Have the groups decide what equipment they will need, where they will locate their businesses, the number of employees they will need, and the wages they will pay.

To make informed decisions, students will need to research the costs of equipment, rent, utilities, and the prevailing wages for the work they require. Have each group prepare a written report.

Discussion Starter

Ask students what their state's unemployment rate is. How does that rate compare with the national rate?

Critical Thinking

Ask students to take a position either for or against open international trade with very few barriers, such as high tariffs on products imported or exported. What effect do they think international trade has on their standard of living? How does it affect unemployment in the United States?

Have students write 150–200 word reports giving their position on the international trade issue and explaining the reason for the position.

 Inflation often leads to business closings. **Why do you think this is true?**

prices of goods and services rise sharply. If prices rise sharply but your wages don't, you cannot buy as much as you used to. Your *standard of living,* a measure of your quality of life based on the amount of goods and services you can buy, declines. Inflation affects the business cycle and can lead to higher unemployment.

Unemployment

A third economic indicator is the unemployment rate. The government figures this rate each month. It identifies the percentage of the labor force that is without work but is actively seeking employment. Low unemployment is a sign the economy is doing well because most people are working, earning wages, and consuming. High unemployment, on the other hand, indicates problems in the economy because many people are out of work. The result is a lower standard of living and personal difficulties for the families involved.

YOU'RE THE BOSS!

✓ *Solving Workplace Problems*

At your busy coffee shop, the cashier usually asks customers how they enjoyed their meal. Today you hear a customer reply with complaints about both the food and the service. You are surprised when your cashier just smiles and says what she always says: "Come back soon!" What will you do?

SECTION 19-1 *Review*

Understanding Key Concepts

Using complete sentences, answer the following questions on a separate sheet of paper.

1. Why do you think the government exercises some control over producers in our free-enterprise system?

2. Why do you think the government keeps track of fluctuations in the economy?

3. What could you infer if the gross domestic product was higher each year for three years in a row?

386 *Unit 6 • Life Skills*

SECTION 19-1 *Review* ANSWERS

1. Citizens choose to have their government protect consumers and promote a healthy economy.

2. Keeping track of what is going on allows it to intervene when necessary to try to prevent problems.

3. You could infer that the economy was growing and that it was probably healthy.

Extending the Illustration

Ask students what other impact inflation may have. (Inflation means that consumers can buy less because products cost more. As businesses sell less, they may have to lay off workers.)

Caption Answer: When prices go up, people tend to buy less. Especially, small businesses are negatively affected and may have to close.

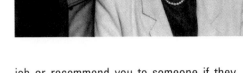

CASE STUDY

Exploring Careers: Communications and Media

Valerie Zavala
Vice President, News
and Public Affairs, KCET

Q: What are the most important skills for a television journalist?

A: Being able to determine immediately the essence of the story is a vital skill. You must be able to make decisions about which questions are the most important to ask in a short interview. You must be able to write a news story under tight deadlines. You also have to be able to present the information with some sense of drama or story.

Q: How does someone begin to get experience in television journalism?

A: Internships are very important. There is nothing like an internship to give you hands-on experience. You can see what it really takes to put a program together. It puts you in contact with people who can give you a job or recommend you to someone if they recognize you as being reliable and bright.

Q: What would you tell someone interested in television journalism?

A: I would advise that person to minor in communications, with a major in another field. A lot of young people going through college are not learning something meaty enough, like the history of the world or our country, or science, or English. Communication is a skill, not a body of knowledge. Intellectual depth can only come when you understand a field of knowledge really well.

Thinking Critically

Would you make a good television journalist? Why or why not?

CAREER FACTS

Nature of the Work:
○ Oversee program planning, editing, and taping; meet with community leaders and freelancers; budget money and time.

Training or Education Needed:
○ Degree in journalism or communications; experience in reporting.

Aptitudes, Abilities, and Skills:
○ Creative-thinking, decision-making, and writing skills; responsibility.

Salary Range:
Starting salary in a small market, about $12,000 to $16,000 a year; anchoring in a small market, about $27,000 to $35,000; higher salary possible in large markets.

Career Path:
Start with an internship; become an assistant to others in the field; advance as a reporter from small, to medium, then to large markets; move into production or management.

Chapter 19 • Economics and the Consumer **387**

Extending the CASE STUDY

Answer: Students who are able to work and make decisions under tight deadlines, and have good communications skills, might make good television journalists.

Further Application: Have students discuss the complementary learning they could do—in or out of college—that would enhance their abilities in their chosen careers. Architects could study painting or sculpture; health professionals could study other sciences; construction workers could study mechanics, cabinetry, or architecture, and so on.

Assessment

Performance

Have each student draw a chart identifying the factors involved in a free enterprise system, then portraying the interactions among them.

Evaluate students' charts for an understanding of the relationship between producers and consumers.

Evaluation

Assign the section review.

Reteaching

Outline this section of the chapter by writing the major headings and subheadings on the chalkboard. Have students explain the meaning of each one and give examples of Key Terms and concepts.

Extending the Content

Assign the appropriate Chapter 19 activities in the *Student Activity Workbook.*

Have students research the economic systems in at least two countries that do not have a free enterprise system. Have students write 200-word reports describing the similarities and differences between the two systems.

CLOSE

Have students complete this sentence: "I'm glad that I live in a free enterprise economy because . . . ." (Answers will vary but students might mention freedom of choice to make decisions about what to do, where to live, and what to buy.)

FOCUS

Bell Ringer

Write these headings on the chalkboard: *Item, Place of Purchase, Reasons for Buying.* Have students complete each category with their last three purchases.

Introducing the Section

Have students share their answers from the Bell Ringer activity. Ask whether the items purchased were name brands or generics. Bring to class several identical products—one name brand and one generic (for example, tissues, laundry soap, paper towels, a food product). Have students compare the unit costs, price, ingredients, and quality of each pair. Discuss which items seem to be the better value, all things considered. Ask students what factors they consider when deciding whether to buy a name brand or generic product.

Motivational Activity

Oral Presentation

Have students make one- or two-minute presentations describing a recent shopping experience in which they were smart shoppers or bought something they really didn't want or need because of sales pressure. Afterwards, have students discuss how they could improve their shopping skills.

You, the Consumer

OBJECTIVES

After studying this section, you will be able to:

- **Identify ways to make wise shopping decisions.**
- **Describe common kinds of consumer fraud.**
- **Identify ways to protect yourself as a consumer.**

KEY TERMS

consumer fraud
bait and switch
warranty

In our free-enterprise system, individuals as well as businesses make choices about earning and spending money. These individual choices are not always easy to make. How can you know the right goods and services to buy? How can you get the best price? If you're like most people, you have only so much money to spend. This makes the right choices very important.

Smart Shopping

Making good choices takes SCANS competencies such as allocating time, allocating money, and acquiring and evaluating information. Consider how these competencies are used when you follow each of these practical tips:

- *Pay attention to quality.* You'll save money in the long run by buying well-made items, especially when you expect to keep your purchases for a long time. Does a high price mean an item has higher quality than a less costly one? Not necessarily. *Generic products*, or products without brand names, usually have plain packaging and are relatively inexpensive.

  Buying generic products can be a smart move. When the quality of such products is high, you save because you are not paying for fancy packaging or expensive advertising.

- *When possible, plan the timing of your purchases.* You will find more bargains at certain times of the year. January and August are good

Implementing Teamwork

Organize students in pairs and have each one design an advertisement to attract teens to a new product or service. They may use any media to design the ads. Once completed, display the ads and ask students in class to select the most appealing advertisements.

Extending the Illustration

(see illustration on top of page 389)

Ask students how peer pressure might cause problems. (If a teen lacks the money to buy the kinds of items his or her friends have, he or she might feel less worthy.)

Caption Answer: Friends can tell you about good products they have purchased and bargains they have found.

sale months because many stores try to sell as much as possible to make room for the next season's goods.

You can also use the law of supply and demand. Instead of rushing out to buy a new videotape or CD, wait a few months. By then, the price may have been marked down because demand has lessened.

- *Take advantage of discount stores.* Discount and "warehouse" stores can offer excellent buys. Do your homework, however, *before* you get to the store because customer service may not be a high priority.

- *Explore on-line options.* On-line prices can be surprisingly low, and

It's easy to be influenced by your friends when you are buying clothes. *In what ways can your friends help you be a responsible consumer?*

you may find electronic shopping very convenient. In addition, product information is often available on the Internet. To protect yourself, however, read about on-line shopping in consumer magazines first. You cannot assume that all the information you get and all the companies you encounter on-line will be trustworthy.

Buyer Beware!

Be a smart consumer. Learn to protect yourself from **consumer fraud,** or dishonest business practices used by people who are trying to trick or cheat you.

Kathleen Coventry of Illinois learned about fraud the hard way. She responded to a telephone work-at-home offer. She

When shopping for clothing, a smart shopping tip is to always make a list. *Why do you think it might be a good idea to look through your wardrobe carefully before you shop for clothing?*

Chapter 19 • Economics and the Consumer **389**

Extending the Illustration

Ask students how making a shopping list can help them stick to a budget. (Buying only what is on their lists helps people avoid impulse purchases.)

Caption Answer: Looking at your wardrobe reminds you of all the different items. When shopping, you might choose one new clothing item over another if it coordinates with several things you already own. Looking at clothes you already have will also keep you from buying duplicates.

389

SECTION 19-2
TEACH

Guided Practice
Teaching Strategies
1. Assign and review Section 19-2.
2. Use the transparency for this section.

Discussion Starter
Give students this scenario. "You're with a friend who wants to buy athletic shoes. The store carries over a dozen kinds. Your friend says, 'These are the most expensive, so I guess that means they're the best.'" What would you say?

Critical Thinking
Have each student find an ad in a magazine that associates a product with a popular idea or person, suggests that use of the product will make one feel a part of a particular group, or suggests that buying the product is "in." Have students discuss their ads in class and identify how such ads affect their buying decisions.

SCANS Foundation Skills Connection

L1 Math
Tell students to keep track of all their expenditures for a week, including small purchases such as soft drinks. At the end of the week, have them determine the two largest categories of expenditures. Ask whether they were surprised at how much they spent in one week. Did they buy on impulse? How could they have spent less?

SCANS Foundation Skills Connection (cont'd.)

L2 Speaking

Have students research and debate on this issue: How much control should government have in protecting consumers and regulating business?

L3 Decision Making

Tell students that their boss has asked them to research and recommend the purchase of a color printer. What facts will they need to gather? What types of information should they include in a report?

SCANS Workplace Competencies Connection

L1 Improving or Designing Systems

Have students advise parents or a friend on specific ways to shop to avoid getting "taken in" by fraudulent advertising.

L2 Negotiating to Arrive at a Decision

Share this scenario: "Pat is working with a photographer, Ben, to publish a brochure. Since they have worked together before, Ben started work without a written contract. Now Ben tells Pat each photo will cost $275, which means Pat will go way over budget." How could Pat negotiate with Ben to lower the costs?

sent a salesperson a check for $153.95, trusting the salesperson's assurance that her money would be refunded if she were unhappy. Kathleen soon received a large envelope full of useless materials that provided only general suggestions such as "Start a home typing business." Kathleen said, "There was no way that any person could read this stuff and actually use the information [to start a home business]."

Kathleen promptly returned the envelope and requested a refund. More than a year later and after follow-up calls and letters, she still had gotten nothing back.

How can you avoid fraud? First, be aware that scams exist. Here are some common tricks of the fraud trade:

- *Fraudulent advertising.* Using a tactic known as **bait and switch,** a retailer advertises a bargain—the bait—to lure people into the store. When the

customers arrive, the store is "out" of the item. A salesperson tries to sell a similar product at a much higher price. This is the switch.

- *Auto repair fraud.* Dishonest mechanics may try to charge you much more than the estimated cost of a repair. They may replace parts that are not defective. To protect yourself, ask for written estimates and request that mechanics keep the old parts and show them to you.

Attitude Counts ✓

Having a positive attitude means expecting the best from yourself, from others, and from the goods and services you select for purchase. Knowing when and how to complain about faulty products and inefficient service is part of being a wise consumer—and part of having a positive attitude.

► Automobile repairs can be expensive. Make sure anyone working on your car explains the recommended repair to your satisfaction. *Why do you think some auto repair shops get away with fraudulent practices?*

► Extending the Illustration

Ask students to brainstorm some steps they could take to help ensure that the auto repair service they take their cars to is reputable. (They might contact the Better Business Bureau and ask about complaints against a business, ask friends and relatives for recommendations, or look for ASE certification.)

Caption Answer: Fraudulent repair shops depend on several factors, including people's need to have autos repaired immediately, customer ignorance about auto repairs, and the fact that breakdowns sometimes occur in unfamiliar places.

- *Phony prize notifications.* "Congratulations! You've just won our grand prize!" This great news may come by mail or phone. To get your prize, all you have to do is send in some money or make a small purchase. Some companies ask you to provide a credit card or checking account number for identification. Beware. Even cautious consumers can fall for this scam.

Most consumer frauds succeed by taking advantage of the consumer's search for a good deal. If an offer sounds too good to be true, it probably is. These tips may save you from becoming a victim: First, *never* give your credit card number over the phone if you didn't place the call. Second, don't send money to any unknown business or organization without checking first to be sure it is legitimate. For information, check with your state or local consumer office or the Better Business Bureau.

Groups That Protect Consumers

Suppose you buy something that breaks the first time you use it. What should you do? First, try to solve the problem by visiting the store where you bought it or by calling the company that produced it. If this doesn't work, you might write a letter of complaint. In your letter, be polite but firm. Be sure to save store receipts, and keep records of your communications with the business. As a last resort, you may need to take legal action. However, help is also available from several other sources.

Government Agencies

Government agencies, specialized organizations within the government, enforce consumer protection laws. They act as watchdogs over certain areas of the marketplace.

- The Federal Trade Commission (FTC) enforces rules about labeling, advertising, and warranties. Thanks to the FTC, the labels in your clothes provide care instructions. This agency also regulates the descriptions of products in ads and commercials to

Career Do's & Don'ts

To Be an Informed Consumer...

Do:
- compare prices.
- plan for and save up for large purchases.
- ask questions about quality.
- find out the store's policy on returning goods.

Don't:
- buy any large purchases on impulse.
- buy anything you aren't sure you will use.
- give in to a good sales pitch—be sure you want the product or service.
- hesitate to point out your rights as a consumer if you are not satisfied with service.

Chapter 19 • *Economics and the Consumer* **391**

MINI QUIZ

Short Answer

1. Those who create goods or services are called ____. (producers)

2. A mall is considered to be a ____ . (marketplace)

3. The price you pay for a pair of jeans is affected by the popularity of that product, in other words, its ____. (demand)

4. If you visit a store to buy an advertised bargain that is no longer available, the store may be guilty of ____ advertising. (bait and switch)

5. A ____ is your guarantee that the product meets certain standards of quality. (warranty)

make sure they are accurate.

A **warranty** is a guarantee that a product meets certain standards of quality. By FTC standards, a warranty must be clearly worded and conveniently placed.

- The Consumer Product Safety Commission (CPSC) helps protect the public against dangerous products. It sets safety standards for equipment and makes sure these standards are met.

- The Food and Drug Administration (FDA) enforces laws about the quality and labeling of food, drugs, and medical devices. It inspects workplaces that produce food and drugs.

Government agencies at the state and local levels also work to protect consumers.

Consumer Groups

Many private groups investigate consumer complaints, educate the public on consumer issues, and try to get consumer legislation passed. Examples of such groups are consumer action panels (CAPs) formed by trade associations, such as MACAP for major appliance manufacturers. A well-known consumer group is Consumers' Union, which publishes *Consumer Reports* and *Consumers' Research*.

Companies are not required by law to offer a warranty, but if they do, they must honor it. *Why would you prefer to buy an appliance that comes with a warranty?*

SECTION 19-2 *Review*

Understanding Key Concepts

Using complete sentences, answer the following questions on a separate sheet of paper.

1. What benefits will you obtain from being a wise shopper?

2. Where might you find information about new types of consumer fraud?

3. How does protecting yourself against consumer fraud help other consumers as well?

Key Terms

economics *(p. 380)*
economic system *(p. 380)*
free enterprise *(p. 381)*
consumers *(p. 381)*
producers *(p. 381)*
marketplace *(p. 383)*
gross domestic product
(GDP) *(p. 385)*
inflation *(p. 385)*

SECTION 19-1 Summary

- The United States has a free-enterprise economic system, in which there is limited governmental intervention in the production, buying, and selling of goods and services.

- The marketplace is the arena where producers and consumers "meet" for buying and selling, even though producers and consumers may be geographically far apart.

- Prices may go up or down, depending on supply and demand, production costs, and competition.

- The economy moves from good times to bad and back to good again. These fluctuations are called the business cycle.

- The condition of the economy can be measured by the gross domestic product, the consumer price index, and the unemployment rate.

Key Terms

consumer fraud *(p. 389)*
bait and switch *(p. 390)*
warranty *(p. 392)*

SECTION 19-2 Summary

- Smart shopping involves paying attention to quality, timing purchases, taking advantage of discount stores, and exploring on-line options when possible.

- Consumers have both rights and responsibilities.

- There are a number of methods of consumer fraud, including fraudulent advertising and phony prize notifications. Consumers need to be aware of fraud schemes and to be on guard against getting cheated.

- Government agencies and private consumer groups protect and educate the consumer as well as handle consumer complaints.

Chapter 19 • Economics and the Consumer **393**

Computer Activity

Have students use a database software package to collect data on products most often purchased by teens. Student may create questionnaires or interview other teens to obtain this information. The product categories are: music, clothing, shoes, fast food, and cars. Ask students to find out the brand names for each product and the number of students who would or have purchased that product. Then prepare a report or listing of the items in order, from the most to least preferred.

Use the Testmaker to create a customized test for Chapter 19.

Reteaching

1. Divide students into three teams. Have each team explain the content and give examples of one of the following topics: *smart shopping, consumer fraud,* or *consumer protection agencies.* Have students use visual aids.

2. Assign and review vocabulary terms, chapter questions, and activities from the Chapter Review.

Extending the Content

Assign the appropriate Chapter 19 activities in the *Student Activity Workbook*.

Fraud or poor automotive repairs are a major concern of consumers. Have students research the National Institute for Automotive Service Excellence, which certifies auto repair technicians. Tell students to survey auto repair companies in your area to see how many of them display the "ASE" certification sign. Have students share their findings in class.

CLOSE

Have students complete this sentence: "Consumers can protect themselves from dishonesty and fraud by . . . ." (Answers will vary but could include being a smart shopper, questioning business offers, and filing complaints.)

Answers

Reviewing Key Terms

Questions and answers will vary but should show an understanding of the terms.

Recalling Key Concepts

1. False: In a free enterprise system, prices and wages are set by individuals and businesses with little or no intervention by the government.

2. False: The more competition there is in the marketplace, the lower prices tend to be.

3. True

4. True

5. False: The Federal Trade Commission enforces those rules.

Thinking Critically

1. Possible answer: There might be fewer entrepreneurs because there would be less chance to rise through one's own hard work; people might not work as hard to create quality products if prices were fixed by the government.

2. Possible answer: If I had to choose between two jackets, I might buy the more expensive one, even if I didn't like it as much, if my friends had that kind of jacket.

3. If the advertised bargain was not in the store, I would not buy a more

---

Reviewing Key Terms

On a separate sheet of paper, write a series of questions and answers that use the following key terms.

economics
economic system
free enterprise
consumers
producers
marketplace
gross domestic
   product
inflation
consumer fraud
bait and switch
warranty

Recalling Key Concepts

On a separate sheet of paper, tell whether each of the following statements is true or false. Rewrite any false statements to make them true.

1. In a free-enterprise system, prices and wages are strictly controlled by government regulations.

2. The presence or absence of competition has no effect on prices.

3. The consumer price index and the unemployment rate are two yardsticks for measuring the economy.

4. Buying generic products when their quality is comparable to brand-name products is one way to save money.

5. The Consumer Product Safety Commission enforces rules about advertising, labeling, and warranties.

Thinking Critically

Using complete sentences, answer each of the following questions on a separate sheet of paper.

---

1. How would life in the United States be different if our economy had much stricter controls?

2. Describe a situation in which your friends might have a negative influence on your shopping choices.

3. How would you deal with a bait-and-switch scam?

4. List three features not mentioned in the text that you think would be important in an effective letter of complaint.

 ## SCANS Foundation Skills and Workplace Competencies

Thinking Skills: *Creative Thinking*

1. You have taken a job with a consumer protection agency. Your first task is to create a poster that provides consumer tips expressed in eye-catching and imaginative ways. Conduct research to come up with 10 tips. Then illustrate each one with drawings or magazine photos. Present your poster to the class.

Information Skills: *Acquiring and Evaluating Information*

2. The Consumer Information Center of the U.S. General Services Administration publishes a booklet called the *Consumer Information Catalog.* Find out the number to call to obtain it, how much the booklet costs, and what information it provides. Prepare a report of your findings.

---

expensive item. I would ask the salesperson for a rain check.

4. Possible answer: a clear statement of the problem, a clear indication of what you would like the company to do about the problem, and specific dates when various related events occurred

 ## SCANS Foundation Skills and Workplace Competencies

1. Posters should include 10 informative tips presented creatively.

2. The catalog is free and can be obtained by calling 719-948-4000 or writing to:

Connecting Academics to the Workplace

Language Arts

1. Adena recently bought an electronic pocket organizer to replace her address book. To her disappointment, the phone numbers keep getting lost. When she tries to recall a name, the number is garbled or has disappeared. Write a letter from Adena to the manufacturer explaining the defect. Tell the manufacturer what kind of action she would like it to take.

Math

2. Allen rents a cart in the business district to sell coffee to people on their way to work. In one week, he spends $17 on coffee, $7 on milk, and $3 on sugar. The rent for the cart is $105 per week. If each cup of coffee is 65¢, how many cups must Allen sell in a week before he begins to make a profit? What would his profit be if he sold 500 cups in one week?

Developing Teamwork and Leadership Skills

Working with a team of other students, find out about one consumer organization in your community. (Coordinate your efforts with other teams so that no two contact the same organization.) As a team, come up with 8 to 10 questions about the organization. Have one team member conduct a telephone or personal interview with a representative of the organization, being sure to get answers to the team's questions. Then write a report on the team's findings, and share it with the class. Divide tasks (such as conducting the interview, writing the report, and sharing the report with the class) equitably among team members.

Real-World Workshop

Select a local government agency that protects consumers. Examples include the health inspector's office and the office of the city building inspector. Interview an agency representative and learn what kinds of consumer protection are provided. Speculate on how you would be affected if the agency did not exist. Discuss your conclusions with the class.

School-to-Work Connection

Choose a consumer product that costs at least $200. Research three sources for the product, such as a department store, a discount warehouse, and the Internet. Write a report that compares prices, services, and other factors that would be involved in obtaining the item through each of the channels you have analyzed. At the end of the report, suggest which source you think would be the best choice.

Individual Career Plan

Write a journal entry describing how what you've learned about economics affects your view of the world of work. Would you like to find out more about starting your own business? Are you interested in fighting consumer fraud? Do you want to learn more about ways of measuring the economy?

Chapter 19 • Economics and the Consumer **395**

---

want the money back; some may request a new pocket organizer.

2. He would have to sell 204 cups to begin making a profit. ($17 + $7 + $3 + $105 = $132; $132 ÷ $0.65 = 203.08 cups) If he sold 500 cups in a week, his profit would be $193. ($500 × $0.65 = $325; $325 − $132 = $193)

Developing Teamwork and Leadership Skills

Teams should divide tasks equally, and the interviews should yield interesting and informative data.

Real-World Workshop

Students should identify ways in which the government agency operates to protect consumers. Students' speculations should demonstrate an understanding of specific effects the agency has on them as consumers.

School-to-Work Connection

Students' reports should reflect good research skills and intelligent analysis of the choices.

Consumer Information Center, Pueblo, CO 81009. The catalog lists approximately 200 free or low-cost federal booklets with helpful information for consumers.

Connecting Academics to the Workplace

1. Letters should be in correct business format and should clearly state the problem, tell when and where Adena bought the product, and indicate what she wants the manufacturer to do about the problem. Most students will probably

Individual Career Plan

Journal entries should demonstrate an understanding of chapter material and an ability to relate an aspect of the material to an individual area of interest.

• • • PLANNING GUIDE • • •
Chapter 20

SECTION 1 *Budgeting*

SECTION OBJECTIVES	SECTION FEATURES	SECTION RESOURCES
• Identify the steps in planning a budget. • Explain how to keep records effectively. • Describe strategies for staying within your budget.	Personal Career Plan, p. 397 Ethics in Action, p. 399 You're the Boss!, p. 401 Career Do's and Don'ts, p. 402 Excellent Business Practices, p. 404 Exploring Careers, p. 408	 Workforce 2000 Videodisc and Videotape Section 20-1 Review, p. 407 Student Activity Workbook

SECTION 2 *Coping with Financial Responsibility*

SECTION OBJECTIVES	SECTION FEATURES	SECTION RESOURCES
• Identify personal changes that might affect your finances. • Discuss ways to adjust to economic change. • List several sources of help for financial problems.		Workforce 2000 Videodisc and Videotape Section 20-2 Review, p. 412 Chapter 20 Review, pp. 414–415 Student Activity Workbook

CHAPTER RESOURCES

- Chapter Transparencies and Lesson Plans
- Chapter 20 Test
- Spanish Resources, Chapter 20
- School-to-Work Activity Handbook, Chapter 20 Activity
- Teacher's Lesson Plans, Chapter 20
- Implementing Block Scheduling, Chapter 20
- Print, Media, and Internet Handbook
- Strategies for Implementing Work-Based Learning
- Strategies for Implementing Connecting Activities

Career Notes

SCANS CORRELATION CHART

Foundation Skills

Basic Skills

| Reading | Writing | Math | Listening | Speaking |

Thinking Skills

| Creative Thinking | Decision Making | Problem Solving | Seeing Things in the Mind's Eye | Knowing How to Learn | Reasoning |

Personal Qualities

| Responsibility | Self-Esteem | Sociability | Self-Management | Integrity/Honesty |

Workplace Competencies

Resources

| Allocating Time | Allocating Money | Allocating Material and Facility Resources | Allocating Human Resources |

Information

| Acquiring and Evaluating Information | Organizing and Maintaining Information | Interpreting and Communicating Information | Using Computers to Process Information |

Interpersonal Skills

| Participating as a Member of a Team | Teaching Others | Serving Clients/ Customers | Exercising Leadership | Negotiating to Arrive at a Decision | Working with Cultural Diversity |

Systems

| Understanding Systems | Monitoring and Correcting Performance | Improving and Designing Systems |

Technology

| Selecting Technology | Applying Technology to Task | Maintaining and Troubleshooting Technology |

Highlighted blocks indicate areas covered in the Chapter.

Additional Activities

 ### Internet Connection

Managing money, credit, and investments are important topics. What information can students find on the Internet to help them? Ask them to look for counseling services, classes, or workshops. They should note at least five resources, the services offered, and the fees charged.

 ### Field Trip Suggestions

Have students go grocery shopping in pairs. At the grocery store, they should look for deceptive packaging or labeling, and compare prices for name brands and generic brands. Have students discuss their experiences in class.

 ### Guest Speaker Suggestions

Invite a teacher in the area who is known to have a flair for teaching living skills. Ask the guest to talk about keeping and balancing a checkbook, shopping, and budgeting. Ask students to prepare at least one question of concern to them.

Key to Ability Levels

Each section gives skill-building activities. Each activity has been labeled for use with students of various learning styles and abilities.

L1 Level 1 activities are basic activities and should be within the range of all students.

L2 Level 2 activities are average activities and should be within the range of average and above average students.

L3 Level 3 activities are challenging activities designed for the ability range of above average students.

School-Based Learning

Chapter Overview

Chapter 20 demonstrates how to plan a budget and keep effective records.

Section 20-1 introduces the concept of planned spending and suggests ways of making and staying on a budget.

Section 20-2 looks at financial responsibility and how to adjust to economic changes and to get help with money-management problems.

Background Information

Write chapter objectives (Sections 20-1 and 20-2) on the chalkboard or use the chapter objective transparency for class discussion.

Choose assignments from the *Student Activity Workbook* and write them on the chalkboard.

Have students preview the chapter, looking at pictures, reading captions, and noting content headings. Ask students to describe what they expect to learn in this chapter.

Preteaching Vocabulary

Write the Key Terms from Sections 20-1 and 20-2 on the chalkboard. Have students describe how each term relates to budgeting and managing one's money.

Meeting SPECIAL Needs

Learning Disabled

Students with learning disabilities can have difficulty processing written or verbal information or both. It is important to help them receive and give information in ways they understand best. Students with difficulty processing written work can get information from other sources such as graphs, charts and tables. Students with problems processing verbal information should read materials before class. Allow them to borrow classmates' notes.

Chapter 20

Managing Your Money

Section 20-1
Budgeting

Section 20-2
Coping with Financial Responsibility

In this video segment, learn why it's important to have a well-planned budget.

Journal
Personal Career Plan

In your journal, write your first responses to these questions:

• Do you think the government should stick to a budget? Why or why not?

• Do you think a small business should stick to a budget? Why or why not?

• Do you think you should stick to a budget? Why or why not?

397

Have each student use the Internet or public library to obtain an annual report for a business that interests him or her. Have each student look at the company's income statement, which is divided into revenue and expenses. Have students note the similarities and the differences between a business income statement and a personal budget.

Work-Based Learning Strategies and Activities

Arrange for each student to interview an accountant or financial officer of a local business, asking questions about the company's use of credit and the impact of the cost of credit on the business's net earnings. Also instruct students to ask the person to discuss the types of budgeting employees do to help the company estimate its earnings and expenses for the year.

Have students write summaries describing their companies' budgeting process.

WORKFORCE 2000 Training Video

Have students view the video and perform the interactive exercises to reinforce important chapter concepts and thinking processes.

Chapter 20

Addressing LEARNING Styles

Logical Learner

Have students record in their journals all the money they spend in a week. They should include every purchase, no matter how small. Have them think about a major purchase they would like to make, such as audio equipment or a car. Ask them to look at their weekly figures and decide what they could give up in order to save for the purchase. How much money could they save each week without really feeling deprived?

FOCUS

Bell Ringer

Tell students they each have $35 to live on for the next two weeks. Have them list what they will buy and how much they will spend on each item. Remind them that they need to buy a birthday gift for a friend.

Introducing the Section

Extend the Bell Ringer activity by asking how many of them would have money left over. If they ran over budget, what purchase would they choose to eliminate?

Ask students to give reasons why they should learn how to manage their money now. Then discuss how budgeting relates to fulfilling both short- and long-term financial goals. Explain that the choices people make can determine whether or not they meet their financial goals.

Motivational Activity
Demonstration

Give students this list of goals and costs: down payment on a new car, $3,000; purchase of a computer and printer, $2,500; purchase of furniture for an apartment, $5,000; down payment on a home, $10,000.

Choose differing savings rates, such as $50 to $200 a month, and work through the amount of time it would take to save for each of these goals.

Budgeting

OBJECTIVES

After studying this section, you will be able to:
- Identify the steps in planning a budget.
- Explain how to keep records effectively.
- Describe strategies for staying within your budget.

KEY TERMS

budget
record keeping

Imagine driving a car with a broken fuel gauge. You wouldn't know how far you could go. You couldn't be sure when your car might sputter and roll to a stop. A fuel gauge enables you to operate for a planned distance. It allows you to balance what you have with how far you want to go. A fuel gauge is a kind of reality check.

Now think about your economic life. To act effectively, you need enough fuel (income) to get where you need to go (to cover your expenses). Your economic fuel gauge is your budget. A **budget** is a plan for saving and spending money based on your income and your expenses. A well-planned budget can give you the same feeling of confidence that a fuel gauge that shows full does. With careful budgeting, you'll be able to handle everyday needs as well as achieve your dreams for the future.

Planning Your Budget

Why take the time to plan a budget? There are many valid reasons. After all, the stakes are pretty high. When you work, you trade valuable assets—your time, knowledge, skills, and effort—for money. You'll want to spend this money on things that are worth the time and effort you've put into earning it.

Begin your planning by asking yourself a few questions.

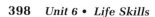

Implementing Teamwork

Organize students into four groups. Have each group check out different college financing programs (for example, grants, scholarships, federal assistance). They should list the requirements to apply and the deadlines. Ask them to write a paragraph on each funding source and present their findings to the class.

Many young couples dream of owning their own home. **What types of costs, other than the actual cost of buying the home, will this couple have to think about as they consider purchasing it?**

- What are your lifestyle goals?
- What's really important to you?
- What do you have, and what do you need?

You'll use your answers to develop a budget plan. You'll also use the SCANS competencies of allocating time, money, material, and human resources.

Defining Goals

The first step in getting anywhere is to decide on your goals. To begin budget planning, make two lists. On one list, write the things you need or want to spend money on now or within the next six months. Perhaps you need new glasses or want to buy a new bicycle. On the other list, put the things you need or want to spend money on in the future. Paying for an education, buying a home, and saving for retirement might go on this list.

The lists identify your financial objectives—at least right now. You aren't locked in to them. You can add or cut out some at any time. Writing down your objectives, however, helps you make plans to achieve them.

ETHICS in Action

You are shopping in the jewelry department of a large department store. While you are discussing a possible purchase with the clerk, you see an older customer slip an expensive watch into her purse and start to walk away. What will you do? Why?

Chapter 20 • Managing Your Money **399**

399

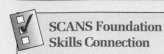
L1 Responsibility

Have students use a monthly calendar to mark the dates their bills are due—for example, car insurance or credit card payments; then have them mark dates they receive income. With that information, have them plan whether they can meet their financial obligations on time. What will they do if they fall short?

L2 Seeing Things in the Mind's Eye

Tell students to imagine themselves five years from now. Have them describe their lifestyles in terms of housing, automobile, personal possessions, vacations, leisure time, and so on. What are they doing now to reach their goals?

L3 Decision Making

Have students list five or six things they would like to buy. Then have them divide their list into *wants* and *needs*. Tell students their needs include anything they must have or do, for instance, repairing a flat tire. Have students write a paragraph describing how they spend their money in order to both meet their needs and satisfy their wants.

Making Choices

You probably have more items on the lists than you have money for. That's why the next step is to prioritize—that is, to put your goals in order of importance. Prioritizing helps you clarify what is most important to you and distinguish between your financial needs and your financial wants. As you prioritize, note a target date for each goal. This will help you keep track of how well you're doing.

Funding your education is a valuable financial goal. **How is money that you put into education an investment?**

Estimating Income and Expenses

The next step in planning your budget is to find out how much money you expect to have coming in (*income*) and how much you think will be going out (*expenses*). Try to estimate these amounts as accurately as you can.

If you have a job, your main source of income is likely to be your earnings. When you are figuring your earnings income, count only *net earnings*, the amount left after taxes and other amounts are taken out. Income also, however, includes tips, gifts of money, and interest on bank accounts.

Your expenses include costs for food, housing, and so on. Sometimes people divide expenses into two types. One type is *fixed expenses*, expenses you have already agreed to pay and that must be paid by a particular date. Rent and car payments are examples of fixed expenses. *Flexible expenses* are the other type. These are expenses that come irregularly or that you may be able to adjust more easily. Medical costs and costs of clothing are examples of flexible expenses.

▶ Extending the Illustration

Ask students if they know the sources of financial aid they might use to pay for an education. If not, schedule a class period for your school's guidance counselor to speak with the class about different types of financial programs available to college students.

Caption Answer: A good education can help you get a better job and be more financially stable. The money you spend on education pays off throughout your life.

Estimating Income and Expenses

Average Monthly Income

Net earnings	$1,188
Interest on savings	5
Gifts	20
	$1,213

Average Monthly Expenses

Rent (my share)	$350
Car loan	220
Car insurance	70
Food	160
Medical and dental care	50
Clothing	80
Transportation	125
Entertainment	60
Gifts and contributions	40
Miscellaneous	40
	$1,195

▲ **Figure 20-1** Here is one person's estimate of her average monthly income and expenses. Which of the expenses listed here vary most from month to month?

Examine your income and expenses for at least a month at a time. Many expenses (such as car or insurance payments) are paid monthly. Some will be paid even less often. For planning purposes, divide these kinds of payments into monthly chunks. For example, if you pay a life insurance premium every three months, or quarterly, divide the payment amount by three and place that number in your expense record as a monthly expense. *Figure 20-1* shows a sample income and expenses worksheet for a single person in her twenties who has a full-time job and shares an apartment with a friend.

Preparing and Following Your Budget

You've identified and prioritized your goals and estimated your income and expenses. Now it's time to get down to preparing your budget. Your budget will be your financial plan of action for the next month or year.

As you draw up your budget, remember to be realistic. Just like a diet that's too strict, a budget that's too strict will be impossible to fulfill. You'll end up feeling resentful. Having a budget doesn't mean doing without all the pleasures in your life. It may mean cutting back, however, and it always requires thinking before you spend.

YOU'RE THE BOSS!

Solving Workplace Problems

Your dry-cleaning business has only two employees, both of whom are hard-working and loyal. One of them tells you she should earn more than her coworker. "He has a wife who works and no children," she explains. "I'm on my own with three children to support. It's only fair that you pay me more." How do you respond?

Chapter 20 • Managing Your Money **401**

SCANS Workplace Competencies Connection

L1 **Applying Technology to Task**

Have students investigate financial software such as Quicken or Microsoft Money. What are the major features of each program? Can software help you to become a better money manager? How? Have students discuss their views in class.

L2 **Allocating Money**

Have students forecast the amount of money it will take for them to get a job in their chosen careers. Tell them to consider the cost of schooling or a training program, living expenses, and transportation. Have students allocate money for each type of expense for the duration of their education or training.

L3 **Acquiring and Evaluating Information**

Have students call several auto insurance companies to find out how much insurance would cost for a 21-year-old individual with a full-time job. Tell students to create tables organizing the information so they can compare quotes from each company.

►► Extending Figure 20-1 ◄◄

Have students look at amounts on the budget in this illustration. How much annual income would students be earning for this budget? ($14,256, not including gifts or interest)

Caption Answer: clothing, car maintenance, health care, and gifts

Teaching YOU'RE THE BOSS!

✓ Possible response: Explain that your workers' salaries are based on their work, not on their need.

Independent Practice

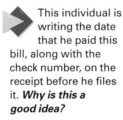 Assign as homework the chapter activity in the *School-to-Work Activity Handbook*.

Reading

Have each student read a current article about money management in a magazine such as *Kiplinger's Personal Finance* or *Money*. Tell students to take notes as they read, listing at least five points they could follow to improve their own money-management skills.

Writing: *Directions*

Tell students they are helping a friend learn how to budget money. Have them write directions for how to estimate income and expenses. They should then set up a budget. Have them include a list of typical expenses and tell how to keep records to track expenses.

Skills Practice

Give students this scenario. "George has been keeping track of his income and expenses. His total income for four months was $600, and his flexible expenses were $350. What were George's average monthly income and his average monthly flexible expenses? (*income*, $150: $600 ÷ 4; *expenses*, $87.50: $350 ÷ 4)

Career Do's & Don'ts

When Keeping Track of Your Money...

Do:
- make a budget and periodically update it.
- keep track of what you spend.
- pay bills when they are due.
- keep receipts of major purchases or anything you might return.

Don't:
- spend more than you make.
- make personal loans.
- put all your savings in long-term investments.
- let someone else be in charge of your money.

Keeping Effective Records

You'll need to get into the habit of **record keeping**, that is, organizing and maintaining records of your income and spending. Records will be useful in many different ways. To estimate income and expenses, for example, you would use records such as a check register, bank account statements, and bill receipts.

A handy and inexpensive way to organize your records is with an accordion folder. If you have a filing cabinet available, that's even better. Record-keeping software allows you to keep records on disk as well in hard copy. Even so, you'll need file folders or an accordion folder to keep your records. Remember, however, that records are useful only if they're kept up-to-date. Here are some tips for good record keeping:

- Keep files where you can get to them easily.

This individual is writing the date that he paid this bill, along with the check number, on the receipt before he files it. **Why is this a good idea?**

Extending the Illustration

It's also a good idea to write account numbers on checks written to pay bills such as mortgages and utility bills. Ask students how many of them follow this practice and discuss why it's a good idea. (So the recipient knows what the payment is for if the statement and the check are separated.)

Caption Answer: If any problem arises with the payment, he will know that he paid the bill, when he paid it, and which cancelled check he should look for, if necessary.

- File bills and records when you receive them.
- Keep a calendar where you can record when bills are due and when they were paid.
- Buy a fireproof box—or rent a safe-deposit box at a bank—to store important documents such as insurance papers, birth certificates, and car titles.

Getting Started

Use a standard form to plan your budget. The form shown in *Figure 20-2* is a good place to start. First, transfer the information from your income and expense estimate into your budget. Your income should be equal to or more than your total expenses. To make this happen, you may need to adjust various categories.

A Budget Form

Categories	Budgeted Monthly Expenses	Actual Monthly Expenses
Savings		
Emergency fund	_____	_____
Savings account	_____	_____
Fixed Expenses		
Rent or mortgage payment	_____	_____
Installment payments	_____	_____
Car loan	_____	_____
Car insurance	_____	_____
Health insurance	_____	_____
Life insurance	_____	_____
Credit card interest	_____	_____
Flexible Expenses		
Food	_____	_____
Utilities	_____	_____
Household supplies	_____	_____
Medical and dental care	_____	_____
Clothing	_____	_____
Transportation	_____	_____
Entertainment	_____	_____
Gifts and contributions	_____	_____
Miscellaneous	_____	_____
Total Spent	_____	_____
Total Income	_____	_____

Figure 20-2 This form is a typical one for planning a budget. How would you use the column at the far right?

Skills Practice

Suzanne's monthly income is $437, and her monthly fixed expenses are 53 percent of her income. What is the dollar amount of her fixed expenses each month? How much does she have left over for flexible expenses? (*fixed*, $231.61: $437 × 0.53; *flexible*, $205.39: $437 − $231.61)

Discussion Starter

Ask students if they've ever found their wallets empty and had no recollection of how they'd spent their money.

Teaching Tip

Tell students that a few dollars spent here and there can add up to a substantial amount over a few weeks. Have them brainstorm ways to keep track of spending. (Possible ways might include keeping a small notebook and jotting down the cost of meals or items bought, or keeping all sales receipts and adding them up periodically.)

Research

Have each student visit a local bank and find out the cost of renting a safe-deposit box in addition to restrictions regarding access to it. Ask them to share their findings in class.

▶▶ Extending Figure 20-2 ◀◀

Have students explore electronic budgeting programs. How might such programs be easier and more convenient than paper programs? (Having entered the categories of income and expenses, a user needs only to update amounts, not create a new budget when a revision is needed.)

Caption Answer: You would use it to record actual expenditures and compare them with estimates to determine whether you are sticking to your budget.

TEACH (cont'd.)

Discussion Starter

Ask students whether they see any problem in using credit cards to help them get through budget crunches.

Teaching Tip

Tell students to work through this example of what happens when you pay only the minimum on a credit card balance each month. Write a beginning balance of $200 and a minimum payment of $20, and these figues, on the chalkboard. The interest rate used is 1.5 percent per month.

Month 1

Beg. balance	$200.00
Less min. payment	20.00
New balance	$180.00

Month 2

Beg. balance	$180.00
Finance charge	2.70
New purchases	100.00
Total	$282.70
Less min. payment	28.00
New balance	$254.70

Month 3

Beg. balance	$254.70
Finance charge	3.82
New purchases	75.00
Total	$333.52
Less min. payment	33.00
New balance	$300.52

Point out that, although the amount of interest looks small, ask what would happen if an individual had thousands of dollars in credit-card debt. (Interest assumes more and more of the payment.)

Notice that there is a category for savings. This should *not* be an afterthought. Get in the habit of considering savings as a type of projected expense. If you establish a plan to save the same way you formulate a plan to pay your bills and make necessary purchases, you'll be more likely to do it. Chapter 21 will explain different savings options.

Your savings plan is your ticket to achieving your goals. There is also another reason to save regularly. Savings can help you create an emergency fund. An *emergency fund* is money you put aside for needs you can't anticipate. Everyone should have an emergency fund. A major illness or the loss of a job can be devastating if you do not have some money put away in an emergency fund.

Fine-Tuning Your Budget

You've prepared a budget, and you're using it as a guide. Is your job done? Of course it isn't. You will always need to make adjustments.

At the end of each month, check to see how you did at staying within your

EXCELLENT BUSINESS PRACTICES

Choose Your Own Benefits

Calvert Group, of Bethesda, Maryland, is a mutual funds company. It invests in companies that make safe products and have good environmental practices.

Calvert provides employees with core benefits that include life insurance, sick leave, disability benefits, holiday pay, and a retirement savings plan. Optional benefits, such as medical coverage and additional disability insurance, are paid for with pretax payroll deductions and with money Calvert gives employees each year for their benefits.

From their overall benefits dollars, employees can choose the level of insurance coverage and other programs. For example, the company gives employees who walk to work up to $120 per year for shoes. Those employees who bike to work are given up to $350 a year for a new bicycle. Employees can be reimbursed up to $3,000 a year for any classes they take. Calvert even allows up to 12 days off a year for community service and sponsors a wide variety of community activities. Since Calvert instituted its benefits plan, the turnover rate dropped from 30 percent to 5 percent.

Thinking Critically

What are the advantages and disadvantages of a flexible benefits program?

Extending EXCELLENT BUSINESS PRACTICES

Answer: *advantages:* offers options that fit various lifestyles and life stages of employees; allows employees to be aware of costs of benefit programs; allows employees to save money by not having to pay for unnecessary benefits

disadvantages: program may be too complicated; an employee's life-style might change unexpectedly, leaving him or her without needed benefits

Further Application: Have students interview a parent or other adult. Have them ask how much health and life insurance they have and how much it costs. If they receive these benefits from a job, how much are they actually receiving in a dollar amount?

Cooking meals at home rather than eating out is one way to cut your expenses. *What is another way you could cut expenses at this point in your life?*

budget. If your income doesn't cover your expenses or barely does, what can you do? You really have only two choices.

- *You can cut back on your expenses.* You may be able to fine-tune your budget by cutting flexible expenses. For example, pack your lunch every day instead of buying it. Save money on gas and parking by carpooling with a coworker.

- *You can increase your income.* You may be able to increase your income by working more hours or getting a better-paying job.

Keep fine-tuning your budget until it fits your needs. Your budget should serve as a guide, but it's not set in concrete. It can be adjusted as your income, expenses, needs, and wants change.

Chapter 20 • Managing Your Money **405**

Extending the Illustration

Have students think about ways they could cut expenses when they are employed and living on their own. (Possibilities include sharing an apartment, living near public transportation and putting off buying a car, or taking lunch to work instead of eating out.)

Caption Answer: Possible answers include waiting until movies are available in rental stores and getting together with friends to rent the movies rather than paying box office prices.

Skills Practice

Sharlene works for a local bank and earns $1,560 a month before taxes. She pays 16 percent in federal taxes and 5 percent in state taxes. She also has a deduction of $27 a month for health insurance. What are her net earnings? ($1,205.40: $1,560 × 0.16 = $249.60; $1,560 × 0.05 = $78; $249.60 + $78 + 27 = $354.60; $1,560 − $354.60)

Critical Thinking

Have students discuss why it is important to "pay yourself first" by setting aside a specific amount for your savings each month. (If you don't, you fail to reach your savings goals.)

Teaching Tip

Tell students to imagine that they lost their only winter coat. It's still winter and they need a new one. Do they have a special fund set aside to cover unexpected expenses?

Discuss the purpose of an emergency fund. Many financial planners suggest that people have three to six months of expenses in their emergency funds. Ask students whether they could cover their expenses for three to six months.

Discussion Starter

Ask students who have part-time jobs if they've ever received a raise. What did they do with the extra money?

Teaching Tip

Explain to students that a budget needs to change as income and expenses change. Also explain that creating a budget is only the first step: they must also monitor it, comparing actual income and expenses to budgeted amounts. If the two sets of figures are different, the budget needs to be adjusted. For example, if expenses are larger than budgeted, you need either to cut back on expenses or find a way to earn extra income.

Critical Thinking

Tell students that they are enrolled in a college or training program. They have a part-time job paying $7.50 an hour, and they're able to work 30 hours a week. Tuition costs are $300 a month. Students must make their own living arrangements; they can either walk or take the bus to school or work. Have them write a paragraph describing what they can afford in terms of rent and utilities, food and entertainment, transportation, and other expenses. Remind students to subtract state and federal taxes from their earnings.

► **Figure 20-3**

Staying Within Your Budget

Following a few simple spending rules can help you stay within your budget.

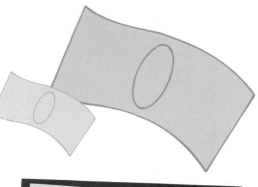

A Keep track of your spending. Carry a small notebook with you at all times. Get in the habit of making a note of every penny you spend. It will help your record keeping, and you will never have to ask yourself where your money went.

B Don't carry around a large amount of cash. You'll be too tempted to spend it on impulse. Just take what you'll need for your trip, along with a little extra for an emergency. Leave your ATM card at home too. This will force you to think before making a purchase.

406 *Unit 6 • Life Skills*

▶▶ **Extending Figure 20-3** ◀◀

Have students write a paragraph describing how overuse of a credit card can undermine a person's budget. (Credit-card interest adds up quickly when a card balance is not paid off in full each month. Too many charges and too few payments can derail any budget.)

Following Your Budget

Your budget can help you only if you follow it. Use your SCANS self-management skills to keep spending within the limits you have set. You'll find some practical hints for staying within the limits of your budget in *Figure 20-3.*

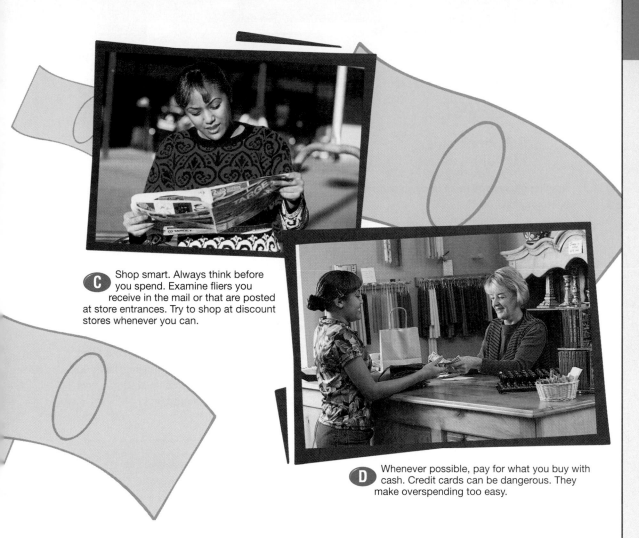

C Shop smart. Always think before you spend. Examine fliers you receive in the mail or that are posted at store entrances. Try to shop at discount stores whenever you can.

D Whenever possible, pay for what you buy with cash. Credit cards can be dangerous. They make overspending too easy.

ASSESS

Assessment

Performance

Have students create a budget by following the monthly earnings and expenses given below. Tell them to identify expenses as fixed or flexible.

Auto insurance, $70
Auto loan, $275
Clothing, $110
Entertainment, $70
Food, $180
Gifts and contributions, $50
Income (net), $1,420
Interest earned, $5
Medical and dental care, $40
Miscellaneous, $50
Rent, $355
Savings, $50
Telephone, $25
Transportation, $110
Utilities, $40

Evaluate students' budgets for accuracy and for inclusion of expenses in the correct category. (Fixed expenses are rent and auto payment; all others are flexible.)

SECTION 20-1 *Review*

Understanding Key Concepts

Using complete sentences, answer the following questions on a separate sheet of paper.

1. Why do you need to examine your financial goals before you create a budget?

2. How might accurate records be useful for tasks other than drawing up a budget?

3. How could you apply skills used in sticking to a budget in your workplace?

Chapter 20 • Managing Your Money **407**

SECTION 20-1 *Review* ANSWERS

1. Once you identify your financial goals, you can plan how you will reach them. You can't assign amounts for spending and saving without goals.

2. Possible answers: Receipts and such provide proof that you have paid for an item; this proof may be necessary when preparing tax forms.

3. To stick to a budget, you use skills such as decision making, problem solving, and self-management.

Evaluation

Assign the section review.

Reteaching

Ask for volunteers to explain budgeting and why it is an important means of planning for and reaching financial goals. Ask for other volunteers to explain the budgets in Figures 20-1 and 20-2. Have them explain why it is important to identify expenses as fixed or flexible. Finally, ask a volunteer to explain some techniques that might be used to follow a budget.

Extending the Content

Assign the appropriate Chapter 20 activities in the *Student Activity Workbook.*

Many financial experts recommend that young people begin saving and investing early in their careers. Have each student talk with a stock broker and ask what an annual savings of $500 invested in the stock market 10 years ago would be worth today. How much would it be worth if the same amount had been invested annually for 20 years?

CLOSE

Have students complete these two sentences: "My short-term financial goals (in the next two to three years) are . . . . My long-term financial goals (five years and beyond) are . . . ." (Answers will vary.)

CASE STUDY

Exploring Careers: Communications and Media

Bob Hernandez Photojournalist

Q: **How long have you been involved with photography?**

A: I was about 12 when I got interested in it through a youth club near my house. Both my older brother and my father were amateur photographers. I started shooting pictures for a community newspaper when I was 13. I got about $2.50 for my first picture and thought I could get rich doing this.

Q: **What's the most important skill for a photojournalist?**

A: Good storytelling ability. It doesn't make any difference whether you're shooting stills or video or film. You have to be able to tell a complete story with the camera, regardless of what the narration is going to be. Composition and the ability to use light will come. Those are skills you can learn.

Q: **How does someone get started as a photojournalist?**

A: A decent audition reel is the best thing you can have. It doesn't lie. It tells what you're capable of doing. You can't see that on a résumé.

Q: **How did you get started?**

A: I got an internship at the television station while I was still in school. I worked hard, won several awards, and made contacts. When the station expanded its programming, I applied for a full-time position. Because I had proved myself during my internship, I earned the support of the newsroom staff and was hired for the full-time position.

Thinking Critically

In what other careers might you be asked to provide more than a résumé as proof of your skills?

CAREER FACTS

Nature of the Work:
Hold meetings to plan stories; call to set up appointments; shoot the story; edit the film; sometimes, write stories.

Training or Education Needed:
Photography/video schools; internships; work at television stations

Aptitudes, Abilities, and Skills:
Listening, speaking, and interpersonal skills; ability to see images in the mind's eye; ability to work with your hands.

Salary Range:
Approximately $20,000 to $25,000 a year to start; higher salary possible with experience.

Career Path:
Start with an internship; work at a community television station or in small markets; work into the market you want.

408 *Unit 6 • Life Skills*

Extending the CASE STUDY

Answer: Architecture, fine art, and graphic art require portfolios; tooling and jewelry-making might require samples or a practical test; music requires demonstration tapes; other fields require a period of practical training, such as student teaching or medical internships.

Further Application: Have students discuss television programs and films that have influenced them in their choices of careers or have changed their thinking about a topic. If you have film students in your class, ask them for their insights on how film presentation can affect how the viewers feel about the film's topic.

Coping with Financial Responsibility

OBJECTIVES

After studying this section, you will be able to:
- **Identify personal changes that might affect your finances.**
- **Discuss ways to adjust to economic change.**
- **List several sources of help for financial problems.**

KEY TERM

financial responsibility

Ellie was feeling good. She'd landed the job she wanted and her salary was fine. She'd had to move and to buy a car, but with her salary, she thought she'd have no trouble making the payments. Unfortunately, several months into her job, Ellie found out that her employers had overextended themselves. They couldn't afford all the new people they had taken on. Laid off, Ellie was faced with high monthly bills and no way to pay them.

What could she have done differently? After all, no one can be expected to see into the future. Should people go through life expecting the worst to happen? Neither option is a good one. There is a middle ground, however, in which you are willing to take some risks but are also prepared for unexpected problems. The key is responsible financial planning.

Adjusting to Personal Change

As you move toward adulthood, your **financial responsibility**, or accountability in money matters, increases. When you were a young child, someone else paid for your food and clothing as well as your wants. When you started getting an allowance or began a part-time job, your financial responsibility may have increased. Perhaps you were expected to pay for some family purchases. In the future, as you move out on your own, your level of financial responsibility will increase even more.

Chapter 20 • Managing Your Money **409**

SECTION 20-2
FOCUS

Bell Ringer

Have students define the term *financial responsibility*.

Introducing the Section

Review students' answers from the Bell Ringer activity. Then ask them to name the things for which they will eventually be financially responsible; write this list on the chalkboard. Tell students that in this lesson, they'll learn ways to adjust to economic changes and strive to attain financial responsibility.

Motivational Activity
Critical Thinking

Tell students to imagine their lives 10 years from today. Where are they living? Are they married? Do they have children? What are their financial responsibilities? How are they meeting their financial goals?

Have students write one or two paragraphs describing themselves and listing the things for which they will be financially responsible.

Addressing Workplace Diversity

To improve relationships with men at work, women should continue their interest in people, relationships and feelings, but reduce the amount of time they talk about these things; learn to talk a bit about sports, business, or money, which men traditionally discuss. (*Genderflex* by Judith Tingley)

Workforce 2000 Trends

When compensation and benefits directors of 300 large corporations were interviewed by a consulting firm, half said that, based on current corporate financial conditions, the average salaried manager won't be able to retire at 65 on the company benefit package.

Teaching Strategies

1. Assign and review Section 20-2.
2. Use the transparency for this section.

Discussion Starter

Ask students how family financial responsibilities have changed in the past 30 years and why this change has occurred.

Teaching Tip

The major change in family financial responsibilities has been the increase in the number of women in the workforce. A majority of families today have two wage earners.

Critical Thinking

Tell students to imagine that they have inherited a lakefront lot; they've learned that the lot is worth less today than when it was purchased five years ago. Ask students whether they would keep the lot or sell it. What factors would they consider in making their decision?

SCANS Foundation Skills Connection

L1 **Creative Thinking**

Tell students that they work as sales representatives. Their total monthly income varies because most of their income is in the form of commission. How would they adjust their budgets to account for such income variations?

Personal Life Changes

Family	Occupation	Health
Marriage	Starting a career	Becoming disabled
Birth or adoption of children	Changing jobs	Growing older
Family member in need of financial help	Starting your own business	Experiencing chronic illness
Aging parents in need of care	Becoming unemployed	Being diagnosed with terminal illness
Death of a spouse or other close family member		
Receipt of an inheritance		
Separation or divorce		

Figure 20-4 This list shows life changes that might require you to alter your financial plans. Choose one item from the list and explain how you could prepare yourself for it ahead of time.

Increasing independence is one type of personal change that requires financial planning skills. You will experience other types as well. Take a look at *Figure 20-4.* It lists life events—some positive, some not—that will require changes in your financial plans. By recognizing these possibilities, you'll be better able to cope with the changes they will bring.

Adjusting to Economic Change

It's not just personal events that can change your financial outlook. Events throughout the nation and the world also can affect your finances.

Inflation and Recession

You may have to refigure your budget during a time of inflation, or a general increase in prices. As long as economic conditions are good, prices tend to edge upward over time, as do wages. What hurts is rapid inflation, when prices go up but wages don't.

During times of inflation, your dollars will buy less than they did before. Some tips for coping with inflation include:

- Cut back on unnecessary expenses.
- Look for a second job to increase income.
- Be a wise shopper. Take advantage of sales, for example, and buy food in bulk whenever possible.

 Extending Figure 20-4

Discuss with students that some life changes can be planned, such as getting married. Other changes are unexpected, such as losing a job. Ask students how financial planning early in their careers might help them deal with unexpected life changes. (Early financial planning may mean that they have funds set aside that could be used for unexpected needs.)

Caption Answer: A possible answer is that you could prepare for becoming unemployed with an emergency fund that would tide you over until you got a job.

During a recession, when the economy does not grow for six months or more, your finances may also be affected. Recessions may be local—as when a major employer in the area closes down or moves away—or national. During a recession, some employers lay off workers. Because of widespread unemployment, workers often find it difficult to land new jobs.

The tips you just read for times of inflation will also be helpful in a recession. In addition, you can do the following:

- Save as much money as possible.
- If you are laid off, accept job placement help if your former employer offers it.
- Talk to a loan officer at your bank to see whether you can refinance any debt to make lower payments.

If you've planned well before the period of inflation or recession, you'll have an emergency fund. That will be a source of help to you.

 Most banks are willing to help with financial planning when a job loss occurs. *How could a bank help you if you lost your job?*

Chapter 20 • *Managing Your Money* **411**

 SECTION 20-2

L2 Self-Management
Have students list four ways they can demonstrate responsible money management. How can they improve their money management skills?

L3 Self-Esteem
Ask students how buying things make them feel. Can they spend less money and still feel good? Have students discuss their feelings in class.

SCANS Workplace Competencies Connection

L1 Teaching Others
Divide students into teams. Have each team member teach the others how he or she manages money. (For example, by reconciling a bank statement or setting up a savings plan.) Students need not divulge amounts of money.

L2 Allocating Money
Have students brainstorm in groups of three or four the kinds of expenses they can anticipate as working adults. Have each team make a list and share with the class.

L3 Applying Technology to Task
Have students use a computer program to design a form they can use to help track their income and expenses over the next year.

Extending the Illustration

Ask students what other businesses should be notified in the case of a job loss. (Utility companies, credit-card companies, and local businesses may all be willing to work with someone who has been a good customer but needs time to pay current bills.)

Caption Answer: A bank could refinance or consolidate debts, offer a home-equity loan to a homeowner, or offer advice about avoiding financial problems.

Independent Practice
Interview

Have students interview a financial manager at a local bank and ask for money management suggestions for someone just beginning a career.

ASSESS

Assessment
Content

Have students write one or two paragraphs listing the factors that could affect their financial stability in the future, and the resources that can help manage their finances.

Evaluate students' papers for an understanding of how economic changes can affect a person's financial situation.

Evaluation

Assign the section review.

MINI QUIZ

True-False

1. Budgeting is a key part of helping people achieve their financial goals. (true)

2. For budgeting purposes, income is classified either as fixed or flexible. (false)

3. Most people do not need an emergency fund. (false)

4. Economic conditions can affect your budget. (true)

5. Several free sources are available to help you learn how to manage money. (true)

Finding Help for Money Management Problems

If you run into trouble managing your finances, help is available. The list that follows highlights sources of help. Remember that many of these sources are good suppliers of financial information even if you aren't having problems.

- *Published sources.* Newspapers often have money management columns that offer timely advice. You can also examine magazines devoted to money matters, such as *Kiplinger's Personal Finance* and *Money*. In addition, most family magazines regularly provide useful tips on money issues. Bookstores carry a comprehensive selection of books on managing your money.

- *On-line sources.* Don't forget the Internet. Financial Web sites may provide informational articles, useful statistics, and practical advice.

- *Schools.* Many continuing education institutions and community colleges offer money management classes. Teachers and counselors may also be available to give you one-on-one advice.

- *Government agencies.* Free or inexpensive booklets providing consumer financial information are available from government agencies. You can find these at local libraries and at federal and county offices.

- *Banks.* Many banks offer free financial advice to their customers. Some even hold seminars on money management.

- *Professionals.* Lawyers, accountants, and financial planners will also provide financial advice. You will have to pay for their services, however.

SECTION 20-2 *Review*

Understanding Key Concepts

Using complete sentences, answer the following questions on a separate sheet of paper.

1. How will having a budget help you cope with personal changes?

2. What could you do to keep yourself informed about possible economic change?

3. Describe how you might use two of the sources listed in the text to help you manage your money now.

SECTION 20-2 *Review* ANSWERS

1. A budget will help you save money to prepare for unexpected costs; also, a budget allows you to adjust to change by showing you where your money is going now.

2. You could read the newspaper or news magazines, watch television news, and check financial news on the Internet.

3. Students may say they might subscribe to a financial magazine or take a course in financial management to find ways to lower expenses or where to invest their savings.

Key Terms

budget *(p. 398)*
record keeping *(p. 402)*

Key Term

financial responsibility
(p. 409)

SECTION 20-1 Summary

- Begin planning your budget by defining your financial goals, prioritizing those goals, and estimating current income and expenses.

- Make your budget realistic. Otherwise, you probably won't follow it.

- Record keeping—organizing and maintaining records of all of your income and spending—is important. Your files should be up-to-date and accessible. Store important documents in a fireproof box or in a safe-deposit box at a bank.

- Your budget will be based on your estimated income and expenses. Be sure to include savings in your budget. You may need to fine-tune your plan by decreasing expenses or increasing income.

- Effective strategies for staying within your budget include paying cash for purchases, shopping wisely, and thinking before spending.

SECTION 20-2 Summary

- Financial responsibility, or accountability in money matters, increases during a person's lifetime. Over time, personal changes also occur that require adjustments to budgets and goals.

- Economic changes such as price increases during times of inflation and economic downturns, or recessions, require effective money management skills. Economic changes also may mean cutting down on expenses, increasing income, and accepting help from others.

- Help for money management problems can come from publications, on-line sources, educational institutions, government agencies, banks, and various types of professionals.

Chapter 20 • Managing Your Money **413**

Computer Activity

Using a spreadsheet software package, ask students to create a weekly expense form and gather data about their personal expenditures. Using this information, ask them to project a monthly budget to meet the fixed and variable expenses. Have them build in formulas to total expenses by category for the month. Ask them to write an explanation if they typically spend more than they earn. Use this information to lead a discussion on budget planning and financial security.

SECTION 20-2

Use the Testmaker to create a customized test for Chapter 20.

Reteaching

1. Have students read through this section again and list the factors that might affect their personal finances, as well as places they could go for help with money management. Then have them research the name of one person or resource under each type of money management resource in your area.

2. Assign and review vocabulary terms, chapter questions, and activities from the Chapter Review.

Extending the Content

Assign the appropriate Chapter 20 activities in the *Student Activity Workbook*. Have each student write a 100-word case study about a person who faced a financial challenge and handled it well by economizing in other areas. Have students share their case studies in class.

CLOSE

Have students complete the following statement: "Personal financial responsibility means . . . ." (Answers will vary but might include being able to take care of all your financial needs.)

Answers

Reviewing Key Terms

Paragraphs will vary but should reflect an understanding of the meanings of the terms.

Recalling Key Concepts

1. c
2. b
3. a
4. b
5. a
6. c

Thinking Critically

1. If you overestimate income or underestimate expenses, you will not be able to stick to your budget. You might experience a false sense of financial security.

2. Both inflation and a recession will cause people to cut expenses and possibly refigure their budgets. During a time of inflation, however, a person might try to get a second job. During a recession, this might not be possible.

3. The reasons probably include embarrassment at not managing money well, fear of the consequences, or lack of knowledge about where to find help.

Reviewing Key Terms

On a separate sheet of paper, write a paragraph about managing your own money. Use the terms below in your paragraph.
   budget
   record keeping
   financial responsibility

Recalling Key Concepts

Choose the correct answer for each item below. Write your answers on a separate sheet of paper.

1. The first step in planning your budget is to ____.
   (a) cut expenses
   (b) obtain budget software
   (c) identify your financial goals

2. You should file your bills ____.
   (a) once a year
   (b) as you receive or pay them
   (c) only after you prepare your taxes

3. One way to help yourself stay within your budget is to ____.
   (a) track your spending
   (b) use credit cards for most purchases
   (c) carry your ATM card at all times

4. Personal changes that affect your finances include ____.
   (a) inflation (b) adopting a child
   (c) recession

5. Inflation, recession, and unemployment are all examples of ____.
   (a) economic change
   (b) flexible expenses
   (c) fixed expenses

414 *Unit 6 • Life Skills*

6. You can usually receive free or low-cost help for financial problems from ____.
   (a) lawyers (b) accountants
   (c) government publications

Thinking Critically

Using complete sentences, answer each of the questions below on a separate sheet of paper.

1. When you are preparing a budget, why is honesty with yourself important in estimating income and expenses?

2. How are the effects of inflation and a recession similar, and how are they different?

3. Why do you think that many people avoid seeking help with financial problems until the problems become serious?

 SCANS Foundation Skills and Workplace Competencies

Thinking Skills: *Problem Solving*

1. Miranda hopes to have her own pottery shop someday. She currently makes and sells planters. This supplements her salary from the grocery store where she works full-time. She is having trouble staying within her budget. List at least three factors that Miranda will have to consider as she seeks to solve her budgeting problem.

Information: *Organizing and Maintaining Information*

2. Assume that you live at home and go to school, have a part-time job, make

 SCANS Foundation Skills and Workplace Competencies

1. Miranda will have to consider factors such as what flexible expenses she might be able to trim, whether she has time to make additional planters and whether there is a market for more of

them, and whether she could increase her hours at the grocery store.

2. Possible answers: Car expenses, Earnings, Entertainment, Food, Miscellaneous, School expenses, Telephone; students may also include files for schedules for school and volunteer work.

payments on a car, pay for your own phone, and volunteer at a hospital. You want to set up a record-keeping system. How will you organize and label your files? Write an alphabetized list of the files you'll want to keep.

Connecting Academics to the Workplace

Math

1. Kim's net earnings are $640 a month. Kim lives at home, paying $100 a month for room and board. She also spends $3 a day on lunch at school, five days a week. She wants to be an electrician and needs to save $120 each month toward classes at a trade school. She's making payments of $220 a month on a used car she bought, and she pays her parents $25 a month toward the insurance. She spends an average of $7 a week on gas. How much does Kim have left over each month for other expenses?

Human Relations

2. Tim works for a large company that has recently experienced financial setbacks. The company plans to cut all salaries by 5 percent. To help employees adjust, the company wants to offer financial counseling. Research resources that could be used in such a program.

Developing Teamwork and Leadership Skills

Work with a team of three. First, agree on a realistic money management problem that might occur in an individual's or a family's life. Then assign each team member one of the sources of financial help listed in Section 20-2. Each team member should find out from the assigned source what help would be available for the problem. Finally, work together to prepare an oral report on the team's findings for presentation to the class.

Real-World Workshop

Describe a hypothetical family that might live in your region. Find out what income, living expenses, transportation costs, and other budget items there might be for this family. Create a monthly budget for the family (use a form similar to the one shown in Figure 20-2), and present it to the class.

School-to-Work Connection

Work with a group of three. Contact a bank, school, or professional organization that helps people with financial planning. Set up an interview to find out what five tips a representative would give to people graduating from high school to avoid financial problems. Within your group, decide how you will present the tips to the class. Possible formats include a skit or a poster.

Individual Career Plan

Choose a career in a business or industry that interests you. Create a list of ways that you think good management of your own finances could help you succeed in this career.

Chapter 20 • Managing Your Money **415**

Developing Teamwork and Leadership Skills

Presentations will vary. Students' oral reports should demonstrate an ability to use the resources effectively to help solve the problem.

Real-World Workshop

Budgets will vary but should be based on current costs in your area as well as the characteristics of the family described.

School-to-Work Connection

Presentations will vary but should be clear and appropriate for the tips given. Teams should display an understanding of the tips and demonstrate effective skills in assigning and completing tasks.

Individual Career Plan

Responses will vary, depending on job choices. However, every job will involve some level of financial responsibility and planning or will utilize the management and problem-solving skills appropriate for personal financial management.

Connecting Academics to the Workplace

1. Kim has $87 left over every month. Her net earnings are $640 a month. ($320 × 2) Her monthly expenses total $553. ($100 + $60 + $120 + $220 + $25 + $28 = $553; $640 − $553 = $87)

2. Students' answers will vary, but students should at least investigate the resources mentioned in the text.

· · · PLANNING GUIDE · · ·
Chapter 21

SECTION 1 *Saving Money*

SECTION OBJECTIVES	SECTION FEATURES	SECTION RESOURCES
• Compare common saving methods. • Explain the characteristics of different retirement plans.	Personal Career Plan, p. 417 You're the Boss!, p. 422	Workforce 2000 Videodisc and Videotape Section 21-1 Review, p. 422 Student Activity Workbook

SECTION 2 *Checking Accounts and Other Banking Services*

SECTION OBJECTIVES	SECTION FEATURES	SECTION RESOURCES
• Shop wisely for a checking account. • Write a check and fill out a check register. • Reconcile a checking account.	Attitude Counts, p. 424 Excellent Business Practices, p. 426 Exploring Careers, p. 428	Workforce 2000 Videodisc and Videotape Section 21-2 Review, p. 427 Student Activity Workbook

SECTION 3 *Using Credit Wisely*

SECTION OBJECTIVES	SECTION FEATURES	SECTION RESOURCES
• Describe different types of credit. • Explain the advantages and disadvantages of using credit. • Explain how to compare credit costs.	Career Do's and Don'ts, p. 431	Workforce 2000 Videodisc and Videotape Section 21-3 Review, p. 432 Chapter 21 Review, pp. 434–435 Student Activity Workbook

CHAPTER 21

CHAPTER RESOURCES

- Chapter Transparencies and Lesson Plans
- Chapter 21 Test
- Spanish Resources, Chapter 21
- School-to-Work Activity Handbook, Chapter 21 Activity
- Teacher's Lesson Plans, Chapter 21
- Implementing Block Scheduling, Chapter 21
- Print, Media, and Internet Handbook
- Strategies for Implementing Work-Based Learning
- Strategies for Implementing Connecting Activities

SCANS CORRELATION CHART

Foundation Skills

Basic Skills	Reading	Writing	Math	Listening	Speaking

Thinking Skills	Creative Thinking	Decision Making	Problem Solving	Seeing Things in the Mind's Eye	Knowing How to Learn	Reasoning

Personal Qualities	Responsibility	Self-Esteem	Sociability	Self-Management	Integrity/Honesty

Workplace Competencies

Resources	Allocating Time	Allocating Money	Allocating Material and Facility Resources	Allocating Human Resources

Information	Acquiring and Evaluating Information	Organizing and Maintaining Information	Interpreting and Communicating Information	Using Computers to Process Information

Interpersonal Skills	Participating as a Member of a Team	Teaching Others	Serving Clients/ Customers	Exercising Leadership	Negotiating to Arrive at a Decision	Working with Cultural Diversity

Systems	Understanding Systems	Monitoring and Correcting Performance	Improving and Designing Systems

Technology	Selecting Technology	Applying Technology to Task	Maintaining and Troubleshooting Technology

Highlighted blocks indicate areas covered in the Chapter.

Additional Activities

 ### Internet Connection

Credit unions are a popular alternative to banks and are available to many people. Ask students to use the Internet to find out more about credit unions—what services they offer, how they differ from banks, and how to become eligible to participate.

 ### Field Trip Suggestions

Send students on a simulated clothes-buying spree. Students will shop for work-appropriate clothes. They should write down each item they "buy" and its price. Post their lists in class and declare the one with the most for his or her money a champion shopper.

 ### Guest Speaker Suggestions

Invite to class a bank representative, a collection agency representative, and a financial advisor who helps people take charge of credit debt. Ask the guests to discuss the pleasures and pitfalls of credit cards, debit cards, and buying on time.

Key to Ability Levels

Each section gives skill-building activities. Each activity has been labeled for use with students of various learning styles and abilities.

L1 Level 1 activities are basic activities and should be within the range of all students.

L2 Level 2 activities are average activities and should be within the range of average and above average students.

L3 Level 3 activities are challenging activities designed for the ability range of above average students.

Banking and Credit

Chapter Overview

Chapter 21 helps students understand banking and how banks can help them manage money.

Section 21-1 compares different types of savings plans.

Section 21-2 teaches students how to use a checking account and on-line banking services.

Section 21-3 describes types and cost of credit.

Background Information

Write chapter objectives (Sections 21-1, 21-2, and 21-3) on the chalkboard or use the chapter objective transparency for class discussion.

Choose assignments from the *Student Activity Workbook* and write them on the chalkboard.

Have students preview the chapter, looking at pictures, reading captions, and noting content headings. Ask students to describe what they expect to learn in this chapter.

Preteaching Vocabulary

Write the Key Terms from all three sections on the chalkboard. Have students describe how each term relates to savings plans, checking accounts, and credit use.

416

Meeting SPECIAL Needs

Limited Proficiency in English

Provide students with limited English ability outlines of lecture notes or planned classroom discussion topics in advance. The opportunity to review lecture notes and look up unfamiliar vocabulary also allows students with limited English skills to prepare responses in advance to questions you might ask.

Chapter 21

Banking and Credit

Section 21-1
Saving Money

Section 21-2
Checking Accounts and Other Banking Services

Section 21-3
Using Credit Wisely

In this video segment, find out about the disadvantages of credit.

Journal
Personal Career Plan

Even though you don't yet have a full-time job, your first credit card— preapproved—has just arrived in the mail. Will you keep the card? Why or why not? If so, how will you use it? Record your responses in your journal.

417

> **School-to-Work Connecting Activities**

Have students research careers available in the banking and finance industries. What skills are needed to work in these careers? What technological skills are needed? What is the occupational outlook over the next five to ten years? Have students write summaries of at least three careers and include the information in their career files.

Work-Based Learning Strategies and Activities

Arrange for students to visit the accounting department of a local business. Have them observe the procedures used to verify and pay regular business expenses. Ask an accountant to explain the business's checking account and the similarities between it and a personal checking account.

Have students write summaries describing their observations, drawing conclusions about money management in a business.

WORKFORCE 2000 Training Video

Have students view the video and perform the interactive exercises to reinforce important chapter concepts and thinking processes.

Chapter 21

Addressing **LEARNING** Styles

Linguistic Learner

Financial terms such as *dividend* and *certificate of deposit* can be confusing. Ask students to choose one of the terms in this chapter. They should define the term, then list all the related words and synonyms they can think of to help classmates remember and understand the term. For example, the term *IRA* could be surrounded by phrases such as "pay later, lower taxes, or after-60-party account." Have students create posters.

FOCUS

Bell Ringer

Ask students what they would do with $500 they earned from a summer job. How could they invest the money and make sure that it grows?

Introducing the Section

Review students' answers from the Bell Ringer activity. Then discuss the value of saving and planning ahead for future financial needs. Explore the concept of compound interest to be sure students understand how compounding works.

Tell students that in this section, they'll learn about various ways of saving and how to evaluate the best plan for their needs.

Motivational Activity

Demonstration

Demonstrate for the class the result of saving $600 each year and investing it for 10 years at a 7 percent return. Using a calculator, multiply $600 times 1.07 for the first year. Add $600, then multiply that amount by 1.07 for the second year. Continue to repeat this process for the third through tenth years. The total will be $8,870.16. Point out to students that they would have earned $2,870.16 on the $6,000 saved over the years.

Discuss with students the impact of saving even larger amounts or investing it for higher returns.

Saving Money

OBJECTIVES

After studying this section, you will be able to:
*   **Compare common saving methods.**
*   **Explain the characteristics of different retirement plans.**

KEY TERMS

dividend
certificate of
    deposit (CD)
401(k) plan
individual
    retirement
    account (IRA)
Keogh plan
simplified employee
    pension (SEP)

It's been termed *moolah, bread, dough, bucks,* and *greenbacks.* In plain language, it's money. Chapter 20 explained how a budget allows you to keep track of money you've worked for. This chapter will give you guidance on how your money can work for you.

Ways to Save

Saving and investing are the way to put your money to work. Most people begin by opening a savings account at a bank, savings and loan association, or credit union. A *credit union* is a not-for-profit financial institution similar to a bank. People who belong to a credit union, however, share a common bond, such as working at the same company.

There are two basic types of savings accounts. With a *passbook account,* you receive a booklet in which transactions are recorded. With a *statement account,* you receive a computerized statement, usually monthly, of transactions.

With either type of account, you deposit money and the institution pays interest. *Interest* is the money that banks pay depositors for the use of their money. Usually, interest is a percentage of the amount deposited.

Normally, interest paid on a savings account is *compounded.* That is, the interest is figured on the amount of money you have deposited *plus* the interest that has accrued on your initial deposit. The effects of compounding are shown in *Figure 21-1.*

Implementing Teamwork

Organize your class into groups of four students and ask each group to form a business partnership. Each group should check into different retirement plans available for a small business. Have each group analyze the information and write a memo to you recommending the best retirement plan.

Computer Activity

Have students use a spreadsheet software package to compare three different savings plans by displaying the earnings potential on a $5,000 investment. Have them show the interest that could be earned in one year, five years, and ten years. Then ask students to make a recommendation about the best savings plan available.

How Compounding Makes $1,000 Grow

Month	Beginning Balance	Monthly Interest at 5%	Ending Balance
January	$ 1,000.00	$ 4.17	$ 1,004.17
February	$ 1,004.17	$ 4.18	$ 1,008.35
March	$ 1,008.35	$ 4.20	$ 1,012.55
April	$ 1,012.55	$ 4.22	$ 1,016.77
May	$ 1,016.77	$ 4.24	$ 1,021.01
June	$ 1,021.01	$ 4.25	$ 1,025.26

▲ Figure 21-1 This table shows how much interest is paid on a $1,000 deposit when the interest rate is 5 percent, compounded monthly. The beginning balance is multiplied by 5 percent and then divided by 12 (because a month is $1/12$ of a year). Why does the interest increase from month to month?

How else can you put your money to work? Following are a few other ways of putting your money to work for you. Use your SCANS decision-making skills to choose the best ones for you.

- *Savings bonds.* When you buy a U.S. savings bond, you are lending money to the government. You buy a bond for half the "face value," which is the amount printed on the bond. Each year the bond grows in value until it has matured, or become payable. You can then *redeem*, or cash it in, for the full face value.

- *Money market deposit accounts or money market mutual funds.* These are other savings options. With a money market account or fund, you deposit money that is pooled with money from other savers and then invested. You are paid a **dividend**, or share of the fund's profits.

- *Certificates of deposit.* With a **certificate of deposit (CD),** you deposit an amount of money for a

fixed amount of time at a stated interest rate. Choosing a longer investment period often ensures you a higher interest rate.

Look at *Figure 21-2* on page 420. It compares these different savings strategies.

Retirement Plans

When should you start putting aside money for your retirement? According to many experts, you should begin when you receive your first paycheck. You may be surprised to learn that Social Security, even combined with retirement plans offered by employers, rarely provides sufficient income for the retirement years. The following are some retirement plan options. Use your SCANS competency of acquiring and interpreting information as you examine them.

Pension Plans

A pension plan is a retirement plan funded, at least in part, by an employer

Chapter 21 • Banking and Credit **419**

►► Extending Figure 21-1 ◄◄

Have students calculate interest on the beginning balance ($1,000) at different rates, for example, 6 percent and 7 percent. Ask students why a part of good financial management is getting the best return on your investment.

Caption Answer: The interest is added to the balance each month. In the following month, interest is paid on the new balance, which includes the previous month's interest.

SECTION 21-1
TEACH

Guided Practice
Teaching Strategies

1. Assign and review Section 21-1.

2. Use the transparency for this section.

Teaching Tip

Ask a representative from a local bank to discuss savings and investment options with the class. Ask the speaker to compare different forms of saving and discuss requirements for each, such as minimum balances and early withdrawal penalties.

Discussion Starter

Have students help you make a list of things they saved money to buy. Then ask how they saved the money. Did they use a savings account? Certificates of deposit?

Critical Thinking

Have students write 100-word papers comparing the retirement savings benefits offered through employer plans and those for self-employed persons.

☑ SCANS Foundation Skills Connection

L1 Writing

Have students search the local newspaper for ads showing current interest rates on savings accounts and certificates of deposit. Have students make charts showing this data for at least five banks or savings institutions.

SCANS Foundation Skills Connection (cont'd.)

L2 **Reasoning**

Have students research the cost of an education at one of your state's four-year schools. How will they pay for their education? Will they consider part-time jobs, assistance from parents, savings, and student loans? Which sources would they use?

L3 **Seeing Things in the Mind's Eye**

Have students picture themselves at retirement age. How old will they be? Have students talk with a financial planner or a bank representative to get an estimate of the annual income they'll need for retirement. How much should they save annually to prepare?

SCANS Workplace Competencies Connection

L1 **Acquiring and Evaluating Information**

Have students survey their friends and families asking how many save money regularly. If they have saving plans, do they invest their money in savings accounts, certificates of deposit, or in mutual funds? What are their reasons for savings? Why did they choose that particular form of savings? Have them share their findings in class.

Comparing Ways to Save

Type of Savings	Characteristics	Advantages	Disadvantages
Savings **Passbook or Statement Account**	• Money deposited in a savings account at a bank, credit union, or savings and loan association • Interest paid on the money in the account	• Can open account with only a few dollars • Easy access • Savings of up to $100,000 often protected by Federal Deposit Insurance Corporation (FDIC)	• Low interest rate • Interest rate not fixed
Certificate of Deposit (CD)	• Purchased at banks and other financial institutions • Money invested for a fixed time, usually six months to several years • Interest paid on money in the account • Traditionally, the longer the term of investment, the higher the interest rate	• Fixed rate of interest guaranteed for term of the deposit • Better interest than regular savings account • Savings of up to $100,000 often protected by FDIC	• Money tied up for fixed period of time • Penalty for early withdrawal • Must invest larger amounts of money, usually $500 or more
Money Market Deposit Account/ Money Market Mutual Fund	• Money market deposit accounts purchased at banks; money market mutual funds sold by mutual funds or insurance companies (a fund is made up of many investors)	• Usually pays higher interest than regular savings account • Money can be withdrawn at any time • Checks usually can be written on account • Savings in money market accounts often insured by FDIC	• Interest rate varies • Requires minimum deposit, which varies with type of account • Bank may not pay interest if balance drops below a minimum amount
U.S. Savings Bond	• Purchased at banks or other financial institutions or directly from the government • Available in set amounts from $50 to $30,000 (face value) • Purchased for half the face value • Grows in value each year; worth face value at maturity	• Can be purchased for as little as $25 • Interest not subject to state or local taxes • Very safe; value guaranteed by the U.S. Treasury	• Money tied up for a period of time • If money is withdrawn early, owner gets less than face value

►► Extending Figure 21-2 ◄◄

Have students obtain from local banks current rates for passbook savings accounts, CDs, money market funds, and U.S. savings bonds.

Caption Answer: They might invest in a plan that is not insured because the interest rate is higher than that of an insured plan.

Figure 21-2 All of these savings plans are relatively safe investments. Savings bonds, which are guaranteed by the U. S. Treasury, along with plans protected by FDIC insurance, are extremely safe. Why might someone invest in a plan that is not insured?

or union. The pension builds up throughout a worker's career. The amount of the pension is based on the employee's salary and the length of service with the company. Here are three common types of pension plans:

- In a *defined-benefit plan*, your company pays you a fixed amount at retirement. You know before you retire what amount you will receive.

- In a *defined-contribution plan*, sometimes called a profit-sharing plan, your employer contributes a set amount to the plan each year. The amount you receive at retirement depends on how much money has built up in the fund.

- In a **401(k) plan**, you put a specific portion of your salary into the plan. Employers often match this contribution, up to a specific amount or salary percentage.

People today are living longer, healthier lives than past generations. *What does this mean for individuals just starting out in their career?*

Chapter 21 • Banking and Credit **421**

Extending the Illustration

Have students research the current life span for males and females in the U.S. What has been the trend over the past several decades?

Caption Answer: They will probably enjoy more years of retirement and therefore should start saving for retirement earlier.

L2 **Organizing and Maintaining Information**

Have students obtain one or more credit applications from a financial institution. Review the applications in class and ask students about similarities and differences. Then have students complete a form, using their own credit history. Students may want to keep these forms for future reference.

L3 **Allocating Material and Facility Resources**

Have students organize filing and storage systems for their financial documents such as bank statements, loan payment books, or school financial aid information.

Independent Practice

Assign as homework the chapter activity in the *School-to-Work Activity Handbook.*

Reading

Have students find an article on personal investment options, such as mutual funds or real estate investments. Have them make note of at least three savings suggestions offered in the article and share their findings in class.

Writing: *Informational*

Have students write letters to a friend explaining the benefits of beginning a savings plan while young.

Assessment

Content

Have each student write a paragraph or two describing various ways to invest personal savings and ways to build funds for retirement.

Evaluate students' paragraphs for clear writing and for inclusion of at least three ways to save and at least three retirement plan options.

Evaluation

Assign the section review.

Reteaching

Divide students into four groups. Assign each group one of the savings methods described in Figure 21-2. Have each group make posters or flip charts to illustrate its topic and then present the information to the class.

Extending the Content

Assign the appropriate Chapter 21 activities in the *Student Activity Workbook*.

Have students research growth in the stock mutual fund industry in the past five years. Have them write at least 250 words describing how to invest in mutual funds and the reasons for their growth.

Have students complete the following statement: "I will begin a savings plan because . . . ." (Answers will vary.)

422

Individual Retirement Accounts

Even if you have a pension plan, you can have an **individual retirement account (IRA)** as well. This is a personal retirement account into which you can put a limited amount of money yearly. The earnings are not taxed until you retire.

Depending on your annual earnings, you can invest up to $2,000 a year in an IRA. One disadvantage of an IRA is that you are charged a penalty if you withdraw the money before you reach the age of 59½.

Plans for the Self-Employed

Do you plan to work for yourself? If so, a Keogh plan or a simplified employee pension may be the right type of plan for you. Both have the tax-deferment advantage of an IRA.

- With a **Keogh plan** (pronounced KEE-oh), you can invest up to 15 percent of your yearly earnings (up to $150,000) each year for retirement. There are special rules for setting up a Keogh account, so you should check with an accountant before you create one.

YOU'RE THE BOSS!

Solving Workplace Problems

The pastry chef in your restaurant is very talented and earns a good salary, but you realize she has trouble managing her money. She often asks you for an advance or wonders about getting a raise, and you've heard her asking the chef for loans. What will you do to help her solve these problems?

- A **simplified employee pension (SEP)** is a simpler tax-deferred retirement plan than the Keogh but one that also offers tax savings. It, too, is for the self-employed. Individuals can set aside as much as 15 percent of their yearly earnings, up to $150,000. (Owner-employees can set aside up to 13 percent.) A SEP account is easier to establish and maintain than a Keogh account, and some people prefer it for that reason.

SECTION 21-1 *Review*

Understanding Key Concepts

Using complete sentences, answer the following questions on a separate sheet of paper.

1. Why might someone who is just starting out prefer a regular savings account to a CD?

2. Explain why you should start contributing to a retirement plan as soon as you can.

SECTION 21-1 *Review* ANSWERS

1. Someone just starting out may not be able to meet the minimum deposit requirements for a CD. Savings accounts and savings bonds are more flexible, even though they offer lower interest rates.

2. Social Security will probably be insufficient for your retirement needs. The sooner you start contributing to a personal retirement plan, the more interest your money will earn.

Checking Accounts and Other Banking Services

OBJECTIVES

After studying this section, you will be able to:

- **Shop wisely for a checking account.**
- **Write a check and fill out a check register.**
- **Reconcile a checking account.**

KEY TERMS

endorse
check register
reconcile

"Will that be cash, check, or charge?" This question is asked countless times each day. Just what are checks, and how do they work?

Checking Accounts

A check is a written document that authorizes the transfer of money from a bank account to a person or business. Most businesses and individuals rely on checks. For paying bills, they are easier and safer than cash. They also simplify record keeping.

Types of Checking Accounts

You open a checking account at a bank or credit union by depositing money into the account. To make a deposit, you fill out a deposit slip. Deposit slips are available in all bank branch offices. You will also receive a supply of deposit slips with your checks.

You can write checks up to the amount of your balance. Whether you gain interest on your balance or have to pay fees depends on the bank and the type of account you have.

A *regular checking account* often requires no minimum balance. However, it rarely earns interest, and you are usually charged a monthly fee for maintaining it. This fee may be a flat monthly rate ($4 to $8

Chapter 21 • Banking and Credit **423**

TEACH

Guided Practice

Teaching Strategies

1. Assign and review Section 21-2.

2. Use the transparency for this section.

3. Assign and review the Case Study.

Discussion Starter

Ask students to think about the number of checks they might write if they were living on their own. Tell them to make a list of expenses. (Students should include rent, utilities, telephone, insurance, and so on.)

Critical Thinking

Have students discuss reasons why they should protect their checks and checking account information. (to avoid fraud and having someone draw money from their accounts)

SCANS Foundation Skills Connection

L1 **Decision Making**

Have students work in small groups to discuss banking services. Prior to the discussion, obtain brochures from several local banks and share them with students. Have each group list services, then rank them in order of importance to the group. Have students share information in class.

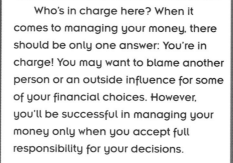

Choices about where to bank depend on many different factors.
What factors do you think are most important in choosing a bank?

a month, for example) or a charge for each check you write. A *NOW account* (negotiable order of withdrawal) pays interest on your deposits. However, you must keep a minimum balance in the account, usually at least $500. A *Super-NOW account* is similar to a NOW account except that the interest rate and minimum balance required are both higher.

Managing Your Checking Account

Having a checking account allows you to write checks when you need to pay bills or buy groceries. When you write a check, you must fill it out completely and accurately. (***Figure 21-3*** shows how to do this.)

Sometimes you will receive checks. Your employer, for example, will probably pay you with a check. Normally, you will take the check to your bank to deposit it or cash it. To complete either transaction, you must **endorse** the check—sign your name on the back.

Attitude Counts ✔

Who's in charge here? When it comes to managing your money, there should be only one answer: You're in charge! You may want to blame another person or an outside influence for some of your financial choices. However, you'll be successful in managing your money only when you accept full responsibility for your decisions.

424   *Unit 6 • Life Skills*

▶ Extending the Illustration

Pose this scenario to students: "A bank has opened a branch in your area. It is offering free checking for the first six months, after which it will charge a fee of $10 a month. Your current bank charges a fee of $7 a month." Which bank offers the better deal for one year? For two years? (one year: the bank charging $10; two years, the bank charging $7)

Caption Answer: Possible answers include a convenient location, convenient hours, good interest rates, and free checking accounts.

► Figure 21-3

Using a Checking Account

A checking account makes paying your bills convenient and safe. It also helps you track your expenses and manage your budget. A check authorizes your bank to take money from your account for payment to someone else. Be sure to write your checks clearly and completely.

Keeping Track of Your Account

If you write checks for more money than you have in your account, the account will be *overdrawn*. Banks charge a high fee for overdrawn checks. They may also send a check back to the business that

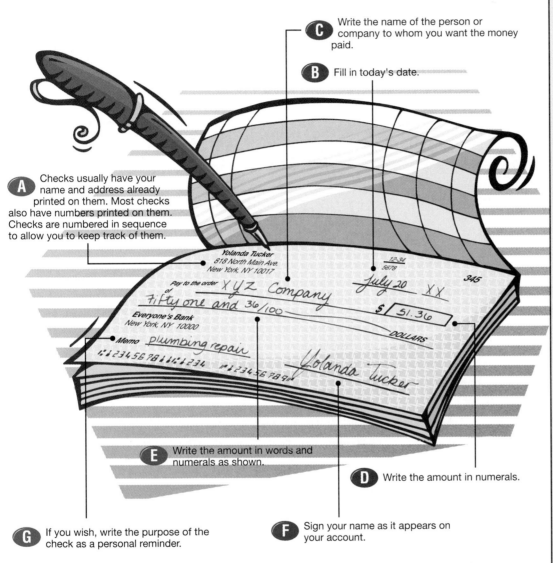

C Write the name of the person or company to whom you want the money paid.

B Fill in today's date.

A Checks usually have your name and address already printed on them. Most checks also have numbers printed on them. Checks are numbered in sequence to allow you to keep track of them.

E Write the amount in words and numerals as shown.

D Write the amount in numerals.

G If you wish, write the purpose of the check as a personal reminder.

F Sign your name as it appears on your account.

Chapter 21 • Banking and Credit **425**

425

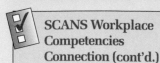
L2 **Selecting Technology**

Tell students they work for a local bank and are responsible for mailing letters about the bank's new electronic banking service to customers. Have students decide what software they would use and how they would accomplish this task.

(Students could create the letter using word processing software, then use a mail merge function to print each letter with the name and address of a customer from the bank's database.)

L3 **Understanding Systems**

Have students research types of commercial loans, such as those for businesses to buy equipment. Have them call the Small Business Administration to find information about loans guaranteed through this organization. Or, information can be accessed on the Internet at: http://www.sba.gov. Have students write 150-word reports about their findings.

Independent Practice
Reading

Have students obtain information from a local bank on investment services. Have them prepare a chart listing the name of each service and giving a brief description.

426

submitted it for payment, causing you embarrassment. For these reasons, keep track of your account.

When you purchase your checks, you will get a **check register**, a small booklet for tracking your account. (See *Figure 21-4.*) Record all checks, deposits, fees, interest charges, and other transactions in the check register. Add and subtract amounts immediately so that you know exactly how much is in your account at any time.

Each month, you will get a statement of your account. You will need to reconcile the statement with your check register. To **reconcile** two items means to make them agree.

Using Other Banking Services

Banks offer additional services to help you manage your money.

- *Electronic fund transfer.* Most banks offer electronic fund transfer (EFT). In most cases, this is accomplished with an ATM card. You'll get a card with a personal identification number (PIN) that will allow you to use an automated teller machine (ATM). This allows you to make deposits and withdrawals to your account electronically—any time of the day or night.

EXCELLENT BUSINESS PRACTICES

A Slice of the Pie

PepsiCo Inc. of Purchase, New York, created a basis for its 470,000 workers to own part of the business. PepsiCo owns such businesses as Pepsi-Cola, Frito-Lay, Taco Bell, Kentucky Fried Chicken, and Pizza Hut. To help employees have a vested interest in the quality of the products and the service, the company offered a stock-option program to workers.

Stock-option plans can help employees accumulate capital over time.

Eligible employees receive the equivalent of 10 percent of their previous year's salary in stock options.

To exercise the option, each year employees can "cash in" 20 percent of the options by buying the stock at the grant price and holding onto it. Or they can sell it at its current value.

Employees who have a monetary interest in the prosperity of a company are more likely to make efforts on a daily basis to serve a good product, treat customers well, identify potential workplace hazards, and make suggestions for improving efficiency.

Thinking Critically

Why do many companies tie in stock options with salaries for top executives' compensation?

426 *Unit 6 • Life Skills*

Extending EXCELLENT BUSINESS PRACTICES

Answer: to provide a link between management's decisions and the company's overall financial success and to encourage executives to keep the company's best interests in mind at all times

Further Application: Have students look up the term *stock*. Discuss the meaning of stock options with students. Ask them if they would prefer such a company benefit.

Check Register

NUMBER	DATE	DESCRIPTION OF TRANSACTION	PAYMENT/DEBIT (-)		√ T	FEE (IF ANY) (-)	DEPOSIT/CREDIT (+)		BALANCE	
									$ 172	16
343	7/15	Bob's Service Station	$ 24	36		$	$		24	36
		oil change							147	80
344	7/15	General Service Co.	72	14					72	14
		heater contract							75	66
	7/16	ATM transfer					200	00	200	00
		from savings							275	66
	7/17	Deposit					424	62	424	62
		paycheck							700	28
345	7/20	XYZ Company	51	36					51	36
		plumbing repair							648	92
	7/20	ATM withdrawal	40	00					40	00
		gift for James							608	92

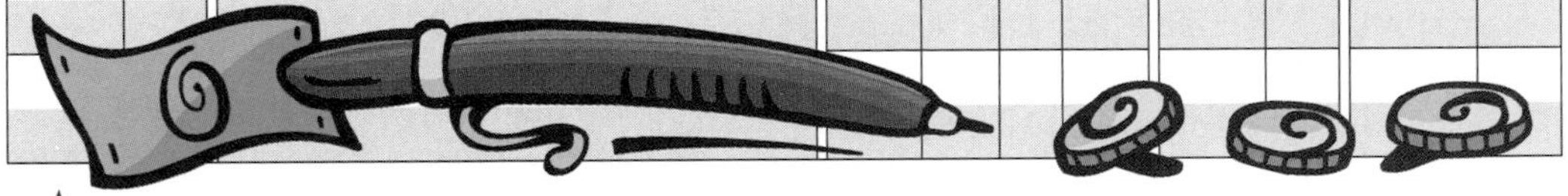

Figure 21-4 Each time you make any transaction involving your checking account, immediately record it in your check register. Add or subtract the transaction from your previous balance in the final column. Why is it important to keep your balance current?

- *Banking on-line.* Another increasingly popular development is banking on-line. This service lets you manage your money from your home computer. Costs for on-line banking are becoming lower each year.

SECTION 21-2 *Review*

Understanding Key Concepts

Using complete sentences, answer the following questions on a separate sheet of paper.

1. Why might you choose a regular checking account instead of a NOW account?
2. Why must you write the amount of a check in both numerals and words?
3. Why is it important to reconcile your check register and bank statement?

SECTION 21-2

Skills Practice

Have students complete this problem. Roberto had a beginning checking account balance of $433.27. He wrote the following checks: $127.44, $15.95, $79.34, and $59.55. Now what is Roberto's new checkbook balance? ($150.99: $433.27 – $127.44 – $15.95 – $79.34 – $59.55)

Interview

Invite a representative from a local computer store to demonstrate checking account software. Have the speaker compare manual and electronic methods for recording checks. Prior to the class visit, have students prepare questions.

Research

Have students research local companies that accept on-line payments of bills. How does this save money for the company? Have students share their findings in class.

ASSESS

Assessment

Content

Have each student write a short informational brochure to be given to fellow students. Students are to describe types of checking accounts, how to maintain a checking account, and electronic banking services.

Evaluate students' brochures for clarity, accuracy of content, and inclusion of the appropriate information from this section.

Extending Figure 21-4

Ask students to describe how keeping their check registers accurate and up-to-date would help them with their budgets. (The register makes it easy to compare actual expenses with budgeted amounts.)

Caption Answer: so that you know how much money is in your account

SECTION 21-2 *Review* ANSWERS

1. A regular account will be better than a NOW account if a person can't keep a minimum balance.
2. Writing the amount both ways allows your bank to be sure of the amount.
3. Reconciling your checking account prevents you from overdrawing your account.

Evaluation

Assign the section review.

Reteaching

Try to find two or three different types of checks for each student so they get used to the variety of formats. Then provide students with voided blank checks and let them practice filling them out, following the steps in Figure 21-3. Also try to obtain sample check registers.

Extending the Content

Assign the appropriate Chapter 21 activities in the *Student Activity Workbook.*

Have students research electronic banking software. They might get information from a local bank, a computer store, or relatives who use such programs. What type of software is needed? What are the advantages of banking from home? Have students share their findings in class.

CLOSE

Have each student write a short paragraph describing how a checking account will be useful to him or her. (Answers will vary but could include when students have full-time jobs and bills to pay.)

Exploring Careers: Manufacturing

Richard J. Kulp
Toolmaker

Q: **How did you get into toolmaking?**

A: I was a helicopter mechanic in the Army. When I got out, I didn't feel I had enough knowledge to go into that field as a civilian. My military training was very specialized. I came to Hoover & Strong as a production worker. Then the company offered me the apprenticeship in toolmaking.

Q: **What does the apprenticeship consist of?**

A: It's different state by state. In Virginia, it's four years long. There are many different classes you have to take, including machining, welding, metalworking and heat treating, hydraulics and pneumatics, and math. Math skills are very important in toolmaking. You have to be very precise.

Q: **What is your job like?**

A: We're designing and making tools for the production of gold jewelry and similar items.

We do everything from designing the tools from scratch to maintaining, sharpening, and cleaning them to keep them in working condition.

Q: **Do you like it?**

A: I like making things. I like taking a chunk of steel and turning it into something that can actually be used for a specific purpose.

Thinking Critically

What skills does a toolmaker have that might transfer into the field of engineering?

CAREER FACTS

○ **Nature of the Work:**
Design and make tools from steel for specific uses; use large machinery and small hand tools.

○ **Training or Education Needed:**
Apprenticeship program through state, union, or private sources; journeyman certificate.

○ **Aptitudes, Abilities, and Skills:**
Very strong math skills; listening skills; problem-solving skills; ability to see things in the mind's eye; self-management skills; ability to use large machinery; ability to work with tools; attention to detail.

Salary Range:
Approximately $12 to $13 an hour in nonunion shops; rates are higher in union shops.

Career Path:
Most journeymen toolmakers usually stay on as toolmakers; other options include becoming a toolroom manager or going into engineering.

428 *Unit 6 • Life Skills*

Extending the CASE STUDY

Answer: math skills, ability to see things in the mind's eye, drawing skills, design skills, understanding of equipment and tools, and enjoyment of making things

Further Application: The salary in many careers depends on the location of the company and whether or not the career or company is unionized. Have students discuss why this is so. (For example, the cost of living—which includes the cost of such items as food, transportation, utilities, housing, child care, and health care—is higher in large cities and in certain states; unions negotiate higher wages with companies, usually in large cities; and high demand exists for workers in certain fields.)

Using Credit Wisely

OBJECTIVES

After studying this section, you will be able to:

- **Describe different types of credit.**
- **Explain the advantages and disadvantages of using credit.**
- **Explain how to compare credit costs.**

KEY TERMS

credit
application fee
down payment
finance charge
annual percentage rate (APR)
credit bureau

Now and then, life has a way of demanding more money than you have on hand. One way to obtain that money is through credit. **Credit** is a sum of money a person can use before having to reimburse the credit lender. It allows the person to receive a good or service now but to pay for it later. When you use credit, you are really taking out a loan.

Understanding Credit

Most businesses that sell a good or service offer credit. Car dealers, department stores, appliance dealers, and even some doctors offer credit. In fact, some companies (such as VISA and MasterCard) are in business just to extend credit.

Types of Credit

The most common type of credit is that offered through a credit card. A *credit card*, issued by a bank or other financial institution, allows the cardholder to charge amounts in many different places. The lender issues you a plastic card stamped with your name and account number. Usually, you are given a *credit limit*. This is the maximum amount you can charge against your account.

Chapter 21 • Banking and Credit **429**

 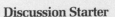

L1 **Knowing How to Learn**

Most large banks offer some type of credit counseling to customers who incur too much debt. Have students learn which banks in your area offer such services, then interview a bank representative. Have students share their findings in class.

L2 **Listening**

A majority of stores accept credit card payments. Have students ask the managers or owners of three such stores why they provide that service. Also have them ask what responsibilities the business has to the company or bank issuing a credit card. Have them take notes and share their information in class.

L3 **Problem Solving**

Have students research credit and how a credit history is established. They might interview someone at a bank and ask for explanations of credit reports and how information is collected by credit reporting agencies. Have students make plans for their own use of credit and decide how they will maintain good credit records.

Many businesses offer consumers charge accounts. A charge account is similar to a credit card account. In this case, the business issues the credit and often a credit card that can be used only at the company, or store, that issued it. When you buy an item, you charge it to your account. Each business sets the terms for its charge accounts.

Loans are another type of credit. People get loans from banks, credit unions, and other financial institutions to make large purchases. Car loans and mortgages are typical consumer loans.

Most loans are *installment loans*, in which you receive the money as a lump sum and pay it back in regular (usually monthly) payments called installments. You may have to pay an **application fee**, an amount of money charged to apply for the loan. Usually, you also have to make a **down payment**, a sum (usually a percentage of the total payment) paid at the time of the purchase.

Secured loans are guaranteed by *collateral*, an asset such as the borrower's home or car. If the borrower defaults on the loan—that is, fails to pay it—the lender can take the collateral. Unsecured loans do not require collateral.

Disadvantages of Credit

While the advantages of credit are clear to most people, credit also has at least two disadvantages. First, lenders charge a **finance charge**, which is a fee based on the amount of money you owe. Finance charges are based on a particular interest rate and can be figured in a number of ways. (The cost of credit is described in the next section.)

The second disadvantage of credit is the risk of overusing it. If you accumulate too much debt, you may not be able to make timely payments. You may lose your collateral on secured loans. Your financial reputation will also suffer.

Use credit when you need to, but avoid overusing it. People with credit problems can find help through organizations such as American Consumer Credit Counseling and the Consumer Credit Counseling Service.

Many stores will be able to process your credit card electronically by passing it through a special machine. *What tasks do you think this machine performs?*

430 *Unit 6 • Life Skills*

Extending the Illustration

Ask students to think of ways they can avoid having credit problems.

Caption Answer: Students may suggest checking the card to see that it has not been reported stolen or is not invalid, or recording the purchase amount for the credit card company.

 Talking with someone from a credit counseling service can help you work out credit problems effectively. *What might be the consequences of ignoring credit problems?*

Career Do's & Don'ts

When Working with Checks and Balances...

Do:
- keep your checking account balanced.
- set up a savings plan for special goals.
- keep charge card receipts and compare them to the bills.
- investigate tax-free savings and retirement plans.

Don't:
- open more than one or two charge cards.
- charge more than you can quickly pay off.
- invest money in any scheme that is not documented as legitimate and sound.
- sign any credit documents that don't clearly state the amount loaned, the length of the loan, and the interest rate.

The Cost of Credit

Credit costs vary widely. Your best bet is to shop around. Not all companies compute costs in the same way or charge the same amounts.

- *Annual fees.* Many credit card companies charge an annual fee or a membership fee. The amount is fixed and is charged to your account no matter how often you use the card.

- *Finance charges.* If you pay off your entire balance every month, you will not incur finance charges, which are interest on your unpaid balance. Finance charges commonly amount to 1.5 percent of your balance per month, or 18 percent per year. The Federal Truth in Lending Act requires lenders to state the cost of the interest as an **annual percentage rate (APR)**. This is the yearly cost of the loan, expressed as a percentage. An APR allows you to compare the costs of credit from different lenders.

Chapter 21 • Banking and Credit **431**

Extending the Illustration

Personal bankruptcy is one consequence of overuse of credit. Have students research the incidence of bankruptcy and how it affects credit card costs. (Bankruptcy increases costs because issuers have to recover their costs from others who manage credit responsibly.)

Caption Answer: A person could get deeper and deeper into debt; his or her credit cards could be invalidated.

431

Assessment

Content

Have each student write a 100-word column for a career newsletter giving advice on using credit. Tell students to explain the types of credit, cost of credit, and credit ratings.

Evaluate students' columns for accurate content and clear writing.

Evaluation

Assign the section review.

MINI QUIZ

True-False

1. Savings earn more with compounded interest than with straight interest. (true)

2. A Keogh plan is an example of a retirement plan for a self-employed person. (true)

3. Checking accounts paying interest usually require a minimum balance. (true)

4. A credit limit requires you to buy a certain amount on credit each month. (false)

5. Finance charges must be paid on all purchases made with a credit card. (false)

Most credit cards have a *grace period*. This is a time during which interest is not charged. With most credit cards, if you pay the entire amount by the due date stated on your first bill, you are not charged interest or any other finance charges.

Credit Agreements and Reports

When you apply for credit, you must complete a *credit application*. This form asks for details about your salary, bank accounts, and credit history. Before your application is approved, the lender will usually check with a credit bureau. A **credit bureau** is an agency that collects information on how promptly people and businesses pay their bills. The credit bureau provides this information, in the form of a credit report, to businesses that request it.

The credit bureau gives you a *credit rating*, a numerical rating that indicates how likely you are to pay your bills. If you have a poor credit rating, you may be denied a car loan or a mortgage. Make a habit of checking your credit rating regularly. You can do this by contacting a credit reporting agency such as Equifax, Trans

It can be tempting to use a credit card to buy items on the spur of the moment. *How could you prevent yourself from overusing credit?*

Union, or TRW and paying a fee. Errors sometimes occur, and you will want to see that the credit bureau corrects them as soon as possible.

SECTION 21-3 *Review*

Understanding Key Concepts

Using complete sentences, answer the following questions on a separate sheet of paper.

1. Why is a credit card more convenient for everyday purchases than a loan?

2. Why is it easy for some people to get into financial trouble when they have credit cards?

3. Why do businesses check with credit bureaus before extending credit to individuals?

SECTION 21-3 *Review* ANSWERS

1. You can use a credit card easily; you have to apply for a loan and wait for approval before the money comes through.

2. Since purchases do not have to be paid for immediately, some people build up a large amount of debt without realizing it.

3. Businesses want to know if people have paid their bills in the past. This is seen as a good indication of how well they will pay them in the future.

Key Terms

dividend *(p. 419)*
certificate of deposit (CD) *(p. 419)*
401(k) plan *(p. 421)*
individual retirement account (IRA) *(p. 422)*
Keogh plan *(p. 422)*
simplified employee pension (SEP) *(p. 422)*

SECTION 21-1 Summary

- Saving your money in an interest-bearing account puts it to work for you. When interest is compounded, your savings will grow even more quickly.

- You can save money by depositing it in a savings account or money market account or fund. You can also buy savings bonds and certificates of deposit.

- You should start saving for your retirement as soon as possible. Participating in a pension plan is a good way to begin. In addition, you will probably want to contribute to an individual retirement account (IRA) or a 401(k) plan. For self-employed people, Keogh plans and simplified employee pension (SEP) plans allow tax-deferred savings.

Key Terms

endorse *(p. 424)*
check register *(p. 426)*
reconcile *(p. 426)*

SECTION 21-2 Summary

- With a checking account, you deposit money and then write checks on your balance.

- Keep track of your checking account with a check register. Reconcile it monthly against your bank statement.

- Electronic fund transfer and banking on-line make banking more convenient.

Key Terms

credit *(p. 429)*
application fee *(p. 430)*
down payment *(p. 430)*
finance charge *(p. 430)*
annual percentage rate (APR) *(p. 431)*
credit bureau *(p. 432)*

SECTION 21-3 Summary

- Credit allows you to buy something now and pay for it later. Credit may be obtained through the use of credit cards, charge accounts, and loans.

- Disadvantages of credit include finance charges and the possibility of taking on too much debt.

- The costs of credit include annual fees and finance charges.

- A credit bureau keeps track of how timely debts are paid.

Chapter 21 • Banking and Credit **433**

Use the Testmaker to create a customized test for Chapter 21.

Reteaching

1. Have students write these headings on paper: *Types of Credit, Disadvantages of Credit, Cost of Credit, Credit Agreements and Reports.* Discuss each topic, asking students for examples. Have students take notes about each topic as you discuss it in class.

2. Assign and review vocabulary terms, chapter questions, and activities from the Chapter Review.

Extending the Content

Assign the appropriate Chapter 21 activities in the *Student Activity Workbook.*

Obtain enough credit card contracts from local stores or banks so that each student can complete one. Have students fill out the forms, using personal and imaginary information.

CLOSE

Have students complete this sentence: "I can use credit responsibly by . . . ." (Answers will vary but might include paying bills on time and avoiding excess use.)

Extending the Illustration

Ask students how the overuse of credit can affect their long-term financial goals. (They may find it difficult to meet goals because their money will go toward paying off debt rather than being invested for the future.)

Caption Answer: Leave your credit card at home except for specific, planned purchases; set a limit on how much to spend each month, and stick to it; or destroy your credit card.

Answers

Reviewing Key Terms

Speeches will vary but should reflect an understanding of the meanings of the key terms included.

Recalling Key Concepts

1. a
2. c
3. a
4. c
5. b

Thinking Critically

1. Factors include how much money you are investing, what percentage of your savings you are investing, whether you have other investments, and how long a period you want to hold the investment.

2. By writing checks for purchases and noting what the checks are for in your check register, you will have a record of expenditures.

3. Credit helps businesses sell more items because it allows people to buy more. Also, stores that offer charge accounts earn income from them.

4. The interest you would earn on a savings account is probably less than the interest you would pay on a credit card debt. It's wiser to eliminate the debt.

Reviewing Key Terms

On a separate sheet of paper, write a brief speech giving advice on banking and credit to a person your age. Use each of the following terms.

dividend
certificate of
  deposit (CD)
401(k) plan
individual
  retirement
  account (IRA)
Keogh plan
simplified
  employee
  pension (SEP)

endorse
check register
reconcile
credit
application fee
down payment
finance charge
annual percentage
  rate (APR)
credit bureau

Recalling Key Concepts

Choose the correct answer for each item below. Write your answers on a separate sheet of paper.

1. You agree to keep your money deposited for a specific length of time in a ____.
   (a) certificate of deposit
   (b) money market mutual fund
   (c) checking account

2. Only self-employed workers can open a ____.
   (a) money market deposit account
   (b) CD (c) Keogh plan

3. When you compare a checking account statement with your check register to make sure they agree, you are ____ your checking account.
   (a) reconciling (b) overdrawing
   (c) transferring

4. The most common type of credit vehicle is a ____.
   (a) SEP (b) charge account
   (c) credit card

5. Credit can be costly because of ____.
   (a) credit bureaus
   (b) high interest rates
   (c) credit ratings

Thinking Critically

Using complete sentences, answer each of the questions below on a separate sheet of paper.

1. What factors might help you choose between a very safe investment with a low interest rate and a riskier investment with a higher interest rate?

2. How can you use your checking account to keep track of your spending habits?

3. Why do you think most businesses offer credit to their customers?

4. Explain which is the wiser strategy: to save $100 a month in a savings account or to repay $100 a month toward a credit card debt of $1,200.

SCANS Foundation Skills and Workplace Competencies

Thinking Skills: *Problem Solving*

1. Imagine that you earn a good salary but have allowed the balances on several credit cards to get too high. Suggest two actions you might take to begin solving your problem.

SCANS Foundation Skills and Workplace Competencies

1. Stop using your credit cards; talk with a credit counselor.

2. I would explain my position diplomatically. I would describe the impact of a loan default on my credit rating and suggest other ways she might accomplish her goal, such as buying a less expensive car.

Connecting Academics to the Workplace

1. The compounded interest after three months will be $7.01. (After first month,

Interpersonal Skills: *Negotiating to Arrive at a Decision*

2. Your sister has asked you to cosign a loan to help her buy a car. By cosigning, you are stating that if she can't repay the loan, you will. You don't think your sister can repay the loan. How do you handle this situation without harming your relationship with your sister?

Connecting Academics to the Workplace

Math

1. Steve's bank pays an annual interest rate of 2.8 percent on savings accounts of less than $5,000. The interest is compounded monthly. If Steve deposits $1,000 in a savings account, how much interest will he earn if he leaves his money in this account for three months?

Family and Consumer Sciences

2. A credit card company has refused to issue Howard a credit card, claiming that he has a bad credit rating. Howard is sure that the credit card company made a mistake about his credit history. What documentation should Howard have in front of him when he makes a call to the credit bureau to check his credit report?

Developing Teamwork and Leadership Skills

Working on a team with three classmates, imagine that you work for a company that does not provide a retirement plan. Your team has been asked to explain to the employees the importance of setting up their own retirement plans. As a team, gather data to show why retirement income in addition to Social Security is needed, and find out what options are available. Then write a presentation to convince other employees to set up their own retirement plans now. Deliver your presentation to the class.

Real-World Workshop

Assume you have $5,000 to invest for one year. Where can you put the money so it will earn the best return? Investigate savings accounts, CDs, money market funds and deposit accounts, and savings bonds. You might check newspaper ads and visit banks and other financial institutions. Choose one or more places to invest the money. Write an explanation of your choice.

School-to-Work Connection

Visit a local bank, credit union, or other financial institution. Interview an employee to learn what advice he or she would give to someone your age about saving money, planning for retirement, and obtaining credit. Ask about special plans that the institution offers for beginning savers, retirement savings, and credit management. Prepare a brief written report on your findings.

Individual Career Plan

Select a career in the banking and credit industry that interests you, such as loan officer or investment counselor. In a paragraph, describe qualities you think would be important for a person in this position.

Chapter 21 • Banking and Credit **435**

payments and the effects of inflation. Groups should describe retirement plans (such as IRAs and SEPs) and explain how they work.

Real-World Workshop

Students should find the best rates possible by comparing options at banks and other financial institutions. Undesirable options would include a regular savings account (because of its low interest rate) or a very risky investment. In most instances, CDs will probably offer the best interest rate of the choices given.

School-to-Work Connection

Reports should demonstrate effective information-gathering techniques and an understanding of the programs the financial institution offers.

Individual Career Plan

Answers will vary, depending on the career chosen. Answers should reflect valuable workplace skills as well as an understanding of the career.

$1,000 × 2.8% ÷ 12 = $2.33; after second month = $2.34, after third month = $2.34; total equals $7.01.)

2. Documentation should include such information as Howard's previous addresses, his Social Security number, the account numbers for any loans, his check register, and the account number and balance of savings or money market accounts.

Developing Teamwork and Leadership Skills

Presentations should include specific data about projections for Social Security

· · · PLANNING GUIDE · · ·
Chapter 22

SECTION 1 *Insurance Basics*

SECTION OBJECTIVES	SECTION FEATURES	SECTION RESOURCES
• Define some common insurance terms. • List some ways to lower insurance costs.	Personal Career Plan, p. 437	⊙ Workforce 2000 Videodisc and Videotape 📁 Section 22-1 Review, p. 440 📓 Student Activity Workbook

CHAPTER RESOURCES
- Chapter Transparencies and Lesson Plans
- Chapter 22 Test
- Spanish Resources, Chapter 22
- School-to-Work Activity Handbook, Chapter 22 Activity
- Teacher's Lesson Plans, Chapter 22
- Implementing Block Scheduling, Chapter 22
- Print, Media, and Internet Handbook
- Strategies for Implementing Work-Based Learning
- Strategies for Implementing Connecting Activities

SECTION 2 *Home and Automobile Insurance*

SECTION OBJECTIVES	SECTION FEATURES	SECTION RESOURCES
• Describe the importance of owning home insurance. • Describe five types of auto insurance coverage. • Explain the factors that influence auto insurance premiums.	Ethics in Action, p. 446 Career Do's and Don'ts, p. 447 Exploring Careers, p. 448	⊙ Workforce 2000 Videodisc and Videotape 📁 Section 21-2 Review, p. 447 📓 Student Activity Workbook

SECTION 3 *Health and Life Insurance*

SECTION OBJECTIVES	SECTION FEATURES	SECTION RESOURCES
• Compare and contrast basic types of health insurance coverage. • Distinguish between group and individual health insurance plans. • Explain the basic types of life insurance.	You're the Boss!, p. 450 Excellent Business Practices, p. 451	⊙ Workforce 2000 Videodisc and Videotape 📁 Section 22-3 Review, p. 452 📁 Chapter 22 Review, pp. 454–455 📓 Student Activity Workbook

SCANS CORRELATION CHART

Foundation Skills

Basic Skills	Reading	Writing	Math	Listening	Speaking

Thinking Skills	Creative Thinking	Decision Making	Problem Solving	Seeing Things in the Mind's Eye	Knowing How to Learn	Reasoning

Personal Qualities	Responsibility	Self-Esteem	Sociability	Self-Management	Integrity/Honesty

Workplace Competencies

Resources	Allocating Time	Allocating Money	Allocating Material and Facility Resources	Allocating Human Resources

Information	Acquiring and Evaluating Information	Organizing and Maintaining Information	Interpreting and Communicating Information	Using Computers to Process Information

Interpersonal Skills	Participating as a Member of a Team	Teaching Others	Serving Clients/ Customers	Exercising Leadership	Negotiating to Arrive at a Decision	Working with Cultural Diversity

Systems	Understanding Systems	Monitoring and Correcting Performance	Improving and Designing Systems

Technology	Selecting Technology	Applying Technology to Task	Maintaining and Troubleshooting Technology

Highlighted blocks indicate areas covered in the Chapter.

Additional Activities

 Internet Connection

Some insurance companies have a presence on the Internet. Ask students to find two or three such companies, research the information given by the company, and compare presentations. Have students discuss which company they might use and how the Web site influenced their decision.

 Field Trip Suggestions

If possible, arrange a visit to an advertising agency. Ask an agency representative to explain to students how ads are created. If the company uses public surveys to rate ads and products, ask if students can take the survey. Ask how advertisers meet health and safety requirements for products.

 Guest Speaker Suggestions

Invite to class a CPA or bookkeeper specializing in taxes. Ask the guest to describe how taxes are filed, what a taxpayer's responsibilities are, and what the penalties are for not handling those responsibilities correctly.

Key to Ability Levels

Each section gives skill-building activities. Each activity has been labeled for use with students of various learning styles and abilities.

L1 Level 1 activities are basic activities and should be within the range of all students.

L2 Level 2 activities are average activities and should be within the range of average and above average students.

L3 Level 3 activities are challenging activities designed for the ability range of above average students.

Chapter 22

Buying Insurance

School-Based Learning

Chapter Overview

Chapter 22 helps students examine insurance policies, such as home, auto, health, and life insurance.

Section 22-1 introduces insurance basics such as policies, coverage, beneficiaries, and deductibles.

Section 22-2 looks at renter's and homeowner's insurance, then focuses on auto insurance.

Section 22-3 explores health and life insurance plans.

Background Information

Write chapter objectives (Sections 22-1, 22-2, and 22-3) on the chalkboard or use the chapter objective transparency for class discussion.

Choose assignments from the *Student Activity Workbook* and write them on the chalkboard.

Have students preview the chapter, looking at pictures, reading captions, and noting content headings. Ask students to describe what they expect to learn in this chapter.

Preteaching Vocabulary

Write the Key Terms from all three sections on the chalkboard. Have students describe how each term relates to home, auto, health, or life insurance.

436

Meeting SPECIAL Needs

Physically Challenged

In order for physically challenged students to participate fully in class, make sure they have access to the classroom. A barrier can be a stair, a curb, a narrow walkway, a heavy door or an elevator door that does not allow time for a wheelchair to exit.

Classroom tables need at least 27½ inches of clearance for a wheelchair to pull up under them. Never assume that a physically challenged student can't do something based on experience with a previous student.

Chapter 22

Buying Insurance

Section 22-1
Insurance Basics

Section 22-2
Home and Automobile Insurance

Section 22-3
Health and Life Insurance

In this video segment, discover why you should budget for insurance.

Journal
Personal Career Plan

Write a short journal entry, identifying the kinds of insurance you now have, and your reasons for having no other kinds of insurance. After you have studied this chapter, reread your journal entry and add a follow-up, explaining the kinds of insurance you expect to buy in the next few years.

437

School-to-Work Connecting Activities

Have students research careers in the insurance industry. Then ask them to interview at least two insurance agents or brokers who sell health, life, homeowner's, or auto insurance. Have them ask about job skills needed, especially interpersonal and technological skills. What will they need to do to prepare for a career in this industry?

Work-Based Learning Strategies and Activities

Arrange for students to visit the regional office of a major insurance company or a broker for a major company. Ask a knowledgeable representative to discuss the office work that supports the insurance industry, such as actuarial, underwriting, claims analysis, and payment systems. Ask the person to discuss skills needed for jobs in each area. After the visit, have students write summaries of what they learned.

WORKFORCE 2000 Training Video

Have students view the video and perform the interactive exercises to reinforce important chapter concepts and thinking processes.

Chapter 22

Addressing **LEARNING** Styles

Kinesthetic Learner

Ask students to work in groups to develop skits that show some of the situations in which insurance would be useful. These might include the obvious: fire, theft, hospitalization. They should also include the not-so-obvious: worker's disability, extended warranty contracts, and trip cancellation. The skits should include the appropriate insurance, the approximate costs, deductibles, and exclusions.

FOCUS

Bell Ringer

Ask students how they would pay for medical or auto repair costs following an accident if they had no insurance.

Introducing the Section

Have students share their thoughts from the Bell Ringer activity. Explain that paying a small amount in premiums protects against paying a much larger amount for a loss.

Motivational Activity

Critical Thinking

Have students write about why most insurance policies have a deductible clause. (A deductible requires a policyholder to share the risk of loss.)

TEACH

Guided Practice

Teaching Strategies

1. Assign and review Section 22-1.
2. Use the transparency  for this section.

Discussion Starter

Discuss how insurance works from the perspectives of the insurer and the insured.

Teaching Tip

Invite a local insurance agent to class to discuss basic terminology. Ask the guest to bring samples of policies.

Critical Thinking

Tell students that they are offering insurance to other students. Have them write papers describing the risks, benefits, and payment method.

438

Insurance Basics

OBJECTIVES

After studying this section, you will be able to:

- **Define some common insurance terms.**
- **List some ways to lower insurance costs.**

KEY TERMS

insurance policy
premium
deductible
claim

When was the last time you made plans, only to have them changed by an unexpected event? One thing is certain in life: No matter how carefully we plan, some things go wrong. A driver backs into your new car. While you are at work, your television set is stolen. You break an arm and need emergency surgery.

How can you plan for life's unexpected events? One way is to buy insurance. When you purchase insurance, you pay an agreed-upon amount of money to an insurance company. The company in turn agrees to pay for losses caused by such events as automobile accidents, theft, or injuries that might otherwise ruin you financially.

The Language of Insurance

Remember when you first used a computer? You had to learn "computerese"—the language of computers. The same is true of insurance. The terms below are part of the language of insurance.

Insurance Policy

When you buy insurance, you'll receive an insurance policy. An **insurance policy** is a legal contract between a person buying insurance (a *policyholder*) and an insurance company. The policy explains:

- who is covered,
- types of losses for which the company will pay,
- amounts the company will pay, and
- the cost of the insurance.

438 *Unit 6 • Life Skills*

Workforce 2000 Trends

In the future, a successful worker will be able to make the transition from individual learner, (as often required in school), to team participant, then team leader. Listening, compromising, mediating, and communication skills will be vital.

An insurance policy is long and technical. In spite of this, you should read it carefully and ask questions about any unclear parts before you sign it.

Insurance Coverage

An insurance policy describes a policyholder's coverage. Insurance *coverage* refers to losses that an insurance company agrees to cover. The amount of coverage is the actual dollar amount that will be paid by the company in case of a loss.

All insurance policies have a list of *exclusions*. These are losses or risks that are not covered.

Benefit and Beneficiary

Money paid by an insurance company for a loss is called the *benefit*. In most cases the benefit is paid to the *beneficiary*, who is usually the policyholder.

Premiums

The amount a policyholder pays an insurance company is known as the **premium**. You can usually pay premiums in installments rather than all at once.

Deductibles

When you buy most types of coverage, you agree to pay a deductible. A **deductible** is the portion of a loss that you pay before the insurance company pays the remaining cost. The higher the deductible that you pay, the lower the cost of your premiums.

Claim

How does an insurance company know to pay you for a loss? You file a **claim**, an oral or written notice to the insurance company.

 Even though it takes time to read an insurance policy, you should understand its terms fully before you buy the coverage it provides. *Why do you think it is as important to understand what a policy does not cover as what it does cover?*

Chapter 22 • Buying Insurance **439**

SCANS Foundation Skills Connection

L1 **Reading**

Have each student read an insurance policy and write down any questions he or she has about it.

L2 **Responsibility**

Have each student write a paragraph explaining why having adequate insurance (life, health, auto) shows responsibility.

L3 **Seeing Things in the Mind's Eye**

Have students imagine themselves at different stages in life and then list the types of insurance they might need.

SCANS Workplace Competencies Connection

L1 **Acquiring and Evaluating Information**

Have each student find an article about current trends and issues in the insurance industry and summarize the main points.

L2 **Improving Systems**

Tell students to think of ways to make their homes or automobiles safer. How can such changes affect insurance premiums?

L3 **Understanding Systems**

Have students research unemployment insurance. Under what circumstances is it available?

Extending the Illustration

Ask students, who drive, how many of them have read their auto insurance policies. Have students find out the coverage they have for auto insurance, and discuss the main points in class.

Caption Answer: Being informed about coverage can save you money in the long run. For example, you might assume, without reading your policy, that your belongings are protected in case of a flood. If such were not the case, you would have to pay to replace your belongings in the event of a flood.

Independent Practice

✍ Assign as homework the chapter activity in the *School-to-Work Activity Handbook.*

Writing: *Journal*

Have students write in their career journals describing the types of insurance they will need in the future.

ASSESS

Assessment

Oral

Have students explain how insurance works. Evaluate their understanding of terms and processes.

Evaluation

Assign the section review.

Reteaching

List basic insurance terms on the chalkboard, and ask students to define them.

Extending the Content

✍ Assign the appropriate Chapter 22 activities in the *Student Activity Workbook.*

CLOSE

Have students write a short paragraph describing why they need insurance.

Kinds of Insurance

You can buy insurance for almost anything. It's possible to purchase marine insurance, space flight insurance, and dread-disease insurance. Professional dancers can have their legs insured. Concert pianists can have their hands insured.

Government Insurance Programs

These programs provide coverage if you lose your job (unemployment insurance), are injured on the job (workers' compensation), or qualify for health coverage (Medicare, Medicaid). See Chapter 23, Types of Benefits.

Holding Down Insurance Costs

How do you shop for big items such as a car or stereo system? Taking time to shop around can save you money when buying insurance. This is where SCANS workplace skills such as reading, math, decision making, problem solving, and reasoning are especially helpful. Here are several tips for controlling insurance costs:

▶ Knowing what type of insurance you want can help you control insurance costs. *What other tips can help you hold down insurance costs?*

- Know what type of insurance you want.
- Call several insurance agencies in your area to ask about coverages and costs.
- Ask about differences in premium costs with different deductibles. Consider paying higher deductibles in order to lower your premium costs.
- Don't buy more coverage than you need or less coverage than you need.

SECTION 22-1 *Review*

Understanding Key Concepts

Using complete sentences, answer the following questions on a separate sheet of paper.

1. Explain the difference between a premium and a deductible.

2. Imagine that you are drawing up a new budget for the coming year. Describe three ways to save money on your insurance costs.

SECTION 22-1 *Review* ANSWERS

1. A premium is an amount of money a policyholder pays to an insurance company for coverage; a deductible is the amount a policyholder pays on a claim before the insurer pays.

2. Possible answers: shop around, buy only the amount of coverage needed, and raise deductibles

---

▶ **Extending the Illustration**

Many employers provide life insurance. What is the major advantage and disadvantage of such coverage? (advantage: low cost or no cost; disadvantage: lost coverage if you leave the job)

Caption Answer: Call several insurance agencies, ask about differences in premium costs, and don't buy more insurance than you need.

Home and Automobile Insurance

OBJECTIVES

After studying this section, you will be able to:

- Describe the importance of owning home insurance.
- Describe five types of auto insurance coverage.
- Explain the factors that influence auto insurance premiums.

KEY TERMS

liability insurance
collision insurance
comprehensive
   insurance

What are your insurance needs? If you're like most people, you'll need only the basics: home, automobile, health, and perhaps life insurance.

You will want to be sure you have the right protection and that you do everything necessary to keep your coverage up-to-date. It is important to understand how insurance works because a great deal of money will be at stake.

Home Insurance

If you decide to rent an apartment, you'll need renter's insurance. This type of insurance covers your belongings up to a set amount, minus your deductible. *Figure 22-1* on page 442 shows one way to keep track of your belongings in case you need to file a claim.

If you decide to buy a house or condominium, you'll purchase homeowner's insurance. This type of coverage protects your house and its contents.

Automobile Insurance

Many states require by law that drivers have insurance. You can find out about a state's requirements from the insurance commissioner or motor vehicle division.

Chapter 22 • Buying Insurance **441**

SECTION 22-2
FOCUS

Bell Ringer

Have students list things they would want covered in an auto insurance policy.

Introducing the Section

As students share their lists from the Bell Ringer activity, write responses on the chalkboard. Students' suggestions should include bodily injury, property damage, and damage to their own or other people's cars. Explain that two of the most costly things people own are their homes and cars; appropriate insurance helps them protect those assets.

Also discuss with students the need to understand the types of losses covered to make sure you're buying the kind of policy you need.

Motivational Activity
Reading

Have students read a typical homeowner's insurance policy. If possible, obtain copies of sample policies from a local insurance agent. As students read policies, have them list the types of losses covered. What are the exceptions to the policy coverage? Have students write 150-word summaries of the main points in the policies.

Implementing Teamwork

Divide the class into pairs and ask each one to research car insurance. First, they should choose a car they want to purchase, then contact an insurance salesperson for pricing. He or she will ask personal information (for example, birth date, driving record, grades).

TEACH

Guided Practice

Teaching Strategies

1. Assign and review Section 22-2.

2. Use the transparency for this section.

3. Assign and review the Case Study.

Discussion Starter

Ask students whether it is discriminatory to charge drivers under 25 more for insurance than older drivers? Why or why not?

Teaching Tip

Invite a local insurance agent or broker to discuss accident rates and costs by gender and age group. Set aside time for students to ask questions.

Critical Thinking

Tell students that they have just been involved in an accident that was not their fault. The other driver refuses to give any information regarding her insurance, stating that she would rather take care of it herself. In your state, however, anyone involved in an accident is legally bound to give out information about his or her insurance. Ask students how they would handle this situation.

(A possible approach is to remind the person of the law. If she still refuses, write down her license plate number, the make and model of the car, and report the incident to the police and to your insurance company.)

Inventory of Personal Property

Item	Purchase Price	Date of Purchase	Item	Purchase Price	Date of Purchase
Electronic items:			Collections:		
TV	_____	_____		_____	_____
CD player	_____	_____		_____	_____
Radio	_____	_____	Other valuables:		
Stereo	_____	_____		_____	_____
Camera	_____	_____		_____	_____
Computer	_____	_____		_____	_____
_____	_____	_____		_____	_____
			Furniture:		
Jewelry:				_____	_____
Watch	_____	_____		_____	_____
Ring	_____	_____		_____	_____
			Silverware, dishes,		
Sports equipment:			glassware:		
_____	_____	_____		_____	_____
_____	_____	_____		_____	_____
_____	_____	_____		_____	_____
			Electrical appliances:		
Musical instruments:				_____	_____
_____	_____	_____		_____	_____
_____	_____	_____		_____	_____
			Linens:		
Clothing:				_____	_____
_____	_____	_____		_____	_____
_____	_____	_____		_____	_____
Tools:					
_____	_____	_____			

▲ **Figure 22-1** When you buy renter's or homeowner's insurance, make an inventory of your possessions and keep receipts for items of value. Update your records annually. What other kinds of items would you include on a list such as this? Why is it also a good idea to photograph or videotape your possessions?

442   *Unit 6 • Life Skills*

▶▶ **Extending Figure 22-1** ◀◀

Have students list from memory all their belongings. Then have them make an actual inventory. Did they forget items they owned?

Caption Answer: Students may name additional items such as bicycles, books, family keepsakes, and so on. If you have to file a claim, the insurance company can easily verify your list of property if you have taken photographs or videotaped your possessions.

Types of Coverage

When you buy a standard automobile insurance policy, you usually buy several different kinds of coverage. Each type of coverage insures your car and you for a different kind of loss, damage, or injury.

Liability Insurance. What if you're involved in an accident that's your fault? **Liability insurance** covers damage or injury for which you're responsible. This includes injuries suffered by the driver and passengers in the other car and by passengers in your car. It also covers property damage to the other car. Liability insurance doesn't cover your injuries or property damage to your car.

Medical Payments Insurance. If you suffer injuries in an auto accident, whether or not it's your fault, *medical payments insurance* will cover your medical expenses. Medical payments insurance also covers medical expenses of your passengers. This insurance is more limited than liability insurance, though. For example, many policies cover only up to $5,000 in medical expenses per person. Liability insurance will cover expenses beyond the maximum amount per person of medical payments coverage.

Liability insurance protects you against claims or lawsuits by people whose cars are damaged and who are injured in an accident that is your responsibility. **Why is it important to have as much auto liability insurance as you can afford?**

Chapter 22 • Buying Insurance **443**

SCANS Foundation Skills Connection

L1 Math

Tell students that they have auto insurance policies with a $500 deductible. If they were in an accident that damaged their cars, what would they have to pay out-of-pocket if the repairs totaled $300? $1,000? $2,000? ($300, $500, $500)

L2 Reasoning

Have students work in pairs to find out which cars are the most expensive to insure. Have them discuss whether having the car you want is worth paying the extra insurance. What other factors might they consider when deciding what car to buy? Have students share their discussions in class.

L3 Listening and Speaking

Have students work in groups of three or four. Tell students that personnel in doctors' offices and hospitals spend a great deal of time handling paperwork and phone calls related to insurance. Have each group interview a person who does this type of work and ask him or her to describe a typical day. What skills does he or she need to be successful on the job? How has the person streamlined the system to make processing insurance papers more efficient? Have groups discuss their findings in class.

Extending the Illustration

Ask students which driver's liability insurance covers damages if they are in an accident and the other driver is at fault. (The other driver's insurance covers damages.)

Caption Answer: Without liability coverage, you could be responsible for hundreds of thousands of dollars in claims by others.

SCANS Workplace
Competencies
Connection

L1 Selecting
Technology

Have students choose a
software program and cre-
ate an electronic file for
recording and maintaining
accurate and up-to-date information on their personal
valuables. Have students
print out copies and share
their work in class.

L2 Acquiring and
Evaluating Information

Many localities offer re-
medial driving courses for
those individuals who re-
ceive traffic tickets. Have
students find out whether
such courses are available
in your area or within 60
miles. Have students learn
the specific details about
the programs and share
their information in class.

L3 Exercising
Leadership

Have students debate
whether they believe insurance coverage should be
mandated by the govern-
ment. For instance, many
states require proof of insurance when registering a
car. Home buyers who take
out a mortgage cannot fi-
nalize the transaction until
they provide proof that
they've purchased home-
owner's insurance. Have
students provide arguments
to support their position.

Collision Insurance. In an accident
that's your fault, **collision insurance** covers the cost of repairs to your car. It also
covers damage to your car if you're in an
accident caused by a driver who is not insured. *Figure 22-2* provides advice on
what to do in case you're involved in an
auto accident.

Comprehensive Insurance. What if
your car is stolen? **Comprehensive insurance** covers your car for reasons other than
a collision. These reasons include theft,
fire, and vandalism.

Uninsured Motorist Insurance. You
can buy *uninsured motorist coverage* to

► **Figure 22-2**

Handling Auto Accidents

Sooner or later, you may be involved in
an automobile accident. If and when this
happens, what should you do?

A When you're involved in an auto accident, try
to stay calm so that you can think clearly.
Move your car to the side of the road, if
possible, away from traffic.

B If you are not injured, get out of your car to see
whether the driver and any passengers in the
other car are injured. Make sure that you are out of
the way of passing vehicles.

444 *Unit 6 • Life Skills*

►► **Extending Figure 22-2** ◄◄

Ask students what they would do if
someone rear-ends them at a time when
police are busy responding to more
serious accidents. (Exchange names,
telephone numbers, and insurance information with the other driver. If possible,
get the names and phone numbers of
eyewitnesses.)

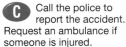

C Call the police to report the accident. Request an ambulance if someone is injured.

D When the police arrive, be prepared to show your driver's license, auto registration, and proof of insurance. As clearly as possible, explain to the police officer the facts as you saw them. If you and the other driver disagree over the incident, avoid arguing. Exchange driver's license numbers and names of auto insurers with the other driver.

E As soon as possible, call your insurance company to report the accident and file a claim.

Chapter 22 • Buying Insurance **445**

Independent Practice
Skills Practice

Have one or two insurance companies send you applications for automobile insurance. Have students work in pairs. Give each pair a copy of an application and have them complete it. The information in the application may be a composite of students' own statistics, or it may be entirely imaginary. Have students share their experiences and questions.

Writing: *Letter*

Have students write to your state's commissioner of insurance and ask for information on the state's minimum requirements for automobile insurance. Tell students to share their responses in class.

Research

Tell students that financial institutions that lend money for mortgages require homeowners to provide proof of adequate insurance. Have students consult with local home insurance agents to learn about the types of homeowner's insurance and how one decides which to buy. Also have students learn about renter's insurance. How does it differ from homeowner's insurance? Have students write 200–250 word reports describing their findings.

Addressing Workplace Diversity

To communicate more effectively with men at work, women should add forcefulness to their speech and power words to their vocabulary; be brief and specific when speaking; use humor, but not self-effacing humor; avoid male-bashing. (*Genderflex* by Judith Tingley)

Discussion Starter

Ask students if it's possible to buy too much auto insurance.

Teaching Tip

Before discussing students' responses to over-insuring a car, you may want to invite an auto insurance agent to talk to your class. Ask the agent to discuss needs at different stages in life and how needs change over time.

Research

Have students find out how much they would save for the discounts described in Figure 22-3. Discuss their findings in class.

Skills Practice

Have students complete this problem. "Jesse lives in a no-fault insurance state. He recently slid off the road during a snow storm. His car had damages of $7,680, and Jesse's medical care cost $1,750. Jesse has collision insurance and a $300 deductible. His insurance policy provides $25,000 for personal injury expenses, $100,000 for total injury claims, and $25,000 for damage to other people's property." How much will the accident cost him? What will the insurance company pay? (Jesse, $300; insurance company, $9,130: $7,680 − $300 = $7,380 + $1,750)

protect yourself against drivers who do not have liability insurance. This coverage is optional. You may not need it if you have medical payments or health coverage.

 ETHICS in Action

You have been involved in a minor automobile accident. There is no damage to your car, but a friend gives you the name of a "good doctor." The friend explains, "This doctor can diagnose whiplash in <u>anyone</u>. Do you know how much insurance you can collect for whiplash!" What will you do?

Systems of Automobile Insurance

When people are in automobile accidents, they sometimes disagree about who is at fault. To limit delays and disagreements, some states have passed laws establishing a *no-fault system*. This means that policyholders have their claims paid by their own insurance companies, no matter who is at fault.

Buying Automobile Insurance

Automobile insurance can be costly. You will want to get the best possible buy

Example Auto Insurance Discounts

Defensive driving courses	10% discount on liability, collision, medical payments, and personal injury protection*
Airbags and other passive restraints	15% discount on medical payments and personal injury protection (driver's side); 30% off medical payments and personal injury protection (both sides)
Drug/alcohol education	5% discount on liability, collision, medical payments, and personal injury protection
Antitheft devices	Reduces comprehensive premium; amount varies by device and county
Two or more cars on a policy	15% discount on liability, collision, medical payments, and personal injury protection

* Personal injury protection pays the same as medical payments, plus 80 percent of lost income and the cost of hiring someone to take on household and caregiver responsibilities of an injured person. The coverage is the same as with medical payments insurance.

Figure 22-3 It pays to check with several insurance companies to find out about available discounts on auto insurance. Why do you think some companies offer discounts for drug and alcohol education?

Teaching **ETHICS** in Action

Have students follow these steps to help them make a decision.

1. What are the ethical issues?
2. What are the alternatives?
3. Who are the affected parties?
4. How do the alternatives affect the parties?
5. What is your decision?

Extending Figure 22-3

Have each student ask two insurance agents about types of discounts offered by insurers in your state.

Caption Answer: Drivers who are aware of the dangers of driving under the influence of drugs or alcohol are likely to be more careful and to have fewer accidents than others.

for the right amount of coverage. There are several ways to control or lower the cost of your auto insurance premiums. They include the following:

- *Shop around.* Try to get prices from at least three different companies.
- *Drive carefully.* Some companies offer safe-driver discounts to policy-holders with good driving records.
- *Take driver education classes.* Some companies give discounts to drivers who take driver education courses.
- *Buy only the coverage you need.* If you have health insurance coverage, you may not need medical payments coverage or uninsured motorist protection. Also, if the premium is more than 10 percent of your car's value, think twice about buying collision coverage.
- *Raise your deductibles.* If you have a good driving record and can afford higher deductibles, this will save you money.
- *Take advantage of insurance discounts.* Some insurance discounts are required by state law; others are optional. ***Figure 22-3*** provides examples of auto insurance discounts.

Career Do's & Don'ts

To Get Value from Insurance...

Do:
- get comparable quotes from several insurers bidding on the same amount of insurance.
- keep all documents and receipts relating to insurance policies and claims.
- carry proof of health and car insurance with you.
- follow up on claims.

Don't:
- buy more or less insurance than you need.
- hesitate to contact your health insurance provider to find out specifically what is covered.
- allow health-care providers or car repair shops to directly bill your insurer without reviewing what they are billing.
- let your insurance coverage lapse.

SECTION 22-2 *Review*

Understanding Key Concepts

Using complete sentences, answer the following questions on a separate sheet of paper.

1. Why is it important to purchase home insurance?

2. Which of the five types of auto insurance coverage would you most likely select if you were buying a new car? Explain your reasoning.

3. How might you influence the cost of your auto insurance premiums even before you buy a car?

Chapter 22 • Buying Insurance **447**

SECTION 22-2 *Review* ANSWERS

1. Renter's insurance would protect you financially if you lost your possessions because of a fire or theft. Homeowner's insurance would protect you financially if you lost your belongings and your home itself.

2. Most students will probably suggest liability coverage, in case of damage to another car; collision coverage, to pay for damage to their car; and comprehensive coverage, in case of car theft.

3. You could reduce costs by taking a driver education class and by driving carefully when using someone else's car.

Research

Have each student contact a local auto insurance agent and find out what penalties the company charges to reckless or accident-prone drivers. Have students write summaries of how they can keep their insurance costs down by driving safely.

Interview

Share this scenario with students. "Suppose you have been involved in a 15-car pileup due to dense fog. No one is seriously hurt, but the police officers on the scene are very busy trying to get traffic moving again." Have each student interview a local police officer, sharing this scenario and asking what they should do in such a situation. Have students share their findings in class.

ASSESS

Assessment
Performance

Assign students to create posters listing the major types of automobile insurance coverage and describing the type of loss or damage each covers. To illustrate each type of coverage, have students cut photos from newspapers or magazines.

Evaluate students' posters for inclusion of these topics: liability, medical payments, collision, comprehensive, and uninsured motorist insurance. Also, evaluate students' posters for accuracy and creativity.

Evaluation

Assign the section review.

Reteaching

Using the posters students created for the section evaluation, discuss each type of insurance coverage. Ask students for examples of how that coverage would apply to them.

Then discuss no-fault insurance and indicate whether your state endorses it. Finally, ask students to list things they could do to reduce the cost of auto insurance.

Extending the Content

Assign the appropriate Chapter 22 activities in the *Student Activity Workbook*.

Have students research the no-fault system and alternatives used in states that do not follow it. Have them find out when no-fault was first introduced and the advantages and disadvantages of such a system. Tell students to write 200–250 word reports, then discuss their findings in class.

CLOSE

Have students write a paragraph or two describing the minimum car insurance coverage they are required to have by state law and the amount they feel they need to be fully protected. (Students' paragraphs will vary but should mention the five major types of coverage.)

CASE STUDY

Exploring Careers: Office and Business

Sylvia Ramirez
Corporate Software Sales

Q: Have you always been in corporate sales?

A: I never thought of myself as a salesperson. I started out in human resources. Part of my job was to recruit people at job fairs. My company's booth was always next to Xerox's booth. Their recruiter recruited me.

Q: What kind of training did you have?

A: I was trained by Xerox. They have an intense sales-training program that is well known throughout the industry. It gave me a solid base to start with. After four years, there was an opening selling software for another company. I worked there selling to large corporate accounts before coming to Microsoft.

Q: What skills are important in sales?

A: Communication skills are the most important. They give you the ability to get your ideas across. You also have to be able to stand up in front of an audience of high-level executives and make your presentation. You have to be able to manage problems tactfully and professionally—and to the customer's satisfaction.

Q: Do you like what you do?

A: I love what I do. When I'm in front of customers and selling, it's exciting and it's fun. I can listen to customer's needs and match them with what my company has to offer.

Thinking Critically

What personal traits should a good salesperson have?

CAREER FACTS

Nature of the Work:
Meet clients; present products; deal with problems in customer satisfaction.

Training or Education Needed:
Bachelor's degree, preferably in business; experience in sales.

Aptitudes, Abilities, and Skills:
Math, listening, speaking, and interpersonal skills; creative-thinking, decision-making, and problem-solving skills; responsibility; self-management skills.

Salary Range:
Salary plus commission; starting level about $20,000; much higher with experience.

Career Path:
Start in an internship or an entry-level position as an account representative; move up through higher-level sales positions.

448 *Unit 6 • Life Skills*

Extending the CASE STUDY

Answer: confidence, self-esteem, persistence, outgoing personality, friendliness, honesty, willingness to learn, among others

Further Application: Have students discuss the ways they might use sales skills in their chosen careers. For example, free-lance writers, artists, photographers, and consultants in all fields sell their services to new clients daily; people in all jobs sell themselves, their ideas, their skills, and their experience to get raises or promotions; health professionals sell necessary treatments to patients.

Health and Life Insurance

OBJECTIVES

After studying this section, you will be able to:

- **Compare and contrast basic types of health insurance coverage.**
- **Distinguish between group and individual health insurance plans.**
- **Explain the basic types of life insurance.**

KEY TERMS

major medical
    coverage
coinsurance
term life
    insurance
face value
cash-value life
    insurance
whole life
    insurance

So far, you've thought about planning for unexpected events involving your belongings and your car. Now you'll consider coverage for your most basic possessions: your health and your life.

Health Insurance

The cost of health care in the United States is rising. How can you ensure that your medical costs stay within your budget? You may be able to participate in a health insurance plan provided by your employer. You can also learn about types of coverage and the advantages and disadvantages of each.

Types of Coverage

As with auto insurance, health insurance coverage varies. Types of health coverage fall within three major categories.

Major Medical Coverage.   As with other types of health insurance, **major medical coverage** includes hospital and surgical expenses, doctor visits, prescription drugs, and medical tests. It differs from other types because it requires you to pay a deductible and **coinsurance,** which is a percentage of your medical expenses. An advantage of major medical coverage, though, is that you're able to choose any hospitals and physicians you prefer.

Chapter 22 • Buying Insurance **449**

Guided Practice

Teaching Strategies

1. Assign and review Section 22-3.
2. Use the transparency for this section.

Discussion Starter

Ask students how their health care needs differ from those of a couple in their thirties with two children.

Teaching Tip

Discuss how health care needs depend upon personal situations. Encourage students to think about their own needs as they move from coverage under a parent's policy to their own plan.

SCANS Foundation Skills Connection

L1 Reading

Have each student find and read an article about managed health care. Tell students to find answers to these questions: What is managed care? What does managed care mean for consumers in terms of accessibility and quality of health care? Have students share their findings in class.

L2 Decision Making

Ask students to decide how important it is to them to have an employer offer and partially pay for a group health insurance plan. Ask whether they would turn down a job that did not include insurance.

Health Maintenance Organizations. Unlike major medical coverage, a *health maintenance organization (HMO)* is a type of health coverage with no deductibles. Members usually pay a small *copayment* for doctor visits. In an HMO, checkups and well-baby care are covered, but your choice of physicians is limited.

Preferred Provider Organizations. Do you prefer a wider choice of doctors than you would have with an HMO? Then a *preferred provider organization (PPO)* may be for you. PPOs offer some of the low-cost advantages of HMOs while allowing more freedom of choice of doctors. With a PPO you often pay higher premiums and higher copayments than you would with HMO coverage.

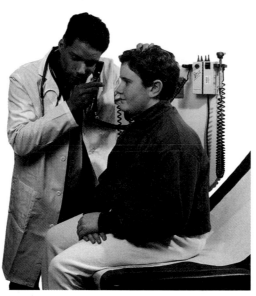

If your health-care insurance pays for annual checkups, take advantage of this coverage. **How can regular checkups help keep you healthy?**

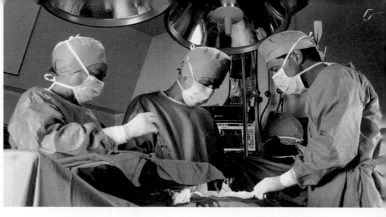

Health-care costs are rising. **What can you do to keep such costs within your budget?**

Types of Plans

You can buy health insurance through a group plan or an individual plan. Most people in the United States belong to group plans, either through their employers or through associations such as trade or alumni associations.

Group Plans. Most group plans are offered through employers. Group plans

---

YOU'RE THE BOSS!

Solving Workplace Problems

The employees at your manufacturing plant are unhappy with the HMO insurance you offer as part of their benefits package. They want a specific PPO, which will give them access to particular doctors in the community. This program will be much more expensive for you. What will you do?

Extending the Illustration

Ask students what other types of regular checkups they should consider as part of their overall health care program. (dental and eye exams)

Caption Answer: Doctors can discover problems before they become serious; they can recommend ways to maintain good health.

Teaching YOU'RE THE BOSS!

Possible responses: Discuss the situation with employees as a group; suggest that they might give up another benefit or even accept slightly lower wages to receive this more expensive benefit; try to find a compromise.

keep premium costs down by spreading the risk over a large number of people. These plans usually have a deductible, coinsurance, and major medical coverage.

Individual Plans. People not enrolled in a group plan can buy insurance coverage through an individual plan. This may include students living on their own, self-employed workers, or retirees. Such coverage can be expensive.

Disability Coverage

Suppose that you become ill and can't return to work for a month or two. How would you pay your bills? Disability insurance pays you a percentage of your salary.

Short-term disability insurance usually covers you for only a few months.

Long-term disability insurance can pay for a lifetime of missed work.

Life Insurance

If others in your household, such as a spouse and children, count on your salary, life insurance will provide money to them in case you die. Some employers offer life insurance as a company benefit.

Types of Life Insurance

There's a wide and confusing array of life insurance choices. It's important to understand each type. The two basic types of life insurance are term life insurance and cash-value life insurance.

EXCELLENT BUSINESS PRACTICES

Reducing Injury on the Job

Kennebec Health Systems of Augusta, Maine, operates a hospital and two nursing homes. The company was experiencing a high injury rate. The injury rate affected the company's bottom line through lost workdays, employee turnover, and expensive premiums for workers' compensation insurance.

Most of the injuries were back injuries sustained when workers were lifting patients. Employees got together to investigate a number of new lifting machines. Kennebec bought the machines the employees liked best. All employees were trained on their proper use and continue to encourage each other to use them.

In a five-year period, the number of days lost because of injury dropped to less than 30 days a year. Annual workers' compensation costs dropped from $1.55 million to $770,000.

Thinking Critically

How does a lower rate of injury and illness affect insurance rates?

Chapter 22 • Buying Insurance **451**

Extending EXCELLENT BUSINESS PRACTICES

Answer: Lower injury rates reduce the overall insurance risk.

Further Application: Have students identify the most common types of injuries

they see at school or at their jobs. Have them talk to the supervisor of the area and find out if there is a policy to help prevent those injuries.

L3 Writing

Assign students to make charts listing local providers for three categories of health insurance: major medical coverage, health maintenance organizations, and preferred provider organizations. Have them list the major features of each program in their charts.

SCANS Workplace Competencies Connection

L1 Understanding Systems

Have students interview an insurance agent to learn why different premiums are charged for different ages. Have them summarize how benefits are determined using life-expectancy data.

L2 Interpreting and Communicating Information

Have each student interview three to five people about concerns they have when buying life insurance. Ask them to draw conclusions about different people's need for life insurance (for example, those with children and without, single, and married).

L3 Applying Technology to Task

Have students identify a major national insurance company on the Internet. Have them find out what services the company offers on-line.

Independent Practice

Writing: *Preparation for Oral Presentation*

Have students write presentations describing types of health insurance coverage and explaining HMO and PPO plans. They should describe the pros and cons for each.

ASSESS

Assessment

Content

Have each student write a short article describing health care coverage and types of providers. Evaluate students' articles for clarity and accuracy.

Evaluation

Assign the section review.

MINI QUIZ

Short Answer

1. A loss not covered by an insurance policy is an ____. (exclusion)

2. An oral or written notice to an insurance company is a ____. (claim)

3. ____ insurance covers the cost of repairing another person's car. (Liability)

4. If your insurance company pays for damages regardless of who causes an accident, you have ____ insurance. (no-fault)

5. Hospital and surgical expenses are paid by ____ insurance. (major medical)

Term Life Insurance. Of the two types of life insurance, term is less costly. **Term life insurance** simply protects your dependents if you die. It has no cash value and provides coverage for a set number of years. If you should die, the beneficiary receives an amount of money known as the **face value** of the policy.

Cash-Value Life Insurance. The second basic type of life insurance, **cash-value life insurance**, is part insurance and part investment. You can borrow money against the total amount of premiums paid on a cash-value policy. One kind of cash-value life insurance is whole life insurance. **Whole life insurance** works in part like term life insurance but has a savings component. With whole life insurance, you can build a reserve of money that you can borrow against or collect when you retire.

Buying Life Insurance

As with other types of insurance, when you buy life insurance, you'll purchase a policy and pay premiums to an insurance company. The company agrees to pay a benefit to your beneficiary if you die. The premium amount will depend on factors such as your age, your health, and the type of policy you buy. Here are some questions to consider before buying life insurance:

- *Should you buy life insurance?* If someone depends on you for your earning power, you should have life insurance. If you have no dependents, you may not need the insurance.

- *How much life insurance do you need?* This depends on how old you are, whether you have dependents, how much your family will need if you die, and how much insurance you can afford.

- *What are some tips on buying life insurance?* Take the time to shop around for life insurance, just as you would when buying a car. Life insurance prices vary widely. Don't make your decision solely on an agent's advice. Talk to others and take advantage of consumer guides.

SECTION 22-3 *Review*

Understanding Key Concepts

Using complete sentences, answer the following questions on a separate sheet of paper.

1. What are the advantages and disadvantages of major medical coverage, HMO coverage, and PPO coverage?

2. If your employer doesn't offer health insurance, what choices do you have in buying health insurance?

3. Explain the difference between term life insurance and whole life insurance.

SECTION 22-3 *Review* ANSWERS

1. An advantage of major medical coverage is freedom to choose a physician; a disadvantage is having to pay a deductible. An advantage of an HMO is low copayment; a disadvantage is limited physician choice. An advantage of PPO is no deductible; a disadvantage is higher premiums.

2. You can buy an individual policy or join an association group policy.

3. Term life insurance pays a beneficiary in case of the policyholder's death; whole life insurance pays a beneficiary but, during the life of a policy, allows money to accumulate in investments.

SECTION 22-1 Summary

- Although insurance policies are long and complex, it pays to learn the language of insurance.
- Most people purchase homeowner's or renter's, auto, health, and life coverage.
- You can hold down your insurance costs by shopping around, buying only the coverage you need, and seeking discounts.

Key Terms

insurance policy *(p. 438)*
premium *(p. 439)*
deductible *(p. 439)*
claim *(p. 439)*

SECTION 22-2 Summary

- The five major types of auto insurance are liability, medical expenses, collision, comprehensive, and uninsured motorist coverage.
- Premium costs for auto insurance are influenced by a driver's age, driving record, location, and type of car, among other factors.
- You can lower your auto insurance premiums by shopping around, maintaining a good driving record, taking driver education courses, buying only the coverage you need, raising your deductibles, and buying a less expensive car.

Key Terms

liability insurance *(p. 443)*
collision insurance *(p. 444)*
comprehensive
    insurance *(p. 444)*

SECTION 22-3 Summary

- The cost of health care is rising, but you have choices in limiting what you pay for coverage.
- Three basic types of health-care coverage are major medical coverage, HMO coverage, and PPO coverage.
- Types of health insurance plans are group and individual plans.
- Life insurance provides for the protection of your dependents.
- Two broad categories of life insurance are cash-value and term life insurance.

Key Terms

major medical
    coverage *(p. 449)*
coinsurance *(p. 449)*
term life insurance *(p. 452)*
face value *(p. 452)*
cash-value life
    insurance *(p. 452)*
whole life insurance *(p. 452)*

Chapter 22 • Buying Insurance **453**

Use the Testmaker to create a customized test for Chapter 22.

Reteaching

1. Write *health insurance* and *life insurance* on the chalkboard. Ask students to describe types of coverage for health care and the different plans. Ask students for examples of each plan and coverage.

   Next, ask students to describe types of life insurance and give examples of each.

2. Assign and review vocabulary terms, chapter questions, and activities from the Chapter Review.

Extending the Content

Assign the appropriate Chapter 22 activities in the *Student Activity Workbook*. Have each student contact a local or state consumer affairs worker and research insurance scams or unnecessary coverage. How can a consumer find out which insurance products are reputable and worthwhile? Have students present their findings in three- to five-minute talks.

CLOSE

Now that students have learned about the different types of insurance plans and coverages, have them complete this sentence: "The primary purpose of life insurance is . . . ." (to provide for people you support after your death)

Computer Activity

Have students use a database program to create a list of health care providers in your community. Tell them that a large business is planning to relocate to their area and needs to identify health care providers currently available. They may list hospitals, clinics, and physicians. Find out what type of insurance plans each provider accepts. (HMO, PPO, major medical) After they have created the database, ask for a list of health care providers alphabetically by category.

Answers

Reviewing Key Terms

Answers will vary. In paragraphs on insurance basics, students should include the terms *insurance policy, premium, deductible,* and *claim.* The paragraph on auto insurance should include the terms *liability insurance, collision insurance,* and *comprehensive insurance.* The paragraph on health insurance should include the terms *major medical coverage* and *coinsurance.* The paragraph on life insurance should include the terms *term life insurance, face value, cash-value life insurance,* and *whole life insurance.*

Recalling Key Concepts

1. b
2. c
3. c
4. a
5. c
6. b

Thinking Critically

1. Deductibles help insurers avoid the time and expense of settling relatively small claims and therefore lower the cost of the insurance.

2. Liability coverage is most important: when an accident is caused by the policyholder, it protects him or her against possible claims or lawsuits brought by the driver of the other vehicle or anyone injured in the accident.

Reviewing Key Terms

On separate paper, write one paragraph each about insurance basics, auto insurance, health insurance, and life insurance. Use the terms below in your paragraphs.

insurance policy	major medical
premium	coverage
deductible	coinsurance
claim	term life
liability	insurance
insurance	face value
collision	cash-value life
insurance	insurance
comprehensive	whole life
insurance	insurance

Recalling Key Concepts

Choose the correct answer for each item below. Write your answers on a separate sheet of paper.

1. Insurance premiums are paid by ____.
   (a) an insurance company
   (b) a policyholder to an insurance company
   (c) an insurance company to a beneficiary

2. One way to lower your insurance costs is to ____.
   (a) raise your risk
   (b) lower your deductibles
   (c) raise your deductibles

3. The type of automobile insurance that covers the cost of repairs to a car that you run into in an accident is ____.
   (a) comprehensive (b) collision
   (c) liability

---

4. You are likely to pay lower auto insurance premiums if you ____.
   (a) buy a less expensive car
   (b) buy more coverage than required by law
   (c) lower your deductibles

5. Which type of health insurance requires policyholders to pay coinsurance? ____.
   (a) an HMO (b) a PPO
   (c) major medical coverage

6. Whole life is a type of ____ life insurance.
   (a) face value (b) cash-value (c) term

Thinking Critically

Using complete sentences, answer each of the questions below on a separate sheet of paper.

1. Why do you think most insurance policies provide for a deductible?

2. Which type of auto insurance coverage do you think is most important?

3. Why should you buy health insurance even if you're well and practice a healthy lifestyle?

SCANS Foundation Skills and Workplace Competencies

Basic Skills: *Writing*

As a writer for a consumer magazine, you are preparing an article on the relationship between lower auto insurance rates and automobile safety features. Research existing safety features on a variety of cars. Include information on

---

3. Unexpected accidents can occur, and even healthy people can develop diseases.

SCANS Foundation Skills and Workplace Competencies

Answers will vary. If students list air bags among safety features, you may want to lead

a discussion of their advantages and disadvantages.

Connecting Academics to the Workplace

1. United States automobile insurance is not valid in Mexico. Mexican auto insurance can be obtained through some U.S.

the development of future auto safety features. Prepare a list of these, with a brief description of their functions.

Connecting Academics to the Workplace

Social Studies

1. Kai is a supervisor for an electronics company. The company wants him to spend a year training new supervisors in its plant in Monterey, Mexico. Kai will use his own car while he lives in Mexico. Use the Internet and sources such as *Birnbaum's Mexico* to research insurance requirements for using your own car in Mexico.

Math

2. On her way to work one morning, Carla slipped on an icy sidewalk and broke her arm. The total cost for medical treatment was $1,000. Carla has major medical coverage through her employer. Her deductible is $500, and coinsurance is 20 percent. Of the medical costs for her broken arm, how much will Carla have to pay?

Developing Teamwork and Leadership Skills

Form groups of four or five. Work as a team to plan a full range of insurance coverage needed by a family of two adults and two young children. You can choose to have the family rent or own their home. Assume that they own at least one automobile. One or both adults can be wage earners for the family. List each type of insurance recommended. Briefly describe the coverage and tell why you recommend it. Choose a leader to share your recommendations with the class.

Real-World Workshop

Working in the same teams as in the previous activity, contact a local insurance company representative. Share your recommendations for the family of four. Ask if there is additional coverage needed by the family. Then find out what the approximate annual cost of complete coverage would be for the family.

School-to-Work Connection

Contact people in charge of employee benefits for three local companies, and discuss with them insurance benefits provided to employees of each company. Ask how the company chooses insurers and provides information on insurance benefits to employees. Then prepare a brief report on your findings.

Individual Career Plan

Research insurance-related careers. Find an area that interests you, and use the Internet to find out more about it. If possible, arrange an interview with a person in your town who works in this career area. Write a paragraph or two about this aspect of the insurance industry.

Developing Teamwork and Leadership Skills

Before students plan family coverage, encourage them to think of additional details about the family, such as the driving records of both adults, types of cars owned, and whether the adults are smokers. Teams should be specific about types of coverage within broad categories, such as auto and life insurance, and about their reasons for selecting each type of coverage.

Real-World Workshop

As students talk to the insurance company representative, have them list factors that influence types and costs of coverage. Have teams compare annual insurance costs for their families of four.

School-to-Work Connection

Students are likely to find that these procedures vary widely among companies. After students have written their reports, you may want to have them assess the various practices, citing those that seem most effective.

Individual Career Plan

Tell students to be specific in their research about the aspects of insurance-related careers that most interest them. Have them refer to their lists of interests, skills, and talents from Chapter 1.

---

agents and in border towns through companies such as Sanborn's Mexico Insurance Service. Most of the Mexican auto insurance policies include collision and upset, fire and theft, property damage, bodily injury, and medical payments. Some agents offer multiple-entry insurance for more than one trip per year; drivers can also purchase insurance for six months or a year at a less expensive rate. Mexican insurers pay for their own insured party's damages no matter who is at fault.

2. Carla will pay the $500 deductible plus 20 percent of $1,000 ($200), for a total of $700.

SECTION 1 *All About Taxes*

SECTION OBJECTIVES	SECTION FEATURES	SECTION RESOURCES
• Identify five characteristics of a good tax system. • Determine whether you owe income tax. • Complete a federal tax return.	Personal Career Plan, p. 457 You're the Boss!, p. 460 Excellent Business Practices, p. 463 Exploring Careers, p. 470	Workforce 2000 Videodisc and Videotape Section 23-1 Review, p. 469 Student Activity Workbook

SECTION 2 *All About Social Security*

SECTION OBJECTIVES	SECTION FEATURES	SECTION RESOURCES
• Describe how the Social Security system works. • Identify four Social Security program benefits and two state social insurance benefits. • Explain the main problem that is facing the Social Security system today.	Career Do's and Don'ts, p. 473 Attitude Counts, p. 474	Workforce 2000 Videodisc and Videotape Section 23-2 Review, p. 474 Chapter 23 Review, pp. 476–477 Student Activity Workbook

CHAPTER 23

CHAPTER RESOURCES

- Chapter Transparencies and Lesson Plans
- Chapter 23 Test
- Spanish Resources, Chapter 23
- School-to-Work Activity Handbook, Chapter 23 Activity
- Teacher's Lesson Plans, Chapter 23
- Implementing Block Scheduling, Chapter 23
- Print, Media, and Internet Handbook
- Strategies for Implementing Work-Based Learning
- Strategies for Implementing Connecting Activities

Career Notes

SCANS CORRELATION CHART

Foundation Skills

Basic Skills | Reading | Writing | Math | Listening | Speaking

Thinking Skills | Creative Thinking | Decision Making | Problem Solving | Seeing Things in the Mind's Eye | Knowing How to Learn | Reasoning

Personal Qualities | Responsibility | Self-Esteem | Sociability | Self-Management | Integrity/Honesty

Workplace Competencies

Resources | Allocating Time | Allocating Money | Allocating Material and Facility Resources | Allocating Human Resources

Information | Acquiring and Evaluating Information | Organizing and Maintaining Information | Interpreting and Communicating Information | Using Computers to Process Information

Interpersonal Skills | Participating as a Member of a Team | Teaching Others | Serving Clients/Customers | Exercising Leadership | Negotiating to Arrive at a Decision | Working with Cultural Diversity

Systems | Understanding Systems | Monitoring and Correcting Performance | Improving and Designing Systems

Technology | Selecting Technology | Applying Technology to Task | Maintaining and Troubleshooting Technology

Highlighted blocks indicate areas covered in the Chapter.

Additional Activities

 Internet Connection

Have students use the Internet to research information about different types of taxes, such as federal income tax, state and local tax, as well as sales tax. What are the differences? Discuss findings in class.

 Field Trip Suggestions

Take students to a stock brokerage firm. Arrange for someone there to explain stocks, bonds, and money markets; show students how the stock market works; explain the risks and returns of buying stocks; and show students how money wisely invested at an early age can help them retire early.

 Guest Speaker Suggestions

Invite to class an insurance representative who specializes in life, health, homeowner's or car insurance. Ask the guest to explain how insurance works, how much coverage a person should have, and how to compare insurance prices and services.

Key to Ability Levels

Each section gives skill-building activities. Each activity has been labeled for use with students of various learning styles and abilities.

L1 Level 1 activities are basic activities and should be within the range of all students.

L2 Level 2 activities are average activities and should be within the range of average and above average students.

L3 Level 3 activities are challenging activities designed for the ability range of above average students.

School-Based Learning

Chapter Overview

Chapter 23 explains the tax system and procedures for filing a federal tax return.

Section 23-1 focuses on the taxes paid to federal, state, and local governments.

Section 23-2 highlights the Social Security program.

Background Information

Write chapter objectives (Sections 23-1 and 23-2) on the chalkboard or use the chapter objective transparency for class discussion.

Choose assignments from the *Student Activity Workbook* and write them on the chalkboard.

Have students preview the chapter, looking at pictures, reading captions, and noting content headings. Ask students to describe what they expect to learn in this chapter.

Preteaching Vocabulary

Write the Key Terms from Sections 23-1 and 23-2 on the chalkboard. Have students describe how each term relates to taxes or Social Security taxes.

456

Meeting SPECIAL Needs

Visually Impaired

One of the ways visually impaired students cope with classroom printed material is by using taped classroom lectures. To that end, think carefully about what you say in class. When writing on the chalkboard while talking, for example, be clear and specific. "This (pointing) plus that (pointing) equals 11," will not mean anything to students listening to a tape. "Four plus seven equals 11," however, is clear.

Taxes and Social Security

Section 23-1
All About Taxes

Section 23-2
All About Social Security

In this video segment, find out how the government uses your tax dollars.

Journal
Personal Career Plan

Who pays taxes? Why? Who benefits from taxes? How? Record your responses in a journal entry.

457

Addressing **LEARNING** Styles

Linguistic Learner

After discussing the different types of taxes, ask students to consider a world without taxes. Ask them to write a short essay that shows how tax-based services, such as education, law enforcement, and mail service would be paid for. They should consider the advantages and disadvantages of such a system on individuals and on society. You might ask a history or economics teacher to discuss economic systems that have eliminated taxes.

FOCUS

Bell Ringer

Have students answer this question: As a citizen and a wage earner, do you have a responsibility to pay taxes? Why or why not?

Introducing the Section

Review students' answers from the Bell Ringer activity. Explore students' feelings about paying taxes for things they either do not use or do not approve of. For example, should tax dollars of citizens who disapprove of space exploration go toward supporting NASA? Should people who do not have children in school have their tax money support public schools? Explain that taxes have always been, and probably always will be, a controversial issue. Introduce the concept of social responsibility and the importance of doing what is best for the good of all.

Motivational Activity
Critical Thinking

Have students write 200-word papers describing what they would term "ideal" government services and how to pay for them. Urge students to be creative in thinking of needs and ways to raise money. Have students compare their tax systems in class.

All About Taxes

OBJECTIVES

After studying this section, you will be able to:

- **Identify five characteristics of a good tax system.**
- **Determine whether you owe income tax.**
- **Complete a federal tax return.**

KEY TERMS

Internal Revenue Service (IRS)
withhold
income tax return
exemption
deduction

What do you think of when you hear the word *taxes*? The extra charge that's added to your bill when you buy a CD? The money your employer takes out of your paycheck each week? It's all money that comes out of your pocket and goes to the government, and it really adds up. You do get a great deal out of the taxes you pay, though. Think about it. What benefits from paying taxes can you name? How many have you enjoyed today?

Understanding Taxes

You may think that the whole topic of taxes is confusing. Actually, the general structure and workings of our tax system are easy to understand.

First of all, *taxes* are payments that you make to support the government and to pay for government services. There are three levels of government: federal, state, and local. The federal government runs the country as a whole. State governments manage the 50 states. Local governments govern counties, cities, and towns. All three levels of government need money to operate, so you must pay taxes to all three.

The **Internal Revenue Service**, or **IRS**, is the agency that collects federal taxes and oversees the federal tax system. Taxes paid to the IRS go into the U.S. Treasury.

Implementing Teamwork

Divide your class into teams of four and ask them to research the tax implications of running a small business. Students may need to talk to other small business owners or a representative from the Small Business Association. Ask each group to make a presentation to the class with its findings.

Addressing Workplace Diversity

To communicate more effectively with women at work, men should replace offensive terms such as lady or gals with woman or women; use humor but not aggressive, sexual humor; use a win-win style of communication not a win-lose. (*Genderflex* by Judith Tingley)

The federal government has spent billions of tax dollars on space exploration. ***Do you think this is a wise use of funds? Why or why not?***

Types of Taxes

There are many kinds of taxes. The following are common ones.

- *Income taxes.* You pay income tax on your income, or the money you make. This income may come from working or from other sources, such as the interest your bank pays you on your savings, or it may come from

profit you make on selling real estate. Income taxes are the federal government's main source of money.

Income tax is calculated as a percentage of the taxable income you earn. (*Taxable income* is your income after you subtract certain permitted amounts.) At the present time, the federal income tax ranges from 15 to 39.6 percent. In general, the greater your taxable income, the higher the rate of income tax you must pay. Your employer will **withhold**, or take out, money from your paychecks to pay income tax due on your wages.

In most states, people also pay state income tax. Many cities also have income taxes. State and local income tax rates vary, but they're generally much lower than federal rates.

- *Social Security taxes.* Workers pay Social Security taxes so that they can receive benefits when they retire. (You'll read more about Social Security on pages 471–474.) Like income taxes, Social Security taxes are figured as a percentage of the money you earn.

Employers withhold money from paychecks to pay Social Security taxes, just as they do for

---

▶ Extending the Illustration

Space exploration also provides a number of jobs. Have students brainstorm a list of other interesting or unusual government jobs. (Some examples might be forestation experts, park rangers, geolgists, or interpreters.)

Caption Answer: Some students may feel that money could be better spent elsewhere. Many, however, will probably feel that it's a wise use of funds because it provides valuable scientific information.

TEACH

Guided Practice
Teaching Strategies

1. Assign and review Section 23-1.
2. Use the transparency for this section.
3. Assign and review the Case Study.

Discussion Starter

Ask students to think about the last time they paid taxes. (If you live in a state with a sales tax, it would have been the last time they bought a taxable item.)

Teaching Tip

Write the words *federal, state,* and *local* on the chalkboard. Discuss income taxes as a type levied by all three levels of government. Explain that one pays a percentage of earnings as federal income taxes. Write the percentages for your state and local taxes under those headings.

Continue explaining types of taxes. Write *Social Security* under the *federal* heading and explain that students will learn more about that tax in the next section. Write *sales taxes* under *state* and *local*, and list the percentages for your area.

Critical Thinking

Prior to the American Revolution, James Otis, a colonist from Massachusetts, reportedly said, "Taxation without representation is tyranny." Have students write a paragraph explaining what Otis meant and its relevance today.

TEACH (cont'd.)

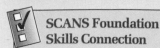

SCANS Foundation Skills Connection

L1 Listening

Have students interview five or six people and ask them about their top four financial concerns (for example, saving for a child's education), ranking concerns from one to four, one being the most important. Have students compare their findings in class.

L2 Knowing How to Learn

Have each student talk to a financial planner or a tax accountant. Tell students to ask about the three most common mistakes people make when preparing their tax returns, sharing what they learn in class. How can students avoid these mistakes when filing their own tax returns?

L3 Reasoning

Divide the class into groups of three or four. Then have each group discuss the benefits derived from taxes paid to various branches of government. Have groups list each government level and the corresponding benefits.

Figure 23-1 <u>Gross pay</u> is the total amount you earn. <u>Net pay</u>, sometimes called take-home pay, is the amount that remains after money has been deducted for various taxes. How much money did the employer withhold from this paycheck? If you are preparing a monthly budget, should you plan on using your gross pay or your net pay? Why?

YOU'RE THE BOSS!

✓ Solving Workplace Problems

Your gardening service is doing well, and you're ready to hire an assistant. The most promising applicant says, "I'd love to have this job, but I don't really need any benefits, and I certainly don't need to pay any taxes. Can't you just pay me in cash every week? Then we won't need to worry about all those forms." How do you respond?

---

income taxes. Your paycheck stub shows the money withheld in a box labeled "FICA." This stands for Federal Insurance Contribution Act. See **Figure 23-1.**

- *Sales taxes.* When you buy something, the salesperson may add sales tax to the price. This tax goes to the state or local government. Almost every state has a sales tax.

  Sales tax is calculated as a percentage of the price of an item. The tax rate varies from state to state. See **Figure 23-2,** which shows the various state sales tax rates. In addition to state taxes, local sales taxes may be.added to the cost of items you purchase.

►► Extending Figure 23-1 ◄◄

Use the current minimum wage and have students calculate earnings for a 40-hour week. Have them subtract deductions of $17 for health insurance and 15 percent for taxes.

Caption Answer: $39.97; you should plan on using your net pay because this is the amount of money you will actually have in hand

Teaching YOU'RE THE BOSS!

✓ Possible responses: Discuss with the applicant the importance of participating in the tax and Social Security systems.

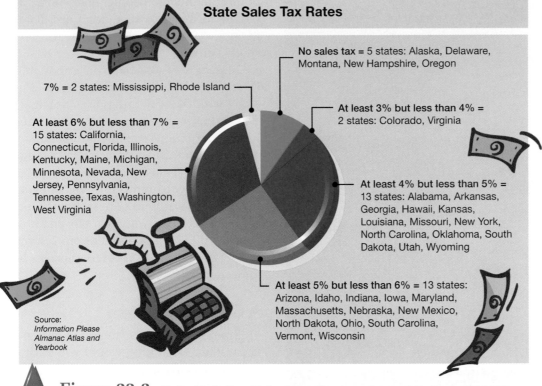

State Sales Tax Rates

No sales tax = 5 states: Alaska, Delaware, Montana, New Hampshire, Oregon

7% = 2 states: Mississippi, Rhode Island

At least 3% but less than 4% = 2 states: Colorado, Virginia

At least 6% but less than 7% = 15 states: California, Connecticut, Florida, Illinois, Kentucky, Maine, Michigan, Minnesota, Nevada, New Jersey, Pennsylvania, Tennessee, Texas, Washington, West Virginia

At least 4% but less than 5% = 13 states: Alabama, Arkansas, Georgia, Hawaii, Kansas, Louisiana, Missouri, New York, North Carolina, Oklahoma, South Dakota, Utah, Wyoming

At least 5% but less than 6% = 13 states: Arizona, Idaho, Indiana, Iowa, Maryland, Massachusetts, Nebraska, New Mexico, North Dakota, Ohio, South Carolina, Vermont, Wisconsin

Source: *Information Please Almanac Atlas and Yearbook*

Figure 23-2 Sales tax is the chief source of revenue for most state governments. Sales tax is calculated on purchase price. For example, if you buy a $10.00 book and the sales tax rate is 5 percent, you'll pay $10.00 plus 50¢ (5% × $10 = 0.50), or $10.50. In some states, some items (for example, clothing or other necessities) are free from sales tax. What's the tax rate in your state?

- *Property taxes.* The main source of money for local governments is property taxes. These taxes are based on the value of property—generally land and buildings.

Where Do Your Tax Dollars Go?

Each year, federal, state, and local governments take in billions of dollars in taxes. Where does this money go? Here's just a partial list of services paid for in full, or in part, by your tax dollars:

- *education*, including public schools and libraries;
- *transportation*, ranging from roadways and mass transit to dams and airports;
- *safety*, including law enforcement and fire protection;
- *health*, ranging from hospitals to medical research studies;
- *military services*; and
- *postal services*.

Chapter 23 • Taxes and Social Security **461**

 SCANS Workplace Competencies Connection

L1 **Creative Thinking**

Although many people see the need for taxes, they don't like paying them. Assign students to groups of four or five and have each group design and write an ad that will encourage people to pay taxes. Have each group display its ad.

L2 **Interpreting and Communicating Information**

Have students research, possibly on the Internet, their state legislature's current slate of bills and find out whether any pending legislation affects taxes. Have students write a summary of their findings, then share the information in class.

L3 **Working with Cultural Diversity**

Working in pairs, tell students to imagine that one of them is a foreigner; have the other ask questions about the U.S. system of taxation and explain the various taxes that are deducted from an employee's earnings and the reason for such deductions.

▶▶ **Extending Figure 23-2** ◀◀

Ask students what the sales tax rate is for your local area. Give students three or four amounts and have them calculate the sales tax.

Caption Answer: Students should find the tax rate for their state.

Skills Practice

Divide students into small groups. Have all groups review the section entitled "Where Do Your Tax Dollars Go?" Then either assign or allow groups to select a service organization in your area that receives tax money. Have each group interview the organization's personnel to learn how the organization spends its tax money. Tell each group to prepare a five- to ten-minute presentation.

Discussion Starter

Ask students to explain why the government cannot increase services and lower taxes at the same time.

Teaching Tip

Tell students that there is always a conflict between increased government services and lower taxes—the more services, the higher the taxes. Controversy often revolves around the issue of *who* pays the taxes and *how much* is paid.

Independent Practice

Assign as homework the chapter activity in the *School-to-Work Activity Handbook.*

Local services, such as fire and police protection, are paid for primarily through local taxes. *What other services does your community provide?*

It's Your Responsibility

When you go out to eat with friends, you split the bill. As a citizen, you also have to split the bill for the services the government provides.

Since we all share in the benefits, we should all contribute our fair share of taxes. That seems reasonable. The problem is that people disagree on what's fair. Some taxpayers think that rich people should pay a larger share of their income than low

or middle income people. Some object to paying for services they don't use. Some disagree with the way the government spends money.

Making everyone happy is impossible. Does that mean that you just have to go along with the way things are? Not at all. You can influence how federal, state, and local governments spend your tax money. You can also influence the tax laws themselves. How? That's easy: vote.

Voters elect representatives at every level of government. These lawmakers decide what taxes you must pay and how your tax money is spent. It's your responsibility as a citizen to vote for officials who represent your beliefs.

A Good Tax System

Suppose it were up to you to design a tax system. What kind would you create? Lawmakers have argued over this question for decades, and the debate goes on. Still, most people agree that a good tax system has certain features.

- A tax system should be fair. Everyone who is able to pay should pay his or her fair share.

- Tax laws should be clear and simple. Many people think that the present system is too complicated. There are too many rules and tax forms.

- Taxes should be collected at a convenient time when most people are able to pay.

- A tax system should be stable. Taxpayers should know in advance how much they'll owe. If tax laws are always changing, people can't predict how much money to budget for taxes.

▶ Extending the Illustration

Obtain information on calculating property taxes for your area and have students calculate taxes using an average home cost in the area.

Caption Answer: Possible answers include trash collection, water, schools, sewage treatment, mass transit, libraries, sidewalks, and community health services.

- A tax system should be flexible. When necessary, the government should be able to adjust the tax system to bring in more or less income. For example, during a war, the government may need to raise more money.

Understanding Federal Income Tax Returns

You've probably heard stories about people who got in trouble over their taxes. Maybe they didn't file their tax return on time. Maybe an audit, or review of their taxes by the IRS, revealed that they had failed to report some of their income. These kinds of mistakes can lead to hefty fines. So should you worry about your taxes? No, but you should understand that the IRS takes tax paying seriously. You've got to do it, and you need to do it right. If you make an honest effort, though, you have little to worry about.

To pay federal income tax, you must complete and file an income tax return each year. An **income tax return** is a form that shows how much you earned from working and made from other sources. It also shows how much tax you owe. If your employer withheld more money from your paychecks than you owe, you'll get a tax refund. If your employer didn't withhold enough, you'll have to pay the difference.

EXCELLENT BUSINESS PRACTICES

Protecting Your Privacy

Atmel Corporation is a San Jose, California, company that manufactures specialized semiconductors. The company has established procedures to ensure that human resources data doesn't fall into the wrong hands.

Records of Atmel's 3,000 employees are stored in locked file cabinets. They can't be looked at by anyone other than an approved clerk. Medical records are kept in separate locked cabinets to keep sensitive medical information from becoming public.

On all employee files, the company uses an employee number rather than the Social Security number, which could be used for financial fraud and other invasions of privacy. Prospective employees are briefed on security and privacy issues concerning their coworkers and on the confidentiality of information pertaining to the company.

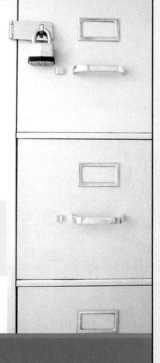

Thinking Critically

How can private information be used against a person?

Extending EXCELLENT BUSINESS PRACTICES

Answer: It can be used to start rumors, put pressure on someone, block promotions, or steal from someone.

Further Application: Have students discuss ways to protect private personnel or medical records kept at their school or job.

Reading

Have each student read an article describing the federal income tax and current tax rates. Tell students to take notes and be prepared to discuss what they read in class.

Writing: *Informational*

Have each student write a message to a foreign friend describing the U.S. tax system. In their messages, students should explain the different types of taxes and which level of government collects them.

Critical Thinking

Tell students to decide whether they support fewer services and lower taxes or the same level of services and either current tax rates or higher taxes on some items. Have them prepare arguments to support their positions. Then hold a debate between the opposing groups.

Discussion Starter

Why is the federal income tax system so complicated? How could it be simplified?

Teaching Tip

In responding to the Discussion Starter, some students may mention the flat tax rate as a possible way to simplify federal income taxes. Another possibility to discuss is the elimination of special tax breaks, such as interest on a home mortgage or write-offs for investment losses.

SECTION 23-1

TEACH (cont'd.)

Teaching Tip

Tell students to prepare a list of questions they would like to ask a tax attorney or an accountant. Invite such individuals to class.

Aside from delivering government services, taxes also provide jobs for many people. Help students explore tax-related careers, brainstorming a list of possible careers. Students will probably mention accountants, tax preparers, tax assessors, and auditors. Less obvious careers include people who design tax forms, publish tax booklets, print documents, assist people in filling out forms, or answer tax questions on the telephone.

Skills Practice

Janet bought a blouse for \$27.95, slacks for \$55.55, and a jacket for \$104.39. How much is her total purchase? At 6 percent, how much will Janet pay for sales taxes? (total sale, \$187.89: \$27.95 + \$55.55 + \$104.39; taxes, \$11.27: \$187.89 × 0.06)

Chuck plans to buy a new car for \$18,595. The sales tax in his area is 6.5 percent. How much will Chuck pay in taxes? What is the total cost of the car? (\$1,208.68: \$18,595 × 0.065; total cost, \$19,803.68: \$18,595 + \$1,208.68)

Personal Allowances Worksheet

A Enter "1" for **yourself** if no one else can claim you as a dependent . . . . . A ____

B Enter "1" if: { • You are single and have only one job; or • You are married, have only one job, and your spouse does not work; or • Your wages from a second job or your spouse's wages (or the total of both) are \$1,000 or less. } . . B ____

C Enter "1" for your **spouse.** But, you may choose to enter -0- if you are married and have either a working spouse or more than one job (this may help you avoid having too little tax withheld) . . . . . C ____

D Enter number of **dependents** (other than your spouse or yourself) you will claim on your tax return . . . . D ____

E Enter "1" if you will file as **head of household** on your tax return (see conditions under **Head of Household** above) . E ____

F Enter "1" if you have at least \$1,500 of **child or dependent care expenses** for which you plan to claim a credit . . F ____

G Add lines A through F and enter total here. **Note:** This amount may be different from the number of exemptions you claim on your return ▶ G ____

For accuracy, do all worksheets that apply. { • If you plan to **itemize or claim adjustments to income** and want to reduce your withholding, see the Deductions and Adjustments Worksheet on page 2. • If you are **single** and have **more than one job** and your combined earnings from all jobs exceed \$30,000 OR if you are **married** and have a **working spouse or more than one job,** and the combined earnings from all jobs exceed \$50,000, see the Two-Earner/Two-Job Worksheet on page 2 if you want to avoid having too little tax withheld. • If **neither** of the above situations applies, **stop here** and enter the number from line G on line 5 of Form W-4 below. }

Cut here and give the certificate to your employer. Keep the top portion for your records.

Form **W-4** Department of the Treasury Internal Revenue Service — **Employee's Withholding Allowance Certificate** — OMB No. 1545-0010

▶ **For Privacy Act and Paperwork Reduction Act Notice, see reverse.**

1 Type or print your first name and middle initial: Lisa N. — Last name: Michaels — 2 Your social security number: 123 45 6789

Home address (number and street or rural route): 33 Clark Lane — 3 ☒ Single ☐ Married ☐ Married, but withhold at higher Single rate. *Note: If married, but legally separated, or spouse is a nonresident alien, check the Single box.*

City or town, state, and ZIP code: Greenville, MA 01234 — 4 If your last name differs from that on your social security card, check here and call 1-800-772-1213 for a new card . . . . ▶ ☐

5 Total number of allowances you are claiming (from line G above or from the worksheets on page 2 if they apply) . 5 0

6 Additional amount, if any, you want withheld from each paycheck . . . . . 6 \$

7 I claim exemption from withholding for 1996 and I certify that I meet **BOTH** of the following conditions for exemption:
• **Last year I had a right to a refund of ALL Federal income tax withheld because I had NO tax liability; AND**
• **This year I expect a refund of ALL Federal income tax withheld because I expect to have NO tax liability.**
If you meet both conditions, enter "EXEMPT" here . . . . ▶ 7

Under penalties of perjury, I certify that I am entitled to the number of withholding allowances claimed on this certificate or entitled to claim exempt status.

Employee's signature ▶ Lisa N. Michaels — **Date** ▶ 8/10/

8 Employer's name and address (Employer: Complete 8 and 10 only if sending to the IRS) — 9 Office code (optional) — 10 Employer identification number

Cat. No. 10220Q

Figure 23-3 All employees must fill out a Form W-4. Why is it important to complete this form accurately?

How does your employer know how much to withhold? Simple: by looking at the information you provide on a Form W-4, like the one in ***Figure 23-3.*** Completing this form is easy.

- Fill in your name, address, and Social Security number. Indicate whether you are married or single.
- Write the number of *allowances*, or deductions, you are allowed to claim. The higher the number, the less tax withheld. Use the "Personal Allowances Worksheet" on the Form W-4 .
- Indicate whether you are *exempt*—excused—from having to pay tax.
- Sign and date the form.

Extending Figure 23-3

Ask students how often they should fill out a new Form W-4 or what events might require a change in their withholding amounts. (Examples include when they change employers, when they marry or have children.)

Caption Answer: The employer uses the information on Form W-4 to determine how much money to withhold for taxes.

How Do You File a Return?

In general, if you're single and earn at least $6,400 in a calendar year, you must file an income tax return. This figure changes from time to time, however. Check with the IRS for the current figure. You have to mail your tax return to the IRS by April 15.

To prepare your return, you'll need Form W-2. See ***Figure 23-4.*** Your employer will send this form to you. It shows how much money you earned and how much your employer withheld for taxes.

There are three basic federal income tax forms: 1040EZ, 1040A, and 1040. Form 1040EZ is the simplest one to fill out. It will probably work for you. These key terms will help you understand the tax forms:

- An **exemption** is a fixed amount of money that is excused from taxes. For example, in one recent year the IRS let each taxpayer claim a $2,500 personal exemption.
- A *dependent* is someone whom you support, such as a child.

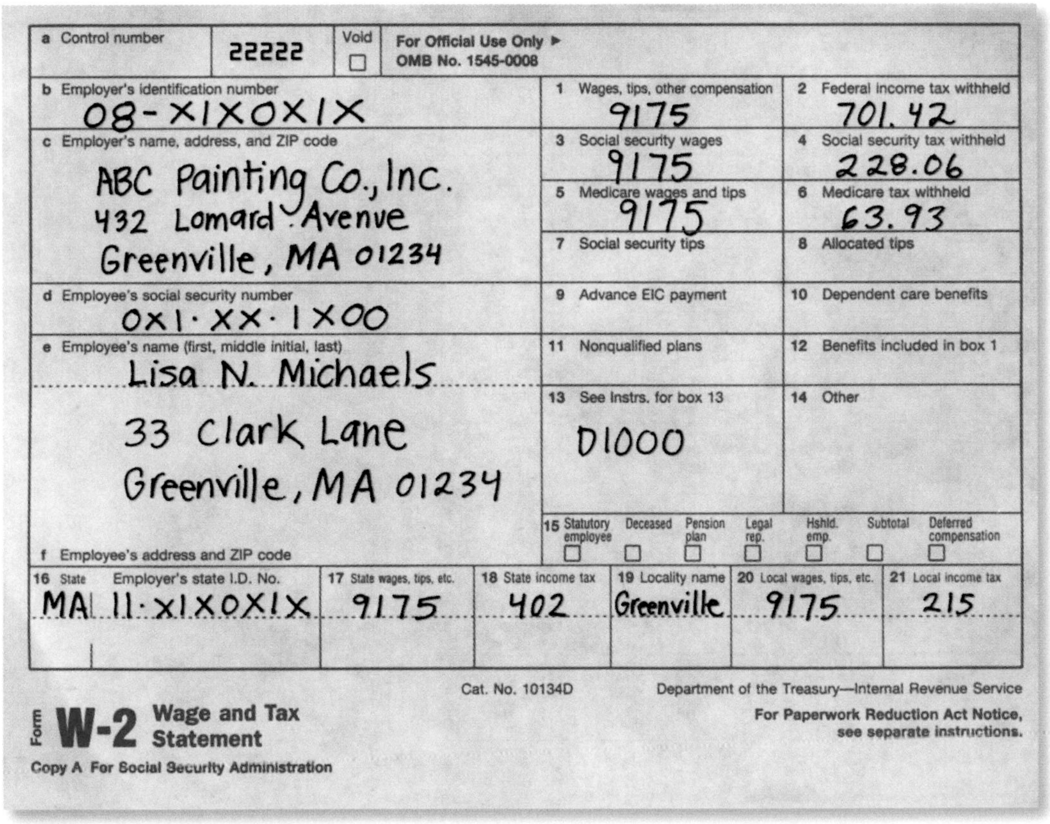

a Control number: 22222	Void ☐	For Official Use Only ▶ OMB No. 1545-0008	
b Employer's identification number: 08-X1X0X1X		1 Wages, tips, other compensation: 9175	2 Federal income tax withheld: 701.42
c Employer's name, address, and ZIP code: ABC Painting Co., Inc. 432 Lomard Avenue Greenville, MA 01234		3 Social security wages: 9175	4 Social security tax withheld: 228.06
		5 Medicare wages and tips: 9175	6 Medicare tax withheld: 63.93
		7 Social security tips	8 Allocated tips
d Employee's social security number: 0X1·XX·1X00		9 Advance EIC payment	10 Dependent care benefits
e Employee's name (first, middle initial, last): Lisa N. Michaels		11 Nonqualified plans	12 Benefits included in box 1
33 Clark Lane Greenville, MA 01234		13 See Instrs. for box 13: D1000	14 Other
f Employee's address and ZIP code		15 Statutory employee ☐ Deceased ☐ Pension plan ☐ Legal rep. ☐ Hshld. emp. ☐ Subtotal ☐ Deferred compensation ☐	

16 State	Employer's state I.D. No.	17 State wages, tips, etc.	18 State income tax	19 Locality name	20 Local wages, tips, etc.	21 Local income tax
MA	11·X1X0X1X	9175	402	Greenville	9175	215

Cat. No. 10134D

Department of the Treasury—Internal Revenue Service

For Paperwork Reduction Act Notice, see separate instructions.

Form **W-2** Wage and Tax Statement

Copy A For Social Security Administration

Figure 23-4 Your employer will send you a Form W-2 in January. What information on this form will help you prepare your income tax return?

Extending Figure 23-4

Ask students who work what they should do if they have not received a Form W-2 from their employers by the end of January. (Telephone the employer's payroll department to report the missing form and ask for another copy to be sent immediately.)

Caption Answer: Form W-2 shows how much money you earned and how much was withheld for taxes, which will help you prepare your income tax return.

SECTION 23-1

Research

Have students learn about the local agencies that deal with taxes. For example, who assesses and collects property taxes? Who handles estate and gift taxes? Which agencies issue special licenses? Have each student choose a local agency and interview personnel to learn what the agency does and the job skills required for that work. Have students share their findings.

Teaching Tip

Obtain blank copies of Form W-4 and have students practice filling them out. Most students should have Social Security numbers; if a student does not, obtain forms needed to apply for a Social Security number and have him or her fill it out. Discuss with students the requirements to apply for a number. (He or she must be a citizen or a legal resident.)

Interview

Have students who work interview their employers to learn about the process followed to complete payroll and tax forms. Tell students who do not work to choose a local company and interview someone in the accounting department. Have students ask how the company keeps track of payroll and tax data, when it sends taxes to the government, and when it prepares tax forms for employees. Have students write summaries of their findings for class discussion.

TEACH *(cont'd.)*

Discussion Starter

Tell students that some people refuse to pay federal income taxes because they object to some government spending (for example, funding for the military). Such tax resistance is illegal. Ask students whether they think refusal to pay taxes for ethical reasons should be legal? Why or why not? What if everyone objected to some form of government spending?

Teaching Tip

Obtain a blank copy of Form 1040EZ for each student to fill out. Those who have part-time jobs may want to use their own information; others could use the current minimum wage, a 20-hour work week during the school year and 40 hours during the summer weeks. Have students use your state's income tax rate and a federal withholding rate of 15 percent. Work through these calculations prior to the activity.

Critical Thinking

Have students respond to this question: If the federal tax code were so simplified that everyone could file a Form 1040EZ, what would happen to those who prepare tax returns and assist in answering questions? Discuss responses in class.

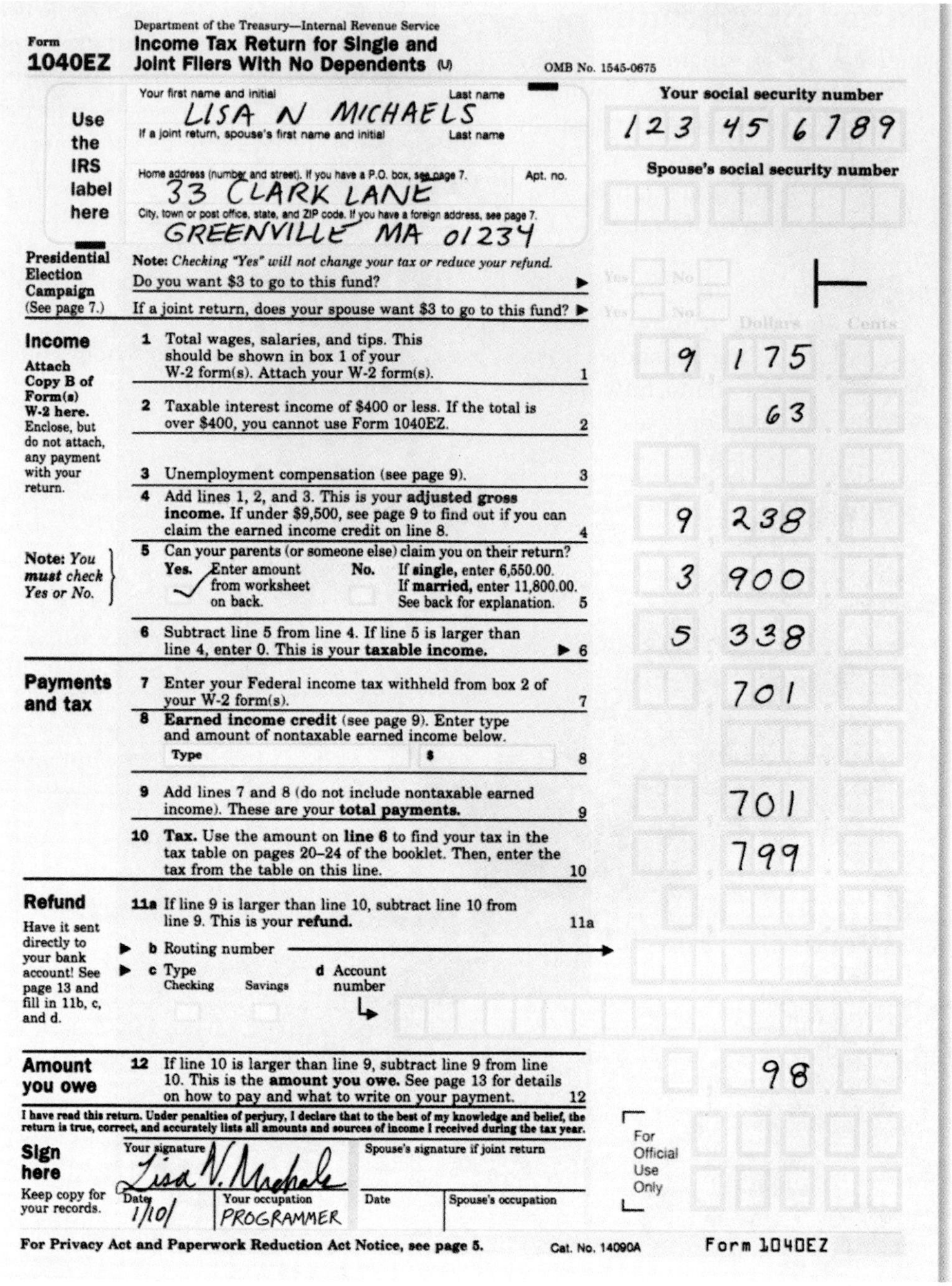

Form 1040EZ
Department of the Treasury—Internal Revenue Service
Income Tax Return for Single and Joint Filers With No Dependents (U)
OMB No. 1545-0675

Use the IRS label here
Your first name and initial: LISA N — Last name: MICHAELS
If a joint return, spouse's first name and initial — Last name
Home address (number and street). If you have a P.O. box, see page 7. Apt. no.: 33 CLARK LANE
City, town or post office, state, and ZIP code. If you have a foreign address, see page 7.: GREENVILLE MA 01234

Your social security number: 123 45 6789
Spouse's social security number

Presidential Election Campaign (See page 7.)
Note: *Checking "Yes" will not change your tax or reduce your refund.*
Do you want $3 to go to this fund? Yes No
If a joint return, does your spouse want $3 to go to this fund? Yes No

Dollars Cents

Income
Attach Copy B of Form(s) W-2 here. Enclose, but do not attach, any payment with your return.

1 Total wages, salaries, and tips. This should be shown in box 1 of your W-2 form(s). Attach your W-2 form(s). 1 — 9 175
2 Taxable interest income of $400 or less. If the total is over $400, you cannot use Form 1040EZ. 2 — 63
3 Unemployment compensation (see page 9). 3
4 Add lines 1, 2, and 3. This is your **adjusted gross income.** If under $9,500, see page 9 to find out if you can claim the earned income credit on line 8. 4 — 9 238

Note: *You must check Yes or No.*
5 Can your parents (or someone else) claim you on their return?
Yes. Enter amount from worksheet on back. ✓
No. If **single**, enter 6,550.00. If **married**, enter 11,800.00. See back for explanation. 5 — 3 900
6 Subtract line 5 from line 4. If line 5 is larger than line 4, enter 0. This is your **taxable income.** 6 — 5 338

Payments and tax
7 Enter your Federal income tax withheld from box 2 of your W-2 form(s). 7 — 701
8 **Earned income credit** (see page 9). Enter type and amount of nontaxable earned income below. Type $ 8
9 Add lines 7 and 8 (do not include nontaxable earned income). These are your **total payments.** 9 — 701
10 **Tax.** Use the amount on **line 6** to find your tax in the tax table on pages 20–24 of the booklet. Then, enter the tax from the table on this line. 10 — 799

Refund
Have it sent directly to your bank account! See page 13 and fill in 11b, c, and d.
11a If line 9 is larger than line 10, subtract line 10 from line 9. This is your **refund.** 11a
b Routing number
c Type Checking Savings
d Account number

Amount you owe
12 If line 10 is larger than line 9, subtract line 9 from line 10. This is the **amount you owe.** See page 13 for details on how to pay and what to write on your payment. 12 — 98

I have read this return. Under penalties of perjury, I declare that to the best of my knowledge and belief, the return is true, correct, and accurately lists all amounts and sources of income I received during the tax year.

Sign here
Keep copy for your records.
Your signature: Lisa N. Michaels — Spouse's signature if joint return
Date: 1/10/ — Your occupation: PROGRAMMER — Date — Spouse's occupation

For Official Use Only

For Privacy Act and Paperwork Reduction Act Notice, see page 5. Cat. No. 14090A Form 1040EZ

Figure 23-5 Most young taxpayers can use Form 1040EZ for at least the first few years they file tax returns. What form do you need to attach to Form 1040EZ?

Extending Figure 23-5

Have students review Form 1040EZ. Ask them what would happen if they had a savings account that earned $480 in interest last year. (They could not use Form 1040EZ since interest income for this form is limited to $400.)

Caption Answer: Form W-2

1040EZ Tax Table—

If Form 1040EZ, line 6, is—		And you are—	
At least	But less than	Single	Married filing jointly
		Your tax is—	

11,000

At least	But less than	Single	Married filing jointly
11,000	11,050	1,654	1,654
11,050	11,100	1,661	1,661
11,100	11,150	1,669	1,669
11,150	11,200	1,676	1,676
11,200	11,250	1,684	1,684
11,250	11,300	1,691	1,691
11,300	11,350	1,699	1,699
11,350	11,400	1,706	1,706
11,400	11,450	1,714	1,714
11,450	11,500	1,721	1,721
11,500	11,550	1,729	1,729
11,550	11,600	1,736	1,736
11,600	11,650	1,744	1,744
11,650	11,700	1,751	1,751
11,700	11,750	1,759	1,759
11,750	11,800	1,766	1,766
11,800	11,850	1,774	1,774
11,850	11,900	1,781	1,781
11,900	11,950	1,789	1,789
11,950	12,000	1,796	1,796

▲ **Figure 23-6** Using a tax table is easy. First, find the line that corresponds to your taxable income. Then find the column that corresponds to your status—single or married, for example. Your tax is the amount shown where the income line and status column meet. If you're single and your taxable income was $11,200, how much tax would you owe?

- A **deduction** is an expense that you are allowed to subtract from your income. Examples may include medical or business expenses. The less taxable income you have, the less tax you'll have to pay. The *standard deduction* is an amount set by the IRS.

You can probably file Form 1040EZ if you meet the following qualifications.

- You're single and earned less than $50,000 during the year. (Check each year with the IRS about the current figure.)

- You had no other income, such as taxable interest or dividends totaling more than $400 each.

- You are not claiming an exemption for being over 65 or for being blind.

- You have no dependents.

There are some additional requirements for using Form 1040EZ but they will probably not apply to you. Check with the IRS to be sure.

Figure 23-5 shows Form 1040EZ. Completing this form involves several basic steps.

- Add up your total income from working and from other sources.

- Subtract your standard deduction and personal exemption.

- Use the tax table to find out how much tax is due on your income. *Figure 23-6* shows a portion of the table. By comparing this amount with the taxes withheld on your Form W-2, you'll see whether you owe more taxes or will get a refund.

Chapter 23 • Taxes and Social Security **467**

Reading

Have each student find and read an article on how to minimize taxes, taking notes and deciding at what point in their lives the advice might be useful.

Skills Practice

Have students complete these problems, referring to Figures 23-5 and 23-6.

Andrea is single and has a taxable income of $11,570. She has already paid $1,840 in federal taxes. Determine how much she owes in taxes. ($0: Andrea will get a refund of $104 because her tax is $1,736 and she has already paid in $1,840.)

Marc earned $18,520 last year, and $1,710 were withheld for federal taxes. Marc is single and supports himself. What is his taxable income and total federal income tax? Does he owe money? (taxable income, $11,970: $17,520 − $6,550; tax, $1,796; Marc owes $86: $1,796 − $1,710)

Critical Thinking

Ask students whether a flat tax rate with no exemptions or deductions would make it easier to fill out a tax return. Also have them think about advantages and disadvantages of a flat rate. Discuss in class.

▶▶ **Extending Figure 23-6** ◀◀

Obtain a larger tax table or several pages of tax tables for the current tax year. Give students examples of different taxable incomes and have them find the tax amount for each.

Caption Answer: $1,684

Writing: *Directions*

Have students write a step-by-step description of how to fill out a Form 1040EZ, citing line numbers in the form when describing where to write specific information.

Research

Have students research the federal tax systems in at least two countries, listing the major features and comparing each system to our own. What conclusions might they draw about the fairness or efficiency of the systems researched? Are the systems more or less fair than the U.S. system? Have students prepare three- to five-minute presentations.

Teaching Tip

If students are having difficulty with Form 1040EZ, have them work in pairs. Tell each pair to create a taxpayer, providing name, age, job, and one or more bank accounts earning interest.

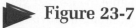

Figure 23-7

Filing a Federal Tax Return

Filing a federal tax return is not difficult if you organize your information and follow instructions.

As ***Figure 23-7*** shows, figuring your taxes isn't hard if you're organized. Need help? Don't worry. The IRS provides free publications that will help. You can also get help over the phone, via the Internet, and from tax-help books at the library. If you have a computer, you might try tax-preparation software. Alternatively, you can pay a tax-preparation service to prepare your forms for you.

A Gather the necessary information. For example, you'll need Form W-2 and records of any other earnings, such as a statement of interest from your bank. If you've filed a tax return before, have a copy of your previous return on hand for reference.

B Obtain the tax form you'll need, such as a Form 1040EZ or 1040A, and the corresponding IRS instruction booklet. You can find forms and booklets at post offices, libraries, and most banks. You can also get them from the IRS. (The IRS even has a site on the World Wide Web from which you can download forms.) If you use a tax-preparation computer program, the software will probably include the forms you need.

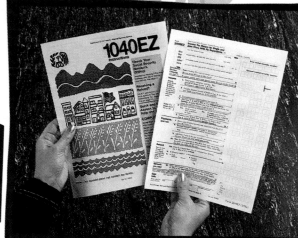

▶▶ Extending Figure 23-7 ◀◀

Obtain copies of the current year's tax booklet (available from the Internal Revenue Service or your local public library). Have students look through the booklet to see the type of information it contains. Go through the basic instructions with students and answer questions.

Workforce 2000 Trends

In the future, 40 percent of all employees will work with data. Most new jobs will be in computer- and other data-based industries. In 1994, more people worked in the computer industry as a whole than in the auto, auto parts, steel, mining and petroleum-refining industries combined.

C Take your time completing the forms. Read instructions carefully. Get help if you need it. Be sure to provide all the required information. Double-check your math.

D Keep a photocopy of the completed tax return for your records. Attach any necessary forms (such as the W-2) to the original return, and send it to the IRS by April 15.

SECTION 23-1 *Review*

Understanding Key Concepts

Using complete sentences, answer the following questions on a separate sheet of paper.

1. List five characteristics of a good tax system. Why are these desirable features?

2. How does the amount of money you earn and the amount withheld determine whether you owe income tax?

3. How will understanding such terms as *exemption, dependent,* and *deduction* help you complete a tax return?

Chapter 23 • Taxes and Social Security **469**

SECTION 23-1 *Review* ANSWERS

1. fairness, simplicity, convenience, stability, and flexibility; such features are desirable because they serve the needs of both people and government

2. The government stipulates how much income tax you must pay, according to how much you earn. If your employer doesn't withhold this much money, you owe income tax. If your employer withholds more than this amount, you will get a refund from the government.

3. Understanding such terms will help you determine whether part of your income is exempt from taxes.

ASSESS (cont'd.)

Reteaching

Divide students into two groups. Have one group create a bulletin board display of the U.S. tax system, including taxes for all three levels of government, clipping newspaper or magazine photos to illustrate.

Have the second group create a display explaining the federal tax return and giving instructions for how to complete it. Have students obtain copies of necessary tax forms from the local public library.

Extending the Content

Assign the appropriate Chapter 23 activities in the *Student Activity Workbook*.

Have students explore software for keeping financial records and filing a personal federal tax return. Tell students to read magazine articles evaluating such software, or visit computer stores and ask a salesperson to describe top-selling programs. Have students share their information in class.

CLOSE

Have students complete this statement: "It's the responsibility of every able citizen to pay his or her fair share of taxes because . . . ." (we all share in the benefits)

CASE STUDY

Exploring Careers: Manufacturing

Joshua Boughton
Production/Administrative Lead
Bullseye Glass

Q: How did you start at Bullseye Glass?

A: I started pulling glass out of bins, packing it into crates that we built ourselves, and shipping it out. Later I worked in quality control. Now I'm in an administrative position and training to be a glass technologist.

Q: Is starting at the bottom best?

A: I don't think anybody should be afraid to take an entry-level position. Then you should try to see if this is the place you want to work. A lot of people don't take into consideration what I call psychic pay: enjoying where they work, liking the people they work with, liking the product, believing in what they are doing.

Q: What's your educational background?

A: I come from a single-parent family of seven children. We didn't have money for schooling. I found out what kind of government-funded programs I could get into while I was in school. I think people should be more aggressive about being educated.

Q: What do you advise students starting out?

A: Don't do only what you're required to do. Look at how your job could be done better. Try to find out where the firm is going, how it has performed in the past. Find out what training your company will fund. Keep yourself "market-ready".

Thinking Critically

Bullseye makes glass for artists. What skills learned in glass production might transfer to other manufacturing fields?

CAREER FACTS

Nature of the Work:
Control quality of glass by analysis, process tracking, and testing; collect and disseminate information to staff.

Training or Education Needed:
Art training in any medium; knowledge of chemistry; glass-working experience.

Aptitudes, Abilities, and Skills:
Math skills; listening, speaking, and interpersonal skills; problem-solving and decision-making skills; computer skills; ability to see things in the mind's eye; ability to work with your hands; ability to learn.

Salary Range:
Approximately $7 to $8 an hour to start; higher as experience increases.

Career Path:
Start in an entry-level position and work your way up; obtain glass technology training; move into an administrative position.

---

470 *Unit 6 • Life Skills*

Extending the CASE STUDY

Answer: computer use; development of procedure documentation; quality control; packing, shipping, receiving, accounting, tracking; teamwork; communication

Further Application: Have students discuss ways they can maximize their education. (For example, seeking tutors; being willing to work above their class level; working with counselors to find out what extra training is available; taking summer classes to improve skills and to move ahead; or getting involved in internships.)

All About Social Security

OBJECTIVES

After studying this section, you will be able to:

- Describe how the Social Security system works.
- Identify four Social Security program benefits and two state social insurance benefits.
- Explain the main problem that is facing the Social Security system today.

KEY TERMS

work credits
disabled worker
Medicare
unemployment
   insurance
workers'
   compensation

What does the term *Social Security* mean to you? Do you think of retired workers who depend on their Social Security checks to live? That's part of it, but there's more to Social Security than that. It's a program that provides benefits for people of all ages. For example, if a worker becomes disabled, Social Security will help his or her family cope with the loss of income.

How the Social Security Program Works

Where does the money that pays for Social Security benefits come from? Most of it comes from Social Security taxes. Both workers and employers pay these taxes. As you read earlier, employers deduct Social Security tax from your paycheck. Your employer matches your contribution. If you're self-employed, you must pay both the employee's and employer's share of the tax. (Currently, however, self-employed workers may deduct half of their Social Security tax from their federal income tax.)

Your Social Security Number

Do you know your Social Security number? Your parent or guardian probably got one for you when you were little. This is your permanent identification number. The government uses it to keep track of your contributions and work history. Your employer will ask you for this number. You'll also need to put it on tax forms.

Chapter 23 • Taxes and Social Security **471**

Bell Ringer

Have students explain their attitude toward the Social Security program.

Introducing the Section

Determine the number of students who support and do not support Social Security. Have students share reasons. For those opposed, ask them who should take care of the elderly poor, those too ill to work, and those disabled by illness or accident. Some of them may say family should care for these people, but who should care for them if they have no family?

Explain that Social Security is intended as a sort of safety net.

Motivational Activity
Reading

Have students read one or more articles describing ways to improve or change the Social Security system. Tell them to write a brief summary of each article to discuss in class. After discussions, have students take a vote on the changes they would like to see made in the Social Security program.

Computer Activity

Using a software program, create a spreadsheet to calculate net income. Have students assume they are self-employed. Ask them to contact an accountant or a financial planner to get the figures for Social Security and state tax deductions. Tell them to assume they will gross $25,000 their first year. Remind them that most self-employed people pay taxes on a quarterly basis. You may want them to show a tax payment per quarter and the total net income for the quarter and the year.

Guided Practice

Teaching Strategies

1. Assign and review Section 23-2.
2. Use the transparency 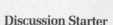 for this section.

Discussion Starter

Ask students why they should pay Social Security taxes if there's a chance the benefits will be decreased by the time they get ready for retirement.

Critical Thinking

Ask students whether they think Social Security benefits paid to wealthy retirees should be taxed.

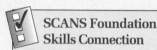

SCANS Foundation Skills Connection

L1 Writing

Have students research the benefits of Social Security and prepare one-page brochures that explain benefits in terms the average person can understand.

L2 Knowing How to Learn

Have students explore the difference between Social Security and an annuity. Tell each to create a table showing typical amounts available at age 65 under each system.

(Payments from an annuity depend on amounts paid into the annuity fund. Social Security guarantees a minimum and is not directly tied to amounts paid in.)

Many people lost their jobs during the Great Depression of the 1930s. Families suffered severe hardship. Congress passed the Social Security Act of 1935 to aid families whose members lost their jobs, were unable to work, or were retired. ***Whom do you know who receives Social Security benefits?***

Becoming Eligible for Benefits

Once you begin working, you start to earn work credits. **Work credits** are measurements of how long you've worked. You must earn a certain number of credits to get Social Security benefits. You earn work credits for each year you work and pay Social Security taxes.

Types of Benefits

There are many different kinds of Social Security benefits. Some are for eligible people of any age.

- *Disability benefits* are paid to disabled workers. A **disabled worker** is someone who cannot work because of a physical or mental condition.

472　*Unit 6 • Life Skills*

The amount of the benefit is based on the worker's average earnings.

- *Survivors' benefits* are paid to the family of a worker who dies.
- *Retirement benefits* are paid to workers who retire. Up to a certain amount, the higher your average yearly earnings, the higher your benefits. The retirement age for reduced benefits is now 62. The retirement age for full benefits is now 65. That age will gradually rise to 67 by 2027.
- *Health insurance benefits* are paid to people who need hospitalization or other medical care. These benefits, called **Medicare**, cover nearly everyone who is 65 or older.

Extending the Illustration

Ask students to discuss how society would be affected if Social Security did not exist.

Caption Answer: Students may mention family members, friends, or neighbors who are retired or disabled, or the family of a deceased worker.

Social Security is a federal program. As a worker, you're also entitled to benefits from two state-run social insurance programs. These are similar to Social Security. Their rules vary from state to state, however.

- **Unemployment insurance** provides temporary income to workers who have lost their jobs. To be eligible, you generally must have worked for a certain length of time and not have lost your job through your fault. Unemployment insurance is funded by taxes both the employer and employee pay.

Career Do's & Don'ts

When Paying Taxes...
Do:
- be sure the right amount of taxes are being taken out of your paycheck.
- use professional help if tax forms are too complicated for you or if you are eligible for deductions.
- keep copies of tax returns and other related documents.

Don't:
- freely give out your social security number.
- wait until the last moment to file your tax returns.
- allow an employer to pay you without withholding taxes and paying the appropriate share.

- **Workers' compensation** benefits are paid to workers injured on the job and to dependents of workers killed on the job. These benefits may include medical care, disability income, and other benefits. Workers' compensation is funded by taxes the employer pays.

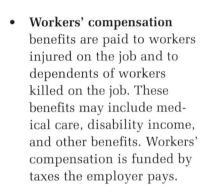

 Medicare helps people who are 65 and older meet the high costs of medical care. **Who pays for Medicare? How?**

Chapter 23 • *Taxes and Social Security*   **473**

Extending the Illustration

Have students find out the current Social Security and Medicare tax rates. Tell students who work to calculate the amount of money they pay toward Medicare each month. Have students who do not work use the current minimum wage and a 20-hour work week to calculate the same.

Caption Answer: Workers and employers pay for Medicare through taxes based on total employee earnings.

Independent Practice

Interview

Have each student interview at least five people and ask what benefits they get in return for paying taxes. Have students share results in class.

ASSESS

Assessment

Content

Have each student write a one-page flyer describing Social Security benefits and who is eligible for them. Evaluate students' flyers for accuracy, clarity, and correct grammar.

Evaluation

Assign the section review.

MINI QUIZ

True-False

1. The IRS is responsible for collecting all types of taxes. (false)

2. Sales taxes are withheld from your paycheck. (false)

3. Property taxes are the main support for public schools. (true)

4. An exemption allows you to reduce the taxes you pay. (true)

5. Work credits are measurements of how long you've worked. (true)

Attitude Counts ✓

Knowing how and when you like to get things done is a big advantage. Still, it's important not to get too tied to your own methods and your own schedule. As you work toward your goals, you'll find that flexibility can be an important asset, too. You'll accomplish more—and enjoy the process more—if you remain flexible.

 It is the U.S. Congress's responsibility to solve the problem with Social Security. *What can you do to influence the decisions that are made?*

The Future of Social Security

If you follow the news, you know that Social Security is a "hot issue" these days. That's because the system has a big problem: it's going broke.

The Social Security taxes you pay provide benefits for workers who have already retired. When it's your turn to retire, younger workers will pay the taxes to fund *your* retirement.

Well, maybe. Here's the problem: People are living longer, and many are retiring earlier. As a result, more workers will collect more years of benefits. At the same time, the U.S. birthrate is declining. This means that there will be fewer young workers around to support retired people in the future. The situation will worsen as the large number of workers now in their 40s and 50s reach retirement age. Before long, the money being paid out will exceed the amount coming in.

There are many proposed solutions to this problem. Some would increase taxes. Others would cut benefits. One way or another, the system needs changes. You can play a part in making these changes by staying informed and voting.

SECTION 23-2 *Review*

Understanding Key Concepts

Using complete sentences, answer the following questions on a separate sheet of paper.

1. Why is it important to build up work credits?

2. Why is the program of benefits discussed in this section called Social Security?

3. What may happen to Social Security by the time you retire if the system isn't changed soon?

474 *Unit 6 • Life Skills*

SECTION 23-2 *Review* ANSWERS

1. If you don't build up work credits, you won't get Social Security benefits.

2. It provides security through benefits paid to people in our society who need them.

3. It will run out of money, and you won't receive any benefits.

Teaching Attitude Counts ✓

Have students write journal entries about their own scheduling habits.

- Which routines help you accomplish the most?

- Do you need to improve your ability to meet schedules or to remain flexible? Why? How?

SECTION 23-1 **Summary**

- Taxes are payments that people must make to support federal, state, and local governments. Common taxes include income taxes, Social Security taxes, sales taxes, and property taxes.

- Tax dollars pay for a wide range of services, such as education, transportation, and military services.

- You can influence the way that tax dollars are spent by voting for officials who represent your views.

- A good tax system should be fair, simple, convenient, stable, and flexible.

- Your income tax return shows how much income you received and how much tax you owe. If your employer withholds more money than you owe, you'll get a tax refund. If your employer withholds too little, you'll have to pay the difference.

Key Terms

Internal Revenue Service (IRS) *(p. 458)*
withhold *(p. 459)*
income tax return *(p. 463)*
exemption *(p. 465)*
deduction *(p. 467)*

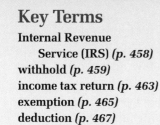

Key Terms

work credits *(p. 472)*
disabled worker *(p. 472)*
Medicare *(p. 472)*
unemployment insurance *(p. 473)*
workers' compensation *(p. 473)*

SECTION 23-2 **Summary**

- The money for Social Security benefits comes chiefly from Social Security taxes paid by workers and employers.

- The government uses your Social Security number to keep track of your contributions and work history.

- You earn work credits each year that you work and pay Social Security taxes. You must earn a certain number of credits to become eligible for Social Security benefits.

- Social Security benefits include disability benefits, survivors' benefits, retirement benefits, and health insurance benefits.

- Two state-run programs that provide benefits for workers are unemployment insurance and workers' compensation.

- The Social Security system must be changed to keep the amount of money being paid out from exceeding the amount coming in.

Chapter 23 • Taxes and Social Security **475**

SECTION 23-2

Use the Testmaker to create a customized test for Chapter 23.

Reteaching

1. Obtain brochures describing Social Security from the SSA. Have students discuss the content in class. A portion of tax dollars pay for printing such brochures to help educate the public. Do students think this a good use of money?

2. Assign and review vocabulary terms, chapter questions, and activities from the Chapter Review.

3. Assign and review the Unit Project on the unit opener pages.

Extending the Content

Assign the appropriate Chapter 23 activities in the *Student Activity Workbook*.

Have students research the social care systems used in at least two countries. Tell each student to create a chart listing benefits and describing who pays for them. Have students draw conclusions about the advantages and disadvantages of each system.

CLOSE

See the Unit Closure and Unit Evaluation located on page 377.

▶ Extending the Illustration

Have students research current positions on Social Security held by your state's U.S. representatives and senators.

Caption Answer: Write letters to or call your representatives and senators to express your views, vote for candidates whose opinions you share, and talk with friends about the issues.

Answers

Reviewing Key Terms

Paragraphs will vary but should include all of the key terms.

Recalling Key Concepts

1. c
2. a
3. c
4. a
5. b

Thinking Critically

1. Most students will probably agree. They should support their responses with clear and specific explanations.

2. Each citizen can vote for a candidate who shares his or her views.

3. The government uses a person's Social Security number to keep track of that person's earnings and work history.

4. If there aren't enough younger workers, there may not be enough money to cover older workers' benefits.

 SCANS Foundation Skills and Workplace Competencies

1. You spent $284.96. ($274 + $10.96; $274 × .04) If the tax rate had been 6 percent, the tax would have been $16.44 ($274 × .06), costing you an additional $5.48. ($16.44 − $10.96)

Reviewing Key Terms

Write one paragraph about taxes and one paragraph about Social Security. Use the terms below.

Internal Revenue
  Service (IRS)
withhold
income tax
  return
exemption
deduction

work credits
disabled worker
Medicare
unemployment
  insurance
workers'
  compensation

Recalling Key Concepts

Choose the correct answer for each item below. Write your answers on a separate sheet of paper.

1. Which of the following is *not* a characteristic of a good tax system?

   (a) Everyone pays his or her fair share.

   (b) Tax rules are clear and simple.

   (c) Taxes are collected at the beginning of each year.

2. You'll have to pay additional income tax if ____.

   (a) your employer withholds too little tax

   (b) your employer withholds too much tax

   (c) you don't receive a Form W-2

3. Social Security taxes are paid by ____.

   (a) workers (b) employers

   (c) both workers and employers

4. Which one of the following benefits is *not* part of the Social Security program?

   (a) workers' compensation

   (b) survivors' benefits (c) Medicare

5. One reason why the Social Security system is in trouble is that ____.

   (a) fewer people are retiring

   (b) the birthrate is declining

   (c) the birthrate is increasing

Thinking Critically

Using complete sentences, answer each of the questions below on a separate sheet of paper.

1. Do you agree that because everyone shares the benefits of tax dollars, everyone should pay a fair share of taxes? Explain.

2. How does voting give all citizens an equal voice in deciding how their government spends tax dollars?

3. Suppose you discover that your employer has recorded the wrong Social Security number for you. Why is it important to correct the error?

4. What is the drawback of having the Social Security taxes of younger workers pay for the benefits that go to older workers?

 SCANS Foundation Skills and Workplace Competencies

Basic Skills: *Math*

1. Suppose you bought an exercise machine for $161, books for $36, CDs for $32, and a watch for $45. If the state sales tax is 4 percent, how much did you spend? Suppose the sales tax had been 6 percent. How much more would you have spent?

2. Some students may suggest getting help from the IRS via phone, Internet, or printed publications. Others may suggest tax-help books or a tax-preparation service. In any case, students should explain the reason for the choice.

Connecting Academics to the Workplace

1. Answers will vary. Students should be able to identify several tax-preparation programs. However, some students may

Information: *Acquiring and Evaluating Information*

2. Over the past year, you held several different part-time jobs. Now it's time to file an income tax return. However, you're not sure which form to complete or how to complete it. Describe two ways in which you could get answers to your questions. Which way would probably be better? Explain.

Connecting Academics to the Workplace

Computer Science

1. Amy works in the human resources department of a large corporation. Her supervisor has asked her to help run a workshop for new employees. Part of the workshop will focus on taxes. Amy wants to include information about tax-preparation software. Research tax-preparation programs in the library, via the Internet, or by speaking to taxpayers who have used such programs. Are there any that you think Amy should recommend? Why or why not?

Math

2. In 1995, Daniel earned $22,490 as a paralegal aide. He got paid every two weeks. His employer withheld Social Security tax at a rate of 7.65 percent. How much Social Security tax did Daniel's employer withhold from each paycheck?

Developing Teamwork and Leadership Skills

Divide into teams of four. Assume that you all work in the human resources department of a major company. You've been asked to make a wall chart briefly summarizing the six kinds of benefits workers are generally eligible for: disability benefits, survivors' benefits, retirement benefits, health benefits, unemployment benefits, and workers' compensation. Work together to make the chart. You may use pictures as well as words.

Real-World Workshop

Obtain a paycheck stub. List the categories for which money was deducted. Which deduction was the largest? Which was the smallest?

School-to-Work Connection

Accountants and bookkeepers handle many financial duties, including tax-related matters. Identify a worker in the accounting department of a company. Discuss with the person the challenges of his or her work. Ask how the person uses computer technology. Summarize your discussion in a brief report.

Individual Career Plan

Look into the future. Imagine that you have pursued your career for about 45 years. You're thinking about retiring. However, you enjoy your work and don't want to stop working entirely. List your options for remaining active in your field. You may want to talk with several adults to hear their ideas.

Real-World Workshop

Categories may vary. Typical categories include federal, state, and local income taxes; Social Security tax (FICA); and Medicare tax. The largest deduction is usually for federal income tax. The smallest of the taxes listed here is usually Medicare tax.

School-to-Work Connection

Most students are likely to learn that computers play a key role in the work of accountants and bookkeepers, regardless of company size.

Individual Career Plan

Students' lists will vary. Some students may suggest remaining on staff and working part-time. Others may suggest becoming an independent consultant and working as many or as few hours as desired. Still others may propose becoming a volunteer, helping others get started in the business.

feel that these programs are difficult for inexperienced taxpayers.

2. Daniel earned $22,490, or $865 every two weeks. His employer withheld 7.65 percent of $865, or $66.17.

Developing Teamwork and Leadership

Charts should present all six kinds of benefits in a clear, easy-to-grasp manner. Some teams may choose to set Social Security benefits apart from unemployment insurance and workers' compensation.

Aspects of Industry: Finance

Students who are fairly sure of their future careers may use the Labs to investigate all the aspects of industry for one career. Other students may want to investigate a different job cluster with each Lab.

STEP A

As usual, students may select jobs from existing lists of jobs, brainstorm with other students, or research the possibilities in the *Occupational Outlook Handbook (OOH)* or other career references.

Have students consider the flexibility of financing available to small entrepreneurs versus that available to a large, established company. Companies with large assets may be able to get money more easily from traditional sources, such as banks. Individual ownership, however, requires a great deal more creativity when financing a new business or expanding an existing one.

STEP B

While students explore the criteria on which business loans are granted, they should bear in mind the criteria on which personal loans, such as car or home loans, are made; for example, proper use of credit in the past, timeliness of loan payments, overall debt obligation, current income, and financial stability.

Before students talk to loan officers, you might want to discuss business plans and financial statements. If you live in a small town, you might want to

ASPECTS OF INDUSTRY:
Finance

Overview

In Unit Six, you learned about making wise consumer decisions, managing your money through savings and budgeting, and using credit carefully. Businesses, too, must use money responsibly. In this Unit Lab, you will use what you have learned about budgeting, buying, paying taxes, and banking while exploring another aspect of industry: **Finance.**

Business finance involves keeping track of sales and expenditures, planning for future purchases, deciding when a product is not profitable, and raising money to start or expand a business. Even if you are not making financial decisions for your company, you should understand what underlies those decisions.

Tools

1. Internet

2. Trade and business magazines

3. Books on starting a business

478

Procedures

STEP A

Choose two careers that interest you from the 15 job clusters outlined in Figure 3-1 in Chapter 3.

Using trade publications, books on business, and the Internet, research the kinds of financing available to a corporation that wants to expand. Then look at the kind of money available to an entrepreneur who wants to start a business.

Keep copies of what you read or take careful notes. You will need this information for your report and for the interviews in Steps B and C.

STEP B

Make an appointment to interview a loan officer at a local bank. You may want to do this in teams of two or three. Explain to the loan officer that you are working on a class project and would like information on business loans.

Some of the questions you might ask are:

1. What criteria does a bank use to determine whether or not a business is loan worthy?

2. How do these criteria differ if the request is for a new business or for expansion of an existing business?

identify which loan officers in town would be willing to talk to students in small groups. Or, to save time, you might invite a loan officer to class to discuss business loans.

STEP C

As an alternative to having students talk to entrepreneurs on their own, you might want to

have a panel discussion in class. Through your local Chamber of Commerce, women's business groups, ethnic organizations, and local community college placement offices, have students identify entrepreneurs who have used unusual financing methods to start their businesses. Have students invite some of these people to participate in a panel discussion in class.

3. Does it make a difference whether the business is a sole proprietorship or a corporation? Why?

4. What is the most common reason a bank refuses a business loan?

STEP C

For each job you chose in Step A, find two businesses that employ people in that job. One should be a large company or corporation, the other a small business.

Make an appointment with a financial officer from the larger company and with the owner of the small business. Explain that you would like to ask a few questions on business finance for a class project.

Some of the questions you might ask are:

1. When does each company seek credit?

2. How does each determine the financial impact on its business when expanding the product line or eliminating a product?

3. What is the company's most common source of funding?

4. What is the most common reason for being turned down for a loan?

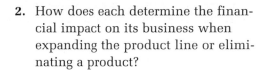

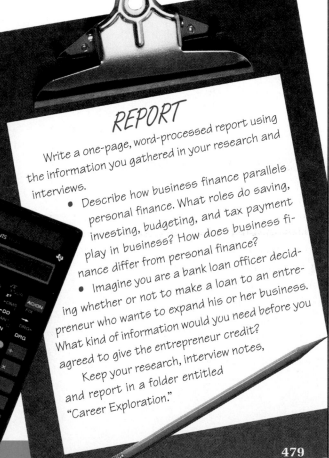

REPORT

Write a one-page, word-processed report using the information you gathered in your research and interviews.

• Describe how business finance parallels personal finance. What roles do saving, investing, budgeting, and tax payment play in business? How does business finance differ from personal finance?

• Imagine you are a bank loan officer deciding whether or not to make a loan to an entrepreneur who wants to expand his or her business. What kind of information would you need before you agreed to give the entrepreneur credit?

Keep your research, interview notes, and report in a folder entitled "Career Exploration."

479

UNIT 6 LAB

Divide students into groups. As a group, have them write one of the panelists a thank-you note mentioning the information they found most interesting or helpful.

Report

Students should come to understand that the principles of money management basically do not change, whether one is managing ones bank accounts or helping a company make a major purchase. Before students write their reports, you might want to have a class discussion on how personal finance techniques are simply expanded in business finance. Discuss how and why individuals and businesses go bankrupt.

Also discuss in class the criteria banks use to decide whether or not to extend credit to businesses. Show students how that parallels a bank's decision to extend credit to individuals. By having students explore the bank's position on credit, help them understand the importance of handling personal credit wisely.

(The number of participants will depend on the space and time you have available.)

Before the discussion, have students prepare questions based on their research in Step A. Questions might include: What kind of alternative financing did you use and how did you locate it? Why did you seek alternative financing? Did you face discrimination from traditional loan sources because of the type or size of your business, or because of your ethnic background, gender, or previous credit history? Would you use this type of financing again?

Allow time at the end of the panel discussion for students to talk individually with the entrepreneurs, if they so desire.

Unit Overview

Unit 7 provides information students will need to be able to live on their own (for example, managing careers, making decisions about whether a job is meeting their needs, and gaining job skills). They are also presented with factors to consider when setting up their own households, as well as balancing work, family, and community responsibilities.

Introducing the Unit

Many students may already have assumed adult responsibilities while others probably have done quite a bit of thinking about them. To orient students toward the goal of living independently, have them brainstorm a list of decisions they would need to make. Write their ideas on the chalkboard.

Unit Project

Have students imagine that a local employer is reviewing five-minute videotapes of job applicants. Have students write a script for their own tapes in which they promote themselves and their qualifications. Tell them to be creative and describe the setting they will use, the props, how they will dress, documents they will show, and what they will say.

UNIT 7
Lifelong Learning

Chapter 24
Adapting to Change

Chapter 25
*Balancing Work
and Personal Life*

480

Developing Community Involvement

Recycling is of growing importance in many communities. Students might want to develop a recycling project with the school, a local retirement home, apartment complex, or industrial complex. Students should contact local recyclers to determine guidelines. Students might use brochures or posters to advertise the project. They should provide containers, and monitor the containers to see that the recycled materials are hauled away on a regular basis.

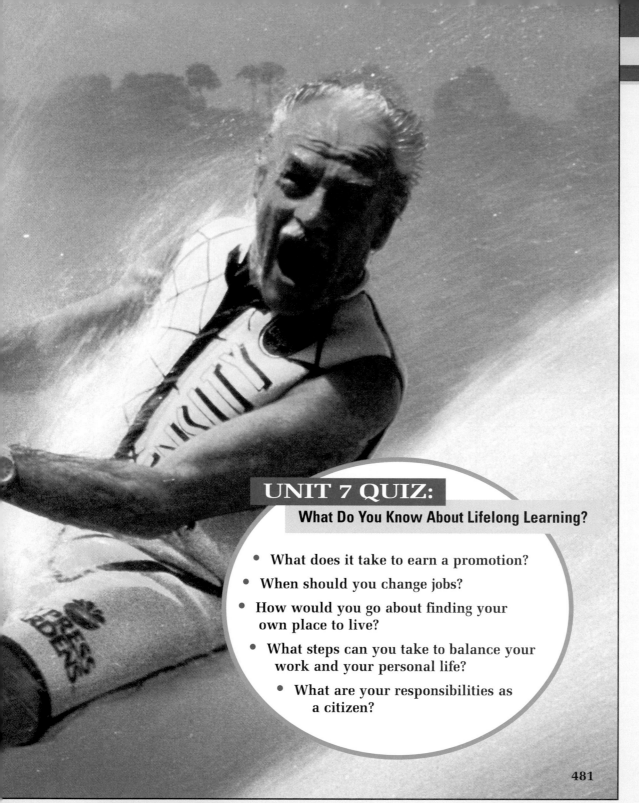

UNIT 7 QUIZ:

What Do You Know About Lifelong Learning?

- What does it take to earn a promotion?
- When should you change jobs?
- How would you go about finding your own place to live?
- What steps can you take to balance your work and your personal life?
- What are your responsibilities as a citizen?

481

Resources for Enrichment

Books

- *Career Book* by Kennedy
- *Clicking* by Popcorn
- *Lifetime Employability* by Hyatt
- *Dare to Change Your Job and Your Life* by Kanchier

Magazines

American Demographics, Environmental Opportunities (newsletter), *The Futurist*

Organizations

- Association on Higher Education and Disability
- Local volunteer organizations

Internet

Career Magazine—Career and company profiles: http://www.careermag.com/careermag

Hoover's Career Page—Company & industry profiles: http://www.hoovers.com/careers.html

IdeaList—Information on nonprofit organizations: http://www.contact.org

Servenet—Volunteer programs by ZIP code: http://www.servenet.org

Unit Closure

Have students present their videotapes to the class.

Unit Evaluation

Administer the reproducible test for Unit 7, which you will find in your Performance Assessment Binder, or construct your own test using the IBM Testmaker Software.

Building Partners in Industry

As you establish contact with local employers through your school-to-work program, don't forget the government. That's right—local government agencies or (depending on your location) state and even federal government agencies may be eager to participate by providing job shadowing, mentoring, and volunteer or paid part-time employment for students.

• • • PLANNING GUIDE • • •
Chapter 24

SECTION 1 *Managing Your Career*

SECTION OBJECTIVES	SECTION FEATURES	SECTION RESOURCES
• Identify ways to prepare yourself for the future. • Describe actions and behaviors that lead to promotions.	Personal Career Plan, p. 483 Excellent Business Practices, p. 487 Exploring Careers, p. 490	Workforce 2000 Videodisc and Videotape Section 24-1 Review, p. 489 Student Activity Workbook

SECTION 2 *Changing Jobs or Careers*

SECTION OBJECTIVES	SECTION FEATURES	SECTION RESOURCES
• Explain why workers may want to change jobs. • Describe strategies for seeking a new job or career. • Describe steps to take if you lose your job.	Ethics in Action, p. 492 Career Do's and Don'ts, p. 495 You're the Boss!, p. 498	Workforce 2000 Videodisc and Videotape Section 24-2 Review, p. 498 Chapter 24 Review, pp. 500-501 Student Activity Workbook

CHAPTER RESOURCES

- Chapter Transparencies and Lesson Plans
- Chapter 24 Test
- Spanish Resources, Chapter 24
- School-to-Work Activity Handbook, Chapter 24 Activity
- Teacher's Lesson Plans, Chapter 24
- Implementing Block Scheduling, Chapter 24
- Print, Media, and Internet Handbook
- Strategies for Implementing Work-Based Learning
- Strategies for Implementing Connecting Activities

Career Notes

SCANS CORRELATION CHART

Foundation Skills

Basic Skills	Reading	Writing	Math	Listening	Speaking

Thinking Skills	Creative Thinking	Decision Making	Problem Solving	Seeing Things in the Mind's Eye	Knowing How to Learn	Reasoning

Personal Qualities	Responsibility	Self-Esteem	Sociability	Self-Management	Integrity/Honesty

Workplace Competencies

Resources	Allocating Time	Allocating Money	Allocating Material and Facility Resources	Allocating Human Resources

Information	Acquiring and Evaluating Information	Organizing and Maintaining Information	Interpreting and Communicating Information	Using Computers to Process Information

Interpersonal Skills	Participating as a Member of a Team	Teaching Others	Serving Clients/Customers	Exercising Leadership	Negotiating to Arrive at a Decision	Working with Cultural Diversity

Systems	Understanding Systems	Monitoring and Correcting Performance	Improving and Designing Systems

Technology	Selecting Technology	Applying Technology to Task	Maintaining and Troubleshooting Technology

Highlighted blocks indicate areas covered in the Chapter.

Additional Activities

Internet Connection

Volunteering for community projects is a great way to gain skills or to meet people. Ask students to use the Internet to find information about volunteer programs that interest them. They should list at least five volunteer programs they would like to apply for, and tell what the program would involve.

Field Trip Suggestions

Arrange to take students to a company in your area known for its job-training program. Ask a representative to explain what is involved in the program, the skills, education, and attitude it looks for in new employees, and the training and education benefits available.

Guest Speaker Suggestions

Through the local paper, identify a worker who started his or her own business after being "downsized." Have the guest discuss the feelings that go with job loss, the decision to start a business, and how the person chose his or her venture.

Key to Ability Levels

Each section gives skill-building activities. Each activity has been labeled for use with students of various learning styles and abilities.

L1 Level 1 activities are basic activities and should be within the range of all students.

L2 Level 2 activities are average activities and should be within the range of average and above average students.

L3 Level 3 activities are challenging activities designed for the ability range of above average students.

School-Based Learning

Chapter Overview

Chapter 24 encourages students to manage their careers by evaluating jobs and developing skills they can use in future jobs.

Section 24-1 focuses on continuously assessing what students need to know to be successful.

Section 24-2 helps students spot characteristics of jobs that don't prepare them for the future.

Background Information

Write chapter objectives (Sections 24-1 and 24-2) on the chalkboard or use the chapter objective transparency for class discussion.

Choose assignments from the *Student Activity Workbook* and write them on the chalkboard.

Have students preview the chapter, looking at pictures, reading captions, and noting content headings. Ask students to describe what they expect to learn in this chapter.

Preteaching Vocabulary

Write the Key Terms from Sections 24-1 and 24-2 on the chalkboard. Have students describe how each term relates to how to manage a career and make wise decisions about when to change jobs.

482

Meeting SPECIAL Needs

Limited Proficiency in English

Students who do not speak English as their native language face special challenges when dealing with large numbers. It is usually not the mathematical calculation that causes problems but the tendency native speakers have of saying numbers very quickly, blurring the sounds. Be sure to write the numbers on the chalkboard along with the sign indicating the operation being performed.

Chapter 24

Adapting to Change

Section 24-1
Managing Your Career

Section 24-2
Changing Jobs or Careers

In this video segment, explore ways to prepare for your changing role.

Journal
Personal Career Plan

Imagine that you have had the same job for four years. This job is an important step—but only a step—toward your career goal. Now you've been offered a promotion that will take you away from your familiar responsibilities and friendly colleagues. In your journal, list the advantages and disadvantages of this job change.

483

School-to-Work Connecting Activities

Have students research the topic of job change and lifetime employability. Several books should be available in your public library; career and general interest magazines also have articles related to job change. Have students identify at least three recommendations or strategies to follow in managing their careers. Have them write 150–200 word reports describing such techniques.

Work-Based Learning Strategies and Activities

Arrange for students to observe activities and talk to workers at a local company that has either downsized or converted a portion of its operation from a manual to a computerized process. Have students ask what assistance employees who were laid off were given. Also, have them ask workers what retraining they were given and what new skills they learned. Have students write 100–150 word summaries.

WORKFORCE 2000 Training Video

Have students view the video and perform the interactive exercises to reinforce important chapter concepts and thinking processes.

Chapter 24

Addressing LEARNING Styles

Logical and Kinesthetic Learner

Alert students that for one week there will be changes in your classroom. One day, change the seating arrangement. On a second, assign one topic but discuss another. At the end of the week, ask students to describe how the changes affected them and their ability to learn. How did it affect their stress levels? Have them think about how more difficult changes—loss of work, moving to a new city—can affect their lives.

FOCUS

Bell Ringer

Tell students to think about space travel as portrayed in movies like *Star Trek*. Forty years ago, the U.S. space program was in its infancy. Today, the idea of space travel is almost a reality. Have students list things technology may enable them to do in the next forty years. (For example, they might be space mechanics or laser tool designers.)

Introducing the Section

Have students share their ideas from the Bell Ringer activity. Ideas may range from medical improvements to living and working in space. Explain that since modern technology is accelerating change at an astonishing pace, students must keep their skills up to fit the minute-by-minute changing marketplace.

Motivational Activity
Critical Thinking

Have students create a marketing campaign, featuring themselves as job candidates. Have them consider the following four factors: product (their skills), promotion (connecting skills to job needs), place (where they want to be), and price (what their skills are worth in the job market).

Managing Your Career

OBJECTIVES

After studying this section, you will be able to:

• **Identify ways to prepare yourself for the future.**
• **Describe actions and behaviors that lead to promotions.**

KEY TERMS

downsizing
promotion
seniority
perseverance

Think back over your high school years. How have you changed? In the years ahead, changes will continue to occur. Your skills and interests will keep expanding in new directions. New career possibilities will emerge. The world of work will change, too. Changes at work may open even more doors. Can you predict these changes? No. You *can*, however, prepare yourself to respond to them.

Preparing for the Future

Today's workplace offers challenges that earlier generations of workers did not face. First of all, the job market changes quickly. Jobs that once employed a majority of the population have become much less significant. *Figure 24-1* shows the 12 jobs that experts predict will grow fastest through the year 2005.

Tracking employment trends is one way to prepare for the future. What else can you do?

Thinking in New Ways

You may know people who took jobs when they were young and stayed with the same company for their entire working lives. Forty years ago, that was typical. Today it is not. As you learned in the first chapter of this book, the average American has at least seven jobs before he or she reaches age 30. People can expect to change employers several—perhaps many— more times before they retire. What does this mean?

484   *Unit 7 • Lifelong Learning*

Workforce 2000 Trends

In the future, technology and communication systems will allow collaboration between distant offices. For example, a company may take mail orders in one state, deliver stock from another, and have its bookkeeping done overseas.

It means that your career and your job security are in your own hands. That can be to your advantage—if you use your SCANS self-management skills.

The new world of work is a leaner place than ever before. Many companies have gone through **downsizing**, the elimination of jobs in a company to promote efficiency or to cut costs. Some people end up losing their jobs from downsizing. Everyone, however, is affected. When, for example, management jobs are cut, individual workers acquire additional responsibilities. That can mean more job satisfaction. Yet it can also mean more work and greater demands on those workers.

Keeping Up

Luckily, the company you work for wants you to meet these demands at least as much as you do. To help workers, many of today's companies invest heavily in employee training and education. AT&T, for example, spends about $1 billion annually on training. The average AT&T employee receives a little more than a week of training every year. At your job, make use of all opportunities to keep your skills and knowledge up-to-date. In other words, become a *lifelong learner*.

The competitive global market puts added demands on workers. Businesses want to maintain the state of the art. These

The 12 Fastest Growing Occupations: 1992–2005

Occupation	Employment in 1992	Projected Employment in 2005	Percentage Change 1992–2005
Home health aides	347,000	827,000	138.1
Human services workers	189,000	445,000	135.9
Personal and home-care aides	127,000	293,000	129.8
Computer engineers and scientists	211,000	447,000	111.9
Systems analysts	455,000	956,000	110.1
Physical and corrective therapy assistants and aides	61,000	118,000	92.7
Physical therapists	90,000	170,000	88.0
Paralegals	95,000	176,000	86.1
Occupational therapy assistants and aides	12,000	21,000	78.1
Electronic pagination systems workers	18,000	32,000	77.9
Special education teachers	358,000	625,000	74.4
Medical assistants	181,000	308,000	70.5

Source: U. S. Bureau of Labor Statistics, *Monthly Labor Review*, November 1993.

Figure 24-1 This table shows the 12 jobs that experts believe will grow fastest through the year 2005. Which job is expected to grow at the highest rate? Even if the prediction is accurate, why can't a person count on a job in this field?

Chapter 24 • Adapting to Change **485**

**SCANS Foundation
Skills Connection**

L1 Problem Solving

Have students think of a time when they had to persevere to reach a goal or solve a problem. Tell them to describe the situation and how they overcame self-doubt or setbacks. What did they do to overcome obstacles? Have them write brief summaries. What would they do differently now?

L2 Self-Esteem

Ask students to identify personal traits that help them succeed in school. In what class or extracurricular activity do they excel? Have them analyze how these traits will help them succeed on the job.

L3 Seeing Things in the Mind's Eye

Have students ask one or both parents to share their career histories and decisions they made along the way. Ask students to visualize their parents during that time. Then have them imagine how their own career paths might compare to their parents' careers. How can they use their parents' experiences to make good decisions?

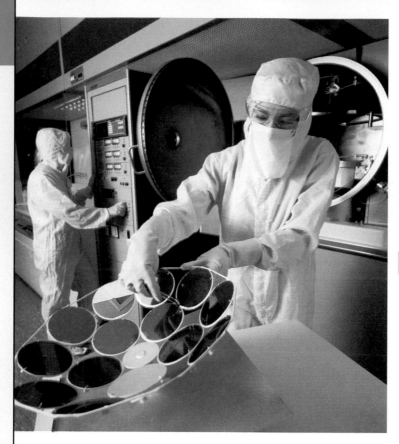

In the past, little was expected of factory employees. They were taught one simple step in a complex process. They repeated that step countless times each day without thinking much about it. Today, employees perform complicated tasks requiring advanced skills. *How has this change benefited workers?*

companies require workers with state-of-the-art knowledge and skills.

Since no one can predict with certainty what new technology will appear, master the SCANS skills in reading, writing, math, speaking, and listening. These skills will give you the basic tools for absorbing new technology.

When new technology appears in your workplace, get involved right away. Volunteer for training sessions or tasks that will give you hands-on training. Take technology courses at community colleges and vocational and technical centers. Many companies offer paid tuition for employees who want to take courses in areas related to their jobs.

Growing in Your Job

Continuing to update and improve your skills and knowledge will make you valuable to your employer. It may also help you earn a promotion. A **promotion** is a job advancement to a position of greater responsibility and authority. Promotions will offer new challenges. Usually promotions also bring increased income.

Who Gets Promoted?

The people who earn promotions are the people who have shown their supervisors that they can handle additional responsibility and authority. What qualities and behaviors do employers look for?

Extending the Illustration

Have students interview one or more people who work in a local factory. How has their work changed over the past few years? What new skills have they learned as a result?

Caption Answer: Workers can become more involved in their work. The work is more challenging and interesting.

- *Seniority.* **Seniority** is the position or prestige you achieve by working for an employer for a sustained length of time. Greater seniority is usually thought of as indicating greater experience and dependability.

- *Knowledge and competence.* Employers want workers who know how to do their jobs, even if the new job requires different skills. Employers also look for workers who go a step beyond this—workers who excel. These employees are likely to do well in jobs with more responsibility.

- *Willingness to learn.* Employers promote workers who show they want to increase their knowledge and skills.

- *Initiative.* You'll probably advance in your career if you make it clear to your supervisor that advancement is an important goal for you. A good time to talk about career goals is during your performance evaluation. Avoid giving the impression that you want to get out of your current job, however. Emphasize that you want more responsibility and challenge.

L1 Acquiring and Evaluating Information

Working in groups, have students clip five ads from the employment section of a Sunday newspaper, underlining key skills and educational requirements. Have groups discuss their ads, then write a profile of an ideal candidate for each job.

L2 Participating as a Member of a Team

Divide students into teams of five. Have each team search for job leads from advertisements, personnel referrals, employment agencies, university placement offices, and the Internet. Have teams report to the class about the advantages and disadvantages of each.

L3 Teaching Others

Divide students into pairs to role-play an interview. Tell interviewers to ask questions about education, job skills, employment history, and why the person wants to work for your company. Tell interviewees to demonstrate professional behavior and give appropriate answers to questions. Afterwards, ask interviewers to give positive feedback. Have students switch roles and repeat the role-plays with their partner.

EXCELLENT BUSINESS PRACTICES

Environmental Concerns

Pitney Bowes Inc. of Stamford, Connecticut, provides mailing, messaging, and document-handling products; software; and business and financial services.

To better serve the environment, Pitney Bowes has maximized energy conservation at its facilities and has eliminated or drastically reduced chemicals that produce hazardous waste, with a goal of completely eliminating the use of hazardous waste. All suppliers must comply with environmental requirements before Pitney Bowes purchases from them.

Pitney Bowes also keeps the environment in mind while designing products. Such factors as energy consumption, ease of disassembly, recycled and recyclable content, and the use of hazardous materials are considered in manufacturing.

A Pitney Bowes fax machine, for example, powers down when not in use and every piece of the machine can be recycled. The company also set up a program to help keep toner cartridges out of landfills. For every cartridge returned, the company makes a financial donation to the United Way.

Thinking Critically

How has environmental awareness caused companies to change?

Chapter 24 • Adapting to Change **487**

Extending EXCELLENT BUSINESS PRACTICES

Answer: Companies must consider all factors related to the environment, including manufacturing, everyday issues involved with running the company, and how consumers will use products safely.

Further Application: Have students find out what recycling programs are available in their community. Have them create an awareness campaign aimed at getting consumers to recycle.

Teaching Tip

Have students read the descriptions of qualities and behaviors that employers look for in employees. Then have them do a self-assessment, rating themselves from 1 to 5 on each quality, 5 being the highest. Omit seniority from the list. Have students use their ratings to decide what skills they need to work on to become high-quality employees.

Independent Practice

 Assign as homework the chapter activity in the *School-to-Work Activity Handbook.*

Reading

Have each student read an article about a future technology, such as digital interactive television. As students read, tell them to think about how technology might affect their careers or how they acquire new skills. (For example, digital televisions connected to the Internet could be used for taking courses to upgrade skills.) Have students discuss their readings in class.

Writing: *Persuasion*

Tell each student to think of a job he or she really wants. Then have him or her write a letter requesting an interview to an actual company offering such a position.

- *Perseverance.* **Perseverance** is the quality of finishing what you start. Employers want to know that you will see a job through to completion.

- *Cooperativeness.* When you have more responsibility, you'll have to cooperate with more people. Employers want people who can get along well with others.

- *Thinking skills.* When considering whom to promote, employers look for people who can think through situations and solve problems.

- *Adaptability.* Business is constantly changing. Employers want workers who can adapt to new situations and get a job done.

- *Education and training.* Employers promote people who have the skills and education needed for the new job.

Handling Your New Responsibilities

Getting a promotion may change your work life in many ways. Often it means you'll become a supervisor. Then you will be responsible for both your own work and the work of others. Look back at Chapter 14 to remind yourself of the qualities of a good supervisor.

Be aware that as a supervisor your relationships with your former coworkers will change. You'll be the boss. You must oversee their work and give direction. You will review their performance. It may be difficult to have close friendships with people you supervise. Be sure you are prepared for these changes.

Learning should not end with high school or even college. Workers must keep up-to-date on the latest information in their fields. *How can further education give you greater confidence?*

Extending the Illustration

Have students brainstorm a list of products that were not in wide use 20 years ago (such as the microwave, desktop computer, cellular phones). Then have them list types of changes they may encounter during the next 20 years. How might those changes affect their job skills?

Caption Answer: Taking classes can help you keep on top of trends in your field. Education can help you do a better job and thus instill confidence.

 If you want to decline a promotion, talk to your supervisor face-to-face. **Why do you think this is important?**

Declining a Promotion

Being offered a promotion is always a good thing. It shows you've earned your employer's trust and appreciation. Not every promotion, however, is right for you. Perhaps the promotion requires too many personal sacrifices. For example, you might be asked to travel more than you want or to take on responsibilities you don't feel ready for.

It's OK to decline a promotion. Avoid closing the door on future offers, however. Even if this promotion is not right, the next one might be. Let your supervisor know your specific reasons for declining a promotion. Leave your supervisor with the impression that you like your work and want to be considered for future promotions.

SECTION 24-1 *Review*

Understanding Key Concepts

Using complete sentences, answer the following questions on a separate sheet of paper.

1. How will continuing your education help you be prepared for changes in the workplace?

2. Why is it important to let your supervisor know you're interested in a promotion?

Evaluation

Assign the section review.

Reteaching

Divide students into eight groups to make posters to be used at a career fair. Each poster should focus on one of these qualities: *knowledge and competence, willingness to learn, initiative, perseverance, cooperativeness, thinking skills, adaptability,* or *education and training.* Have each group illustrate its poster and present it to the class.

Extending the Content

Assign the appropriate Chapter 24 activities in the *Student Activity Workbook.*

Have students think about the future by researching projections for the next decade. What will work be like? How will technology change what people do and where they do it? Have students prepare and deliver two- to three-minute presentations.

CLOSE

Have students complete this sentence: "Personal skills that will be important to me in my future career are . . . ." (Answers will vary but might include willingness to learn, initiative, perseverance, cooperativeness, thinking skills, adaptability, positive attitude.)

CASE STUDY

Exploring Careers: Environment

**Brad Nanke
Corporate Environmental
Manager**

Q: **What does your job involve?**

A: I have the responsibility for seeing that my company complies with all environmental regulations. I take care of permits pertaining to water and air quality, hazardous waste handling, and waste-water discharge. I also take care of all the reports that go with the regulations. I report to the state fire marshal on the chemicals we use and on our emergency response procedures. I work with the city on water quality.

Q: **Do you have environmental training?**

A: I've learned along the way. I've never gotten a degree. Even if you have a degree in environmental science or engineering, you don't necessarily become a regulations expert.

I'm a certified hazardous materials manager. The certification was developed for people like me, who have come up through the field. We are recognized for what we know.

Q: **Will there be a demand for environmental managers in the future?**

A: Yes, especially among small companies that don't have a health or environmental staff.

Q: **Is there anything you don't like about your job?**

A: I don't like the legal liability. Because I sign the permits, I could go to jail if someone else does something wrong. You have to make sure that people know what the permits actually mean and that they don't operate outside the limits of those permits.

Thinking Critically —————

Would you be interested in an environmental career? Why or why not?

CAREER FACTS

Nature of the Work:
Oversee issuing of permits, environmental impact, and compliance with state, local, and federal environmental regulations.

Training or Education Needed:
Bachelor's degree in chemistry, chemical or civil engineering, or environmental science; experience in the field.

Aptitudes, Abilities, and Skills:
Computer skills; ability to learn; read blueprints; self-management skills; detail orientation.

Salary Range:
Approximately $30,000 with bachelor's degree and one year of experience.

Career Path:
Start in an entry-level position; move up to a position with more responsibility.

490 *Unit 7 • Lifelong Learning*

Extending the CASE STUDY

Answer: Students should list skills and interests that would make them suited or not suited for this career.

Further Application: Have students discuss the personal responsibilities that go with their chosen careers. Health-care providers are legally, morally, and ethically responsible for the health of their patients; engineers are responsible for the safety and trustworthiness of their structures and machinery; and auto mechanics are responsible for the cars they fix.

Changing Jobs or Careers

OBJECTIVES

After studying this section, you will be able to:

- **Explain why workers may want to change jobs.**
- **Describe strategies for seeking a new job or career.**
- **Describe steps to take if you lose your job.**

KEY TERM
notice

As you know, you are likely to change employers several times during your work career. Sometimes you may choose the change because you want to seek new opportunities. At other times, the change may be forced on you by events beyond your control.

Why Change Jobs?

Changing your job should never be a snap decision. Before making a change, you should analyze what is missing from your current job and what you want from a new one. Always make sure you have thought through the change carefully. This section will help you clarify possible reasons for a job change. The next sections will help you make the transition.

Because You're Not Happy

When you are unhappy at work, a job change may be one solution. *Figure 24-2* on page 492 is a checklist of danger signs. Use it to evaluate your situation.

Before giving up on your job, however, consider whether there might be a way to stay and solve the problem. Ask advice from an experienced coworker or friend. If you decide to stay, set work goals for yourself. What do you want to achieve in your job—a pay raise, a promotion, new responsibilities or challenges? How long will you give yourself to reach your goals?

Chapter 24 • Adapting to Change **491**

Guided Practice

Teaching Strategies

1. Assign and review Section 24-2.

2. Use the transparency for this section.

Discussion Starter

Ask students whether they think a person should play it safe by staying in a career that offers good pay and opportunities, even if he or she is not particularly interested in that career.

Teaching Tip

Have students discuss the idea of job satisfaction. Then ask what role attitude plays in job satisfaction. Have them consider whether someone with a positive attitude might be more apt to find a satisfying job than someone with a negative attitude.

Critical Thinking

Have each student talk with at least three people who have left an employer to work for another. Tell students to take notes on reasons why people changed jobs. Have them analyze reasons, since they may apply to their own career plans. Are there steps they can take now to avoid such problems? Discuss in class.

Signs of Trouble Checklist

☐ Do my coworkers ignore me or leave me out?

☐ Do I feel that I'm wasting my time?

☐ Do I find myself daydreaming what my life would be like without this job?

☐ Is being sick a relief to me because I don't have to go to work?

☐ Do I seem to be always making someone at work angry or upset?

☐ Do I feel as if I don't have a future with the company or a chance for advancement?

☐ Do I have trouble sleeping because I'm worrying about my job?

► Figure 24-2

Use this checklist to evaluate your level of job satisfaction. Answering yes to any of these questions indicates that you should reassess your situation.

Changing your job isn't necessarily the answer, however. How might you solve a work problem if you plan to stay?

Because You Want to Grow

Is there a good time to change jobs? Yes! It is possible to outgrow your job. Perhaps you feel unfulfilled and unchallenged. Perhaps you have discovered that what you are doing isn't really what you want to do. In these cases, a job change may be what you need.

Because Your Job Is Terminated

There are times, of course, when a job change is forced on you. People can no longer count on keeping their jobs until retirement. Downsizing, corporate restructuring, and global economic factors have created a working world in which little is constant except change.

As illogical as it sounds, you *can* prepare for an unexpected job loss. How is this possible? Stay alert. Keep your ears open at work for signs of trouble. These include signals that your supervisor is displeased with your work or that the company is not doing well. Read newspaper articles and magazines about your industry to detect trends. Read the front page of the newspaper, too. Is there anything happening in the world that might affect the industry in which you work?

ETHICS in Action

You've been offered a new job that doesn't begin for another two months. You plan to keep working at your old job until your new job begins. Your best friend tells you that you should plan to tell your employer you will be leaving two weeks before you actually leave. Your coworker says you should give your employer more notice since you know what you are going to do so far in advance. What will you do?

▶▶ Extending Figure 24-2 ◀◀

Have students discuss in pairs how self-evaluation can help them manage their careers. (By assessing their skills and job needs, they will be better able to decide how to change their attitude toward a current job or to seek a new job that is more challenging or improves their skills.)

Caption Answer: You could discuss the situation with coworkers or a supervisor to clear up misunderstandings. You could reevaluate your own goals. You could look for ways to make non-work time more fulfilling.

Making the Change

When you decide to make a career or job change, put your SCANS decision-making skills to work. First you have to define your needs or wants.

Focusing Your Search

Consider where you want to look for a new job. Here are three possible ways to focus your search.

- *Same job, new company.* If you like what you're doing, explore similar positions with other companies. You already know you have the right skills for the job. A different company, however, may offer better opportunities.

- *New job, new company.* What if you have the right skills for your

job but you really don't like it? That happened to Lisa Von Drasek. She was working in book sales when a layoff forced her to do some rethinking. She suddenly realized she didn't feel fulfilled in her career. She wanted a job that would allow her to make a difference in the world. When a friend suggested library school, Von Drasek was skeptical. After talking with several librarians, however, she signed up for a master's program.

Today she's a children's librarian at the Brooklyn Public Library. Every day, she sees young teen mothers, recent immigrants, and others discover the world of books. She has even developed her own children's

SCANS Foundation Skills Connection

L1 **Decision Making**

Tell students to list things that will make them happy on the job (for example, money, the kinds of people they want to work with, whether they prefer a slow or fast pace, amount of noise, working alone or dealing with the public, working inside or outdoors). Based on this information, have students identify one or two careers that meet their needs.

L2 **Self-Management**

Have students trace their personal growth over the past four years. (For example, have they developed a more patient attitude?) Tell them to think not just in terms of mechanical skills, but also to consider attitudes and personal traits that show maturity. Then have students visualize how they want to grow in the next four years.

L3 **Speaking**

Working in pairs, have students identify skills that are most important to employers. One person should take the position that technical skills matter the most; while the other argues that interpersonal skills are more important. Have both partners substantiate their positions.

Keeping up with business news can bring early warnings of trouble in your industry or company. It can also bring news of better times to come. **What are some examples of business news that could affect employment in your area?**

Chapter 24 • Adapting to Change **493**

Teaching ETHICS in Action

Have students follow these steps to help them make a decision.

1. What are the ethical issues?
2. What are the alternatives?
3. Who are the affected parties?
4. How do the alternatives affect the parties?
5. What is your decision?

Extending the Illustration

Have students create a list of resources they might use to keep up with business news. Tell them to list specific titles. (Examples might include *The Wall Street Journal* or business magazines such as *Business Week*, *Forbes*, or *Fortune*.)

Caption Answer: business openings or closings; or changes in interest rates

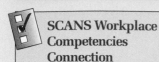
L1 Organizing and Maintaining Information

Have students list at least five people they've met or talked with before that they might call on to talk about job possibilities.

L2 Exercising Leadership

Have each student in the class choose a class office or a school club position to which he or she would like to be elected. Tell students to prepare and deliver two-minute speeches to the class, describing their skills and the programs they would work on if elected.

L3 Allocating Human Resources

Have students imagine they own a small company. Have them list qualities and skills they would want a supervisor to have. Would they promote someone who had most of these skills but not all of them? Discuss in class.

writing program. "The kids run up to my desk and say, 'When are we going to write?'" she says. "I make a difference."

- *Starting over.* A third possibility is to turn a hobby or interest into a career. Geoffrey Macon had spent 17 years in the banking industry. When a combination of health problems and corporate restructuring cost him his job, he turned his career in a different direction. Macon had always had a passionate interest in ethnic art. He became an entrepreneur designing, manufacturing, and selling plates and other tableware based on ethnic designs.

What's Different This Time Around?

In this book, you have been introduced to many job search strategies. Chapter 2, for example, talked about career decision making. Chapter 3 gave tips on researching careers. Chapter 6 provided basic

These entrepreneurs have turned a personal interest into a way of making a living. ***What interest of yours might you turn into a business?***

▶ Extending the Illustration

Have students discuss whether it is better to begin one's career as an entrepreneur or to first work for another business. What are some advantages and disadvantages of each approach? (An advantage of immediate entrepreneurship is that you're doing what you want; a disadvantage is lack of business experience. An advantage of working for someone else is learning skills that will help in running a business; a disadvantage is not being able to be your own boss.)

Caption Answer: Answers will vary. Students might suggest an artistic or musical interest, an interest in writing, or an interest in sewing.

information on finding and applying for a job. Chapter 7 covered interview techniques. The main focus in these chapters was on choosing your career and landing your first job. The advice is just as useful when you are finding a new job or changing your career. In addition, consider the following points:

- Because you've been out in the world of work, you have much more data available to you. What are your work skills? Which tasks have you enjoyed most? Which have you enjoyed least?

- Consider how you can use proven skills in new ways. Suppose you have been a receptionist. Your telephone skills could be used in marketing. Your ability to remain in control when all the lines are flashing could be valuable in retail sales.

- List jobs or careers that you might like. Then analyze them. What are the pros and cons of each? How can your current skills and interests be applied to them?

- Research jobs in which you are interested. You have probably built up a network of people at your current job. Use these contacts to explore new directions.

- Try to arrange your interviews so that you don't miss work.

- Don't burn your bridges with your present employer. You don't want to lose your current job until you've landed a new one. Besides, you never know when your old contacts will once again be valuable to you.

Career Do's & Don'ts

When Preparing for Change...

Do:
- take initiative.
- be flexible.
- keep physically active.
- maintain your sense of humor.

Don't:
- focus on the negative aspects of change.
- overlook your strengths and long-term goals.
- make change too big in your mind.

- When you've found a new job, give proper notice to your current employer. **Notice** is an official written statement that you are leaving the company. Most people prepare a formal letter of resignation. Businesses usually have a policy stating how long they expect employees to work after giving notice. This period of time gives the employer time to find a replacement.

- Don't tell coworkers about your job hunt. They don't need to know. Always inform coworkers about the new job *after* you've given notice.

- Don't lose steam at work. Perhaps you've worked long hours for five years. Unfortunately, people will

Chapter 24 • Adapting to Change **495**

Addressing Workplace Diversity

Diversity awareness programs often concentrate on the concerns of women and minorities, leaving white males feeling resentful and defensive. Companies such as AT&T address this anger by conducting workshops aimed at preventing white males being categorized as the "bad guys."

Independent Practice

Reading

Have students find and read information on the Americans with Disabilities Act. How has this law made it easier for people with disabilities to find jobs?

Skills Practice

Share this scenario with students. "Selena works for an advertising agency as an administrative assistant. She has been taking classes at night to learn the computer and graphics software programs the agency uses in preparing campaigns. She wants to be promoted to assistant designer." Have students write what Selena might say to her supervisor to ask for the promotion. Discuss in class.

Research

Selma Burke is an African-American sculptor whose bust of President Franklin Roosevelt appears on the U.S. dime. As a black woman in a society that limited her options, Burke never considered exploring all the possibilities open to her.

Have students research her life and write 200-word papers about her attitude toward her career. Tell students to draw conclusions about how commitment and perseverance apply to their own future careers. You may also choose to have students select other successful persons to research—perhaps someone in a career area of interest to them.

Discussion Starter

Have students imagine that their boss has just told them that 100 jobs must be cut and asks why theirs should be one of those exempted. What would they say?

Teaching Tip

Explain that changes in company policies are a fact of life; a new president can decide to cut costs by closing a plant or shutting down a department. Employees have no control over such decisions; they can only show how they feel about change and how they react to it. Tell students that controlling feelings and actions is a key part of self-management.

Skills Practice

Eva is stressed out by a part-time job. She is thinking of quitting, even though she needs the money. A friend says that job hassles are just part of life. Ask students what they would say to Eva.

Larry has worked for a local manufacturer for three years. Yesterday, he was told that the company is downsizing and 50 workers will be laid off; Larry is one of them. Ask students what advice they would give Larry.

remember if you slack off during your last two weeks. Leave a good impression.

- Let people outside the company know what's happening. Tell clients or other business contacts that you are leaving. Don't criticize the

▶ Figure 24-3

Losing a Job

If you lose your job, you may think you have nothing to do. That's not true! You'll be working full-time getting a new job.

A Your first response to the news of the job loss may be a powerful negative emotion such as anger or sadness. As soon as you have your emotions under control, talk with your supervisor. Ask about job-search services available through your employer, severance pay (money that may be offered to employees who are dismissed), funds from profit-sharing or pension plans, payment for unused vacation time, and terms for extension of your health insurance coverage.

B Next review your financial situation. Figure out how much money you have to live on. Then prepare a budget so you know you can pay for the things you must have. Find ways to cut back on your expenses.

C In most cases, workers who lose their jobs can get unemployment benefits. These checks will help you get by until you find your next job. Every state has its own guidelines for applying for unemployment compensation. Make your application as soon as possible.

▶▶ Extending Figure 24-3 ◀◀

Tell students that losing a job may create new opportunities. Ask students how. (A person may evaluate skills and decide to gain more education or pursue a career in a different field.)

company, however, no matter how disappointed or angry you feel. Doing so will only make you seem petty, and it could lose you a future job.

D Update and improve your résumé. Remember that it should be brief and to the point. Ask several people to read it over, and consider having it printed professionally. Use every strategy you can think of in your job search. These include networking, contacting employment agencies, and reading the classified ads.

E Stay positive as you go for interviews. Remember that a job loss can be a good opportunity to find a better job or to follow your dreams.

Dealing with a Job Loss

Most people are laid off or have their jobs terminated at least once during their working careers (See **Figure 24-3**). It is always a painful experience. If it happens to you, you may feel depressed, embarrassed, resentful, angry, afraid, or discouraged.

These are valid emotions, and you shouldn't be ashamed of feeling them. However, don't let them overwhelm you.

Chapter 24 • Adapting to Change **497**

Implementing Teamwork

Divide the class into groups of five or six. Ask each group to set up a job counseling service. Each group should brainstorm the types of assistance it could provide (for example, training, assessment, interview skills) and the career target areas. Ask each group to give a presentation about its counseling service.

Discussion Starter

Read this quote from economist John Kenneth Galbraith to students: "Faced with the choice between changing one's mind and proving that there is no need to do so, almost everybody gets busy on the proof." Ask students why so many people are resistant to change.

Teaching Tip

Discuss students' ideas about change. Then explain that change will be a part of every career. Technological changes will eventually affect almost everyone. Tell students that learning to adapt to change and using it to enhance their job skills will help make them valuable employees.

Despite good job skills, people still lose their jobs. Have students discuss each step in Figure 24-3; then have them write a summary for their career journals describing how to deal with losing a job.

Interview

Have each student interview a representative of the local unemployment office to find out how to apply for unemployment benefits. What are the requirements for eligibility? How long are benefits paid? Who pays into the unemployment benefits fund? Tell students to write 100-word summaries.

Role-Play

Divide students into pairs and have each pair role-play a conversation between a supervisor and an employee, who gives notice.

Skills Practice

Tell students that their employer is going out of business and is giving each employee three weeks severance pay. Students earn $8.70 an hour. How much would each employee receive before taxes and deductions? ($1,044: $8.70 × 40 × 3)

ASSESS

Assessment
Content

Have students write 150-word advice columns on points to consider before quitting a job. Evaluate students' columns for clarity and inclusion of appropriate content.

Evaluation

Assign the section review.

MINI QUIZ

True-False

1. One of the fastest-growing occupations is that of home health aide. (true)

2. Adaptability will help people who are downsized find new jobs. (true)

3. People who turn down a promotion probably will not be offered another one. (false)

4. Once you start a job, you won't need to get more education or training. (false)

5. If you lose a job due to downsizing, you can collect unemployment benefits. (true)

Try to remain positive. Look on the event as an opportunity to start over. Perhaps, like Lisa Von Drasek or Geoffrey Macon, you may be able to do what you've always wanted. You may even be able to earn a better income than you did before.

> Try to be open-minded when you are looking for a new job. You might find that your skills apply to some very interesting jobs. *What kinds of skills would be important in the job pictured here?*

YOU'RE THE BOSS!

✓ *Solving Workplace Problems*

You own and run a small, busy travel agency. Your best agent, who has worked for you for seven years, expresses an interest in "moving up." However, you aren't looking for a partner, and there aren't any senior positions left to fill. What will you do? Why?

SECTION 24-2 *Review*

Understanding Key Concepts

Using complete sentences, answer the following questions on a separate sheet of paper.

1. Why is the desire for personal growth a good reason to change jobs?

2. What are some of the unique aspects of looking for a job when you already have one?

3. Why is it important to keep a positive attitude when you have lost your job?

SECTION 24-2 *Review* ANSWERS

1. People should find personal fulfillment in their jobs. Feeling unfulfilled can lead to stress and poor job performance.

2. Students may mention such positive aspects as knowledge of one's skills or confidence in one's abilities. They may also mention such negative aspects as difficulty keeping the job search confidential or scheduling interviews.

3. Negative feelings will affect your ability to present yourself well.

SECTION 24-1 **Summary**

- You can prepare for the future by tracking employment trends and managing your own career.
- Many businesses are downsizing, or eliminating jobs to cut costs. Some employees lose their jobs, and others gain new responsibilities.
- Businesses help employees meet the demands of the workplace by offering training and paying for education.
- Continuing to update your skills and knowledge may also help you get a promotion.
- Employers look for many different qualities and behaviors when selecting employees to promote, including competence, willingness to learn, initiative, and adaptability.
- Getting a promotion may change your relationships with coworkers. Be prepared for this change.
- If a promotion is not right for you, decline it. Keep your options open, however. Let your employer know you are open to future offers.

Key Terms

downsizing *(p. 485)*
promotion *(p. 486)*
seniority *(p. 487)*
perseverance *(p. 488)*

Key Term

notice *(p. 495)*

SECTION 24-2 **Summary**

- You may choose to change jobs for a number of reasons, including unhappiness in your job, the desire to grow, or termination of your job.
- Focus your job search. You might look for a job like the one you have but with a different company. You might look for a job that will use your current skills but in a different field. You might look for a job that involves a hobby or personal interest that you have.
- You will use many of the job search strategies that you learned in previous chapters. This time, however, you have more information about yourself and your skills.
- If you lose your job, first find out what your former employer is offering to you at termination. Then assess your financial situation, and arrange for unemployment benefits. Update and improve your résumé. Stay positive as you go for interviews.

Chapter 24 • Adapting to Change **499**

SECTION 24-2

Use the Testmaker to create a customized test for Chapter 24.

Reteaching

1. Invite a career counselor to class to discuss the key points of this section. Set aside time for students to ask questions.
2. Assign and review vocabulary terms, chapter questions, and activities from the Chapter Review.

Extending the Content

Assign the appropriate Chapter 24 activities in the *Student Activity Workbook*.

Have students research jobs of the future, some of which may not exist yet. Two references are *New Emerging Careers: Today, Tomorrow, and in the 21st Century* by Norman Feingold & Maxine Atwater, or *Careers Tomorrow: The Outlook for Work in a Changing World* by Edward Cornish. Have students choose two future careers and write a paragraph on each, describing the skills they think will be needed for those careers.

CLOSE

Have students complete this sentence: "Some steps I will take to manage my career are . . . ." (Answers will vary but could include choosing a job for satisfaction rather than economic security, gaining new job skills, learning how to use a computer, and so on.)

▶ Extending the Illustration

Have students brainstorm a list of the most unusual jobs they can think of. (An example of an unusual job might include milking snake venom for medical use.)

Caption Answer: Skills might include an interest in working with animals, a calming influence, a knowledge of animal habitats and ecological issues.

Teaching YOU'RE THE BOSS!

✓ Possible responses: Discuss the situation with this employee and explore various possibilities, including changing your mind and taking on a partner, or expanding into a second location with this employee as the manager.

Answers
Reviewing Key Terms

Checklists will vary, but students should use all the terms.

Recalling Key Concepts

1. True
2. False: Businesses invest heavily in training programs to help employees keep their skills current.
3. True
4. False: You may be able to resolve the problems and keep your job.
5. True

Thinking Critically

1. If you know which jobs are predicted to grow fastest in the next 10 years, you can choose a career in a field that will give you a better chance for employment.
2. They enable you to understand what you read and hear. When you are being trained in a new type of technology, these skills will help you absorb and use information.
3. Possible benefits/drawbacks of quitting: You might get a better job. You will get away from a bad situation. You might feel as if you gave up. You might lose a chance to improve things. Possible benefits/drawbacks of staying: You might learn important

---

Reviewing Key Terms

On a separate sheet of paper, write a checklist of ways to manage your own career. Use each of the following terms.

downsizing   perseverance
promotion   notice
seniority

Recalling Key Concepts

On a piece of paper, tell whether each statement is true or false. Rewrite any false statements to make them true.

1. In today's workplace, your career and your job security are mainly in your own hands.
2. Businesses do little to help employees keep their job skills current.
3. When promoting workers, employers consider such factors as seniority, initiative, and perseverance.
4. If you have problems with your coworkers or supervisor, the only thing you can do is find a new job.
5. Emotions such as fear or sadness are normal when you lose your job.

Thinking Critically

Using complete sentences, answer each of the questions below on a separate sheet of paper.

1. How can tracking employment trends help you manage your own career?
2. How can the SCANS skills in reading, writing, math, speaking, and listening help you keep up with new technology?

---

3. You have learned that you can either adjust to a negative work situation or decide to make a job change. List two possible benefits and two drawbacks to each choice.
4. Suppose you find a new job, and you know that you will never want to work for your former employer again. Why is it still a good policy not to criticize your former employer?
5. Why should you examine your financial situation soon after finding out about a job loss?

 SCANS Foundation Skills and Workplace Competencies

Basic Skills: *Writing*

1. Write a letter of resignation that includes a gracious opening, a body stating the reason for leaving and notification of the last day you plan to be on the job, and a cordial closing.

Interpersonal Skills: *Exercising Leadership*

2. You have received a promotion, and you now supervise Carrie, a coworker who is also a good friend. Carrie has begun coming in to work late, leaving early, and not performing as well on the job as before. When you talk with her, she says: "What's the big deal? I thought you were my friend. You sure have changed since you became a boss." What should you say?

---

skills. You might gain the respect of others. You might be unhappy. You might get fired.

4. Your new employer may decide that your criticism indicates poor judgment.
5. It is a good idea to know exactly how much money you have and how long it will last.

SCANS Foundation Skills and Workplace Competencies

1. Letters should demonstrate proper business form and style; the writing should be clear and the grammar should be correct.

Connecting Academics to the Workplace

Human Relations

1. Margo is an admissions clerk in a health-care center. She has held the job for three years. A better position in the department has become available, and Margo thinks she is qualified for the promotion. Her supervisor, however, has not offered the position to her. Margo feels overlooked and also a little angry. What should she do?

Computer Science

2. Miguel is an equipment specialist for a construction firm. His supervisor has asked him to recommend a laptop computer that engineers can take with them to the work site. Create a list of features Miguel might look for in a laptop that would make it suitable.

Developing Teamwork and Leadership Skills

Work with a group of three or four classmates. Together, decide on one technological device or a group of technological devices that are currently being developed and marketed for business or industrial use. Do research to learn about the technology and how it may be used in the next 5 or 10 years. Present your findings to the class.

Real-World Workshop

Work with a classmate. First choose a type of company that you might work for and a job that you might have in the company. Then role-play the following situation. An employee has been offered a promotion but does not want to accept it. (You and your partner must decide what the employee's reasons are.) Perform two role-plays. In one, you should be the employee and your partner should be the supervisor; in the other, your roles should be switched. Show through the role-plays either two good ways to decline a promotion or a good way and a poor way to decline a promotion. Present your role-plays to the class.

School-to-Work Connection

Select a local company for which you might like to work. Interview the human resources manager or a department supervisor. Ask what qualities or behaviors this individual looks for when considering employees for promotions. Ask also what training opportunities the company provides to help employees develop the skills needed for promotion. Prepare a brief report on your findings.

Individual Career Plan

Choose a job or career you wish to pursue. Do research to learn about trends in that field. Find answers to questions such as the following: How will the field be affected by new technology? What kind of an impact will globalization have? What are the predictions for future employment growth (or decline) in the field? Outline a plan for keeping your knowledge and skills current. Include formal training and education as well as individual efforts you might make, such as reading specialized magazines or volunteering for jobs using new technology.

Chapter 24 • Adapting to Change **501**

---

2. Features could include durability and protection or resistance to jarring, dust, and moisture.

Developing Teamwork and Leadership Skills

Students should report on technology that has direct business or industrial use. Encourage teams to speculate on technology for the more distant future.

Real-World Workshop

Students' role-plays will vary. They should demonstrate an understanding of how an employee might decline a promotion gracefully.

School-to-Work Connection

Reports will vary, depending on the individual and the company selected.

Individual Career Plan

Student plans will vary. However, students should cite specific actions they can take that will prepare them for changes in their field.

---

2. You should kindly but firmly point out that your new position requires you to correct situations in which employees are not fulfilling their responsibilities, no matter who is involved.

Connecting Academics to the Workplace

1. She should have a calm discussion with her supervisor explaining why she thinks she is qualified for the job and how she would handle it. If she is not happy with her supervisor's response, she may want to consider looking for a job with another company.

• • • PLANNING GUIDE • • •
Chapter 25

SECTION 1	*Setting Up Your Own Household*

SECTION OBJECTIVES	SECTION FEATURES	SECTION RESOURCES
• Decide on a place to live. • Organize your living space. • Establish good housekeeping habits.	Personal Career Plan, p. 503 Attitude Counts, p. 506 Exploring Careers, p. 510	• Workforce 2000 Videodisc and Videotape • Section 25-1 Review, p. 509 • Student Activity Workbook

SECTION 2	*Managing Work, Family, and Community Life*

SECTION OBJECTIVES	SECTION FEATURES	SECTION RESOURCES
• Describe ways of balancing your work life and your personal life. • Identify some strategies for meeting family responsibilities. • Identify some family-friendly employment practices. • Participate in your community as a voter and as a volunteer.	You're the Boss!, p. 516 Excellent Business Practices, p. 517 Career Do's and Don'ts, p. 518	• Workforce 2000 Videodisc and Videotape • Section 25-2 Review, p. 518 • Chapter 25 Review, pp. 520–521 • Student Activity Workbook

CHAPTER 25

CHAPTER RESOURCES

- Chapter Transparencies and Lesson Plans
- Chapter 25 Test
- Spanish Resources, Chapter 25
- School-to-Work Activity Handbook, Chapter 25 Activity
- Teacher's Lesson Plans, Chapter 25
- Implementing Block Scheduling, Chapter 25
- Print, Media, and Internet Handbook
- Strategies for Implementing Work-Based Learning
- Strategies for Implementing Connecting Activities

Career Notes

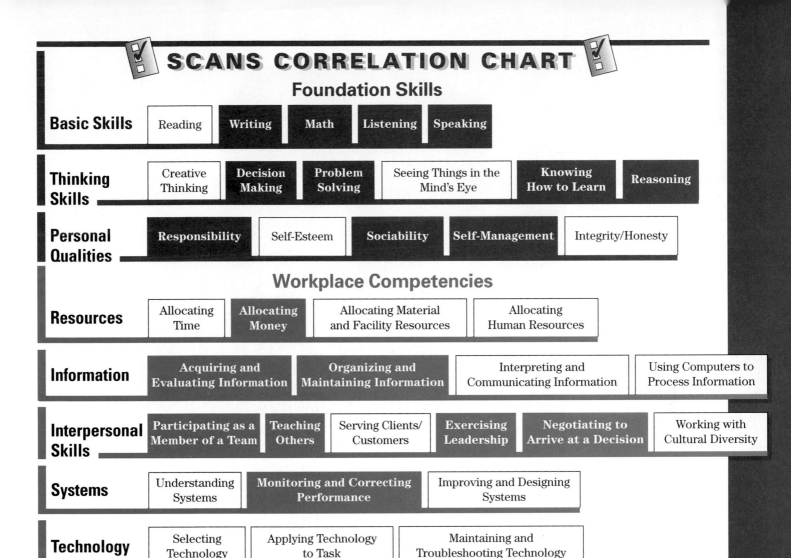

SCANS CORRELATION CHART

Foundation Skills

Basic Skills

| Reading | Writing | Math | Listening | Speaking |

Thinking Skills

| Creative Thinking | Decision Making | Problem Solving | Seeing Things in the Mind's Eye | Knowing How to Learn | Reasoning |

Personal Qualities

| Responsibility | Self-Esteem | Sociability | Self-Management | Integrity/Honesty |

Workplace Competencies

Resources

| Allocating Time | Allocating Money | Allocating Material and Facility Resources | Allocating Human Resources |

Information

| Acquiring and Evaluating Information | Organizing and Maintaining Information | Interpreting and Communicating Information | Using Computers to Process Information |

Interpersonal Skills

| Participating as a Member of a Team | Teaching Others | Serving Clients/ Customers | Exercising Leadership | Negotiating to Arrive at a Decision | Working with Cultural Diversity |

Systems

| Understanding Systems | Monitoring and Correcting Performance | Improving and Designing Systems |

Technology

| Selecting Technology | Applying Technology to Task | Maintaining and Troubleshooting Technology |

Highlighted blocks indicate areas covered in the Chapter.

Additional Activities

 Internet Connection

A citizen's vote is one of his or her most powerful forms of expression. Ask students to use the Internet to find voting information. They should look into registering to vote, political parties, candidates, party policies, and platforms. Ask them to discuss the information they find in class.

 Field Trip Suggestions

Arrange to visit a local recycling center. Have a representative discuss with students what items are recycled and how, what products use recycled materials, how recycling has grown in the past 10 years, the sources of recycled materials, and the future of the recycling business.

 Guest Speaker Suggestions

Invite to class a financial consultant specializing in retirement counseling. Ask the guest to talk to students about preparing for retirement; retirement plans, such as 401(k), saving and investing, the Social Security system; and women and retirement.

Key to Ability Levels

Each section gives skill-building activities. Each activity has been labeled for use with students of various learning styles and abilities.

L1 Level 1 activities are basic activities and should be within the range of all students.

L2 Level 2 activities are average activities and should be within the range of average and above average students.

L3 Level 3 activities are challenging activities designed for the ability range of above average students.

School-Based Learning

Chapter Overview

This chapter prepares students to venture forth on their own.

Section 25-1 explores living arrangements for students to consider.

Section 25-2 encourages students to balance work, family, and community life.

Background Information

Write chapter objectives (Sections 25-1 and 25-2) on the chalkboard or use the chapter objective transparency for class discussion.

Choose assignments from the *Student Activity Workbook* and write them on the chalkboard.

Have students preview the chapter, looking at pictures, reading captions, and noting content headings. Ask students to describe what they expect to learn in this chapter.

As a study aid, have students outline the chapter using the chapter headings.

Preteaching Vocabulary

Write the Key Terms from Sections 25-1 and 25-2 on the chalkboard. Have students describe how each term relates to setting up a household and balancing work and family life.

502

Meeting SPECIAL Needs

Limited Proficiency in English

The telephone presents special obstacles to people who are not native speakers of English and prevents them from fully participating in the business world. Encourage non-native students to practice speaking on the phone. Encourage students to ask for clarification, saying, for example: "Would you mind repeating that last sentence, please?" or "Could you spell that name for me?"

Balancing Work and Personal Life

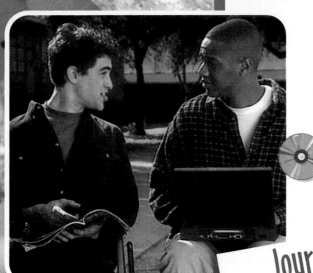

Section 25-1
Setting Up Your Own Household

Section 25-2
Managing Work, Family, and Community Life

In this video segment, see why it's important to plan for the future.

Journal
Personal Career Plan

After years of living with parents or other adults who have taken responsibility for you, you will soon be living on your own. What are the most exciting and interesting aspects of this change? Which aspects do you expect to find most difficult? Why? Write a journal entry describing your ideas and your feelings.

503

Addressing LEARNING Styles

All Learners

Have each student choose which learning style best suits him or her. Students may work individually or in teams to describe how they envision their balance among home, community, and career. Visual learners may work with musical learners to make a slide show with music; linguistic learners may write a short story; kinesthetic and interpersonal learners may create a diorama or produce a skit. Encourage teamwork whenever possible, but allow intrapersonal learners to pursue their own projects.

SECTION 25-1

Setting Up Your Own Household

OBJECTIVES

After studying this section, you will be able to:
- **Decide on a place to live.**
- **Organize your living space.**
- **Establish good housekeeping habits.**

KEY TERMS

commute
utilities
security deposit

You've planned your career, you've landed your first job, you've drawn your first paycheck. What's the next step? For many people, it's finding their own place to live. One of the most exciting decisions you'll ever make is choosing where you'll live.

To Move or Not to Move

Depending on your personal situation, you may be ready to move into a place of your own. Before settling on this plan, though, weigh the pros and cons of living at home.

As you may have guessed, living at home is much less expensive. Even if your parent(s), relative(s), or guardian(s) charge you room and board, you'll still probably be paying less than you would to rent an apartment. In addition, you won't have to buy your own furniture, and you can probably save money on food and laundry as well. On the negative side, living at home means you won't be able to make all your own decisions, and privacy may become a serious issue.

Now consider the pros and cons of having your own place. For most people, being more independent is the number one factor. The challenge of being on your own, the enjoyment of fixing up your own place, your sense of individual pride and responsibility— these are part of the joy of drawing a paycheck!

When you move into a place of your own, you accept new responsibilities and face new problems. It can be a stressful time. *How can your parents and friends help you through such a time?*

On the other hand, you'll have to pay the monthly rent, although you might reduce the expense by having roommates who will split the cost. Even good roommates, though, will complicate your life. The dwelling won't be yours alone. You'll have to adapt to other people's personalities and habits. *Figure 25-1* provides a questionnaire you might use to assess a potential roommate.

If you decide to move, choose the location carefully. These questions may help you evaluate possible areas:

- How far will I have to **commute,** or travel, to get to my job?
- Is the area safe?
- Is it close to public transportation?

Roommate Questionnaire

- Do you have a regular income?
- What hours do you work?
- When do you go to bed? Wake up?
- Do you drink alcohol?
- Do you smoke?
- Will you ever have friends or family staying with you? If so, who?
- Do you like to cook?
- Do you watch a lot of television? What programs? What hours?
- Do you listen to music much? If so, what kind(s) of music?

- Do you play a musical instrument? What kind(s) of music? Do you practice at home? If so, when?
- Do you have a pet or want one? If so, what kind?
- Do you enjoy time alone? If so, how much time and when?
- What kind of parties do you like to have and how often?
- What kind of housekeeper are you?
- How long do you think you'll want to share a place?

Figure 25-1 Learning details about a potential roommate before sharing an apartment is essential. Why would it be helpful to ask these questions even of someone you know?

Chapter 25 • Balancing Work and Personal Life **505**

Guided Practice
Teaching Strategies
1. Assign and review Section 25-1.
2. Use the transparency for this section.
3. Assign and review the Case Study.

Discussion Starter
Ask students to list the decisions their parents now make for them that they will have to make for themselves once they're on their own.

Teaching Tip
Collect enough home furnishings catalogs to give to several small groups. Assign students to groups and have each group list the furnishings they would need for a one-bedroom apartment (excluding a stove and refrigerator). Tell each group to use the catalog to select furnishings, list prices, and total costs. Have each group present its choices to the class. Discuss cost and ways of lowering costs, such as buying used furniture or renting furniture.

Critical Thinking
Have each student obtain a lease for an apartment and review its terms, noting his or her responsibilites and the landlord's responsibilities. Discuss in class.

▶ Extending Figure 25-1 ◀
Have students answer the questions in the figure. Does each think he or she would be a good roommate? Why or why not?

Caption Answer: Living with someone is different from just being friends. You may not have had the occasion to observe certain types of behavior or habits.

SCANS Foundation Skills Connection

L1 **Writing**

Ask each student to write a description of his or her ideal roommate. Tell students to consider personal qualities such as willingness to accept responsibility, neatness, and sociability.

L2 **Knowing How to Learn**

Tell each student to choose a city where he or she would like to live and work someday. Have them use maps, almanacs, books, and the Internet to learn about the city (for example, climate, businesses and industries, recreational opportunities, cost of a typical apartment, and general cost of living). Have students create profiles in table format.

L3 **Responsibility**

Have students list their current responsibilities. Then have each student create a bar graph or pie chart showing how he or she allocates time for each. Have them evaluate the percentage of their time that is spent on useful versus frivolous activities. Then have them discuss how allocation of time will change when they are living on their own.

- Is it close to my friends and family?
- Is it near places I go to for recreation and entertainment?

Money Matters

After you find a place you like, prepare a budget. Estimate how much you will have to spend each month to live on your own. You may want to review budgeting in Chapter 20.

Remember that the amount you budget needs to include more than the monthly rent. You may have to pay a monthly maintenance fee. You'll also have to pay for **utilities**—services for your dwelling, including the cost of electricity, gas or oil heat, and perhaps water. In addition, you will have telephone costs and probably cable TV costs.

You can't predict exactly how much your utility costs will be. Some may be included in your monthly rent, and heating and electricity costs can vary widely.

However, most utility companies can provide you with estimates based on other households in your neighborhood. Talk to your friends and neighbors, too, so that your monthly bills don't turn out to be an unpleasant surprise. Use your estimated monthly expenses as a guide to identify places you can afford.

Remember one of the most important elements you've learned about decision making—gather all the information you can. Before deciding on a place to live, inspect it thoroughly. *Figure 25-2* presents a useful checklist of things to look for.

When young people move into their first apartment, they often don't have a lot of money. *What can you do if you can't afford a place where you would feel comfortable and safe?*

Attitude Counts ✓

It's tough to be a good loser. You may not realize, though, that it's probably even more difficult—and certainly as important—to be a good winner. Although you feel like celebrating, remember to think about the people around you. Whatever else happens, be sure to avoid bragging about your good work or your good luck.

Extending the Illustration

Have students obtain copies of apartment rental publications for your area. Tell students to make a list of the features they want in an apartment and choose three apartments that interest them.

Caption Answer: You can get a roommate or stay in your parents' home while you save money or until you get a better-paying job.

Rental Property Checklist

Inside Areas

- Halls and stairways
  - _____ What condition are they in?
  - _____ Can you use them safely and conveniently when your arms are loaded with groceries?
  - _____ Does someone clean them regularly?
  - _____ Are there at least two exits?
- Cleanliness
  - _____ Is the apartment clean?
  - _____ Is the rental property clean?
- Room configuration
  - _____ Do you like the floor plan?
  - _____ Will there be enough privacy if you have a roommate?
- Storage
  - _____ Is there enough storage space?
  - _____ How many closets are there?
- Kitchen
  - _____ Do all appliances work?
  - _____ Do cabinet doors and drawers work?
  - _____ Is there enough space in the cabinets?
  - _____ Are the faucets and sink in good condition?
- Bathroom
  - _____ Is there a shower?
  - _____ Is there a bath?
  - _____ Are the faucets, sink, shower/bath in good condition?

- _____ Is there good water pressure?
- _____ Will there be plenty of hot water?
- Windows and screens
  - _____ Do the windows fit snugly and work smoothly?
  - _____ Do the windows have locks?
  - _____ Are there screens?
- Doors
  - _____ Are the doors sturdy and secure?
  - _____ Do they have deadbolts?
- Laundry facilities
  - _____ Are there washers and dryers in the building or in the complex?

Outside Areas

- Neighborhood
  - _____ Is it safe?
  - _____ Is it quiet?
  - _____ Is it clean?
- Parking
  - _____ Is there enough parking?
  - _____ Is parking convenient?
  - _____ Is the parking area safe?
- Safety
  - _____ Is the area around your building or complex well lighted?
  - _____ Is the general area safe at night?

Figure 25-2 Make copies of this checklist, and complete them as you visit different rental properties. Use the checklist to compare places that interest you. Which items are most important to you? Why?

Use it to compare places and to choose the one that's best for you.

When you're ready to sign on the dotted line, be sure you understand the following items:

- _Lease._ Usually, owners will ask you to sign a lease. This written agreement spells out the responsibilities

of the owner and _tenant_, or the person renting the property.

- _Rent and due date._ How much is the rent? When is it due? Is there a penalty for late payment?
- _Security deposit._ How much is the security deposit? A **security deposit** is money you pay the owner before

Chapter 25 • Balancing Work and Personal Life **507**

SCANS Workplace Competencies Connection

L1 Allocating Money

Tell students that they share an apartment with two other people. Rent is $525 a month. They share the following monthly costs: $58 for utilities, $20 for household supplies, and $270 for food. How much must each person contribute each month for communal expenses? ($291: $525 + $58 + $20 + $270 = $873 ÷ 3)

L2 Organizing and Maintaining Information

Over the next week, have students take an inventory of possessions they won't take with them when they're out on their own. Have them list items they'll need to purchase for an apartment and price them at a local store.

L3 Teaching Others

Divide students into groups. Have each person learn about adjustments people make when they move from their parents' home to live on their own by talking with friends or relatives who have made such a move. Tell group members to teach others in the group about adjusting to new living arrangements.

Teaching Attitude Counts ✓

Let students work with partners to role-play these "winning and losing" situations:

- you land the starring role in a play
- you are elected class president
- you get a great part-time job.

Have students discuss what they learned from these role-plays.

Extending Figure 25-2

Have students re-create this checklist in an electronic file so they will have it for future use. Ask students how using such a checklist will help them assess apartments.

Caption Answer: Answers will vary, depending on students' priorities.

Independent Practice

 Assign as homework the chapter activity in the *School-to-Work Activity Handbook*.

Reading

Have students look at apartment rental ads and choose three apartments that appeal to them. Have them call to find out the rent, estimated monthly utilities, and security deposit for each one.

Skills Practice

Paul pays $1.25 to wash and $1.00 to dry each load of laundry. If he does three loads a week, how much does he pay to do laundry? ($6.75: $1.25 + $1 = $2.25 × 3)

Pam wants to buy a comforter at $115, one flat and one fitted sheet at $28 each, two pillows at $19 each, and two pillowcases at $17 each. What is the total cost of the bedding? ($243: $115 + ($28 × 2) + ($19 × 2) + ($17 × 2))

Dexter has found a sofa and matching armchair on sale. The original prices are $579 for the sofa and $359 for the armchair. If both are marked down 35 percent, what is the total sale price? ($609.70: $579 + $359 = $938; $938 × 0.35 = $328.30; $938 − $328.30)

you move in; often, it's equal to one or two months' rent. The deposit is held to cover potential damage while you live in the dwelling. If no damage occurs, the security deposit should be returned to you when you move out.

- *Landlord's responsibilities.* Which repairs and maintenance jobs (such as cleaning hallways) are the landlord's responsibility? Which are your responsibility?

- *Utilities.* Are any of the utilities included in the monthly rent?

Settling In and Getting Connected

As soon as possible after signing your lease, measure the rooms and begin deciding where your furniture will go.

 On graph paper, draw a floor plan to scale of an apartment you'd like. Draw your pieces of furniture on separate sheets of paper so that you can move them around on the floor plan. *How will creating a scale model drawing of your apartment help save you time and trouble on moving day?*

Although moving is hard work, it can be fun. *What are some advantages in getting friends to help with the move?*

You might try drawing the rooms to scale on paper. For example, an inch on paper might equal a foot of floor space. By measuring your furniture and drawing it to scale, you can plan where the largest pieces will fit and decide on new items you'll need to buy.

You'll also have to make arrangements with your utility companies, telephone company, cable TV company, and so on to have services turned on. Call

508 *Unit 7 • Lifelong Learning*

Extending the Illustration

Have each student call a local company that rents vans or trailers. Have students decide what size vehicle they would need to move their things and learn how much it would cost to rent it for a day.

Caption Answer: A possible answer is that friends ease the stress of moving. The more people, the easier the move. Friends can help with decisions about where furniture, pictures, and so on look best.

each company as soon as you sign your lease. Tell their representatives when you want service to begin and schedule appointments so that you can be present when the service people arrive.

Don't forget to report your new address to the post office. Your mail will be forwarded to your new address, beginning on the date you specify. You might also want to get a stack of postcards from the post office and send your new address to family, friends, and business acquaintances.

Housekeeping Habits

What makes a household work on an everyday basis? Routines are a large part of the answer. One of the biggest favors you can do for yourself is to establish a few basic housekeeping habits.

At the top of the list—pay your bills on time. Most bills arrive with a due date, the date by which the payment must be received. Don't bury your bills under piles of other mail. Consider buying a file or bill holder so that envelopes don't get lost or forgotten. Paying your monthly bills on time not only gives you a good credit record (valuable when you need a loan), but it will also undoubtedly save

you money on late fees and credit card finance charges.

Set aside a small amount of time on a regular basis for housecleaning. If you wait until you need a bulldozer to straighten up your rooms, the job will seem much harder than it really is. You can raise the quality of your life a great deal by regularly seeing to such simple jobs as washing the dishes and sweeping the floor.

The same basic rule applies to doing the laundry. Don't wait until the pile looks like Mt. Everest. Doing a load of laundry every few days will not only keep your living space looking better, you'll actually have more choices of clothes to wear!

Cook healthful meals and try to eat at regular times. A steady diet of fast food will not only rob you of energy, but it will also cost much more than cooking for yourself. Keep a list handy of groceries and other household items you need to buy. Jot things down when you notice you need them. That way, you won't run out of necessary items, and when you shop for groceries, you'll know what you need and won't buy items you already have. You'll be surprised at how these few housekeeping routines can actually save you time and money.

SECTION 25-1 *Review*

Understanding Key Concepts

Using complete sentences, answer the following questions on a separate sheet of paper.

1. Which items on the checklist used to compare places to live are most important to you? Why?

2. Why should you call the utility, telephone, and cable TV companies as soon as you sign your lease?

3. Which housekeeping habits do you think are the easiest to maintain? Which ones may be more difficult?

Chapter 25 • Balancing Work and Personal Life **509**

Extending the Illustration

Have students obtain the floor plan of an apartment they would like to rent. Then have them use graph paper to plan how much and what types of furniture they would need for this apartment.

Caption Answer: You'll know where your things will fit. You can place them there immediately instead of moving them around.

SECTION 25-1 *Review* ANSWERS

1. Answers will vary. Students should give reasons for their choices.
2. Those companies will need time to initiate service at the new residence.
3. Answers will vary, but students should recognize the value of the habits.

SECTION 25-1

Writing: *Informational*

Have each student write a letter to a business, such as a bank or savings and loan institution, notifying the recipient that the student has a new address. Ask volunteers to share letters. Discuss the key information to include in such a letter.

Interview

Have each student write questions to interview a rental manager or agent of an apartment complex. Have them find out details such as specific restrictions (no pets), facilities (exercise room, laundry, etc.), if utilities are included, parking arrangement, and the amount of security deposit. Discuss findings in class.

ASSESS

Assessment

Process

Have students write about the processes they would follow in deciding future living arrangements, commenting on personal, financial, legal, and practical issues.

Evaluate students' papers for inclusion of appropriate actions taken for each aspect of deciding where and how to live.

Evaluation

Assign the section review.

ASSESS (cont'd.)

Reteaching

As you discuss the topics in this section, have students create their own checklists for questions they will need to answer in deciding where to live. Tell students to write the headings *Personal*, *Financial*, *Legal*, and *Practical* on one or two sheets of paper. Under each topic, have them write questions related to that topic. For example, under *Financial* they might write, "How much rent can I afford?"

Extending the Content

Assign the appropriate Chapter 25 activities in the *Student Activity Workbook*.

Different cities have landlord/tenant associations. If there is one in your area, have students interview a representative of the association. Tell students to ask about a landlord's and tenant's rights and responsibilities. Have students write 100-word summaries of their findings.

CLOSE

Have students complete this sentence: "I would (not) prefer to live with a roommate because . . . ." (Answers will vary.)

CASE STUDY

Exploring Careers: Public Service

Raymond C. Byrd
Police Officer

Q: How did you become a police officer?

A: When I went into the military, one of the choices the recruiter gave me was the opportunity to become a military police officer.

Q: Was the training for military police different from that for civilian police?

A: In the military, we spent more time on our combat role. In civilian training, we learned more about the law. We have to work within state, local, and federal laws, so we dealt more with that aspect of police work.

Q: What is your work like?

A: I'm assigned to the detective section of the department. I'm also the liaison officer for all the schools. I handle criminal calls in the schools, such as thefts or fights, but I'm also the school resource officer. I try to open myself up so the students know that they can talk to me and that I will do everything I can to protect them. I surprised them one day when

I was asked if I would give my life for them and I said I would.

Q: That's a pretty strong commitment to service.

A: I really do feel that value. It's a personal thing with me. I come from a military family. I wanted to be a soldier since I was five years old. There has never been a question that my life was for service. I think it's a mind-set you have to have to do this job.

Thinking Critically

Why are communication skills important to a police officer?

CAREER FACTS

Nature of the Work:
Answer phone calls about crime and accidents; take care of the paperwork related to those calls; work with the community.

Training or Education Needed:
Police academy training; ongoing training to update techniques; a bachelor's degree is often required in order to receive promotions.

Aptitudes, Abilities, and Skills:
Self-management skills; ability to learn; good judgment, honesty, and integrity.

Salary Range:
Approximately $1,500 to $3,000 a month to start; more with experience.

Career Path:
Start as a patrol officer; seek promotion through the ranks; may become a detective.

510 *Unit 7 • Lifelong Learning*

Extending the CASE STUDY

Answer: may need to give instructions to people in stressful situations when the people are not paying close attention; may need to calm people in criminal or accident situations; may need to deal with people of all backgrounds; may need to inspire trust and confidence in people

Further Application: Have students discuss what values they cherish. How are those values reflected in their career choices? The responses will vary depending on the student and the career choice. A paramedic may want to help save lives; a lawyer may want to ensure justice; a farmer may seek a more wholesome lifestyle.

Managing Work, Family, and Community Life

OBJECTIVES

After studying this section, you will be able to:

- **Describe ways of balancing your work life and your personal life.**
- **Identify some strategies for meeting family responsibilities.**
- **Identify some family-friendly employment practices.**
- **Participate in your community as a voter and as a volunteer.**

KEY TERM
register

A job can take up a good deal of your time and energy. However, just as you wouldn't eat only one kind of food, you shouldn't let one aspect of your life dominate all the others. Balance is as essential to your personal life as it is to your diet. Knowing how to balance your work and your personal life is key to successfully managing your career.

Enriching Your Personal Life

You have a responsibility to yourself as well as to your job. Fulfilling that personal responsibility can bring about the feeling of life success that you value most of all. Here's a good rule of thumb: No matter what happens at work, don't forget what you're working for.

Strive to balance your work life and your commitments to yourself, your family, friends, and the community. By doing so, you will be successful in reaching your career goals as well as your personal goals in life. The pressures of a job can sometimes seem to overshadow the other aspects of your life, but in the long run, the time you spend outside of work will prove at least as valuable as the time you spend on the job. The right balance will make you happier, healthier, and probably even more satisfied with your work.

Chapter 25 • Balancing Work and Personal Life **511**

Bell Ringer

Have students think about their lives and list what they'd like to have. Wants should include both tangibles and intangibles (good friends, a car, a good job, a top-notch computer, peace of mind).

Introducing the Section

Have students share their ideas from the Bell Ringer activity. Ask students how they would create a social life if they took a job in a city where they knew no one outside of work. Also discuss the added responsibilities created by marriage and children. Ask students to envision life several years in the future. How are they spending their time?

Motivational Activity
Critical Thinking

Tell students to imagine themselves married. Both husband and wife work and have a three-year-old child. Who takes care of her when they're at work? How do they spend time individually and as a family outside of work? Have students write 100-word papers describing how they would handle this situation.

Workforce 2000 Trends

In the 21st century, offices may disappear due to fax machines, modems, cell phones, and laptops. Employees will be able to work at home, in a hotel, or in their cars, yet all will have access to company files stored in a central database.

Implementing Teamwork

Divide the class into four teams and ask them to research college housing costs for four institutions: a community college, a state university, a private college, and an out-of-state university. Have each group develop a flyer to inform students of the costs for college housing.

Guided Practice

Teaching Strategies

1. Assign and review Section 25-2.
2. Use the transparency  for this section.

Discussion Starter

Ask students to identify their personal goals.

Teaching Tip

Discuss setting career goals and how the process can also be used for setting personal goals. Have students focus on what will make them happy. Remind them that writing down goals and the steps needed to accomplish them may help bring them to life.

Critical Thinking

Have students imagine they're attending a class reunion in 2010. Have students write 50-word paragraphs describing what they want to be able to say about themselves at a future high school reunion.

People must have time to play in order to remain mentally and physically healthy. *Why is it important to make time for physical activities such as soccer or dancing?*

Expand Your Circle of Friends

Since you spend so much time at work, you'll form friendships with coworkers. That's good, but you should also focus on developing friendships outside of work. This is a key to avoid keeping work at the center of your life. How can you expand your circle of friends?

Join a group. Get involved with an organization that interests you, such as an environmental association, arts group, or charity. Sign up for a sports league. Join a book group at a local bookstore. Take up a hobby or enroll in evening classes at a local community college.

Family Responsibilities

The biggest challenge for working parents is finding time for both work and home. They're torn between job responsibilities and the needs of their children. Life often becomes a delicate balancing act, and every hour can seem accounted for. When anything happens to upset the balance, there's a scramble to pick up the pieces. It can be tough on the parents and on the children. Magda Cosner knows about these difficulties.

Cosner is a Miami police officer. After returning to work from maternity leave, her schedule worked well—for a while. Now her department is going to change her schedule. "I'm going to have to start coming in at 6:30 in the morning instead of 8:30," Cosner explains. "That's going to cause a problem with the kids—they'll have to be up at 5:30. My husband's very helpful with the kids … but he's a police officer, too, and with my new schedule, we're not going to have a day off together anymore."

512   *Unit 7 • Lifelong Learning*

▶ Extending the Illustration

Have students allocate time for physical activities for one hour, three times a week. Tell them they work a 40-hour week and spend 45 minutes commuting to work each way. What other activities would students need to consider to balance their lives? (spending time with friends and family, doing household chores, or perhaps taking an evening class)

Caption Answer: Physical activities keep your body fit. They also provide an outlet for emotions and relieve stress.

There are no easy solutions to problems such as these. However, careful planning and communication are a start. They can enable families to build on the love for one another that is the foundation of their relationship.

People Need People

Everyone needs to share thoughts and feelings. The very act of talking and listening creates a bond between people and makes it easier to deal with problems. Make listening to the needs of your spouse or roommate a major priority. Communication is the key. Listen to what others have to say, what problems they're facing, what interests them. When work and other obligations present problems, keep the lines of communication open.

Be considerate of each other. Pay attention to the little things that can make life more pleasant for everyone in your household. This can mean anything from turning off lights to adjusting mealtimes. If you know that someone has a pet peeve, do what you can to avoid it.

Don't forget how good it feels to receive praise and encouragement. An enthusiastic word goes a long way toward keeping a relationship strong.

Children have many needs. They need to be fed, clothed, bathed, taken to activities, and helped with homework. That's just part of it. They need to be loved, and love takes time and energy. Make time for talking, playing, and being together.

Caring for children's emotional needs is as important as caring for their physical needs. *Why is it important for parents to play with their children every day, not just on weekends?*

 SCANS Foundation Skills Connection

L1 Listening

Have students talk to at least three adults whose opinions they respect and ask what advice each would give regarding a career search. Have students take notes and write summaries of comments for their career journals.

L2 Reasoning

Ask students whether they have ever participated in a school money-making project (a bake sale or car wash). In what ways are school-based efforts similar to money-making activities of community organizations? Why are these types of activities necessary?

L3 Responsibility

Ask students whether they keep informed about what's going on at school and in their community. How do they stay informed? How could they become more active citizens regarding school or community? Ask students how staying informed about activities affecting an employer might help them on the job. Tell students to summarize their thoughts in a paragraph or two.

Extending the Illustration

Have students visit a day care center and spend at least an hour observing the children. What needs do children have that would be their responsibility as parents? (physical care, learning and emotional development)

Caption Answer: Children need to play to be happy and healthy. Playtime must not be limited to weekends.

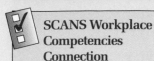

☑ **SCANS Workplace Competencies Connection**

L1 Monitoring and Correcting Performance

Tell students to think about a good friend. In what ways does he or she demonstrate friendship? Is there anything he or she could do to be a better friend? What do friendships add to students' lives?

L2 Negotiating to Arrive at a Decision

Working in pairs, have students brainstorm the types of issues that have to be negotiated when both members of a couple have a career. What compromises might need to be made? (For example, what would happen if one person had the opportunity to advance by moving to another city, but the other person was successful staying put?) What factors might be important to each person?

L3 Exercising Leadership

Ask students whether they think it's possible to work from home and produce quality work. Or do they think people who work at home produce less? Have them write one or two paragraphs justifying their positions.

514

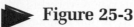

Figure 25-3

Balancing Your Job and Family Responsibilities

Putting extra effort into balancing work and family responsibilities will undoubtedly lead to greater personal satisfaction.

A Be realistic. Accept the fact that you will have to make compromises in your job and in your family life in order to make time for both.

B Share family duties and household chores so that no one person has to do them all.

C Don't overschedule your nonwork time. Allow for free time to spend doing something you enjoy with your family.

A Balancing Act

There are no easy rules for balancing your responsibilities to your job and to your family. Everyone's situation is different. However, *Figure 25-3* provides a few hints that you can apply in your own way.

▶ Extending Figure 25-3 ◀

Have students interview their parents to learn how they balance work and family responsibilities. Tell students to ask for tips they can use in their own lives, even though they may not yet be balancing work and personal relationships.

Addressing Workplace Diversity

Family-oriented diversity programs often treat men as second-class members; they tend to emphasize women's roles in parenting. Companies that want to relieve gender tension take care that programs aimed at the concerns of families consider males.

Help from Employers

You might think your company is the last place to look for help in managing your family life. In fact, employers are realizing that it is to their benefit to help families. Studies show that employees who are under less family stress are more loyal and more productive. What kind of help do employers offer? Benefits vary from company to company, but here are a few:

- *Flextime.* You can work the schedule that's best for you and your family.

- *On-site day care.* It's sometimes easier to bring children to work with

E Don't build up resentment. Do at least some of the things you want to do.

Tot Care

D Keep your promises. If you say you'll be somewhere or do something, stick to your word.

Chapter 25 • Balancing Work and Personal Life **515**

Independent Practice

Reading

Have each student find and read an article on the most desirable employers. Business and general interest magazines frequently publish such rankings. Have each student make a chart identifying the reasons why at least five of the companies were chosen. Have students discuss the companies in class. Would students want to work for one of these companies? Why or why not?

Discussion Starter

Write the word *compromise* on the chalkboard and ask students to suggest definitions. Remind students that compromise is a human-relations skill—a way of getting along with others. Compromising is also a way of balancing job and family responsibilities.

Research

Have students research the best places to live in the U.S. The public library should have references that rate U.S. cities on livability. Have students write 200-word reports describing the criteria used, choosing one location that interests them. Tell students to give reasons for their choice.

▶ Extending the Illustration

(see illustration on page 516)

Have each student contact a local day care center and find out what it costs for a week. What are the hours of operation? What is the youngest age accepted? Is the group licensed? What are the requirements to become licensed?

Caption Answer: When parents know their children are nearby, they worry less about their welfare; parents' stress is reduced so that they can better attend to their jobs.

Skills Practice

Divide students into groups of three or four. Have groups discuss the stress that may result from trying to balance work and family responsibilities. Have each group brainstorm ways to relieve stress.

Research

Have students choose two environmental careers to research. Ask students what role citizens play in taking care of the environment.

Discussion Starter

Ask students how many of them followed the most recent local election. Had they been old enough, would they have voted in that election? Why or why not?

Writing: *Persuasion*

Tell students that voting patterns show that older people are far more likely to vote than people in their twenties. Ask students why they think younger people fail to vote. How could they be encouraged to do so? Have students write 100-word messages to their peers persuading them to follow political issues and vote.

 On-site day care centers are one of the most popular employee benefits for working parents. ***How do such day care centers help parents concentrate on their jobs?***

YOU'RE THE BOSS!

Solving Workplace Problems

You want to promote an employee to manage your plumbing business. You've narrowed your choice to two good workers: one is an older man with years of experience but only moderate people skills; the other is a young, less-experienced plumber who's unusually good at dealing with people. Which employee will you choose? Why?

you than to take them elsewhere. You can also visit them during your breaks or at lunchtimes.

- *Family-friendly training for managers.* Many companies train their managers to be sensitive to the family needs of their staff. As a result, you may find it easier to make special arrangements to balance your job responsibilities and your family's needs.

Your Responsibilities as a Citizen

As you move into the world of work and get your own place to live, your responsibilities as a citizen will grow. You'll be a working adult, a taxpayer, and a voter.

Being Informed

As a citizen, your community is your responsibility. You need to stay informed on issues and events.

Read the newspaper. Listen to radio and television news reports. Talk to your neighbors to learn what they think about issues. The SCANS skills of reading, listening, and speaking and the SCANS competencies of acquiring and using information will help you as a citizen. Then you can put your knowledge to work by voting.

Voting

Voting is your most important obligation as a citizen. Your vote helps decide who our leaders will be and what laws we will live by. Don't let other people make these decisions for you.

Teaching YOU'RE THE BOSS!

Possible responses: the older man, because he would be offended and might even quit if a less experienced employee were promoted; or the younger man, because his people skills will make him a good manager

Extending the Illustration

Have students discuss why they should be informed about local, state, and national issues. Ask them how politicians' decisions affect their lives. (Voting allows citizens to influence who gets to make the political decisions.)

Caption Answer: Answers will vary. Guide students in a discussion of the importance of everyone voting.

Before you can vote, you must be at least 18 years old and **register,** or officially sign up as a qualified voter. Methods for registering vary from place to place. To find out how it is done in your area, call the League of Women Voters, your county election commission, or the county registrar's office. Any of these sources can tell

 To cast an informed vote, you have to prepare for an election by learning about the candidates and issues. *How important is your vote? Will it matter in an election in which thousands or millions of people vote? Explain.*

EXCELLENT BUSINESS PRACTICES

Career Management

To help its 40,000 employees maintain a high level of skill awareness, Chicago-based Amoco Corporation has a career management program.

Employees go through a self-assessment process to identify their skills, establish goals, and add competencies. They work with team leaders to focus on career planning and to create an individual development plan.

The company has an interactive database that lists jobs available in the worldwide organization. Employees can review and apply for jobs electronically from their own computers. The database also provides information about emerging skills and competencies.

The program allows individuals to align their abilities and aspirations with company

requirements and strategic planning. Together, employees and management share the responsibility of preparing for the future.

Thinking Critically

What are the advantages of a career management program?

Chapter 25 • *Balancing Work and Personal Life* 517

SECTION 25-2

Discussion Starter

Ask students how they'd react if local officials asked citizens to vote for a one percent increase in local income tax in order to build new government offices.

After discussing the issue, tell students that since the school system is operating in the red, an increase in property taxes will also be placed on the ballot. What would students decide?

Research

Tell students that as citizens, they have the right to express their views to lawmakers. Have students create charts identifying elected officials representing them. Tell them to include local officials, and state and federal representatives, writing each person's name, position, party affiliation, telephone and fax numbers, address, and E-mail address. Tell students to update charts when new elections are held.

For students who have access to computers, suggest that they create a database for elected officials.

Extending EXCELLENT BUSINESS PRACTICES

Answer: If employees' skills are up-to-date, time can be saved in on-the-job training, employee self-confidence will be high, employees can more easily move up in the organization and be prepared for new responsibilities.

Further Application: Have students review the classified section of the Sunday edition of a major city newspaper. Ask them to choose a page or two of the help-wanted ads and note the requirements for jobs being advertised. Then have students make a list of 25 separate skills included in those requirements.

Assessment

Content

Have students write a paragraph on each of these topics: how to create a personal life, issues to consider in balancing job and family responsibilities, your rights and responsibilities as a citizen.

Evaluate students' paragraphs for an understanding of the need for personal and professional relationships and the role of citizens as voters, taxpayers, and community members.

Evaluation

Assign the section review.

MINI QUIZ

Short Answer

1. Services for electricity, gas, and perhaps water are called ____ costs. (utility)

2. Signing a ____ obligates you to pay rent on specified dates. (lease)

3. A ____ is usually equal to one or two months' rent. (security deposit)

4. Among benefits some employers offer are ____, on-site day care, and family-friendly training for managers. (flextime)

5. Your responsibilities as a citizen include paying taxes, ____, and participating in your community. (voting)

---

you how, when, and where you can go to register and what documents you'll need to take along.

Doing Your Part

Actively participating in your community is not only a responsibility, it's also a way to genuinely enrich your life. By engaging in volunteer work, you'll widen your circle of friends, learn new skills, and make your community a better place in which to live.

How can you get involved? Think of the activities you enjoy and the concerns that are important to you. Call the organizations that promote those activities and ask if they offer volunteer opportunities. Talk to people, ask questions, attend some meetings. Just remember that whether you're interested in restoring old buildings, reading to the blind, or coaching basketball, you've got a lot to give.

One Final Word: Give It All You've Got!

Whatever career you follow, whatever your family situation, live as fully as you can. Your job and your loved ones may

Career Do's & Don'ts

When Designing Your Life's Path...

Do:
- take charge of your life.
- ask for more responsibilities in your current position and seek ways to change your role in the organization.
- Volunteer to participate in team projects or short-term tasks.
- regularly update your goals.

Don't:
- be afraid to take a lower level job at another company or in another industry if you're unhappy with your present position.
- be satisfied with your work because it's easy for you to do.
- doubt yourself.
- stop challenging yourself.

take you to places you can't even imagine now. Above all, enjoy what you do. At work and at home, you get out of life as much as you put into it.

SECTION 25-2 *Review*

Understanding Key Concepts

Using complete sentences, answer the following questions on a separate sheet of paper.

1. How can making time for yourself make you more productive at work?

2. Why should you treat time scheduled with your family with the same importance as you treat work?

3. Why are people frequently more productive when they work for a family-friendly company?

SECTION 25-2 *Review* ANSWERS

1. It will relieve stress and help you get a fresh perspective so that you can approach your work with a positive attitude and increased energy.

2. You may create family problems that will impact all aspects of your life.

3. Family-friendly companies allow workers to better manage family situations. As a result, employees work more effectively because they have fewer domestic worries.

Key Terms

commute *(p. 505)*
utilities *(p. 506)*
security deposit *(p. 507)*

SECTION 25-1 Summary

- Setting up your own household is a major life change. Before moving out, be sure that staying at home for a while isn't better for you.

- Staying home will cost less, but in your own place, you'll have more independence and pride of ownership.

- If you have roommates, you'll have lower rent payments, but you'll have to adapt to other people.

- Prepare a budget to estimate how much you'll have to spend on your own place.

- Choose a location that fits your needs, values, and budget.

- Make your life easier by establishing some good house-keeping habits.

 Use the Testmaker to create a customized test for Chapter 25.

Reteaching

1. Draw a circle on the chalkboard and divide it into three equal sections: *Work, Personal Life, Citizenship.* Discuss each section. (For example, work takes up a significant part of our lives. Personal relationships and family bring happiness. Being a good citizen means voting and participating in the community.) Redraw the lines to make one section much larger than others to convey imbalance. Stress the need to balance various aspects of one's life.

2. Assign and review vocabulary terms, chapter questions, and activities from the Chapter Review.

Key Term

register *(p. 517)*

SECTION 25-2 Summary

- Balance your work time and your personal time.
- Develop friends outside of work by joining groups.
- Fulfilling responsibilities to both your job and your family can be difficult. Communication is the key. A few rules of thumb include being realistic, sharing family duties, and keeping your promises.
- Employers sometimes help people manage their family lives by offering flexible work schedules and on-site day care centers.
- Voting is a citizen's most important duty. Before you can vote, you must register.
- Participate in your community by joining volunteer organizations.

Extending the Content

 Assign the appropriate Chapter 25 activities in the *Student Activity Workbook*.

Have each student choose a local volunteer organization and interview the person who leads it. Tell students to ask about the person's ideas regarding community service and why he or she volunteers. Have students share their findings in class.

CLOSE

See the Unit Closure and Unit Evaluation located on page 481.

Chapter 25 • Balancing Work and Personal Life **519**

Computer Activity

Using a database software package, have students create a listing of non-profit organizations or special-interest clubs in your community. Ask students to find at least two organizations or clubs for each of these categories: youth-related, civic, religious, professional development, and artistic. Once the database is created, have them sort by subject and print a directory of information.

Answers
Reviewing Key Terms

Paragraphs will vary but should include all the key terms.

Recalling Key Concepts

1. True
2. False: Many housekeeping chores are best done in small increments throughout the week.
3. False: Your responsibilities to yourself and to your family are as important as your responsibilities to your job.
4. True
5. False: Your responsibilities also include keeping informed about issues and being involved in your community.

Thinking Critically

1. If you can't get along or put up with each other's habits and behavior, living together will be difficult.
2. Answers will vary. Students should give reasons for their choices.
3. Possible answers: It makes work the center of your life. If friendships at work go sour, you don't have another support group to rely on.
4. Your life will be thrown out of balance. Spending time with family and friends may give you a perspective on work and will probably make you

Reviewing Key Terms

On a separate sheet of paper, write a paragraph describing how you will handle finding and living in your own place. Use the terms below in your paragraph.

commute   security deposit
utilities   register

Recalling Key Concepts

On a separate sheet of paper, tell whether each statement is true or false. Rewrite any false statements to make them true.

1. There are some advantages to living at home for a while after graduating from high school.
2. It's wiser to leave all housekeeping chores for the weekend.
3. Your responsibilities at work are the most important ones you have.
4. Having coworkers as friends is good, but you should try to have friends outside of work too.
5. Your only responsibility as a citizen is to vote.

Thinking Critically

Using complete sentences, answer each of the questions below on a separate sheet of paper.

1. Why should you carefully evaluate anyone whom you are considering as a roommate?
2. Which is most important to you when choosing a place to live—being close to work, the amount of the rent, or living in a safe neighborhood? Why?

3. What's wrong with making friends from work the center of your social life?
4. When a job takes up a good deal of your time, why is it especially important to schedule time with your family and friends?
5. Why do you need to be well informed to fulfill your responsibility as a voter?

SCANS Foundation Skills and Workplace Competencies

Basic Skills: *Knowing How to Learn*

1. Imagine that a proposition is on the ballot for the next election. The proposition calls for a special tax to support state parks. What are three sources of information you might use to form your decision about how to vote on this issue?

Resources: *Allocating Money*

2. You have take-home pay of $1,600 per month. You have a monthly car payment of $150. Your car insurance is $650 every six months. Estimate additional expenses for food, entertainment, clothes, gas and repairs for your car, laundry, and so on. (Refer to Figure 20-2 for any expense categories you may have forgotten.) Base your estimates on your actual spending habits. Use these figures to create a personal budget. Use the budget to figure out how much you can afford to spend on rent and utilities each month.

happier, healthier, and more satisfied with work.

5. If you're not informed, you won't know which candidates and issues to vote for.

SCANS Foundation Skills and Workplace Competencies

1. Possible answers: newspaper reports and editorials; friends or neighbors who

are informed on the issue; an organization, such as a conservation group or a state park association

2. Answers will vary, depending on students' estimated personal expenses. Estimated expenses should be realistic, and all relevant expenses should be accounted for.

Connecting Academics to the Workplace

Math

1. You and your roommate have just rented an apartment together. The only furniture you have is bedroom furniture, which you each brought from home. You each have $500 to contribute toward furnishing the new apartment. What should you buy? Make a list of items you need. Then go shopping to find the best prices on those items. Finally, select the items you need most and can afford to buy right now.

Social Studies

2. Sandra has recently taken a job that requires her to move to your city. Except for her new coworkers, she doesn't know anyone there. She has decided she will join an organization or club in order to make new friends. Sandra enjoys dancing, photography, and art. What organizations might she join? Do research to find those related to her interests.

Developing Teamwork and Leadership Skills

Work as a team with three or four classmates. Individually, choose a firm in your area where you might like to work. Then imagine that you and the members of your team have decided to become roommates. Divide up responsibilities and search for a place to live. Estimate your income.

Determine a location and the cost of an actual place. Find out how much it will cost to move in. Interview the landlord to obtain realistic estimates on utility costs.

Real-World Workshop

Imagine that you and a classmate have decided to become roommates. Role-play an interview with each other. Use the checklist shown in Figure 25-1 as a basis for the interview. Then decide if you would get along as roommates.

School-to-Work Connection

Make a list of your interests and hobbies. Then identify a local organization or club that reflects your interests. Visit the organization and talk with some members. Then write your reaction to the group. Tell whether this is a group that you would be interested in joining. Could it be a source of new friendships?

Individual Career Plan

How ready are you to move into an apartment of your own? First, make a list of the furnishings you now have that you could take with you. Then make a second list of all the things you would need to get to move into an unfurnished apartment. Assume that the apartment has a stove and refrigerator. Don't forget items such as pots and pans, dinnerware, silverware, towels, sheets, and so on.

Chapter 25 • Balancing Work and Personal Life **521**

Developing Teamwork and Leadership Skills

Teams should identify an actual place to live. The location should be based on criteria discussed in the text and should take into account where each roommate will work. The place chosen should be affordable in terms of their projected incomes.

Real-World Workshop

Students should have candid discussions with their classmates to determine whether they would be compatible as roommates.

School-to-Work Connection

Answers will vary, depending on the organizations students select. Students should explain what they do or do not like about the organizations, whether they would be interested in joining, and whether the organizations could be a source of new friendships.

Individual Career Plan

Answers will vary, depending on what items students may already have. The list should include furniture and other items needed in a kitchen, bathroom, bedroom, or living room.

Connecting Academics to the Workplace

1. Answers will vary, depending on students' priorities and local prices. They should shop around to find the best prices. Most students will probably settle for a dining table and chairs, a couch, and perhaps an easy chair.

2. Answers will vary, depending on students' research and the types of organizations in their city. Possibilities include a singles social group, a camera club, and a museum volunteer group.

Aspects of Industry: Community Issues

Students who are fairly sure of their future careers may use the Labs to investigate all the aspects of industry for one career. Other students may want to investigate a different job cluster with each Lab.

STEP A

As previously stated, students may select jobs by brainstorming with other students, or research the possibilities in the *Occupational Outlook Handbook (OOH)* or other career references.

Encourage students to look at how seemingly disparate career clusters and individual jobs actually relate and overlap. Encourage students to make their groups of individuals whose chosen jobs for this Lab may seem diverse but actually complement each other. This kind of thinking will help them in the future to survive when their jobs disappear or they feel they need to change jobs.

STEP B

Have students brainstorm in class the questions they will ask community leaders. Emphasize that the person they are interviewing is more likely to give them in-depth answers if their questions are based on solid research. Each person will want to know that the students understand the industry and the issues they are asking about.

Emphasize that students' attitudes to everyone they talk to should be respectful and non-confrontational, even if the

ASPECTS OF INDUSTRY:
Community Issues

Overview

In Unit Seven, you learned about how changes may affect your work life, and about balancing your work and personal lives. In this Unit Lab, you will use what you have learned about change and balance while exploring another aspect of industry: **Community Issues.**

Like people, businesses interact with the communities around them. Their factories may be eyesores to the people living near them, their wastes may pollute the air and water. If a company is a major employer in a community, the community may be crippled if the company closes. On the other hand, industries may contribute to the health of a community through fund-raising, donations, or education programs. Conversely, the community—people who live near the business, other businesses, community organizations, and government—also affects industries.

522

Tools

1. Internet
2. Trade and business magazines
3. News magazine
4. Newspapers

Procedures

STEP A

Choose a career that interests you from the 15 job clusters outlined in Figure 3-1 in Chapter 3. Working with two or more classmates who have chosen careers in your job cluster or have chosen related jobs in other clusters, brainstorm positive and negative ways industries and communities interact. For example: pollution, poor employee benefits, or financial help following natural disasters.

Using the Internet and trade, business, and news publications, examine how your chosen industry could affect the community. How do decisions made by government, social and environmental organizations, and other businesses affect your industry?

STEP B

As a team, interview a community leader such as a city councilperson, an environmental affairs expert, or social services specialist.

students' personal views differ from those of the person they are interviewing. Remind students that every industry has its strengths and weaknesses; each is made up of organizations that are made up of individuals. Each industry can have positive or negative impacts on a community.

You may want to have students role-play the interviews with members of each team playing the interviewee and interviewer, using information obtained from their library research.

STEP C

To help students prepare for their business interviews, you might want to have them discuss in class the information they got from

Using the information you obtained from your library research, develop questions to get the person's perspective on how your chosen industry affects the community, both positively and negatively. Also ask how the larger community—government, other industries, and organizations—affects the industry.

Try to balance your questions so that you see both positive and negative sides to the industry. The responses will probably vary according to whom you interview.

STEP C

Next, as a team interview a business person in your chosen industry. You should not choose someone you have already interviewed. Explain that you are doing a class project and want to ask how the particular business deals with environmental, cultural, and social concerns in the community.

Based on your library research and previous interviews, develop questions that address both the positive and negative influences of the industry on the community.

Businesspeople may be sensitive to questions about the negative impact of their industry on the community. Be sure you ask about the positive impacts as well.

As always, dress appropriately, be prompt and courteous, and follow up the appointment with a thank-you note.

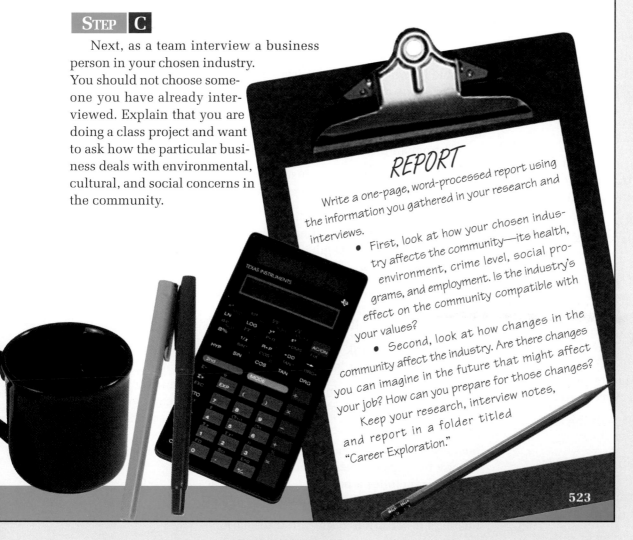

REPORT

Write a one-page, word-processed report using the information you gathered in your research and interviews.

- First, look at how your chosen industry affects the community—its health, environment, crime level, social programs, and employment. Is the industry's effect on the community compatible with your values?
- Second, look at how changes in the community affect the industry. Are there changes you can imagine in the future that might affect your job? How can you prepare for those changes?

Keep your research, interview notes, and report in a folder titled "Career Exploration."

523

their previous interviews with community leaders. What kinds of issues seemed to come up repeatedly in their interviews? If your community has particular concerns about education, job losses, crime, or pollution, you may want to have students focus on these issues in their interviews. It will help students explain their purpose more fully to the persons if they

can say, "We are studying how local industries can affect the issue of crime," or unemployment or pollution. If there are several areas of concern among community leaders, you might want to break the class into groups, each group focusing on one concern and how their chosen industry can influence that concern.

Encourage students to think locally. Encourage them to look at how small local decisions—where to place a park, where to place stoplights, repairing roads—can all affect local businesses, and the jobs they provide. Students should look at their jobs in the larger context of the community.

Report

A person's enjoyment of his or her work may be affected by whether or not an industry's values are compatible with an employee's. This is not often something a person considers when starting out in the working world. Yet students should be aware that compatibility of values can contribute to long-term happiness in a field.

Students should also be aware that changes in the larger community can affect an industry and cause job losses. In the 1980s, for example, a slowdown in the economy and high interest rates meant fewer houses were being built. This in turn contributed to a slowdown in the lumber industry of the Northwest and many job layoffs. Students should be aware of how sensitive their industries—and their jobs—are to changes they cannot control. You might want to have students discuss in class the ways their chosen industries can be affected by change beyond their control.

Glossary

A

ability　A skill a person has already developed. (p. 36)

access　To find and use information. (p. 367)

active listening　Listening with full attention. (p. 300)

addiction　The physical or psychological need for a substance. (p. 217)

affirmative action　Action to give those who have suffered discrimination a fair chance. (p. 238)

agenda　A list of items to be addressed at a meeting. (p. 288)

allowances　Deductions. (p. 464)

analogy　A problem-solving strategy in which a person says one thing is like another in order to suggest a solution. (p. 328)

annual percentage rate (APR)　The amount of interest for one year, expressed as a percentage. (p. 431)

application fee　An amount of money charged to apply for a loan. (p. 430)

application letter　A cover letter that accompanies a résumé. (p. 125)

apprentice　Someone who learns how to do a job through hands-on experience under the guidance of a skilled worker. (p. 99)

aptitude　One's potential for learning a certain skill. (p. 36)

arbitration　A hearing at which both sides present evidence and witnesses to an arbitrator, who issues a written decision, just as a judge or jury would do. (p. 245)

arrogance　An excessive display of self-regard. (p. 201)

assertiveness　The confident presentation of oneself and one's abilities. (p. 200)

assumptions　Beliefs a person takes for granted. (p. 328)

attitude　A person's basic outlook on life. (p. 194)

audience　One or more persons who receive information. (p. 297)

B

bait and switch　The fraudulent practice of advertising a bargain item that is not available for sale in the advertiser's store; when customers arrive, a salesperson tries to talk them into a more expensive item. (p. 390)

beneficiary　The person who receives a benefit from an insurance company. (p. 439)

benefit　Money paid by an insurance company for a loss or some occurrence. (p. 439)

block style　A style of written communication in which all lines begin at the left margin. (p. 308)

body language　The posture, gestures, and eye contact people use to express themselves nonverbally. (p. 136)

brainstorm　To think creatively without evaluating ideas until later. (p. 327)

budget　A plan for saving and spending money based on one's income and expenses. (p. 398)

business cycle　The movement of the economy from good times to bad and back to good; includes a peak or boom, a contraction, a trough, and an expansion. (p. 384)

business description　Specific information about a business's product(s), location, employees, and competitors. (p. 80)

C

cafeteria plan A plan that allows employees to choose the benefits they want. (p. 167)

career A series of related jobs built on a foundation of interest, knowledge, training, and experience. (p. 5)

cash-value life insurance Part insurance and part investment, in which you can borrow money against the total amount of premiums paid on a cash-value life insurance policy. (p. 452)

cause and effect What happened and what made it happen. (p. 299)

certificate of deposit (CD) A type of investment in which a person deposits a specific amount of money for a fixed amount of time at a stated interest rate. (p. 419)

check register A small booklet that allows one to keep track of the money in one's checking account. (p. 426)

chronological résumé A résumé organized in reverse time order. (p. 122)

civil law The type of law that pertains to arguments in which one person (or company) claims that another person (or company) has violated rights or neglected responsibilities. (p. 242)

claim An oral or written notice given to an insurance company to collect for a loss or a certain occurrence. (p. 439)

coinsurance The percentage of major medical expenses that a policyholder is required to pay. (p. 449)

cold call A blind telephone call, or a call that is not the result of a lead or a referral, that is made to discover whether there is a job opening or to gain a contact. (p. 116)

collateral An asset such as a house or a car that could be taken by the lender if a loan is not repaid as promised. (p. 430)

collective bargaining Using the power of numbers (the workers in a union) to negotiate for better wages, increased benefits, better safety rules, and other job improvements. (p. 236)

collision insurance Insurance that covers damage to a policyholder's car caused by an accident. (p. 444)

commission Earnings based on how much a worker sells. (p. 165)

communication The exchange of information between senders and receivers. (p. 296)

commute To travel to and from one's job. (p. 505)

company culture The behavior, attitudes, values, and habits of the employees and owners of a company that are unique to that particular company. (p. 156)

comparison and contrast The pointing out of similarities and differences. (p. 299)

compensatory time Paid time off from work, instead of cash, in exchange for working overtime. (p. 235)

compounded Paid interest on money originally invested and also on any interest that has already been added. (p. 418)

comprehensive insurance Insurance that covers damage to a policyholder's car for reasons other than a collision. (p. 444)

compromise To settle a dispute by having each party give up something. (p. 268)

Glossary

confidentiality The keeping of secrets from people who are not supposed to know them. (p. 185)

conflict resolution A problem-solving strategy for settling disputes. (p. 268)

consequence An effect or outcome. (p. 319)

constructive criticism Criticism presented in a way that can lead to learning and growth. (p. 204)

consume To buy and use goods and services. (p. 381)

consumer fraud Dishonest business practices used by people trying to trick or cheat consumers. (p. 389)

consumers Individuals who buy and use goods and services. (p. 381)

contact list A list of people one knows and will contact to build a network. (p. 113)

contingency fee A lawyer's fee based on a percentage of the amount of money that a client wins in a court case. (p. 248)

continuing education Programs offered by high schools, colleges, and universities that are geared toward adult students. (p. 101)

convenience benefits Fringe benefits that make workers' lives easier. (p. 167)

cooperativeness A willingness to work well with everyone on the job to reach a common goal. (p. 174)

cooperative program A program combining school and work in which a local employer teams with a school, hiring students to perform jobs that are taught in school classes. (p. 54)

copayment The amount of money an HMO member pays for each service from a health-care provider. (p. 450)

copyright The legal right of authors or other creators of works to control the reproduction and use of their works. (p. 350)

corporation A business owned by people who buy part of, or shares in, the company. (p. 79)

coverage Losses or events that an insurance company will insure against. (p. 439)

cover letter A letter a job seeker sends along with a résumé to introduce the job seeker to an employer. (p. 125)

credit A sum of money a person can use before having to reimburse the credit lender. (p. 429)

credit application A form that a person must complete when seeking credit; it asks for details about the person's job, salary, bank account(s), and credit history. (p. 432)

credit bureau An agency that collects information on how promptly people and businesses pay their bills. (p. 432)

credit card A card usually issued by a bank or other financial institution that allows the holder to charge amounts of purchases in many different places. (p. 429)

credit limit The maximum amount of money a person can charge against an account. (p. 429)

credit rating An estimate made by a credit bureau that tells how likely an individual is to pay his or her bills. (p. 432)

credit union A not-for-profit financial institution similar to a bank; people who belong share a common bond. (p. 418)

criminal law The type of law under which the government charges an individual or organization with committing a crime. (p. 246)

criteria Standards of judgment. (p. 318)

cross-functional team   A group of people from two or more departments or areas of expertise who work together toward a common business goal. (p. 278)

customer relations   The use of communication skills to meet the needs of business customers or clients. (p. 296)

D

data   Information, knowledge, ideas, facts, words, symbols, figures, statistics. (p. 34)

database   A software program in which information is stored in tables and can be sorted and combined in different ways. (p. 345)

decision-making process   A logical series of steps used to identify and evaluate possibilities and arrive at a workable choice. (p. 24)

deductible   The portion of the cost of a loss that an insurance policyholder pays before the insurance company pays the remaining cost. (p. 439)

deduction   An expense, such as certain medical or business costs, that taxpayers are allowed to subtract from their income when figuring the amount of tax they must pay. (p. 467)

defensiveness   The guarding of oneself emotionally against negative opinions. (p. 205)

defined-benefit plan   A type of pension plan that provides a fixed amount of money at a person's retirement. (p. 421)

defined-contribution plan   A type of pension plan in which the employer contributes a set amount of money to the plan each year. (p. 421)

delegating   Assigning tasks to other people. (p. 364)

deliberate   Purposeful. (p. 243)

dependent   Someone, such as a child, who relies on another person for support. (p. 465)

depression   A very serious recession, or downturn in the economy. (p. 384)

desktop publishing   The use of computers and special software to create professional-looking printouts; uses include reports, brochures, newsletters, invitations, and greeting cards. (p. 346)

directory   A special computer file that contains the names of a group of files on a broad topic; also called a folder. (p. 370)

disabilities   Conditions that include visual or hearing impairment, mental illness, or paralysis. (p. 238)

disabled worker   Someone who cannot work because of a physical or mental condition. (p. 472)

discrimination   Unequal treatment based on such factors as race, religion, nationality, gender, age, or physical appearance. (p. 237)

disputes   Disagreements. (p. 242)

distributing   Making goods and services available, such as by selling or delivering, to the people who need or want them. (p. 380)

diversity   Variety. (p. 269)

dividend   A portion of a fund or an organization's profits. (p. 419)

down payment   The amount of money paid at the time something is purchased through an installment loan. (p. 430)

downsizing   The elimination of jobs in a company to promote efficiency or to cut costs. (p. 485)

downtime   Periods of time when nothing is scheduled. (p. 362)

drug-testing programs   Programs designed to detect illegal drug use. (p. 218)

Glossary

E

economics The study of how a group produces, distributes, and uses its goods and services. (p. 380)

economic system A country's way of using resources to provide the goods and services people want and need. (p. 380)

economy The ways in which a group produces, distributes, and consumes its goods and services. (p. 11)

E-mail Electronic mail; messages sent from computer to computer. (p. 307)

emergency fund Money people put aside for needs they cannot anticipate. (p. 404)

emoticons Groups of keyboard symbols designed to show Internet users' feelings. (p. 349)

empathize To see someone else's point of view and to imagine oneself in his or her situation. (p. 263)

endorse To sign one's name on the back of a check before depositing or cashing it. (p. 424)

enthusiasm Lively interest or eagerness. (p. 198)

entrepreneur Someone who starts and then runs a business. (p. 68)

enumeration The listing or citing of key points when speaking or writing. (p. 299)

enunciation The clear and separate vocalization of each sound in a word. (p. 300)

ergonomics The applied science that attempts to design work areas that are safe, comfortable, and efficient. (p. 223)

ethics The moral rules of society; the values that help people decide what is right and what is wrong. (p. 181)

etiquette Good manners; the rules of polite behavior in dealing with other people. (p. 266)

evaluation The comparison and contrast of data or possible outcomes to decide which is the best choice. (p. 88)

exclusions Losses or risks not covered by an insurance company. (p. 439)

exempt Excused from something, such as having to pay taxes. (p. 464)

exempt employees Workers who are not eligible to earn overtime pay; generally, those who earn salaries. (p. 165)

exemption A fixed amount of money that is excused from taxes. (p. 465)

expenses Money that must be paid out. (p. 400)

exploratory interview A short, informal talk with someone who works in a career one finds appealing. (p. 54)

F

face value The amount of a death benefit that an insurance company pays. (p. 452)

facilitator A leader who helps a team work more smoothly by coordinating its tasks. (p. 280)

fax Facsimile; a copy or replica of a message received over telephone lines. (p. 307)

felony A serious crime, such as murder or rape. (p. 246)

finance charges Fees that lenders charge that are usually based on the amount of money owed. (p. 430)

financial plan A description of a business's start-up costs, operating expenses, and other costs for its first few months of operation. (p. 81)

financial responsibility   Accountability in money matters. (p. 409)

first aid   Actions taken in a physical emergency before help arrives. (p. 224)

fixed expenses   Expenses that people have already agreed to pay and that must be paid by a particular date. (p. 400)

flexible expenses   Expenses that come irregularly or that people can adjust more easily than fixed expenses. (p. 400)

flextime   An arrangement in which workers construct their own work schedules. (p. 59)

fluctuate   To go up or down, as prices do in a free-enterprise system. (p. 383)

Food Guide Pyramid   A guideline created by the U.S. Department of Health and Human Services to show people the nutrients they need each day. (p. 215)

401(k) plan   A type of pension plan in which an employee contributes a specific portion of his or her salary to the plan each year; employers may match the contribution. (p. 421)

franchise   The legal right to sell a company's goods or services in a particular area. (p. 75)

free enterprise   A type of economic system in which individuals or individual businesses buy and sell and set prices with little intervention by the government. (p. 381)

fringe benefits   Forms of reward for employment beyond salary, including health insurance, vacation and holiday time, and retirement plans. (p. 61)

functional team   A group of people from one company department or area of expertise who work together toward a common business goal. (p. 278)

G

gender   Sex, either male or female. (p. 237)

generality   A broad or indefinite statement. (p. 298)

generalization   A broad law, statement, or principle. (p. 299)

generic products   Products without brand names that usually have plain packaging and are not advertised as brand-name products are. (p. 388)

global economy   The worldwide linkage of national economies. (p. 11)

globalization   The establishment of worldwide communication links between people and groups. (p. 337)

goods   Items that people buy. (p. 11)

goods-producing industries   Industries that provide goods, such as stereo systems, cars, and buildings. (p. 17)

goodwill   The loyalty of existing customers. (p. 75)

gossip   Idle talk or rumor, especially about the personal affairs of others. (p. 207)

grace period   A time during which interest is not charged on a loan. (p. 432)

gross domestic product (GDP)   The total dollar value of all goods and services produced in a country during one year. (p. 385)

gross pay   The total amount of money a person earns. (p. 460)

gross profit   The difference between the cost of a good or service and its selling price. (p. 82)

Glossary

H

health maintenance organization (HMO)   A health-care plan that has no deductibles but that usually requires a copayment and offers limited physician choice. (p. 450)

hot call   A telephone call made to a referral or to follow up on a lead. (p. 115)

hourly wages   Pay that is based on a fixed rate for each hour worked. (p. 164)

I

income   Money one receives. (p. 400)

income statement   A document showing how much money a business earned or lost during a specified period of time. (p. 82)

income tax return   A form that shows how much income a person received from working and other sources and how much tax that person must pay. (p. 463)

indictment   Under criminal law, a list of charges the government brings against an individual or organization. (p. 246)

individual career plan   The final step in the decision-making process leading to a career. (p. 93)

individual retirement account (IRA)   A personal retirement account into which a working person can put a limited amount of money each year; a portion or all of this money may be tax deferred until the person retires, depending on his or her annual earnings. (p. 422)

inflation   A sharp increase in the average price of goods and services. (p. 385)

inflection   A change in the pitch or loudness of one's voice, often used for emphasis. (p. 299)

initiative   A willingness to do what is necessary without having to be told to do it. (p. 176)

installment loans   Loans in which people receive money in a lump sum and pay it back in installments, or regularly scheduled payments. (p. 430)

insurance policy   A legal contract between a person buying insurance and an insurance company. (p. 438)

interest   The money that banks pay depositors for the use of their money. (p. 418)

interests   Favorite activities. (p. 4)

Internal Revenue Service (IRS)   The government agency that collects federal taxes and oversees the federal tax system. (p. 458)

Internet   A worldwide electronic community in which millions of computers and computer users are linked. (p. 117)

Internet job services   Web sites, newsgroups, and bulletin boards created by trade organizations, companies, and individuals specifically for job recruitment and career research. (p. 53)

internship   A formally defined temporary position, usually unpaid, that often requires a longer-term commitment than volunteering. (p. 55)

interpret   To make sense of; to translate. (p. 300)

interview   A formal meeting in which a job seeker and an employer meet face-to-face to discuss possible employment. (p. 132)

J

jargon   The vocabulary of a particular trade, profession, or group. (p. 306)

job   Work that a person does for pay. (p. 5)

job application   A document that job seekers fill out so that employers can use it to screen applicants. (p. 120)

job lead   Information about a job opening. (p. 112)

job market   The demand for particular jobs. (p. 11)

job shadowing   Following a worker on the job for a few days to learn the routine. (p. 55)

K

Keogh plan   A retirement plan for self-employed people in which a certain percentage of one's earnings can be invested and is tax deferred until one retires. (p. 422)

keywords   Descriptive words that tell a computer what to search for. (p. 117)

L

laptop   A small, portable computer with a screen and a keyboard. (p. 339)

layoff   Job termination that results when a company's business becomes slow. (p. 168)

leadership style   How a person behaves when he or she is in charge of other people. (p. 286)

learning styles   The different ways that people naturally think and learn. (p. 37)

lease   A contract to use something for a specified period of time. (p. 74)

liability insurance   Insurance that covers damage or injury for which a policyholder is responsible. (p. 443)

liable   Responsible. (p. 243)

lifelong learner   A person who makes use of all opportunities to keep his or her skills and knowledge up-to-date. (p. 485)

lifestyle   The way a person uses his or her time, energy, and resources. (p. 6)

lifestyle goals   The ways in which a person wants to spend his or her time, energy, and resources in the future. (p. 30)

M

major medical coverage   Insurance that covers hospital and medical expenses, allowing for full choice of hospitals and doctors but requiring a deductible and coinsurance. (p. 449)

marketing   The process of getting goods and services to consumers; includes the packaging, shipping, advertising, and selling of goods and services. (p. 383)

market outlook   The potential for future sales. (p. 75)

marketplace   The entire realm of trade and business; the "place" where buying and selling go on. (p. 383)

mediation   A process in which two opposing people or organizations present their cases to a neutral panel or person who helps them reach a compromise or an agreement. (p. 245)

medical payments insurance   Insurance that covers medical expenses of a policyholder and his or her passengers involved in an auto accident. (p. 443)

Medicare A part of the Social Security program that provides health insurance benefits to people who need hospitalization or other medical care. (p. 472)

mentors Experienced coworkers who act as guides or informal teachers for new employees. (p. 159)

minimum wage The lowest hourly wage that an employer can legally pay for a worker's services. (p. 234)

minutes The written record of what is said and done during a meeting, kept by the secretary. (p. 288)

misdemeanor A crime, such as shoplifting, that is less serious than a felony. (p. 246)

mission A company's overall goal. (p. 278)

modem A device that translates digital signals from a computer into sounds that can travel over telephone lines. (p. 307)

N

negligence Disregard. (p. 243)

net pay The amount of income left after taxes and other deductions are taken out. (p. 460)

netiquette Accepted rules of conduct when using the Internet. (p. 349)

net profit The amount of money left after operating costs are subtracted from the gross profit. (p. 82)

networking Communicating with people one knows or can get to know to share information and advice. (p. 112)

new business Any topic brought before the participants of a meeting for the first time. (p. 289)

no-fault system A system of insurance in which insurance companies pay for their policyholders' damage no matter who is at fault in an accident. (p. 446)

nonexempt employees Workers who are covered by a law that entitles them to earn overtime pay. (p. 165)

notice An official written statement that one is leaving a company. (p. 495)

NOW account A negotiable order of withdrawal; a type of checking account that pays interest on deposits but requires a minimum balance. (p. 424)

nutrients The substances in food that the body needs to produce energy and stay healthy. (p. 215)

O

Occupational Safety and Health Administration (OSHA) The branch of the Department of Labor that sets job safety standards and inspects job sites. (p. 222)

on-the-job training On-site instruction in how to perform a job. (p. 99)

operating expenses The costs of doing business. (p. 81)

orientation A program that introduces new employees to their new company and its policies, procedures, values, and benefits. (p. 158)

outsourcing A practice in which businesses hire other companies or individuals to produce their services or goods. (p. 15)

overdrawn An account in which checks have been written for more money than is in the account. (p. 425)

overtime Extra pay for each hour worked in excess of 40 hours per week. (p. 164)

P

parliamentary procedure Strict rules of order for conducting a meeting. (p. 287)

partnership A business arrangement in which two or more people share ownership. (p. 78)

passbook account A savings account with which one receives a booklet in which to record transactions. (p. 418)

pending Temporarily on hold. (p. 367)

pension plan A benefit that builds a retirement fund for each worker. (p. 167)

performance bonuses Rewards given to workers for high levels of performance. (p. 166)

performance reviews Meetings between an employee and his or her supervisor to evaluate how well the employee is doing his or her job. (p. 167)

perseverance The quality of finishing what one starts. (p. 488)

personal career profile form A chart in which one can arrange what one has learned about oneself and what one has learned about a possible career side by side, along with a number indicating how closely the two match. (p. 89)

personality The combination of an individual's attitudes, behaviors, and characteristics. (p. 37)

policyholder A person who buys insurance. (p. 438)

positive self-talk The use of positive statements to "outtalk" one's negative inner voice. (p. 197)

preferred provider organization (PPO) A health-care plan similar to an HMO, with more choice of physicians but with higher premium and copayment costs. (p. 450)

prejudice An unjustifiable negative attitude toward a person or group. (p. 187)

premium The amount of money a policyholder pays for insurance. (p. 439)

previewing Reading only the parts of a document that outline or summarize its contents. (p. 309)

prioritize To put in order from first to last or from most important to least important. (p. 321)

probation The period after an employee is first hired, when he or she is "on trial." (p. 168)

problem solving A technique involving the use of thinking skills to suggest solutions to problems or situations, such as theoretical ones posed by an interviewer. (p. 141)

procrastinate To put off deciding or acting. (p. 321)

producers Companies or individuals who make or provide goods and services. (p. 381)

producing Creating goods or services. (p. 380)

professionalism A mature approach and appropriate behavior in regard to one's job. (p. 203)

profit-sharing plan A program that gives workers a portion of their company's profits. (p. 166)

promotion A job advancement to a position of greater responsibility and authority. (p. 486)

pronunciation How the sounds and stresses of a word are voiced. (p. 300)

purpose An overall goal or aim. (p. 297)

Glossary

R

recession   A six-month or longer period when the economy does not grow. (p. 384)

reconcile   To compare items and make them agree; used to refer to a checking account statement and check register. (p. 426)

record keeping   Organizing and maintaining records, often of one's income and spending. (p. 402)

redeem   To cash in. (p. 419)

references   People who will recommend applicants to an employer. (p. 121)

referral   Someone to whom one has been directed who may have information about a job or job opening. (p. 113)

register   To officially sign up as a qualified voter. (p. 517)

regular checking account   A type of checking account that usually does not require a minimum balance but generally charges service fees. (p. 423)

repetitive stress injuries   Injuries caused when the same motions are performed over and over. (p. 223)

resources   Time, money, material, information, facilities, and people needed to get a job done. (p. 317)

responsibility   A willingness to accept an obligation and to be accountable for an action or situation. (p. 177)

résumé   A brief summary of a job seeker's personal information, education, skills, work experience, activities, and interests. (p. 122)

revenue   Income from sales. (p. 82)

role-playing   Acting out a role in a make-believe situation, usually at the request of another person for the purpose of evaluation. (p. 140)

S

salary   A fixed amount of pay for a certain period of time, usually a month or a year. (p. 165)

scan   A method of electronically copying a document into a computer. (p. 124)

schedule   A list or chart showing when tasks must be completed. (p. 359)

school-to-work programs   Programs that bring local schools and businesses together so that students can gain work experience and training. (p. 115)

security deposit   Money a tenant pays a property owner before moving in, usually equal to one or two months' rent. (p. 507)

sedentary   A type of activity in which most of one's time is spent sitting. (p. 215)

self-concept   The way one sees oneself. (p. 37)

self-directed   Responsible for choosing one's own methods for reaching a goal. (p. 276)

self-esteem   Recognition and regard for oneself and one's abilities. (p. 197)

self-management   The act of making oneself do what is necessary to build a better career. (p. 178)

self-starters   Workers who do not always have to be told what to do. (p. 277)

seniority   A position or prestige achieved by working for an employer for a sustained length of time. (p. 487)

service learning   Programs in which students do community service—such as helping to clean up urban neighborhoods—as part of their schoolwork. (p. 55)

service-producing industries   Industries that provide services for a fee. (p. 17)

services   Activities done for others for a fee. (p. 11)

settlement   A mutual agreement that does not state that either party in a dispute is right or wrong. (p. 244)

sexual harassment   Any unwelcome behavior of a sexual nature. (p. 239)

shareholders   The owners of a company who buy shares, or parts, of the company and earn a profit based on the number of shares they own. (p. 79)

simplified employee pension (SEP)   A tax-deferred retirement plan for the self-employed that is simpler and easier to set up and maintain than a Keogh plan. (p. 422)

skills   Developed abilities. (p. 4)

skills résumé   A résumé organized around skills and accomplishments rather than time order. (p. 122)

skimming   Reading quickly for main ideas and key points. (p. 310)

small-claims court   A court that handles disputes over relatively small amounts of money and does not require lawyers. (p. 244)

Social Security   A government program that provides benefits for people of all ages. (p. 471)

Social Security number   A number issued by the federal government that one needs in order to get a job. (p. 120)

sole proprietorship   A business that is completely owned by one person. (p. 78)

spreadsheet   A software program that arranges data in rows and columns; often used for keeping accounts payable records and projecting expenses. (p. 345)

standard deduction   A set amount of money taxpayers may subtract from their income when figuring how much tax they must pay; amount is set by the IRS and based on itemized deductions claimed by thousands of "average" taxpayers. (p. 467)

standard English   The form of writing and speaking taught in school and used in newspapers and on television news programs. (p. 120)

standard of living   A measure of quality of life based on the amount of goods and services individuals can buy. (p. 386)

start-up costs   The expenses involved in beginning a business. (p. 73)

statement account   A savings account with which a person receives a computerized statement of transactions, usually monthly. (p. 418)

stereotype   An oversimplified and distorted belief about a person or group without attention to individual differences. (p. 269)

stress   Emotional and physical tension resulting from the body's natural response to conflict. (p. 142)

style   An individual way of expressing oneself. (p. 306)

subdirectories   Smaller groupings of files within a computer directory. (p. 370)

subject   A main topic or key idea. (p. 298)

summons   An order to appear in court. (p. 244)

Super-NOW account   An enhanced version of the NOW account; a checking account that pays a higher interest rate than a NOW account but also requires a higher minimum balance. (p. 424)

Glossary

T

tact The ability to say and do things in a way that will not offend other people. (p. 259)

taxable income A person's income after he or she subtracts certain permitted amounts of money for tax-figuring purposes. (p. 459)

taxes Payments made to support the government and to pay for government services. (p. 458)

team An organized group that sets goals, makes decisions, and implements actions. (p. 15)

team planning A process that involves setting goals, assigning roles, and communicating regularly. (p. 278)

technological literacy Knowing about and being able to use technology effectively. (p. 341)

telecommuting Using modern technology—especially computers, fax machines, and telephones—to perform a job at home. (p. 16)

teleconferencing Holding discussions among people in different locations by electronic means. (p. 337)

tenant A person renting a property. (p. 507)

terminate To end a worker's employment. (p. 168)

term life insurance Insurance that provides money to the policyholder's dependents or other beneficiaries if he or she dies. (p. 452)

time line A type of chart that shows the order in which events occur in time. (p. 359)

tone Manner or mood, as in writing. (p. 305)

total quality management (TQM) A theory of management that carefully coordinates company efforts to achieve customer satisfaction and continuous product improvement. (p. 282)

tracking schedule A chart that identifies the people who will be working on each part of a project and when they will start and finish. (p. 280)

trade school A privately run institution that trains students for particular types of jobs. (p. 100)

U

unemployment insurance A state-run social insurance program that provides some temporary income to workers who have lost their jobs. (p. 473)

unfinished business Any topic brought before the participants of a meeting for at least the second time. (p. 289)

uninsured motorist coverage Insurance that provides coverage for damage or injuries caused by a driver who is at fault in an auto accident and does not have liability insurance. (p. 444)

utilities Services for one's dwelling, including electricity, heat, and water. (p. 506)

V

values The principles a person wants to live by and the beliefs that are important to that person. (p. 31)

viruses Programs that can damage computer files and even hard drives. (p. 344)

vocational-technical center A school that offers a variety of skills-oriented programs. (p. 99)

W

warranty A guarantee that a product meets certain standards of quality. (p. 392)

whole life insurance A type of cash-value insurance with a savings component, which can build a reserve of money that a policyholder can borrow against or collect when he or she retires. (p. 452)

withhold Deduct, as money from a paycheck. (p. 459)

word processing Using any software program that creates text-based documents. (p. 344)

work credits Measurements of how long a person has worked, a certain number of which the person must earn in order to become eligible for Social Security benefits. (p. 472)

work environment The social and physical surroundings of a job, which can affect a worker's well-being. (p. 59)

workers' compensation A state-run social insurance program that provides benefits to workers injured on the job and to dependents of workers killed on the job. (p. 222, 473)

work permit A document needed by workers under 16 and sometimes by those under 18, showing that the young person knows about restrictions on the hours young people can work and the kinds of jobs they can hold. (p. 120)

Index A

Page numbers in *italics* refer to illustrations.

A

ABCs (airway, breathing, circulation) of emergency response, 225
Abilities, 36–37, *139*
  defined, 36
  matching careers to, 37
  research on, 59–60
  teamwork and, 280
  techniques for identifying, 36–37
Acceptance letters, 145
Access, 367
Achievement, 32
Active listening, 300–301
Adaptability, 488
Addiction, 217–218
Address change, 509
Advertising, fraudulent, 390
Advertising Age, 115
Affirmative action, 238–239
Age
  antidiscrimination laws and, 238
  buddy system and, 159
  generational distinctions and, 270
Age Discrimination Act of 1967, 238
Agenda of meeting, 288–289
Agribusiness and natural resources careers, *51,* 92
A-I-D, 224
AIDS, questions about, 142
Allowances, tax, 464
American Consumer Credit Counseling, 430
American Express Financial Advisors, 263
Americans with Disabilities Act (ADA), 238
America Online, 117
America's Job Bank, 117
Analogy, 328
Anger, 208
Annual fees, 431
Annual percentage rate (APR), 431
Answering machines, 300
Antidiscrimination laws, 238–239
Apollo 13, 324
Application fee, 430

Apprenticeship, 99
Aptitudes, 36–37, *39*
  defined, 36
  matching careers to, 37
  in personal career profile form, *89*
  research on, 59–60
  techniques for identifying, 36–37
Arbitration, *268*
Arrests, on job application, 122
Arrogance, 201
Art exercises, 43, 65, 105, 231
Assertiveness, 200–201
Associate's degree, 60, 100
Association of Trial Lawyers of America, 247
Assumptions, 328
Attitude, 194–201
  assertiveness, 200–201
  building positive, *196–197*
  dealing with mistakes, 198–199
  defined, 194
  enthusiasm, 198
  in interviews, 136
  positive thinking, 6, 195–197
  self-esteem. *See* Self-esteem
Audience
  speaking to, 297–298
  for written communication, 305
Audits, tax, 463
Automated teller machine (ATM), 336, 426
Automobile accidents, handling, *444–445*
Automobile insurance, 441–447
  buying, 446–447
  collision, 444
  comprehensive, 444
  discounts for, *446,* 447
  liability, 443
  medical payments, 443
  systems of, 446
  uninsured motorist, 444–445
Automobile repair fraud, 390
Automotive customer service adviser, 265

B

Bachelor's degree, 60, 100
Bait and switch, 390
Banking services, 423–427

checking accounts. *See* Checking accounts
electronic fund transfer, 426
financial advice, 412
on-line banking, 427
savings accounts, 418, *420*
Bank statements, 426
Bar association, 247
Basic payment methods, 164–165
Basic skills, 13. *See also* Listening skills; Math skills; Reading skills; Speaking skills; Writing skills
Beliefs, 31
Benefits, insurance, 439
Beneficiaries, insurance, 439
Better Business Bureau, 391
Biologist/senior interpreter, 56
Black Enterprise, 115
Block style letter, *308*
Bodily/kinesthetic learning style, *38*
Body language
  assertive, 200
  coworker interaction and, 263
  in interviews, 136–137, *138–139*
  "listening" to, 301
  speaking and, 299
Books
  on career information, 52
  on money management, 412
Bottom line, 319
Bragging, 6, 506
Brainstorming, *326,* 328
  description of, 327
  on international careers, 62
  on lifestyle goals, 30
Budget, 398–407
  defined, 398
  defining goals for, 399
  do's & don'ts, 402
  estimating income and expenses in, 400–401
  fine-tuning, 404–405
  household, 506–508
  planning, 398–401
  prioritizing in, 400
  record keeping and, 402–403
  staying within, *406–407*
Budget form, *403*

Building contractor, 118

Bureau of Labor Statistics, U.S., 385

Business and office careers, *51*, 343, 448

Business and office education exercises, 353

Business cycle, 384, *384*, 386

Business description, 80–81

Business magazines, 53

Business ownership, 73–76, 78–82. *See also* Entrepreneurship; Self-employment
buying a franchise, 75
buying an existing business, 74–75
financing of, 80–81
forms of legal, 78–79
location importance in, 75, 79–80
operation in, 81–82
starting a new business, 73–74
taking over the family business, 75–76
working at home, 80

Business school, 60

Business Week, 53

C

Cafeteria plans, 167

Caffeine, 217

Career clusters, 50
agribusiness and natural resources, *51*, 92
business and office, *51*, 343, 448
communications and media, 35, *51*, 221, 387, 408
construction, *51*, 118, 241
environment, *51*, 490
family and consumer services, *51*, 265
fine arts and humanities, *51*, 180, 284
health, *51*, 163
hospitality and recreation, *51*, 77, 365
manufacturing, *51*, 428, 470
marine science, *51*, 56
marketing and distribution, *51*, 202
personal service, *51*, 143
public service, 9, *51*, 304, 510
transportation, *51*, 323

Careers, 5–6, 484–489. *See also* Jobs

changing, 491–498
data, people, or things in, *33*, 34, 58, *58, 89*, 91
decision-making process in, 27–29
defined, 5
do's & don'ts for finding right, 100
evaluating choices in, 88–91
goals for, 36–40
handling new responsibilities in, 488
hobbies as, 494
international outlook for, 62, 178
keeping up in, 485–486
making decision on, 91
matching aptitudes and abilities to, 37
need to grow in, 492
outlook for, 61
personality and learning styles in, 37–38, *39*
researching. *See* Research
twelve fastest growing, *485*

Cash-value life insurance, 451, 452

Casual Fridays, 157

Cause and effect, *299*

Certificates of deposit (CDs), 419, *420*

Certified insurance claims assistant, 343

Change
adjusting to economic, 410–411
adjusting to personal, 409–410, *410*
anticipating in career, 484–485
career or job, 491–498
in financial responsibility, 409–410
keeping up with, 10
technological, *14–15*, 14–16, 336–342
in women's roles, 95
in worker expectations, *165*
in workplace, 10–18

Charge accounts, 430

Checking accounts, 423–426
do's & don'ts, 431
keeping track of, 425–426
managing, 424
using, *425*

Check register, 426, *427*

Child labor laws, 235

Chiropractor, 163

Choices
evaluation of, 25, *26*, 29, 316, 319–320
identifying, 25, *26*, 29, 316, 318

Chronological résumé, 122, *123*

Citizen responsibilities, 516–518

Civil law, 242–246
defined, 242
legal assistance and, 248

Civil Rights Act of 1964, 238

Claim, insurance, 439

Classified ads, 115

Cluster diagram, *327*

Clustering, 327

Coaching (leadership style), 286

Coinsurance, 449, 451

Cold calls, 116

Collateral, 430

Collective bargaining, 236

Colleges, 100

Collision insurance, 444

Color coding
of folders, 369
of schedule, 360

Commissions, 165

Communications and media careers, 35, *51*, 221, 387, 408

Communication skills. *See also* Basic skills
applying for a job and, 120
defined, 296
family and, 513
leadership and, 290
teamwork and, 277, 281

Community colleges, 100

Commuting, 505

Company culture, 156–157

Company policies, 162

Comparison and contrast, *299*

Compassion, 32

Compensatory time, 235

Competence, 487

Competition
for existing business, 75
in free-enterprise system, 384
global economy and, 12

Compounded interest, 418, *419*

Comprehensive insurance, 444

CompuServe, 117

Computers, 336. *See also* Computer software; Technology
banking via, 427
career search on, 53
importance of learning to

Index

use, 16
laptop, 339
organizing information on, 370
privacy in, 267
résumés on, 124–125
Computer science exercises, 129, 272–273, 344–350, 352–353, 373, 477, 501
Computer software, 344–350
database, 345
desktop publishing, 346
maintenance and troubleshooting, 346–347
record-keeping, 402
spreadsheet, 345
tax preparation, 468
viruses and, 344
word processing, 344
Computerworld, 115
Confidence, 119
Confidentiality, 185–186
Conflict resolution, 267–268
steps in, *268*
Consequences, 319–320
Construction careers, *51*, 118, 241
Consumer action panels (CAPs), 392
Consumer Credit Counseling Service, 430
Consumer fraud, 389–391
Consumer groups, 392
Consumer price index (CPI), 385–386
Consumer Product Safety Commission (CPSC), 392
Consumer Reports, 392
Consumers, 381–383, 388–392. *See also* Customers
defined, 381
do's & don'ts, 391
main goal of, 383
organizations protecting, 391–392
shopping tips for, 388–389
spending by, *17*
Consumers' Research, 392
Consumers' Union, 392
Contact list, 113
Contingency fee, 248
Continuing education, 100–101
Convenience benefits, 167
Cooperativeness, 174–175
defined, 174
promotions based on, 488
Cooperative programs, 54
Copyright, 350

Corporate environmental manager, 490
Corporate software sales, 448
Corporations, 79, *79*
Courage, 32
Courtesy, 266
Cover letters, *125,* 125–126
Coworkers
becoming an effective, 261–264
communicating with, 264
conflict resolution and, 267–268
job change and, 495
privacy of, 267
remembering names of, 156
representing oneself to, 200
respect for, 262
sense of humor and, 264
understanding, 262–263
unethical practices in, 187
Creative thinking, 13, 326–328, 394
Credit, 429–432
cost of, 431–432
defined, 429
disadvantages of, 430
types of, 429–430
Credit application, 432
Credit bureau, 432
Credit cards, 429, 509
safeguarding number of, 391
Credit limit, 429
Credit rating, 432, 509
Credit reports, 432
Credit unions, 418
Criminal law, 246, 248
Criteria, 318
Critical thinking exercises, 20, 42, 64, 84, 104, 128, 148, 170, 190, 210, 230, 250, 272, 292, 312, 332, 352, 372, 394, 414, 434, 454, 476, 500, 520
Criticism, 203–207
constructive, 204–205, *205*
responding to, 205–207
from supervisors, 267
Cross-functional teams, 278, *279*
Cultural distinctions, 270
Customer relations, 296
Customers. *See also* Consumers
communication skills and, 296
handling complaints, *302–303*
total quality management and, 282
unethical practices in, 187

D

Data, careers related to, *33*, 34, 58, *58, 89*, 91
Database programs, 345
Deadlines, 359
Decision-making process, 24–29, *28*
analyzing resources in, 25, *26*, 28, 316, 317–318
in automobile purchase, *26*
in career choice, 27–29
defining needs and wants in, 25, *26*, 28, 316, 317
in entrepreneurship, 72
evaluation of choices in, 25, *26*, 29, 316, 319–320
gathering information in, 25, *26*, 29, 316, 319
living arrangements, 506–507
on-the-job, 316–322
seven steps in, 24–29
Deductibles, 439
for automobile insurance, 447
for health insurance, 449, 451
Deductions, tax, 464, 467
Deep breathing, 219
Defensiveness, 205, 267
Defined-benefit plans, 421
Defined-contribution plans, 421
Delegating defined, 364
do's & don'ts, 262
Delegating leadership style, 286
Deliberate injury, 243
Department of Health and Human Services, U.S., 215
Department of Labor, U.S., 5, 52, 53, 222. *See also* SCANS
Dependents, 465
Deposit slips, 423
Desktop publishing, 346
Dictionary of Occupational Titles, 33, 52
Dictionary use, 305
Directing (leadership style), 286
Directions, willingness to follow, 175
Directories, 370
Disability benefits, Social Security, 471, 472
Disability insurance, 451
Disabled workers
antidiscrimination laws for, 238
estimated number of, *238*
Social Security benefits for, 471, 472

Discount stores, 389
Discrimination
    laws on, 237–239
Distributed workforce, 339
Distributing, defined, 380
Diversity, 269–270
    businesses encouraging, 13
    cultural distinctions in, 270
    defined, 269
    employee networking and, 263
    future projections for, *269*
    gender distinctions in, 270
    generational distinctions in, 270
    school-to-work connection on, 273
Dividend, 419
Doubt, overcoming, 197–198
Down payment, 430
Downsizing, 485, 492
Downtime, 362
Downward spirals, 205, 262
Dress
    for interviews, 134, *135*
    for the job, 157–158, 266
Driver, 323
Driver education classes, 447
Drug tests, 126, 157, 218

E

Earthquakes, 227
Eating habits, 214–215, 509
Economics, defined, 380
Economic systems, 380–386
    consumer price index in, 385–386
    defined, 380
    free-enterprise. *See* Free-enterprise system
    gross domestic product in, 385
    unemployment as indicator of, 386
Economy, 11
    measuring, 385–386
    pattern of, *382*
Editing, 306
Education
    continuing, 100–101
    employee, 485–486
    employer satisfaction and, *98*
    in personal career profile form, *89*
    promotions based on, 488
    research on requirements for, 60

taxes used for, 461
types of post-high school, 98–101
Electronic fund transfer, 426
Electronic résumé, 124–125
Elementary school teacher, 304
E-mail, 267, 307
Emergencies, 224–225
Emergency fund, 404, 411
Emoticons, 349, *349*
Empathy, 263
Employers, 164–168.
        See also Jobs
    help in balancing family and job, 515–516
    honest and fair treatment from, 167
    performance reviews and, 167–168
    respecting property of, 185
    safety and, 223
    unethical practices in, 188
Employment agencies, 116–117
Empty words, 299–300
Endorsement, 424
Enthusiasm, 198
Entrepreneur, 53
Entrepreneurship, 68–72.
        See also Business ownership;
        Self-employment
    advantages of, 68
    defined, 68
    disadvantages of, 69
    do's & don'ts, 72
    traits needed in, 70–72
Enumeration, *299*
Enunciation, 300
Environmental careers, *51*, 490
Environmental protection, 223
Equal Employment Opportunity Commission, 240
Equal Pay Act of 1963, 239
Equal rights laws, 239
Equifax, 432
Ergonomics, 223
Ethics, 181–188. *See also*
        Unethical behavior
    confidentiality in, 185–186
    defined, 181
    do's & don'ts in, 186
    fairness vs. prejudice in, 187
    in interpersonal interactions, 185–187
    quiz in, *187*
    respecting employers' property, 185
    technology and, 350

Etiquette
    Internet, 349
    workplace, 266–267
Evaluation
    of career choices, 88–91
    of choices, 25, *26*, 29, 316, 319–320
    forms of, 88
    of job performance, 167–168
Exclusions, 439
Exempt employees, 165
Exemptions, tax, 464, 465
Exercise, 215–216, 220
Existing business, buying, 74–75
Expenses
    cutting, 405
    estimating, 400–401
    fixed, 400
    flexible, 400, 405
    relationship to income, 403
Exploratory interviews, 53–54
Eye contact, 136, 299

F

Face value
    of insurance policy, 452
    of savings bonds, 419
Facilitators, 280
Facsimile. *See* Faxes
Facts
    opinion vs., 301
    specific, 298
Fair Labor Standards Act (FLSA), 234–235
Fairness
    from employers, 167
    prejudice vs., 187
Family and consumer services, *51*, 265
Family and consumer services exercises, 435
Family and Medical Leave Act, 237
Family business, 75–76
Family-friendly training, 516
Family responsibilities, 512–516
Farrier, 92
Faxes, 267, 307
Federal Insurance Contribution Act (FICA), 460
Federal Job Openings, 117
Federal taxes, 458
Federal Trade Commission (FTC), 391–392
Federal Truth in Lending Act, 431
Feedback, 179

Felony, 246
    on job application, 122
FICA (Federal Insurance
        Contribution Act), 460
Filing, 367, 368–369, 402
Finance charge, 430, 431
Financial plan, 80, 81
Financial responsibility,
        409–412
    adjusting to economic
        change and, 410–411
    adjusting to personal
        change and, 409–410
    help for problems, 412
Financial Web, 412
Financing, of business, 80–81
Fine arts and humanities careers,
        51, 180, 284
Fire, 226–227
First aid, 224
Fixed expenses, 400
Flexibility, 474
    in career choice, 91, 102
    in time management, 362
Flexible expenses, 400, 405
Flextime, 182, 515
    defined, 59
Follow-up letters, 144, *145*
Food and Drug Administration
        (FDA), 392
Food Guide Pyramid, 215, *216*
Forbes, 53
Foreign language exercises, 171
Foresight, 70–71
Form 1040, 465
Form 1040A, 465
Form 1040EZ, 465, *466*, 467
Form W-2, 465, *465*, 467
Form W-4, 464, *464*
Formal research, 52–54
401(k) plan, 421
Four-year colleges and
        universities, 100
Franchises, 75
Fraudulent advertising, 390
Free-enterprise system,
        381–384, 388
    marketplace in, 383
    pattern of economy in, *382*
    price fluctuations in,
        383–384
    role of producers and
        consumers in, 381–383
Friends, 512
Fringe benefits, *60*
    research on, 61
    types of, 166–167

Frustration, 208
Functional teams, 278, *279*, 280
Future Business Leaders of
        America, 288

G

Gender discrimination, 237
Gender distinctions, 270
Generalization/generalities, 298,
        299
Generational distinctions, 270
Generic products, 388
Glass maker, 470
Global economy, 11–13, 62
Globalization, 337–338
Global market, 485
Goals
    aptitudes and abilities in,
        36–37
    budget, 399
    career, 36–40
    lifestyle. *See* Lifestyle goals
    long-term, 96, 102, 279, 322
    medium-term, 96, 102, 279
    personality and learning
        style in, 37–38
    plan for reaching, 25, *26*, 29,
        94–97, 316, 321–322
    positive thinking and, 196
    realistic, 36–40, 94–95
    self-esteem and, 198
    short-term, 96, 102, 279, 322
    specific, 94
    stepping–stone. *See*
        Stepping–stone goals
    in teamwork, 278–280
    traditional, 95
Goods, 11
    producers of, 381
Goods-producing industries, 17,
        17
Goodwill, *74*, 75
Gossip, 207, 267
Government
    consumer protection
        agencies of, 391–392
    financial advice from
        agencies of, 412
    in free-enterprise system,
        381
    insurance programs of, 440
    safety and, 222
Grace period, 432
Graphic designer, 180
Gross domestic product (GDP),
        385
Gross pay, *460*

Gross profit, 82
Group plans (insurance),
        450–451
*Guide for Occupational
        Exploration*, 53–54

H

Hairstylist, 143
Handshake, 136
Hazardous waste disposal, 223
Health, 214–220
    addiction and, 217–218
    do's & don'ts, 228
    eating habits and, 214–215
    exercise and, 215–216
    positive thinking and, 197
    sleep and, 216–217
    stress management and,
        218–220
    taxes used for, 461
Health careers, *51,* 163
Health education exercises, 21,
        171, 211
Health insurance, 166, 449–451
    disability, 451
    group plans, 450–451
    health maintenance
        organizations, 450
    individual plans, 451
    major medical coverage,
        449, 451
    preferred provider
        organizations, 450
    Social Security benefits, 472
    types of coverage, 449–450
    types of plans, 450–451
Health maintenance
        organizations (HMOs),
        450
Hispanic Business, 115
Hobbies, as careers, 494
Home, working at, 80, 182, 339.
        See also Telecommuting
Homeowners insurance, 441
Honesty, 13, 181–185, 259
    about money, 183–184
    about time, 182
    from employers, 167
    in interviews, 139
Hospitality and recreation
        careers, *51*, 77, 365
Hot calls, 115–116
Hourly wages, 164–165
Household, setting up, 504–509
    budget for, 506–508
    first tasks, 508–509
    housekeeping habits in, 509
    pros and cons of, 504–505

roommates in, 505, 513
Human relations exercises, 85, 149, 210–211, 273, 293, 333, 415, 501
Human rights office, 240
Hurricanes, 227–228

I

Illegal immigrants, 237
Immigration Reform and Control Act of 1990, 237
Incentive plans, 166
Income, 400
  estimating, 400–401
  increasing, 405
  taxable, 459
Income statement, 82, *82*
Income taxes, 459
Income tax returns, 463–469
  filing, 465–468, *468–469*
  help with, 468
Indictment, 246
Individual career plan, 93–102, *102*
  committing to paper, 101–102
  defined, 93
  education and training in, 98–101
  realistic, 94–95
  specific, 94
Individual career plan exercises, 21, 43, 65, 85, 105, 129, 149, 171, 191, 211, 231, 251, 273, 293, 313, 333, 353, 373, 415, 435, 455, 477, 501, 521
Individual retirement accounts (IRAs), 422
Inflation, 385–386, 410–411
Inflection, 299, 300, 301
Informal research, 50
Information
  acquiring and evaluating, 190, 332–333, 394, 477
  interpreting and communicating, 91, 290, 296–302, 307–308, 347–350
  organizing and maintaining, 42–43, 94–97, 99–102, 336–369, 370, 372, 414–415
  using computers to process 117, 336–339, 340–341, 344–350, 370
Information gathering, 25, *26*, 29, 316, 319

Initiative, 176–177, 267, 487
Installment loans, 430
Insurance, 438–440
  automobile. *See* Automobile insurance
  do's & don'ts, 447
  government plans, 440
  health. *See* Health insurance
  holding down costs, 440
  home, 441
  homeowners, 441
  inventory of personal property in, *442*
  life. *See* Life insurance
  renter's, 441
  terminology in, 438–439
  types of, 440
Insurance coverage, 439
Insurance policy, 438–439
Integrity, 13, 259
Interest, 418
  on checking accounts, 423, 424
  compounded, 418, *419*
Interests, 7, 18, *39*
  defined, 4
  determining, 33–34
  in personal career profile form, *89*, 90
Interest surveys, 34
Internal Revenue Service (IRS), 458, 468
International companies/careers, 62, 178
Internet, 347–349
  etiquette for, 349
  financial advice on, 412
  getting on, 117
  job leads on, 117
  job services on, 53
  navigating, 117
  researching prospective employers on, 132
  résumé sent via, 122
  shopping on, 389
  tax help on, 468
  terminology of, *348*
  uses of, 349
Internet marketing specialist, 202
Internet surfer, 339
Internships, 55
Interpersonal learning style, *38*
Interpersonal skills, 266–270
  conflict resolution and, 267–268
  ethics in, 185–187
  exercising leadership, 149, 285, 286–290, 292, 500
  negotiating to arrive at a

decision, 24–26, 88–90, 435
  participating as a member of a team, 15, 104–105, 210, 276–277, 278, 282
  personal traits in. *See* Personal traits
  positive thinking and, 195
  respect for privacy, 267
  serving clients/customers, 84, 296, 302–303
  teaching others, 20–21, 280, 313
  working with cultural diversity, 269, 270, 271, 272
Interpersonal skills exercises, 20–21, 85, 104–105, 149, 210, 272, 292, 435, 500
Interviews, 132–149
  accepting job, 145
  attitude in, 136
  body language in, 136–137, *138–139*
  do's & don'ts, 135
  dress for, 134, *135*
  exploratory, 53–54
  following up, 144–146
  handling rejection, 146
  illegal questions in, 142
  rehearsing for, 133–134
  rejecting job, 145–146
  research prior to, 132–133
  role-playing in, 140–141
  speaking skills in, 137–138
  stress during, 142
  tough questions in, 140
  typical questions in, 138–139
Intrapersonal learning style, *38*
Inventory of personal property, *442*
Investments, 418–419

J

Jealousy, 262
Jeans days, 157
Job application, 119–126
  communicating effectively in, 120
  cover letters in, 125–126
  filling out form, 120–121
  illegal questions in, 121–122
  preparation for, 120
  résumé and, 122–125
  tests given in, 126
Job leads, 112–117
  breakdown of types, *113*
  from classified ads, 115

do's & don'ts, 115
from employment
    agencies, 116–117
from the Internet, 117
from networking, 112–114
from school resources,
    114–115
from telephone calls, 115–116
Job market, 11–13
    changes in, 484
Jobs. *See also* Careers; Employers
    accepting, 145
    average number held in
      lifetime, 5–6, 484
    balancing family
      responsibilities and,
      514–515
    changing, 491–498
    changing worker
      expectations in, *165*
    company culture in, 156–157
    company policies in, 162
    defined, 5
    do's & don'ts in new, 162
    dress for, 157–158, 266
    first day on, 156–157
    focus of search for new,
      493–494
    orientation in, 158–161,
      160–161
    outlook for, 16–18
    preparing for new,
      156–162
    questions in new, 161
    rejecting, 145–146
    resigning from, 491–496
    searching for while still
      employed, 494–497
    sedentary, 215–216
    signs of trouble checklist,
      492
    termination from. *See*
      Termination
    unhappiness in as reason
      to change, 491–492
Job safety. *See* Safety
Job satisfaction, 277
Job security, *165*
Job shadowing, 55
Journal keeping, 38, 179, 200,
    261

K

Keogh plans, 422
Keywords, on Internet, 117
Kiplinger's Personal Finance,
    412
Knowing how to learn, 13,
    128, 170, 210, 520

Knowledge, promotions
    based on, 487
Knowledge workers, 339

L

Labor laws, 234–237
    child, 235
    on illegal immigrants,
      237
    on unions, 235–236
    on work and pay,
      234–235
Labor unions, 235–236
Landlords, responsibilities of,
    508
Language arts exercises, 129,
    251, 313, 333, 395
Laptop computers, 339
Laws, 234–240. *See also*
    Legal system
    antidiscrimination,
      237–239
    civil. *See* Civil law
    criminal, 246, 248
    do's & don'ts for
      protecting rights
      under, 240
    equal rights, 239–240
    labor. *See* Labor laws
    on overtime pay, 165
    technology and, 350
Lawyers, 246–248
    fees of, 248
Layoffs, 168, 411
Leadership, 285–290
    communication and, 290
    do's & don'ts, 277
    leading a meeting and,
      287–289
    personal qualities for,
      285, *286*
    styles of, 286–287
League of Women Voters, 517
Learning, willingness in,
    176, 487
Lease, business, 74
Legal Aid Society, 248
Legal ownership, forms of, 78–79
Legal services, 246–248
Legal system, 242–248. *See also*
    Laws
    avoiding trials in,
      244–245
    settlement in, 244–245
    using services in,
      246–248
Letters
    acceptance, 145

block style, *308*
common business forms
    of, 307, *308*
cover, 125–126
follow-up, 144, *145*
Liability, 243
Liability insurance, 443
Libraries, 52–53, 132
Life insurance, 451–452
    cash-value, 451, 452
    term, 451, 452
    whole, 452
Lifelong learners, 485
Lifestyle, 6
    do's and don'ts for, 518
Lifestyle goals, 30–34
    values in, 31–33
Linguistic learning style, *38*
Listening skills, *12*
    active, 300–301
    do's & don'ts, 301
    following directions and,
      175
    in interviews, 137
    job time spent on, *297*
    note taking and, 301–302
    in teamwork, 264
Listening skills exercises, 84
Lists
    of abilities and successes,
      198
    in budget planning, 399
    task, 357, 360
Live Your Dreams (Brown), 196
Loans
    business, 80–81
    installment, 430
    secured, 430
    unsecured, 430
Local taxes, 458, 459
Location
    of business, 75, 79–80
    of household, 505–506
Logical/mathematical learning
    style, *38*
Long-term goals, 96, 102, 279,
    322
Loyalty, 179

M

MACAP, 392
Magazines
    business, 53
    career information in, 53
    classified ads in, 115
    money management advice
      in, 412

Index

Major medical coverage, 449, 451

Managers. *See also* Supervisors
family-friendly training for, 516
middle, 15

Manners, 137

Manufacturing careers, *51*, 428, 470

Marine science careers, *51*, 56

Marketing, 383

Marketing and distribution careers, *51*, 202

Market outlook, 75

Marketplace, 383

Market system, 383

Maternity leave, 242–243

Mathematics skills, 82, 95

Mathematics skills exercises, 20, 21, 43, 65, 85, 129, 149, 171, 190–191, 273, 293, 353, 395, 415, 435, 455, 476, 477, 521

Maturing, of savings bonds, 419

Mediation, *268*

Medicaid, 440

Medical payments insurance, 443

Medicare, 440, 472

Medium-term goals, 96, 102, 279

Meetings, 287–289

Memorandum (memo), *307, 308*

Mentors, 159–160

Messages, taking and leaving, 300

Military service, 101
taxes used for, 461

Minimum wage, 234–235

Minutes of meeting, 288–289

Misdemeanor, 246

Mission, 161, 278–279

Mistakes, dealing with, 198–199

Modems, 307

Money. *See also* Salary
honesty about, 183–184
as motivation for work, 7

Money, 412

Money management. *See* Budget; Financial responsibility

Money market deposit accounts, 419, *420*

Money market mutual funds, 419, *420*

Motivation, 70

Murphy's Law, 346

Musical learning style, *38*

Music exercises, 211

N

Names
addressing people by, 299
remembering, 156

National Business Employment Weekly, 115

National Labor Relations Act, 235–236

Natural disasters, 225–228

Near-far rule, 366

Neatness, 367

Needs, defining, 25,26,28, 316, 317

Negligence, 243

Net earnings/pay, 400, *460*

Netiquette, 349

Net profit, 82

Networking, 112–114
associations in successful, *114*
employee, 263

New business, starting, 73, 74

Newspapers
job listings in, 53, 115
money management advice in, 412

No-fault system of automobile insurance, 446

Nonexempt employees, 165

Nonwords, 299

Note taking, 175, 301–302, 310

Notice, 492, 495

NOW (negotiable order of withdrawal) checking accounts, 424

Nutrients, 215

O

Occupational Outlook Handbook, 52

Occupational Outlook Quarterly, 53

Occupational Safety and Health Administration (OSHA), 222, 224

Occupations. *See* Careers; Jobs

Office of Education, U.S., 50

Online Career Center, 117

On-site day care, 515–516

On-the-job training, 99, 176

Opening of letter, 125

Operating expenses, 81

Opportunities, problems as, 70–71, 72

Organization, 366–370
of computer information, 370
of information, 367–369
of work area, 366–367

Orientation, 158–161, *160–161*

Outsourcing, 15

Overdrawn accounts, 425

Overtime, 164–165, 179, 235

P

Parliamentary procedure, 287–289
terminology in, *287*

Partnerships, 78–79, *79*

Part-time work, 54–55

Passbook accounts, 418, *420*

Payment, 164–166
basic methods of, 164–165
incentive plans, 166
laws regulating, 234–235

Pending file, 367

Pension plans, 167, 419–421
defined-benefit, 421
defined-contribution, 421
401(k), 421
for self-employed, 422

People, careers related to, *33*, 34, 58, *58, 89*, 91

Performance bonuses, 166

Performance reviews, 167–168

Performance tests, 126

Perseverance, 488

Persistence, *137*

Personal career profile form, *89*, 89–91

Personal identification number (PIN), 426

Personality, 37–38, *39*
and leadership, 285–287

Personal life. *See also* Family responsibilities
citizenship in, 516–518
enriching, 511–512

Personal qualities, 13, 18, 258–264. *See also* Honesty; Integrity; Responsibility; Self-esteem; Self-management; Sociability
communicating with others and, 264
desirable in employees, 174–179
improving, 260–261, *260–261*

for leadership, 285, *286*
respect for others and, 262
self-awareness in, 259–260
sense of humor, 264
understanding others
and, 262–263
Personal qualities exercises, 64,
129, 148, 170, 272, 352
Personal service careers, *51*, 143
Photojournalist, 408
Physical education exercises,
171, 211
Pilot, 9
Planners, 359
Planning, 278–282, 298–299
Plan of action. *See* Individual
career plan
Plumber, 241
Police officer, 510
Polygraph tests, 126
Positive self-talk, 197–198
Positive thinking, 6, 195–197
Posture, 299
Preferred provider organizations
(PPO), 450
Prejudice, 187
Premiums, 439
Pressure, *206*, 207. *See also*
Stress
Previewing, 309
Price fluctuations, 383–384
Principles, 31
Prioritizing
in budget, 400
in decision-making, 321–322
steps in, *320–321*
in time management,
357–358
Privacy, 264, 267
Private employment agencies,
116
Prize notifications, phony, 391
Probation, job, 168
Problems
as opportunities, *70–71*, 72
positive thinking and, 196
shape of, 327
Problem solving, 324–330
channeling anger into, 208
cluster diagram on, *327*
decide on best solution,
324, 329
do's & don'ts, 328
evaluate probable
consequences of
solutions, 324, 328
evaluate the results, 324, 330
generate alternative

solutions, 324, 326–328
identification and
clarification of
problem, 324, 324–326
implement the solution,
324, 329–330
in interviews, 141
Procrastination, 321, 362
Prodigy, 117
Producers, 381–383
defined, 381
Producing, defined, 380
Production costs, 383–384
Professionalism, 203–208
accepting criticism, 203–207
controlling anger, 208
do's & don'ts, 208
handling gossip, 207
handling pressure, *206*, 207
Profit, 382
gross, 82
net, 82
Profit-sharing plans, 166, 421
Promotions, 486
declining, 489
reasons for, 486–488
self-awareness and, 259–260
Pronunciation, 300
Proofreading, 306
Property, respecting, 185
Property taxes, 461
Public defender, 248
Public employment agencies,
116
Public relations department, 132
Public relations specialist, 35
Public service careers, 9, *51*, 304,
510
Punctuality, 266–267, 358
Purpose
in listening, 301
in speaking, 297
in written communication,
305

Q

Questions
about career goals, 101
illegal, 121–122, 142
in new job, 161
preparing answers to
typical, 134
tough, 140
typical, 138–139
Quitting job, 491–496

R

Racism, 187
*Reader's Guide to Periodical
Literature,* 53
Reading skills, 309–310
note taking as, 310
previewing, 309
skimming, 310
Reading skills exercises, 250
Real-world workshops exercises,
21, 43, 65, 85, 105, 129,
149, 171, 191, 211, 231,
251, 273, 293, 313, 333,
353, 373, 415, 435, 455,
477, 501, 521
Reasoning, 13
Recession, 410–411
Recognition, 32
Reconciling statements, 426
Record keeping, 402–403
Recycling, 223
Redeeming, of savings bonds,
419
References, 121, 122, 135
Referrals, 113–114
Refinancing of debts, 411
Refund, tax, 463, 467
Registration for voting, 517
Regular checking accounts,
423–424
Rehabilitation Act of 1973, 238
Rejection, handling, 146
Relationships, as a value, 31
Relaxation techniques, 219–220
Renter's insurance, 441
Renting, 507–508
property checklist for, *507*
Repetitive stress injuries, 223
Reports, *308*
Representing oneself, 200
Rescue breathing, *226–227*
Research, 50–55, 57–62.
See also Information
gathering
on aptitudes and abilities,
59–60
on career outlook, 61
education and training
considered in, 60
exploratory interviews in,
53–54
formal, 52–54
informal, 50
on international careers, 62
library, 52–53
part-time work as, 54–55

on salary and fringe benefits, *60*, 61
on tasks and responsibilities, 58
values considered in, 57
on work environment, 59
on work hours, 59
Resigning from job, 491–496
Resources, 317
allocating human resources, 13, 58, 114, 317
allocating material and facility resources, 50–56, 58, 80, 99–101, 112–117, 317
allocating money, 61, 317, 398–400, 401–405, 406, 520
allocating time, 64, 129, 317
analyzing, 25, *26*, 28, 316, 317–318
Resources exercises, 64, 129, 520
Respect, 185, 262
Responsibilities, 58
citizen, 516–518
family. *See* Family responsibilities
Responsibility, 13, 258
defined, 177
financial. *See* Financial responsibility
for tax payment, 462
as a value, 31
willingness to take on more, 177–178
Résumé, 122–125
chronological, 122, *123*
electronic, 124–125
at interview, 135
skills, 122, 124, *124*
Retirement benefits, Social Security, 472
Retirement plans, 167, 419–422. *See also* Pension plans
Revenue, 82
Role-playing, 140–141
Roommates, 505, 513
questionnaire, *505*

S

Safe-driver discounts, 447
Safety, 222–228
do's & don'ts, 228
emergency response, 224–225
employers' roles in, 223
government's role in, 222
natural disasters and, 225–228

rules and regulations on, 222–224
taxes used for, 461
workers' responsibility for, 223–224
Salary, *60*, 165
changing expectations, *165*
on job application, 121
research on, 61
Sales, 388–389
Sales taxes, 460, *461*
Saving money, 418–422
budget category for, 404
comparison of methods, *420*
for inflation and recession, 411
methods of, 418–419
Savings accounts, 418, *420*
Savings bonds, 419, *420*
SCANS (Secretary's Commission on Achieving Necessary Skills), 13. *See also* Basic Skills; Information; Interpersonal skills; Personal qualities; Resources; Systems; Technology; Thinking Skills
Schedules, 359–362, *360–361*
School food service manager, 365
Schools, resources at, 114–115
School-to-work connection exercises, 21, 43, 85, 105, 129, 149, 171, 191, 211, 231, 251, 273, 293, 313, 333, 353, 373, 415, 435, 455, 501, 521
School-to-work programs, 115
Science exercises, 105, 191, 211
Sculptor, 284
Secretary's Commission on Achieving Necessary Skills. *See* SCANS
Secured loans, 430
Security deposit, 507–508
Sedentary jobs, 215–216
Seeing things in the minds eye, 13, 359
Self-concept, 37
Self-directed teams, 276, 280
Self-employment. *See also* Business ownership; Entrepreneurship
Self-esteem, 13, 64, 148, 258
overcoming doubt, 197–198
teamwork and, 277
Self-fulfillment, 7–8

Self-improvement, 260–261, *260–261*
Self-management, 13, 178–179, 259, 272
Self-starters, 277
Seniority, 487
Sense of humor, 264
Service learning, 55
Service-producing industries defined, 17
outlook for, *16*, 16–17, 61
Services, 11
producers of, 381
Settlement, 244–245
Seven-step decision-making process. *See* Decision-making process
Sexism, 187, 270
Sexual harassment, 239–240, 270
Shareholders, 79
Shopping tips, 388–389
Short-term goals, 96, 102, 279, 322
Simplified employee pension (SEP), 422
Skills, 4, 7, 13, 18
Skills résumé, 122, 124, *124*
Skimming, 310
Small-claims court, 244
Sociability, 13, 170, 259
Social Security, 471–474
disability benefits, 471, 472
eligibility for benefits, 472
future of, 474
health insurance benefits, 472
insufficient income provided by, 419
retirement benefits, 472
survivors' benefits, 472
Social Security number, 120, 135, 471
Social Security taxes, 459–460, 471, 474
Social studies exercises, 21, 43, 65, 85, 129, 149, 191, 215, 251, 293, 313, 373, 455
Sole proprietorship, 78, *79*
Spatial learning style, *38*
Speaking skills, 296–300
audience for, 297–298
do's & don'ts, 301
good habits in, 299–300
in interviews, 137–138
job time spent on, *297*
organizing material, 298–299, *299*
planning in, 298–299

Index

purpose in, 297
subject in, 298
teamwork and, 264
Speaking skills exercises, 42, 148, 332
Spending, breakdown of, *7*
Spider maps, 327
Spreadsheet programs, 345
Standard deduction, 467
Standard English, 120, 137
Standard of living, 386
Start-up costs, 73
Statement accounts, 418
State taxes, 458, 459
Stepping-stone goals, 96–97, *96–97*, 98
for teams, 279–280
Stereotypes, 187, 269–270
Stress, 218–220.
See also Pressure
in interviews, 142
in new job, 156
positive and negative, 218
Subdirectories, 370
Subject
in speaking, 298
in written communication, 305
Summons, 244
Super-NOW accounts, 424
Supervisors. *See also* Managers
getting to know, 200
leadership tips for, 290
maintaining a good relationship with, 267
Supply and demand, 383, 389
Supporting (leadership style), 286
Survivors' benefits, 472
Systems
improving and designing systems, 287–289, 338–339
monitoring and correcting performance, 286, 346
understanding systems, 336–339, 340–341

T

Task lists, 357, 360
Tasks, 58
Taxable income, 459
Taxes, 458–469. *See also* Income tax returns
do's & don'ts, 473

federal, 458
income, 459
on individual retirement accounts, 422
local, 458, 459
property, 461
qualities of good system, 462–463
refund of, 463, 467
responsibility for payment, 462
sales, 460, *461*
on simplified employee pension, 422
Social Security, 459–460, 471, 474
state, 458, 459
Tax tables, 467, *467*
Teamwork, 276–283
communication in, 264
cross-functional teams in, 278, *279*
experiential training and, 281
functional teams in, 278, *279*, 280
goal setting in, 278–280
planning in, 278–282
potential obstacles in, 281–282
providing value in, 282
reasons for encouraging, 276–277
Technical schools, 60, 100
Technology, 336–342. See also Computers
applying technology to task, 14–15, 336–339, 342
business partnerships with schools, 347
changing, *14–15*, 14–16, 336–342
do's & don'ts, 342
efficiency promoted by, *14–15*
exercises, 352–353
globalization and, 337–338
impact on workers, 16
impact on workplace skills requirements, *340–341*
impact on work situations, 338–339
legal and ethical issues in, 350
literacy in, 340–341
maintaining and troubleshooting technology, 231, 346–347
risks fostered by emerging, 223
selecting technology, 64, 170, 352
volunteering for training in, 486

Technology skills exercises, 64, 170, 231, 352
Telecommuting, 16, 59, 339
Teleconferencing, 337
Telephone skills
interview requests and, 133
job hunting and, 115–116
time management and, 362, *363*
tips for, 300
Television journalist, 387
Termination. *See also* Unemployment
action following, *496–497*
dealing with, 497–498
drug test failure and, 218
preparing for, 492
reasons for, 168
Term life insurance, 451, 452
Tests, 126, 157, 218
Things, careers related to, *33, 34, 58, 58, 89*, 91
Thinking skills. *See also* Creative thinking; Decision-making process; Knowing how to learn; Problem solving; Reasoning; Seeing things in the mind's eye
Thinking skills exercises, 104, 128, 148, 170, 210, 230–231, 250, 372, 394, 414, 434, 520
Time, honesty about, 182
Time clocks, *165*, 290
Time lines, 359
Time management, 356–364
breaking projects into steps, 358–359
do's & don'ts, 364
estimates in, 359–362
list making in, 357, 360
prioritizing in, 357–358
schedules in, 359–362
wise use of other people's time, 363–364
wise use of own time, 362–363
Time-out, taking a, 219–220
Tone, in writing, 305
Toolmaker, 428
Tornadoes, 228
Total quality management (TQM), 282, *283*, 318
Tracking schedules, 280
Trade magazine editor, 221
Trade schools, 100
Trade with foreign countries. *See* Global economy

Training. *See* Education

Transportation
    careers in, *51*, 323
    taxes used for, 461

Trans Union, 432

Travel agent, 77

Treasury, U. S., 458

Trials, avoiding, *244–245*

Troubleshooting, computer, 346–347

TRW, 432

U

Understanding others, 262–263

Unemployment, 386, 411. *See also* Termination

Unemployment insurance, 236, 440
    eligibility for, 473

Unethical behavior
    effects of, *182–183*
    handling, 187–188
    observed, *184*

Uninsured motorist insurance, 444–445

Universities, 100

Unsecured loans, 430

Upward spirals, 196, 197, 205, 261

Utilities, 506, 508

V

Values, 31–33, *39*, 88, 90, 207

VCR resources, 53

Viruses, computer, 344

Visualization, 219

Vocational education exercises, 105

Vocational-technical centers, 99–100

Voice mail, 267, 300

Volkswagen, 279

Volunteering, 200

Volunteer work, 55, 518

Voting, 462, 474, 516–518
    registration for, 517

W

Wagner Act, 235–236

Warehouse stores, 389

Warranty, 392

Whole life insurance, 452

Willingness to follow directions, 175

Willingness to learn, 176, 487

Willingness to take on more responsibility, 177–178

Withholding, 459–460, 463

Women
    changing role of, 95
    growing percentage in workforce, *239*
    legal protection for rights of, 239

Word processing programs, 344

Work, 4–9. *See also* Careers; Jobs; Workplace
    amount of time spent at, 4
    lifestyle impact of, 6–7
    meaning of, 5
    part-time, 54–55
    reasons for, 7–8

Work area, organization of, 366–367

Work credits, 472

Work environment, 59

Workers' compensation, 222, 440
    eligibility for, 473

Work experience programs, 54–55

Work habits, 359–360

Work hours, 59
    laws regulating, 235

Work permit, 120

Workplace, 10–18
    do's & don'ts when entering, 12
    etiquette in, 266–267
    global economy and, 11–13
    job market and, 11–13

World Wide Web, 53

Writing skills. *See also* Letters
    basic, 305–306
    in business communications, 307, *308*
    in E-mail and fax communications, 307
    style in, 306
    tone in, 305

Writing skills exercises, 104, 250, 292, 312, 332, 454–455, 500

Written records
    of sexual harassment, 240
    of unethical practices, 188

Y

Yellow Pages, 116

School-to-Work Applications and Connections

A

Academics
art, 43, 65, 105, 231
business and office
education, 353
computer science, 129,
272–273, 352, 373, 477,
501
family and consumer
science, 435
foreign language, 171
health and physical
education, 21, 171, 211
human relations, 85, 149,
210–211, 273, 293, 333,
415, 501
language arts, 129, 251, 313,
333, 395
math, 21, 43, 65, 85, 129,
149, 171, 273, 293, 353,
395, 415, 435, 455, 477,
521
music, 211
science, 105, 191, 211, 231
social studies, 21, 43, 65, 85,
129, 149, 191, 251, 293,
313, 373, 455, 521
vocational education, 105

**Acquiring and evaluating
information.** *See*
SCANS

Art. See Academics

Aspects of industry
community issues, 522–523
finance, 478–479
health, safety, and
environmental issues,
252–253
management, 150–151
planning, 106–107
technical and production
skills, 44–45
underlying principles of
technology, 374–375

Attitude
assertiveness, 200-201
bragging, 506
confidence, 338
dealing with mistakes,
198-199
defined, 194
enthusiasm, 198
exercise, 220
failure, 55
flexibility, 474

Golden Rule, 264
in interviews, 135, 136, 146
money management, 424
perfection, 90
positive thinking,
6, 195–197, 390
speaking, 298
unpleasant jobs, 185

B

Basic skills. *See* SCANS

Business and office education.
See Academics

C

Career clusters: case studies
agribusiness and natural
resources, 92
business and office, 343, 448
communications and
media, 35, 221, 387, 408
construction, 118
environment, 490
family and consumer
services, 265
fine arts and humanities,
180, 284
health, 163
hospitality and
recreation, 77, 365
manufacturing, 428, 470
marine science, 56
marketing and
distribution, 202
personal service, 143
public service, 9, 304, 510
transportation, 323

Career do's and don'ts
career choice, 100
career path, 60
consumerism, 391
delegating, 262
ethics, 186
insurance, 447
interview, 146
job change, 495
job search, 115
leadership, 277
legal interests, 240
lifestyle, 518
money, 402, 431
new job, 162
own business, 72
positive thinking, 208
professionalism, 301

safety, 228
self-awareness, 40
taxes, 473
technology, 342
time management, 364
workplace, 12, 328

Computer science. *See*
Academics

Cooperative learning. *See*
Teamwork/Leadership
skills

Creative thinking. *See* SCANS

Critical thinking
anger, 210, 272
art, 284
attitude and age, 159
attitudes, 190
auto service adviser, 265
being hired, 128
benefits, 170, 404
budgeting, 414, 434
business ownership, 84
career choice, 20, 42, 121
career goals, 104
career management, 516
career research, 64
child care, 369
chiropractic, 163
communication skills, 312
consumerism, 385, 394
contractor, 118
coworkers, 263, 343
decision making and
problem solving, 332
disabilities, 309
diversity, 13, 250, 272
economic systems, 394
editor, 221
educational interpreter, 56
emergencies, 9, 230
entering job or career, 20
environmentalism, 487, 490
ethics, 178, 190
farrier, 92
financial responsibility, 414
food service, 365
graphic design, 180
health and physical fitness,
225, 230
insurance, 454
Internet marketing, 202
interpersonal skills, 272
interview performance, 148
job application, 128
job change, 500
job interview, 148
job shadowing, 61, 64

job swap, 318
journalism, 387
leadership, 292
legal rights, 250
legal system, 237, 250
lifestyle, 20, 27, 520
listening/speaking skills, 312
money management, 434
new employees, 170
operating own business, 84
organization skills, 332
personal life, 520
personal service, 143
plumber, 241
positive attitude, 210
privacy, 463
problem solving, 241
sales, 404
self-esteem, 190, 210, 272
skills transfer, 428, 470
stock options, 426
stress, 205, 230, 265
succeeding at new job, 170
taxes and Social Security, 476
teaching, 304
teamwork, 281, 292
technology, 309, 347, 352
time management, 372
transportation career, 323
travel agency, 77
values, 64, 81, 104
volunteering, 141
work and personal life, 20, 42, 95
writing skills, 221

D

Decision making. *See* SCANS

E

Ethics
competition, 69, 126
confidentiality in, 185–186
cooperation, 174, 362
defined, 181
do's & don'ts in, 186
drug test, 157
ethical behavior, 181
employee qualities, 174
fairness vs. prejudice in, 187
fraud, 446
giving notice, 492
in interpersonal interactions, 185–187
legal action, 247
privacy, 322
quiz in, 187
recognition for work, 201
respecting employers'

property, 185
supervisor, 290
technology and, 350
theft, 34, 399
unethical behavior, 182–184, 187–188
Excellent business practices
buddy system, 159
career management program, 517
contributing to worthy causes, 81
dispute-resolution program, 237
diverse workplace, 13
electronic job recruitment, 121
employee networking, 263
employee training schools, 385
environmental concerns, 487
fitness screenings, 225
flexible benefits program, 404
internship program for volunteers, 141
on-site child care, 369
privacy protection, 463
providing a second chance, 95
reaching the global marketplace, 178
reducing on-the-job injury, 451
stock options, 426
stress reduction, 204
teamwork through experiential training, 281
technology partnerships with schools, 347
total quality management, 318
tourism career opportunities, 61
wants coordinators, 27
working with visual impairments, 309

F

Family and consumer science. *See* Academics

Foreign language. *See* Academics

H

Health and physical education. *See* Academics

Human relations. *See* Academics

I

Individual career plan
banking, 435
career plan, 105
company research, 129
computers, 353
decisions, 333
diversity, 273
exploratory interview, 65
financial management, 415
goals, 105
health and fitness, 231
household move, 521
industry research, 21
insurance, 455
interests, 43
lifelong learning, 501
listening/speaking skills, 313
own business, 85, 395
personal assessment, 191, 211
retirement, 477
teamwork, 293
thank-you letter, 149
time management, 373
wardrobe, 171
work eligibility forms, 251

Information competency. *See* SCANS

Interpersonal skills. *See* SCANS

J

Journal writing
budget, 397
career goals, 94
consumerism, 379
credit, 417
entrepreneurship, 67
ethics, 173
goals, 87
health, 213
insurance, 437
interview, 131
job change, 483
job leads, 111
leadership, 275
legal system, 233, 237
living on one's own, 503
moods, 193
personality traits, 257
reading skills, 309
self-description, 40
self-fulfillment, 8
speaking, 295

School-to-Work Applications and Connections Index

starting new job, 155
taxes, 457
technology, 335
thinking skills, 315
time, 355
values and interests, 23

K

Knowing how to learn. *See* SCANS

L

Language arts. *See* Academics

Leadership. *See* Teamwork/
Leadership skills

Learning styles
bodily/kinesthetic, 38,
136–139, 200, 299
interpersonal, 20–21, 38, 85,
104–105, 149, 210, 272,
292, 435, 500
intrapersonal, 38, 64, 70,
259, 260–261
logical/mathematical, 20, 21,
38, 43, 65, 85, 129, 149,
171, 190–191, 273, 293,
353, 395, 415, 435, 455,
476, 477, 521
musical/rhythmic, 38, 84
verbal/linguistic, 38, 42,
104, 148, 250, 292, 312,
332, 454–455, 500
visual/spatial, 38, 65

Listening. *See* SCANS

M

Math. *See* Academics; SCANS

Music. *See* Academics

O

**Organizing and communicating
information.** *See* SCANS

P

Personal qualities. *See* SCANS

**Problem solving in the
workplace.** *See also* SCANS

conflict resolution, 263
customer service, 17, 91, 386
dissatisfaction with job, 198
emergencies, 215
employees, 25, 158, 178,
282, 330, 516
health insurance, 450
hiring, 116, 142
income, 401
job growth, 498
legal matters, 248
money management, 422
taxes, 460
technology, 347
time management, 358
values, 80
writing skills, 310

R

Reading. *See* SCANS

Real-world workshops
abilities, 43
budget, 415
career choice, 105
company culture, 171
conflict resolution, 273
decision making, 333
deductions from pay, 477
government agencies, 395
insurance, 455
investing, 435
job experience, 21
job interview, 149
job security, 191
labor laws, 251
office environment, 211
parliamentary procedure, 293
part-time work, 65
promotions, 501
résumés, 129
roommates, 521
safety, 231
speaking, 313
starting a business, 85
telecommuting, 353
use of time, 373

Reasoning. *See* SCANS

Resources, allocating.
See SCANS

S

**SCANS (Secretary's Commission
on Achieving Necessary
Skills)**
basic skills
listening, 12, 84, 137,
175, 264, 297, 300–301
math, 20, 21, 43, 65, 82,
85, 95, 129, 149, 171,
190–191, 273, 293, 353,
395, 415, 435, 455, 476,
477, 521
reading, 250, 309, 310
speaking, 42, 148,
137–138, 264, 297, 298,
299, 300, 301, 332
writing, 104, 125, 126,
144, 145, 250, 292,
305–308, 312, 332,
454–455, 500
information competency
acquiring and evaluating
information, 24–27,
50–56, 88–90, 190, 332,
394, 477
interpreting and
communicating
information, 91, 290,
296–302, 307–308,
347–350
organizing and
maintaining
information, 42–43,
94–97, 99–102,
336–369, 370, 372,
414–415
using computers to
process information,
117, 336–339, 340–341,
344–350, 370
interpersonal skills
exercising leadership,
149, 285, 286–290, 292,
500
negotiating to arrive at a
decision, 24–26, 88–90,
435
participating as a member
of a team, 15, 104–105,
210, 276–277, 278, 282
serving clients/customers,
84, 296, 302–303
teaching others, 20–21,
280, 313
working with cultural
diversity, 269, 270, 271,
272
personal qualities
integrity/honesty, 13,
129, 139, 167, 181–185,
259, 286, 352
responsibility, 13, 31, 58,
90, 177–178, 258, 286,
462, 488, 516–518
self-esteem, 13, 64, 148,
197, 198, 258, 277
self-management, 13,
178–179, 259, 272
sociability, 13, 170, 259
resources competency
allocating human
resources, 13, 58, 114,
317
allocating material and
facility resources,
50–56, 58, 80, 99–101,
112–117, 317

allocating money, 61, 317, 398–400, 401–405, 406, 520

allocating time, 64, 129, 317

systems

improving and designing systems, 287–289, 338–339

monitoring and correcting performance, 286, 346

understanding systems, 336–339, 340–341

thinking skills

creative thinking, 13, 326–327, 328, 394

decision making, 13, 24, 25, 26, 27, 29, 72, 104, 316, 317, 318, 319, 320, 321, 322

knowing how to learn, 13, 128, 170, 210, 520

problem solving, 13, 25, 40, 62, 80, 91, 116, 128, 142, 158, 170, 198, 210, 215, 230, 248, 250, 263, 282, 310, 324–330, 346, 358, 386, 401, 414, 434, 450, 460, 498, 516, 520

reasoning, 13, 148, 317

seeing things in the mind's eye, 13, 39, 359, 372

technology competency

applying technology to task, 14–15, 336–339, 342

maintaining and troubleshooting technology, 231, 346–347

selecting technology, 64, 170, 352

School-to-work connection activities

accounting, 477

conservation, 231

consumerism, 395

court system, 251

diversity, 273

financial planning, 415, 435

friendships, 521

fringe benefits, 171

global economy, 21

hiring practices, 43

insurance, 455

interviews, 149

job application, 129

job shadowing, 65, 313

new employees, 191, 211

parliamentary procedure, 293

problem solving, 333

promotions, 501

small business, 85

technology, 21, 353

time management, 373

training, 105

Science. *See* Academics

Seeing things in mind's eye. *See* SCANS

Social studies. *See* Academics

Speaking. *See* SCANS

T

Team participation. *See* SCANS; Teamwork/ Leadership skills

Teamwork/Leadership skills

benefits, 477

career research, 65

consumerism, 395

design of work space, 373

emergency preparedness, 231

employer/supervisor conflict, 211

goal setting, 105

hiring, 149

insurance coverage, 455

interpersonal relationships, 273

job description, 21

job fair presentation, 191

job search, 129

legal responsibility handbook, 251

living on one's own, 521

money management, 415

newscast, 313

orientation program, 171

planning event, 293

planning strategy, 333

retirement plans, 435

starting a business, 85

technology, 353, 501

values, 43

Technology. *See* SCANS

Thinking skills. *See* SCANS

Time management

breaking projects into steps, 358–359

do's & don'ts, 364

estimates in, 359–362

list making in, 357, 360

prioritizing in, 357–358

schedules in, 359–362

wise use of other people's time, 363–364

wise use of own time, 362–363

V

Vocational education. *See* Academics

W

Writing. *See* SCANS

Acknowledgments

Chapter 4: Excerpt from "The Young and Entrepreneur-ial." From *Occupational Outlook Quarterly,* Fall 1994, a publication of the U.S. Department of Labor. Public Domain. Excerpt from "Overcoming Isolation" by Don Wallace. Reprinted with permission from *Home Office Computing Magazine.* Copyright ©1995.

Chapter 6: Excerpt from "Secrets of Highly Successful Job Hunters" by Annette Foglino. *Glamour,* October 1995. Reprinted by permission of Condé Nast. Excerpt from "How to Find a Job when 'There Aren't Any'" by E. Bingo Wyer, from *Cosmopolitan,* Spring 1992. Reprinted by permission of the author.

Chapter 7: Excerpt from "Into the Loop" by Charlie Drozdyk from *Rolling Stone,* March 23, 1995. Copyright © by Straight Arrow Publishers Company L.P., 1995. All Rights Reserved. Reprinted by Permission. Excerpt with permission from *Inc.* magazine, June 1996. Copyright ©1996 by Goldhirsh Group, Inc., 38 Commercial Wharf, Boston, MA 02110.

Chapter 9: Excerpt from *The 100 Best Jobs for the 1990s and Beyond* by Carol Kleiman. Copyright ©1992 by Carol Kleiman. Published by Dearborn Financial Publishing, Inc./ Chicago. Reprinted by permission. All rights reserved. Excerpt from "Finding, Training and Keeping the Best Service Workers" by Ronald Henkoff. *Fortune,* October 3, 1994. Reprinted by permission. Excerpt from "Office Ethics." First appeared in *Working Woman* in December 1991. Written by Catherine Fredman. Reprinted with the permission of *Working Woman* magazine. Copyright ©1991 by *Working Woman* magazine.

Chapter 10: Excerpt from "How to Get what You Want in '95" from Johnson Publishing Co. (Ebony).

Chapter 11: Excerpt from "Time Out" by John Marks. Copyright © December 11, 1995, *U.S. News & World Report.* Excerpt from *The American Red Cross First Aid & Safety Handbook.* Courtesy of the American Red Cross. All Rights Reserved in all Countries.

Chapter 12: Excerpt from *Sexual Harassment on the Job* by Attorneys William Petrocelli and Barbarea Kate Repa. Copyright ©1995 by William Petrocelli and Barbara Kate Repa, published by Nolo Press.

Chapter 14: Excerpt from *Taking the Mystery Out of TQM* by Peter Capezio and Debra Morehouse. Copyright ©1993. Reprinted by permission of The Career Press, Franklin Lakes, NJ.

Chapter 24: Excerpt from "What I Do for Love" first appeared in *Working Woman* in December 1995. Written by Katherine Griffin. Reprinted with permission of *Working Woman* magazine. Copyright ©1995 by MacDonald Communications Corporation. Excerpt from "Reinvent Yourself" by Caroline V. Clarke. *Black Enterprise,* February 1994. Reprinted by permission of Earl G. Graves Publishing Co., Inc.

Chapter 25: Excerpt from *Business Education Forum,* April 1996. Reprinted by permission. Excerpt from "How's the Job?" by Katie Monagle. *Ms. Magazine,* September/October 1995. Reprinted by permission.

Photo Credits

Lori Adamski Peek/Tony Stone Images 421, 433T; Charles Allen/The Image Bank 279, 291B; Kevin Anderson/Tony Stone Images 212; Bill Aron/Photo Edit 76, 83B; Bruce Ayers/Tony Stone Images 90, 103T, 204T, 209B, 218, 270, 294, 325, 331T, 416, 494, 499B; Paul Berger/Tony Stone Images 480–481; Bokelberg/The Image Bank 172; Daniel Bosler/Tony Stone Images 48, 259B, 298, 311T, 319, 329, 331B, 338, 351T; Tim Brown/Tony Stone Images 357; Peter Cade/Tony Stone Images 223; Giovanni Canitano/LGI Photo Agency 381; Melanie Carr/Zephyr 246; Comstock xx–1, 22, 46–47,152–153, 314, 326, 436, 443, 453M; Corbis-Bettmann 472, 475B; Dennis Cody/FPG International 432; Stewart Cohen/Tony Stone Images 301, 339, 378; Joe Cornish/Tony Stone Images 256; Robert E. Daemmrich/Tony Stone Images 141T; ET Archive, London/Superstock 99L; Jon Feingersh/ The Stock Market 300; Bruce Forster/Tony Stone Images 367, 371B; Tony Freeman/Photo Edit 113, 127T; Tim Fuller Photography 5, 6, 8, 11, 12, 19(2), 25, 27, 31B, 32, 37, 41(3), 52, 53, 54, 63T, 74B, 75, 116, 117, 122, 126, 157, 158, 165, 175, 177, 179, 185, 189T, 195, 201, 262, 267, 271(2), 322, 346, 358 369T, 370, 371T, 383(2)L, 389B, 390, 392, 393B, 402, 413T, 439, 453T, 489, 493, 505, 506, 508(2); Michael Goldman/FPG International 345; Mark Green/FPG International 168; Peter Grindley/FPG International 243, 249B; Charles Gupton/Tony Stone Images 278, 517T; H.M.S. Images/ The Image Bank 309; Craig Hammell/The Stock Market 206; David Hanover/Tony Stone Images 502; Michael Hart/FPG International 225; Dallas & John Heaton/Westlight 31T; Lewis Hines/Corbis-Bettmann, NY 235, 249T; Ted Horowitz/The Stock Market 224, 229B; Index Stock 167, 369B, 473, 499T, 513; Gary Irving/Tony Stone Images 462, 475T; Fernand Ivaldi/Tony Stone Images 159T, 169T; Bonnie Kamin/Photo Edit 82; Jeff Kaufman/FPG International 450B; James Kelly/ Globe Photos 474; Ken Lax Photography 133, 134, 137, 140(2), 146, 147(3); Alan Levenson/Tony Stone Images 192; Llewellyn/Uniphoto 396; Dick Luria/FPG International 74T, 83C; David Madison/Tony Stone Images 376–377; Scott Markewitz/FPG International 217T, 229T; Rich Meyer/The Stock Market 186, 189B; Benn Mitchell/The Image Bank 176; Art Montes de Oca/FPG International 486; Jonathan Nourok/ Photo Edit 247; Dennis O'Clair/Tony Stone Images 334; Gabe Palmer/The Stock Market 277, 291T; Reggie Parker/FPG International 399; Steven Peters/Tony Stone Images 66, 69, 83T; Photo Edit 2, 256; Joseph Pobereskin/Tony Stone Images 456; Jon Riley/Tony Stone Images 274, 389, 430; Michael Rosenfeld/Tony Stone Images 337; Pete Saloutos/The Stock Market 18, 450T, 453B; Juan Silva/The Image Bank 448; Frank Siteman/Tony Stone Images 199, 209T; Stephen Simpson/FPG International 88; Ariel Skelley/The Stock Market 59, 63B, 516; Don Smetzer/Tony Stone Images 98, 103B, 108–109, 386; Philip & Karen Smith/Tony Stone Images 62; G. Steiner/ Westlight 15; Dag Sunberg/The Image Bank 178; Superstock 94, 101, 110, 166, 169B, 204B, 228, 232, 236, 259T, 280, 306, 311B, 317, 364, 405, 411, 413B, 424, 433C, 440, 482, 488; William Taufic/The Stock Market 99R; Siegfried Tauquer/Leo de Wys 80; Telegraph Colour Library/FPG International 459; Charles Thatcher/Tony Stone Images 121; Ron Thomas/FPG International 141B; Tim Thompson/Tony Stone Images 498; Arthur Tilley/FPG International 431, 433B; Tony Stone Images 154; Robert Torrez/Tony Stone Images 400; Roger Tully/Tony Stone Images 362; Uniphoto 130, 354; Stephen Whalen/ Zephyr Pictures 115; Dana White/Photo Edit 120, 127B; Lee White Photography 13, 27, 61, 81, 95, 145, 159B, 200, 201, 207, 215, 217B, 237, 263, 281, 310, 318, 347, 351B, 359, 385, 404, 426, 451, 463, 487, 517B. 519T; Marshall Williams/ Zephyr Pictures 184; Zane Williams/Tony Stone Images 383R, 393T; David Young-Wolff/Tony Stone Images 319, 512, 519B.